The Wisdom of Arthur W. Pink Vol. I

The Holy Spirit
The Attributes of God
The Sovereignty of God

The Wisdom of Arthur W. Pink
by Arthur W. Pink

Start Publishing PD LLC
Copyright © 2024 by Start Publishing PD LLC

All rights reserved, including the right to reproduce this book or portions thereof in any form whatsoever.

Start Publishing PD is a registered trademark of Start Publishing PD LLC
Manufactured in the United States of America

Cover art: Shutterstock/Taisiya Kozorez

Cover design: Jennifer Do

10 9 8 7 6 5 4 3 2 1

ISBN 979-8-8809-2273-4

The Holy Spirit

Table of Contents

The Holy Spirit. 7
The Personality of the Holy Spirit. 11
The Deity of the Holy Spirit. 15
The Titles of the Holy Spirit. 19
The Covenant-Offices of the Holy Spirit. 23
The Holy Spirit During the Old Testament Ages. 27
The Holy Spirit and Christ. 31
The Advent of the Spirit. 38
The Work of the Spirit. 51
The Holy Spirit Regenerating. 58
The Spirit Quickening. 64
The Spirit Enlightening. 72
The Spirit Convicting. 79
The Spirit Comforting. 86
The Spirit Drawing. 93
The Spirit Working Faith. 99
The Spirit Uniting to Christ. 102
The Spirit Indwelling. 105
The Spirit Teaching. 111
The Spirit Cleansing. 118
The Spirit Leading. 126

The Spirit Assuring. 133
The Spirit Witnessing. 140
The Spirit Sealing.. 150
The Spirit Assisting. 154
The Spirit Interceding. 161
The Spirit Transforming.. 168
The Spirit Preserving. 181
The Spirit Confirming. 188
The Spirit Fructifying.. 193
The Spirit Endowing. 199
Honoring the Spirit. 206

The Holy Spirit

In the past having given consideration to the attributes of God our Father, and then to a contemplation of some of the glories of God our Redeemer, it now seems fitting that these should be followed by this series on the Holy Spirit. The need for this is real and pressing, for ignorance of the Third Person of the Godhead is most dishonoring to Him, and highly injurious to ourselves. The late George Smeaton of Scotland began his excellent work upon the Holy Spirit by saying, "Wherever Christianity has been a living power, the doctrine of the Holy Spirit has uniformly been regarded, equally with the Atonement and Justification by faith, as the article of a standing or falling church. The distinctive feature of Christianity as it addresses itself to man's experience, is the work of the Spirit, which not only elevates it far above all philosophical speculation, but also above every other form of religion."

The Importance of Studying the Holy Spirit

Not at all too strong was the language of Samuel Chadwick when he said, "The gift of the Spirit is the crowning mercy of God in Christ Jesus. It was for this all the rest was. The Incarnation and Crucifixion, the Resurrection and Ascension were all preparatory to Pentecost. Without the gift of the Holy Spirit all the rest would be useless. The great thing in Christianity is the gift of the Spirit. The essential, vital, central element in the life of the soul and the work of the Church is the Person of the Spirit" (Joyful News, 1911).

The great importance of a reverent and prayerful study of this subject should be apparent to every real child of God. The repeated references made to the Spirit by Christ in His final discourse (John 14 to 16) at once intimates this. The particular work which has been committed to Him furnishes clear proof of it. There is no spiritual good communicated to anyone but by the Spirit; whatever God in His grace works in us, it is by the Spirit. The only sin for which there is no forgiveness is one committed against the Spirit. How necessary is it then that we should be well instructed in the Scripture doctrine concerning Him! The great abuse there has been in all ages under the pretense of His holy name, should prompt us to diligent study. Finally, the awful ignorance which now so widely prevails upon the Spirit's office and operations, urges us to put forth our best efforts.

Yet important as is our subject, and prominent as is the place given to it in Holy Writ, it seems that it has always met with a considerable amount of neglect and perversion. Thomas Goodwin commenced his massive work on The Work of the Holy Spirit in Our Salvation (1660) by affirming, "There is a general omission in the saints of God, in their not giving the Holy Spirit that glory that is due to His Person and for His great work of salvation in us, insomuch that we have in our hearts almost forgotten this Third Person." If that could be said in the midst of the balmy days of the Puritans, what language would be required to set forth the awful spiritual ignorance and impotency of this benighted 20th century!

In the Preface to his Lectures on "The Person, Godhead, and Ministry of the Holy Spirit" (1817), Robert Hawker wrote, "I am the more prompted to this service, from contemplating the present awful day of the world. Surely the 'last days' and the 'perilous times,' so expressly spoken of by the Spirit, are come (1 Tim. 4:1). The flood gates of heresy are broken up, and are pouring forth their deadly poison in various streams through the land. In a more daring and open manner the denial of the Person, Godhead, and Ministry of the Holy Spirit is come forward and indicates the tempest to follow. In such a season it is needful to contend, and that, 'earnestly, for the faith once delivered unto the saints.' Now in a more awakened manner ought the people of God to remember the words of Jesus, and 'to hear what the Spirit saith unto the churches.'"

So again, in 1880, George Smeaton wrote, "We may safely affirm that the doctrine of the Spirit is almost entirely ignored." And let us add, Wherever little honor is done to the Spirit, there is grave cause to suspect the genuineness of any profession of Christianity. Against this, it may he replied, Such charges as the above no longer hold good. Would to God they did not, but they do. While it be true that during the past two generations much has been written and spoken on the person of the Spirit, yet, for the most part, it has been of a sadly inadequate and erroneous character. Much dross has been mingled with the gold. A fearful amount of unscriptural nonsense and fanaticism has marred the testimony. Furthermore, it cannot be denied that it is no longer generally recognized that supernatural agency is imperatively required in order for the redemptive work of Christ to be applied to sinners.

The Holy Spirit

Rather do actions show it is now widely held that if unregenerate souls are instructed in the letter of Scripture their own willpower is sufficient to enable them to "decide for Christ."

The Problem: Effort in the Flesh

In the great majority of cases, professing Christians are too puffed up by a sense of what they suppose they are doing for God, to earnestly study what God has promised to do for and in His people. They are so occupied with their fleshly efforts to "win souls for Christ" that they feel not their own deep need of the Spirit's anointing. The leaders of "Christian" (?) enterprise are so concerned in multiplying "Christian workers" that quantity, not quality, is the main consideration. How few today recognize that if the number of "missionaries" on the foreign field were increased twenty-fold the next year, that that, of itself, would not ensure the genuine salvation of one additional heathen? Even though every new missionary were "sound in the faith" and preached only "the Truth," that would not add one iota of spiritual power to the missionary forces, without the Holy Spirit's unction and blessing! The same principle holds good everywhere. If the orthodox seminaries and the much-advertised Bible institutes turned out 100 times more men than they are now doing, the churches would not be one bit better off than they are, unless God vouchsafed a fresh outpouring of His Spirit. In like manner, no Sunday School is strengthened by the mere multiplication of its teachers.

o my readers, face the solemn fact that the greatest lack of all in Christendom today is the absence of the Holy Spirit's power and blessing. Review the activities of the past 30 years. Millions of dollars have been freely devoted to the support of professed Christian enterprises. Bible institutes and schools have turned out "trained workers" by the thousands. Bible conferences have sprung up on every side like mushrooms. Countless booklets and tracts have been printed and circulated. Time and labors have been given by an almost incalculable number of "personal workers." And with what results? Has the standard of personal piety advanced? Are the churches less worldly? Are their members more Christ-like in their daily walk? Is there more godliness in the home? Are the children more obedient and respectful? Is the Sabbath Day being increasingly sanctified and kept holy? Has the standard of honesty in business been raised?

The Need

Those blest with any spiritual discernment can return but one answer to the above questions. In spite of all the huge sums of money that have been spent, in spite of all the labors which has been put forth, in spite of all the new workers that have been added to the old ones, the spirituality of

Christendom is at a far lower ebb today than it was 30 years ago. Numbers of professing Christians have increased, fleshly activities have multiplied, but spiritual power has waned. Why? Because there is a grieved and quenched Spirit in our midst. While His blessing is withheld there can be no improvement. What is needed today is for the saints to get down on their faces before God, cry unto Him in the name of Christ to so work again, that what has grieved His Spirit may be put away, and the channel of blessing once more be opened.

Until the Holy Spirit is again given His rightful place in our hearts, thoughts, and activities, there can be no improvement. Until it be recognized that we are entirely dependent upon His operations for all spiritual blessing, the root of the trouble cannot be reached. Until it be recognized that it is "'Not by might, (of trained workers), nor by power (of intellectual argument or persuasive appeal), but by MY SPIRIT,' saith the Lord" (Zech. 4:6), there will be no deliverance from that fleshly zeal which is not according to knowledge, and which is now paralyzing Christendom. Until the Holy Spirit is honored, sought, and counted upon, the present spiritual drought must continue. May it please our gracious God to give the writer messages and prepare the hearts of our readers to receive that which will be to His glory, the furtherance of His cause upon earth, and the good of His dear people. Brethren, pray for us.

The Personality of the Holy Spirit

If we were asked to state in a comprehensive form what constitutes (according to our views of Scripture) the blessedness of the Lord's people on earth, after His work of grace is begun in their souls, we would not hesitate to say that it must be wholly made up of the personal knowledge of and communion with the glorious Trinity in their Persons in the Godhead—for as the church is chosen to be everlastingly holy and everlastingly happy, in uninterrupted communion with God in glory when this life is ended, the anticipation of it now by faith must form the purest source of all present joy. But this communion with God in the Trinity of His Persons cannot be enjoyed without a clear apprehension of Him. We must know under Divine teaching God in the Trinity of His Persons, and we must also know from the same source the special and personal acts of grace by which each glorious Person in the Godhead has condescended to make Himself known unto His people before we can be said to personally enjoy communion with each and all.

We offer no apology, then, for devoting a separate chapter to the consideration of the personality of the Holy Spirit, for unless we have a right conception of His glorious being, it is impossible that we should entertain right thoughts about Him, and therefore impossible for us to render to Him that homage, love, confidence, and submission, which are His due. To the Christian who is given to realize that he owes to the personal operations of the Spirit every Divine influence exercised upon him from the first moment of regeneration until the final consummation in glory, it cannot be a matter of little importance for him to aspire after the fullest apprehension of Him that his finite faculties are capable of—yea, he will consider no effort too great to obtain spiritual views of Him to whose Divine grace and power the effectual means of his salvation through Christ are to be ascribed. To those who are strangers to the operations of the blessed Spirit in the heart, the theme of this chapter is likely to be a matter of unconcern, and its details wearisome.

Figurative or Literal Personality

Some of our readers may be surprised to hear that there are men professing to be Christians who flatly deny the personality of the Spirit. We will not sully these pages by transcribing their blasphemies, but we will mention one detail to which appeal is made by the spiritual seducers, because some of our friends have possibly experienced a difficulty with it. In the second chapter of Acts the Holy Spirit was said to be "poured out" (v. 18) and "shed abroad" (v. 33). How could such terms be used of a Person? Very easily: that language is figurative, and not literal; literal it cannot be for that which is spiritual is incapable of being materially "poured out." The figure is easily interpreted: as water "poured out" descends, so the Spirit has come from Heaven to earth; as a "pouring" rain is a heavy one, so the Spirit is freely given in the plentitude of His gifts.

Aspects of Personality

Having cleared up, we trust, what has given difficulty to some, the way is now open for us to set forth some of the positive evidence. Let us begin by pointing out that a "person" is an intelligent and voluntary entity, of whom personal properties may be truly predicated. A "person" is a living entity, endowed with understanding and will, being an intelligent and willing agent. Such is the Holy Spirit: all the elements which constitute personality are ascribed to and found in Him. "As the Father hath life in Himself, and the Son has life in Himself, so has the Holy Spirit: since He is the Author of natural and spiritual life to men, which He could not be unless He had life in Himself; and if He has life in Himself, He must subsist in Himself" (John Gill).

1. Personal properties are predicated of the Spirit. He is endowed with understanding or wisdom, which is the first inseparable property of an intelligent agent: "the Spirit searcheth all things, even the deep things of God" (1 Cor. 2:10). Now to "search" is an act of understanding, and the Spirit is said to "search" because He "knoweth" (v. 11). He is endowed with will, which is the most eminently distinguishing property of a person: "All these things worketh that one and selfsame Spirit, dividing unto every man as He will" (1 Cor. 12:11)—how utterly meaningless would be such language were the Spirit only an influence or energy! He loves: "I beseech you, brethren, for the Lord Jesus Christ's sake, and for the love of the Spirit" (Rom. 15:30)—how absurd would it be to speak of the "love of the Spirit" if the Spirit were nothing but an impersonal breath or abstract quality!

2. Passive personal properties are ascribed to the Holy Spirit: that is to say, He is the Object of such actions of men as none but a person can be. "Ye agree together to tempt the Spirit of the Lord" (Acts 5:9)—rightly did John Owen say, "How can a quality, an accident, an emanation from God be

The Holy Spirit

tempted? None can possibly be so but he that hath an understanding to consider what is proposed unto him, and a will to determine upon the proposals made." In like manner, Ananias is said to, "lie to the Holy Spirit" (Acts 5:3)—none can lie unto any other but such a one as is capable of hearing and receiving a testimony. In Ephesians 4:30 we are bidden not to grieve the Holy Spirit"—how senseless would it be to talk about "grieving" an abstraction, like the law of gravity. Hebrews 10:29 warns us that He may be "done despite unto."

3. Personal actions are attributed to Him. He speaks: "The Spirit speaketh expressly" (1 Tim. 4:1); "he that bath an ear, let him hear what the Spirit saith unto the churches" (Rev. 2:7). He teaches: "The Holy Spirit shall teach you in the same hour what ye ought to say" (Luke 12:12); "He shall teach you all things" (John 14:26). He commands or exercises authority: a striking proof of this is found in Acts 13:2, "The Holy Spirit said, Separate unto me Barnabas and Saul for the work whereunto I have called them"—how utterly misleading would such language be if the Spirit were not a real person! He intercedes: "The Spirit itself maketh intercession for us" (Rom. 8:26)—as the intercession of Christ proves Him to be a person, and a distinct one from the Father, unto whom He intercedes, so the intercession of the Spirit equally proves His personality, even His distinct personality.

4. Personal characters are ascribed to Him. Four times over the Lord Jesus referred to the Spirit as "The Comforter," and not merely as "comfort"; inanimate things, such as clothes, may give us comfort, but only a living person can be a "comforter." Again, He is the Witness: "The Holy Spirit also is a witness to us" (Heb. 10:15); "The Spirit itself beareth witness with our spirit that we are the children of God" (Rom. 8:16)—the term is a forensic one, denoting the supplying of valid evidence or legal proof; obviously, only an intelligent agent is capable of discharging such an office. He is Justifier and Sanctifier: "But ye are sanctified, but ye are justified in the name of the Lord Jesus, and by the Spirit of God" (1 Cor. 6:11).

5. Personal pronouns are used about Him. The word "pneuma" in the Greek, like "spirit" in the English, is neuter, nevertheless the Holy Spirit is frequently spoken of in the masculine gender: "The Comforter, which is the Holy Spirit, whom the Father will send in My name, He shall teach you all things" (John 14:26)—the personal pronoun could not, without violating grammar and propriety, be applied to any other but a person. Referring again to Him, Christ said, "If I depart, I will send Him unto you" (John 16:7)—there is no other alternative than to regard the Holy Spirit as a Person, or to be guilty of the frightful blasphemy of affirming that the Savior

employed language which could only mislead His Apostles and bring them into fearful error. "I will pray the Father that he shall give another Comforter" (John 14:16)—no comparison would be possible between Christ (a Person) and an abstract influence.

Borrowing the language of the revered J. Owen, we may surely say, "By all these testimonies we have fully confirmed what was designed to be proved by them, namely, that the Holy Spirit is not a quality, as some speak, residing in the Divine nature; not a mere emanation of virtue and power from God; not the acting of the power of God in and unto our sanctification, but a holy, intelligent subsistent, or Person." May it please the Eternal Spirit to add His blessings to the above, apply the same to our hearts, and make His adorable Person more real and precious to each of us. Amen.

The Deity of the Holy Spirit

In the last chapter we endeavored to supply from the testimony of Holy Writ abundant and clear evidence that the Holy Spirit is a conscious, intelligent, personal Being. Our present concern is the nature and dignity of His Person. We sincerely trust that our present inquiry will not strike our readers as being a superfluous one: surely any mind which is impressed with a due reverence for the subject we are upon will readily allow that we cannot be too minute and particular in the investigation of a point of such infinite importance. While it be true that almost every passage which we brought forward to demonstrate the Spirit's personality also contained decisive proof of His Godhead, yet we deemed the present aspect of our subject of such importance as to be justly entitled to a separate regard—the more so, as error at this point is fatal to the soul.

Deity or Not Deity

Having shown, then, that God's Word expressly and unequivocally teaches that the Spirit is a Person, the next question to be considered is, Under what character are we to consider Him? What rank does He occupy in the scale of existence? It has been truly said that, "He is either God, possessing, in a distinction of Person, an ineffable unity of the Divine nature with the Father and the Son, or He is the creature of God, infinitely removed from Him in essence and dignity, and having no other than a derivative excellence in that rank to which He is appointed in creation. There is no medium betwixt the one and the other. Nothing intermediate between the Creator and created can be admissible. So that were the Holy Spirit to be placed at the top of all creation, even as high above the highest angel as that angel transcends the lowest reptile of animated life, the chasm would be still infinite; and He, who is emphatically called the Eternal Spirit, would not be God" (Robert Hawker).

We will now endeavor to show from the Word of Truth that the Holy Spirit is distinguished by such names and attributes, that He is endowed with such a plentitude of underived power, and that He is the Author of such works as to altogether transcend finite ability, and such as can belong to none but God Himself. However mysterious and inexplicable to human reason the existence of a distinction of Persons in the essence of the Godhead may be, yet if we submissively bow to the plain teachings of the Divine Oracles, then the conclusion that there subsists three Divine Persons who are co-essential, co-eternal, and co-equal is unavoidable. He of whom such works as the creation of the universe, the inspiration of the Scriptures, the formation of the humanity of Christ, the regeneration and sanctification of the elect, is, and must be, GOD; or, to use the language of 2 Corinthians 3:17 "Now the Lord is that Spirit."

Proofs of the Spirit's Deity

1. The Holy Spirit is expressly called God. To Ananias Peter said, "Why hath Satan filled thine heart to lie to the Holy Spirit?" and then in the very next verse, he affirms "thou hast not lied unto men, but unto God" (Acts 5:3, 4): if, then, lying to the Holy Spirit is lying to God, it necessarily follows that the Spirit must be God. Again, the saints are called "the temple of God," and the reason proving this is that, "the Spirit of God dwelleth in you" (1 Cor. 3:16). In like manner, the body of the individual saint is designated, "the temple of the Holy Spirit," and then the exhortation is made, "therefore glorify God in your body" (1 Cor. 6:19, 20). In 1 Corinthians 12, where the diversity of His gifts, administrations, and operations are mentioned, He is spoken of severally as "the same Spirit" (v. 4), "the same Lord" (v. 5), "the same God" (v. 6). In 2 Corinthians 6:16 the Holy Spirit is called "the living God."

2. The Holy Spirit is expressly called Jehovah, a name that is utterly incommunicable to all creatures, and which can be applied to none except the Great Supreme. It was Jehovah who spoke by the mouth of all the holy Prophets from the beginning of the world (Luke 1:68, 70), yet in 2 Peter 1:20 it is implicitly declared that those Prophets all spoke by "the Holy Spirit" (see also 2 Sam. 23:2, 3, and compare Acts 1:16)! It was Jehovah whom Israel tempted in the wilderness, "sinning against God and provoking the Most High" (Ps. 78:17, 18), yet in Isaiah 63:10 this is specifically termed, "rebelling against and vexing the Holy Spirit"! In Deuteronomy 32:12 we read, "The Lord alone did lead them," yet speaking of the same people, at the same time, Isaiah 63:14 declares, "the Spirit of the Lord did lead them." It was Jehovah who bade Isaiah, "Go and tell this people, hear ye indeed" (6:8, 9), while the Apostle declared, "well spake the Holy Spirit by Isaiah the Prophet, saying, Go unto the people and say, Hear ye indeed..." (Acts 28:25, 26)! What could more plainly establish the identity of Jehovah and the Holy Spirit? Note that the Holy Spirit is called "the Lord" in 2 Thessalonians 3:5.

The Holy Spirit

3. The perfections of God are all found in the Spirit. By what is the nature of any being determined but by its properties? He who possesses the properties peculiar to an angel or man is rightly esteemed one. So He who possesses the attributes or properties which belong alone to God, must be considered and worshipped as God. The Scriptures very clearly and abundantly affirm that the Holy Spirit is possessed of the attributes peculiar to God. They ascribe to Him absolute holiness. As God is called "Holy," "the Holy One," being therein described by that superlatively excellent property of His nature wherein He is "glorious in holiness" (Ex. 15:1 1); so is the Third Person of the Trinity designated "the Spirit of Holiness" (Rom. 1:4) to denote the holiness of His nature and the Deity of His Person. The Spirit is eternal (Heb. 9:14). He is omnipresent: "Whither shall I flee from thy Spirit?" (Ps. 139:7). He is omniscient (see 1 Cor. 2:10, 11). He is omnipotent: being termed "the Power of the Highest" (Luke 1:35; see also Micah 2:8, and compare Isa. 40:28).

4. The absolute sovereignty and supremacy of the Spirit manifest His Godhead. In Matthew 4:1 we are told, "Then was Jesus led up of the Spirit into the wilderness": who but a Divine Person had the right to direct the Mediator? and to whom but God would the Redeemer have submitted! In John 3:8 the Lord Jesus drew an analogy between the wind which "bloweth where it listeth" (not being at the disposal or direction of any creature), and the imperial operations of the Spirit. In 1 Corinthians 12:11 it is expressly affirmed that the Holy Spirit has the distribution of all spiritual gifts, having nothing but His own pleasure for His rule. He must, then, be "God over all, blessed forever." In Acts 13:2-4 we find the Holy Spirit calling men unto the work of the ministry, which is solely a Divine prerogative, though wicked men have abrogated it unto themselves. In these verses it will be found that the Spirit appointed their work, commanded them to be set apart by the church, and sent them forth. In Acts 20:28 it is plainly declared that the Holy Spirit set officers over the church.

5. The works ascribed to the Spirit clearly demonstrate His Godhead. Creation itself is attributed to Him, no less than to the Father and the Son: "By the Spirit lie hath garnished the heavens" (Job 26: 13): "the Spirit of God hath made me" (Job 33:4). He is concerned in the work of providence (Isa. 40:13-15; Acts 16:6, 7). All Scripture is given by inspiration of God (2 Tim. 3:16), the source of which is the Spirit Himself (2 Peter 1:21). The humanity of Christ was miraculously formed by the Spirit (Matthew 1:20). Christ was anointed for His work by the Spirit (Isa. 61:1; John 3:34). His miracles were performed by the Spirit's power (Matthew 12:3 8). He was raised from the

dead by the Spirit (Rom. 8:11). Who but a Divine person could have wrought such works as these!?

Reader, do you have a personal and inward proof that the Holy Spirit is none other than God? Has He wrought in you that which no finite power could? Has He brought you from death unto life, made you a new creature in Christ, imparted to you a living faith, filled you with holy longings after God? Does He breathe into you the spirit of prayer, take of the things of Christ and show them unto you, apply to your heart both the precepts and promises of God? If so, then, these are so many witnesses in your own bosom of the deity of the Blessed Spirit.

The Titles of the Holy Spirit

Correct views of the Divine character lie at the foundation of all genuine and vital godliness. It should, then, be one of our chief quests to seek after the knowledge of God. Without the true knowledge of God, in His nature and attributes, we can neither worship Him acceptably nor serve Him aright.

"Names" Describe Character

Now the three Persons in the Godhead have graciously revealed Themselves through a variety of names and titles. The Nature of God we are utterly incapable of comprehending, but His person and character may be known. Each name or title that God has appropriated unto Himself is that whereby He reveals Himself unto us, and whereby He would have us know and own Him. Therefore whatever any name of God expresses Him to be, that He is, for He will not deceive us by giving Himself a wrong or false name. On this account He requires us to trust in His Name, because He will assuredly be found unto us all that His Name imports.

The names of God, then, are for the purpose of expressing Him unto us; they set forth His perfections and make known the different relations which He sustains unto the children of men and unto His own favored people. Names are given for this intent, that they might declare what the thing is to which the name belongs. Thus, when God created Adam and gave him dominion over this visible world, He caused the beasts of the field and the fowls of the air to pass before him, that they might receive names from him (Gen. 2:19). In like manner, we may learn of what God is through the names and titles He has taken. By means of them, God spells out Himself to us, sometimes by one of His perfections, sometimes by another. A very wide field of study is here introduced to us, yet we can now say no more than that the prayerful and diligent searcher will find it a highly profitable one to investigate.

What has been said above serves to indicate the importance of the present aspect of our subject. What the Holy Spirit is in His Divine Person and ineffable character is made known unto us by means of the many names and varied titles which are accorded to Him in Holy Writ. A whole volume, rather than a brief chapter, might well be devoted to their contemplation. May we be Divinely guided in using the limited space which is now at our disposal in writing that which will both magnify the Third Person in the blessed Trinity, and serve as a stimulus unto our readers to give more careful study and holy meditation to those titles of His which we cannot here consider. Possibly, we can help our friends most by devoting our attention to those which are more difficult to apprehend.

Concurrence in the Trinity

The Holy Spirit is designated by a great many names and titles in Scripture which clearly evince both His personality and Deity. Some of these are peculiar to Himself, others He has in common with the Father and the Son, in the undivided essence of the Divine nature. While in the wondrous scheme of redemption the Father, the Son, and the Holy Spirit are revealed unto us under distinct characters, by which we are taught to ascribe certain operations to one more immediately than to another, yet the agency of each is not to be considered as so detached but that They cooperate and concur. For this reason the Third Person of the Trinity is called the Spirit of the Father (John 14:26) and the Spirit of the Son (Gal. 4:6), because, acting in conjunction with the Father and the Son, the operations of the one are in effect the operations of the others—and altogether result from the indivisible essence of the Godhead.

Titles Used in Scripture

First, He is designated "The Spirit," which expresses two things. First, His Divine nature, for "God is Spirit" (John 4:24); as the Thirty-Nine Articles of the Episcopal Church well express it, "without body, parts, or passions." He is essentially pure, incorporeal Spirit, as distinct from any material or visible substance. Second, it expresses His mode of operation on the hearts of the people of God, which is compared in Scripture to a "breath," or the movement of the "wind"—both of which adumbrate Him in this lower world; suitably so, inasmuch as they are invisible, and yet vitalizing elements. "Come from the four winds, 0 Breath, and breathe upon these slain, that they may live" (Ezek. 37:9). Therefore was it that in His public descent on the day of Pentecost, "suddenly there came a sound from Heaven of a rushing, mighty wind, and it filled all the house where they were sitting" (Acts 2:2).

Second, He is called by way of eminency "The Holy Spirit" which is His most usual appellation in the New Testament. Two things are included. First, respect is had unto His nature. As Jehovah is distinguished from all false gods thus, "Who is like unto thee, O LORD, among the gods; who is like thee, glorious in holiness" (Ex. 15:11); so is the Spirit called Holy to denote the holiness of His nature. This appears plainly in Mark 3:29, 30, "He that shall blaspheme against the Holy Spirit hath never forgiveness; because they said, he hath an unclean spirit"—thus opposition is made between His immaculate nature and that of the unclean or unholy spirit. Observe, too, how this verse also furnishes clear proof of His personality, for the "unclean spirit" is a person, and if the Spirit were not a Person, no comparative opposition could be made between them. So also we see here His absolute Deity, for only God could be "blasphemed"! Second, this title views His operations and that in respect of all His works, for every work of God is holy—in hardening and blinding, equally as in regenerating and sanctifying.

Third, He is called God's "good Spirit" (Neh. 9:20). "Thy Spirit is good" (Ps. 143:10). He is so designated principally from His nature, which is essentially good for "there is none good but one, that is God" (Matthew 19:17); so also from His operations, for "the fruit of the Spirit is in all goodness, and righteousness, and truth" (Eph. 5:9).

Fourth, He is called the "free Spirit" (Ps. 5 1:12), so designated because He is a most munificent Giver, bestowing His favors severally as He pleases, literally, and upbraiding not; also because it is His special work to deliver God's elect from the bondage of sin and Satan, and bring them into the glorious liberty of God's children.

Fifth, He is called "the Spirit of Christ" (Rom. 8:9) because sent by Him (Acts 2:33), and as furthering His cause on earth (John 16:14).

Sixth, He is called "the Spirit of the Lord" (Acts 8:29) because He possesses Divine authority and requires unhesitating submission from us.

Seventh, He is called, "the Eternal Spirit" (Heb. 9:14). "Among the names and titles by which the Holy Spirit is known in Scripture, that of 'the eternal Spirit' is His peculiar appellation—a name, which in the very first face of things, accurately defines His nature, and carries with it the most convincing proof of Godhead. None but 'the High and Holy One, inhabiteth eternity,' can be called eternal. Of other beings, who possess a derivative immortality, it may be said that as they are created for eternity, they may enjoy, through the benignity of their Creator, a future eternal duration. But this differs as widely as the east is from the west, when applied to Him of whom we are speaking. He alone, who possesses an underived, independent, and necessary self-existence, 'who was, and is, and is to come,' can be said, in exclusion of all other beings, to be eternal" (Robert Hawker).

Eighth, He is called "the Paraclete" or "the Comforter" (John 14:16) than which no better translation can be given, providing the English meaning of the word be kept in mind. Comforter means more than Consoler. It is derived from two Latin words, com "along side of" and fortis "strength." Thus a "comforter" is one who stands alongside of one in need, to strengthen. When Christ said He would ask the Father to give His people "another Comforter," He signified that the Spirit would take His own place, doing for the disciples, what He had done for them while He was with them on earth. The Spirit strengthens in a variety of ways: consoling when cast down, giving grace when weak or timid, guiding when perplexed.

We close this subject with a few words from the pen of the late J. C. Philpot (1863), "Nor let anyone think that this doctrine of the distinct Personality of the Holy Spirit is a mere strife of words, or unimportant matter, or an unprofitable discussion, which we may take or leave, believe or deny, without any injury to our faith or hope. On the contrary, let this be firmly impressed on your mind, that if you deny or disbelieve the Personality of the blessed Spirit, you deny and disbelieve with it the grand foundation truth of the Trinity. If your doctrine be unsound, your experience must be a delusion, and your practice an imposition."

The Covenant-Offices of the Holy Spirit

The ground which we are now to tread, will, we fear, be new and strange to most of our readers. In the January and February 1930 issues of Studies in the Scriptures, we wrote two rather lengthy articles upon "The Everlasting Covenant." There we dwelt principally upon it in connection with the Father and the Son; here we shall contemplate the relation of the Holy Spirit unto the same. His covenant-offices are intimately connected with and indeed flow from His Deity and Personality, for if He had not been a Divine Person in the Godhead, He would not and could not have taken a part in the Covenant of Grace. Before proceeding further, let us define our terms.

Definitions

By the "Covenant of Grace," we refer to that holy and solemn compact entered into between the august Persons of the Trinity on behalf of the elect, before the foundation of the world. By the word "offices" we understand the whole of that part of this sacred compact which the Holy Spirit undertook to perform. Lest some should suppose that the application of such a term to the Third Person of the Godhead be derogatory to His ineffable majesty, let us point out that it by no means implies subordination or inferiority. It signifies literally a particular charge, trust, duty, or employment, conferred for some public or beneficial end. Hence we read of "the priest's office" (Ex. 28:1; Luke 1:8), the apostolic "office" (Rom. 11:13), etc.

There is then no impropriety in using the word "office" to express the several parts which the Son and the blessed Spirit undertook in the Covenant of Grace. As Persons in the Trinity they were equal; as covenanting Parties they were equal; and as They in infinite condescension, undertook to communicate to the church unutterable favors and blessings, Their kind offices, so graciously and voluntarily entered into, neither destroy nor diminish that original equality in which They from all eternity subsisted in the perfection and glory of the Divine Essence. As Christ's assumption of the "office" of "Servant" in no way tarnished or canceled His equality as the Son, so the Spirit's free undertaking the office of applying the benefits of the Everlasting Covenant (Covenant of Grace) to its beneficiaries in no way detracts from His essential and personal honor and glory.

The word "office," then, as applied to the covenant-work of the Holy Spirit, denotes that which He graciously undertook to perform by way of stipulated engagement and sets forth, under one comprehensive term, the whole of His blessed pledging and performances on behalf of the election of grace. To an enlightened understanding and a believing heart, there is in the Covenant itself—in the fact of it, and the provisions of it—something singularly marvelous and precious. That there should have been a Covenant at all—that the three Persons in the Godhead should have deigned to enter into a solemn compact on behalf of a section of the fallen, ruined, and guilty race of mankind should fill our minds with holy wonderment and adoration. How firm a foundation was thus laid for the salvation of the church. No room was allowed for contingencies, no place left for uncertainties; her being and well-being was forever secured by unalterable compact and eternal decree.

The Spirit's Covenant-Office: Sanctification

Now the "office-work" of the Holy Spirit in connection with this "everlasting Covenant, ordered in all things and sure" (2 Sam. 23:5), may be summed up in a single word, sanctification. The Third Person of the Holy Trinity agreed to sanctify, the objects of the Father's eternal choice, and of the Son's redemptive satisfaction. The Spirit's work of sanctification was just as needful, yea, as indispensable for the church's salvation, as was the obedience and blood-shedding of Christ. Adam's fall plunged the church into immeasurable depths of woe and wretchedness. The image of God in which her members had been created was defaced. Sin, like a loathsome leprosy, infected them to the very heart's core. Spiritual death spread itself with fatal effect over her every faculty. But the gracious Holy Spirit pledged Himself to sanctify such wretches, and frame and fit them to be partakers of holiness, and live forever in God's spotless presence.

Without the Spirit's sanctification the redemption of Christ would avail no man. True, a perfect atonement was made by Him and a perfect righteousness brought in, and so the persons of the elect are legally reconciled to God. But Jehovah is holy as well as just, and the employments and enjoyment of His dwelling-place are holy too. Holy angels there minister whose unceasing cry is, "Holy, holy, holy is the Lord of hosts" (Isa. 6:3). How then could unholy, unregenerated, unsanctified sinners dwell in that ineffable place into which "there shall in no way enter anything that defileth, neither whatsoever worketh abomination, or maketh a lie" (Rev. 21:27)? But O the wonder of covenant grace and covenant love! The vilest of sinners, the worst of wretches, the basest of mortals, can and will enter through the gates into the Holy City: "And such were some of you, but ye are washed, but ye are sanctified, but ye are justified in the name of the Lord Jesus and by the Spirit of our God" (1 Cor. 6:11).

From what has been said in the last paragraph it should be clear that sanctification is as indispensable as justification. Now there are many phases presented in Scripture of this important Truth of sanctification, into which we cannot here enter. Suffice it to say that aspect of it which is now before us is the blessed work of the Spirit upon the soul, whereby He internally makes the saints meet for their inheritance in the light (Col. 1:12): without this miracle of grace none can enter Heaven. "That which is born of the flesh is flesh" (1 John 3:6): no matter how it be educated and refined, no matter how disguised by religious ornamentation, it remains still flesh. It is like everything else which earth produces: no manipulation of art can change the original nature of the raw material.

No process of manufacture can transmute cotton into wool, or flax into silk: draw, twist, spin or weave, bleach and surface all we may, its nature remains the same. So men-made preachers and the whole corps of creature religionists may toil night and day to change flesh into spirit, they may work from the cradle to the grave to fit people for Heaven, but after all their labors to wash the Ethiopian white and to rub the spots out of the leopard, flesh is flesh still and cannot by any possibility enter the kingdom of God. Nothing but the supernatural operations of the Holy Spirit will avail. Not only is man polluted to the very core by sin original and actual, but there is in him an absolute incapability to understand, embrace or enjoy spiritual things (1 Cor. 2:14).

The imperative necessity, then, of the Spirit's work of sanctification lies not only in the sinfulness of man, but in the state of spiritual death whereby he is as unable to live, breathe, and act Godward as the corpse in the graveyard is unable to leave the silent tomb and move among the busy haunts of men. We indeed know little of the Word of God and little of our own hearts if we need proof of a fact which meets us at every turn; the vileness of our nature and the thorough deathliness of our carnal heart are so daily and hourly forced upon us that they are a such a matter of painful consciousness to the Christian, as if we should see the sickening sight of a slaughterhouse, or smell the death taint of a corpse.

Suppose a man is born blind: he has a natural incapacity of sight. No arguments, biddings, threats, or promises can make him see. But let the miracle be wrought: let the Lord touch the eyes with His Divine hand; he sees at once. Though he cannot explain how or why, he can say to all objectors, "One thing I know, that whereas I was blind, now I see" (John 9:25). And thus it is in the Spirit's work of sanctification, begun at regeneration, when a new life is given, a new capacity imparted, a new desire awakened. It is carried forward in his daily renewing (2 Cor. 4:16) and is completed at glorification. What we would specially emphasize is that whether the Spirit is convicting us, working repentance in us, breathing upon us the spirit of prayer, or taking of the things of Christ and showing them unto our joyful hearts, He is discharging His covenant-offices. May we render unto Him the praise and worship which is His due.

For most of the above we are indebted to some articles by the late J. C. Philpot.

The Holy Spirit During the Old Testament Ages

Much ignorance prevails today concerning this aspect of our subject. The crudest ideas are now entertained as to the relation between the Third Person of the Godhead and the Old Testament saints. Yet this is scarcely to be wondered at in view of the fearful confusion which obtains respecting their salvation, many supposing that they were saved in an entirely different way from what we are now. Nor need we be surprised at that, for this, in turn, is only another of the evil effects produced by the misguided efforts of those who have been so eager to draw as many contrasts as possible between the present dispensation and those which preceded it, to the disparaging of the earlier members of God's family. The Old Testament saints had far more in common with the New Testament saints than is generally supposed.

A verse which has been grossly perverted by many of our moderns is John 7:39, "The Holy Spirit was not yet given, because that Jesus was not yet glorified." It seems passing strange that with the Old Testament in their hands, some men should place the construction which they do upon those words. The words "was not yet given" can no more be understood absolutely than "Enoch was not" (Gen. 5:24); they simply mean that the Spirit had not yet been given in His full administrative authority. He was not yet publicly manifested here on earth. All believers, in every age, had been sanctified and comforted by Him, but the "ministration of the Spirit" (2 Cor. 3:8) was not at that time fully introduced; the outpouring of the Spirit, in the plentitude of His miraculous gifts, had not then taken place.

In Relation to Creation

Let us first consider, though very briefly, the work of the Spirit in connection with the old or material creation. Before the worlds were framed by the Word of God, and things which are seen were made out of things which do not appear (Heb. 11:3), when the whole mass of inanimate matter lay in one undistinguished chaos, "without form and void," we are told that, "the Spirit of God moved upon the face of the waters" (Gen. 1:2). There are other passages which ascribe the work of creation (in common with the Father and the Son), to His immediate agency. For example, we are told, "by His Spirit He hath garnished the heavens" (Job 26:13). Job was moved to confess, "The Spirit of God hath made me, and the breath of the Almighty hath given me life" (33:4). "Thou sendest forth Thy Spirit, they are created: and Thou renewest the face of the earth" (Ps. 104:30).

In Relation to Adam

Let us next contemplate the Holy Spirit in relation to Adam. As so much darkness now surrounds this subject, we must enter into it in greater detail. "Three things were required to render man fit unto that life to God for which he was made. First, an ability to discern the mind and wisdom of God with respect unto all the duty and obedience that God requires of him; as also for to know the nature and properties of God, as to believe Him the only proper object of all acts and duties of religious obedience, and an all-sufficient satisfaction and reward in this world, and to eternity. Secondly, a free, uncontrolled, unentangled, disposition to every duty of the law of his creation for living unto God. Thirdly, an ability of mind and will, with a readiness of compliance in his affections, for a regular performance of all duties and abstinence from all sin. These things belonged unto the integrity of his nature, with the uprightness of the state and condition wherein he was made. And all these things were the peculiar effects of the immediate operation of the Holy Spirit.

"Thus Adam may be said to have had the Spirit of God in his innocence. He had Him in these peculiar effects of His power and goodness, and he had Him according to the tenor of that covenant, whereby it was possible that he should utterly lose Him, as accordingly it came to pass. He had Him not by especial inhabitation, for the whole world was then the temple of God. In the Covenant of Grace, founded in the Person and on the mediation of Christ, it is otherwise. On whomsoever the Spirit of God is bestowed for the renovation of the image of God in him, He abides with him forever" (J. Owen, 1680).

The three things mentioned above by that eminent Puritan constituted the principal part of that "image of God" wherein man was created by the Spirit. Proof of this is seen in the fact that at regeneration the Holy Spirit restores those abilities in the souls of God's elect: "And hath put on the new man, which is renewed in knowledge, after the image of Him that created him" (Col. 3:10): that is, the spiritual knowledge which man lost at the Fall is, potentially, restored at the new birth; but it could not be restored or "renewed" if man had never possessed it!

The Holy Spirit

The "knowledge" with which the Holy Spirit endowed Adam was great indeed. Clear exemplification of this is seen in Genesis 2:19. Still, more conclusive evidence is found in Genesis 2:21-23: God put Adam into a deep sleep, took a rib out of his side, formed it into a woman, and then set her before him. On sight of her Adam said, "This is now bone of my bones, and flesh of my flesh." He knew who she was and her origin, and forthwith gave her a suitable name; and he could only have known all this by the Spirit of revelation and understanding.

That Adam was, originally, made a partaker of the Holy Spirit is quite evident to the writer from Genesis 2:7, "The Lord God formed man of the dust of the ground, and breathed into his nostrils the breath of life." If those words were interpreted in the light of the Analogy of Faith, they can mean nothing less than that the Triune God imparted the Holy Spirit unto the first man. In Ezekiel 37 we have a vivid parabolic picture of the regenerating of spiritual Israel. There we are told, "Prophesy unto the Wind, prophesy, son of man, and say to the Wind, Thus saith the LORD God, Come from the four winds, O Breath, and breathe upon these slain, that they may live. So I prophesied as He commanded me, and the Breath came unto them, and they lived" (vv. 9, 10). Again, we find the Savior, after His resurrection, "Breathed on them (the Apostles), and saith unto them, Receive ye the Holy Spirit" (John 20:22): that was the counterpart of Genesis 2:7: the one the original gift, the other the restoration of what was lost.

Rightly has it been said that "The doctrine that man was originally, though mutably, replenished with the Spirit, may be termed the deep fundamental thought of the Scripture doctrine of man. If the first and second Adam are so related that the first man was the analogue or figure of the second, as all admit on the authority of Scripture (Rom. 5:12-14), it is clear that, unless the first man possessed the Spirit, the last man, the Healer or Restorer of the forfeited inheritance, would not have been the medium of giving the Spirit, who was withdrawn on account of sin, and who could be restored only on account of the everlasting righteousness which Christ (Rom. 8:10) brought in" (G. Smeaton, 1880).

In Relation to the Nation Israel

Let us next observe the relation of the Holy Spirit unto the nation of Israel. A very striking and comprehensive statement was made by Nehemiah, when he reviewed the Lord's dealings with His people of old: "Thou gavest also Thy good Spirit to instruct them" (Neh. 8:20). He was, until quenched, upon the members of the Sanhedrin (Num. 11:16, 17). He came upon the judges (Judges 3:10; 6:34; 11:29; 15:14), upon the kings (1 Sam. 11:6; 16:13), and the Prophets. But note it is a great mistake to say, as many have done, that the Holy Spirit was never in any believer before Pentecost: Numbers 27:18, Nehemiah 9:30, 1 Peter 1:11 clearly prove otherwise. But alas, Israel "rebelled and vexed his Holy Spirit" (Isa. 63:10), as Stephen declared, "Ye do always resist the Holy Spirit: as your fathers did, so do ye" (Acts 7:51).

That the Holy Spirit indwelt saints under the Legal economy is clear from many considerations: how otherwise could they have been regenerated, had faith, been enabled to perform works acceptable to God? The Spirit prompted true prayer, inspired spiritual worship, produced His fruit in the lives of believers then (see Zech. 4:6) as much as He does now. We have "the same Spirit of faith" (2 Cor. 4:13) as they had. All the spiritual good which has ever been wrought in and through men must be ascribed unto the Holy Spirit. The Spirit was given to the Old Testament saints prospectively, as pardon of sin was given in view of the satisfaction which Christ was to render unto God.

The Holy Spirit and Christ

We are afraid that our treatment of the particular aspect of this many-sided theme which is now before us is rather too abstruse for some of our readers to follow, yet we trust they will kindly bear with us as we endeavor to write for those who are anxious for help on the deeper things of God.

The Deeper Things of God

As stated before, we are seeking to minister unto widely different classes, unto those with differing capacities, and therefore we wish to provide a varied spiritual menu. He who is hungry will not leave the table in disgust because one dish thereon appeals not to him. We ask their forbearance while we seek to give something like completeness to our exposition of the subject as a whole.

"As the humanity of Christ was assumed into the Hypostatic union, we may fitly say, on the one hand, that the Person of Christ was anointed, so far as the call to office was concerned; while we bear in mind, on the other hand, that it is the humanity that is anointed in as far as we contemplate the actual supplies of God's gifts and graces, aids and endowments, necessary to the execution of His office. But that we may not be engulfed in onesidedness, it must be also added that the Holy Spirit, according to the order of the Trinity, interposes His power only to execute the will of the Son

as to the unction of the Lord Jesus by the Spirit, it was different according to the three grades successively imparted. The first grade was at the incarnation; the second coincided with His baptism, the third and highest grade was at the ascension, when He sat down on His mediatorial throne, and received from the Father the gift of the Spirit to bestow upon His Church in abundant measure" (G. Smeaton).

The Spirit in the Incarnation and Baptism of Christ

We have already contemplated the first anointing of the Lord Jesus when, in His mother's womb, His humanity was endowed with all spiritual graces, and when through childhood and up to the age of 30 He was illuminated, guided, and preserved by the immediate operations of the Third Person in the Godhead. We come now to briefly consider His second anointing, when He was formally consecrated unto His public mission and Divinely endowed for His official work. This took place at the River Jordan, when He was baptized by His forerunner. Then it was, while emerging from the waters, that the heavens were opened, the Holy Spirit descended upon Him in the form of a dove, and the voice of the Father was heard testifying unto His infinite pleasure in His incarnate Son (Matthew 3:16, 17). All the references to that unique transaction call for close examination and prayerful study.

The first thing that is recorded after this is, "And Jesus being full of the Holy Spirit, returned from Jordan, and was led by the Spirit into the wilderness" (Luke 4:14). The reason why we are told this seems to be for the purpose of showing us that Christ's humanity was confirmed by the Spirit and made victorious over the devil by His power. Hence it is we read that right after the temptation, "And Jesus returned in the power of the Spirit into Galilee" (Luke 4:14). Next we are told that He entered the synagogue at Nazareth and read from Isaiah 61, "The Spirit of the Lord is upon Me, because He hath anointed Me to preach the Gospel to the poor; He hath sent Me to heal the broken-hearted, to preach deliverance to the captives, and recovering of sight to the blind, to set at liberty them that are bruised; to preach the acceptable year of the Lord," and declared, "This day is this Scripture fulfilled in your ears" (Luke 4:18, 19, 21).

Here, then, is to be seen the leading distinction between the first and second "grades" of Christ's "unction" from the Spirit. The first was for the forming of His human nature and the enduing it with perfect wisdom and faultless holiness. The second was to endow Him with supernatural powers for His great work. Thus the former was personal and private, the latter official and public; the one was bestowing upon Him of spiritual graces, the other imparting to Him ministerial gifts. His need for this double "anointing" lay in the creature-nature He had assumed and the servant-place which He had taken; and also as a public attestation from the Father of His acceptance of Christ's Person and His induction into His mediatorial office. Thus was fulfilled that ancient oracle, "The Spirit of the Lord shall rest upon Him, the Spirit of wisdom and understanding, the Spirit of counsel and might, the Spirit of knowledge and of the fear of the LORD; and shall make Him of quick understanding" (Isa. 11:2, 3).

"For He whom God hath sent speaketh the words of God; for God giveth not the Spirit by measure unto Him" (John 3:34). This at once brings out the pre-eminence of Christ, for He receives the Spirit as no mere man could. Observe the contrast pointed out by Ephesians 4:7, "But unto everyone of us is given grace according to the measure of the gift of Christ." In none but the

Mediator did "all the fullness of the Godhead" dwell "bodily" (Col. 2:9). The uniqueness of the Spirit's relation to our Lord comes out again in Romans 8:2, "For the law of *the Spirit of life in Christ Jesus* hath made me free from the law of sin and death." Note carefully the words we have italicized: not only does this statement reveal to us the source of all Christ's actions, but it intimates that more habitual grace dwells in Him than in all created beings.

The Spirit in the Ascension of Christ

The third degree of Christ's unction was reserved for His exaltation, and is thus described, "Therefore being by the right hand of God exalted, and having received of the Father the promise of the Holy Spirit, He hath shed forth this, which ye now see and hear" (Acts 2:33). This highest ride of unction, when Christ was "anointed with the oil of gladness above his fellows" (Ps. 45:7) and which became apparent at Pentecost, was an ascension-gift. The declaration which Peter gave of it was but a paraphrase of Psalm 68:18, "Thou hast ascended on high, Thou hast led captivity captive: Thou hast received gifts for men; yea, for the rebellious also, that the LORD might dwell among them." That bountiful supply of the Spirit was designed for the erecting and equipping of the New Testament church, and it was fitly bestowed after the ascension upon those for whom the Spirit was purchased.

Christ Bestows the Spirit

As Mediator, the Lord Jesus was anointed with the Holy Spirit for the execution of all His offices, and for the performance of all His mediatorial work. His right to send the Spirit into the hearts of fallen men was acquired by His atonement. It was the well-earned reward of all His toil and sufferings. One of the chief results of the perfect satisfaction which Christ offered to God on behalf of His people, was His right now to bestow the Spirit upon them. Of old it was promised Him, "By His knowledge shall My righteous Servant justify many, for He shall bear their iniquities: therefore will I divide Him a portion with the great, and He shall divide the spoil with the strong; because He hath poured out His soul unto death" (Isa. 53:11, 12). So, too, His forerunner had announced, "He shall baptize you with the Holy Spirit and fire" (Matthew 3:11).

What has just been said above is further borne out by Galatians 3:13, 14. "Christ hath redeemed us from the curse of the law, being made a curse for us ... that the blessing of Abraham might come on the Gentiles through Jesus Christ, that we might receive the promise of the Spirit through faith." The promised Spirit followed the great work of canceling the curse as the effect follows the cause. To give the Holy Spirit to men, clearly implied that their sins had been put away; see Leviticus 14:1-3, 17 for the type of this—the "oil" (emblem of the Spirit) placed upon the "blood"! Not only does Christ's right to bestow the Holy Spirit upon His redeemed intimate the cancellation of their sins, but it also clearly argues His Divine dignity, for no mere servant, however exalted his station, could act thus or confer such a Gift!

A Joint Mission

From the varied quotations which have been made from Scripture in reference to Christ's unction for all His offices, it sometimes appears as if He were in the subordinate position of needing direction, aid, and miraculous power for the purposes of His mission (Isa. 11:1-3; 61:1, 2, etc.); at other times He is said to have the Spirit (Rev. 3:1), to give the Spirit (Acts 2:33), to send the Spirit (John 15:26) as if the Spirit's operations were subordinated to the Son. But all difficulty is removed when we perceive, from the whole tenor of Scripture, that there was a conjoined mission in which the Son and the Spirit act together for the salvation of God's elect. The Son effected redemption—the Spirit reveals and applies it to all for whom it was purchased.

In writing on the Holy Spirit and Christ, it is to be understood that we are not now contemplating our Lord as the Second Person of the Trinity, but rather as the God-man Mediator, and the Holy Spirit not in His Godhead abstractly considered, but in His official discharge of the work assigned Him in the Everlasting Covenant. This is undoubtedly the most difficult aspect of our subject, yet it is very important that we should prayerfully strive after clear scriptural views thereof. To apprehend aright, even according to our present limited capacity, the relation between the Holy Spirit and the Redeemer, throws much light on some difficult problems, supplies the key to a number of perplexing passages in Holy Writ, and better enables us to understand the work of the Spirit in the saint.

"Come ye near unto Me, hear ye this; I have not spoken in secret from the beginning: from the time that it was, there am I: and now the Lord God and his Spirit hath sent Me" (Isa. 48:16). This remarkable verse presents to us the Lord Jesus speaking of old by the spirit of prophecy. He declares that He had always addressed the Nation in the most open manner, from the time when He appeared unto Moses at the burning bush and called Himself, "I am that I am" (Ex. 3); and He was constantly present with Israel as their Lord and Deliverer. And now the Father and the Spirit had sent Him to effect the promised spiritual deliverance of His people; sent Him in the likeness of sin's flesh, to preach the Gospel, fulfill the Law, and make a perfect satisfaction unto Divine justice for His church. Here, then, is a glorious testimony unto a Trinity of Persons in the Godhead: the Son of God is sent in human nature and as Mediator; Jehovah the Father and the Spirit are the Senders, and so is a proof of Christ's mission, commission, and authority, who came not of Himself, but was sent of God (John 8:42).

"The Lord hath created a new thing in the earth: A woman shall compass a man" (Jer. 31:22). Here we have one of the prophetic announcements of the wonder of the Divine incarnation, the eternal Word becoming flesh, a human body and soul being prepared for Him by the miraculous intervention of the Holy Spirit. Here the Prophet intimates that the creating power of God was to be put forth under which a woman was to compass a Man. The virgin Mary, under the overshadowing power of the Highest (Luke 1:35) was to conceive and bring forth a Child, without the help or cooperation of man. This transcendent wonder Isaiah calls a "sign" (7:14); Jeremiah "a new thing in the earth"; the New Testament record of which is, "When as his mother Mary was espoused to Joseph, before they came together, she was found with child of the Holy Spirit" (Mathew 1:18).

"And the Child grew, and waxed strong in spirit, filled with wisdom, and the grace of God was upon Him. And Jesus increased in wisdom and stature, and in favor with God and man" (Luke 2:40, 52). Not only was the humanity of Christ supernaturally begotten by the Holy Spirit, but it was "anointed" by Him (cf. Lev. 2:1 for the type), endued with all spiritual races. All the progress in the Holy Child's mental and spiritual development, all His advancement in knowledge and holiness must be ascribed unto the Spirit. "Progress," in the human nature which He deigned to assume, side by side with His own Divine perfection, is quite compatible, as Hebrews 2:14, 17 plainly intimate. As George Smeaton has so helpfully pointed out in his book, the Spirit's operations "formed the link between Christ's deity and humanity, perpetually imparting the full consciousness of personality, and making Him inwardly aware of His Divine Sonship at all times."

Thus the Spirit, at the incarnation, became the great guiding principle of all Christ's earthly history, and that, according to the order of operation that ever belongs to the Holy Trinity: all proceeds from the Father, through the Son, and is by the Holy Spirit. It was the Spirit who formed Christ's human nature, and directed the whole tenor of His earthly life. Nothing was undertaken but by the Spirit's directing, nothing was spoken but by His guidance, nothing executed but by His power. Unless this be steadfastly maintained, we are in grave danger of confounding the two natures of Christ, absorbing the one in the other instead of keeping them separate and distinct in our thoughts. Had His Deity been absorbed by His humanity, then grief, fear, and compassion had been impossible. The right use of the faculties of His soul owed their exercise to the Holy Spirit who fully controlled Him.

"From birth to baptism the Spirit directed His mental and moral development, and strengthened and kept Him through all the years of preparation and toil. He was in the Carpenter as truly as in the Messiah, and the work at the bench was as perfect as the sacrifice on the Cross" (S. Chadwick). At first sight, such a statement may seem to derogate from the personal honor of the Lord Jesus, but if we perceive that, according to the order of the Trinity, the Spirit exercises His power only to execute the will of the Father and the Son, then the seeming difficulty disappears. So far is the interposition of the Spirit's operations from interfering with the glory of the Son, it rather reveals Him the more conspicuously: that in the work of redemption the activities of the Spirit are next in order to those of the Son.

Misguided Theories

To this we may add another excerpt from G. Smeaton: "The two natures of our Lord actively concurred in every mediatorial act. If He assumed human nature in the true and proper sense of the term into union with His Divine Person, that position must be maintained. The Socinian objection that there could be no further need for the Spirit's agency, and, in fact, no room for it—if the Divine nature was active in the whole range of Christ's mediation—is meant to perplex the question, because these men deny the existence of any Divine nature in Christ's Person. That style of reasoning is futile, for the question simply is, What do the Scriptures teach? Do they affirm that Christ was anointed by the Spirit (Acts 10:38)? that He was led out into the wilderness by the Spirit? that He returned in the power of the Spirit to begin His public ministry? that He performed His miracles by the Spirit? and that, previously to His ascension, He gave commandments by the Spirit to His disciples whom He had chosen (Acts 1:2)?

"No warrant exists for anything akin to the Kenotic theory which denudes Him of the essential attributes of His Godhead, and puts His humanity on a mere level with that of other men. And as little warrant exists for denying the Spirit's work on Christ's humanity in every mediatorial act which He performed on earth or performs in Heaven. The unction of the Spirit must be traced in all His personal and official gifts. In Christ the Person and office coincide. In His Divine Person He was the substance of all the offices to which He was appointed, and these He was fitted by the Spirit to discharge. The offices would be nothing apart from Himself, and could have neither coherence nor validity without the underlying Person."

If the above still appears to derogate from the glory of our Lord's Person, most probably the difficulty is created by the objector's failing to realize the reality of the Son's humanity. The mystery is indeed great, and our only safeguard is to adhere strictly unto the several statements of Scripture thereon. Three things are to be kept steadily in view. First, in all things (sin excepted) the eternal Word was "made like unto his brethren" (Heb. 2:17): all His human faculties developed normally as He passed through infancy, childhood and youth. Second, His Divine nature underwent no change or modification when He became incarnate, yet it was not merged into His humanity, but preserved its own distinctness. Third, He was "anointed with the Spirit" (Acts 10:38), nay, He was the absolute receiver of the Spirit, poured on Him in such a plentitude, that it was not by measure (John 3:34).

The Advent of the Spirit

It is highly important we should closely observe how each of the Eternal Three has been at marked pains to provide for the honor of the other Divine Persons, and we must be as particular to give it to Them accordingly. How careful was the Father to duly guard the ineffable glory of the Darling of His bosom when He laid aside the visible insignia of His Deity and took upon Him the form of a servant: His voice was then heard more than once proclaiming, "This is my beloved Son." How constantly did the incarnate Son divert attention from Himself and direct it unto the One who had sent Him. In like manner, the Holy Spirit is not here to glorify Himself, but rather Him whose vicar and Advocate He is (John 16:14). Blessed is it then to mark how jealous both the Father and the Son have been to safeguard the glory and provide for the honor of the Holy Spirit.

The Importance of the Advent of the Spirit

"'If I go not away, the Comforter will not come' (John 16:7); He will not do these works while I am here, and I have committed all to Him. As My Father hath visibly 'committed all judgment unto the Son: that all men should honor the Son, even as they honor the Father' (John 5:22, 23), so I and my Father will send Him having committed all these things to Him, that all men might honor the Holy Spirit, even as they honor the Father and the Son. Thus wary and careful are everyone of the Persons to provide for the honor of each other in our hearts" (T. Goodwin, 1670).

The public advent of the Spirit, for the purpose of ushering in and administering the new covenant, was second in importance only unto the incarnation of our Lord, which was in order to the winding up of the old economy and laying the foundations of the new. When God designed the salvation of His elect, He appointed two great means: the gift of His Son for them, and the gift of His Spirit to them; thereby each of the Persons in the Trinity being glorified. Hence, from the first entrance of sin, there were two great heads to the promises which God gave His people: the sending of His Son to obey and die, the sending of His Spirit to make effectual the fruits of the former. Each of these Divine gifts was bestowed in a manner suited both to the august Giver Himself and the eminent nature of the gifts. Many and marked are the parallels of correspondence between the advent of Christ and the advent of the Spirit.

Parallels in the Advents of Christ and of the Spirit

1. God appointed that there should be a signal coming accorded unto the descent of Each from Heaven to earth for the performance of the work assigned Them. Just as the Son was present with the redeemed Israelites long before His incarnation (Acts 7:37, 38; 1 Cor. 10:4), yet God decreed for Him a visible and more formal advent, which all of His people knew of—so though the Holy Spirit was given to work regeneration in men all through the Old Testament era (Neh. 9:20, etc.), and moved the Prophets to deliver their messages (2 Peter 1:21), nevertheless God ordained that He should have a coming in state, in a solemn manner, accompanied by visible tokens and glorious effects.

2. Both the advents of Christ and of the Spirit were the subjects of Old Testament prediction. During the past century much has been written upon the Messianic prophecies, but the promises which God gave concerning the coming of the Holy Spirit constitute a theme which is generally neglected. The following are among the principal pledges which God made that the Spirit should be given unto and poured out upon His saints: Psalm 68:18; Proverbs 1:23; Isaiah 32:15; Ezekiel 36:26, 39:29; Joel 2:28; Haggai 2:9: in them the descent of the Holy Spirit was as definitely announced as was the incarnation of the Savior in Isaiah 7:14.

3. Just as Christ had John the Baptist to announce His incarnation and to prepare His way, so the Holy Spirit had Christ Himself to foretell His coming, and to make ready the hearts of His own for His advent.

4. Just as it was not until "the fullness of time had come" that God sent forth His Son (Gal. 4:4), so it was not until "the day of Pentecost was fully come" that God sent forth His Spirit (Acts 2:1).

5. As the Son became incarnate in the holy land, Palestine, so the Spirit descended in Jerusalem.

6. Just as the coming of the Son of God into this world was auspiciously signalized by mighty wonders and signs, so the descent of God the Spirit was attended and attested by stirring displays of Divine power. The advent of Each was marked by supernatural phenomena: the angel choir (Luke 2:13) found its counterpart in the "sound from Heaven" (Acts 2:1), and the Shekinah "glory" (Luke 2:9) in the "tongues of fire" (Acts 2:3).

7. As an extraordinary star marked the "house" where the Christ-child was (Matthew 2:9), so a Divine shaking marked the "house" to which the Spirit had come (Acts 2:2).

8. In connection with the advent of Christ there was both a private and a public aspect to it: in like manner, too, was it in the giving of the Spirit. The birth of the Savior was made known unto a few, but when He was to "be made manifest to Israel" (John 1:31), He was publicly identified, for at His baptism the heavens were opened, the Spirit descended upon Him in the form of a dove, and the voice of the Father audibly owned Him as His Son. Correspondingly, the Spirit was communicated to the Apostles privately, when the risen Savior "breathed on, and said unto them, Receive ye the Holy Spirit" (John 20:22); and later He came publicly on the day of Pentecost when all the great throng then in Jerusalem were made aware of His descent (Acts 2:32-36).

9. The advent of the Son was in order to His becoming incarnate, when the eternal Word was made flesh (John 1:14); so, too, the advent of the Spirit was in order to His becoming incarnate in Christ's redeemed: as the Savior had declared to them, the Spirit of truth "shall be in you" (John 14:17). This is a truly marvelous parallel. As the Son of God became man, dwelling in a human "temple" (John 2:19), so the Third Person of the Trinity took up His abode in men, to whom it is said, "Know ye not that ye are the temple of God, and that the Spirit of God dwelleth in you?" (1 Cor. 3:16). As the Lord Jesus said to the Father, "A body hast Thou prepared Me" (Heb. 10:5), so the Spirit could say to Christ, "A body hast Thou prepared Me" (see Eph. 2:22).

10. When Christ was born into this world, we are told that Herod "was troubled and all Jerusalem with him" (Matthew 2:3); in like manner, when the Holy Spirit was given we read, "And there were dwelling at Jerusalem Jews, devout men out of every nation under heaven. Now when this was noised abroad, the multitude came together, and were troubled in mind" (Acts 2:5, 6).

11. It had been predicted that when Christ should appear He would be unrecognized and unappreciated (Isa. 53), and so it came to pass. In like manner, the Lord Jesus declared, "The Spirit of truth, whom the world cannot receive, because it seeth Him not, neither knoweth Him" (John 14:17).

12. As the Messianic claims of Christ were called into question, so the advent of the Spirit was at once challenged: "They were all amazed and were in doubt, saying one to another, What meaneth this?" (Acts 2:12).

13. The analogy is yet closer: as Christ was termed "a winebibber" (Matthew 11:19), so of those filled with the Spirit it was said, "These men are full of new wine" (Acts 2:13)!

14. As the public advent of Christ was heralded by John the Baptist (John 1:29), so the meaning of the public descent of the Spirit was interpreted by Peter (Acts 2:15-36).

15. God appointed unto Christ the executing of a stupendous work, even that of purchasing the redemption of His people; even so to the Spirit has been assigned the momentous task of effectually applying to His elect the virtues and benefits of the atonement.

16. As in the discharge of His work the Son honored the Father (John 14:10), so in the fulfillment of His mission the Spirit glorifies the Son (John 16:13, 14).

17. As the Father paid holy deference unto the Son by bidding the disciples, "hear ye him" (Mart. 17:5), in like manner the Son shows respect for His Paraclete by saying, "He that hath an ear, let him hear what the Spirit saith unto the churches" (Rev. 2:7).

18. As Christ committed His saints into the safe-keeping of the Holy Spirit (John 16:7; 14:16), so the Spirit will yet deliver up those saints unto Christ, as the word "receive" in John 14:3 plainly implies. We trust that the reader will find the same spiritual delight in perusing this chapter as the writer had in preparing it.

The Meaning of the Advent of the Spirit

At Pentecost the Holy Spirit came as He had never come before. Something then transpired which inaugurated a new era for the world, a new power for righteousness, a new basis for fellowship. On that day the fearing Peter was transformed into the intrepid evangelist. On that day the new wine of Christianity burst the old bottles of Judaism, and the Word went forth in a multiplicity of Gentile tongues. On that day more souls seem to have been truly regenerated, than during all the three and one half years of Christ's public ministry. What had happened? It is not enough to say that the Spirit of God was given, for He had been given long before, both to individuals and the nation of Israel (Neh. 9:20; Hag. 2:5); no, the pressing question is, In what sense was He then given? This leads us to carefully consider the meaning of the Spirit's advent.

1. It was the fulfillment of the Divine promise. First, of the Father Himself. During the Old Testament dispensation, He declared, again and again, that He would pour out the Spirit upon His people (see Prov. 1:23; Isa. 32:15; Joel 2:28, etc.), and now these gracious declarations were accomplished. Second,

of John the Baptist. When he was stirring the hearts of multitudes by his call to repentance and his demand of baptism, many thought he must be the long-expected Messiah, but he declared unto them, "I indeed baptize you with water, but one mightier than I cometh, the latchet of whose shoes I am not worthy to unloose: He shall baptize you with the Holy Spirit and with fire" (Luke 3:15, 16). Accordingly He did so on the day of Pentecost, as Acts 2:32, 33 plainly shows. Third, of Christ. Seven times over the Lord Jesus avowed that He would give or send the Holy Spirit: Luke 24:49; John 7:37-39; 14:16-19; 14:26; 15:26; 16:7; Acts 1:5, 8. From these we may particularly notice, "When the Comforter is come, whom I will send unto you from the Father ... He shall testify of Me" (John 15:26): "It is expedient for you that I go away; for if I go not away, the Comforter will not come unto you; but if I depart, I will send Him unto you" (John 16:7).

That which took place in John 20:22 and in Acts 2 was the fulfillment of those promises. In them we behold the faith of the Mediator: He had appropriated the promise which the Father had given Him, "Therefore being by the right hand of God exalted, and having received of the Father the promise of the Holy Spirit, He hath shed forth this, which ye now see and hear" (Acts 2:33)—it was by faith's anticipation the Lord Jesus spoke as He did in the above passage.

"The Holy Spirit was God's ascension gift to Christ, that He might be bestowed by Christ, as His ascension gift to the church. Hence Christ had said, 'Behold, I send the promise of My Father upon you.' This was the promised gift of the Father to the Son, and the Savior's promised gift to His believing people. How easy now to reconcile the apparent contradiction of Christ's earlier and later words: 'I will pray the Father and He shall give you another Comforter'; and then, afterward, 'If I depart I will send Him unto you.' The Spirit was the Father's answer to the prayer of the Son; and so the gift was transferred by Him to the mystical body of which He is the head" (A. T. Pierson in The Acts of the Holy Spirit).

2. It was the fulfillment of an important Old Testament type. It is this which explains to us why the Spirit was given on the day of "Pentecost," which was one of the principal religious feasts of Israel. Just as there was a profound significance to Christ's dying on Passover Day (giving us the antitype of Ex. 12), so there was in the coming of the Spirit on the 50th day after Christ's resurrection. The type is recorded in Leviticus 23, to which we can here make only the briefest allusion. In Leviticus 23:4 we read, "These are the feasts of the Lord."

The Holy Spirit

The first of them is the Passover (v. 5) and the second "unleavened bread" (v. 6, etc.). The two together speaking of the sinless Christ offering Himself as a sacrifice for the sins of His people. The third is the "wave sheaf" (v. 10, etc.) which was the "firstfruits of the harvest" (v. 10), presented to God "on the morrow after the (Jewish) Sabbath" (v. 11), a figure of Christ's resurrection (1 Cor. 15:23).

The fourth is the feast of "weeks" (see Ex. 34:22; Deut. 16:10, 16) so-called because of the seven complete weeks of Leviticus 23:15; also known as "Pentecost" (which means "Fiftieth") because of the "fifty days" of Leviticus 23:16. It was then the balance of the harvest began to be gathered in. On that day Israel was required to present unto God "two wave loaves," which were also designated "the first-fruits unto the Lord" (Lev. 23:17). The antitype of which was the saving of the 3,000 on the day of Pentecost: the "firstfruits" of Christ's atonement, compare James 1:18. The first loaf represented those redeemed from among the Jews, the second loaf was anticipatory and pointed to the gathering in of God's elect from among the Gentiles, begun in Acts 10.

3. ft was the beginning of a new dispensation. This was plainly intimated in the type of Leviticus 23, for on the day of Pentecost Israel was definitely required to offer a "new meal offering unto the Lord" (v. 16). Still more clearly was it fore-announced in a yet more important and significant type, namely, that of the beginning of the Mosaic economy, which took place only when the nation of Israel formally entered into covenant relationship with Jehovah at Sinai. Now it is exceedingly striking to observe that just 50 days elapsed from the time when the Hebrews emerged from the house of bondage till they received the Law from the mouth of Moses. They left Egypt on the 15th of the first month (Num. 33:3), and arrived at Sinai the first of the third month (Ex. 19:1, note "the same day"), which would be the forty-sixth. The next day Moses went up into the mount, and three days later the law was delivered (Ex. 19:11)! And just as there was a period of 50 days from Israel's deliverance from Egypt until the beginning of the Mosaic economy, so the same length of time followed the resurrection of Christ (when His people were delivered from Hell) to the beginning of the Christian economy!

That a new dispensation commenced at Pentecost further appears from the "tongues like as office" (Acts 2:1). When John the Baptist announced that Christ would baptize, "with the Holy Spirit and with fire," the last words might have suggested material burning to any people except Jews, but in their minds far other thoughts would be awakened. To them it would recall the scene when their great progenitor asked God, who promised he should inherit that land wherein he was a stranger, "Lord, whereby shall I know that I shall inherit it?" The answer was "Behold a smoking furnace and a burning lamp . . ." (Gen. 15:17). It would recall the fire which Moses saw in the burning bush. It would recall the "pillar of fire" which guided by night, and the Shekinah which descended and filled the tabernacle. Thus, in the promise of baptism by fire they would at once recognize the approach of a new manifestation of the presence and power of God!

Again—when we read that, "there appeared unto them cloven tongues like as of fire, and it sat upon each of them" (Acts 2:2), further evidence is found that a new dispensation had now commenced. "The word 'sat' in Scripture marks an ending and a beginning. The process of preparation is ended and the established order has begun. It marks the end of creation and the beginning of normal forces. 'In six days the Lord made Heaven and earth, the sea, and all that in them is, and rested the seventh day.' There is no weariness in God. He did not rest from fatigue: what it means is that all creative work was accomplished. The same figure is used of the Redeemer. Of Him it is said 'when He had made purification for sins (He) sat down on the right hand of the Majesty on high.' No other priesthood had sat down. The priests of the Temple ministered standing because their ministry was provisional and preparatory, a parable and prophecy. Christ's own ministry was part of the preparation for the coming of the Spirit. Until He 'sat down' in glory, there could be no dispensation of the Spirit . . . When the work of redemption was complete, the Spirit was given, and when He came he 'sat.' He reigns in the Church as Christ reigns in the Heavens" (S. Chadwick in *The Way to Pentecost*).

"There are few incidents more illuminating than that recorded in 'the last day of the feast' in John 7:37-39. The feast was that of Tabernacles. The feast proper lasted seven days, during which all Israel dwelt in booths. Special sacrifices were offered and special rites observed. Every morning one of the priests brought water from the pool of Siloam, and amidst the sounding of trumpets and other demonstrations of joy, the water was poured upon the altar. The rite was a celebration and a prophecy. It commemorated the miraculous supply of water in the wilderness, and it bore witness to the expectation of the coming of the Spirit. On the seventh day the ceremony of the poured water ceased, but the eighth was a day of holy convocation, the greatest day of all.

"On that day there was no water poured upon the altar, and it was on the waterless day that Jesus stood on the spot and cried, saying: 'If any man thirst, let him come unto Me and drink.' Then He added those words: 'He that believeth on Me, as the Scripture has said, from within him shall flow rivers of living water.' The Apostle adds the interpretative comment: 'But this spake He of the Spirit, which they that believe on Him were to receive: for the Spirit was not given because Jesus was not yet glorified.' 'As the scripture hath said.' There is no such passage in the Scripture as that quoted, but the prophetic part of the water ceremony was based upon certain Old Testament symbols and prophecies in which water flowed forth from Zion to cleanse, renew, and fructify the world. A study of Joel 3:18 and Ezekiel 47 will supply the key to the meaning both of the rite and our Lord's promise.

"The Holy Spirit was 'not yet given,' but He was promised, and His coming should be from the place of blood, the altar of sacrifice. Calvary opened the fountain from which poured forth the blessing of Pentecost" (S. Chadwick).

4. It was the Grace of God flowing unto the Gentiles. We have considered the meaning of the Spirit's descent, and pointed out that it was the fulfillment of Divine promise, the accomplishment of Old Testament types, and the beginning of a new dispensation. It was also the Grace of God flowing unto the Gentiles. But first let us observe and admire the marvelous grace of God extended unto the Jews themselves. In His charge to the Apostles, the Lord Jesus gave orders that "repentance and remission of sins should be preached in His name among all nations, beginning at Jerusalem" (Luke 24:47), not because the Jews had any longer a covenant standing before God—for the Nation was abandoned by Him before the crucifixion—see Matthew 23:38—but in order to display His matchless mercy and sovereign benignity. Accordingly, in the Acts we see His love shining forth in the midst of the rebellious city. In the very place where the Lord Jesus had been slain the full Gospel was now preached, and 3,000 were quickened by the Holy Spirit.

But the Gospel was to be restricted to the Jews no longer. Though the Apostles were to commence their testimony in Jerusalem, yet Christ's glorious and all-efficacious Name was to be proclaimed "among all nations." The earnest of this was given when "devout men out of every nation under heaven" (Acts 2:5) exclaimed, "How hear we every man in his own tongue?" (v. 8). It was an entirely new thing. Until this time, God had used Hebrew, or a modification of it. Thus Bullinger's view that a new "Jewish" dispensation (the "Pentecostal") was then inaugurated is Divinely set aside. What occurred in Acts 2 was a part reversal and in blessed contrast from what is recorded in Genesis 11. There we find "the tongues were divided to destroy an evil unity, and to show God's holy hatred of Babel's iniquity." In Acts 2 we have grace at Jerusalem, and a new and precious unity, suggestive of another building (Mathew 16:18), with living stones—contrast the 'bricks' of Genesis

11:3 and its tower (P. W. Heward). In Genesis the dividing of tongues was in judgment; in Acts 2 the cloven tongues were in grace; and in Revelation 7:9, 10 we see men of all tongues in glory.

The Purpose of the Advent of the Spirit

We next consider the purpose of the Spirit's descent.

1. To witness unto Christ's exaltation. Pentecost was God's seal upon the Messiahship of Jesus. In proof of His pleasure in and acceptance of the sacrificial work of His Son, God raised Him from the dead, exalted Him to His own right hand, and gave Him the Spirit to bestow upon His Church (Acts 2:33). It has been beautifully pointed out by another, that, on the hem of the ephod worn by the high priest of Israel were golden bells and pomegranates (Ex. 28:33, 34). The sound of the bells (and that which gave them sound was their tongues) furnished evidence that he was alive while serving in the sanctuary. The high priest was a type of Christ (Heb. 8:1); the holy place was a figure of Heaven (Heb. 9:24); the "sound from Heaven" and the speaking "in tongues" (Acts 2:2, 4) were a witness that our Lord was alive in Heaven, ministering there as the High Priest of His people.

2. To take Christ's place. This is clear from His own words to the Apostles, "And I will pray the Father, and He shall give you another Comforter, that He may abide with you forever" (John 14:16). Until then, Christ had been their "Comforter," but He was soon to return to Heaven; nevertheless, as He went on to assure them, "I will not leave you orphans, I will come to you" (marginal rendering of John 14:18); He did "come" to them corporately after His resurrection, but He "came" to them spiritually and abidingly in the Person of His Deputy on the day of Pentecost. The Spirit, then, fills the place on earth of our absent Lord in Heaven, with this additional advantage, that, during the days of His flesh the Savior's body confined Him unto one location, whereas the Holy Spirit—not having assumed a body as the mode of His incarnation—is equally and everywhere resident in and abiding with every believer.

3. To further Christ's cause. This is plain from His declaration concerning the Comforter: "He shall glorify Me" (John 16:14). The word "Paraclete" (translated "Comforter" all through the Gospel) is also rendered "Advocate" in I John 2:1, and an "advocate" is one who appears as the representative of another. The Holy Spirit is here to interpret and vindicate Christ, to administer for Christ in His Church and Kingdom. He is here to accomplish His redeeming purpose in the world. He fills the mystical Body of Christ, directing its movements, controlling its members, inspiring its wisdom, supplying its strength. The Holy spirit becomes to the believer individually

and the church collectively all that Christ would have been had He remained on earth. Moreover, He seeks out each one of those for whom Christ died, quickens them into newness of life, convicts them of sin, gives them faith to lay hold of Christ, and causes them to grow in grace and become fruitful.

It is important to see that the mission of the Spirit is for the purpose of continuing and completing that of Christ's. The Lord Jesus declared, "I am come to send fire on the earth: and what will I, if it be already kindled? But I have a baptism to be baptized with; and how am I straitened till it be accomplished!" (Luke 12:49, 50). The preaching of the Gospel was to be like "fire on the earth," giving light and warmth to human hearts; it was "kindled" then, but would spread much more rapidly later. Until His death Christ was "straitened": it did not consist with God's purpose for the Gospel to be preached more openly and extensively; but after Christ's resurrection, it went forth unto all nations. Following the ascension, Christ was no longer "straitened" and the Spirit was poured forth in the plenitude of His power.

4. To endue Christ's servants. "Tarry ye in Jerusalem until ye be endued with power from on high" (Luke 24:49) had been the word of Christ to His Apostles. Sufficient for the disciple to be as his Master. He had waited, waited till He was 30, ere He was "anointed to preach good tidings" (Isa. 61:1). The servant is not above his Lord: if He was indebted to the Spirit for the power of His ministry, the Apostles must not attempt their work without the Spirit's unction. Accordingly they waited, and the Spirit came upon them. All was changed: boldness supplanted fear, strength came instead of weakness, ignorance gave place to wisdom, and mighty wonders were wrought through them.

Unto the Apostles whom He had chosen, the risen Savior "commanded them that they should not depart from Jerusalem, but wait for the promise of the Father," assuring them that "Ye shall receive power after that the Holy Spirit is come unto you; and ye shall be witnesses unto Me both in Jerusalem, and in all Samaria, and unto the uttermost part of the earth" (Acts 1:2, 4, 8). Accordingly, we read that, "And when the day of Pentecost was fully come, they were all with one accord in one place" (Acts 2:1): their unity of mind evidently looked back to the Lord's command and promise, and their trustful expectancy of the fulfillment thereof. The Jewish "day" was from sunset unto the following sunset, and as what took place here in Acts 2 occurred during the early hours of the morning—probably soon after sunrise—we are told that the day of Pentecost was "fully come." The Outward Marks of the Spirit's Advent

The outward marks of the Spirit's advent were three in number: the "sound from Heaven as of a rushing mighty wind," the "cloven tongues as of fire," and the speaking "with other tongues as the Spirit gave them utterance." Concerning the precise signification of these phenomena, and the practical bearing of them on us today, there has been wide difference of opinion, especially during the past 30 years. Inasmuch as God Himself has not seen fit to furnish us with a full and detailed explanation of them, it behooves all interpreters to speak with reserve and reverence. According to our own measure of light, we shall endeavor briefly to point out some of those things which appear to be most obvious.

First, the "rushing mighty wind" which filled all the house was the collective sign, in which, apparently, all the 120 of Acts 1:15 shared. This was an emblem of the invincible energy with which the Third Person of the Trinity works upon the hearts of men, bearing down all opposition before Him, in a manner which cannot be explained (John 3:8), but which is at once apparent by the effects produced. Just as the course of a hurricane may be clearly traced after it has passed, so the transforming work of the Spirit in regeneration is made unmistakably manifest unto all who have eyes to see spiritual things.

Second, "there appeared unto them cloven tongues like as of fire, and it sat upon each of them" (Acts 2:3), that is, upon the Twelve, and upon them alone. The proof of this is conclusive. First, it was to the Apostles only that the Lord spoke in Luke 24:49. Second, to them only did He, by the Spirit, give commandments after His resurrection (Acts 1:2). Third, to them only did He give the promise of Acts 1:8. Fourth, at the end of Acts 1 we read, "he (Matthias) was numbered with the eleven Apostles." Acts 2 opens with "And" connecting it with 1:26 and says, "they (the Twelve) were all with one accord in one place" and on them the Spirit now "sat" (Acts 2:3). Fifth, when the astonished multitude came together they exclaimed, "Are not all these which speak Galileans?" (Acts 2:7), namely, the "men (Greek, "males") of Galilee" of 1:11! Sixth, in Acts 2:14, 15, we read, "But Peter standing up with the eleven lifted up his voice and said unto them, "Ye men of Galilee and all ye that dwell in Judea, be this known unto you and hearken unto my words: For these are not drunk"—the word "these" can only refer to the "eleven" standing up with Peter!

These "cloven tongues like as of fire" which descended upon the Apostles was the individual sign, the Divine credential that they were the authorized ambassadors of the enthroned Lamb. The baptism of the Holy Spirit was a baptism of fire. " 'Our God is a consuming fire.' The elect sign of His presence is the fire unkindled of earth, and the chosen symbol of His approval is the sacred flame: covenant and sacrifice, sanctuary and dispensation were sanctified and approved by the descent of fire. 'The God that answereth by fire, he is the God' (1 Kings 18:24). That is the final and universal test of Deity. Jesus Christ came to bring fire on the earth. The symbol of Christianity is not a Cross, but a Tongue of Fire" (Samuel Chadwick).

Third, the Apostles, "speaking with other tongues" were the public sign. 1 Corinthians 14:22 declares "tongues are for a sign, not to them that believe, but to them that believe not," and as the previous verse (where Isa. 28:11 is quoted) so plainly shows, they were a sign unto unbelieving Israel. A striking illustration and proof of this is found in Acts 11, where Peter sought to convince his skeptical brethren in Jerusalem that God's grace was now flowing forth unto the Gentiles: it was his description of the Holy Spirit's falling upon Cornelius and his household (Acts 11:15-18 and cf. 10:45, 46) which convinced them. It is highly significant that the Pentecostal type of Leviticus 23:22 divided the harvest into three degrees and stages: the "reaping" or main part, corresponding to Acts 2 at Jerusalem; the "corners of the field" corresponding to Acts 10 at "Caesarea Philippi," which was in the corner of Palestine; and the "gleaning" for "the stranger" corresponding to Acts 19 at Gentile Ephesus! These were the only three occasions of "tongues" recorded in Acts.

Signs in Relation to "The Pentecostal Movement"

It is well known to some of our readers that during the last generation many earnest souls have been deeply exercised by what is known as "the Pentecostal movement," and the question is frequently raised as to whether or not the strange power displayed in their meetings, issuing in unintelligible sounds called "tongues," is the genuine gift of the Spirit. Those who have joined the movement—some of them godly souls, we believe—insist that not only is the gift genuine, but it is the duty of all Christians to seek the same. But surely such seem to overlook the fact that it was not any "unknown tongue" which was spoken by the Apostles: foreigners who heard them had no difficulty in understanding what was said (Acts 2:8).

If what has just been said be not sufficient, then let our appeal be unto 2 Timothy 3:16, 17. God has now fully revealed His mind to us: all that we need to "thoroughly furnish" us "unto all good works" is already in our hands! Personally the writer would not take the trouble to walk into the next room to hear any person deliver a message which he claimed was inspired by the Holy Spirit; with the completed Scriptures in our possession, nothing more is required except for the Spirit to interpret and apply them. Let it also be duly observed that there is not a single exhortation in all the Epistles of the New Testament that the saints should seek "a fresh Pentecost," no, not even to the carnal Corinthians or the legal Galatians.

As a sample of what was believed by the early "fathers" we quote the following: "Augustine saith, 'Miracles were once necessary to make the world believe the Gospel, but he who now seeks a sign that he may believe is a wonder, yea a monster.' Chrysostom concludeth upon the same grounds that, 'There is now in the Church no necessity of working miracles,' and calls him 'a false prophet' who now takes in hand to work them" (From W. Perkins, 1604).

In Acts 2:16 we find Peter was moved by God to give a general explanation of the great wonders which had just taken place. Jerusalem was, at this time of the feast, filled with a great concourse of people. The sudden sound from Heaven "as of a rushing mighty wind," filling the house where the Apostles were gathered together, soon drew there a multitude of people; and as they, in wonderment, heard the Apostles speak in their own varied languages, they asked, "What meaneth this?" (Acts 2:12). Peter then declared, "This is that which was spoken of by the Prophet Joel." The prophecy given by Joel (2:28-32) now began to receive its fulfillment, the latter part of which we believe is to be understood symbolically.

Application

And what is the bearing of all this upon us today? We will reply in a single sentence: the advent of the Spirit followed the exaltation of Christ: if then we desire to employ more of the Spirit's power and blessing, we must give Christ the throne of our hearts and crown Him the Lord of our lives.

Having dwelt upon the doctrinal and dispensational aspects of our subject, next we hope to take the "practical" and "experimental" bearings of it.

The Work of the Spirit

It is a great mistake to suppose that the works of the Spirit are all of one kind, or that His operations preserve an equality as to degree. To insist that they are and do would be ascribing less freedom to the Third Person of the Godhead than is enjoyed and exercised by men. There is variety in the activities of all voluntary agents: even human beings are not confined to one sort of work, nor to the production of the same kind of effects; and where they design so to do, they moderate them as to degrees according to their power and pleasure. Much more so is it with the Holy Spirit. The nature and kind of His works are regulated by His own will and purpose. Some He executes by the touch of His finger (so to speak), in others He puts forth His hand, while in yet others (as on the day of Pentecost) He lays bare His arm. He works by no necessity of His nature, but solely according to the pleasure of His will (1 Cor. 12: 11).

Upon Both the Unsaved and the Saved

Many of the works of the Spirit, though perfect in kind and fully accomplishing their design, are wrought by Him upon and within men who, nevertheless, are not saved. "The Holy Spirit is present with many as to powerful operations, with whom He is not present as to gracious inhabitation. Or, many are made partakers of Him in His spiritual gifts, who are not made partakers of Him in His saving grace: Matthew 7:22, 23" (John Owen on Heb. 6:4). The light which God furnishes different souls varies considerably, both in kind and degree. Nor should we be surprised at this in view of the adumbration in the natural world: how wide is the difference between the glimmering of the stars from the radiance of the full moon, and that again from the shining of the midday sun. Equally wide is the gulf which separates the savage with his faint illumination of conscience from one who has been educated under a Christian ministry, and greater still is the difference between the spiritual understanding of the wisest unregenerate professor and the feeblest babe in Christ; yet each has been a subject of the Spirit's operations.

"The Holy Spirit works in two ways. In some men's hearts He works with restraining grace only, and the restraining grace, though it will not save them, is enough to keep them from breaking out into the open and corrupt vices in which some men indulge who are totally left by the restraints of the Spirit . ... God the Holy Spirit may work in men some good desires and feelings, and yet have no design of saving them. But mark, none of these feelings are things that accompany salvation, for if so, they would be continued. But He does not work Omnipotently to save, except in the persons of His own elect, whom He assuredly bringeth unto Himself. I believe, then, that the trembling of Felix is to be accounted for by the restraining grace of the Spirit quickening his conscience and making him tremble" (C. H. Spurgeon on Acts 24:25).

The Holy Spirit has been robbed of much of His distinctive glory through Christians failing to perceive His varied workings. In concluding that the operations of the blessed Spirit are confined unto God's elect, they have been hindered from offering to Him that praise which is His due for keeping this wicked world a fit place for them to live. Few today realize how much the children of God owe to the Third Person of the Trinity for holding in leash the children of the Devil, and preventing them from utterly consuming Christ's church on earth. It is true there are comparatively few texts which specifically refer to the distinctive Person of the Spirit as reigning over the wicked, but once it is seen that in the Divine economy all is from God the Father, all is through God the Son, and all is by God the Spirit, each is given His proper and separate place in our hearts and thoughts.

The Spirit's Operation in the Non-elect

Let us, then, now point out a few of the Spirit's general and inferior operations in the non-elect, as distinguished from His special and superior works in the redeemed.

1. In restraining evil. If God should leave men absolutely to their own natural corruptions and to the power of Satan (as they fully deserve to be, as He will in Hell, and as He would now but for the sake of His elect), all show of goodness and morality would be entirely banished from the earth: men would grow past feeling in sin, and wickedness would swiftly and entirely swallow up the whole world. This is abundantly clear from Genesis 6:3, 4, 5, 12. But He who restrained the fiery furnace of Babylon without quenching it, He who prevented the waters of the Red Sea from flowing without changing their nature, now hinders the working of natural corruption without mortifying it. Vile as the world is, we have abundant cause to adore and praise the Holy Spirit that it is not a thousand times worse.

The Holy Spirit

The world hates the people of God (John 15:19): why, then, does it not devour them? What is it that holds back the enmity of the wicked against the righteous? Nothing but the restraining power of the Holy Spirit. In Psalm 14:1-3 we find a fearful picture of the utter depravity of the human race. Then in verse 4 the Psalmist asks, "Have all the workers of iniquity no knowledge? who eat up my people as they eat bread, and call not upon the Lord." To which answer is made, "There were they in great fear: for God is in the generation of the righteous" (v. 5). It is the Holy Spirit who places that "great fear" within them, to keep them back from many outrages against God's people. He curbs their malice. So completely are the reprobate shackled by His almighty hand, that Christ could say to Pilate, "thou couldest have no power against me, except it were given thee from above" (John 19:11)!

2. In inciting to good actions. All the obedience of children to parents, all the true love between husbands and wives, is to be attributed unto the Holy Spirit. Whatever morality and honesty, unselfishness and kindness, submission to the powers that be and respect for law and order which is still to be found in the world, must be traced back to the gracious operations of the Spirit. A striking illustration of His benign influence is found in 1 Samuel 10:26, "Saul also went home to Gibeah: and there went with him a band of men, whose hearts God (the Spirit) had touched." Men's hearts are naturally inclined to rebellion, are impatient against being ruled over, especially by one raised out of a mean condition among them. The Lord the Spirit inclined the hearts of those men to be subject unto Saul, gave them a disposition to obey him. Later the Spirit touched the heart of Saul to spare the life of David, melting him to such an extent that he wept (1 Sam. 24:16). In like manner, it was the Holy Spirit who gave the Hebrews favor in the eyes of the Egyptians—who hitherto had bitterly hated them—so as to give earrings to them (Ex. 12:35, 36).

3. In convicting of sin. Few seem to understand that conscience in the natural man is inoperative unless stirred up by the Spirit. As a fallen creature, thoroughly in love with sin (John 3:19), man resists and disputes against any conviction of sin. "My Spirit shall not always strive with man, for that he also is flesh" (Gen. 6:3): man, being "flesh," would never have the least distaste of any iniquity unless the Spirit excited those remnants of natural light which still remain in the soul. Being "flesh," fallen man is perverse against the convictions of the Spirit (Acts 7:51), and remains so forever unless quickened and made "spirit" (John 3:6).

4. In illuminating. Concerning Divine things, fallen man is not only devoid of light, but is "darkness" itself (Eph. 5:8). He had no more apprehension of spiritual things than the beasts of the field. This is very evident from the state of the heathen. How, then, shall we explain the intelligence which is found in thousands in Christendom, who yet give no evidence that they are new creatures in Christ Jesus? They have been enlightened by the Holy Spirit (Heb. 6:4). Many are constrained to inquire into those scriptural subjects which make no demand on the conscience and life; yea, many take great delight in them. Just as the multitudes took pleasure in beholding the miracles of Christ, who could not endure His searching demands, so the light of the Spirit is pleasant to many to whom His convictions are grievous.

The Spirit's Operation in the Elect

We have dwelt upon some of the general and inferior operations which the Holy Spirit performs upon the non-elect, who are never brought unto a saving knowledge of the Truth. Now we shall consider His special and saving work in the people of God, dwelling mainly upon the absolute necessity for the same. It should make it easier for the Christian reader to perceive the absoluteness of this necessity when we say that the whole work of the Spirit within the elect is to plant in the heart a hatred for and a loathing of sin as sin, and a love for and longing after holiness as holiness.

This is something which no human power can bring about. It is something which the most faithful preaching as such cannot produce. It is something which the mere circulating and reading of the Scripture does not impart. It is a miracle of grace, a Divine wonder, which none but God can or does perform.

Total Depravity Apart from the Spirit

Of course if men are only partly depraved (which is really the belief today of the vast majority of preachers and their hearers, never having been experimentally taught by God their own depravity), if deep down in their hearts all men really love God, if they are so good-natured as to be easily persuaded to become Christians, then there is no need for the Holy Spirit to put forth His Almighty power and do for them what they are altogether incapable of doing for themselves. And again: if "being saved" consists merely in believing I am a lost sinner and on my way to Hell, and by simply believing that God loves me, that Christ died for me, and that He will save me now on the one condition that I "accept Him as my personal Savior" and "rest upon His finished work," then no supernatural operations of the Holy Spirit are required to induce and enable me to fulfill that condition—self-interest moves me to, and a decision of my will is all that is required.

But if, on the other hand, all men hate God (John 15:23, 25), and have minds which are "enmity against Him" (Rom. 8:7), so that "there is none that seeketh after God" (Rom. 3:11), preferring and determining to follow their own inclinations and pleasures. If instead of being disposed unto that which is good, "the heart of the sons of men is fully set in them to do evil" (Eccl. 8:11). And if when the overtures of God's mercy are made known to them and they are freely invited to avail themselves of the same, they "all with one consent begin to make excuse" (Luke 14:1 8)—then it is very evident that the invincible power and transforming operations of the Spirit are indispensably required if the heart of a sinner is thoroughly changed, so that rebellion gives place to submission and hatred to love. This is why Christ said, "No man can come to me, except the Father (by the Spirit) which hath sent me draw him" (John 6:44).

Again—if the Lord Jesus Christ came here to uphold and enforce the high claims of God, rather than to lower or set them aside. If He declared that "strait is the gate and narrow is the way that leadeth unto Life, and few there be that find it," rather than pointing to a smooth and broad road which anyone would find it easy to tread. If the salvation which He has provided is a deliverance from sin and self-pleasing, from worldliness and indulging the lusts of the flesh, and the bestowing of a nature which desires and determines to live for God's glory and please Him in all the details of our present lives—then it is clear beyond dispute that none but the Spirit of God can impart a genuine desire for such a salvation. And if instead of "accepting Christ" and "resting upon His finished work" be the sole condition of salvation, He demands that the sinner throw down the weapons of his defiance, abandon every idol, unreservedly surrender himself and his life, and receive Him as His only Lord and Master, then nothing but a miracle of grace can enable any captive of Satan's to meet such requirements.

Objections to Total Depravity Proved False

Against what has been said above it may be objected that no such hatred of God as we have affirmed exists in the hearts of the great majority of our fellow-creatures—that while there may be a few degenerates, who have sold themselves to the Devil and are thoroughly hardened in sin, yet the remainder of mankind are friendly disposed to God, as is evident by the countless millions who have some form or other of religion. To such an objector we reply, The fact is, dear friend, that those to whom you refer are almost entirely ignorant of the God of Scripture: they have heard that He loves everybody, is benevolently inclined toward all His creatures, and is so easy-going that in return for their religious performances will wink at their sins. Of course, they have no hatred for such a "god" as this! But tell them something of the character of the true God: that He hates "all the workers of iniquity" (Ps. 5:5), that He is inexorably just and ineffably holy, that He is an uncontrollable Sovereign, who "hath mercy on whom He will have mercy, and whom He will He hardeneth" (Rom. 9:18), and their enmity against Him will soon be manifested—an enmity which none but the Holy Spirit can overcome.

It may be objected again that so far from the gloomy picture which we have sketched above being accurate, the great majority of people do desire to be saved (from having to suffer a penalty for their sin), and they make more or less endeavor after their salvation. This is readily granted. There is in every human heart a desire for deliverance from misery and a longing after happiness and security, and those who come under the sound of God's Word are naturally disposed to be delivered from the wrath to come and wish to be assured that Heaven will be their eternal dwelling-place—who wants to endure the everlasting burnings? But that desire and disposition is quite compatible and consistent with the greatest love to sin and most entire opposition of heart to that holiness without which no man shall see the Lord (Heb. 12:14). But what the objector here refers to is a vastly different thing from desiring Heaven upon God's terms, and being willing to tread the only path which leads there!

The instinct of self-preservation is sufficiently strong to move multitudes to undertake many performances and penances in the hope that thereby they shall escape Hell. The stronger men's belief of the truth of Divine revelation, the more firmly they become convinced that there is a Day of Judgment, when they must appear before their Maker, and render an account of all their desires, thoughts, words and deeds, the most serious and sober will be their minds. Let conscience convict them of their misspent lives, and they are ready to turn over a new leaf; let them be persuaded that Christ stands ready as a Fire-escape and is willing to rescue them, though the world still claims their hearts, and thousands are ready to "believe in Him." Yes, this is done by multitudes who still hate the true character of the Savior, and reject with all their hearts the salvation which He has. Far, far different is this from an unregenerate person longing for deliverance from self and sin, and the impartation of that holiness which Christ purchased for His people.

All around us are those willing to receive Christ as their Savior, who are altogether unwilling to surrender to Him as their Lord. They would like His peace, but they refuse His "yoke," without which His peace cannot be found (Matthew 11:29). They admire His promises, but have no heart for His precepts. They will rest upon His priestly work, but will not be subject to His kingly scepter. They will believe in a "Christ" who is suited to their own corrupt tastes or sentimental dreams, but they despise and reject the Christ of God. Like the multitudes of old, they want His loaves and fishes, but for His heart-searching, flesh-withering, sin-condemning teaching, they have no appetite. They approve of Him as the Healer of their bodies, but as the Healer of their depraved souls they desire Him not. And nothing but the miracle-working power of the Holy Spirit, can change this bias and bent in any soul.

It is just because modern Christendom has such an inadequate estimate of the fearful and universal effects which the Fall has wrought, that the imperative need for the supernatural power of the Holy Spirit is now so little realized. It is because such false conceptions of human depravity so widely prevail that, in most places, it is supposed all which is needed to save half of the community is to hire some popular evangelist and attractive singer. And the reason why so few are aware of the awful depths of human depravity, the terrible enmity of the carnal mind against God and the heart's inbred and inveterate hatred of Him, is because His character is now so rarely declared from the pulpit. If the preachers would deliver the same type of messages as did Jeremiah in his degenerate age, or even as John the Baptist did, they would soon discover how their hearers were really affected toward God; and then they would perceive that unless the power of the Spirit attended their preaching they might as well be silent.

The Holy Spirit Regenerating

Self-Regeneration Is Impossible

The absolute necessity for the regenerating operation of the Holy Spirit in order for a sinner's being converted to God lies in his being totally depraved. Fallen man is without the least degree of right disposition or principles from which holy exercises may proceed. He is completely under a contrary disposition: there is no right exercise of heart in him, but every motion of his will is corrupt and sinful. If this were not the case, there would be no need for him to be born again and made "a new creature." If the sinner were not wholly corrupt he would submit to Christ without any supernatural operation of the Spirit; but fallen man is so completely sunk in corruption that he has not the faintest real desire for God, but is filled with enmity against Him (Rom. 8:7). Therefore does Scripture affirm him to be "dead in trespasses and sins" (Eph. 2:1).

"But as many as received Him, to them gave He power to become the sons of God, to them which believe on His name: Which were born, not of blood, nor of the will of the flesh, nor of the will of man, but of God" (John 1:12, 13). The latter verse expounds the former. There an explanation is given as to why any fallen descendant of Adam ever spiritually receives Christ as His Lord and Master, and savingly believes on His name.

First, it is not because grace runs in the blood—as the Jews supposed. Holiness is not transmitted from father to son. The child of the most pious parents is by nature equally as corrupt and is as far from God as is the offspring of infidels. Second, it is not because of any natural willingness—as Arminians contend: "nor of the will of the flesh" refers to man in his natural and corrupt state. He is not regenerated by any instinct, choice, or exertion of his own; he does not by any personal endeavor contribute anything towards being born again; nor does he cooperate in the least degree with the efficient cause: instead, every inclination of his heart, every exercise of his will, is in direct opposition thereto.

Third, the new birth is not brought about by the power and influence of others. No sinner is ever born again as the result of the persuasions and endeavors of preachers or Christian workers. However pious and wise they are, and however earnestly and strenuously they exert themselves to bring others to holiness, they do in no degree produce the effect. "If all the angels and saints in Heaven and all the godly on earth should join their wills and endeavors and unitedly exert all their powers to regenerate one sinner, they could not effect it; yea, they could do nothing toward it. It is an effect infinitely beyond the reach of finite wisdom and power: 1 Corinthians 3:6, 7" (S. Hopkins).

Regeneration Is the Sole Work of the Spirit

In regeneration one of God's elect is the subject, and the Spirit of God is the sole agent. The subject of the new birth is wholly passive: he does not act, but is acted upon. The sovereign work of the Spirit in the soul precedes all holy exercises of heart—such as sorrow for sin, faith in Christ, love toward God. This great change is wrought in spite of all the opposition of the natural heart against God: "So then it is not of him that willeth, nor of him that runneth, but of God that showeth mercy" (Rom. 9:16). This great change is not a gradual and protracted process, but is instantaneous: in an instant of time the favored subject of it passes from death unto life.

In regeneration the Spirit imparts a real, new, and immortal life; a life not such as that which was inherited from the first Adam, who was "a living soul," but such as is derived from the last Adam, who is "a quickening Spirit" (1 Cor. 15:45). This new creation, though as real as the first, is widely different from it; that was an original or primary creation in the dust of the earth becoming man by the word of God's power; this is the regeneration of an actual and existing man—fallen and depraved, yet rational and accountable—into an heir of God and joint-heir with Christ. The outcome is "a new man," yet it is the same person, only "renewed."

"Regeneration consists in a new, spiritual, supernatural, vital principle, or habit of grace infused into the soul, the mind, the will and affections, by the power of the Holy Spirit, disposing and enabling them in whom it is, unto spiritual, supernatural, vital actings and spiritual obedience" (John Owen). No new faculties are created, but instead, the powers of the soul are spiritualized and made alive unto God, fitted to enjoy God and hold communion with Him. Regeneration consists in a radical change of heart, for there is implanted a new disposition as the foundation of all holy exercises; the mind being renovated, the affections elevated, and the will emancipated from the bondage of sin. The effect of this is that the one who is born again loves spiritual things as spiritual, and values spiritual blessings on account of their being purely spiritual.

Regeneration of Existing (Not New) Faculties

In view of a certain school of teaching upon "the two natures in the believer," some readers may experience difficulty over our statement above that at regeneration no new faculties are created, the soul remaining, substantially, the same as it was before. No, not even in the glorified state will any addition be made to the human constitution, though its faculties will then be completely unfettered and further enlarged and elevated. Perhaps this thought will be the more easily grasped if we illustrate it by a striking case recorded in 2 Kings 6:17, "Elisha prayed, and said, LORD, I pray Thee, open his eyes, that he may see. And the LORD opened the eyes of the young man, and he saw; and, behold, the mountain was full of horses and chariots of fire round about Elisha."

No new faculties were communicated unto Elisha's servant, but the powers of his vision were so enlarged that he was now able to discern objects which before were invisible to him. So it is with our understandings at regeneration: the mind (abstractly considered) is the same in the unregenerate as in the regenerate, but in the case of the latter, the Spirit has so quickened it that it is now able to take in spiritual objects and act toward them. This new spiritual visive (i.e., of vision) power with which the understanding is endowed at the new birth is a quality, super-added to the original faculties. As this is a point of importance, yet one which some find it difficult to grasp, we will proceed to dwell upon it a moment longer.

The bodily eye of the saint after resurrection will be elevated to see angels (which are now invisible), and therefore may be rightly termed a new eye, yea, a spiritual eye—even as the whole body will be a "spiritual body" (1 Cor. 15:44)—yet that change will be but the super-induction of new spiritual qualities for the eye (and the whole body) unto spiritual objects. In like manner, the entire being of one who is born again is so spiritualized or endued with "spirit" (John 3:6) as to be styled a "new man," a spiritual man; nevertheless, it is but the original man "renewed," and not the creating of a new being.

After regeneration things appear in an altogether new light, and the heart exercises itself after quite a new manner. God is now seen as the sum of all excellence. The reasonableness and spirituality of His law is so perceived that the heart approves of it. The infinite evil of sin is discerned. The one born again judges, condemns, and loathes himself, and wonders that he was not long ago cast into Hell. He marvels at the grace of God in giving Christ to die for such a wretch. Constrained by the love of Christ, he now renounces the ways of sin and gives himself up to serve God. Hereby we may discover what it is which persons are to inquire after in order to determine whether they have been born again, namely, by the exercises of their hearts, and the influence and effects these have upon their conduct.

We have pointed out that at regeneration the faculties of the soul are spiritually enlivened, grace putting into them a new ability so that they are capable of performing spiritual acts. At the new birth the Holy Spirit communicates principles of spiritual life, whereby the soul is qualified to act as a supernatural agent and produce supernatural works. The need for this should be evident; God and Christ, as they are revealed in the Gospel, are supernatural objects to the natural faculties or powers of the soul, and there is no proportion between them—not only such a disproportion as the bat's eye has unto the sun, but as a blind man's eye to the sun. Thus there is a greater necessity for the soul to be given new principles and abilities to act in a holy and spiritual manner than at the first creation to act naturally.

Manifestations of Regeneration

Holiness in the heart is the main and ultimate birth brought forth in regeneration, for to make us partakers of God's holiness is the sum and scope of His gracious purpose toward us, both of His election (Eph. 1:4), and of all His dealings afterward (Heb. 12:10), without which "no man shall see the Lord" (Heb. 12:14). Not that finite creatures can ever be partakers of the essential holiness that is in God, either by imputation, or much less by real transubstantiation. We can be no otherwise partakers of it than in the image thereof—"which after God (as pattern or prototype) is created in righteousness and true holiness" (Eph. 4:24); "after the image of Him that created him" (Col. 3:10).

Regeneration is the first discovery and manifestation of election and redemption to the persons for whom they were intended: "But after the kindness and love of God our Savior toward man appeared" (Titus 3:4); and how and when did it appear? "According to His mercy He saved us by the washing of regeneration and renewing of the Holy Spirit" (v. 5). "God's eternal love, like a mighty river, had from everlasting run, as it were underground. When Christ came, it took its course through His heart, hiddenly ran through it, He bearing on the Cross the names of them whom God had given Him; but was yet still hidden from us, and our knowledge of it. But the first breaking of it forth, and particular appearing of it in and to the persons, is when we are converted, and is as the first opening of a fountain" (T. Goodwin).

There is a great display of God's power apparent in our regeneration; yea, an "exceeding greatness" thereof, no less than that which raised up Christ from the dead (Eph. 1:19, 20). Because the work of regeneration is often repeated, and accomplished in a trice, as seen in the dying thief and Paul, and often accomplished (apparently) by a few words from one frail mortal falling on the ears of another, we are apt to lose sight of the omnipotent working of the Holy Spirit in the performing thereof. Indeed the Spirit so graciously hides the exceeding greatness of His power working in sinners' hearts, by using such sweet persuasive motives and gent)e inducements—drawing with "the cords of a man" (Hosea 11:4)-that His might is inadequately recognized, owned, and adored by us.

The marvel of regeneration is the bringing of a soul out of spiritual death into spiritual life. It is a new creation, which is a bringing of something out of nothing. Moreover the new creation is a far greater wonder than is the old—in the first creation there was nothing to oppose, but in the new all the powers of sin and Satan are set against it. Regeneration is not like the changing of water into wine, but of contrary into contrary—of hearts of stone into flesh (Ezek. 36:26), of wolves into lambs (Isa. 11:6). This is greater than any miracle Christ showed, and therefore did He tell His Apostles that, under the mighty endowment of the Holy Spirit, they should work "greater works" than He did (John 14:12).

Not only is there a wondrous exhibition of His power when the Spirit regenerates a soul, but there is also a blessed manifestation of His love. In the exercise of His gracious office towards God's elect and in His work in them, the Holy Spirit proves to a demonstration that His love toward the heirs of glory is ineffable and incomprehensible. As the principal work of the Spirit consists in making our souls alive to God, in giving us to apprehend the transactions of the Father and the Son in the Everlasting Covenant, and in imparting to them spiritual principles whereby they are fitted to enjoy and commune with God, it is internal—hence it is that His work being within us, we are more apt to overlook Him, and are prone to neglect the giving to Him the glory which is distinctly His due, and most sadly do we fail to praise and adore Him for His gracious work in us.

Thus it is with all believers: they find themselves more disposed to think on the love of Christ, or on the Father's love in the gift of Him than in exercising their minds spiritually in soul-inflaming and heartwarming meditations on the love and mercy of the Holy Spirit towards them, and His delight in them. Yet all that they really know and enjoy of the Father's love by faith in the finished work of the Son, is entirely from the inward teaching and supernatural influences of the eternal Spirit. This is too plainly evident in our neglect to ascribe distinctive glory to Him as a Divine person in the Godhead as God and Lord.

The Holy Spirit

Summary

"For God hath not appointed us to wrath, but to obtain salvation by our Lord Jesus Christ, Who died for us, that, whether we wake or sleep, we should live together with Him" (1 Thess. 5:9, 10). Yet, the Father's appointment and the Son's redemption, with all the unspeakable blessings thereof, remained for a season quite unknown to us. In their fallen, sinful, and guilty state, Christians lay "dead in trespasses and sins," without hope. To bring them out of this state, and raise them from a death of sin into a life of righteousness is the great and grand work reserved for the Holy Spirit, in order to display and make manifest thereby His love for them.

The Holy Spirit is fully acquainted with the present and everlasting virtue and efficacy of the Person and work of Immanuel, and what His heart was set upon when He made His soul an offering for sin, and how infinitely and eternally well pleased was Jehovah the Father with it, who has it in perpetual remembrance. The Father and the Son having committed the revelation and application of this great salvation unto the persons of all the elect to the Holy Spirit, He is pleased therefore, out of the riches of His own free and sovereign grace, to work in due season in all the heirs of glory. And as Christ died but once—His death being all-sufficient to answer every design to be effected by it—so the Holy Spirit by one act works effectually in the soul, producing a spiritual birth and changing the state of its partaker once and for all, so that the regenerated are brought out of and delivered from the power of death and translated into the kingdom of God's dear Son. Without this spiritual birth we cannot see spiritual objects and heavenly blessings in their true worth and excellence.

The effect of the new birth is that the man born again loves spiritual things as spiritual and values spiritual blessings on account of their being purely spiritual. The spring of life from Christ enters into him, and is the spring of all his spiritual life, the root of all his graces, the perpetual source of every Divine principle within him. So says Christ: "But whosoever drinketh of the water that I shall give him shall never thirst; but the water that I shall give him shall be in him a well of water springing up into everlasting life" (John 4:14). This regeneration introduces the elect into a capacity for the enjoyments which are peculiar to the spiritual world, and makes the one alteration in their state before God which lasts forever. All our meetness for the heavenly state is wrought at our regeneration (Col. 1:12, 13). Regeneration is one and the same in all saints. It admits of no increase or diminution. All grace and holiness are then imparted by the Spirit: His subsequent work is but to draw it forth into exercise and act.

The Spirit Quickening

We shall now confine ourselves to the initial operation of the Spirit within the elect of God. Different writers have employed the term "regeneration" with varying latitude: some restricting it unto a single act, others including the whole process by which one becomes a conscious child of God. This has hindered close accuracy of thought, and has introduced considerable confusion through the confounding of things which, though intimately related, are quite distinct. Not only has confusion of thought resulted from a loose use of terms, but serious divisions among professing saints have issued therefrom. We believe that much, if not all, of this would have been avoided had theologians discriminated more sharply and clearly between the principle of grace (spiritual life) which the Spirit first imparts unto the soul, and His consequent stirrings of that principle into exercise.

Quickening Is the Initial Operation of the Spirit

In earlier years we did not ourselves perceive the distinction which is pointed by John 6:63 and 1 Peter 1:23: the former referring unto the initial act of the Spirit in "quickening" the spiritually-dead soul, the latter having in view the consequent "birth" of the same. While it is freely allowed that the origin of the "new creature" is shrouded in impenetrable mystery, yet of this we may be certain, that life precedes birth. There is a strict analogy between the natural birth and the spiritual: necessarily so, for God is the Author of them both, and He ordained that the former should adumbrate the latter. Birth is neither the cause nor the beginning of life itself: rather is it the manifestation of a life already existent: there had been a Divine "quickening" before the child could issue from the womb. In like manner, the Holy Spirit "quickens" the soul, or imparts spiritual life to it, before its possessor is "brought forth" (as James 1:18 is rightly rendered in the R.V.) and "born again" by the Word of God (1 Pet. 1:23).

James 1:18, 1 Peter 1:23, and parallel passages, refer not to the original communication of spiritual life to the soul, but rather to our being enabled to act from that life and induced to love and obey God by means of the Word of Truth—which presupposes a principle of grace already planted in the heart. In His work of illumination, conviction, conversion, and sanctification, the Spirit uses the Word as the means thereto, but in His initial work of "quickening" He employs no means, operating immediately or directly upon the soul. First there is a "new creation" (2 Cor. 5:17; Eph. 2:10), and then the "new creature" is stirred into exercise. Faith and all other graces are wrought in us by the Spirit through the instrumentality of the Word, but not so with the principle of life and grace from which these graces proceed.

Quickening Imparts Life

In His work of "quickening," by which we mean the impartation of spiritual life to the soul, the Spirit acts immediately from within, and not by applying something from without. Quickening is a direct operation of the Spirit without the use of any instrument: the Word is used by Him afterwards to call into exercise the life then communicated. "Regeneration is a direct operation of the Holy Spirit upon the human spirit. It is the action of Spirit upon spirit, of a Divine Person upon a human person, whereby spiritual life is imparted. Nothing, therefore, of the nature of means or instruments can come between the Holy Spirit and the soul that is made alive. God did not employ an instrument or means when He infused physical life into the body of Adam. There were only two factors: the dust of the ground and the creative power of God which vivified that dust. The Divine omnipotence and dead matter were brought into direct contact, with nothing interposing. The dust was not a means or instrument by which God originated life. So in regeneration there are only two factors: the human soul destitute of spiritual life, and the Holy Spirit who quickens it.

"The Word and Truth of God, the most important of all the means of grace, is not a means of regeneration, as distinct from conviction, conversion and sanctification. This is evident when we remember that it is the office of a means or instrument to excite or stimulate an already existing principle of life. Physical food is a means of physical growth, but it supposes physical vitality. If the body is dead, bread cannot be a means or instrument. Intellectual truth is a means of intellectual growth, but it supposes intellectual vitality. If the mind be idiotic, secular knowledge cannot be a means or instrument. Spiritual truth is a means of spiritual growth, in case there be spiritual vitality. But if the mind be dead to righteousness, spiritual truth cannot be a means or instrument.

"The unenlightened understanding is unable to apprehend, and the unregenerate will is unable to believe. Vital force is lacking in these two principal factors. What is needed at this point is life and force itself. Consequently, the Author of spiritual life Himself must operate directly, without the use of means or instruments; and outright give spiritual life and power from the dead: that is, ex nihilo. The new life is not imparted because man perceives the truth, but he perceives the truth because the new life is imparted. A man is not regenerated because he has first believed in Christ, but he believes in Christ because he has been regenerated" (W. T. Shedd, Presbyterian, 1889).

First the Work of the Spirit, Then the Word

Under the guise of honoring the written word, many have (no doubt unwittingly) dishonored the Holy Spirit. The idea which seems to prevail in "orthodox" circles today is that all which is needed for the salvation of souls is to give out the Word in its purity, God being pledged to bless the same. How often we have heard it said, "The Word will do its own work." Many suppose that the Scriptures are quite sufficient of themselves to communicate light to those in darkness and life to those who are dead in sins. But the record which we have of Christ's life ought at once to correct such a view. Who preached the Word as faithfully as He, yet how very few were saved during His three and a half years' ministry?!

The parable of the Sower exposes the fallacy of the theory now so widely prevailing. The "seed" sown is the Word. It was scattered upon various kinds of ground, yet notwithstanding the purity and vitality of the seed, where the soil was unfavorable, no increase issued therefrom. Until the ground was made good, the seed yielded no increase. That seed might be watered by copious showers and warmed by a genial sum, but while the soil was bad there could be no harvest. The ground must be changed before it could be fertile. Nor is it the seed which changes the soil: what farmer would ever think of saying, The seed will change the soil! Make no mistake upon this point: the Holy Spirit must first quicken the dead soul into newness of life before the Word obtains any entrance.

To say that life is communicated to the soul by the Spirit's application of the Word, and then to affirm that it is the principle of life which gives efficacy to the Word, is but to reason in a circle. The Word cannot profit any soul spiritually until it be "mixed with faith" (Heb. 4:2), and faith cannot be put forth unless it proceeds from a principle of life and grace; and therefore that principle of life is not produced by it.

"We might as well suppose that the presenting of a picture to a man who is blind can enable him to see, as we can suppose that the presenting of the Word in an objective way is the instrument whereby God produces the internal principle by which we are enabled to embrace it" (Thomas Ridgley,

Presbyterian, 1730—quoted by us to show we are not here inculcating some new doctrine.)

Yet notwithstanding what has been pointed out above, many are still likely to insist upon the quickening power which inheres in the Word itself, reminding us that its voice is that of the Almighty. This we freely and fully acknowledge, but do not all the unregenerate resist, and refuse to heed that Voice? How, then, is that opposition to be removed? Take an illustration. Suppose the window of my room is darkened by an iron wall before it. The sun's beams beat upon it, but still the wall remains. Were it of ice, it would melt away, but the nature of iron is to harden and not soften under the influence of heat. How, then, is the sun to enter my room? Only by removing that wall: a direct power must be put forth for its destruction. In like manner, the deadly enmity of the sinner must be removed by the immediate operation of the Spirit, communicating life, before the Word enters and affects him.

"The light of the body is the eye: if therefore thine eye be single, thy whole body shall be full of light. But if thine eye be evil, thy whole body shall be full of darkness" (Matthew 7:22, 23). By the "eye" is not here meant the mind only, but the disposition of the heart (cf. Mark 7:22). Here Christ tells us in what man's blindness consists, namely, the evil disposition of his heart, and that the only way to remove the darkness, and let in the light, is to change the heart. An "evil eye" is not cured or its darkness removed merely by casting light upon it, any more than the rays of the sun communicate sight unto one whose visive faculty is dead. The eye must be cured, made "single," and then it is capable of receiving the light.

"It is said the Lord opened the heart of Lydia, that she attended unto the things that were spoken by Paul (Acts 16:14). It would be a contradiction, and very absurd, to say that God's Word spoken by Paul was that by which her heart was opened; for she knew not what he did speak, until her heart was opened to attend to his words and understand them. Her heart was first opened in order for his words to have any effect or give any light to her. And this must be done by an immediate operation of the Spirit of God on her heart. This was the regeneration now under consideration, by which her heart was renewed, and formed unto true discerning like the single eye" (Samuel Hopkins, 1792).

The soul, then, is quickened into newness of life by the direct and supernatural operation of the Spirit, without any medium or means whatever. It is not accomplished by the light of the Word, for it is His very imparting of life which fits the heart to receive the light. This initial work of the Spirit is absolutely indispensable in order to have spiritual illumination. It is depravity or corruption of heart which holds the mind in darkness, and it is in this that unregeneracy consists. It is just as absurd to speak of illumination being conveyed by the Word in order to have a change of heart, or the giving of a relish for spiritual things, as it would be to speak of giving the capacity to a man to taste the sweetness of honey while he was devoid of a palate.

No, men are not "quickened" by the Word, they must be quickened in order to receive and understand the Word. "And I will give them a heart to know me, that I am the LORD; and they shall be My people, and I will be their God" (Jer. 24:7): that statement would be quite meaningless if a saving knowledge of or experimental acquaintance with God were obtained through the Word previous to the "new heart" or spiritual life being given, and was the means of our being quickened. "The fear of the Lord is the beginning of knowledge" (Prov. 1:7); the "fear of the Lord" or Divine grace communicated to the heart (spiritual life imparted) alone lays the foundation for spiritual knowledge and activities.

Characteristics of Quickening

"For as the Father raiseth up the dead, and quickeneth, even so the Son quickeneth whom He will" (John 5:21); "It is the Spirit that quickeneth: the flesh profiteth nothing" (John 6:63). All the Divine operations in the economy of salvation proceed from the Father, are through the Son, and are executed by the Spirit. Quickening is His initial work in the elect. It is that supernatural act by which He brings them out of the grave of spiritual death on to resurrection ground. By it He imparts a principle of grace and habit of holiness; it is the communication of the life of God to the soul. It is an act of creation (2 Cor. 5:17). It is a Divine "workmanship" (Eph. 2:10). All of these terms denote an act of Omnipotency. The origination of life is utterly impossible to the creature. He can receive life; he can nourish life; he can use and exert it; but he cannot create life.

In this work the Spirit acts as sovereign. "The wind bloweth where it listeth (or "pleaseth") ... so is everyone that is born of the Spirit" (John 3:8). This does not mean that He acts capriciously, or without reason and motive, but that He is above any obligation to the creature, and is quite uninfluenced by us in what He does. The Spirit might justly have left everyone of us in the hardness of our hearts to perish forever. In quickening one and not another, in bringing a few from death unto life and leaving the mass still dead in trespasses and sins, the Spirit has mercy "on whom He will have mercy." He is absolutely free to work in whom He pleases, for none of the fallen sons of Adam have the slightest claim upon Him.

The Holy Spirit

The quickening of the spiritually dead into newness of life is therefore an act of amazing grace: it is an unsought and unmerited favor. The sinner, who is the chosen subject of this Divine operation and object of this inestimable blessing, is infinitely ill-deserving in himself, being thoroughly disposed to go on in wickedness till this change is wrought in him. He is rebellious, and will not hearken to the Divine command; he is obstinate and refuses to repent and embrace the Gospel. However terrified he may be with the fears of threatened doom, however earnest may be his desire to escape misery and be happy forever, no matter how many prayers he may make and things he may do, he has not the least inclination to repent and submit to God. His heart is defiant, full of enmity against God, and daily does he add iniquity unto iniquity. For the Spirit to give a new heart unto such an one is indeed an act of amazing and sovereign grace.

This quickening by the Spirit is instantaneous: it is a Divine act, and not a process; it is wrought at once, and not gradually. In a moment of time the soul passes from death unto life. The soul which before was dead toward God, is now alive to Him. The soul which was completely under the domination of sin, is now set free; though the sinful nature itself is not removed nor rendered inoperative, yet the heart is no longer en rapport (in sympathy) with it. The Spirit of God finds the heart wholly corrupt and desperately wicked, but by a miracle of grace He changes its bent, and this by implanting within it the imperishable seed of holiness. There is no medium between a carnal and a spiritual state: the one is what we were by nature, the other is what we become by grace, by the instantaneous and invincible operation of the Almighty Spirit.

This initial work of quickening is entirely unperceived by us, for it lies outside the realm and the range of human consciousness. Those who are dead possess no perception, and though the work of bringing them on to resurrection ground is indeed a great and powerful one, in the very nature of the case its subjects can know nothing whatever about it until after it has been accomplished. When Adam was created, he was conscious of nothing but that he now existed and was free to act: the Divine operation which was the cause of his existence was over and finished before he began to be conscious of anything. This initial operation of the Spirit by which the elect become new creatures can only be known by its effects and consequences. "The wind bloweth where it listeth," that is first; then "thou hearest the sound thereof" (John 3:8): it is now made known, in a variety of ways, to the conscience and understanding.

Under this work of quickening we are entirely passive, by which is meant that there is no co-operation whatever between the will of the sinner and the act of the Holy Spirit. As we have said, this initial work of the Spirit is effected by free and sovereign grace, consisting of the infusion of a principle of spiritual life into the soul, by which all its faculties are supernaturally renovated. This being the case, the sinner must be entirely passive, like clay in the hands of a potter, for until Divine grace is exerted upon him he is utterly incapable of any spiritual acts, being dead in trespasses and sins. Lazarus co-operated not in his resurrection: he knew not that the Savior had come to his sepulcher to deliver him from death. Such is the case with each of God's elect when the Spirit commences to deal with them. They must first be quickened into newness of life before they can have the slightest desire or motion of the will toward spiritual things; hence, for them to contribute the smallest iota unto their quickening is utterly impossible.

The life which the Spirit imparts when He quickens is uniform in all its favored subjects. "As seed virtually contains in it all that afterwards proceeds from it, the blade, stalk, ear, and full corn in the ear, so the first principle of grace implanted in the heart seminally contains all the grace which afterwards appears in all the fruits, effects, acts, and exercises of it" (John Gill). Each quickened person experiences the same radical change, by which the image of God is stamped upon the soul: "that which is born of the Spirit is spirit" (John 3:6), never anything less, and never anything more. Each quickened person is made a new creature in Christ, and possesses all the constituent parts of "the new man." Later, some may be more lively and vigorous, as God gives stronger faith unto one than to another; yet there is no difference in their original: all partake of the same life.

While there is great variety in our perception and understanding of the work of the Spirit within us, there is no difference in the initial work itself. While there is much difference in the carrying on of this work unto perfection in the growth of the "new creature"—some making speedy progress, others thriving slowly and bringing forth little fruit—yet the new creation itself is the same in all. Each alike enters the kingdom of God, becomes a vital member of Christ's mystical body, is given a place in the living family of God. Later, one may appear more beautiful than another, by having the image of his heavenly Father more evidently imprinted upon him, yet not more truly so. There are degrees in sanctification, but none in vivification. There has never been but one kind of spiritual quickening in this world, being in its essential nature specifically the same in all.

Only the Beginning

The Holy Spirit

Let it be pointed out in conclusion that the Spirit's quickening is only the beginning of God's work of grace in the soul. This does not wholly renew the heart at once: no indeed, the inner man needs to be "renewed day by day" (2 Cor. 4:16). But from that small beginning, the work continues— God watering it "every moment" (Isa. 27:3)—and goes on to perfection; that is, till the heart is made perfectly clean and holy, which is not accomplished till death. God continues to work in His elect, "both to will and to do of His good pleasure," they being as completely dependent upon the Spirit's influence for every right exercise of the will after, as for the first. "Being confident of this very thing, that He which bath begun a good work within you will finish it until the day of Jesus Christ" (Phil. 1:6).

The Spirit Enlightening

Darkness by Nature

By nature fallen man is in a state of darkness with respect unto God. Be he ever so wise, learned, and skillful in natural things, unto spiritual things he is blind. Not until we are renewed in the spirit of our minds by the Holy Spirit can we see things in God's light. But this is something which the world cannot endure to hear of, and when it be insisted upon, they will hotly deny the same. So did the Pharisees of Christ's day angrily ask, with pride and scorn, "Are we blind also?" (John 9:40), to which our Lord replied by affirming that their presumption of spiritual light and knowledge only aggravated their sin and condemnation (v. 41); unhesitatingly, He told the blind leaders of religion, that, notwithstanding all their boasting, they had never heard the Father's voice "at any time" (John 5:37).

There is a twofold spiritual darkness, outward and inward. The former, is the case with those who are without the Gospel until God sends the external means of grace to them: "The people which sat in darkness saw a great light" (Matthew 4:16). The latter, is the case with all, until God the Spirit performs a miracle of grace within the soul and quickens the dead into newness of life: "And the light shineth in darkness, and the darkness comprehended it not" (John 1:5). No matter how well we are acquainted with the letter of Scripture, no matter how sound and faithful is the preaching we sit under and the books we read, until the soul be Divinely quickened it has no spiritual discernment or experimental perception of Divine things. Until a man be born again, he cannot "see" the kingdom of God (John 3:3).

Inward Darkness: Active Opposition to God

This inward darkness which fills the soul of the natural man is something far more dreadful than a mere intellectual ignorance of spiritual things. Ignorance is a negative thing, but this spiritual "darkness" is a positive thing—an energetic principle which is opposed to God. The "darkness" which rests upon the human soul gives the heart a bias toward evil, prejudicing it against holiness, fettering the will so that it never moves God-wards. Hence we read of "the power of darkness" (Col. 1:13): so great

The Holy Spirit

is its power that all under it love darkness "rather than light" (John 3:19). Why is it that men have little difficulty in learning a business and are quick to discover how to make money and gratify their lusts, but are stupid and unteachable in the things of God? Why is it that men are so prone and ready to believe religious lies, and so averse to the Truth? None but the Spirit can deliver from this terrible darkness. Unless the Sun of righteousness arises upon us (Mal. 4:2), we are shut up in "the blackness of darkness forever" (Jude 13).

Because of the darkness which rests upon and reigns within his entire soul, the natural man can neither know, admire, love, adore, or serve the true God in a spiritual way. How can God appear infinitely lovely to one whose every bias of his heart prompts unto hatred of the Divine perfections? How can a corrupt soul be charmed with a Character which is the absolute opposite of its own? What fellowship can there be between darkness and Light; what concord can there be between sin and Holiness; what agreement between a carnal mind and Him against whom it is enmity? False notions of God may charm even an unregenerate heart, but none save a Divinely-quickened soul can spiritually know and love God. The true God can never appear as an infinitely amiable and lovely Being to one who is dead in trespasses and sins and completely under the dominion of the Devil.

Enlightenment Presupposes Turning from Self

"It is true that many a carnal man is ravished to think that God loves him, and will save him; but in this case, it is not the true character of God which charms the heart: it is not God that is loved. Strictly speaking, he can only love himself, and self-love is the source of all his affections. Or, if we call it 'love' to God, it is of no other kind than sinners feel to one another: 'for sinners also love those that love them' (Luke 6:32). The carnal Israelites gave the fullest proof of their disaffection to the Divine character (in the wilderness), as exhibited by God Himself before their eyes, yet were once full of this same kind of 'love' at the side of the Red Sea" (Joseph Bellamy).

My reader, the mere fact that your heart is thrilled with a belief that God loves you, is no proof whatever that God's true character would suit your taste had you right notions of it. The Galatians loved Paul while they considered him as the instrument of their conversion; but on further acquaintance with him, they turned his enemies, for his character, rightly understood, was not at all congenial to them. If God is "of purer eyes than to behold evil" and cannot but look upon sin with infinite detestation (Hab. 1:13); if all those imaginations, affections, and actions which are so sweet to the taste of a carnal heart, are so infinitely odious in the eyes of God as to appear to Him worthy of the eternal pains of Hell, then it is utterly impossible for a carnal heart to see any beauty in the Divine character until it perceives its own character to be infinitely odious.

There is no spiritual love for the true God until self be hated The one necessarily implies the other. I cannot look upon God as a lovely Being, without looking upon myself as infinitely vile and hateful. When Christ said to the Pharisees, "Ye serpents, ye generation of vipers, how can ye escape the damnation of Hell?" (Matthew 23:33), those words determined His character in their eyes. And it implies a contradiction to suppose that Christ's character might appear lovely to them, without their own appearing odious, answerable to the import of His words. There was nothing in a Pharisee's heart to look upon his own character in such a detestable light, and therefore all the Savior's words and works could only exasperate them. The more they knew of Christ, the more they hated Him; as it was natural to approve of their own character, so it was natural to condemn His.

The Pharisees were completely under the power of "darkness," and so is every human being till the Spirit quickens him into newness of life. If the fault were not in the Pharisees, it must have been in Christ; and for them to own it was not in Christ, was to acknowledge they were "vipers" and worthy of eternal destruction. They could not look upon Him as lovely, until they looked upon themselves as infinitely odious; but that was diametrically opposite to every bias of their hearts. Their old heart, therefore, must be taken away, and a new heart be given them, or they would never view things in a true light. "Except a man be born again, he cannot see the kingdom of God" (John 3:3).

Enlightenment Follows Quickening

"Darkness was upon the face of the deep" (Gen. 1:2)—fallen man's state by nature. "And the Spirit of God moved upon the face of the waters" (Gen. 1:2)—adumbrating His initial work of quickening. "And God said, Let there be light, and there was light" (Gen. 1:3). Natural light was the first thing produced in the making of the world, and spiritual light is the first thing given at the new creation: "But God, who commanded the light to shine out of darkness, hath shined in our hearts, to give the light of the knowledge of the glory of God in the face of Jesus Christ" (2 Cor. 4:6). This Divine light shining into the mind, occasions new apprehensions of what is presented before it. Hitherto the favored subject of it had heard much about Christ: "by the hearing of the ear," but now his eye sees Him (Job 42:5): he clearly apprehends a transcendent excellence in Him, an extreme necessity of Him, a complete sufficiency in Him.

"In Thy light shall we see light" (Ps. 36:9). This is of what spiritual illumination consists. It is not a mere informing of the mind, or communication of intellectual knowledge, but an experimental and efficacious consciousness of the reality and nature of Divine and spiritual things. It is capacitating the mind to see sin in its real hideousness and heinousness, and to perceive "the beauty of holiness" (Ps. 96:9) so as to fall heartily in love with it. It is a spiritual light super-added to all the innate conceptions of the human mind, which is so pure and elevated that it is entirely beyond the power of the natural man to reach unto. It is something which the natural heart cannot even conceive of, but the knowledge of which is communicated by the Spirit's enlightenment (1 Cor. 2:9, 10).

A dead man can neither see nor hear: true alike naturally and spiritually. There must be life before there can be perception: the Spirit must quicken the soul before it is capable of discerning and being affected by Divine things in a spiritual way. We say "in a spiritual way," because even a blind man may obtain an accurate idea of objects which his eye has never beheld; even so the unregenerate may acquire a natural knowledge of Divine things. But there is a far greater difference between an unregenerate man's knowledge of Divine things—no matter how orthodox and Scriptural be his views—and the knowledge possessed by the regenerate, than there is between a blind man's conception of a gorgeous sunset and what it would appear to him were sight communicated and he were permitted to gaze upon one for himself. It is not merely that the once-blind man would have a more correct conception of the Creator's handiwork, but the effect produced upon him would be such as words could not describe.

The Spirit's quickening of the dead soul into newness of life lays the foundation for all His consequent operations. Once the soul is made the recipient of spiritual life, all its faculties are capacitated unto spiritual exercises: the understanding to perceive spiritually, the conscience to feel spiritually, the affections to move spiritually, and the will to act spiritually. Originally, God formed man's body out of the dust of the ground, and it then existed as a complete organism, being endowed with a full set of organs and members; but it was not until God "breathed into" him the "breath of life" (Gen. 2:7) that Adam was able to move and act. In like manner, the soul of the natural man is vested with all these faculties which distinguish him from the beasts, but it is not until the Spirit quickens him that he is capable of discerning and being affected by Divine things in a spiritual way.

Once the Spirit has brought one of God's dead elect on to resurrection ground, He proceeds to illumine him. The light of God now shines upon him, and the previously-blind soul, having been Divinely empowered to see, is able to receive that light. The Spirit's enlightenment commences immediately after quickening, continues throughout the Christian's life, and is consummated in glory: "The path of the just is as the shining light, that shineth more and more unto the perfect day" (Prov. 4:18). As we stated in a previous chapter, this spiritual enlightenment is not a mere informing of the mind or communication of spiritual knowledge, but is an experimental and efficacious consciousness of the Truth. It is that which is spoken of in 1 John 2:20, 27, "But ye have an unction from the Holy One, and ye know all things . . . But the anointing which ye have received of Him abideth in you, and ye need not that any man teach you."

Manifestations of Enlightenment

By this "anointing" or enlightenment the quickened soul is enabled to perceive the true nature of sin—opposition against God, expressed in self-pleasing. By it he discerns the plague of his own heart, and finds that he is a moral leper, totally depraved, corrupt at the very center of his being. By it he detects the deceptions of Satan, which formerly made him believe that bitter was sweet, and sweet bitter. By it he apprehends the claims of God: that He is absolutely worthy of and infinitely entitled to be loved with all his heart, soul, and strength. By it he learns God's way of salvation: that the path of practical holiness is the only one which leads to Heaven. By it he beholds the perfect suitability and sufficiency of Christ: that He is the only One who could meet all God's claims upon him. By it he feels his own impotence unto all that is good, and presents himself as an empty vessel to be filled out of Christ's fullness.

A Divine light now shines into the quickened soul. Before, he was "darkness," but now is he "light in the Lord" (Eph. 5:8). He now perceives that those things in which he once found pleasure, are loathsome and damnable. His former concepts of the world and its enjoyments, he now sees to be erroneous and ensnaring, and apprehends that no real happiness or contentment is to be found in any of them. That holiness of heart and strictness of life which before he criticized as needless preciseness or puritanical extreme, is now looked upon not only as absolutely necessary, but as most beautiful and blessed. Those moral and religious performances he once prided himself in and which he supposed merited the approval of God, he now regards as filthy rags. Those whom he once envied, he now pities. The company he once delighted in now sickens and saddens him. His whole outlook is completely changed.

The Holy Spirit

Divine illumination, then, is the Holy Spirit imparting to the quickened soul accurate and spiritual views of Divine things. To hear and understand is peculiar to the "good-ground" hearer (Matthew 13:23). None but the real "disciple" knows the Truth (John 8:31, 32). Even the Gospel is "hid" from the lost (2 Cor. 4:4). But when a quickened soul is enlightened by the Spirit, he has a feeling realization of the excellence of the Divine character, the spirituality of God's Law, the exceeding sinfulness of sin in general and of his own vileness in particular. It is a Divine work which capacitates the soul to have real communion with God, to receive or take in spiritual objects, enjoy them, and live upon them. It is in this way that Christ is "formed in us" (Gal. 4:19). Thus, at times, the Christian is able to say: "Thy shining grace can cheer, This dungeon where I dwell. 'Tis paradise when Thou art here, If Thou depart, 'tis Hell."

Characteristics of Enlightenment

In closing, let us seek to define a little more definitely some of the characteristics of this Divine enlightenment.

First, it is one which gives certainty to the soul. It enables its favored possessor to say, "One thing I know, that, whereas I was blind, now I see" (John 9:25). And again, "I know whom I have believed, and am persuaded that He is able to keep that which I have committed unto Him against that day" (2 Tim. 1:12). Later, Satan may be permitted to inject unbelieving and atheistic thoughts into his mind, but it is utterly impossible for him to persuade any quickened and enlightened soul that God has no existence, that Christ is a myth, that the Scriptures are a human invention. God in Christ has become a living reality to him, and the more He appears to the soul the sum of all excellence, the more is He loved.

Second, this Divine enlightenment is transforming. Herein it differs radically from a natural knowledge of Divine things, such as the unregenerate may acquire intellectually, but which produces no real and lasting impression upon the soul. A spiritual apprehension of Divine things is an efficacious one, stamping the image thereof upon the heart, and molding it into their likeness: "But we all, with open face beholding as in a glass the glory of the Lord, are changed into the same image from glory to glory, by the Spirit of the Lord" (2 Cor. 3:18). Thus this spiritual illumination is vastly different from a mere notional and inoperative knowledge of Divine things. The Spirit's enlightenment enables the Christian to "show forth the praises of him who hath called him out of darkness into his marvelous light" (1 Pet. 2:9).

Third, this Divine enlightenment is a spiritual preservative. This is evident from 1 John 2:20, though to make it fully clear unto the reader an exposition of that verse in the light of its context is required. In 1 John 2:18 the Apostle had mentioned the "many antichrists" (to be headed up in the antichrist), which were to characterize this final dispensation: seducers from the Faith were numerous even before the close of the first century AD. In 1 John 2:19 reference is made to those who had fallen under the spell of these deceivers, and who had in consequence, apostatized from Christianity. In sharp contrast therefrom, the Apostle affirms, "But ye have an unction from the Holy One, and ye know all things" (v. 20). Here was the Divine preservative: the Spirit's enlightenment ensured the saints from being captured by Satan's emissaries. Apostates had never been anointed by the Spirit; renewed souls are, and this safeguards them. The voice of a stranger "will they not follow" (John 10:5). It is not possible to fatally "deceive" one of God's elect (Matthew 24:24). The same precious truth is found again in 1 John 2:27: the Spirit indwells the Christian "forever" (John 14:16), hence the "anointing" he has received "abideth in him" and thus guarantees that he shall "abide in Christ."

The Spirit Convicting

Though man in his natural estate is spiritually dead, that is, entirely destitute of any spark of true holiness, yet is he still a rational being and has a conscience by which he is capable of perceiving the difference between good and evil, and of discerning and feeling the force of moral obligation (Rom. 1:32; 2:15). By having his sins clearly brought to his mind and conscience, he can be made to realize what his true condition is as a transgressor of the holy Law of God. This sight and sense of sin, when aroused from moral stupor, under the common operations of the Holy Spirit, is usually termed "conviction of sin"; and there can be no doubt that the views and feelings of men may be very clear and strong even while they are in an unregenerate state. Indeed, they do not differ in kind (though they do in degree), from what men will experience in the Day of Judgment, when their own consciences shall condemn them, and they shall stand guilty before God (Rom. 3:19).

Not "Conviction of Sin"

But there is nothing whatever in the kind of conviction of sin mentioned above which has any tendency to change the heart or make it better. No matter how clear or how strong such convictions are, there is nothing in them which approximates to those that the Spirit produces in those whom He quickens. Such convictions may be accompanied by the most alarming apprehensions of danger, the imagination may be filled with the most frightful images of terror, and Hell may seem almost uncovered to their terrified view. Very often, under the sound of the faithful preaching of Eternal Punishment, some are aroused from their lethargy and feelings of the utmost terror are awakened in their souls, while there is no real spiritual conviction of the exceeding sinfulness of sin. On the other hand, there may be deep and permanent spiritual convictions where the passions and the imagination are very little excited.

Solemn is it to realize that there are now in Hell multitudes of men and women who on earth were visited with deep conviction of sin, whose awakened conscience made them conscious of their rebellion against their

Maker, who were made to feel something of the reality of the everlasting burnings, and the justice of God meting out such punishment to those who spurn His authority and trample His laws beneath their feet. How solemn to realize that many of those who experienced such convictions were aroused to flee from the wrath to come, and became very zealous and diligent in seeking to escape the torments of Hell, and who under the instinct of self-preservation took up with "religion" as offering the desired means of escape. And how unspeakably solemn to realize that many of those poor souls fell victim to men who spoke "smooth things," assuring them that they were the objects of God's love, and that nothing more was needed than to "receive Christ as your personal Savior." How unspeakably solemn, we say, that such souls look to Christ merely as a fire-escape, who never—from a supernatural work of the Spirit in their hearts—surrendered to Christ as Lord

Does the reader say, "Such statements as the above are most unsettling, and if dwelt upon would destroy my peace." We answer, O that it may please God to use these pages to disturb some who have long enjoyed a false peace. Better far, dear reader, to be upset, yea, searched and terrified now, than die in the false comfort produced by Satan, and weep and wail for all eternity. If you are unwilling to be tested and searched, that is clear proof that you lack an "honest heart." An "honest" heart desires to know the Truth. An "honest" heart hates pretense. An "honest" heart is fearful of being deceived. An "honest" heart welcomes the most searching diagnosis of its condition. An "honest" heart is humble and tractable, not proud, presumptuous, and self-confident. O how very few there are who really possess an "honest heart."

Characteristics of the Spirit's True Conviction

The "honest" heart will say, "If it is possible for an unregenerate soul to experience the convictions of sin you have depicted above, if one who is dead in trespasses and sins may, nevertheless, have a vivid and frightful anticipation of the wrath to come, and engage in such sincere and earnest endeavors to escape from the same, then how am I to ascertain whether my convictions have been of a different kind from theirs?" A very pertinent and a most important question, dear friend. In answering the same, let us first point out that, soul terrors of Hell are not, in themselves, any proof of a supernatural work of God having been wrought in the heart: it is not horrifying alarms of the everlasting burnings felt in the heart which distinguishes the experience of quickened souls from that of the un-quickened; though such alarms are felt (in varying degrees) by both classes.

In His particular saving work of conviction, the Holy Spirit occupies the soul more with sin itself than with punishment. This is an exercise of the mind to which fallen men are exceedingly averse: they had rather meditate on almost anything than upon their own wickedness: neither argument, entreaty, nor warning will induce them to do so; nor will Satan suffer one of his captives—till a mightier One comes and frees him—to dwell upon sin, its nature, and vileness. No, he constantly employs all his subtle arts to keep his victim from such occupation, and his temptations and delusions are mixed with the natural darkness and vanity of men's hearts so as to fortify them against convictions; so that he may keep "his goods in peace" (Luke 11:21).

It is by the exceeding greatness of His power that the Holy Spirit fixes the mind of a quickened and enlightened soul upon the due consideration of sin. Then it is that the subject of this experience cries, "my sin is ever before me" (Ps. 51:3), for God now reproves him and "sets his sins in order" before his eyes (Ps. 50:21). Now he is forced to behold them, no matter which way he turns himself. Feign would he cast them out of his thoughts, but he cannot: "the arrows" of God stick in his heart (Job 6:4), and he cannot get rid of them. He now realizes that his sins are more in number than the hairs of his head (Ps. 40:12). Now it is that "the grass withereth, the flower fadeth; because the Spirit of the Lord bloweth upon it" (Isa. 40:7).

The Spirit occupies the quickened and enlightened soul with the exceeding sinfulness of sin. He unmasks its evil character, and shows that all our self-pleasing and self-gratification are but a species of sinfulness—of enmity against Him—against His Person, His attributes, His government. The Spirit makes the convicted soul feel how grievously he has turned his back upon God (Jer. 32:33), lifted up his heel against Him and trampled His laws underfoot. The Spirit causes him to see and feel that he has forsaken the pure Fountain for the foul stream, preferred the filthy creature above the ineffable Creator, a base lust to the Lord of glory.

The Spirit convicts the quickened soul of the multitude of his sins. He realizes now that all his thoughts, desires and imaginations, are corrupt and perverse; conscience now accuses him of a thousand things which hitherto never occasioned him a pang. Under the Spirit's illumination the soul discovers that his very righteousnesses are as "filthy rags," for the motive which prompted even his best performances were unacceptable to Him who "weigheth the spirits." He now sees that his very prayers are polluted, through lack of pure affections prompting them. In short, he sees that "from the sole of the foot even unto the head there is no soundness in him; but wounds, and bruises, and putrefying sores" (Isa. 1:6).

The Spirit brings before the heart of the convicted one the character and claims of God Sin is now viewed in the light of the Divine countenance, and he is made to feel what an evil and bitter thing it is to sin against God. The pure light of God, shining in the conscience over against vile darkness, horrifies the soul. The convicted one both sees and feels that God is holy and that he is completely unholy; that God is good and he is vile; that there is a most awful disparity between Him and us. He is made to feelingly cry, "How can such a corrupt wretch like I ever stand before such a holy God, whose majesty I have so often slighted?" Now it is that the soul is made to realize how it has treated God with the basest ingratitude, abusing His goodness, perverting His mercies, scorning his best Friend. Reader, has this been your experience?

Summary of Differences in "Conviction"

In summary, there is a very real and radical difference between that conviction of sin which many of the unregenerate experience under the common operations of the Spirit, and that conviction of sin which follows His work of quickening and enlightening the hearts of God's elect. We have pointed out that in the case of the latter, the conscience is occupied more with sin itself than with its punishment; with the real nature of sin, as rebellion against God; with its exceeding sinfulness, as enmity against God; with the multitude of sins, every action being polluted; with the character and claims of God, as showing the awful disparity there is between Him and us. Where the soul has not only been made to perceive, but also to feel—to have a heart-horror and anguish over the same—there is good reason to believe that the work of Divine grace has been begun in the soul.

Many other contrasts may be given between that conviction which issues from the common operations of the Spirit in the unregenerate and His special work in the regenerate. The convictions of the former are generally light and uncertain, and of short duration, they are sudden frights which soon subside; whereas those of the latter are deep, pungent and lasting, being repeated more or less frequently throughout life. The former work is more upon the emotions; the latter upon the judgment. The former diminishes in its clarity and efficacy, the latter grows in its intensity and power. The former arises from a consideration of God's justice; the latter are more intense when the heart is occupied with God's goodness. The former springs from a horrified sense of God's power; the latter issues from a reverent view of His holiness.

Unregenerate souls regard eternal punishment as the greatest evil, but the regenerate look upon sin as the worst thing there is. The former groan under conscience's presages of damnation; the latter mourn from a sense of their lack of holiness. The greatest longing of the one is to be assured of escape from the wrath to come; the supreme desire of the other is to be delivered from the burden of sin and conformed to the image of Christ. The former, while he may be convicted of many sins, still cherishes the conceit that he has some good points; the latter is painfully conscious that in his flesh there "dwelleth no good thing," and that his best performances are defiled. The former greedily snatches at comfort, for assurance and peace are now regarded as the highest good; the latter fears that he has sinned beyond the hope of forgiveness, and is slow to believe the glad tidings of God's grace. The convictions of the former harden, those of the latter melt and lead to submission. (The above two paragraphs are condensed from the Puritan, Charnock).

The Means of the Spirit's Convicting: Use of the Law

The great instrument which the Holy Spirit uses in this special work of conviction is the law, for that is the one rule which God has given whereby we are to judge of the moral good or evil of actions, and conviction is nothing more or less than the formal impression of sin by the law upon the conscience. Clear proof of this is found in the passages that follow. "By the law is the knowledge of sin" (Rom. 3:20): it is the design of all laws to impress the understanding with what is to be done, and consequently with man's deviation from them, and so absolutely necessary is the law for this discernment, the Apostle Paul declared, "I had not known sin but by the law" (Rom. 7:7)—its real nature, as opposition to God; its inveterate enmity against Him; its unsuspected lustings within. "The law entered that sin might abound" (Rom. 5:20): by deepening and widening the conviction of sin upon the conscience.

Now it is that God holds court in the human conscience and a reckoning is required of the sinner. God will no longer be trifled with, and sin can no longer be scoffed at. Thus a solemn trial begins: the law condemns, and the conscience is obliged to acknowledge its guilt. God appears as holy and just and good, but as awfully insulted, and with a dark frown upon His brow. The sinner is made to feel how dreadfully he has sinned against both the justice and goodness of God, and that his evil ways will no longer be tolerated. If the sinner was never solemn before, he is solemn now: fear and dismay fills his soul, death and destruction seem his inevitable and certain doom. When the Lord Almighty Himself appears in the court of conscience to vindicate His honor, the poor criminal trembles, sighs for mercy, but fears that pardoning mercy cannot justly be granted such a wretch.

Now it is that the Holy Spirit brings to light the hidden things of darkness. The whole past life is made to pass in review before the convicted soul. Now it is that he is made to experimentally realize that "the Word of God is quick and powerful, and sharper than any two-edged sword, piercing even to the dividing asunder of soul and spirit, and of the joints and marrow, and is a discerner of the thoughts and intents of the heart" (Heb. 4:12). Secret things are uncovered, forgotten deeds are recalled; sins of the eyes and sins of the lips, sins against God and sins against man, sins of commission and sins of omission, sins of ignorance and sins against light, are brought before the startled gaze of the enlightened understanding. Sin is now seen in all its excuselessness, filthiness, heinousness, and the soul is overwhelmed with horror and terror.

Whatever step the sinner now takes, all things appear to be against him; his guilt abounds, and his soul tremblingly sinks under it; until he feels obliged, in the presence of a heart-searching God, to sign his own death-warrant, or in other words, freely acknowledge that his condemnation is just. This is one of "the solemnities of Zion" (Isa. 32:20). As to whether this conviction is experienced at the beginning of the Christian life (which is often though not always the case), or at a later stage; as to how long the sinner remains under the spirit of bondage (Rom. 8:15); as to what extent he feels his wretchedness and ruin, or how deeply he sinks into the mire of despair, varies in different cases. God is absolute sovereign, and here, too, He acts as He sees good. But to this point every quickened soul is brought: to see the spirituality of God's Law, to hear its condemning sentence, to feel his case is hopeless so far as all self-help is concerned.

Here is the fulfillment of Deuteronomy 30:6, "The Lord thy God will circumcise thine heart." The blessed Spirit uses the sharp knife of the Law, pierces the conscience, and convicts of the exceeding sinfulness of sin. By this Divine operation the hardness of the heart is removed, and the iniquity of it laid open, the plague and corruption of it discovered, and all is made naked to the soul's view. The sinner is now exceedingly pained over his rebellions against God, is broken down before Him, and is filled with shame, and loathes and abhors himself. "Ask ye now, and see whether a man doth travail with child: wherefore do I see every man with his hands on his loins, as a woman in travail, and all faces are turned into paleness? Alas! for that day is great, so that none is like it: it is even the time of Jacob's trouble; but he shall be saved out of it" (Jer. 30:6, 7)—such is, sooner or later, the experience of all God's quickened people.

Of ourselves we could never be truly convicted of our wretched state, for "the heart is deceitful above all things," and God alone can search it (Jer. 17:9). O the amazing grace of the Holy Spirit that He should rake into such foul and filthy hearts, amid the dunghill of putrid lusts, of enmity against God, of wickedness unspeakable! What a loathsome work it must be for the Holy Spirit to perform! If God the Son humbled Himself to enter the virgin's womb and be born in Bethlehem's manger, does not God the Spirit humble Himself to enter our depraved hearts and stir up their vile contents in order that we may be made conscious thereof?! And if praise is due unto the One for the immeasurable humiliation which He endured on our behalf, is not distinctive praise equally due unto the Other for His amazing condescension in undertaking to convict us of sin?! Thanksgiving, honor and glory for ever be ascribed unto Him who operates as "the Spirit of judgment" and "the Spirit of burning" (Isa. 4:4).

The Spirit Comforting

Several Sequential Steps

The saving work of the Spirit in the heart of God's elect is a gradual and progressive one, conducting the soul step by step in the due method and order of the Gospel to Christ. Where there is no self-condemnation and humiliation there can be no saving faith in the Lord Jesus: "Ye repented not afterward, that ye might believe Him" (Matthew 21:32) was His own express affirmation. It is the burdensome sense of sin which prepares the soul for the Savior: "Come unto Me all ye that labors and are heavy laden" (Matthew 11:28). Without conviction there can be no contrition and compunction: he that sees not his wickedness and guilt never mourns for it; he that feels not his filthiness and wretchedness never bewails it.

Never was there one tear of true repentance seen to drop from the eye of an unconvicted sinner. Equally true is it that without illumination there can be no conviction, for what is conviction but the application to the heart and conscience of the light which the Spirit has communicated to the mind and understanding: Acts 2:37. So, likewise, there can be no effectual illumination until there has been a Divine quickening, for a dead soul can neither see nor feel in a spiritual manner. In this order, then, the Spirit draws souls to Christ: He brings them from death unto life, shines into their minds, applies the light to their consciences by effectual conviction, wounds and breaks their hearts for sin in compunction, and then moves the will to embrace Christ in the way of faith for salvation.

These several steps are more distinctly discerned in some Christians than in others. They are more clearly to be traced in the adult convert, than in those who are brought to Christ in their youth. So, too, they are more easily perceived in such as are drawn to Him out of a state of profaneness than those who had the advantages of a pious education. Yet in them, too, after conversion, the exercises of their hearts—following a period of declension and backsliding—correspond thereto. But in this order the work of the Spirit is carried on, ordinarily, in all—however it may differ in point of clearness in the one and in the other. God is a God of order both in nature and in grace, though He be tied down to no hard and fast rules.

Weaned from the World

By His mighty work of illumination and conviction, with the humiliation which is wrought in the soul, the Spirit effectually weans the heart forever from the comfort, pleasure, satisfaction or joy that is to be found in sin, or in any creature, so that his soul can never be quiet and contented, happy or satisfied, till it finds the comfort of God in Christ. Once the soul is made to feel that sin is the greatest of all evils, it sours for him the things of the world, he has lost his deep relish for them forever, and nothing is now so desirable unto him as the favor of God. All creature comforts have been everlastingly marred and spoiled, and unless he finds comfort in the Lord there is none for him anywhere.

"Therefore, behold, I will allure her, and bring her into the wilderness, and speak comfortably unto her" (Hosea 2:14). When God would win His church's heart to Him, what does He do? He brings her into "the wilderness," that is, into a place which is barren or devoid of all comforts and delights; and then and there He "speaks comfort to her." Thus, too, He deals with the individual. A man who has been effectually convicted by the Spirit is like a man condemned to die: what pleasure would be derived from the beautiful flowers as a murderer was led through a lovely garden to the place of execution! Nor can any Spirit-convicted sinner find contentment in anything till he is assured of the favor of Him whom he has so grievously offended. And none but God can "speak comfortably" to one so stricken.

The Nature of the Spirit's Comforting in Suffering

Though God acts as a sovereign, and does not always shine in the same conspicuous way into the hearts of all His children, nevertheless, He brings them all to see light in His light: to know and feel that there can be no salvation for them but in the Lord alone. By the Spirit's powerful illuminating and convicting operations the sinner is made to realize the awful disparity there is between God and himself, so that he feebly cries, "How can a poor wretch like me ever stand before such a holy God, whose righteous Law I have broken in so many ways, and whose ineffable majesty I have so often insulted?" By that light the convicted soul, eventually, is made to feel its utter inability to help itself, or take one step toward the obtainment of holiness and happiness. By that light the quickened soul both sees and feels there can be no access to God, no acceptance with Him, save through the Person and blood of Christ; but how to get at Christ the stricken soul knows not.

"And I will give her vineyards from thence, and the valley of Achor for a door of hope" (Hosea 2:15): such is the comforting promise of God to the one whom He proposes to "allure" or win unto Himself. First, He hedges up the sinner's way with "thorns" (Hosea 2:6), piercing his conscience with the sharp arrows of conviction. Second, He effectually battles all his attempts to drown his sorrows and find satisfaction again in his former lovers (v. 7). Third, He discovers his spiritual nakedness, and makes all his mirth to cease (vv. 10, 11). Fourth, He brings him into "the wilderness" (v. 14), making him feel his case is desperate indeed. And then, when all hope is gone, when the poor sinner feels there is no salvation for him, "a door of hope" is opened for him even in "the valley of Achor" or "trouble," and what is that "door of hope" but the mercy of God!

It is by putting into his mind thoughts of God's mercy that the Spirit supports the fainting heart of the convicted sinner from sinking beneath abject despair. Now it is that the blessed Spirit helps his infirmities with "groanings that cannot be uttered," and in the midst of a thousand fears he is moved to cry, "God be merciful to me a sinner." But "we must through much tribulation enter into the kingdom of God" (Acts 14:22)—true alike of the initial entrance into the kingdom of grace and the ultimate entrance into the kingdom of glory. The Lord heard the "groaning" of the poor Hebrews in Egypt, and "had respect unto them" (Ex. 2:23-25), nevertheless, He saw it was good for them to pass through yet sorer trials before He delivered them. The deliverer was presented to them and hope was kindled in their hearts (Ex. 4:29-31), yet the time appointed for their exodus from the house of bondage had not yet arrived.

And why was the deliverance of the Hebrews delayed after Moses had been made manifest before them? Why were they caused to experience yet more sorely the enmity of Pharaoh? Ah, the Lord would make them to feel their impotence as well as their wretchedness, and would exhibit more fully His power over the enemy. So it is very often (if not always) in the experience of the quickened soul. Satan is now permitted to rage against him with increased violence and fury (Zech. 3:1). The Devil accuses him of his innumerable iniquities, intensifies his remorse, seeks to persuade him that he has committed the unpardonable sin, assures him he has transgressed beyond all possibility of Divine mercy, and tells him his case is hopeless. And, my reader, were the poor sinner left to himself, the Devil would surely succeed in making him do as Judas did!

But, blessed be His name, the Holy Spirit does not desert the convicted soul, even in its darkest hour: He secretly upholds it and grants at least

The Holy Spirit

temporary respites, as the Lord did the Hebrews in Egypt. The poor Satan-harassed soul is enabled "against hope to believe in hope" (Rom. 4:18) and to cry, "Let the sighing of the prisoner come before Thee: according to the greatness of Thy power, preserve Thou those that are appointed to destruction" (Ps. 79:11). Yet before deliverance is actually experienced, before that peace which passeth all understanding is communicated to his heart, before the redemption "which is in Christ Jesus" becomes his conscious portion, the soul is made to feel its complete impotence to advance one step toward the same, that it is entirely dependent upon the Spirit for that faith which will enable him to "lay hold of Christ."

No Place for a "Decision" to Be Saved

One would naturally suppose that the good news of a free Savior and a full salvation would readily be embraced by a convicted sinner. One would think that, as soon as he heard the glad tidings, he could not forbear exclaiming, in a transport of joy, "This is the Savior I want! His salvation is every way suited to my wretchedness. What can I desire more? Here will I rest." But as a matter of fact this is not always the case, yea, it is rarely so. Instead, the stricken sinner, like the Hebrews in Egypt after Moses had been made manifest before them, is left to groan under the lash of his merciless taskmasters. Yet this arises from no defect in God's gracious provision, nor because of any inadequacy in the salvation which the Gospel presents, nor because of any distress in the sinner which the Gospel is incapable of relieving; but because the workings of self-righteousness hinder the sinner from seeing the fullness and glory of Divine grace.

Strange as it may sound to those who have but a superficial and non-experimental acquaintance with God's Truth, awakened souls are exceedingly backward from receiving comfort in the glorious Gospel of Christ. They think they are utterly unworthy and unfit to come to Christ just as they are, in all their vileness and filthiness. They imagine some meetness must be wrought in them before they are qualified to believe the Gospel, that there must be certain holy dispositions in their hearts before they are entitled to conclude that Christ will receive them. They fear that they are not sufficiently humbled under a sense of sin, that they have not a suitable abhorrence of it, that their repentance is not deep enough; that they must have fervent breathings after Christ and pantings after holiness before they can be warranted to seek salvation with a well-grounded hope of success. All of which is the same thing as hugging the miseries of unbelief in order to obtain permission to believe.

Burdened with guilt and filled with terrifying apprehensions of eternal destruction, the convicted sinner yet experimentally ignorant of the perfect righteousness which the Gospel reveals for the justification of the ungodly, strives to obtain acceptance with God by his own labors, tears, and prayers. But as he becomes better acquainted with the high demands of the Law, the holiness of God, and the corruptions of his own heart, he reaches the point where he utterly despairs of being justified by his own strivings. "What must I do to be saved?" is now his agonized cry. Diligently searching God's Word for light and help, he discovers that "faith" is the all-important thing needed, but exactly what faith is, and how it is to be obtained, he is completely at a loss to ascertain. Well-meaning people, with more zeal than knowledge, urge him to "believe," which is the one thing above all others he desires to do, but finds himself utterly unable to perform.

If saving faith were nothing more than a mere mental assent to the contents of John 3:16, then any man could make himself a true believer whenever he pleased—the supernatural enablement of the Holy Spirit would be quite unnecessary. But saving faith is very much more than a mental assenting to the contents of any verse of Scripture; and when a soul has been Divinely quickened and awakened to its awful state by nature, it is made to realize that no creature-act of faith, no resting on the bare letter of a text by a "decision" of his own will, can bring pardon and peace. He is now made to realize that "faith" is a Divine gift (Eph. 2:8, 9), and not a creature work; that it is wrought by "the operation of God" (Col. 2:12), and not by the sinner himself. He is now made conscious of the fact that if ever he is to be saved, the same God who invites him to believe (Isa. 45:22), yea, who commands him to believe (1 John 3:23), must also impart faith to him (Eph. 6:23).

Cannot you see, dear reader, that if a saving belief in Christ were the easy matter which the vast majority of preachers and evangelists of today say it is, that the work of the Spirit would be quite unnecessary? Ah, is there any wonder that the mighty power of the Spirit of God is now so rarely witnessed in Christendom?—He has been grieved, insulted, quenched, not only by the skepticism and worldliness of "Modernists," but equally so by the creature-exalting free-willism and self-ability of man to "receive Christ as his personal Savior" of the "Fundamentalists"!! Oh, how very few today really believe those clear and emphatic words of Christ, "No man can come to me, except the Father which hath sent me (by His Spirit) draw him" (John 6:44).

Ah, my reader, when GOD truly takes a soul in hand, He brings him to the end of himself He not only convicts him of the worthlessness of his own works, but He convinces him of the impotence of his will. He not Only strips him of the filthy rags of his own self-righteousness, but He empties him of all self-sufficiency. He not only enables him to perceive that there is "no good thing" in him (Rom. 7:18), but he also makes him feel he is "without strength" (Rom. 5:6). Instead of concluding that he is the man whom God will save, he now fears that he is the man who must be lost forever. He is now brought down into the very dust and made to feel that he is no more able to savingly believe in Christ than he can climb up to Heaven.

We are well aware that what has been said above differs radically from the current preaching of this decadent age; but we will appeal to the experience of the Christian reader. Suppose you had just suffered a heavy financial reverse and were at your wits' end to know how to make ends meet: bills are owing, your bank has closed, you look in vain for employment, and are filled with fears over future prospects. A preacher calls and rebukes your unbelief, bidding you lay hold of the promises of God. That is the very thing which you desire to do, but can you by an act of your own will? Or, a loved one is suddenly snatched from you: your heart is crushed, grief overwhelms you. A friend kindly bids you to, "sorrow not even as others who have no hope." Are you able by a "personal decision" to throw off your anguish and rejoice in the Lord? Ah, my reader, if a mature Christian can only "cast all his care" upon the Lord by the Holy Spirit 's gracious enablement, do you suppose that a poor sinner who is yet "in the gall of bitterness and the bond of iniquity" can lay hold of Christ by a mere act of his own will?

Just as to trust in the Lord with all his heart, to be anxious for nothing, to let the morrow take care of its own concerns, is the desire of every Christian, but "how to perform that which is good" he "finds not" (Rom. 7:18), until the Holy Spirit is pleased to graciously grant the needed enablement. The one supreme yearning of the awakened and convicted sinner is to lay hold of Christ, but until the Spirit draws him to Christ, he finds he has no power to go out of himself, no ability to embrace what is proffered him in the Gospel. The fact is, my reader, that the heart of a sinner is as naturally indisposed for loving and appropriating the things of God, as the wood which Elijah laid on the altar was to ignite, when he had poured so much water upon it, as not only to saturate the wood, but also to fill the trench round about it (1 Kings 18:33)-a miracle is required for the one as much as it was for the other.

The fact is that if souls were left to themselves—to their own "free will"—after they had been truly convicted of sin, none would ever savingly come to Christ! A further and distinct operation of the Spirit is still needed to actually "draw" the heart to close with Christ Himself. Were the sinner left to himself, he would sink in abject despair; he would fall victim to the malice of Satan. The Devil is far more powerful than we are, and never is his rage more stirred than when he fears he is about to lose one of his captives: see Mark 9:20. But blessed be His name, the Spirit does not desert the soul when His work is only half done: He who is "the Spirit of life" (Rom. 8:2) to quicken the dead, He who is "the Spirit of truth" (John 16:13) to instruct the ignorant, is also "the Spirit of faith" (2 Cor. 4:13) to enable us to savingly believe.

How the Spirit Comforts

And how does the Spirit work faith in the convicted sinner's heart? By effectually testifying to him of the sufficiency of Christ for his every need; by assuring him of the Savior's readiness to receive the vilest who come to Him. He effectually teaches him that no good qualifications need to be sought, no righteous acts performed, no penance endured in order to fit us for Christ. He reveals to the soul that conviction of sin, deep repenting, a sense of our utter helplessness, are not grounds of acceptance with Christ, but simply a consciousness of our spiritual wretchedness, rendering relief in a way of grace truly welcome. Repentance is needful not as inducing Christ to give, but as disposing us to receive. The Spirit moves us to come to Christ in the very character in which alone He receives sinners—as vile, ruined, lost. Thus, from start to finish "Salvation is of the Lord" (Jonah 2:9)—of the Father in ordaining it, of the Son in purchasing it, of the Spirit in applying it.

The Spirit Drawing

There seems to be a pressing need for a clear and full exposition of the Spirit's work of grace in the souls of God's people. It is a subject which occupies a place of considerable prominence in the Scriptures—far more so than many are aware—and yet, sad to say, it is grievously neglected by most preachers and writers of today; and, in consequence, the saints are to a large extent ignorant upon it.

Reasons for Ignorance of the Spirit's Drawing

The supernatural and special work of the Holy Spirit in the soul is that which distinguishes the regenerate from the unregenerate.

1. The religion of the vast majority of people today consists merely in an outward show, having a name to live among men, but being spiritually dead toward God. Their religion comprises little more than bare speculative notions, merely knowing the Word in its letter; in an undue attachment to some man or party; in a blazing zeal which is not according to knowledge; or in censoriously contending for a certain order of things, despising all who do not rightly pronounce their particular shibboleths. The fear of God is not upon them, the love of God does not fill and rule their hearts, the power of God is not working in their souls—they are strangers to it. They have never been the favored subjects of the Spirit's quickening operation.

"No man can come to Me, except the Father which hath sent Me draw him; and I will raise him up at the last day" (John 6:44). This emphatic and man-humbling fact is almost universally ignored in Christendom today, and when it is pressed upon the notice of the average preacher or "church member," it is hotly denied and scornfully rejected. The cry is at once raised, "If that were true, then man is nothing more than a machine, and all preaching is useless. If people are unable to come to Christ by an act of their own will, then evangelistic effort is needless, worthless." No effort is made to understand the meaning of those words of our Lord: they clash with modern thought, they rile the proud flesh, so they are summarily condemned and dismissed. No wonder the Holy Spirit is now "quenched" in so many places, and that His saving power is so rarely in evidence.

2. With others the supernatural agency of the Spirit is effectually shut out by the belief that Truth will prevail: that if the Word of God be faithfully preached, souls will be truly saved. Far be it from us to undervalue the Truth, or cast the slightest reflection on the living Word of God; yet modern ideas and present conditions demand that we plainly point out that it is not the Truth, the Scriptures, the Gospel, which renews the soul; but instead, the power and operations of the Holy Spirit. "You may teach a man the holiest of truths, and yet leave him a wretched man. Many who learn in childhood that 'God is love,' live disregarding, and die blaspheming God. Thousands who are carefully taught, 'Believe on the Lord Jesus Christ, and thou shalt be saved,' neglect so great salvation all their days. Some of the most wicked and miserable beings that walk the earth are men into whose consciences, when yet youthful and unsophisticated, the truth was carefully instilled.

"Unmindful of this, and not considering the danger of diverting faith from the power to the instrument, however beautiful and perfect the instrument may be, many good men, by a culpable inadvertence, constantly speak as if the Truth had an inherent ascendance over man, and would certainly prevail when justly presented. We have heard this done till we have been ready to ask, 'Do they take men for angels, that mere Truth is to captivate them so certainly?' yes, and even to ask 'Have they ever heard whether there be any Holy Spirit?'

"The belief that Truth is mighty, and by reason of its might must prevail, is equally fallacious in the abstract, as it is opposed to the facts of human history, and to the Word of God. We should take the maxim, the Truth must prevail, as perfectly sound, did you only give us a community of angels on whom to try the Truth. With every intellect clear and every heart upright, doubtless Truth would soon be discerned, and, when discerned, cordially embraced. But, Truth, in descending among us, does not come among friends. The human heart offers ground whereon it meets Truth at an immeasurable disadvantage. Passions, habits, interests, yes, nature itself, lean to the side of error; and though the judgment may assent to the Truth, which, however, is not always the case, still error may gain a conquest only the more notable because of this impediment. Truth is mighty in pure natures, error in depraved ones.

"Do they who know human nature best, when they have a political object to carry, trust most of all to the power of Truth over a constituency, or would they not have far more confidence in corruption and revelry? The whole history of man is a melancholy reproof to those who mouth about the mightiness of Truth. 'But,' they say, 'Truth will prevail in the long run.' Yes, blessed be God, it will; but not because of its own power over human nature, but because the Spirit will be poured out from on high, opening blind eyes and unstopping deaf ears.

"The sacred writings, while ever leaving us to regard the Truth as the one instrument of the sinner's conversion and the believer's sanctification, are very far from proclaiming its power over human nature, merely because it is Truth. On the contrary, they often show us that this very fact will enlist the passions of mankind against it, and awaken enmity instead of approbation. We are ever pointed beyond the Truth to HIM who is the Source and Giver of Truth; and, though we had Apostles to minister the Gospel, are ever lead not to deem it enough that it should be 'in word only, but in demonstration of the Spirit and in power'"(William Arthur, 1859).

It Is the Spirit Who Draws

John the Baptist came preaching "the baptism of repentance for the remission of sins" (Mark 1:4), but by what, or rather Whose power was it, that repentance was wrought in the hearts of his hearers? It was that of the Holy Spirit! Of old it was said, "He shall go before Him in the spirit and power of Elijah" (Luke 1:17). Now the "spirit and power of Elijah" was that of the Holy Spirit, as is clear from Luke 1:15, "he (the Baptist) shall be filled with the Holy Spirit." Similarly, it should be duly observed that when Christ commissioned His Apostles to preach in His name among all nations (Luke 24:47), that He added, "Behold, I send the promise of my Father upon you: but tarry ye in the city of Jerusalem, until ye be endued with power from on high" (v. 49). Why was the latter annexed to the former, and prefaced with a "Behold" but to teach them (and us) that there could be no saving repentance produced by their preaching, except by the mighty operations of the Third Person of the Godhead?

None will ever be drawn to Christ, savingly, by mere preaching; no, not by the most faithful and Scriptural preaching: there must first be the supernatural operations of the Spirit to open the sinner's heart to receive the message? And how can we expect the Spirit to work among us while He is so slighted, while our confidence is not in Him, but in our preaching? How can we expect Him to work miracles in our midst, while there is no humble, earnest, and trustful praying for His gracious activities? Most of us are in such a feverish rush to "win souls," to do "personal work," to preach, that we have no time for definite, reverent, importunate crying unto the Lord for His Spirit to go before us and prepare the soil for the Seed. Hence it is that the converts we make are but "man made," and their subsequent lives make it only too apparent unto those who have eyes to see that the Holy Spirit does not indwell them nor produce His fruits through them. O brethren, join the writer in contritely owning to God your sinful failure to give the Spirit His proper place.

The renewed heart is moved and melted when it contemplates the holy Savior having our iniquities imputed to Him and bearing "our sins in His own body on the tree." But how rarely is it considered that it is little less wonderful for the Holy Spirit to exercise Himself with our sins and hold them up to the eyes of our understanding. Yet this is precisely what He does: He rakes in our foul hearts and makes us conscious of what a stench they are in the nostrils of an infinitely pure God. He brings to light and to sight the hidden and hideous things of darkness and convicts us of our vile and lost condition. He opens to our view the "horrible pit" in which by nature we lie, and makes us to realize that we deserve nothing but the everlasting burnings. O how truly marvelous that the Third Person of the Godhead should condescend to stoop to such a work as that!

"No man can come to Me, except the Father which hath sent Me draw him" (John 6:44). No sinner ever knocks (Matthew 7:7) at His door for mercy, by earnest and importunate prayer, until Christ has first knocked (Rev. 3:20) at his door by the operations of the Holy Spirit!

The Natural Man Rejects God

As the Christian now loves God "because he first loved" him (1 John 4:19), so he sought Christ, because Christ first sought him (Luke 19:10). Before Christ seeks us, we are well content to lie fast asleep in the Devil's arms, and therefore does the Lord say, "I am found of them that sought Me not" (Isa. 65:1). When the Spirit first applies the Word of Conviction, He finds the souls of all men as the angel found the world in Zechariah 1:11; "all the earth sitteth still, and is at rest." What a strange silence and midnight stillness there is among the unsaved! "There is none that seeketh after God" (Rom. 3:11).

It is because of failure to perceive the dreadful condition in which the natural man lies, that difficulty is experienced in seeing the imperative need for the Spirit's drawing power if he is to be brought out of it. The natural man is so completely enslaved by sin and enchained by Satan that he is unable to take the first step toward Christ. He is so bent on having his own way and so averse to pleasing God, he is so in love with the things of this world and so out of love with holiness that nothing short of Omnipotence can produce a radical change of heart in him, so that he will come to hate the things he naturally loved, and love what he previously hated. The Spirit's "drawing" is the freeing of the mind, the affections, and the will from the reigning power

The Holy Spirit

of depravity; it is His emancipating of the soul from the dominion of sin and Satan.

Prior to that deliverance, when the requirements of God are pressed upon the sinner, he in every case, rejects them. It is not that he is averse from being saved from Hell—for none desire to go there—but that he is unwilling to 'forsake" (Prov. 28:13; Isa. 55:7) his idols—the things which hold the first place in his affections and interests. This is clearly brought out in our Lord's parable of "The Great Supper." When the call went forth, "Come for all things are now ready," we are told, "they all with one consent began to make excuse" (Luke 14:18). The meaning of that term "excuse" is explained in what immediately follows: they preferred other things; they were unwilling to deny themselves; they would not relinquish the competitive objects—the things of time and sense ("a piece of ground," "oxen," "a wife") were their all-absorbing concerns.

Had nothing more been done by "the Servant"—in this parable the Holy Spirit—all had continued to "make excuse" unto the end: that is, all had gone on cherishing their idols, and turning a deaf ear to the holy claims of God. But the Servant was commissioned to "bring in hither" (v. 21), yea, to "compel them to come in" (v. 23). It is a holy compulsion and not physical force which is there in view—the melting of the hard heart, the wooing and winning of the soul to Christ, the bestowing of faith, the imparting of a new nature, so that the hitherto despised One is now desired and sought after: "I drew them with cords of a man (using means and motives suited to a rational nature) with bands of love" (Hosea 11:4). And again, God says of His people "with loving-kindness have I drawn thee" (Jer. 31:10).

The Spirit's Drawing the Elect

Even after the elect have been quickened by the Spirit, a further and distinct work of His is needed to draw their hearts to actually close with Christ. The work of faith is equally His operation, and therefore is it said, "we having received (not "exercised"!) the same Spirit of faith" (2 Cor. 4:13) i.e., "the same" as Abraham, David, and the other Old Testament saints received, as the remainder of the verse indicates. Hence, observe the careful linking together in Acts 6:5, where of Stephen we read that, he was "a man full of faith and of the Holy Spirit"; full of "faith," because filled with the Spirit. So of Barnabas we are told, "he was a good man, and full of the Holy Spirit and of faith" (Acts 11:24). Seek to realize more definitely, Christian reader, that spiritual faith is the gift of the Spirit, and that He is to be thanked and praised for it. Equally true is it that we are now entirely dependent upon Him to call it into exercise and act.

The Divine Drawer is unto God's people "the Spirit of grace and of supplications" (Zech. 12:10). Of grace, in making to their smitten consciences and exercised hearts a wondrous discovery of the rich grace of God unto penitent rebels. Of supplications, in moving them to act as a man fleeing for his life, to seek after Divine mercy. Then it is He leads the trembling soul to Calvary, "before whose eyes Jesus Christ" is now "evidently (plainly) set forth crucified" (Gal. 3:1), beholding the Savior (by faith) bleeding for and making atonement for his sins—more vividly and heart affectingly than all the angels in Heaven could impart. And hence it follows in Zechariah 12:10, "they shall look upon Me whom they have pierced." Then it is that their eyes are opened to see that which was hitherto hidden from them, namely the "Fountain opened. . .for sin and for uncleanness" (Zech. 13:1), into which they are now moved to plunge for cleansing.

Yes, that precious "Fountain" has to be opened to us, or, experimentally, we discern it not. Like poor Hagar, ready to perish from thirst, knowing not that relief was near to hand, we—convicted of our fearful sins, groaning under the anguish of our lost condition—were ready to despair. But as God opened Hagar's eyes to see the "well," or "fountain" (Gen. 21:19), so the Spirit of God now opens the understanding of the awakened soul to see Christ, His precious blood, His all-sufficient righteousness. But more—when the soul is brought to see the Fountain or Well, he discovers it is "deep" and that he has "nothing to draw with" (John 4:11). And though he looks in it with a longing eye, he cannot reach unto it, so as to wash in it. He finds himself like the "impotent man" of John 5, desirous of "stepping in," but utterly without strength to do so. Then it is the Holy Spirit applies the atonement, "sprinkling the conscience" (Heb. 10:23), effectually granting a realization of its cleansing efficacy (see Acts 15:8, 9; 1 Cor. 6:11—it is Christ's blood, but the Spirit must apply it.)

And when the awakened and convicted soul has been brought to Christ for cleansing and righteousness, who is it that brings him to the Father, to be justified by Him? Who is it that bestows freedom of access unto Him from whom the sinner had long been absent in the "far country"? Ephesians 2:18 tell us, "for through Him (Christ, the Mediator) we both (regenerated Jews and Gentiles, Old Testament and New Testament saints alike) have access by one Spirit unto the Father." Ah, dear reader, it was nothing but the secret and invincible operations of the blessed Spirit which caused you—a wandering prodigal—to seek out Him, whom before you dreaded as a "consuming fire." Yes, it was none other than the Third Person of the Holy Trinity who drew you with the bands of love, and taught you to call God, "Father" (Rom. 8:15)!

The Spirit Working Faith

The principal bond of union between Christ and His people is the Holy Spirit; but as the union is mutual, something is necessary on our part to complete it, and this is faith. Hence, Christ is said to dwell in our hearts "by faith" (Eph. 3:17). Yet, let it be said emphatically, the faith which unites to Christ and saves the soul is not merely a natural act of the mind assenting to the Gospel, as it assents to any other truth upon reliable testimony, but is a supernatural act, an effect produced by the power of the Spirit of grace, and is such a persuasion of the truth concerning the Savior as calls forth exercises suited to its Object. The soul being quickened and made alive spiritually, begins to act spiritually, "The soul is the life of the body, faith is the life of the soul, and Christ is the life of faith" (John Flavel).

What Is "Saving Faith"

It is a great mistake to define Scriptural terms according to the narrow scope and meaning which they have in common speech. In ordinary conversation, "faith" signifies credence or the assent of the mind unto some testimony. But in God's Word, so far from faith—saving faith, we mean—being merely a natural act of the mind, it includes the concurrence of the will and an action of the affections: it is "with the heart," and not with the head, "that man believeth unto righteousness" (Rom. 10:10). Saving faith is a cordial approbation of Christ, an acceptance of Him in His entire character as Prophet, Priest, and King; it is entering into covenant with Him, receiving Him as Lord and Savior. When this is understood, it will appear to be a fit instrument for completing our union with Christ, for the union is thus formed by mutual consent.

Were people to perceive more clearly the implications and the precise character of saving faith, they would be the more readily convinced that it is "the gift of God," an effect or fruit of the Spirit's operations on the heart. Saving faith is a coming to Christ, and coming to Christ necessarily presupposes a forsaking of all that stands opposed to Him. It has been rightly said that, "true faith includes in it the renunciation of the flesh as well as the reception of the Savior; true faith admires the precepts of holiness as well as the glory of the Savior" (J. H. Thornwell, 1850). Not until these facts are recognized, enlarged upon, and emphasized by present-day preachers is there any real likelihood of the effectual exposure of the utter inadequacy of that natural "faith" which is all that thousands of empty professors possess.

Saving Faith Is the Work of the Spirit

"Now He which stablisheth us with you in Christ, and hath anointed us, is God" (2 Cor. 1:21). None but God (by His Spirit) can "stablish" the soul in all its parts—the understanding, the conscience, the affections, the will. The ground and reason why the Christian believes the Holy Scriptures to be the Word of God is neither the testimony nor the authority of the church (as Rome erroneously teaches), but rather the testimony and power of the Holy Spirit. Men may present arguments which will so convince the intellect as to cause a consent—but establish the soul and conscience so as to assure the heart of the Divine authorship of the Bible, they cannot. A spiritual faith must be imparted before the Word is made, in a spiritual way, its foundation and warrant.

1. Faith In the Word: The same blessed Spirit who moved holy men of old to write the Word of God, works in the regenerate a faith which nothing can shatter. That Word is the Word of God. The stablishing argument is by the power of God's Spirit, who causes the quickened soul to see such a Divine Majesty shining forth in the Scriptures that the heart is established in this first principle. The renewed soul is made to feel that there is such a pungency in that Word that it must be Divine. No born-again soul needs any labored argument to convince him of the Divine inspiration of the Scriptures: he has proof within himself of their Heavenly origin. Faith wrought in the heart by the power of the Spirit is that which satisfies its possessor that the Scriptures are none other than the Word of the living God.

2. Faith in Christ: Not only does the blessed Spirit work faith in the written Word—establishing the renewed heart in its Divine veracity and authority—but He also produces faith in the personal Word, the Lord Jesus Christ. The imperative necessity for this distinct operation of His was briefly shown in a previous chapter upon "The Spirit Comforting," but a further word thereon will not here be out of place. When the soul has been Divinely awakened and convicted of sin, it is brought to realize and feel its depravity and vileness, its awful guilt and criminality, its utter unfitness to approach a holy God. It is emptied of self-righteousness and self-esteem, and is brought into the dust of self-abasement and self-condemnation. Dark indeed is the cloud which now hangs over it; hope is completely abandoned, and despair fills the heart. The painful consciousness that Divine goodness has been

abused, Divine Law trodden under foot, and Divine patience trifled with, excludes the expectation of any mercy.

How the Spirit Works Saving Faith

When the soul has sunk into the mire of despair no human power is sufficient to lift it out and set it upon the Rock. Now that the renewed sinner perceives that not only are all his past actions transgressions of God's Law, but that his very heart is desperately wicked—polluting his very prayers and tears of contrition—he feels that he must inevitably perish. If he hears the Gospel, he tells himself that its glad tidings are not for such an abandoned wretch as he; if he reads the Word he is assured that only its fearful denunciations and woes are his legitimate portion. If godly friends remind him that Christ came to seek and to save that which was lost, he supposes they are ignorant of the extremities of his case—should they urge him to believe or cast himself on the mercy of God in Christ, they do but mock him in his misery, for he now discovers that he can no more do this of himself than he can grasp the sun in his hands. All self-help, all human aid, is useless.

In those in whom the Spirit works faith, He first blows down the building of human pretensions, demolishes the walls which were built with the untempered mortar of man's own righteousness, and destroys the foundations which were laid in self-flattery and natural sufficiency, so that they are entirely shut up to Christ and God's free grace. Once awakened, instead of fondly imagining I am the man whom God will save, I am now convinced that I am the one who must be damned. So far from concluding I have any ability to even help save myself, I now know that I am "without strength" and no more able to receive Christ as my Lord and Savior than I can climb up to Heaven. Evident it is, then, that a mighty supernatural power is needed if I am to come to Him who "justifieth the ungodly." None but the all-mighty Spirit can lift a stricken soul out of the gulf of despair and enable him to believe to the saving of his soul.

To God the Holy Spirit be the glory of His sovereign grace in working faith in the heart of the writer and of each Christian reader. You have attained peace and joy in believing, but have you thanked that peace-bringer—"the Holy Spirit" (Rom. 15:13)? All that "joy unspeakable and full of glory" (1 Peter 1:8) and that peace which "passeth all understanding" (Phil. 4:7)—to whom is it ascribed? The Holy Spirit. It is particularly appropriated to Him: "peace and joy in the Holy Spirit" (Rom. 14:17 and cf. 1 Thess. 1:6). Then render unto Him the praise which is His due.

The Spirit Uniting to Christ

Two Kinds of Union

One of the principal ends or designs of the Gospel is the communication to God's elect of those benefits or blessings which are in the Redeemer; but the communication of benefits necessarily implies communion, and all communion as necessarily presupposes union with His Person. Can I be rich with another man's money, or advanced by another man's honors? Yes, if that other be my surety (one who pledges himself as liable for my debt), or my husband. Peter could not be justified by the righteousness of Paul, but both could be justified by the righteousness of Christ imputed to them, seeing they are both knit to one common Head. Principal and surety are one in obligation and construction of law. Head and members are one body; branch and stock are one tree, and a slip will live by the sap of an-other stock when once engrafted into it. We must, then, be united to Christ before we can receive any benefits from Him.

Now there are two kinds of union between Christ and His people: a judicial and a vital, or a legal and a spiritual. The first is that union which was made by God between the Redeemer and the redeemed when He was appointed their federal Head. It was a union in law, in consequence of which He represented them and was responsible for them, the benefits of His transactions redounding to them. It may be illustrated by the case of suretyship among men: a relation is formed between the surety and that person for whom he engages, by which the two are thus far considered as one—the surety being liable for the debt which the other has contracted, and his payment is held as the payment of the debtor, who is thereby absolved from all obligation to the creditor. A similar connection is established between Christ and those who had been given to Him by the Father.

But something farther was necessary in order to the actual enjoyment of the benefits procured by Christ's representation. God, on whose sovereign will the whole economy of grace is founded, had determined not only that His Son should sustain the character of their Surety, but that there should be also a vital as well as legal relation between them, as the foundation of communion with Him in all the blessings of His purchase. It was His good pleasure that as they were one in law, they should be also one spiritually, that Christ's merit and grace might not only be imputed, but also imparted to them, as the holy oil poured on the head of Aaron descended to the skirt of his garments. It is this latter, this vital and spiritual union, which the Christian has with Christ, that we now purpose to treat of.

Internal "Drawing"

The preaching of the Gospel by the ambassadors of the Lord Jesus is the instrument appointed for the reconciling or bringing home of sinners to God in Christ. This is clear from Romans 10:14 and 1 Corinthians 1:21, and more particularly from 2 Corinthians 5:20, "Now then we are ambassadors for Christ, as though God did beseech you by us: we pray you in Christ's stead, be ye reconciled to God." But, as we have pointed out, the mere preaching of the Word—no matter how faithfully—will never bring a single rebel to the feet of Christ in penitence, confidence, and allegiance. No, for that there must be the special and supernatural workings of the Holy Spirit: only thus are any actually drawn to Christ to receive Him as Lord and Savior: and only as this fact is carefully kept prominently before us does the blessed Spirit have His true place in our hearts and minds.

"Thy people shall be willing in the day of Thy power" (Ps. 110:3). It is by moral persuasion—"with cords of a man" (Hosea 11:4)—that the Holy Spirit draws men to Christ. Yet by moral persuasion we must not understand a simple and bare proposal or tender of Christ, leaving it still to the sinner's choice whether he will comply with it or not. For though God does not force the will contrary to its nature, nevertheless He puts forth a real efficacy when He "draws," which consists of an immediate operation of the Spirit upon the heart and will whereby its native rebellion and reluctance is removed, and from a state of unwillingness the sinner is made willing to come to Christ. This is clear from Ephesians 1:19, 20 which we quote below.

"And what is the exceeding greatness of His power to us-ward who believe, according to the working of His mighty power, which He wrought in Christ, when He raised Him from the dead, and set Him at His own right hand in the heavenly places." Here is much more than a mere proposal made to the will: there is the putting forth of Divine power, great power, yea the exceeding greatness of God's power; and this power has a sure and certain efficacy ascribed to it: God works upon the hearts and wills of His people "according to the working of His mighty power, which He wrought in Christ, when He raised Him from the dead"—both are miracles of Divine might. Thus God fulfills "all the good pleasure of His goodness, and the work of faith with power" (2 Thess. 1:11). Unless the "arm of the LORD" is revealed (Isa. 53:1) none believe His "report."

Spiritual Union

Spiritual union with Christ, then, is effected both by the external preaching of the Gospel and the internal "drawing" of the Father. Let us now take note of the bands by which Christ and the believer are knit together. These bands are two in number, being the Holy Spirit on Christ's part, and faith on our part. The Spirit on Christ's part is His quickening us with spiritual life, whereby Christ first takes hold of us. Faith on our part, when thus quickened, is that whereby we take hold of Christ. We must first be "apprehended" (laid hold of) by Christ, before we can apprehend Him:

Philippians 3:12. No vital act of faith can be exercised until a vital principle is first communicated to us. Thus, Christ is in the believer by His Spirit; the believer is in Christ by faith. Christ is in the believer by inhabitation; the believer is in Christ by implantation (Rom. 6:3-5). Christ is in the believer as the head is in the body; we are in Christ as the members are in the head.

"He that is joined unto the Lord is one spirit" with Him (1 Cor. 6:17). The same Spirit which is in the Head is in the members of His mystical body, a vital union being effected between them. Christ is in Heaven, we upon earth, but the Spirit being omnipresent is the connecting link. "For by one Spirit are we all baptized into one body, whether we be Jews or Gentiles" (1 Cor. 12:13)—what could be plainer than that? "Hereby know we that we dwell in Him, and He in us, because He hath given us of His Spirit" (1 John 4:13). Thus, Christ is unto His people a Head not only of government, but also of influence. Though the ties which connect the Redeemer and the redeemed are spiritual and invisible, yet are they so real and intimate that He lives in them and they live in Him, for "the Spirit of life in Christ Jesus hath made me free from the law of sin and death" (Rom. 8:2).

"But if the Spirit of Him that raised up Jesus from the dead dwell in you, He that raised up Christ from the dead shall also quicken your mortal bodies by His Spirit that dwelleth in you" (Rom. 8:11), and this, because the Spirit is the bond of union between us and Christ. Because there is the same Spirit in the Head and in His members, He will therefore work the same effects in Him and in us. If the Head rise, the members will follow after, for they are appointed to be conformed unto Him (Rom. 8:29)—in obedience and suffering now, in happiness and glory hereafter. Christ was raised by the Spirit of holiness (Rom. 1:4), and so shall we be—the earnest of which we have already received when brought from death unto life.

The Spirit Indwelling

The Spirit and Christ Go Together

"But ye are not in the flesh, but in the Spirit, if so be that the Spirit of God dwell in you. Now if any man have not the Spirit of Christ, he is none of His" (Rom. 8:9). The possession of the Holy Spirit is the distinguishing mark of a Christian, for to be without the Spirit is proof positive that we are out of Christ—"none of His": fearful words! And, my reader, if we are not Christ's, whose are we? The answer must be, Satan's, for there is no third possessor of men. In the past all of us were subjects of the kingdom of darkness, the slaves of Satan, the heirs of wrath. The great questions which each one of us needs to accurately answer are, Have I been taken out of that terrible position? Have I been translated into the kingdom of God's dear Son, made an heir of God, and become indwelt by His Holy Spirit?

Observe that the Spirit and Christ go together: if we have Christ for our Redeemer, then we have the Holy Spirit for our Indweller. But if have not the Spirit, we are not Christ's. We may be members of His visible "Church," we may be externally united to Him by association with His people, but unless we are partakers of that vital union which arises from the indwelling of the Spirit, we are His only by name. "The Spirit visits many who are unregenerate, with His motions, which they resist and quench; but in all that are sanctified He dwells: there He resides and rules. He is there as a man at his own house, where he is constant and welcome, and has the dominion. Shall we put this question to our hearts, Who dwells, who rules, who keeps house there? Which interest has the ascendant?" (Matthew Henry).

The Spirit belongs to Christ (Heb. 1:9, Rev. 3:1) and proceeds from Him (John 1:33; 15:26; Luke 24:49). The Spirit is sent by Christ as Mediator (Acts 2:33). He is given to God's people in consequence of Christ's having redeemed them from the curse of the Law (Gal. 3:13, 14). We have nothing but what we have in and from the Son. The Spirit is given to Christ immediately, to us derivatively. He dwells in Christ by radication, in us by operation. Therefore is the Spirit called "the Spirit of Christ" (Rom. 8:9) and "the Spirit of His Son" (Gal. 4:6); and so it is Christ who "liveth in" us (Gal.

2:20). Christ is the great Fountain of the waters of life, and from Him proceeds every gift and grace. It is our glorious Head who communicates or sends from Himself that Spirit who quickens, sanctifies, and preserves His people.

What high valuation we set upon the blessed Person and work of the Holy Spirit when we learn that He is the gift, yea the dying legacy which Christ bequeathed unto His disciples to supply His absence. "How would some rejoice if they could possess any relic of anything that belonged unto our Savior in the days of His flesh, though of no use or benefit unto them. Yea, how great a part of men, called Christians, do boast in some pretended parcels of the tree whereon He suffered. Love abused by superstition lies at the bottom of this vanity, for they would embrace anything left them by their dying Savior. But He left them no such things, nor did ever bless and sanctify them unto any holy or sacred ends; and therefore hath the abuse of them been punished with blindness and idolatry. But this is openly testified unto in the Gospel: when His heart was overflowing with love unto His disciples and care for them, when He took a holy prospect of what would be their condition, work, and temptations in the world, and thereon made provision of all that they could stand in need of, He promised to leave and give unto them His Holy Spirit to abide with them forever" (John Owen).

Plain and express are the declarations of Holy Writ on this wondrous and glorious subject. "Know ye not that ye are the temple of God, and that the Spirit of God dwelleth in you?" (1 Cor. 3:16). "Because ye are sons, God hath sent forth the Spirit of His Son into your hearts, crying, Abba, Father" (Gal. 4:6). "Observe where the Spirit is said to dwell: not in the understanding—the fatal error of many—but in the heart. Most certainly He enlightens the understanding with truth, but He does not rest there. He makes His way to, and takes up His abode in the renewed and sanctified heart. There He sheds abroad the love of God. There He inspires the cry of "Abba, Father." And be that cry never so faint, it yet is the breathing of the indwelling Spirit, and meets a response in the heart of God.

"How affecting are Paul's words to Timothy, 'That good thing which was committed unto thee by the Holy Spirit which dwelleth in us.' "

The Basis for the Spirit's Indwelling

The basis upon which the Spirit takes up His abode within the believer is twofold: first, on the ground of redemption. This is illustrated most blessedly in the cleansing of the leper—figure of the sinner. "And the priest shall take some of the blood of the trespass offering, and the priest shall put it upon the tip of the right ear of him that is to be cleansed, and upon the thumb of his right hand, and upon the great toe of his right foot ... And of the rest of the oil that is in his hand shall the priest put upon the tip of the right ear of him that is to be cleansed, and upon the thumb of his right hand, and upon the great toe of his right foot, upon the blood of the trespass offering" (Lev. 14:14, 17). Wondrous type was that: the "oil" (emblem of the Holy Spirit) was placed "upon the blood"—only on the ground of atonement accomplished could the Holy Spirit take up His abode in sinners: this at once sets aside human merits.

There must be moral fitness as well. The Spirit of God will not tabernacle with unbelieving rebels. "After (or "when") that ye believed, ye were sealed with that Holy Spirit of promise" (Eph. 1:13). It is to those who obey the command, "Be ye not unequally yoked together" that God promises, "I will dwell in them" (2 Cor. 6:16). When by repudiating all idols, receiving Christ as Lord, trusting in the merits of His sacrifice, the heart is prepared—the Spirit of God enters to take possession for Christ's use. When we give up ourselves to the Lord, He accepts the dedication by making our bodies the temples of the Holy Spirit, there to maintain His interests against all the opposition of the Devil.

In considering the Spirit indwelling believers we need to be on our guard against entertaining any conception of this grand fact which is gross and dishonoring to His Person. He does not so indwell as to impart His essential properties or perfections—such as omniscience or omnipotence—it would be blasphemy so to speak. But His saving and sanctifying operations are communicated to us as the sun is said to enter a room, when its bright beams and genial warmth are seen and felt therein. Further, we must not think that the graces and benign influences of the Spirit abide in us in the selfsame manner and measure they did in Christ: no, for God "giveth not the Spirit by measure unto Him" (John 3:34)—in Him all fullness dwells.

This lays the basis for the most solemn appeal and powerful exhortation. Is my body a temple of the Holy Spirit? then how devoted should it be to God and His service! Am I indwelt by the Spirit of Christ? then how I ought to lend my ear to His softest whisper, my will to His gentlest sway, my heart to His sacred influence. In disregarding His voice, in not yielding to His promptings, He is grieved, Christ is dishonored, and we are the losers. The greatest blessing we possess is the indwelling Spirit: let us seek grace to conduct ourselves accordingly.

What "Indwelling" Denotes

"But ye are not in the flesh, but in the Spirit, if so be that the Spirit of God dwell in you" (Rom. 8:9). Three things are denoted by the Spirit's "indwelling." First, intimacy. As the inhabitant of a house is more familiar there than elsewhere, so is the Spirit in the hearts of Christ's redeemed. God the Spirit is omnipresent, being everywhere essentially, being excluded nowhere: "Whither shall I go from Thy Spirit? or whither shall I flee from Thy presence?" (Ps. 139:7). But as God is said more especially to be there where He manifests His power and presence, as Heaven is "His dwelling place," so it is with His Spirit. He is in believers not simply by the effects of common Providence, but by His gracious operations and familiar presence. "Even the Spirit of truth; whom the world cannot receive, because it seeth Him not, neither knoweth Him: but ye know Him; for He dwelleth with you, and shall be in you" (John 14:17). The world of natural men are utter strangers to the Spirit of God, not being acquainted with His sanctifying operations, but He intimately discovers His presence to those who are quickened by Him.

Second, constancy: "dwelling" expresses a permanent abode. The Spirit does not affect the regenerate by a transient action only, or come "upon" them occasionally as He did the Prophets of old, when He endowed them for some particular service above the measure of their ordinary ability—but He abides in them by working such effects as are lasting. He comes to the believer not as a Visitor, but as an Inhabitant: He is within us "a well of water springing up into everlasting life" (John 4:14). He lives in the renewed heart, so that by His constant and continual influence He maintains the life of grace in us. By the blessed Spirit Christians are "sealed unto the day of redemption" (Eph. 4:30).

Third, sovereignty: this is also denoted under the term "dwell." He is owner of the house, and not an underling. From the fact that the believer's body is the temple of the Holy Spirit, the Apostle points out the necessary implication that he is "not his own" (1 Cor. 6:19). Previously he was possessed by another owner, even Satan—the evil spirit says, "I will return into my house" (Matthew 12:44). But the Spirit has dispossessed him, and the sanctified heart has become His "house," where He commands and governs after His own will. Take again the figure of the sanctuary: "Know ye not that ye are the temple of God, and that the Spirit of God dwelleth in you?" (1 Cor. 3:16). A "temple" is a sacred dwelling, employed for the honor and glory of God, where He is to be revered and worshipped, and from which all idols must be excluded.

What the Indwelling Spirit Is

The indwelling Spirit is the bond by which believers are united to Christ. If, therefore, we find the Holy Spirit abiding in us, we may warrant-ably conclude we have been 'joined to the Lord." This is plainly set forth in those words of the Savior's, "And the glory which Thou gavest Me I have given them; that they may be one, even as We are one: I in them, and Thou in Me, that they may be made perfect in one" (John 17:22, 23). The "glory" of Christ's humanity was its union with the Godhead. How was it united? By the Holy Spirit. This very "glory" Christ has given His people: "I in them," which He is by the sanctifying Spirit—the bond of our union with Him.

The indwelling Spirit is the sure mark of the believer's freedom from the Covenant of Works, under which all Christless persons stand. And our title to the special privileges of the new covenant, in which none but Christ's are interested is but another way of saying. they are "not under the law, but under grace" (Rom. 6:14). This is plain from the Apostle's reasoning in Galatians 4:6, 7, "Because ye are sons, God hath sent forth the Spirit of His Son into your hearts, crying, Abba, Father. Wherefore thou art no more a servant, but a son." The spirit of the old covenant was a servile one, a spirit of fear and bondage, and those under the same were not "sons," but servants. The spirit of the new covenant is a free one, that of children, inheriting the blessed promises and royal immunities contained in the charter of grace.

The indwelling Spirit is the certain pledge and earnest of eternal salvation. The execution of the eternal decree of God's electing love—"drawn" (Jer. 31:3), and the application of the virtues and benefits of the death of Christ by the Spirit (Gal. 3:13, 14), is sure evidence of our personal interest in the Redeemer. This is plain from 1 Peter 1:2: "Elect according to the foreknowledge of God the Father, through sanctification of the Spirit, unto obedience and sprinkling of the blood of Jesus Christ." God's eternal decree is executed and the blood of Christ is sprinkled upon us when we receive the Spirit of sanctification. The Spirit's residing in the Christian is the guarantee and earnest of the eternal inheritance: "Who hath also sealed us, and given the earnest of the Spirit in our hearts" (2 Cor. 1:22).

The Evidences of the Spirit's Indwelling

What are the evidences and fruits of the Spirit's inhabitation? First, wherever the Spirit dwells, He does in some degree mortify and subdue the evils of the soul in which He resides. "The Spirit (lusts) against the flesh" (Gal. 5:17), and believers "through the Spirit do mortify the deeds of the body" (Rom. 8:13). This is one special part of His sanctifying work. Though He kills not sin in believers, He subdues it—though He does not subdue the flesh as that it never troubles or defiles them any more, its dominion is taken away. Perfect freedom from its very presence awaits them in Heaven; but even now, animated by their holy Indweller, Christians deny themselves and use the means of grace which God has appointed for deliverance from the reigning power of sin.

Second, wherever the Spirit dwells, He produces a spirit of prayer and supplication. "Likewise the Spirit also helpeth our infirmities: for we know not what we should pray for as we ought: but the Spirit itself maketh intercession for us with groanings which cannot be uttered" (Rom. 8:26). The two things are inseparable: wherever He is poured out as the Spirit of grace, He is also poured out as the Spirit of supplication (Zech. 12:10). He helps Christians before they pray by stirring up their spiritual affections and stimulating holy desires. He helps them in prayer by teaching them to ask for those things which are according to God's will. He it is who humbles the pride of their hearts, moves their sluggish wills, and out of weakness makes them strong. He helps them after prayer by quickening hope and patience to wait for God's answers.

Third, wherever the Spirit dwells He works a heavenly and spiritual frame of mind. "They that are after the flesh do mind the things of the flesh; but they that are after the Spirit the things of the Spirit. For to be carnally minded is death; but to be spiritually minded is life and peace" (Rom. 8:5-6). The workings of every creature follow the being and bent of its nature. If God, Christ, Heaven, engage the thoughts and affections of the soul, the Spirit of God is there. There are times in each Christian's life when he exclaims, "How precious also are Thy thoughts unto me, O God! how great is the sum of them! If I should count them, they are more in number than the sand: when I awake, I am still with Thee" (Ps. 139:17, 18)—such holy contemplation is the very life of the regenerate.

But, says the sincere Christian, If the Spirit of God dwelt in me, could my heart be so listless and averse to spiritual duties? Answer, The very fact that you are exercised and burdened over this sad state evidences the presence of spiritual life in your soul. Let it be borne in mind that there is a vast difference between spiritual death and spiritual deadness: the former is the condition of the unregenerate, the latter is the disease and complaint of thousands of the regenerate. Note it well that nine times over, David, in a single Psalm, prayed, "Quicken me!" (119). Though it be so often, it is not so always with you: there are seasons when the Lord breaks in upon your heart, enlarges you affections, and sets your soul at liberty—clear proof you are not deserted by the Comforter!

The Spirit Teaching

Taught of the Spirit

"But the Comforter, which is the Holy Spirit, whom the Father will send in My name, He shall teach you all things" (John 14:26). Those words received their first fulfillment in the men to whom they were immediately addressed—the Apostles were so filled and controlled by the Holy Spirit that their proclamation of the Gospel was without flaw, and their writings without error. Those original ambassadors of Christ were so taught by the Third Person in the Trinity that what they delivered was the very mind of God. The second fulfillment of the Savior's promise has been in those men whom He called to preach His Gospel throughout the Christian era. No new revelations have been made to them, but they were, and are, according to their varied measure, and the particular work assigned to them, so enlightened by the Spirit that the Truth of God has been faithfully preached by them. The third and widest application of our Lord's words are unto the entire Household of Faith, and it is in this sense we shall now consider them.

It is written, "And all Thy children shall be taught of the LORD" (Isa. 54:13 and cf. John 6:45). This is one of the great distinguishing marks of the regenerate: all of them are "taught of the LORD." There are multitudes of unregenerate religionists who are taught, numbers of them well taught, in the letter of the Scriptures. They are thoroughly versed in the historical facts and doctrines of Christianity; but their instruction came only from human media—parents, Sunday School teachers, or through reading religious books. Their intellectual knowledge of spiritual things is considerable, sound, and clear; yet is it unaccompanied by any heavenly unction, saving power, or transforming effects. In like manner, there are thousands of preachers who abhor the errors of "Modernists" and who contend earnestly for the Faith. They were taught in Bible Institutes, and theological schools, yet it is to be feared that many of them are total strangers to a miracle of grace being wrought in the heart. How it behooves each of us to test ourselves rigidly at this point!

It is a common fact of observation—which anyone may test for himself—that a very large percentage of those who constitute the membership of evangelical denominations were first taken there in childhood by their parents. The great majority in the Presbyterian churches today had a father or mother who was a Presbyterian and who instructed the offspring in their beliefs. The same is true of Baptists, the Methodists, and those who are in fellowship at the Brethren assemblies. The present generation has been brought up to believe in the doctrines and religious customs of their ancestors. Now we are far from saying that because a man who is a Presbyterian today had parents and grandparents that were Presbyterians and who taught him the Westminster Catechism, that therefore all the knowledge he possesses of Divine things is but traditional and theoretical. No indeed. Yet we do say that such a training in the letter of the Truth makes it more difficult, and calls for a more careful self-examination, to ascertain whether or not he has been taught of the Lord.

Though we do not believe that Grace runs in the blood, yet we are convinced that, as a general rule, (having many individual exceptions), God does place His elect in families where at least one of the parents loves and seeks to serve Him, and where that elect soul will be nurtured in the fear and admonition of the Lord. At least three-fourths of those Christians whom the writer has met and had opportunity to question, had a praying and Scripture-reading father or mother. Yet, on the other hand, we are obliged to acknowledge that three-fourths of the empty professors we have encountered also had religious parents, who sent them to Sunday School and sought to have them trained in their beliefs: and these now rest upon their intellectual knowledge of the Truth, and mistake it for a saving experience of the same. And it is this class which it is the hardest to reach: it is much more difficult to persuade such to examine themselves as to whether or not they have been taught of God, than it is those who make no profession at all.

Let it not be concluded from what has been pointed out that, where the Holy Spirit teaches a soul, He dispenses with all human instrumentality. Not so. It is true the Spirit is sovereign and therefore works where He pleases and when He pleases. It is also a fact that He is Almighty, tied down to no means, and therefore works as He pleases and how He pleases. Nevertheless, He frequently condescends to employ means, and to use very feeble instruments. In fact, this seems to generally characterize His operations: that He works through men and women, and sometimes through little children. Yet, let it be said emphatically, that no preaching, catechizing or reading produces any vital and spiritual results unless God the Spirit is pleased to bless and apply the same unto the heart of the individual. Thus there are many who have passed from death unto life and been brought to love the Truth under the Spirit's application of a pious parent's or Sunday School teacher's instruction—while there are some who never enjoyed such privileges yet have been truly and deeply taught by God.

Tests for the Spirit's Teaching

From all that has been said above a very pertinent question arises, How may I know whether or not my teaching has been by the Holy Spirit? The simple but sufficient answer is, By the effects produced. First, that spiritual knowledge which the teaching of the Holy Spirit imparts is an operative knowledge. It is not merely a piece of information which adds to our mental store, but is a species of inspiration which stirs the soul into action. "For God, who commanded the light to shine out of darkness, hath shined in our hearts, to give the light of the knowledge of the glory of God in the face of Jesus Christ" (2 Cor. 4:6). The light which the Spirit imparts reaches the heart. It warms the heart, and sets it on fire for God. It masters the heart, and brings it into allegiance to God. It molds the heart, and stamps upon it the image of God. Here, then, is a sure test: how far does the teaching you have received, the knowledge of Divine things you possess, affect your heart?

Second, that knowledge which the teaching of the Spirit imparts is a soul-humbling knowledge. "Knowledge puffeth up" (1 Cor. 8:1), that is a notional, theoretical, intellectual knowledge which is merely received from men or books in a natural way. But that spiritual knowledge which comes from God reveals to a man his empty conceits, his ignorance and worthlessness, and abases him. The teaching of the Spirit reveals our sinfulness and vileness, our lack of conformity to Christ, our unholiness; and makes a man little in his own eyes. Among those born of women was not a greater than John the Baptist: wondrous were the privileges granted him, abundant the light he was favored with. What effect had it on him? "He it is, who coming after me is preferred before me, whose shoe's latchet I am not worthy to unloose" (John 1:27). Who was granted such an insight into heavenly things as Paul! Did he herald himself as "The greatest Bible teacher of the age"? No. "Unto me, who am less than the least of all saints" (Eph. 3:8). Here, then, is a sure test: how far does the teaching you have received humble you?

Third, that knowledge which the teaching of the Holy Spirit imparts is a world-despising knowledge. It makes a man have poor, low, mean thoughts of those things which his unregenerate fellows (and which he himself, formerly) so highly esteem. It opens his eyes to see the transitoriness and comparative worthlessness of earthly honors, riches and fame. It makes him perceive that all under the sun is but vanity and vexation of spirit. It brings him to realize that the world is a flatterer, a deceiver, a liar, and a murderer which has fatally deceived the hearts of millions. Where the Spirit reveals eternal things, temporal things are scorned. Those things which once were gain to him, he now counts as loss; yea, as dross and dung (Phil. 3:4-9). The teaching of the Spirit raises the heart high above this poor perishing world. Here is a sure test: does your knowledge of spiritual things cause you to hold temporal things with a light hand, and despise those baubles which others hunt so eagerly?

Fourth, the knowledge which the teaching of the Spirit imparts is a transforming knowledge. The light of God shows how far, far short we come of the standard Holy Writ reveals, and stirs us unto holy endeavors to lay aside every hindering weight, and run with patience the race set before us. The teaching of the Spirit causes us to "deny ungodliness and worldly lusts," and to "live soberly, righteously, and godly, in this present world" (Titus 2:12). "We all, with open face beholding as in a glass the glory of the Lord, are changed into the same image from glory to glory, even as by the Spirit of the Lord" (2 Cor. 3:18). Here, then, is a sure test: how far does my knowledge of spiritual things influence my heart, govern my will, and regulate my life? Does increasing light lead to a more tender conscience, more Christlike character and conduct? If not, it is vain, worthless, and will only add to my condemnation.

The Spirit Applies Knowledge to the Heart

"But the Comforter, which is the Holy Spirit, whom the Father will send in My name, He shall teach you all things" (John 14:26). How urgently we need a Divine Teacher! A natural and notional knowledge of Divine things may be obtained through men, but a spiritual and experimental knowledge of them can only be communicated by God Himself. I may devote myself to the study of the Scriptures in the same ways as I would to the study of some science or the mastering of a foreign language. By diligent application, persevering effort, and consulting works of reference (commentators, etc.), I may steadily acquire a comprehensive and accurate acquaintance with the letter of God's Word, and become an able expositor thereof. But I cannot obtain a heart-affecting, a heart-purifying, and a heart-molding knowledge thereof. None but the Spirit of truth can write God's Law on my heart, stamp God's image upon my soul, and sanctify me by the Truth.

Conscience informs me that I am a sinner; the preacher may convince me that without Christ I am eternally lost; but neither the one nor the other is

The Holy Spirit

sufficient to move me to receive Him as my Lord and Savior. One man may lead a horse to the water, but no 10 men can make him drink when he is unwilling to do so. The Lord Jesus Himself was "anointed to preach the Gospel" (Luke 4:18), and did so with a zeal for God's glory and a compassion for souls such as none other ever had; yet He had to say to His hearers, "Ye will not come to Me, that ye might have life" (John 5:40). What a proof is that, that something more is required above and beyond the outward presentation of the Truth. There must be the inward application of it to the heart with Divine power if the will is to be moved. And that is what the teaching of the Spirit consists of: it is an effectual communication of the Word which works powerfully within the soul.

Why is it that so many professing Christians change their view so easily and quickly? What is the reason there are so many thousands of unstable souls who are "tossed to and fro, and carried about with every wind of doctrine, by the sleight of men, and cunning craftiness, whereby they lie in wait to deceive" (Eph. 4:14)? Why is it that this year they sit under a man who preaches the Truth and claim to believe and enjoy his messages; while next year they attend the ministry of a man of error and heartily embrace his opinions? It must be because they were never taught of the Spirit. "I know that, whatsoever God doeth, it shall be forever: nothing can be put to it, nor any thing taken from it" (Eccl. 3:14). What the Spirit writes on the heart remains: "The anointing which ye have received of Him abideth in you" (1 John 2:27), and neither man nor devil can efface it.

Why is it that so many professing Christians are unfruitful? Month after month, year after year, they attend upon the means of grace, and yet remain unchanged. Their store of religious information is greatly increased, their intellectual knowledge of the Truth is much advanced, but their lives are not transformed. There is no denying of self, taking up their cross, and following a despised Christ along the narrow way of personal holiness. There is no humble self-abasement, no mourning over indwelling sin, no mortification of the same. There is no deepening love for Christ, evidenced by a running in the way of His commandments. Such people are "ever learning, and never able to come to the knowledge of the truth" (2 Tim. 3:7), i.e. that "knowledge" which is vital, experimental, affecting, and transforming. They are not taught of the Spirit.

Why is it in times of temptation and death that so many despair? Because their house is not built upon the Rock. Hence, as the Lord Jesus declared, "the rain descended, and the floods came, and the winds blew, and beat upon that house; and itself" (Matthew 7:27). It could not endure the testing: when trouble and trial, temptation and tribulation came, its insecure foundation was exposed. And note the particular character Christ there depicted: "Everyone that heareth these sayings of Mine, (His precepts in the much-despised "Sermon on the Mount") and doeth them not, shall be likened unto a foolish man, which built his house upon the sand" (v. 26). Men may go on in worldly courses, evil practices, sinful habits, trusting in a head-knowledge of Christ to save them; but when they reach "the swelling of Jordan" (Jer. 12:5) they will prove the insufficiency of it.

Ah, dear reader, a saving knowledge is not a knowledge of Divine things, but is a Divinely-imparted knowledge. It not only has God for its Object, but God for its Author. There must be not only a knowledge of spiritual things, but a spiritual knowledge of the same. The light which we have of them must be answerable to the things themselves: we must see them by their own light. As the things themselves are spiritual, they must be imparted and opened to us by the Holy Spirit. Where there is a knowledge of the Truth which has been wrought in the heart by the Spirit, there is an experimental knowledge of the same, a sensible consciousness, a persuasive and comforting perception of their reality, an assurance which nothing can shake. The Truth then possesses a sweetness, a preciousness, which no inducement can cause the soul to part with it.

What the Spirit Teaches

Now as to what it is which the Spirit teaches us, we have intimated, more or less, in previous chapters. First, He reveals to the soul "the exceeding sinfulness of sin" (Rom. 7:13), so that it is filled with horror and anguish at its baseness, its excuselessness, its turpitude. It is one thing to read of the excruciating pain which the gout or gall stones will produce, but it is quite another thing for me to experience the well-nigh unbearable suffering of the same. In like manner, it is one thing to hear others talking of the Spirit convicting of sin, but it is quite another for Him to teach me that I am a rebel against God, and give me a taste of His wrath burning in my conscience. The difference is as great as looking at a painted fire, and being thrust into a real one.

Second, the Spirit reveals to the soul the utter futility of all efforts to save itself. The first effect of conviction in an awakened conscience is to attempt the rectification of all that now appears wrong in the conduct. A diligent effort is put forth to make amends for past offenses, painful penances are readily submitted to, and the outward duties of religion are given earnest attendance. But by the teaching of the Spirit the heart is drawn off from resting in works of righteousness which we have done (Titus 3:5), and this, by His giving increasing light, so that the convicted soul now perceives he is a mass of corruption within, that his very prayers are polluted by selfish motives, and that unless God will save him, his case is beyond all hope.

Third, the Spirit reveals to the soul the suitability and sufficiency of Christ to meet its desperate needs. It is an important branch of the Spirit's teaching to open the Gospel to those whom He has quickened, enlightened, and convicted—and to open their understanding and affections to take in the precious contents of the Gospel. "He shall glorify Me" said the Savior, "for He shall receive of Mine, and shall show it unto you" (John 16:14). This is His prime function: to magnify Christ in the esteem of "His own." The Spirit teaches the believer many things, but His supreme subject is Christ: to emphasize His claims, to exalt His Person, to reveal His perfections, to make Him superlatively attractive. Many things in Nature are very beautiful, but when the sun shines upon them, we appreciate their splendor all the more. Thus it is when we are enabled to view Christ in the light of the Spirit's teaching.

The Spirit continues to teach the regenerate throughout the remainder of their lives. He gives them a fuller and deeper realization of their own native depravity, convincing them that in the flesh there dwells no good thing, and gradually weaning them from all expectation of improving the same. He reveals to them "the beauty of holiness," and causes them to pant after and strive for an increasing measure of the same. He teaches them the supreme importance of inward piety.

The Spirit Cleansing

The title of this chapter may possibly surprise some readers who have supposed that cleansing from sin is by the blood of Christ alone. Judicially it is so, but in connection with experimental purging, certain distinctions need to be drawn in order to a clearer understanding. Here, the gracious operation of the Holy Spirit is the efficient cause, the blood of Christ is the meritorious and procuring cause, faith's appropriation of the Word is the instrumental cause. It is by the Holy Spirit our eyes are opened to see and our hearts to feel the enormity of sin, and thus are we enabled to perceive our need of Christ's blood. It is by the Spirit we are moved to betake ourselves unto that "fountain" which has been opened for sin and for uncleanness. It is by the Spirit we are enabled to trust in the sufficiency of Christ's sacrifice now that we realize what Hell-deserving sinners we are. All of which is preceded by His work of regeneration whereby He capacitates the soul to see light in God's light and appropriate the provisions of His wondrous mercy.

It is now our purpose to trace out the various aspects of the Spirit's work in purging the souls of believers, for we do not wish to anticipate too much the ground we hope to yet cover in our articles upon "Sanctification," yet this present topic would be incomplete were we to pass by this important phase of the Spirit's operations. We shall therefore restrict ourselves unto a single branch of the subject, which is sufficiently comprehensive as to include in it all that we now feel led to say thereon, namely, that of mortification. Nor shall we attempt to discuss in detail the varied ramifications of this important Truth, for if we are spared we hope some day ere very long to devote a series of articles to its separate consideration, for it is far too weighty and urgent to be dismissed with this brief notice of it.

"For if ye live after the flesh, ye shall die: but if ye through the Spirit do mortify' the deeds of the body, ye shall live" (Rom. 8:13). A most solemn and searching verse is this, and one which we greatly fear has very little place in present-day preaching. Five things in it claim attention. First, the persons addressed. Second, the awful warning here set before them. Third, the duty enjoined upon them. Fourth, the efficient Helper provided. Fifth, the promise made. Those here addressed are regenerated believers, Christians, as is evident from the whole context: the Apostle denominates them "brethren" (v. 12).

The Awful Warning

Our text, then, belongs to the Lord's own people, who "are debtors, not to the flesh, to live after the flesh" (Rom. 8:12); rather are they "debtors" to Christ (who redeemed them) to live for His glory, "debtors" to the Holy Spirit (who regenerated them) to submit themselves to His absolute control. But if an apprehension of their high privilege (to please their Savior) and a sense of their bounded duty (to Him who has brought them from death unto life) fail to move them unto godly living, perhaps an apprehension of their awful danger may influence them thereto: "For if ye live after the flesh, ye shall die"—die spiritually, die eternally, for "life" and "death" in Romans always signifies far more than natural life and death. Moreover, to restrict "ye shall die" to physical dissolution would be quite pointless, for that experience is shared by sinners and saints alike.

It is to be noted that the Apostle did not say, "If ye have lived after the flesh ye shall die," for everyone of God's children did so before He delivered them from the power of darkness and translated them into the kingdom of His dear Son. No, it is, "If ye live after the flesh," now. It is a continual course, a steady perseverance in the same, which is in view. To "live after the flesh" means to persistently follow the inclinations and solicitations of inward corruption, to be wholly under the dominion of the depravity of fallen human nature. To "live after the flesh" is to be in love with sin, to serve it contentedly, to make self-gratification the trade and business of life. It is by no means limited to the grosser forms of wickedness and crime, but includes as well the refinement, morality, and religiousness of the best of men, who yet give God no real place in their hearts and lives. And the wages of sin is death.

"For if ye live after the flesh, ye shall die." That is a rule to which there is no exception. No matter what your experience or profession, no matter how certain of your conversion or how orthodox your belief: "Be not deceived; God is not mocked: for whatsoever a man soweth, that shall he also reap. For he that soweth to his flesh shall of the flesh reap corruption; but he that soweth to the Spirit shall of the Spirit reap life everlasting" (Gal. 6:7, 8). O the madness of men in courting eternal death rather than leave their sinful pleasures and live a holy life. O the folly of those who think to reconcile God and sin, who imagine they can please the flesh, and yet be happy in eternity notwithstanding. "How much she hath glorified herself, and lived deliciously, so much torment and sorrow give her" (Rev. 18:7)— so much as the flesh is gratified, so much is the soul endangered. Will you, my reader, for a little temporal satisfaction run the hazard of God's eternal wrath? Heed this solemn warning, fellow-Christian: God means what He says, "IF ye live after the flesh, ye shall die."

The Duty to Mortify Sin

Let us now consider the duty which is here enjoined—"do mortify the deeds of the body." In this clause, "the body" is the same as "the flesh" in the previous one, they are equivalent terms for the corruption of nature. The emphasis is here placed upon the body because it is the tendency of in-dwelling sin to pamper and please our baser part. The soul of the unregenerate acts for no higher end than does the soul of a beast—to gratify his carnal appetites. The "deeds of the body," then, have reference not only to the outward actions, but also the springs from which they proceed. Thus, the task which is here assigned the Christian is to "mortify" or put to death the solicitations to evil within him. The life of sin and the life of grace are utterly inconsistent and repellent: we must die to sin in order to live unto God.

Now there is a threefold power in sin unto which we must die. First, its damning or condemning power, whereby it brings the soul under the wrath of God. This power it has from the Law, for "the strength of sin is the law" (1 Cor. 15:56). But, blessed be God, the sentence of the Divine Law is no longer in force against the believer, for that was executed and exhausted upon the head of his Surety: consequently, "we are delivered from the law" (Rom. 7:6). Though sin may still hale Christians before God, accuse them before Him, terrify the conscience and make them acknowledge their guilt, yet it cannot drag them to Hell or adjudge them to eternal wrath. Thus, by faith in Christ sin is "mortified" or put to death as to its condemning power (John 5:24).

Second, sin has a ruling and reigning power, whereby it keeps the soul under wretched slavery and continual bondage. This reign of sin consists not in the multitude, greatness, or prevalence of sin, for all those are consistent with a state of grace, and may be in a child of God, in whom sin does not and cannot reign. The reign of sin consists in the in-being of sin unopposed by a principle of grace. Thus, sin is effectually "mortified" in its reigning at the first moment of regeneration, for at the new birth a principle of spiritual life is implanted, and this lusts against the flesh, opposing its solicitations, so that sin is unable to dominate as it would (Gal. 5:17); and this breaks it tyranny. Our conscious enjoyment of this is dependent, mainly, upon our obedience to Romans 6:11.

Third, sin has an indwelling and captivating power, whereby it continually assaults the principle of spiritual life, beating down the Christian's defenses, battering his armor, routing his graces, wasting his conscience, destroying his peace, and at last bringing him into a woeful captivity unless it be mortified. Corruption does not lie dormant in the Christian: though it reigns not supreme (because of a principle of grace to oppose it) yet it molests and often prevails to a very considerable extent. Because of this the Christian is called upon to wage a constant warfare against it: to "mortify" it, to struggle against its inclinations and deny its solicitations, to make no provision for it, to walk in the Spirit so that he fulfill not the lusts of the flesh.

Unless the Christian devotes all his powers to a definite, uncompromising, earnest, constant warfare upon indwelling sin: unless he diligently seeks to weaken its roots, suppress its motions, restrain its outward eruptions and actions, and seeks to put to death the enemy within his soul, he is guilty of the basest ingratitude to Christ. Unless he does so, he is a complete failure in the Christian life, for it is impossible that both sin and grace should be healthy and vigorous in the soul at the same time. If a garden is overrun with weeds, they choke and starve the profitable plants, absorbing the moisture and nourishment they should feed upon. So, if the lusts of the flesh absorb the soul, the graces of the Spirit cannot develop. If the mind is filled with worldly or filthy things, then meditation on holy things is crowded out. Occupation with sin deadens the mind for holy duties.

But who is sufficient for such a task? Who can expect to gain the victory over such a powerful enemy as indwelling sin? Who can hope to put to death that which defies every effort the strongest can make against it? Ah, were the Christian left entirely to himself the outlook would be hopeless, and the attempt useless. But, thank God, such is not the case. The Christian is provided with an efficient Helper: "greater is He that is in you, than he that is in the world" (1 John 4:4). It is only "through the Spirit" we can, in any measure, successfully "mortify the deeds of the body."

True Mortification

Though the real Christian has been delivered from condemnation and freed from the reigning power of sin, yet there is a continual need for him to "mortify" or put to death the principle and actings of indwelling corruption. His main fight is against allowing sin to bring him into captivity to the lusts of the flesh. "Have no fellowship with the unfruitful works of darkness"—enter into no truce, form no alliance with—"but rather reprove them" (Eph. 5:11). Say with Ephraim of old, "What have I to do any more with idols?" (Hosea 14:8). No real communion with God is possible while sinful lusts remain unmortified. Allowed sin draws the heart from God, entangles the affections, discomposes the soul, and provokes God to close His ears against our prayers: see Ezekiel 14:3.

Now it is most important that we should distinguish between mock mortification and true, between the counterfeit resemblances of this duty and the duty itself. There is a pagan "mortification," which is merely suppressing such sins as nature itself discovers and from such reasons and motives as nature suggests (Rom. 2:14). This tends to hide sin rather than mortify it. It is not a recovering of the soul from the world unto God, but only acquiring a fitness to live with less scandal among men. There is a Popish and superstitious "mortification," which consists in the neglect of the body, abstaining from marriage, certain kinds of meat, and apparel. Such things have "a show of wisdom" and are highly regarded by the carnal world, but not being commanded by God they have no spiritual value whatsoever. They macerate the natural man instead of mortifying the old man. There is also a Protestant "mortification" which differs nothing in principle from the Popish: certain fanatics eschew some of God's creatures; others demand abstinence when God requires temperance.

True mortification consists, first, in weakening sin's root and principle. It is of little avail to chop off the heads of weeds while their roots remain in the ground—nor is much accomplished by seeking to correct outward habits while the heart be left neglected. One in a high fever cannot expect to lower his temperature while he continues to eat heartily, nor can the lusts of the flesh be weakened so long as we feed or "make provision for" them. Second, in suppressing the risings of inward corruptions: by turning a deaf ear to their voice, by crying to God for grace so to do, by pleading the blood of Christ for deliverance. Make conscience of evil thoughts and imaginations: do not regard them as inevitable, still less cherish them; turn the mind to holy objects. Third, in restraining its outward actings: "denying ungodliness," etc. (Titus 2:12).

Our Helper

Though grace be wrought in the hearts of the regenerate, it is not in their power to act it: He who implanted it must renew, excite, and marshal it. "If ye through the Spirit do mortify" (Rom. 8:13). First, He it is who discovers the sin that is to be mortified, opening it to the view of the soul, stripping it of its deceits, exposing its deformity. Second, He it is who gradually weakens sin's power, acting as "the Spirit of burning" (Isa. 4:4), consuming the dross. Third, He it is who reveals and applies the efficacy of the Cross of Christ, in which there is contained a sin-mortifying virtue, whereby we are "made conformable unto His death" (Phil. 3:10). Fourth, He it is who strengthens us with might in the inner man, so that our graces—the opposites of the lusts of the flesh—are invigorated and called into exercise.

The Holy Spirit is the effective Helper. Men may employ the aids of inward rigor and outward severity, and they may for a time stifle and suppress their evil habits; but unless the Spirit of God work in us, nothing can amount to true mortification. Yet note well it is not, "If the Spirit do mortify," nor even, "If the Spirit through you do mortify," but, "If ye through the Spirit do mortify"! The Christian is not passive, but active in this work. We are bidden to "cleanse ourselves from all filthiness of the flesh and spirit" (2 Cor. 7:1). We are exhorted to "build up yourselves on your most holy faith" and "keep ourselves in the love of God" (Jude 20, 21). Paul could say, "I keep under my body, and bring it into subjection" (I Cor. 9:27). It is by yielding to the Spirit's impulses, heeding His strivings, submitting ourselves unto His government, that any measure of success is granted us in this most important work.

The believer is not a cipher in this work. The gracious operations of the Spirit were never designed to be a substitute for the Christian's discharge of his duty. True, His influence is indispensable, though it relaxes us not from our individual responsibility. "Little children, keep yourselves from idols" (1 John 5:21) emphasizes our obligation, and plainly intimates that God requires from His people something more than a passive waiting for Him to stir them into action. O my reader, beware of cloaking a spirit of slothful indolence under an apparent jealous regard for the honor of the Spirit. Is no self-effort required to escape the snares of Satan by refusing to walk in those paths which God has forbidden? Is no self-effort to be made in breaking away from the evil influence of godless companions? Is no self-effort called for to dethrone an unlawful habit? Mortification is a task to which every Christian must address himself with prayerful and resolute earnestness. Nevertheless it is a task far transcending our feeble powers.

It is only "through the Spirit" that any of us can acceptably and effectually (in any degree) "mortify the deeds of the body." He it is who works in us a loathing of sin, a mourning over it, a turning away from it. He it is who presses upon us the claims of Christ, reminding us that inasmuch as He died for sin, we must spare no efforts to die to sin—"striving against sin" (Heb. 12:4), confessing it (1 John 1:9), forsaking it (Prov. 28:13). He it is who preserves us from giving way to despair, and encourages us to renew the conflict, assuring us that ultimately we shall be more than conquerors through Him that loved us. He it is who deepens our aspirations after holiness, causing us to cry, "Create in me a clean heart, O God" (Ps. 51:10), and moving us to "forget those things which are behind, and reach forth unto those things which are before" (Phil. 3:13).

The Promise

"If ye through the Spirit do mortify the deeds of the body, ye shall live" (Rom. 8:13). Here is the encouraging promise set before the sorely-tried contestant. God will be no man's debtor: He is a rewarder of them that diligently seek Him (Heb. 11:6). If, then, by grace, we deny the flesh and cooperate with the Spirit, if we strive against sin and strive after holiness, richly shall we be recompensed. To say that Christians are unable to concur with the Spirit is to deny there is any real difference between the renewed and those who are dead in sin. It is true that without Christ we can do nothing (John 15:5), yet it is equally true (though far less frequently quoted) that "I can do all things through Christ which strengtheneth me" (Phil. 4:13). Mortification and vivification are inseparable: dying to sin and living unto God are indissolubly connected: the one cannot be without the other. If we through the Spirit do mortify the deeds of the body, then, but only then, we shall "live"—live a life of grace and comfort here, and live a life of eternal glory and bliss hereafter.

Some have a difficulty here in that Romans 8:13 conditions "life" upon our performance of the duty of mortification. "In the Gospel there are promises of life upon the condition of our obedience. The promises are not made to the work, but to the worker, and to the worker not for his work, but for Christ's sake according to his work. As for example, promise of life is made not to the work of mortification, but to him that mortifieth the flesh, and that not for his mortification, but because he is in Christ, and his mortification is the token or evidence thereof And therefore it must be remembered that all promises of the Gospel that mention works include in them reconciliation with God in Christ" (W. Perkins, 1604). The conditionality of the promise, then, is neither that of causation or uncertainty, but of coherence and connection, or means and end. The Highway of Holiness is the only path that leads to Heaven: "He that soweth to the Spirit shall of the Spirit reap life everlasting" (Gal. 6:8).

But let it be pointed out that the sowing of a field with grain is not accomplished in a few minutes, it is a lengthy and laborious task, calling for diligence and patience. So it is with the Christian: mortification is a lifelong task. A neglected garden is neither easily nor quickly rid of weeds and much care is required for the cultivation of herbs and flowers. Nor is a long-neglected heart, with its indwelling corruptions and powerful lusts, brought into subjection to the Spirit by a few spasmodic efforts and prayers.

The Holy Spirit

It calls for painful and protracted effort, the daily denying of self, application of the principles of the Cross to our daily walk, earnest supplication for the Spirit's help. So "Be not weary" (Gal. 6:9).

In conclusion let us seek to meet the objection of the discouraged Christian. "If a true mortification must be not only a striving against the motions of inward corruptions, but also the weakening of its roots, then I fear that all my endeavors have been in vain. Some success I have obtained against the outbreakings of lust, but still I find the temptation of it as strong as ever. I perceive no decays in it, but rather does it grow more violent each day." Answer, "That is because you are more conscious and take more notice of corruption than formerly. When the heart is made tender by a long exercise of mortification, a small temptation troubles it more than a greater one did formerly. This seeming strengthening of corruption is not a sign that sin is not dying, but rather an evidence that you are spiritually alive and more sensible of its motions" (condensed from Ezekiel Hopkins, 1680, to whom we are indebted for several leading thoughts in the first part of this chapter).

The Spirit Leading

"For as many as are led by the Spirit of God, they are the sons of God" (Rom. 8:14). This verse presents to us another aspect of the varied work of the blessed Holy Spirit. In addition to all His other functions, He performs the office of Guide unto the godly. Nor is this peculiar to the present dispensation: He so ministered during the Old Testament times. This is brought out clearly in Isaiah 63, "Where is He that brought them up out of the Sea with the shepherd of His flock? where is He that put His holy Spirit within him? That led them by the right hand of Moses with His glorious arm, dividing the water before them, to make Himself an everlasting name? That led them through the deep, as an horse in the wilderness, that they should not stumble? As a beast goeth down into the valley, the Spirit of the LORD caused him to rest: so didst Thou lead Thy people, to make Thyself a glorious name" (vv. 11-14). Moses was no more able, by his own power, to induce the Hebrews to pass between the divided waters of the Red Sea and to cross the trackless desert, than by the mere extending of the rod he could divide those waters. Moses was simply the human instrument: the Holy Spirit was the efficient Agent.

Divinely Drawn

In the above passage we have more than a hint of how the Holy Spirit "leads": it is by means of an inward impulse, as well as by external directions. Among his comments upon Romans 8:14 Matthew Henry says, "Led by the Spirit as a scholar in his learning is led by his tutor, as a traveler in his journey is led by his guide, as a soldier in his engagements is led by his captain." But such analogies are inadequate, for they present only the external side, leaving out of account the internal operations of the Spirit, which are even more essential. "O LORD, I know that the way of man is not in himself: it is not in man that walketh to direct his steps" (Jer. 10:23). By nature we are not only ignorant of God's way, but reluctant to walk therein even when it is shown us, and therefore we find the Church praying "Draw me, we will run after Thee" (Song. 1:4). Ah, we never seek unto God, still less "run after Him," till we are Divinely drawn.

This humbling truth was well understood by David of old. First, he prayed, "Teach me, O LORD, the way of Thy statutes . . . Give me understanding" (Ps. 119:33, 34). But second, he realized that something more than Divine illumination was needed by him: therefore did he add, "Make me to go in the path of Thy commandments . . . Incline my heart unto Thy testimonies," (vv. 35, 36). By nature our hearts are averse from God and holiness. We can be worldly of ourselves, but we cannot be heavenly of ourselves. The power of sin lies in the love of it, and it is only as our affections are Divinely drawn unto things above that we are delivered from sin's dominion. Moreover, our wills are perverse, and only as supernatural grace is brought to bear upon them are they "inclined" Godwards. Thus, to be "led by the Spirit of God" is to be governed by Him from within, to be subject unto His secret but real impulses or strivings.

Not only are our hearts inclined by nature unto temporal, material, worldly, and evil things, rather than unto eternal, spiritual, heavenly and holy things, but they are by inveterate custom too. As soon as we are born we follow the bent of our natural appetites, and the first few years of our life are governed merely by sense; and the pleasures begotten by gratifying our senses become deeply ingrained in us. Moreover, by constant living in the world and long contact with material things, the tendency increases upon us and we become more strongly settled in a worldly frame. "Can the Ethiopian change his skin, or the leopard his spots? then may ye also do good, that are accustomed to do evil" (Jer. 13:23). Custom becomes a "second nature" to us: the more we follow a certain course of life, the more we delight in it, and we are only weaned from it with very great difficulty.

Natural lusts and appetites being born and bred in us from infancy, continue to cry out for indulgence and satisfaction. The will has become bent to a carnal course and the heart craves material pleasures. Hence, when the claims of God are presented to us, when the interests of our souls and the things of eternity are brought before us, when the "beauty of holiness" is presented to our view, they find our wills already biased in the contrary direction and our heart prepossessed with other inclinations, which by reason of long indulgence bind us to them. The heart being deeply engaged with and delighting in temporal and worldly things, is quite unable to respond to the dictates of reason and set itself upon that which is heavenly and Divine; and even the voice of conscience is unheeded by the soul, which prefers the insidious lullaby of Satan. Nothing but the Almighty power of the Holy Spirit can turn ("lead") the heart in a contrary direction.

Now the heart is inclined toward God when the habitual bent of our affections is more to holiness than to worldly things. As the power of sin lies in the love of it, so it is with indwelling grace. Grace prevails over us when we so love the things of God that the bent of the will and the strength of our affections is carried after them. When the course of our desires and endeavors, and the strength and stream of our souls runs out after holiness, then the heart is "inclined" Godwards. And how is this brought to pass, how does God reduce our rebellious hearts and mold them to the obedience of His will? The answer is, by His Word and by His Spirit; or putting it another way, by moral persuasion and by gracious power.

"And I will put My Spirit within you, and cause you to walk in My statutes" (Ezek. 36:27). God does this by combining together invincible might and gentle inducements. God works upon us morally, not physically, because He will preserve our nature and the principles thereof. He does not force us against our wills, but sweetly draws us. He presents weighty reasons, casting into the mind one after another, till the scales be turned and then all is made efficacious by His Spirit. Yet this is not a work which He does in the soul once and for all, but is often renewed and repeated; and that because the "flesh" or sinful nature remains in us, unchanged, even after regeneration. Therefore do we need to ask God to continue inclining our hearts toward Himself.

This brings us to notice the intimate connection which exists between our present text and the verse immediately preceding it. "For if ye live after the flesh, ye shall die: but if ye through the Spirit do mortify the deeds of the body, ye shall live" (Rom. 8:13):—if we yield ourselves to the Spirit's impulses to restrain our evil propensities and our proneness to indulge them, then Heaven will be our portion, "For as many as are led by the Spirit of God, they are the sons of God" (v. 14). Thus Romans 8:14 is said in confirmation and amplification of verse 13: only those who are ruled by the Spirit give evidence that they are the "sons of God." To be "led by the Spirit," then, means, as the whole context clearly shows, to "walk not after the flesh, but after the Spirit" (v. 4), to "mind the things of the Spirit" (v. 5), to "through the Spirit mortify the deeds of the body" (v. 13). Suitably did Calvin remark on Romans 8:14, "Thus the empty boasting of hypocrites is taken away, who without any reason assume the title of sons of God."

Thus we are "led by the Spirit" both actively and passively: actively, with respect to His prompting; passively on our part, as we submit to those promptings; actively, by His pressing upon us the holy requirements of the Scriptures; passively, as we yield ourselves unto those requirements. The

Spirit is our Guide, but we must obey His motions. In the immediate context it is His restraining motives which are in view, moving us to the mortifying of sin. But His "leading" is not to be restricted to that: He exercises inviting motives, encouraging us unto the perfecting of holiness. And this being guided and governed by the Holy Spirit is an infallible proof that we are living members of God's family.

Active Guidance

It is the office of Jehovah the Spirit in the covenant of redemption, after He has called the elect out of the world, to place Himself at their head and undertake their future guidance. He knows the only path which leads to Heaven. He knows the difficulties and dangers which beset us, the intricate maze of life's journey, the numerous false routes by which Satan deceives souls, and the proneness of the human heart to follow that which is evil; and therefore does He, in His infinite grace, take charge of those who are "strangers and pilgrims" in this scene, and conduct them safely to the Celestial Country. O what praise is due unto this heavenly Guide! How gladly and thankfully should we submit ourselves unto His directions! How hopeless would be our case without Him! With what alacrity should we follow His motions and directions!

As we have already pointed out, the blessed Spirit of God "leads" both objectively and subjectively: by pointing us to the directive precepts of the Word, that our actions may be regulated thereby: and by secret impulses from within the soul, impressing upon us the course we should follow—the evils to be avoided, the duties to be performed. The Spirit acts upon His own life in the renewed soul. He works in the Christian a right disposition of heart relating to Truth and duty. He maintains in the believer a right disposition of mind, preparing and disposing him to attend unto the revealed will of God. He speaks effectually to the conscience, enlightens the understanding, regulates the desires, and orders the conduct of those who submit themselves unto His holy suggestions and overtures. To be "led by the Spirit of God" is to be under His guidance and government.

A Caution

The wayward child and the self-willed youth is guided by his own unsanctified and unsubdued spirit. The man of the world is controlled by "the spirit of the world." The wicked are governed by Satan "the spirit that now worketh in the children of disobedience" (Eph. 2:2). But the Christian is to yield himself unto "the still small voice" of the Holy Spirit. Yet a word of caution is needed at this point, for in our day there are many fanatics and impious people who do that which is grossly dishonoring to God under the plea that they were "prompted by the Spirit" so to act. To be "led by the Spirit of God" does not mean being influenced by unaccountable suggestions and uncontrollable impulses which result in conduct displeasing to God, and often injurious to ourselves and others. No, indeed: not so does the Spirit of God "lead" anyone.

There is a safe and sure criterion by which the Christian may gauge his inward impulses, and ascertain whether they proceed from his own restless spirit, an evil spirit, or the Spirit of God. That criterion is the written Word of God, and by it all must be measured. The Holy Spirit never prompts anyone to act contrary to the Scriptures. How could He, when He is the Author of them! His promptings are always unto obedience to the precepts of Holy Writ. Therefore, when a man who has not been distinctly called, separated, and qualified by God to be a minister of His Word, undertakes to "preach," no matter how strong the impulse, it proceeds not from the Holy Spirit. When a woman "feels led" to pray in public where men are present, she is moved by "another spirit" (2 Cor. 11:4), or if one claimed "guidance" in assuming an unequal yoke by marrying an unbeliever, 2 Corinthians 6:14 would prove conclusively that it was not the "guidance" of the Holy Spirit.
Divine Direction

The Holy Spirit fulfills His office of Guide by three distinct operations. First, He communicates life and grace, a new "nature"; second, He stirs that life unto action, and gives "more grace"; third, He directs the action into performance of duty. Life, motion, and conduct are inseparable in nature and grace alike. First, the Holy Spirit quickens us into newness of life, infusing gracious habits into the soul. "A new heart also will I give you, and a new spirit will I put within you" (Ezek. 36:26). Second, He moves upon the soul and assists the new nature to act according to its own gracious habits and principles: He "worketh in you both to will and to do of His good pleasure" (Phil. 2:13). Third, He directs our actions by enlightening our understandings, guiding our inclinations, and moving our wills to do that which is pleasing unto God. It is the last two we are now considering.

Divine direction is promised the saints: "The meek will He guide in judgment: and the meek will He teach His way" (Ps. 25:9): and this not only by general directions, but by particular excitations. "I am the LORD thy God which teacheth thee to profit, which leadeth thee by the way that thou shouldest go" (Isa. 48:17). Divine guidance is desired by the saints as a great and necessary blessing: "Show me Thy ways, O LORD; teach me Thy paths. Lead me in Thy truth, and teach me: for Thou art the God of my salvation; on Thee do I wait all the day" (Ps. 25:4, 5). Mark the earnestness of this prayer: "show me, teach me, lead me." Note the argument: "Thou art the God of my salvation," and as such, pledged to undertake for me. Observe the importunity: "on Thee do I wait all the day," as if he would not be left for a moment to his own poor wisdom and power. Even the "new nature" is utterly dependent upon the Holy Spirit.

Though the children of God are "light in the Lord" (Eph. 5:8) and have a general understanding of the way of godliness, yet much ignorance and darkness still remains in them, and therefore in order to a steady and constant course of obedience they need to be guided by the Holy Spirit, so that their light may be both directive and persuasive. Though Christians have a general understanding of their duty, much grace from God is needed to perform it by them. If left to themselves, their own corruptions would blind and govern them, and therefore do they pray, "Order my steps in Thy Word: and let not any iniquity have dominion over me" (Ps. 119:133). The way to Heaven is a "narrow" one, hard to find and harder still to be kept, except God teach us daily by His Spirit. Wisdom from on High is continually needed to know how to apply the rules of Scripture to all the varied details of our lives. The Holy Spirit is the only fountain of holiness, and to Him we must constantly turn for directions.

But something more than knowledge is needed by us: the Spirit must persuade and incline our hearts, and move our wills. How strong are our inclinations to sin, how easily fleshly impulses override our better judgment, how weak we are before temptation! We know what we should do, but are carried away by corrupt affections to the contrary. It is at this point the Holy Spirit governs from within. First, by His restraining motions, bidding us to avoid and mortify sin; second, by His quickening motions, inviting us to the pursuit of holiness. And just so far as we yield to His "strivings" are we "led by the Spirit of God." As moral agents we are responsible to co-operate with the Spirit and respond to His gentle sway over us. Alas, we so often fail to do so. But though He allows this up to a certain point—for our humbling—yet by His invincible power He prevents our making shipwreck of the faith, and after many chastenings, conducts us safely to Glory.

Knowing We Are Led by the Spirit

In conclusion we will seek to supply answer to the following question: How may Christians know whether they be among those who are "led by the Spirit of God"? In general, those who are directed by this Divine Guide are moved to examine their hearts and take frequent notice of their ways, to mourn over their carnality and perverseness, to confess their sins, to earnestly seek grace to enable them to be obedient. They are moved to search the Scriptures daily to ascertain the things which God has prohibited and the things which He enjoins. They are moved to an increasing conformity to God's holy Law, and an increasing enablement to meet its requirements is wrought in them by the Spirit blessing to them the means of grace. But to be more specific.

First, just so far as we are governed by the Spirit of God are we led from ourselves: from confidence in our own wisdom, from dependence upon our own strength, and from trust in our own righteousness. We are led from self-aggrandizement, self-will, self-pleasing. The Spirit conducts away from self unto God. Yet let it be pointed out that this weaning us from ourselves is not accomplished in a moment, but is a perpetual and progressive thing. Alas, God has at best but a portion of our affections. It is true there are moments when we sincerely and ardently desire to be fully and unreservedly surrendered to Him, but the ensnaring power of some rival object soon confirms how partial and imperfect our surrender has been.

Second, just so far as we are governed by the Spirit of God are we brought to occupation with Christ. To whom else, in our deep need, can we go? Who so well-suited to our misery and poverty? Having severed us in some degree from ourselves, the Spirit brings us into a closer realization of our union with the Savior. Are we conscious of our filth and guilt?—the Spirit leads us to the blood of Christ. Are we sorely tried and oppressed?— the Spirit leads us to Him who is able to succour the tempted. Are we mourning our emptiness and barrenness?—the Spirit leads us to the One in whom dwelleth all the fullness of the Godhead bodily. It is the special office of the Spirit to take of the things of Christ and show them unto us.

Third, just so far as we are governed by. the Spirit of God are we conducted along the highway of holiness. The Spirit leads the Christian away from the vanities of the world to the satisfying delight which is to be found in the Lord. He turns us from the husks which the swine feed upon unto spiritual realities, drawing our affections unto things above. He moves us to seek after more intimate and more constant communion with God, which can only be obtained by separation from that which He abhors. His aim is to conform us more and more to the image of Christ. Finally, He will conduct us to Heaven, for of it the Spirit is both the pledge and the earnest.

The Spirit Assuring

We do not propose to treat of the Spirit assuring in a topical and general way, but to confine ourselves to His inspiring the Christian with a sense of his adoption into the family of God, limiting ourselves unto two or three particular passages which treat specifically thereof. In Romans 8:15 we read, "For ye have not received the spirit of bondage again to fear; but ye have received the Spirit of adoption, whereby we cry, Abba, Father." The eighth chapter of Romans has ever been a great favorite with the Lord's people, for it contains a wide variety of cordials for their encouragement and strengthening in the running of that heavenly race which is marked out and set before them in the Word of God. The Apostle is there writing to such as have been brought, by the grace and power of the Holy Spirit, to know and believe on the Lord Jesus, and who by their communion with Him are led to set their affection upon things above.

First, let us observe that Romans 8:15 opens with the word "For," which not only suggests a close connection with that which precedes, but intimates that a proof is now furnished of what had just been affirmed. In the verse, the Apostle had said, "Therefore, brethren, we are debtors, not to the flesh, to live after the flesh": the "Therefore" being a conclusion drawn from all the considerations set forth in verses 1-11. Next, the Apostle had declared, "For if ye live after the flesh, ye shall die: but if ye through the Spirit do mortify the deeds of the body, ye shall live" (v. 13); which means, first, ye shall continue to "live" a life of grace now; and second, this shall be followed by a "life" of glory throughout eternity. Then the Apostle added, "For as many as are led by the Spirit of God, they are the sons of God" (v. 14), which is a confirmation and amplification of verse 13: none live a life of grace save those who are "led by the Spirit of God"—are inwardly controlled and outwardly governed by Him: for they only are "the sons of God."

"Not Received the Spirit of Bondage"

Now, in verse 15, the Apostle both amplifies and confirms what he had said in verse 14: there he shows the reality of that relationship with God which our regeneration makes manifest—obedient subjection to Him as dear children. Here he brings before us further proof of our Divine sonship—deliverance from a servile fear, the exercise of a filial confidence. Let us consider the negative first: "For ye have not received the spirit of bondage again to fear." By nature we were in "bondage" to sin, to Satan, to the world; yet they did not work in us a spirit of "fear," so they cannot be (as some have supposed) what the Apostle had reference to; rather is it what the Spirit's convicting us of sin wrought in us. When He applies the Law to the conscience our complacency is shattered, our false peace is destroyed, and we are terrified at the thought of God's righteous wrath and the prospect of eternal punishment.

When a soul has received life and light from the Spirit of God, so that he perceives the infinite enormity and filthiness of sin, and the total depravity and corruption of every faculty of his soul and body, that spirit of legality which is in all men by nature, is at once stirred up and alarmed, so that the mind is possessed with secret doubts and suspicions of God's mercy in Christ to save. Thereby the soul is brought into a state of legal bondage and fear. When a soul is first awakened by the Holy Spirit, it is subject to a variety of fears; yet it does not follow from thence that He works those fears or is the Author of them: rather are they to be ascribed unto our own unbelief. When the Spirit is pleased to convict of sin and gives the conscience to feel the guilt of it, it is to show him his need of Christ, and not to drive unto despair.

No doubt there is also a dispensational allusion in the passage we are now considering. During the Mosaic economy, believing Israelites were to a considerable extent under the spirit of legal bondage because the sacrifices and ablutions of the Levitical institutions could not take away sins. The precepts of the ceremonial law were so numerous, so various, so burdensome, that the Jews were kept in perpetual bondage. Hence, we find Peter referring to the same as "a yoke which neither our fathers nor we were able to bear" (Acts 15:10). Much under the Old Testament dispensation tended to a legal spirit. But believers, under the Gospel, are favored with a clearer, fuller, and more glorious display and revelation of God's grace in the Person and work of the Lord Jesus Christ, the Evangel making known the design and sufficiency of His finished work, so that full provision is now made to deliver them from all servile fear.

"Received the Spirit of Adoption"

Turning now to the positive side: believers have "received the Spirit of adoption, whereby they cry, Abba, Father": they have received that unspeakable Gift which attests and makes known to them their adoption by God. Before the foundation of the world God predestined them "unto the adoption of children by Jesus Christ to Himself" (Eph. 1:5). But more—the elect were not only predestined unto the adoption of children—to actually and openly enjoy this inestimable favor in time—but this blessing was itself provided and bestowed upon them in the Everlasting Covenant of grace, in which they not only had promise of this relationship, but were given in that Covenant to Christ under that very character. Therefore does the Lord Jesus say, "Behold I and the children which God hath given Me" (Heb. 2:13).

It is to be carefully noted that God's elect are spoken of as "children" previous to the Holy Spirit's being sent into their hearts: "Because ye are sons, God hath sent forth the Spirit of his Son into your hearts" (Gal. 4:6). They are not, then, made children by the new birth. They were "children" before Christ died for them: "he prophesied that Jesus should die for that nation; and not for that nation only, but that also He should gather together in one the children of God that were scattered abroad" (John 11:51, 52). They were not, then, made children by what Christ did for them. Yea, they were "children" before the Lord Jesus became incarnate: "Forasmuch then as the children are partakers of flesh and blood, He also Himself likewise took part of the same" (Heb. 2:14). Thus it is a great mistake to confound adoption and regeneration: they are two distinct things; the latter being both the effect and evidence of the former. Adoption was by an act of God's will in eternity—regeneration is by the work of His grace in time.

Had there been no adoption, there would be no regeneration: yet the former is not complete without the latter. By adoption the elect were put into the relation of children; by regeneration they are given a nature suited to that relation. So high is the honor of being taken into the family of God, and so wondrous is the privilege of having God for our Father, that some extraordinary benefit is needed by us to assure our hearts of the same. This we have when we receive the Spirit of adoption. For God to give us His Spirit is far more than if He had given us all the world, for the latter would be something outside Himself, whereas the former is Himself! The death of Christ on the Cross was a demonstration of God's love for His people, yet that was done without them; but in connection with what we are now considering, "the love of God is shed abroad in our hearts by the Holy Spirit which is given unto us" (Rom. 5:5).

Wondrous and blessed fact that, God manifests His love to the members of His Church in precisely the same way that He evidenced His love unto its Head when He became incarnate, namely, by the transcendent gift of His Spirit. The Spirit came upon Jesus Christ as the proof of God's love to Him and also as the visible demonstration of His Sonship. The Spirit of God descended like a dove and abode upon Him, and then the Father's voice was heard saying, "This is My Beloved Son, in whom I am well pleased"—compare John 3:34, 35. In fulfillment of Christ's prayer, "I have declared unto them Thy name, and will declare it: that the love wherewith Thou hast loved Me may be in them" (John 17:26) the Spirit is given to His redeemed, to signify the sameness of the Father's love unto His Son and unto His sons. Thus, the inhabitation of the Spirit in the Christian is both the surest sign of God's fatherly love and the proof of his adoption.

Inclining Hearts to Love God

"Because ye are sons, God hath sent forth the Spirit of His Son into your hearts, crying, Abba, Father" (Gal. 4:6). Because they had been eternally predestined unto the adoption of sons (Eph. 1:4, 5), because they were actually given to Christ under that character in the Everlasting Covenant (John 17:2; Heb. 2:13), at God's appointed time the Holy Spirit is sent unto their hearts to give them a knowledge of the wondrous fact that they have a place in the very family of God and that God is their Father. This it is which inclines their hearts to love Him, delight in Him, and place all their dependence on Him. The great design of the Gospel is to reveal the love of God to His people, and thereby recover their love to God, that they may love Him again who first loved them. But the bare revelation of that love in the Word will not secure this, until "the love of God is shed abroad in our hearts by the Holy Spirit which is given unto us" (Rom. 5:5).

It is by the gracious work of the Holy Spirit that the elect are recovered from the flesh and the world unto God. By nature they love themselves and the world above God; but the Holy Spirit imparts to them a new nature, and Himself indwells them, so that they now love God and live to Him. This it is which prepares them to believe and appropriate the Gospel. The effects of the Spirit's entering as the Spirit of adoption are liberty, confidence, and holy delight. As they had "received" from the first Adam "the spirit of bondage"—a legalistic spirit which produced "fear"; their receiving the Spirit of adoption is all the more grateful: liberty being the sweeter because of the former captivity. The Law having done its work in the conscience, they can now appreciate the glad tidings of the Gospel—the revelation of the amazing love and grace of God in Jesus Christ. A spirit of love is now bred in them by the knowledge of the same.

The blessed fruit of receiving the Spirit of adoption is that there is born in the heart a childlike affection toward God and a childlike confidence in Him: "Whereby we cry, Abba, Father." The Apostle employs in the original two different languages, "Abba" being Syrian and "Father" being Greek, the one familiar to the Jews, the other to the Gentiles. By so doing he denotes that believing Jews and Gentiles are children of one family, alike privileged to approach God as their Father. "Christ, our peace, having broken down the middle wall of partition between them; and now, at the same mercy-seat, the Christian Jew and the believing Gentile both one in Christ Jesus, meet, as the rays of light converge and blend in one common center—at the feet of the reconciled Father" (O. Winslow).

A Filial Spirit

As the Spirit of adoption, the Holy Spirit bestows upon the quickened soul a filial spirit: He acts in unison with the Son and gives a sense of our relationship as sons. Emancipating from that bondage and fear which the application of the Law stirred up within us, He brings us into the joyous liberty which the reception of the Gospel bestows. O the blessedness of being delivered from the Covenant of Works! O the bliss of reading our sentence of pardon in the blood of Immanuel! It is by virtue of our having received the Spirit of adoption that we cry "Father! Father!" It is the cry of our own heart, the desire of our soul going out unto God. And yet our spirit does not originate it: without the immediate presence, operation, and grace of the Holy Spirit we neither would nor could know God as our "Father." The Spirit is the Author of everything in us which goes out after God.

This filial spirit which the Christian has received is evidenced in various ways. First, by a holy reverence for God our Father, as the natural child should honor or reverence his human parent. Second, by confidence in God our Father, as the natural child trusts in and relies upon his earthly parent. Third, by love for our Father, as the natural child has an affectionate regard for his parent. Fourth, by subjection to God our Father, as the natural child obeys his parent. This filial spirit prompts him to approach God with spiritual freedom, so that he clings to Him with the confidence of a babe, and leans upon Him with the calm repose of a little one lying on its parent's breast. It admits to the closest intimacy. Unto God as his "Father" the Christian should repair at all times, casting all his care upon Him, knowing that He cares for him (1 Pet. 5:7). It is to be manifested by an affectionate subjection (obedience) to Him "as dear children" (Eph. 5:1).

"The Spirit of adoption is the Spirit of God, who proceedeth from the Father and the Son, and who is sent by Them to shed abroad the love of God in the heart, to give a real enjoyment of it, and to fill the soul with joy and peace in believing. He comes to testify of Christ; and by taking of the things which are His, and showing them to His people, He draws their heart to Him; and by opening unto them the freeness and fullness of Divine grace, and the exceeding great and precious promises which God has given unto His people, He leads them to know their interest in Christ; and helps them in His name, blood, and righteousness, to approach their heavenly Father with holy delight" (S. E. Pierce).

John Gill observes that the word "Abba" reads backwards the same as forwards, implying that God is the Father of His people in adversity as well as prosperity. The Christian's is an inalienable relationship: God is as much his "Father" when He chastens as when He delights, as much so when He frowns as when He smiles. God will never disown His own children or disinherit them as heirs. When Christ taught His disciples to pray He bade them approach the mercy-seat and say, "Our Father which art in Heaven." He Himself, in Gethsemane, cried, "Abba, Father" (Mark 14:36)—expressive of His confidence in and dependence upon Him. To address God as "Father" encourages faith, confirms hope, warms the heart, and draws out its affections to Him who is Love itself

Respective of Care

Let it next be pointed out that this filial spirit is subject to the state and place in which the Christian yet is. Some suppose that if we have received the Spirit of adoption there must be produced a steady and uniform assurance, a perpetual fire burning upon the altar of the heart. Not so. When the Son of God became incarnate, He condescended to yield unto all the sinless infirmities of human nature, so that He hungered and ate, wearied and slept. In like manner, the Holy Spirit deigns to submit Himself unto the laws and circumstances which ordinarily regulate human nature. In Heaven the man Christ Jesus is glorified; and in Heaven the Spirit in the Christian will shine like a perpetual star. But on earth, He indwells our hearts like a flickering flame; never to be extinguished, but not always bright, and needing to be guarded from rude blasts, or why bid us "quench not the Spirit" (1 Thess. 5:19)?

The Spirit, then, does not grant the believer assurance irrespective of his own carefulness and diligence. "Let your loins be girded about, and your lights burning" (Luke 12:35): the latter being largely determined by the former. The Christian is not always in the enjoyment of a child-like confidence. And why? Because he is often guilty of "grieving" the Spirit, and then, He withholds much of His comfort. Hereby we may ascertain our communion with God and when it is interrupted, when He be pleased or displeased with us—by the motions or withdrawings of the Spirit's consolation. Note the order in Acts 9:31, "Walking in the fear of the Lord, and in the comfort of the Holy Spirit"; and again in Acts 11:24, "He was a good man, and full of the Holy Spirit."

Hence, when our confidence toward "the Father" is clouded, we should search our ways and find out what is the matter.

Empty professors are fatally deluded by a false confidence, a complacent taking for granted that they are real Christians when they have never been born again. But many true possessors are plagued by a false diffidence, a doubting whether they be Christians at all. None are so inextricably caught in the toils of a false confidence as they who suspect not their delusion and are unconscious of their imminent danger. On the other hand, none are so far away from that false confidence as those who tremble lest they be cherishing it. True diffidence is a distrust of myself True confidence is a leaning wholly upon Christ, and that is ever accompanied by utter renunciation of myself. Self-renunciation is the heart-felt acknowledgment that my resolutions, best efforts, faith and holiness, are nothing before God, and that Christ must be my All.

In all genuine Christians there is a co-mingling of real confidence and false diffidence, because as long as they remain on this earth there is in them the root of faith and the root of doubt. Hence their prayer is "Lord, I believe; help Thou mine unbelief" (Mark 9:24). In some Christians faith prevails more than it does in others; in some unbelief is more active than in others. Therefore some have a stronger and steadier assurance than others. The presence of the indwelling Spirit is largely evidenced by our frequent recourse to the Father in prayer-often with sighs, sobs, and groans. The consciousness of the Spirit of adoption within us is largely regulated by the extent to which we yield ourselves unto His government.

The Spirit Witnessing

The Holy Spirit is first a witness for Christ, and then He is a witness to His people of Christ's infinite love and the sufficiency of His finished work. "But when the Comforter is come, whom I will send unto you from the Father, even the Spirit of truth, which proceedeth from the Father, He shall testify (bear witness) of Me" (John 15:26). The Spirit bears His testimony for Christ in the Scriptures; He bears His testimony to us in our renewed minds. He is a Witness for the Lord Jesus by all that is revealed in the Sacred Volume concerning Him. He bears witness to the abiding efficacy of Christ's offering: that sin is effectually put away thereby, that the Father hath accepted it, that the elect are forever perfected thereby, and that pardon of sins is the fruit of Christ's oblation.

The sufficiency of the Spirit to be Witness for Christ unto His people appears first, from His being a Divine Person; second, from His being present when the Everlasting Covenant was drawn up; third, from His perfect knowledge of the identity of each member of the election of grace. When the ordained hour strikes for each one to be quickened by Him, He capacitates the soul to receive a spiritual knowledge of Christ. He shines upon the Scriptures of Truth and into the renewed mind. He enables the one born again to receive into his heart the Father's record concerning His beloved Son, and to give full credit to it. He enables him to realize that the Father is everlastingly well pleased with every one who is satisfied with the Person, righteousness, and atonement of His co-equal Son, and who rests his entire hope and salvation thereon. Thereby He assures him of the Father's acceptance of him in the Beloved.

Objective and Subjective Witness

Now the Spirit is a Witness unto God's people both objectively and subjectively: that is to say, He bears witness to them, and He also bears witness in them—such is His wondrous grace toward them. His witness to them is in and through and by means of the Scriptures. "By one offering He hath perfected forever them that are sanctified. Whereof the Holy Spirit also is a Witness to us" (Heb. 10:14, 15), which is explained in what immediately follows. A quotation is made from the Prophet Jeremiah, who had spoken as he was moved by the Holy Spirit (2 Pet. 1:21). The Lord declares of His people "their sins and iniquities will I remember no more" (Heb. 10:17). Whereupon the Holy Spirit points out, "Now where remission of these is, there is no more offering for sin" (v. 18). Thus does He witness to us, through the Word, of the sufficiency and finality of Christ's one offering.

But something more is still required by God's needy people, for they are the subjects of many fears, and Satan frequently attacks their faith. It is not that they have any doubt about the Divine inspiration of the Scriptures, or the unerring reliability of every thing recorded therein. Nor is it that they are disposed for a moment to call into question the infinite sufficiency and abiding efficacy of the sacrifice of Christ. No—that which occasions them such deep concern is, whether they have a saving interest therein. They are aware that there is a faith (such as the demons have—James 2:19) which obtains no salvation. They perceive that the faith of which many empty professors boast so loudly is not evidenced by their works. And they discover so much in themselves that appears to be altogether incompatible with their being new creatures in Christ, until they often fear their own conversion was but a delusion after all.

When an honest soul contemplates the amazing greatness of the honor and the stupendousness of the relation of regarding itself as a joint-heir with Christ, it is startled and staggered. What, me a child of God! God my Father! Who am I to be thus exalted into the Divine favor? Surely it cannot be so. When I consider my fearful sinfulness and unworthiness, the awful depravity of my heart, the carnality of my mind, such rebellion of will, so prone to evil every moment, and such glaring flaws in all I undertake—surely I cannot have been made a partaker of the Divine nature. It seems impossible; and Satan is ever ready to assure me that I am not God's child. If the reader be a stranger to such tormenting fears, we sincerely pity him. But if his experience tallies with what we have just described, he will see how indispensable it is that the Holy Spirit should bear witness to him within.

But there are some who say that it is a sin for the Christian to question his acceptance with God because he is still so depraved, or to doubt his salvation because he can perceive little or no holiness within. They say that such doubting is to call God's Truth and faithfulness into question, for He has assured us of His love and His readiness to save all who believe in His Son. They affirm it is not our duty to examine our hearts, that we shall never obtain any assurance by so doing; that we must look to Christ alone, and rest on His naked Word. But does not Scripture say, "For our rejoicing is this, the testimony of our conscience, that in simplicity and godly sincerity, not with fleshly wisdom, but by the grace of God, we have had our conversation in the world" (2 Cor. 1:12)? And again we are told, "Let us not love in word, neither in tongue; but in deed and in truth. And hereby we know that we are of the truth, and shall assure our hearts before Him" (1 John 3:18, 19).

Doubting and Professing Christians

But it is insisted that Scripture forbids all doubting: "O thou of little faith, wherefore didst thou doubt?" (Matthew 14:31). Yes, but Christ was not there blaming Peter for doubting his spiritual state, but for fearing he would be drowned. Yet Christ "upbraided them with their unbelief" (Mark 16:14): true, for not believing He was risen from the dead—not for calling into question their regeneration! But Abraham is commended because "against hope (all appearances) he "believed in hope" (Rom. 4:18): yes, and that was that he should have a son!—how is that relevant to what we are now discussing? But "we walk by faith, not by sight" (2 Cor. 5:7): yes, the conduct of the Apostles was governed by a realization of that which is to come (see v. 11). But "whatsoever is not of faith is sin" (Rom. 14:23): but this is nothing to the purpose; if a man does not believe it is right to do some act, and yet ventures to do it, he sins.

Let us define more closely the point now under discussion. We may state it thus: Does God require anyone to believe he has been born again when he has no clear evidence that such is the case? Surely the question answers itself: the God of Truth never asks anyone to believe a lie. If my sins have not been pardoned, then the more firmly convinced I am that they have been, the worse for me; and very ready is Satan to second me in my self-deception! The Devil would have me assured that all is well with me, without a diligent search and thorough examination for sufficient evidence that I am a new creature in Christ. O how many he is deceiving by making them believe it is wrong to challenge their profession and put their hearts to a real trial!

True, it is a sin for a real Christian so to live that his evidences of regeneration are not clear; but it is no sin for him to be honest and impartial, or to doubt when, in fact, his evidences are not clear. It is sin to darken my evidences, but it is no sin to discover that they are darkened. It is a sin for a man, by rioting and drunkenness, to make himself ill; but it is no sin to feel he is sick, if there be grounds for it, to doubt if he will survive his sickness. Our sins bring upon us inward calamities as well as outward, but these are chastisements rather than sins. It is the Christian's sin which lays the foundation for doubts, which occasions them; yet those doubtings are not themselves sins.

But it will be said, Believers are exhorted to "hold fast the confidence and the rejoicing of the hope firm unto the end" (Heb. 3:6) and that "we are made partakers of Christ, if we hold the beginning of our confidence steadfast unto the end" (v. 14). Yes, but that "confidence" is that Jesus is the Christ, together with a true faith in Him, as is clear from the whole context there. Nothing is more absurd than to say that professing Christians are made partakers of Christ by holding fast the confidence that they are saved, for that is what many a deceived soul does, and does to the very end (Matthew 7:22). There can be no well-grounded confidence unless it rests upon clear evidence or reliable testimony. And for that, there must be not only "the answer of a good conscience" (1 Pet. 3:21), but the confirmatory witness of the Spirit.

The Office of Witness

The Holy Spirit who dwells in Christ, the great and eternal Head of His people, dwells also in all the living members of His mystical Body, to conform them to Him and to make them like Him in their measure. He it is who takes possession of every quickened soul, dwelling in them as the Spirit of life, of grace, of holiness, of consolation, of glory. He who made them alive in the Lord, now makes them alive to the Lord. He gives them to know the Father in the Son, and their union with Christ. He leads them into communion with the Father and the Son, and fulfills all the good pleasure of His will in them and the work of faith with power (2 Thess. 1:11). In the carrying on of His "good work" in the soul—commenced in regeneration, and manifested in conversion to the Lord—the Spirit is pleased to act and perform the office of Witness: "The Spirit itself beareth witness with our spirit, that we are the children of God" (Rom. 8:16).

Now the office of a "witness" is to bear testimony or supply evidence for the purpose of adducing proof. The first time this term occurs is in the Epistle to the Romans in 2:15, "Which show the work of the law written in their hearts, their conscience also bearing witness, and their thoughts the mean while accusing or else excusing." The reference is to the Heathen: though they had not received from God a written revelation (like the Jews had), nevertheless, they were His creatures, responsible creatures, subject to His authority, and will yet be judged by Him. The grounds upon which God holds them accountable are, first, the revelation which He has given them of Himself in creation, which renders them "without excuse" (Rom. 1:19, 20); and second, the work of His Law written in their hearts, that is, their rationality or "the light of nature." But not only do their moral instincts instruct them in the difference between right and wrong, and warn them of a future day of reckoning, but their conscience also bears witness—it is a Divine monitor within, supplying evidence that God is their Governor and Judge.

But while the Christian ever remains a creature accountable to his Maker and Ruler, he is also a child of God, and, normally (that is, while he is sincerely endeavoring to walk as such), his renewed conscience bears witness to—supplies evidence of—the fact. We say "renewed conscience," for the Christian has been renewed throughout the whole of his inner man. The genuine Christian is able to say, "We trust we have a good conscience, in all things willing to live honestly" (Heb. 13:18)—the bent of his heart is for God and obedience to Him. Not only is there a desire to please God, but there are answerable endeavors: "Herein do I exercise myself, to have always a conscience void of offense toward God, and men" (Acts 24:16). When these endeavors are carried on there is inward assurance of our state: "For our rejoicing is this, the testimony of our conscience" (2 Cor. 1:12).

Thus, the Christian's sincerity is evidenced by his conscience. It is true that there is also "another law in his members, warring against the law of his mind, and bringing him into captivity to the law of sin" (Rom. 7:23); yet that is his grief, and not his joy; his burden and not his satisfaction. It is true that "to will is present with him; but how to perform that which is good (how to attain unto what he ardently desires and prays for) he finds not." Yea, the good that he loves to do, he often does not; and the evil which he hates, he often falls into (Rom. 7:18, 19). Even so; yet, blameworthy and lamentable though such things are, it in no way alters the fact that the one whose experience it is, can call God Himself to witness that he wishes with all his heart it were otherwise; and his own conscience testifies to his sincerity in expressing such a desire.

What He Bears Witness To

It is most important that the Christian should be quite clear as to what it is his own "spirit" or conscience bears witness to. It is not to the eradication of evil from his heart, nor is it to any purification of or improvement in his carnal nature—anyone whose conscience bears witness to that, bears witness to a lie, for "if we say that we have no sin, we deceive ourselves, and the truth is not in us" (1 John 1:8). So long as the Christian remains on earth, "the flesh (the principle of sin) lusteth against the Spirit"—the principle of grace (Gal. 5:17). Moreover, the more our thoughts are formed by the Word, the more do we discover how full of corruption we are; the closer we walk with God, the more light we have, and the more are the hidden (unsuspected) things of darkness within discovered to our horrified gaze. Thus, the Christian's assurance that he is a regenerate person by no means signifies he is conscious that he is more and more dying to the presence and activities of indwelling sin. God does not intend that we should be in love with ourselves.

That which the renewed conscience of the Christian bears witness to is the fact that he is a child of God. Side by side with the sink of iniquity which indwells the believer—of which he becomes increasingly conscious, and over which he daily groans—is the spirit of adoption which has been communicated to his heart. That filial spirit draws out his heart in love to God, so that he craves after the conscious enjoyment of His smiling countenance, and esteems fellowship with Him high above all other privileges. That filial spirit inspires confidence toward God, so that he pleads His promises, counts on His mercy, and relies on His goodness. That filial spirit begets reverence for God, so that His ineffable majesty is held in awe. His high authority is respected, and he trembles at His Word. That filial spirit produces subjection to God, so that he desires to obey Him in all things, and sincerely endeavors to walk according to His commands and precepts.

Now here are definite marks by which the Christian may test himself. True, he is yet very far from being what he should be, or what he would be could his earnest longings only be realized; nevertheless, is not his present case very different from what it once was? Instead of seeking to banish God from your thoughts, is it not now the desire of your heart for your mind to be stayed upon Him, and is it not a joy to meditate upon His perfections? Instead of giving little or no concern as to whether your conduct honored or dishonored the Lord, is it not now your sincere endeavor to please Him in all your ways? Instead of paying no attention to indwelling sin, has not the plague of your heart become your greatest burden and grief? Well, then, these very things evidence you are a child of God. They were not in your nature, so they must have been implanted by the Holy Spirit. Those graces may be very feeble, yet their presence struggling amid corruptions—are marks of the new birth.

If with honesty of purpose, lowliness of heart, and prayerful inquiry, I find myself breathing after holiness, panting after conformity to Christ, and mourning over my failures to realize the same, then so far from it being presumption for me to conclude I am a child of God, it would be willful blindness to refuse to recognize the work of the Spirit in my soul. If my conscience bears witness to the fact that I honestly desire and sincerely endeavor to serve and glorify God, then it is wrong for me to deny, or even to doubt, that God has "begun a good work" in me. Take note of your health, dear reader, as well as of your disease. Appropriate to yourself the language of Christ's Spouse, "I sleep, but my heart waketh" (Song. 5:2)—grace is to be acknowledged amid infirmities; that which is a cause for humiliation must not be made a ground for doubting.

But notwithstanding the evidences which a Christian has of his Divine sonship, he finds it no easy matter to be assured of his sincerity, or to establish solid comfort in his soul. His moods are fitful, his frames variable. Grace in the best of us is but small and weak, and we have just cause to mourn the feebleness of our faith, the coldness of our love, and the grievous imperfections of our obedience. But it is at this very point the blessed Spirit of God, in His wondrous grace and infinite condescension, helps our infirmities—He adds His witness to the testimony of our renewed conscience, so that (at times) the conviction is confirmed, and the trembling heart is assured. It is at such seasons the Christian is able to say, "My conscience also bearing me witness in the Holy Spirit" (Rom. 9:1).

The question which most deeply exercises a genuine saint is not, have I repented, have I faith in Christ, have I any love for God? but rather, are my repentance, faith and love sincere and genuine? He has discovered that Scripture distinguishes between repentance (1 Kings 21:27) and repentance "not to be repented of" (2 Cor. 7:10); between faith (Acts 8:13) and "faith unfeigned" (1 Tim. 1:5), between love (Matthew 26:49) and "love in sincerity" (Eph. 6:24); and only by the gracious enabling of the Holy Spirit can any soul discern between them. He who bestowed upon the Christian repentance and faith must also make him to know the things which are freely given to him of God (1 Cor. 2:12). Grace can only be known by grace, as the sun can only be seen in its own light. It is only by the Spirit Himself that we can be truly assured we have been born of Him.

Errors in Subjective Witness

Rightly did Jonathan Edwards affirm, "Many have been the mischiefs that have arisen from that false and delusory notion of the witness of the Spirit, that it is a kind of inward voice, suggestion, or revelation from God to man, that he is beloved of Him, and that his sins are pardoned—sometimes accompanied with, sometimes without, a text of Scripture; and many have been the false and vain (though very high) affections that have arisen from hence. It is to be feared that multitudes of souls have been eternally undone by it." Especially was this so in the past, when fanaticism made much of the Spirit witnessing to souls.

An affectionate and dutiful child has within his own bosom the proof of the peculiar and special relationship in which he stands to his father. So it is with the Christian: his filial inclinations and aspirations after God prove that he is His child. In addition to this, the Holy Spirit gives assurance of the same blessed fact by shedding abroad in his heart the love of God (Rom. 5:5). The Holy Spirit's indwelling of the Christian is the sure mark of his adoption. Yet the Spirit cannot be discerned by us in His essence: only by means of His operations is He to be known. As we discern His work, we perceive the Worker; and how His work in the soul can be ascertained without diligent examination of our inward life and a careful comparison of it with the Scriptures, we know not. The Spirit reveals Himself to us by that spirit which He begets in us.

"The Spirit itself beareth witness with our spirit, that we are the children of God" (Rom. 8:16). Let it be carefully noted that this verse does not say the Spirit bears witness to our spirit (as it is so often misquoted), but "with"—it is a single word in the Greek (a compound verb) "beareth witness with." It is deeply important to notice this distinction: the witness of the Spirit is not so much a revelation which is made to my spirit, considered as the recipient of the testimony, as it is a confirmation made in or with my spirit, considered as co-operating in the testimony. It is not that my spirit bears witness that I am a child of God, and that then the Spirit of God comes in by a distinguishable process with a separate testimony, to say Amen to my assurance; but it is that there is a single testimony which has a conjoint origin.

The "witness" of the Spirit, then, is not by means of any supernatural vision nor by any mysterious voice informing me I am a child of God—for the Devil tells many a hypocrite that. "This is not done by any immediate revelation or impulse or merely by any text brought to the mind (for all these things are equivocal and delusory); but by coinciding with the testimony of their own consciences, as to their uprightness in embracing the Gospel, and giving themselves up to the service of God. So that, whilst they are examining themselves concerning the reality of their conversion, and find Scriptural evidence of it, the Holy Spirit from time to time shines upon His own work, excites their holy affections into lively exercise, renders them very efficacious upon their conduct, and thus puts the matter beyond all doubt" (Thomas Scott).

Guidelines for Subjective Witness

First, the Spirit's witness is in strict accord with the teaching of Holy Writ. In the Word He has given certain marks by which the question may be decided as to whether or not I am a child of God: He has described certain features by which I may identify myself—see John 8:39, Romans 4:12 and 8:14 and contrast John 8:44 and Ephesians 2:2, 3. It is by the Truth that the Spirit enlightens, convicts, comforts, feeds, and guides the people of God; and it is by and through the Truth that He bears witness with their spirit. There is a perfect harmony between the testimony of Scripture and the varied experiences of each renewed soul, and it is by revealing to us this harmony, by showing us the correspondence between the history of our soul and the testimony of the Word that He persuades us we are born again: "Hereby we know that we are of the truth, and shall assure our hearts before Him" (1 John 3:19).

Second, He works such graces in us as are peculiar to God's children, and thereby evidences our interest in the favor of God. He makes the Christian to feel "poor in spirit," a pauper dependent upon the charity of God. He causes him to "mourn" over much which gives the worldling no concern whatever. He bestows a spirit of "meekness" so that the rebellious will is, in part, subdued, and God's will is submitted unto. He gives a "hunger and thirst after righteousness" and gives the soul to feel that the best this perishing world has to offer him is unsatisfying and but empty husks. He makes him "merciful" toward others, counteracting that selfish disposition which is in us by nature. He makes him "pure in heart" by giving him to pant after holiness and hate that which is vile (Matthew 5:3-8, etc.). By His own fruit in the soul, the Spirit makes manifest His indwelling presence.

Third, He helps us to discern His work of grace in our souls more clearly. Conscience does its part, and the Spirit confirms the same. The conjoint witness of the Spirit gives vigor and certainty to the assurance of our hearts. When the flood-waters of a land mingle themselves with a river they make one and the same stream, but it is now more rapid and violent. In like manner, the united testimonies of our own conscience and of the Spirit make but one witness, yet it becomes such as to break down our fears and overcome our doubts. When the blessed Spirit shines upon His own work of grace and holiness in our souls, then in His light we "see light" (Ps. 36:9). Inward holiness, a filial spirit, an humble heart, submission to God, is something that Satan cannot imitate.

Fourth, He helps us not only to see grace, but to judge of the sincerity and reality of it. It is at this point many honest souls are most sorely exercised. It is much easier to prove that we believe, than to be assured that our faith is a saving one. It is much easier to conclude that we love Christ, than it is to be sure that we love Him in sincerity and for what He is in Himself. Our hearts are fearfully deceitful, there are many minglings of faith and unbelief (Mark 9:24), and grace in us is so feeble that we hesitate to pronounce positively upon our state. But when the Spirit increases our faith, rekindles our love, strengthens us with might in the inner man, He enables us to come to a definite conclusion. First He sanctifies and then He certifies.

The deceits of Satan, though often plausible imitations up to a point, are, in their tendency and outcome, always opposed to that which God enjoins. On the other hand, the operations of the Spirit are ever in unison with the written Word. Here, then, is a sure criterion by which we may test which spirit is at work within us. The three truths of Scripture which more directly concern us are, our ruin by nature, our redemption by grace, and the duties we owe by virtue of our deliverance. If then, our beliefs, our feelings, our assurance, tend to exalt depraved nature, depreciate Divine grace, or lead to a licentious life, they are certainly not of God. But if they have quite the opposite tendency, convincing us of our wretchedness by nature, making Christ more precious to us, and leading us into the duties He enjoins, they are of the Holy Spirit.

It only remains for us to ask, Why does not the Holy Spirit grant unto the Christian a strong and comforting assurance of his Divine sonship at all times? Various answers may be given. First, we must distinguish between the Spirit's work and His witness: often it is His office to convict and make us miserable, rather than to impart comfort and joy. Second, His assuring consolation is often withheld because of our slackness: we are bidden to "make your calling and election sure" and "be diligent that ye may be found of Him in peace" (2 Pet. 1:10 and 3:1 4)—the comforts of the Spirit drop not into lazy souls. Third, because of our sins: "The Holy Spirit fell on all them which heard the Word" (Acts 10:44)—not while they were walking in the paths of unrighteousness. His witness is a holy one: He will not put a jewel in a swine's snout (Prov. 11:22). Keep yourselves in the love of God (Jude 21) and the Spirit's witness will be yours.

The Spirit Sealing

Closely connected with the Spirit's work of witnessing with the Christian's spirit that he is a child of God, is His operation in sealing. This appears clearly from 2 Corinthians 1:19-22 and Ephesians 1:13.

The riches of the Christian are found in the promises of God, and these are all "Yea and Amen" in Christ: unless, then, our faith he built upon them, it is worthless. It is not sufficient that the promises he sure, we must he "established" upon them. No matter how firm the foundation (be it solid rock), unless the house he connected therewith, actually built thereon, it is insecure. There must he a double "Amen": one in the promises, and one in us. There must be an echo in the Christian's own heart: God says these things, so they must be true; faith appropriates them and says they are for me. In order to have assurance and peace it is indispensable that we be established in and on the Divine promises.

The Christian's riches lie in the promises of God: his strength and comfort in his faith being built upon them. Now the same Divine power which delivered the Christian from the kingdom of Satan and brought him into a state of grace, must also deliver him from the attacks of the enemy upon his faith and confirm him in a state of grace. Only God can produce stability: only He can preserve that spark of faith amid the winds and waves of unbelief, and this He is pleased to do—"He which bath begun a good work in you will finish it" (Phil. 1:6). Therefore are we told "Now he which stablisheth us with you in Christ... is God." Observe carefully it is not "hath stablished," but "stablisheth" — it is a continuous process throughout the Christian's life on earth.

In what follows the apostle shows us what this "stablishing" consists of, or how it is accomplished: "and bath anointed us ... who bath also sealed us, and given the earnest of the Spirit in our heart" (2 Cor. 1:22). Each of these figures refers to the same thing, and has to do with the "stablishing" or assuring of our hearts. Under the Old Testament economy prophets, priests, and kings were authorized and confirmed in their office by "anointing" (Lev. 8:11; 2 Sam. 5:3; 1 Kings 19:16). Again; contracts and deeds of settlement were ratified by "sealing" (Esther 8:8; Jer. 32:8-10). And a "pledge" or "earnest" secured an agreement or bargain (Gen. 38:17, 18; Deut. 24:10). Thus the sure estate of the Christian is first expressed under the general word "stablisheth," and then it is amplified under these three figurative terms "anointed, sealed, earnest." It is with the second of them we are now concerned.

It may be asked, But what need has the Christian of attestation or confirmation of his state in Christ—is not faith itself sufficient proof? Ah, often our faith and the knowledge we have of our believing in Christ is severely shaken; the activities of indwelling sin stir up a thick cloud of doubt, and Satan avails himself of this to tell us our profession is an empty one. But in His tender grace, God has given us the Holy Spirit, and from time to time He "seals" or confirms our faith by His quickening and comforting operations. He draws out our hearts anew unto God and enables us to cry "Abba, Father." He takes of the things of Christ, shows them to us, and brings us to realize that we have a personal interest in the Same.

The same blessed truth is found again in Ephesians 1:13. It is important to note the order of the three things there predicated of saints: they "heard," they "believed," they were "sealed": thus the sealing is quite distinct from and follows the believing, as the believing does the hearing. There are two things, and two only, upon which the Spirit puts His seal, namely, two mighty and efficacious works: first, the finished work of Christ, whereby He put away sin by the sacrifice of Himself; and second, upon His own work in the hearts of those who believe. In legal documents the writing always precedes the witnessing and sealing: so here, the Spirit writes God's laws on the heart (Heb. 8:10), and then He seals the truth and reality of His own work to the consciousness of the recipient.

The main intent of "sealing" is to assure, to certify and ratify. First, the Holy Spirit conveys an assurance of the truth of God's promises, whereby a man's understanding is spiritually convinced that the promises are from God. Neither the light of reason nor the persuasive power of a fellow-mortal can bring any one to rest his heart upon the Divine promises: in order to do that, there must be the direct working of the Holy Spirit—"Our gospel came not unto you in word only, but also in power, and in the Holy Spirit, and in much assurance" (1 Thess. 1:5): the "much assurance comes last! Second, He gives the believer an assurance of his own personal interest in those promises: and this again is something which none but the Spirit can impart. We do not say that this sealing excludes all doubting, but it is such an assurance as prevails over doubts.

There are many uses of a "seal" such as proprietorship, identification, confirmation, secrecy, security; but in Ephesians 1:13 the immediate thing stated is the sealing of an inheritance: we have obtained an inheritance by faith, and having believed we are "sealed." What is the specific use of a "seal" in connection with an inheritance? It may either be the making of the inheritance sure to a man in itself, or making the man know that it is his—assuring him of the fact. Now it cannot be the former, for nothing is needed to make Heaven sure once a sinner truly believes—the moment he lays hold of Christ, the inheritance is certain. So it must be the latter: to make us sure, to persuade our hearts the inheritance is ours. It is this the Spirit accomplishes in His "seal."

The Holy Spirit is never called a "Seal" as He is an "Earnest" (2 Cor. 5:5): it is only in relation to an act of sealing that this figure is associated with Him; thus it is a distinct operation of His "in our hearts" (2 Cor. 1:22). It is not the stamping of God's image upon the soul (as many of the Puritans supposed) that is referred to in Ephesians 1:13, for that is done before believing, and not after. The order of truth in that verse is very simple and decisive: in the gospel salvation is offered —it may he mine; faith accepts that offer so as to make salvation mine; the Spirit seals or confirms my heart that salvation is mine. Thus in "sealing" the Spirit authenticates, certifies, ratifies.

Observe that He does this in His special character as "the Spirit of promise." He is so designated because, first, the Spirit was the great and grand promise of the New Testament (John 14:26; 15:26, etc.) as Christ was of the Old Testament. Second, because He works by means of the promises. Third, because in His whole work He acts according to the everlasting covenant, which, as it respects the elect, is a Covenant of Promise (Eph. 2:12). When He seals home a sense of the love of God and gives the soul a view of its interest in Christ, it is done by means of the Word of Promise. It was so when He "sealed" Christ (John 6:27) and consecrated Him to the work of redemption. The Father said by an audible voice from Heaven, "This is my beloved Son, in whom I am well pleased": this was repeating what had been pronounced in the purpose of Jehovah the Father concerning the Mediator (Isa. 42:1); this the Holy Spirit brought home in power or "sealed" upon the mind of Jesus at that time.

The "sealing" or assuring operations of the Spirit are known to the believer in two ways. First, inferentially: by enabling him to perceive His work in the soul and from it conclude his regeneration. When I see smoke I must infer a fire, and when I discern spiritual graces (however feeble) I reason back to the Producer of them. When I feel a power within combating my corruptions, and often thwarting my intentions to indulge the lusts of the flesh, I conclude it is the Spirit resisting the flesh (Gal. 5:17). Second, intuitively: by a Divine light in the heart, by a Divine authority felt, by the love of God shed abroad therein. If I have any hope wrought in me, either by looking to Christ's blood or perceiving grace in me, it is by the power of the Spirit (Rom. 15:13).

The Spirit brings to the mind of the Christian the sacred promises. He shows us the good contained in them, the grace expressed in them, the perfection and freeness of Christ's salvation declared by them; and thereby He seals them on our mind and enables us to rest thereon. He shows us the veracity and faithfulness of God in the promises, the immutability of the everlasting covenant, the eternity of God's love, and that He hath by two immutable things (His word and His oath), in which it is impossible for Him to lie, given a firm foundation for strong consolation to us who have fled for refuge to lay hold upon the hope set before us in the gospel (Heb. 6:18). It is in this way that "the God of all grace" doth, by the Spirit, "stablish, strengthen, settle us" (1 Pet. 5:10). It is by the Spirit's operations that the Christian's fears are quietened, his doubts subdued, and his heart assured that a "good work" (Phil. 1:6) has been Divinely begun in him. The Spirit indwelling us is Christ's seal (mark of identification) that we are His sheep; the Spirit authenticating His own blessed work in our souls, by revealing to us our "title" to Heaven, is His sealing us.

The Spirit Assisting

Role of Suffering

A child of God oppressed, suffering sorely, often driven to his wit's end—what a strange thing! A joint-heir with Christ financially embarrassed, poor in this world's goods, wondering where his next meal is coming from—what an anomaly! An object of the Father's everlasting love and distinguishing favor tossed up and down upon a sea of trouble, with every apparent prospect of his frail boat capsizing—what a perplexity! One who has been regenerated and is now indwelt by the Holy Spirit daily harassed by Satan, and frequently overcome by indwelling sin—what an enigma! Loved by the Father, redeemed by the Son, his body made the temple of the Holy Spirit, yet left in this world year after year to suffer affliction and persecution, to mourn and groan over innumerable failures, to encounter one trial after another, often to be placed in far less favorable circumstances than the wicked; to sigh and cry for relief, yet for sorrow and suffering to increase—what a mystery! What Christian has not felt the force of it, and been baffled by its inscrutability.

Now it was to cast light upon this pressing problem of the sorely tried believer that the eighth chapter of Romans was written. There the Apostle was moved to show that "the sufferings of the present time" (v. 18) are not inconsistent with the special favor and infinite love which God bears unto His people. First, because by those sufferings the Christian is brought into personal and experimental fellowship with the sufferings of Christ (v. 17 and cf. Phil. 3:10). Second, severe and protracted as our afflictions may be, yet there is an immeasurable disproportion between our present sufferings and the future Glory (vv. 18-23). Third, our very sufferings provide occasion for the exercise of hope and the development of patience (vv. 24, 25). Fourth, Divine aids and supports are furnished us under our afflictions (vv. 26, 27) and it is these we would now consider.

Help amidst Suffering

"Likewise the Spirit also helpeth our infirmities" (Rom. 8:26). Not only does "hope" (a sure expectation of God's making good His promises) support and cheer the suffering saint, leading him to patiently wait for deliverance from his afflictions, but the blessed Comforter has also been given to him in order to supply help to this very end. By His gracious aid the believer is preserved from being totally submerged by his doubts and fears. By His renewing operations the spark of faith is maintained, despite all the fierce winds of Satan which assail. By His mighty enabling the sorely harassed and groaning Christian is kept from sinking into complete skepticism, abject despair, and infidelity. By His quickening power hope is still kept alive, and the voice of prayer is still faintly heard.

And how is the gracious help of the Spirit manifested? Thus: seeing the Christian bowed down by oppression and depression, His compassion is called forth, and He strengthens with His might in the inner man. Every Christian is a living witness to the truth of this, though he may not be conscious of the Divine process. Why is it, my afflicted brother, my distressed sister, that you have not made shipwreck of your profession long ere this? What has kept you from heeding that repeated temptation of Satan's to totally abandon the good fight of faith? Why has not your manifold "infirmities" annihilated your faith, extinguished your hope, and cast a pall of unrelieved gloom upon the future? The answer is because the blessed Spirit silently, invisibly, yet sympathetically and effectually helped you. Some precious promise was sealed to your heart, some comforting view of Christ was presented to your soul, some whisper of love was breathed into your ear, and the pressure upon your spirit was reduced, your grief was assuaged, and fresh courage possessed you.

Here, then, is real light cast upon the problem of a suffering Christian—the most perplexing feature of that problem being how to harmonize sore sufferings with the love of God. But if God had ceased to care for His child, then He had deserted him, left him to himself Very far from this, though, is the actual case: the Divine Comforter is given to help his infirmities. Here, too, is the sufficient answer to an objection which the carnal mind is ready to make against the inspired reasoning of the Apostle in the context: How can we who are so weak in ourselves, so inferior in power to the enemies confronting us, bear up under our trials which are so numerous, so protracted, so crushing? We could not, and therefore Divine grace has provided for us an all-sufficient Helper. Without His aid we had long since succumbed, mastered by our trials. Hope looks forward to the Glory to come; in the weary interval of waiting, the Spirit supports our poor hearts and keeps grace alive within us.

"Our infirmities": note the plural number, for the Christian is full of them, physically, mentally, and spiritually. Frail and feeble are we in ourselves, for "all flesh is grass, and all the goodliness thereof is as the flower of the field"

(Isa. 40:6). We are "compassed with infirmity" (Heb. 5:2) both within and without. When trials and troubles come we are often bewildered by them and faint beneath them. When opposition and persecution break out against us, because of our cleaving to the Truth and walking with Christ, we are staggered. When the chastening rod of our Father falls upon us, how we fret and fume. What a little thing it takes to disturb our peace, stifle the voice of praise, and cause us to complain and murmur. How easily is the soul cast down, the promises of God forgotten, the glorious future awaiting us lost sight of. How ready are we to say with Jacob, "All these things are against me," or with David, "I shall now perish one day at the hand of Saul."

The "infirmities" of Christians are as numerous as they are varied. Some are weak in faith, and constantly questioning their interest in Christ. Some are imperfectly instructed in the Truth, and therefore ill-prepared to meet the lies of Satan. Some are slow travelers along the path of obedience, frequently lagging in the rear. Others groan under the burden of physical afflictions. Some are harassed with a nervous temperament which produces a state of perpetual pessimism, causing them to look only upon the dark side of the cloud. Others are weighed down with the cares of this life, so that they are constantly depressed. Others are maligned and slandered, persecuted and boycotted, which to those of a sensitive disposition is well-nigh unbearable. "Our infirmities" include all that cause us to groan and render us the objects of the Divine compassion.

But "the Spirit also helpeth our infirmities." Here is a Divine revelation, for we had known nothing about it apart from the Scriptures. We are not left alone to endure our infirmities: we have a helper, a Divine Helper; One not far off, but with us; nay, in us. The Greek word here for "helpeth" is a striking one; it signifies to "take part with" or to "take hold with one." It occurs in only one other passage, namely, "bid Mary therefore that she help me" (Luke 10:40), where the obvious thought is that Martha was asking for her sister's assistance, to share the burden of the kitchen, that she might be eased. The Spirit "helpeth" the Christian's infirmities not only by a sympathetic regard, but by personal participation, supporting him beneath them, like a mother "helps" her child when learning to walk, or a friend gives his arm to an aged person to lean upon.

In his comments on this clause Calvin says, "The Spirit takes on Himself a part of the burden by which our weakness is oppressed, so that He not only succours us, but lifts us up, as though He went under the burden with us." Oh how this should endear the blessed Spirit of God to us. We worship the Father, whence every mercy has its rise; we adore the Son, through whom every blessing flows; but how often we overlook the Holy Spirit, by whom every blessing is actually communicated and applied. Think of His deep compassion, His manifold succourings, His tender love, His mighty power, His efficacious grace, His infinite forbearance; all these challenge our hearts and should awaken praises from us. They would if we meditated more upon them.

The Spirit does not remove our "infirmities," any more than the Lord took away Paul's thorn in the flesh; but He enables us to bear them. Constrained by a love which no thought can conceive, moved by a tenderness no tongue can describe, He places His mighty arm beneath the pressure and sustains us. Though He has been slighted and grieved by us a thousand times, receiving at our hands the basest requital for His tenderness and grace, yet when a sword enters our soul or some fresh trouble bows us down to the ground, He again places beneath us the arms of His everlasting love and prevents our sinking into hopeless despair.

Help in Intercessory Prayer

It is a great infirmity or weakness for the Christian to faint in the day of adversity, yet such is often the case. It is a sad thing when, like Rachel of old weeping for her children, he "refuses to be comforted" (Jer. 31:15). It is most deplorable for all when he so gives way to unbelief that the Lord has to say to him, "How is it that ye have no faith?" (Mark 4:40). Terrible indeed would be his end if God were to leave him entirely to himself. This is clear from what is said in Mark 4:17, "when affliction or persecution ariseth for the Word's sake, immediately they are offended," or as Luke says, "Which for a while believe, and in time of temptation fall away" (8:13). And why does the stony-ground hearer apostatize? Because he is without the assistance of the Holy Spirit! Writer and reader would do the same if no Divine aid were forthcoming!

But thank God, the feeble and fickle believer is not left to himself: "the Spirit also helpeth our infirmities" (Rom. 8:26). That "help" is as manifold as our varied needs; but the Apostle singles out one particular "infirmity" which besets all Christians, and which the blessed Spirit graciously helps: "for we know not what we should pray for as we ought: but the Spirit itself maketh intercession for us." How this Divine declaration should humble us into the dust: so depraved is the saint that in the hour of need he is incapable of asking God aright to minister unto him. Sin has so corrupted his heart and darkened his understanding that, left to himself, he cannot even discern what he should ask God for. Alas, that pride should so blind us to our real condition and our deep, deep need.

In nothing do the saints more need the Spirit's presence and His gracious assistance than in their addresses of the Throne of Grace. They know that God in His Persons and perfections is the Object of their worship; they know that they cannot come unto the Father but by Christ, the alone Mediator; and they know that their access to Him must be by the Spirit (Eph. 2:18). Yet such are their varying circumstances, temptations, and wanderings, so often are they shut up in their frames and cold in their affections, such deadness of heart is there toward God and spiritual things, that at times they know not what to pray for as they ought. But it is here that the Spirit's love and grace is most Divinely displayed: He helps their infirmities and makes intercession for them!

One had thought that if ever there were a time when the Christian would really pray, earnestly and perseveringly, and would know what to ask for, it should be when he is sorely tried and oppressed. Alas, how little we really know ourselves. Even a beast will cry out when suffering severe pain, and it is natural (not spiritual!) that we should do the same. Of degenerate Israel of old God said, "they have not cried unto Me with their heart, when they howled upon their beds" (Hosea 7:14): no, relief from their sufferings was all they thought about. And by nature our hearts are just the same! So long as we are left to ourselves (to try us and manifest what we are: 2 Chron. 32:31), when the pressure of sore trial comes upon us, we are concerned only with deliverance from it, and not that God may be glorified or that the trial may be sanctified to our souls.

Left for himself, man asks God for what would be curses rather than blessings, for what would prove to be snares rather than helps to him spiritually. Have we not read of Israel that, "They tempted God in their heart by asking meat for their lust" (Ps. 78:18); and again, "He gave them their request; but sent leanness into their soul" (Ps. 106:15)! Perhaps someone replies, But they were not regenerate souls. Then have we not read in James, "Ye ask, and receive not, because ye ask amiss, that ye may consume it upon your lusts" (4:3)? Ah, my reader, this is a truth which is very unpalatable to our proud hearts. Did not Moses "ask" the Lord that he might be permitted to enter Canaan (Deut. 3:26, 27)? Did not the Apostle Paul thrice beseech the Lord for the removal of his thorn in the flesh? What proofs are these that "we know not what we should pray for as we ought!"

"The Spirit also helpeth our infirmities." This being so, surely the least that we can do is to seek His aid, to definitely ask Him to undertake for us. Alas, how rarely we do so. As intimated above, when the pressure of trouble first presses upon us, usually it is nature which cries out for relief At other times the soul is so cast down that even the voice of natural "prayer" is stifled. Often there is so much rebellion at work in our hearts against the providential dispensations of God toward us that we feel it would be mockery to seek His face; yea, we are ashamed to do so. Such at least has been the experience of the writer more than once, and that not long ago, though he blushes to acknowledge it. O the infinite patience and forbearance of our gracious God!

Why We Need Help

"We know not what we should pray for as we ought." And why? First, because we are so blinded by self-love that we are unable to discern what will be most for God's glory, what will best promote the good of our brethren (through some of the dross being purged out of us), and what will advance our own spiritual growth. O what wretched "prayers" (?) we put up when we are guided and governed by self-interests, and what cause do we give the Lord to say "ye know not what manner of spirit ye are of" (Luke 9:55). Alas, how often we attempt to make God the Servant of our carnal desires. Shall we ask our heavenly Father for worldly success! Shall we come to Him who was born in a stable and ask Him for temporal luxuries or even comforts!

Why is it that "we know not what we should pray for as we ought"? Second, because our minds are so discomposed by the trial and the suffering it brings, and then we have to say with one of old, "I am so troubled that I cannot speak" (Ps. 77:4): so you see, dear "brother, and companion in tribulation" (Rev. 1:9) that you are not the first to experience spiritual dumbness! But it is most blessed to link with this such a promise as, "For the Holy Spirit shall teach you in the same hour what ye ought to say" (Luke 12:12). Why is it that "we know not what we should pray for as we ought"? Third, because oftentimes our tongues are tied as the result of leanness of our souls. It is "out of the abundance of the heart" that "the mouth speaketh" (Matthew 12:34), and if the Word of Christ be not dwelling in us "richly" (Col. 3:16), how can we expect to have the right petition to present to God in the hour of our need!

"The Spirit also helpeth our infirmities," but He does so silently and secretly, so that we are not conscious of His assistance at the time He renders it. That gracious and effectual help is manifested to us by the effects which it has produced in us; though so perverse are our hearts and so great is our pride, we often attribute those effects to our own will-power or resolution. Have we suddenly, or even gradually, emerged from the slough of despond? It was not because we had "come to our senses" or "regained our poise," rather was it solely due to the Spirit's renewing us in the inner man. Has the storm within us—which God's crossing of our will occasioned—been calmed? It was because the Spirit deigned to subdue our iniquities. Has the voice of true prayer again issued from us? It was because the Spirit had made intercession for us.

Lord God the Spirit, to whom Divine honor and glory belongs, equally as to the Father and the Son, I desire to present unto Thee unfeigned praise and heartfelt thanksgiving. O how deeply am I indebted to Thee: how patiently hast Thou borne with me, how tenderly hast Thou dealt with me, how graciously hast Thou wrought in me. Thy love passeth knowledge, Thy forbearance is indeed Divine. O that I were more conscientious and diligent in seeking not to slight and grieve Thee.

The Spirit Interceding

If left to himself, the believer would never see (by faith) the all-wise hand of God in his afflictions, still less would his heart ever honestly say concerning them, "Thy will be done." If left to himself, he would never seek grace to patiently endure the trial, still less would he hope that afterwards it would produce the peaceable fruit of righteousness (Heb. 12:11). If left to himself, he would continue to chafe and kick like "a bullock unaccustomed to the yoke" (Jer. 31:18) and would curse the day of his birth (Job 3:1). If left to himself, he would have no faith that his sufferings were among the "all things" working together for his ultimate good, still less would he "glory in his infirmity that the power of Christ might rest upon him" (2 Cor. 12:9). No, dear reader, such holy exercises of heart are not the product of poor fallen human nature; instead, they are nothing less than the immediate, gracious, and lovely fruits of the Holy Spirit—brought forth amid such uncongenial soil. What a marvel!

"Likewise the Spirit also helpeth our infirmities: for we know not what we should pray for as we ought" (Rom. 8:26). At no one point is the Christian made more conscious of his "infirmities" than in connection with his prayer-life. The effects of indwelling corruption are such that often prayer becomes an irksome task, rather than the felt delight of a precious privilege; and strive as he may, he cannot always overcome this fearful spirit. Even when he endeavors to pray, he is handicapped by wanderings of mind, coldness of heart, the intrusion of carnal cares; while he is painfully conscious of the unreality of his petitions and unfelt confessions. How cold are the effusions of our hearts in secret devotions, how feeble our supplications, how little solemnity of mind, brokenness of heart. How often the prayer exercises of our souls seem a mass of confusion and contradiction.

"But the Spirit itself maketh intercession for us with groanings which cannot be uttered" (Rom. 8:26). It is particularly the help which the blessed Comforter gives the Christian in his prayer-life, in the counteracting of his "infirmities," which is now to engage our attention. In Zechariah 12:10 He is emphatically styled "The Spirit of grace and of supplications," for He is the

Author of every spiritual desire, every holy aspiration, every outgoing of the heart after God. Prayer has rightly been termed "the breathing of the newborn soul," yet we must carefully bear in mind that its respiration is wholly determined by the stirrings of the Holy Spirit within us. As the Person, work and intercession of Christ are the foundation of all our confidence in approaching the Father, so every spiritual exercise in prayer is the fruit of the Spirit's operations and intercession.

How the Spirit Intercedes

First, when the believer is most oppressed by outward trials and is most depressed by a sense of his inward vileness, when he is at his wit's end and ready to wring his hands in despair, or is most conscious of his spiritual deadness and inability to express the sinfulness of his case, the Spirit stirs him in the depths of his being: "The Spirit itself maketh intercession for us with groanings which cannot be uttered." There has been some difference of opinion as to whether this refers directly to groanings of the Spirit Himself, or indirectly to the spiritual groanings of the Christian, which are prompted and produced by Him. But surely there is no room for uncertainty: the words "cannot be uttered" could not apply to a Divine Person. That which He produces in and through the believer, is ascribed to the Spirit—the "fruit" of Galatians 5:22, and Galatians 4:6 compared with Romans 8:15!

As it is the Spirit who illumines and gives us to see the exceeding sinfulness of sin and the depravity of our hearts, so He is the One who causes us to groan over the same. The conscience is pierced, the heart is searched, the soul is made to feel something of its fearful state. The conscious realization of "the plague of our hearts" (1 Kings 8:38) and its "putrefying sores" (Isa. 1:6), produces unutterable anguish. The painful realization of our remaining enmity against God, the rebellion of our wills, the woeful lack of heart-conformity to His holy Law, so casts down the soul that it is temporarily paralyzed. Then it is that the Spirit puts forth His quickening operations, and we "groan" so deeply that we cannot express our feelings, articulate our woe, or unburden our hearts. All that we can do is to sigh and sob inwardly. But such tears of the heart are precious in the sight of God (Ps. 56:8) because they are produced by His blessed Spirit.

Second, when the soul is so sorely oppressed and deeply distressed, the Spirit reveals to the mind what should be prayed for. He it is who pours oil on the troubled waters, quiets in some measure the storm within, spiritualizes the mind, and enables us to perceive the nature of our particular need. It is the Spirit who makes us conscious of our lack of faith, submissiveness, obedience, courage, or whatever it may be. He it is who gives us to see and feel our spiritual wants, and then to make them known before the Throne of Grace. The Spirit helps our infirmities by subduing our fears, increasing our faith, strengthening our hope, and drawing out our hearts unto God. He grants us a renewed sense of the greatness of God's mercy, the changelessness of His love, and the infinite merits of Christ's sacrifice before Him on our behalf.

Third, the Spirit reveals to cast-down saints that the supplies of grace for their varied needs are all expressed in the promises of God. It is those promises which are the measures of prayer, and contain the matter of it; for what God has promised, all that He has promised, but nothing else are we to ask for. "There is nothing that we really stand in need of, but God hath promised the supply of it, in such a way and under such limitations as may make it good and useful unto us. And there is nothing that God hath promised but we stand in need of it, or are some way or other concerned in it as members of the mystical body of Christ" (John Owen). But at this point also the help of the Spirit is imperative, "that we might know the things that are freely given to us of God" (1 Cor. 2:12).

It is thus that the Spirit bears up the distressed minds of Christians: by directing their thoughts to those promises most suited to their present case, by impressing a sense of them upon their hearts, by giving them to discern that those precious promises contain in them the fruits of Christ's mediation, by renewing their faith so that they are enabled to lay hold of and plead them before God. Real prayer is in faith: faith necessarily respects God's promises: therefore if we understand not the spiritual import of the promises, the suitability of them to our varied cases, and reverently urge the actual fulfillment of them to us, then we have not prayed at all. But for that sight and sense of the promises, and the appropriation of them, we are entirely dependent upon the Holy Spirit.

Fourth, the Spirit helps the Christian to direct his petitions unto right ends. Many prayers remain unanswered because of our failure at this point: "Ye ask, and receive not, because ye ask amiss, that ye may consume it upon your lusts" (Jas. 4:3). The "ask amiss" in that passage means to ask for something with a wrong end in view, and were we left entirely to ourselves, this would always be the case with us. Only three ends are permissible: that God may be glorified, that our spirituality may be promoted, that our brethren may be blessed. Now none but the Spirit can enable us to subordinate all our desires and petitions unto God's glory. None but the Spirit can bring us to make our advancement in holiness our end—the reason why we ask God to grant our requests. This He does by putting into our minds a high valuation of conformity to God, a deep longing in the heart that His image may be more manifestly stamped upon us, a strong inclination of will to diligently seek the same by the use of all appointed means.

It is by the Spirit the sin-troubled Christian is helped to apprehend God as his Father, and his heart is emboldened to approach Him as such. It is by the Spirit we are granted a conscious access to the Throne of Grace. He it is who moves us to plead the infinite merits of Christ. He it is who strengthens us to pray in a holy manner, rather than from carnal motives and sentiments. He it is who imparts any measure of fervor to our hearts so that we "cry" unto God—which respects not the loudness of our voices, but the earnestness of our supplications. He it is who gives us a spirit of importunity, so that we are enabled (at times) to say with Jacob, "I will not let Thee go, except Thou bless me" (Gen. 32:26). And He it is who prepares the heart to receive God's answer, so that what is bestowed is a real blessing to us and not a curse.

In conclusion let it be pointed out that the motions of the Spirit in the saint are a "help" to prayer, but not the rule or reason of prayer. There are some who say that they never attempt to pray unless conscious that he Spirit moves them to do so. But this is wrong: the Spirit is given to help us in the performance of duty, and not in the neglect of it! God commands us to pray: that is our "rule"—"always to pray" (Luke 18:1), "in everything by prayer and supplication" (Phil. 4:6). For many years past, the editor had made it a practice of beginning his prayers by definitely and trustfully seeking the Spirit's aid: see Luke 11:13. Do not conclude that lack of words and suitable expressions is a proof that the Spirit is withholding His help. Finally, remember that He is Sovereign: "the wind bloweth were it listeth" (John 3:8).

The Negative and the Positive

God's Word is designed to have a twofold effect upon the Christian: a distressing and a comforting. As we appropriate the Scriptures to ourselves, pride will be abased and the old man cast down; on the other hand faith will be strengthened and the new man built up. Our poor hearts first need humbling, and then exalting; we must be made to mourn over our sins, and then be filled with praise at the realization of God's amazing grace. Now in Romans 8:26, 27 there is that which should produce both these effects upon us. First, we are reminded of "our infirmities" or weaknesses: note the plural number, for we are full of them—how our apprehension of this should "hide pride from us"! Yet, second, here is also real ground for comfort and hope: "The Spirit also helpeth our infirmities." The frail and erring believer is not left to himself: a gracious, all-powerful, ever-present Helper is given to support and assist him. How this blessed fact should rejoice our hearts!

The tones of Scripture, then, fall upon the ear of God's children in ever alternating keys: the minor and the major. So it is in the passage before us, for next we read "we know not what we should pray for as we ought." What a pride-withering word is that! One which is in direct variance with what is commonly supposed. The general belief is that men do know well enough what they should pray for, but they are so careless and wicked they do not discharge this duty; but God says, they "know not." Nor can the godliest saint or wisest minister help the unregenerate at this point, by drawing up for them a form of words, which suitably expresses their needs, for it is one thing to have Scriptural words upon our lips, but it is quite another for the soul to feel his dire need of what he asks for; it is out of the abundance of the heart the mouth speaketh in prayer, or God will not hear.

But the words of our text are yet more searching and solemn: they refer not to the unregenerate (though of course it is of them), but to the regenerate: "we (Christians) know not what we should pray for as we ought." And again we say what a heart-humbling word is this. Now we are partakers of the Divine nature, now a way has been opened for us into the presence of God, now we have access to the Throne of Grace itself, now we are invited to "make known our requests." Yet so fearfully has sin darkened our judgment, so deceitful and wicked are our hearts, so blind are we as to what would truly promote the manifest glory of God and what would really be for our highest good, that "we know not what we should pray for as we ought." Do you actually believe this, my reader? If you do, it must bring you into the dust before the One with whom we have to do.

"We know not what we should pray for as we ought." No, we "know not" even with the Bible in our hands, in which are full instructions to direct praying souls; in which are so many inspired prayers for our guidance. No, we "know not" even after the Lord Himself has graciously supplied us with a pattern prayer, after which ours should be modeled. Sin has so perverted our judgments, self-love has so filmed our eyes, worldliness has so corrupted our affections, that even with a Divine manual of prayer in our hands, we are quite incapable (of ourselves) of discerning what we should ask for—supplies of Divine grace to minister to our spiritual needs—and are unable to present our suit in a spiritual manner, acceptable to God. How the recognition of this fact should empty our hearts of conceit! How the realization of it should fill us with shame! What need have we to cry, "Lord, teach us to pray!"

But now on the other side: lest we should be utterly cast down by a sense of our excuseless and guilty ignorance, we are Divinely informed "the Spirit itself maketh intercession for us." Wondrous indeed, unspeakably blessed, is this! Instead of turning away from us in disgust because of our culpable ignorance, God has not only provided us with an Intercessor at His right hand (Heb. 7:25). But what is to the writer even more remarkable, God has given His needy people a Divine Intercessor at their right hand, even the Holy Spirit. How this glorious fact should raise our drooping souls, revolutionize our ideas of prayer, and fill our hearts with thanksgiving and praise for this unspeakable Gift. If it be asked, Why has God provided two Intercessors for His people, the answer is: to bridge the entire gulf between Him and us. One to represent God to us, the Other to represent us before God. The One to prompt our prayers, the Other to present them to the Father. The One to ask blessings for us, the Other to convey blessings unto us!

Groanings

It is indeed striking to observe this alternation between the minor and major keys running all through our passage, for next we are told, "the Spirit itself maketh intercession for us with groanings which cannot be uttered." This, as we have seen, refers to the inward anguish which the Spirit produces in the believer. Here, then, is further ground for self-abasement: even when a sense of need has been communicated to us, so sottish are we that our poor hearts are overwhelmed, and all we can do is to sigh and groan. Even when the Spirit has convicted us of our corruptions and imparted a deep yearning for Divine grace, we are incapable of articulating our wants or expressing our longings: rather is our case then like the Psalmist's, "I was dumb with silence" (39:2). If left to ourselves, the distress occasioned by our felt sinfulness would quite disable us to pray.

It may be objected, To what purpose is it that the Spirit should stir up such "groanings," which the Christian can neither understand nor express? Ah, this brings us to the brighter side again: "He that searcheth the hearts knoweth what is the mind of the Spirit" (Rom. 8:27). God knows what those groanings mean, for He discerns the very thoughts and intents of our hearts. How comforting is this: to realize in prayer we are coming to One who thoroughly understands us! How blessed to be assured that God will rightly interpret every motion the Spirit prompts within us. God "knows" the "mind of the Spirit"—His intention in producing our anguish. God is able to distinguish between the moanings of mere nature and the "groanings" of which the Spirit is the Author.

There is a fourfold "spirit" which works in prayer. First, the natural spirit of man, which seeks his own welfare and preservation. This is not sinful, as may be seen from the case of Christ in Gethsemane: the innocent desire of human nature to be delivered from the awful pressure upon Him; and then subjecting His will to the Father's. Second, a carnal and sinful spirit: "your brethren that hated you, that cast you out for My name's sake, said, Let the LORD be glorified" (Isa. 66:5), but God did not answer them in the way they meant. Third, the new nature in the believer, which has holy aspirations, but is powerless of itself to express them. Fourth, "praying in the Holy Spirit" (Jude 20)—by His prompting and power. Now God discerns between the motions of nature, the lustings of the flesh, the longings of grace, and the desires wrought by the Spirit. This it is which explains "The LORD weigheth the spirits" (Prov. 16:2)—the fourfold "spirit" mentioned above.

None but God is able to thus distinguish and interpret the "groanings" of the Spirit in the saint. A striking proof of this is found in, "Now Hannah, she spake in her heart; only her lips moved, but her voice was not heard: therefore Eli thought she had been drunken" (1 Sam 1:13)—even the high priest of Israel was incapable of discerning the anguish of her heart and what the Spirit had prompted within her. "He that searcheth the hearts knoweth what is the mind of the Spirit," (Rom. 8:27), signifies far more than that He understands: God approves and delights in—for this use of the word "know" see Psalm 1:6; Amos 3:2; John 10:14; 1 Corinthians 8:3. And why is it that God thus finds perfect complacency in the mind of our Helper? Because as the Father and the Son are One, so the Father and the Spirit are One—one in nature, in purpose, in glory.

"Because He maketh intercession for the saints according to the will of God" (Rom. 8:27). Here is additional ground for our encouragement. The words "the will of" are in italics, which means they are not in the Greek, but have been supplied by our translators. They interpose a needless limitation. That which the Spirit produces in the saint is, first, in accord with God's nature—spiritual and holy. Second, it is according to God's Word, for the Spirit ever prompts us to ask for what has been revealed or promised. Third, it is according to God's purpose, for the Spirit is fully cognizant of all the Divine counsels. Fourth, it is according to God's glory, for the Spirit teaches us to make that our end in asking. O what encouragement is here: the Spirit creates within us holy desires, the Son presents them, the Father understands and approves them! Then let us "come boldly to the Throne of Grace."

The Spirit Transforming

2 Corinthians 3:18

Just as there are certain verses in the Old Testament and the Gospels which give us a miniature of the redemptive work of Christ for God's people—such, for example, as Isaiah 53:5 and John 3:16—so in the Epistles there are some condensed doctrinal declarations which express in a few words the entire work of the Spirit in reforming, conforming, and transforming believers. 2 Corinthians 3:18 is a case in point: "But we all, with open face beholding as in a glass the glory of the Lord, are changed into the same image from glory to glory, even as by the Spirit of the Lord." This important passage supplies a brief but blessed summary of the progressive work of grace which is wrought in the Christian by the indwelling Spirit. It focuses to a single point the different rays which are emitted by the various graces which He communicates to them, namely, that wherein the saint is slowly but surely conformed unto and transfigured into the very image of the Lord.

There are many parts in and aspects of the Spirit's work in reforming, conforming and transforming the believer, but they are here epitomized in one brief but most comprehensive statement, which we now propose to examine and expound. As an aid to this, let us proceed to ask our verse a number of questions. First, exactly what is meant by "the glory of the Lord," into "the same image" of which all believers "are changed"?—are—not, "shall be." Second, what is "the glass" in which we are beholding this glory? Third, what is denoted in the we are "changed into the same image from glory to glory." Fourth, what is the force of "we all with open face" are beholding this glory? Finally, how does the Spirit of the Lord effect this great change in believers? Are they entirely passive therein, or is there an active co-operation on their part?

Perhaps it will help the reader most if we first give brief answers to these questions and then supply amplifications of the same in what follows. The "glory of the Lord" here signifies His moral perfections, the excellencies of His character. The "glass" in which His glory is revealed and in which those with anointed eyes may behold it, is the Holy Scripture. Our being "changed into

The Holy Spirit

the same image" has reference to our sanctification, viewed from the experimental side; that it is here said to be "from glory to glory" intimates it is a gradual and progressive work. Our beholding that glory with "open face" means that the veil of darkness, of prejudice, of "enmity," which was over our depraved hearts by nature, has been removed, so that in God's light we now see light. The Spirit effects this great change both immediately and mediately, that is, by His direct actions upon the soul and also by blessing to us our use of the appointed means of grace.

"The glory of the Lord." This we have defined as His moral perfections, the excellencies of His character. The best theologians have classified God's attributes under two heads: incommunicable and communicable. There are certain perfections of the Divine Being which are peculiar to Himself, which in their very nature cannot be transmitted to the creature: these are His eternity, His immutability, His omnipotence, His omniscience, His omnipresence. There are other perfections of the Divine Being which He is pleased to communicate, in measure, to the unfallen angels and to the redeemed from among men: these are His goodness, His grace, His mercy, His holiness, His righteousness, His wisdom. Now, obviously, it is the latter which the Apostle has before him in 2 Corinthians 3:18, for believers are not, will not, and cannot be changed into the "same image" of the Lord's omniscience, etc. Compare "we beheld the glory ... full of grace and truth" (John 1: 14)—His moral perfections.

The "Glass"

The "glass" in which the glory of the Lord is revealed and beheld by us is His written Word, as is clear by a comparison with James 1:22-25. Yet let it be carefully borne in mind that the Scriptures have two principal parts, being divided into two Testaments. Now the contents of those two Testaments may be summed up, respectively, in the Law and the Gospel. That which is outstanding in the Old Testament is the Law; that which is preeminent in the New Testament is the Gospel. Thus, in giving an exposition or explanation of the "glass" in which believers behold the Lord's glory, we cannot do better than say, It is in the Law and the Gospel His glory is set before us. It is absolutely essential to insist on this amplification, for a distinctive "glory of the Lord" is revealed in each one, and to both of them is the Christian conformed (or "changed") by the Spirit.

Should anyone say that we are "reading our own thoughts into" the meaning of the "glass" in which the glory of the Lord is revealed, and object to our insisting this signifies, first the Law, we would point out this is fully borne out by the immediate context of 2 Corinthians 3:18, and what is found there obliges us to take this view. The Apostle is there comparing and contrasting the two great economies, the Mosaic and the Christian, showing that the preeminence of the one over the other lay in the former being an external ministration (the "letter"), whereas the latter is internal (the "spirit"), in the heart; nevertheless, he affirms that the former ministration "was glorious" (v. 7), and "if the ministration of condemnation be glorious" (v. 9), "for even that which is made glorious" (v. 10), "if that which was done away was glorious" (v. 11)—all being explained by the fact that the glory of the Lord was exhibited therein.

In the "glass" of the Law the Lord gave a most wondrous revelation of His "glory." The Law has been aptly and rightly designated "a transcript of the Divine nature," though (as is to be expected) some of our modems have taken serious exception to that statement, thereby setting themselves in opposition to the Scriptures. In Romans 8:7 we are told "the carnal mind is enmity against God," and the proof furnished of this declaration is, "for it is not subject to the Law of God," which, manifestly, is only another way of saying that the Law is a transcript of the very character of God. So again we read, "The law is holy, and the commandment holy, and just, and good" (Rom. 7:12): what is that but a summarized description of the Divine perfections! If God Himself is "holy and just and good" and the Law is an immediate reflection of His very nature, then it will itself be "holy and just and good." Again, if God Himself is "love" (1 John 4:8) and the Law is a glass in which His perfections shine, then that which the Law requires, all that is required, will be love, and that is exactly the case: Matthew 22:37-39.

What a word is that in Exodus 24:16, "And the glory of the LORD abode upon Mount Sinai." Yes, the glory of the Lord was as really and truly manifested at Sinai as it is displayed now at Mount Zion—that man in his present state was unable to appreciate the awe-inspiring display which God there made of His perfections, in no way alters that fact, for He is a God to be feared as well as loved. In the "glass" of the Law we behold the glory of the Lord's majesty and sovereignty, the glory of His government and authority, the glory of His justice and holiness. Yes, and the "glory" of His goodness in framing such a Law which requires us to love Him with all our hearts, and for His sake, His creatures, our neighbors as ourselves.

But the "glory of the Lord" is further manifested in the "glass" of the Gospel, in which God has made a fuller and yet more blessed revelation of His moral perfections than He did at Sinai. Now the Gospel necessarily implies or presupposes the following things. First, a broken Law, and its transgressors utterly unable to repair its breach. Second, that God graciously determined to save a people from its curse. Third, that He purposes to do so without making light of sin, without dishonoring the Law, and without compromising His holiness—otherwise, so far from the Gospel being the best news of all, it would herald the supreme calamity. How this is effected, by and through Christ, the Gospel makes known. In His own Son, God shines forth in meridian splendor, for Jesus Christ is the brightness of His glory, the express image of His Person. In Christ the veil is rent, the Holy of Holies is exposed to full view, for now we behold "The light of the knowledge of the glory of God in the face of Jesus Christ" (2 Cor. 4:6).

In the Gospel is displayed not only the amazing grace and infinite mercy, but also and mainly the "manifold wisdom" of God. Therein we learn how grace is exercised righteously, how mercy is bestowed honorably, how transgressors are pardoned justly. God did not deem it suitable to the honor of His majesty to sovereignly pardon sinners without a satisfaction being offered to Himself, and therefore did He appoint a Mediator to magnify the Law and make it honorable. The great design of the incarnation, life and death of Christ, was to demonstrate in the most public manner that God was worthy of all that love, honor and obedience which the Law required, and that sin was as great an evil as the punishment threatened supposed. The heart of the glorious Gospel of Christ is the Cross, and there we see all the Divine perfections fully displayed: in the death of the Lord Jesus the Law was magnified, Divine holiness vindicated, sin discountenanced, the sinner saved, grace glorified, and Satan defeated.

The Unregenerate See It Not

Though the glory of the Lord be so plainly revealed in the two-fold "glass" of the Law and the Gospel, yet the unregenerate appreciate it not: concerning the one it is said, "But even unto this day, when Moses is read, the veil is upon their heart" (2 Cor. 3:15); and of the latter we read, "In whom the god of this world hath blinded the minds of them which believe not, lest the light of the glorious Gospel of Christ, who is the image of God, should shine unto them" (2 Cor. 4:4). The unregenerate are blind to the loveliness of the Divine character: not that they have no eyes to see with, but they have deliberately "closed them" (Matthew 13:15); not that they are not intellectually convinced of the Divine perfections, but that their hearts are unaffected thereby. It is because man is a fallen depraved and vicious creature that he is not won by "the beauty of holiness."

"Except a man be born again, he cannot see the kingdom of God" (John 3:3). Clearest possible proof of this was furnished when the Word became flesh and tabernacled among men. Those who had been "born of God" (John

1:13) could say, "We beheld His glory, the glory as of the Only begotten of the Father, full of grace and truth" (John 1:14). But different indeed was it with those who were left in their natural state—they, notwithstanding their education, culture, and religion, were so far from discerning any form or comeliness in Christ, that they cried, "Thou art a Samaritan, and hast a devil" (John 8:48). Yet it is as plain as a sunbeam that the blindness of the Pharisees was due neither to the lack of necessary faculties nor to the want of outward opportunities, but entirely to the perverted state of their minds and the depraved condition of their hearts—which was altogether of a criminal nature.

From what has just been pointed out, then, it is plain when the Apostle declares, "but we all, with open face beholding as in a glass the glory of the Lord" (2 Cor. 3:18), that a miracle of grace had been wrought in them. As spiritual blindness consists in an absence of relish for holy beauty—which blindness is capable of being greatly increased and confirmed through the exercise and influence of the various corruptions of a wicked heart, and which Satan augments by all means in his power—so spiritual sight is the soul's delighting itself in Divine and spiritual things. In regeneration there is begotten in the soul a holy taste so that the heart now goes out after God and His Christ. This is referred to in Scripture in various ways. It is the fulfillment of that promise "And the LORD thy God will circumcise thine heart, and the heart of thy seed, to love the LORD thy God" (Deut. 30:6).

This new relish for spiritual things which is begotten in the soul by the immediate operations of the Spirit is also the fulfillment of, "A new heart also will I give you, and a new spirit will I put within you: and I will take away the stony heart out of your flesh, and I will give you an heart of flesh" (Ezek. 36:26); and of, "I will give them an heart to know Me, that I am the LORD: and they shall be My people" (Jer. 24:7). So also, "Then the eyes of the blind shall be opened, and the ears of the deaf shall be unstopped" (Isa. 35:5). Of Lydia we read, "Whose heart the Lord opened, that she attended unto the things which were spoken of Paul" (Acts 16:14). To the Corinthian saints the Apostle wrote, "For God, who commanded the light to shine out of darkness, hath shined in our hearts" (2 Cor. 4:6). In consequence thereof, the happy subjects of this work of Divine grace perceive and relish the holy character of God and are enamored with His perfections.

"Changed into the Same Image"

"But we all": that is, all who have been supernaturally brought from death unto life, out of darkness into God's marvelous light. "With open face," or "unveiled face," as it is in the Greek and as the R.V. translates it: that is, with hearts from which "the veil" of prejudice (2 Cor. 3:15) has been removed, from which that "covering cast over all people" (Isa. 25:7), the covering of enmity against God, has been destroyed. "Beholding"—note carefully the present tense, for it is a continuous action which is here in view; "as in a glass" or "mirror," namely, the twofold glass of the Law and the Gospel; "the glory of the Lord," that is His communicable perfections, His moral character; "are changed into the same image," this clause it is which must next engage our careful attention.

Following our usual custom, let us first give a brief definition and then amplify the same. To be changed into "the same image" means that the regenerated soul becomes conformed unto the Divine character, that answerable principles and affections are wrought in his heart, bringing him into harmony with the perfections of God. This must be the case, for since Divinely enlightened souls have such a relish for holy beauty, for such beauty as there is in the character of God, then it necessarily follows that every Divine truth as it comes into their view will appear beautiful, and will accordingly beget and excite holy affections corresponding with its nature. Or, more specifically, as the heart is occupied with the several perfections of God exhibited in the Law and in the Gospel, corresponding desires and determinations will be awakened in and exercised by that soul.

It would imply a contradiction to suppose that any heart should be charmed with a character just the opposite to its own. The carnal mind is enmity against God: resenting His authority, disliking His holiness, hating His sovereignty, and condemning His justice: in a word, it is immediately opposed to His glory as it shines in the glass of the Law and the Gospel. But one who has been Divinely enlightened loves the Truth because he has a frame of heart answerable thereto—just as the unregenerate soul loves the world because it suits his depraved tastes. The regenerate discerns and feels that the Law is righteous in requiring what it does, even though it condemns him for his disobedience. He perceives, too, that the Gospel is exactly suited to his needs and that its precepts are wise and excellent. Thus he is brought into conformity with the one and into compliance with the other.

Universal experience teaches us that characters appear agreeable or disagreeable just as they suit our taste or not. To an angel, who has a taste for holy beauty, the moral character of God appears infinitely amiable; but to the Devil, who is being of a contrary taste, God's moral character appears just the reverse. To the Pharisees, no character was more odious than that of the Lord Jesus; but at the same time Mary and Martha and Lazarus were charmed with Him. To the Jewish nation in general, who groaned under the Roman yoke, and longed for a Messiah to set them at liberty, to make them victorious, rich and honorable—a Messiah in the character of a temporal prince, who had gratified their desires—such an one had appeared glorious in their eyes, and they would have been changed into the same image; that is, every answerable affection had been excited in their hearts.

Now it is this moral transformation in the believer which is the evidence of his spiritual enlightenment: "beholding," he is "changed." Where a soul has been supernaturally illumined there will issue a corresponding conformity to the Divine image. But in so affirming, many of our Christian readers are likely to feel that we are thereby cutting off their hopes. They will be ready to exclaim, Alas, my character resembles the likeness of Satan far more than it does the image of God. Let us, then, ease the tension a little. Observe, dear troubled souls, this transformation is not effected instantaneously, but by degrees: this great "change" is not accomplished by the Spirit in a moment, but is a gradual work. This is plainly signified in the "from glory to glory," which means, from one degree of it to another. Only as this fact is apprehended can our poor hearts be assured before God.

This expression "from glory to glory" is parallel with "the rain also filleth the pools: they go from strength to strength" (Ps. 84:6, 7), which means that under the gracious revivings of the Spirit, believers are renewed again and again, and so go on from one degree of strength to another. So in Romans 1:17 we read of "from faith to faith," which means from little faith to more faith, until sometimes it may be said, "your faith groweth exceedingly" (2 Thess. 1:3). So it is with this blessed "change" which the Spirit works in believers. The first degree of it is effected at their regeneration. The second degree of it is accomplished during their progressive (practical) sanctflcation. The third and last degree of it takes place at their glorification. Thus "the path of the just is as the shining light, that shineth more and more unto the perfect day" (Prov. 4:18).

Summary

For the benefit of clarity we will give a brief digest of our previous exposition of 2 Corinthians 3:18, which is a verse that supplies a comprehensive summary of the Spirit's work in the believer. The "we all" are those that are indwelt by the Holy Spirit. The "with open face" signifies with minds from which their enmity against God has been removed, with hearts that are reconciled to Him. "Beholding" is a repeated act of the soul, which is the effect of its having been supernaturally enlightened. "As in a glass" refers to the revelation which God has made of Himself in the Law and in the Gospel. The "glory of the Lord" connotes His character or moral perfections.

The Holy Spirit

"Are changed into the same image" tells of the transformation which is effected in the believer by the Spirit. The "from glory to glory" announces that this great change of the heart's reformation and conformation to the image of God is produced gradually.

When the Spirit deals with an elect soul, He first brings him face to face with God's Law, for "by the law is the knowledge of sin" (Rom. 3:20). He reveals to him the perfections of the Law: its spirituality, its immutability, its righteousness. He makes him realize that the Law is "holy, and just, and good" (Rom. 7:12) even though it condemns and curses him. He shows that the Law requires that we should love the Lord our God with all our hearts, and our neighbors as ourselves; that it demands perfect and perpetual obedience in thought, word, and deed. He convinces the soul of the righteousness of such a demand. In a word, the one with whom the Spirit is dealing beholds "the glory of the Lord"—His majesty, His holiness, His justice—in the glass of the Law. Only thus is the soul prepared and fitted to behold and appreciate the second great revelation which God has made of His moral perfections.

Next, the Spirit brings before the soul the precious Gospel. He shows him that therein a marvelous and most blessed display is made of the love, the grace, the mercy, and the wisdom of God. He gives him to see that in His eternal purpose God designed to save a people from the curse of the Law, and that, without flouting its authority or setting aside its righteous claims; yea, in such a way that the Law is "magnified and made honorable" (Isa. 42:21) through its demands being perfectly met by the believing sinner's Surety. He unveils to his wondering gaze the infinite condescension of the Father's Beloved, who willingly took upon Him the form of a servant and became obedient unto death, even the death of the Cross. And the Spirit so works in his heart that, though the Cross be a stumbling block to the Jew and foolishness unto the Greek, it appears to him to be the most wondrous, blessed, and glorious object in the universe—and by faith he thankfully rests the entire interests of his soul for time and eternity upon the atoning sacrifice which Christ offered thereon unto God.

Not only does the Spirit give that soul to behold "the glory of the Lord" as it shines first in the "glass" of the Law, and second in the "glass" of the Gospel, but He also causes him to be "changed into the same image," that is, He begets within him corresponding principles and affections, to the one and to the other. In other words, He brings his heart to a conformity to the Law and to a compliance with the Gospel. He causes the believer to "set to his seal" (John 3:33) to the whole Truth of God. He brings him to a full acquiescence with the Law, consenting to its righteous claims upon him, and working in him a desire and determination to adopt the Law as his rule of life or standard of conduct. So, too, the Spirit causes him to gladly embrace the Gospel, admiring the consummate wisdom of God therein, whereby the perfect harmony of His justice and mercy are blessedly exhibited. He brings him to renounce all his own works, and rest alone on the merits of Christ for his acceptance with God.

"Beholding as in a glass" is literally "in a mirror." Now the mirrors to the ancients, unlike ours, were not made of glass, but of highly burnished metal, which reflected images with great brilliancy and distinctness, corresponding to the metal. If the mirror was of silver, a white light would be the result; if of gold, a yellow glow would be suffused. Thus an opaque object reflected the rays of the sun, and so became in a measure luminous. Here the Apostle makes use of this as a figure of the Spirit's transforming the believer. The Law and the Gospel display various aspects of "the glory of the Lord," that is, of God Himself, and as anointed eyes behold the same, the soul is irradiated thereby and an answerable change is wrought in it.

As the soul by faith, with broken heart (and not otherwise), beholds the glory of the Lord, in the mirror of the two Testaments (and not in the New without the Old), he is by the continual operations of the Spirit in him (Phil. 1:6) "changed into the same image." The views thus obtained of the Divine character excite answerable affections in the beholder. Rational argument may convince a man that God is holy, yet that is a vastly different thing from his heart being brought to love Divine holiness. But when the Spirit removes the veil of enmity and prejudice from the mind and enables the understanding to see light in God's light, there is a genuine esteem of and delight in God's character. The heart is won with the excellence of His moral perfections, and he perceives the rightness and beauty of a life wholly devoted to His glory. Thus there is a radical change in his judgment, disposition and conduct.

In the glass of the Law there shines the glory of God's holiness and righteousness, and in the glass of the Gospel the glory of His grace and mercy, and as by the Spirit's enablement the believer is beholding them, there is wrought in him a love for the same, there is given to him an answerable frame of heart. He cordially owns God as righteous in all His ways and holy in all His works. He acknowledges that God is just in condemning him, and equally just in pardoning him. He freely confesses that he is as evil as the Law pronounces him to be, and that his only hope lies in the atoning sacrifice of the Lamb. Christ is now "The Fairest of ten thousand" to his soul. He desires and endeavors to exercise righteousness and truth, grace and mercy, in all his dealings with his fellows. Thus a personal experience of the transforming power of the Law and the Gospel brings its subject into a conformity to their temper and tendency.

This being "changed into the same image" of the glory of the Lord, is but another way of saying that the Law of God is now written on the heart (Heb. 8:10), for as we have said previously, the Law is a transcript of the Divine nature, the very image of God. As the Law was written in indelible characters on the tables of stone by the very finger of God, so at regeneration and throughout the entire process of sanctification, views and dispositions in accord with the nature of the Law become habitual in the heart, through the operations of the Holy Spirit, according to the measure of grace which He supplies. The genuine language of the soul now becomes, "How reasonable it is that I should love with all my heart such an infinitely glorious being as God, that I should be utterly captivated by His supernal excellence. How fitting that I should be entirely for Him and completely at the disposal of Him who is Lord of all, whose rectitude is perfect, whose goodness and wisdom are infinite, and who gave His Son to die for me!"

This being "changed into the same image" of the glory of the Lord, is also the same as Christ being "formed" in the soul (Gal. 4:19). It is having in kind, though not in degree, the same mind that was in the Lord Jesus. It is being imbued with His Spirit, being brought into accordance with the design of His mediatorial work, which was to honor and glorify God. In a word, it is being at heart the very disciples of Christ. This being "changed into the same image" of the glory of the Lord, is to be "reconciled to God" (2 Cor. 5:20). Previously, we were at enmity against Him, hating His sovereignty, His strictness, His severity; but now we perceive the surpassing beauty of His every attribute and are in love with His whole Person and character. No greater change than this can be conceived of: "Ye were sometimes darkness, but now are ye light in the Lord" (Eph. 5:8). This great change is to "come unto" God (Heb. 7:25), causing us to diligently seek daily supplies of grace from Him.

Occupation and Application

"Mine eye affecteth mine heart" (Lam. 3:51). We are influenced by the objects we contemplate, we become ostensibly assimilated to those with whom we have much intercourse, we are molded by the books we read. This same law or principle operates in the spiritual realm: "But we all, with open face beholding as in a glass the glory of the Lord, are changed into the same image from glory to glory, even as by the Spirit of the Lord" (2 Cor.

3:18)—beholding, we are changed. Here, then, is our responsibility: to use the means which God has appointed for our growth in grace, to be daily occupied with spiritual objects and heavenly things. Yet our study and contemplation of the Truth will not, by itself, produce any transformation: there must be a Divine application of the Truth to the heart. Apart from the Divine agency and blessing all our efforts and use of the means amount to nothing, and therefore is it added "We are changed . . . by the Spirit."

Just as surely as Christ's all-mighty power will, on the resurrection morning, transform the bodies of His people from mortality to life and from dishonor to glory, so also does the Holy Spirit now exert a supernatural power in morally transforming the characters of those whom He indwells. The great difference between these two—the future work of Christ upon the bodies of the saints and the present work of the Spirit upon their souls—is that the one will be accomplished instantaneously, whereas the other is effected slowly and gradually. The one we shall be fully conscious of, the other we are largely unconscious of. This being "changed into the same image" of the glory of the Lord is a progressive experience, as the "from glory to glory" plainly intimates—from one degree of it to another. It is begun at regeneration, is continued throughout our sanctification, and will be perfected at our glorification.

Now that which deeply exercises and so often keenly distresses the sincere Christian is that as he seeks to honestly examine himself he discovers so very little evidence that he IS being "changed into" the image of the Lord. He dare not take anything for granted, but desires to "prove" himself (2 Cor. 13:5). The moral transformation of which we have been treating is that which supplies proof of spiritual illumination, and without at least a measure of it, all supposed saving knowledge of the Truth is but a delusion. We shall therefore endeavor now to point out some of the leading features by which this transformation may be identified, asking the reader to carefully compare himself with each one.

Marks of Transformation

First, where the Spirit has begun to transform a soul the Divine Law is cordially received as a Rule of Life, and the heart begins to echo to the language of Psalm 119 in its commendation. Nothing more plainly distinguishes a true conversion from a counterfeit than this: that one who used to be an enemy to God's Law is brought understandingly and heartily to love it, and seek to walk according to its requirements. "Hereby we do know that we know Him, if we keep His commandments" (1 John 2:3). He who has been born again has a new palate, so that he now relishes what he formerly disliked. He now begins to prove that it is not only the fittest, but the happiest thing in the world, to aspire to be holy as God is holy, to love Him supremely and live to Him entirely.

Second, a life of self-loathing. The regenerated soul perceives that complete and constant subjection to God is His due, and that the gift of His beloved Son has laid him under lasting obligations to serve, please, and glorify Him. But the best of God's people are only sanctified in part in this life, and realizing the Law requires, and that God is entitled to sinless perfection from us, what but a life of self-abhorrence must ensue? Once we are supernaturally enlightened to see that "the Law is spiritual," the inevitable consequence must be for me to see and feel that "I am carnal, sold under sin" (Rom. 7:14). And therefore there must be a continued sense of infinite blame, of self-loathing, of godly sorrow, of broken-heartedness, of hungering and thirsting after righteousness; of watching, praying, striving, or mourning because of frequent defeat.

Third, genuine humility. In view of what has just been pointed out, it is easy to see why humility is represented all through Scripture as a dominant feature of those who are quickened by the Spirit. An hypocrite, being experimentally ignorant of Divine Law—never having been slain by it (Rom. 7:9, 11)—then, the more religious he is, the more proud and conceited will he be. But with a true saint it is just the opposite: for if the Law be his rule of duty, and his obligations to conform thereto are infinite, and his blame for every defect is proportionately great—if the fault lie entirely in himself, and his lack of perfect love and obedience to God be wholly culpable-then he must be filled with low and mean thoughts of himself, and have an answerable lowliness of heart.

There is no greater proof that a man is ignorant of the Truth savingly, and a stranger to Christ experimentally, than for spiritual pride to reign in his heart. "Behold, his soul which is lifted up is not upright in him" (Hab. 2:4). The graceless Pharisee, blind to the real character and purport of the Law, was ready to say, "God, I thank Thee, that I am not as other men"; while the penitent Publican, seeing himself in the light of God, dared not lift up his eyes to Heaven, but smote upon his breast (the seat of his spiritual leprosy) and cried "God be merciful to me, the sinner." The proud religionists of Christ's day exclaimed, "Behold, we see" (John 9:41); but the holy Psalmist prayed, "Open Thou mine eyes, that I may behold wondrous things out of Thy Law." Thousands of deluded people who profess to be Christians prate about their consecration, victories, and attainments; but the Apostle Paul said, "I count not myself to have apprehended" (Phil. 3:13).

Fourth, a growing apprehension of the Divine goodness. The more a quickened soul sees himself in the light of God, the more he discovers how much there still is in him which is opposed to His Law, and in how many respects he daily offends. The more clearly he perceives how very far he comes short of the glory of God, and how unlike Christ he is in character and conduct, the deeper becomes his appreciation of the grace of God through the Mediator. The man who is of a humble, broken and contrite heart, finds the promises of the Gospel just fitted to his case. None but One who is "mighty to save" (Isa. 63:1) can redeem such a wretch as he knows himself to be; none but the "God of all grace" (1 Pet. 5:10) would show favor to one so vile and worthless. "Worthy is the Lamb" is now his song. "Not unto us, O LORD, not unto us, but unto Thy name give glory, for Thy mercy, and for Thy Truth's sake" (Ps. 115:1) is his hearty acknowledgment. It is the Spirit's continued application of the Law to the believer's conscience which prepares him to receive the comforts and consolations of the Gospel.

When the mind is thoroughly convinced that God can, consistently with His honor, willingly receive to favor the most naked, forlorn, wretched, guilty, Hell-deserving of the human race, and become a Father and Friend to him, he is happier than if all the world was his own. When God is his sensible Portion, everything else fades into utter insignificance. The fig tree may not blossom, nor any fruits be in the vine, yet he will "joy in the God of his salvation" (Hab. 3:18). The Apostle Paul, although a prisoner at Rome, not in the least dejected, cries, "Rejoice in the Lord alway: and again I say, Rejoice" (Phil. 4:4). When God is chosen as our supreme Good, all earthly idols are rejected, and our treasure is laid up in Heaven. In proportion as grace flourishes in the heart our comforts will remain, let outward things go as they will; yea, it will be found that it is "good to be afflicted" (Ps. 119:71).

Here, then, are some of the principal effects produced by our being "changed," or reformed, conformed, and transformed by the Spirit of God. There is a growing realization of the ineffable holiness of God and of the righteousness and spirituality of the Law, and the extent of its requirements. There is a deepening sense of our utter sinfulness, failure and blameworthiness, and the daily loathing of ourselves for our hard-heartedness, our base ingratitude, and the ill returns we make to God for His infinite goodness to us. There is a corresponding self-abasement, taking our place in the dust before God, and frankly admitting that we are not worthy of the least of His mercies (Gen. 32:10). There is an increasing appreciation of the grace of God and of the provision He has made for us in Christ, with a corresponding longing to be done with this body of death and conformed fully to the lovely image of the Lord; which longings will be completely realized at our glorification.

The Spirit Preserving

During recent years much has been written upon the eternal security of the saints, some of it helpful, but most of it superficial and injurious. Many Scriptures have been quoted, but few of them explained. A great deal has been said about the fact of Divine preservation, but comparatively little on the method thereof. The preservation of the believer by the Father and by the Son has been given considerable prominence, but the work of the Spirit therein was largely ignored. The general impression conveyed to the thoughtful reader has been that, the "final perseverance" of the Christian is a mechanical thing rather than a spiritual process, that it is accomplished by physical force rather than by moral persuasion, that it is performed by external might rather than by internal means—something like an unconscious non-swimmer being rescued from a watery grave, or a fireman carrying a swooning person out of a burning building. Such illustrations are radically faulty, utterly misleading, and pernicious in their tendency.

It may be objected that the principal thing for us to be concerned with is the blessed fact itself, and that there is no need for us to trouble ourselves about the modus operandi: let us rejoice in the truth that God does preserve His people, and not wrack our brains over how He does so. As well might the objector say the same about the redemptive work of Christ: let us be thankful that He did make an atonement, and not worry ourselves over the philosophy of it. But is it of no real importance, no value to the soul, to ascertain that Christ's atonement was a vicarious one, that it was a definite one, and not offered at random; that it is a triumphant one, securing the actual justification of all for whom it was made? Why, my reader, it is at this very point lies the dividing-line between vital truth and fundamental error. God has done something more than record in the Gospels the historical fact of Christ's death: He has supplied in the Epistles an explanation of its nature and design.

So, too, God has given us far more than bald statements in His Word that none of His people shall perish: He has also revealed how He preserves them from destruction, and it is not only highly insulting to Him, but to our own great loss, if we ignore or refuse to ponder carefully what He has made known therein. Was it without reason Paul prayed, "That the God of our Lord Jesus Christ, the Father of glory, may give unto you the spirit of wisdom and revelation in the knowledge of Him: the eyes of your understanding being enlightened; that ye may know . . . what is the exceeding greatness of His power to usward who believe, according to the working of His mighty power, which He wrought in Christ, when He raised Him from the dead, and set Him at His own right hand" (Eph. 1:17-20). Christians are "kept by the power of God" (1 Pet. 1:5), and evidently we can only know what that power is, and the greatness thereof, as we are spiritually enlightened concerning the same.

When we read that we are "kept by the power of God through faith unto salvation ready to be revealed in the last time" (1 Pet. 1:5), or "For it is God which worketh in you both to will and to do of His good pleasure" (Phil. 2:13), in such passages the immediate reference is always to the Holy Spirit—the "immediate," though not the exclusive. In the economy of redemption all is from the Father, through the Son, by the Spirit. All proceeds from the fore-ordination of the Father, all that comes to the believer is through Christ, that is, on account of His infinite merits: all is actually wrought by the Spirit, for He is the Executive of the Godhead, the active Agent in all the works of redemption. The believer is as truly and directly preserved by the Spirit, as he was quickened by Him; and only as this is duly recognized by us will we be inclined to render Him that thanks and praise which is His distinctive due.

Preservation in Holiness

The chief end for which God sends the Spirit to indwell His people is to deliver them from apostasy: to preserve them not only from the everlasting burnings, but from those things which would expose them thereto. Unless that be clearly stated, we justly lay ourselves open to the charge that this is a dangerous doctrine—making light of sin and encouraging careless living. It is not true that if a man has once truly believed in Christ, no matter what enormities he may commit afterwards, nor what course of evil he follow, he cannot fail to reach Heaven. Not so is the teaching of Holy Writ. The Spirit does not preserve in a way of licentiousness, but only in the way of holiness. Nowhere has God promised His favor to dogs who go back to their vomit, nor to swine which return to their wallowing in the mire. The believer may indeed experience a fearful fall, yet he will not lie down content in his filth, any more than David did: "Though he fall, he shall not be utterly cast down: for the LORD upholdeth him with His hand" (Ps. 37:24).

The Holy Spirit

That many Christians have persevered in holiness to the last moment of their lives, cannot be truthfully denied. Now their perseverance must have been obtained wholly of themselves, or partly of themselves and partly by Divine aid, or it must have been wholly dependent on the purpose and power of God. None who profess to believe the Scriptures would affirm that it was due entirely to their own efforts and faithfulness, for they clearly teach that progress in holiness is as much the work of the Spirit as is the new birth itself. To say that the perseverance of the saint is due, in part to himself, is to divide the credit, afford ground for boasting, and rob God of half His rightful glory. To declare that a life of faith and holiness is entirely dependent upon the grace and power of God, is but to repeat what the Lord told His disciples: "without Me ye can do nothing" (John 15:5), and is to affirm with the Apostle, "Not that we are sufficient of ourselves to think any thing as of ourselves; but our sufficiency is of God" (2 Cor. 3:5).

Yet it needs to be pointed out that in maintaining His people in holiness, the power of God operates in quite another manner than it does in the maintenance of a river or the preservation of a tree. A river may (sometimes does) dry up, and a tree may be uprooted: the one is maintained by being replenished by fresh waters, the other is preserved by its being nourished and by its roots being held in the ground; but in each case, the preservation is by physical power, from without, entirely without their concurrence. In the case of the Christian's preservation it is quite otherwise. With him God works from within, using moral persuasion, leading him to a concurrence of mind and will with the Holy Spirit in this work. God deals with the believer as a moral agent, draws him "with cords of a man" (Hosea 11:4), maintains his responsibility, and bids him, "work out your own salvation with fear and trembling, for it is God which worketh in you both to will and to do of His good pleasure" (Phil. 2:12, 13).

Thus there is both preservation on God's part and perseverance in holiness on ours, and the former is accomplished by maintaining the latter. God does not deal with His people as though they were machines, but as rational creatures. He sets before them weighty considerations and powerful motives, solemn warnings and rich rewards, and by the renewings of His grace and the revivings of His Spirit causes them to respond thereto. Are they made conscious of the power and pollution of indwelling sin? then they cry for help to resist its lustings and to escape its defilements. Are they shown the importance, the value, and the need of faith? then they beg the Lord for an increase of it. Are they made sensible of that obedience which is due unto God, but aware, too, of the hindering drag of the flesh? then they cry, "Draw me, we will run after Thee." Do they yearn to be fruitful? then they pray, "Awake, O north wind; and come, thou south; blow upon my garden, that the spices thereof may flow out. Let my Beloved come into His garden, and eat His pleasant fruits" (Song. 4:16).

His understanding having been savingly enlightened, the believer desires to grow in grace and the knowledge of his Lord, that he may abound in spiritual wisdom and good works. Every affection of his heart is stirred, every faculty of his soul called into action. And yet this concurrence is not such as to warrant us saying that his perseverance depends, in any degree on himself, for every spiritual stirring and act on his part is but the effect of the Spirit's operation within him, "He which hath begun a good work in you will finish it" (Phil. 1:6). He who first enlightened, will continue to shine upon the understanding; He who originally convicted of sin, will go on searching the conscience; He who imparted faith will nourish and sustain the same; He who drew to Christ, will continue to attract the affections toward Him.

Regeneration and Preservation

There are two eminent benefits or spiritual blessings which comprehend all others, filling up the entire space of the Christian's life, from the moment of his quickening unto his ultimate arrival in Heaven, namely, his regeneration and his preservation. And as the renowned Puritan Thomas Goodwin says, "If a debate were admitted which of them is the greater, it would be found that no jury of mankind could determine on either side, but must leave it to God's free grace itself, which is the author and finisher of our faith, to decide." As the creating of the world at first and the upholding and governing of all things by Divine power and Providence are yoked together (Heb. 1:2, 3), so are regeneration and preservation. "Faithful is He that calleth you, who also will do it" (1 Thess. 5:24)—i.e., preserve (v. 23). "Blessed be the God and Father of our Lord Jesus Christ, which according to His abundant mercy hath begotten us again unto a lively hope ... to an inheritance incorruptible, and undefiled ... who are kept by the power of God through faith" (1 Pet. 1:3-5).

The same blessed linking together of these eminent benefits is seen in the Old Testament: "Do ye thus requite the LORD, O foolish people and unwise? is not He thy Father that hath bought thee? hath He not made thee and established thee?" (Deut. 32:6); "And even to your old age I am He; and even to hoar hairs will I carry you; I have made and I will bear" (Isa. 46:4); "Which holdeth our soul in life, and suffereth not our feet to be moved" (Ps. 66:9)—the verb has a double meaning, as the margin signifies: "putteth" at the first, and "holdeth" or maintaineth afterwards. How wonderful is this in the natural: delivered from countless dangers, preserved from epidemics and diseases which carried off thousands of our fellows, recovered from various illnesses which had otherwise proven fatal. Still more wonderful is the spiritual preservation of the saint: kept from the dominion of sin which still indwells him; kept from being drawn out of the Narrow Way by the enticements of the world; kept from the horrible heresies which ensnare multitudes on every side; kept from being entirely overcome by Satan, who ever seeks his destruction.

What pleasure it now gives the Christian to hear of the varied and wondrous ways in which God regenerates His people! What delight will be ours in Heaven when we learn of the loving care, abiding faithfulness, and mighty power of God in the preservation of each of His own! What joy will be ours when we learn the details of how He made good His promise, "When thou passest through the waters, I will be with thee; and through the rivers, they shall not overflow thee; when thou walkest through the fire, thou shalt not be burned, neither shall the flame kindle upon thee" (Isa. 43:2)—His Providence working for us externally, His grace operating internally: preserving amid the tossings and tempests of life, recovering from woeful backslidings, reviving us when almost dead.

How the Spirit Preserves

The preservation of God's people through all the vicissitudes of their pilgrim journey is accomplished, immediately, by the Holy Spirit. He it is who watches over the believer, delivering him when he knows it not; keeping him from living in the world's sinks of iniquity, lifting up a standard when the Enemy comes like a flood against him (Isa. 59:19). He it is who keeps him from accepting those fatal heresies which deceive and destroy so many empty professors. He it is who prevents his becoming contented with a mere "letter" ministry or satisfied with head-knowledge and notional religion. And how does the Spirit accomplish the Christian's preservation? By sustaining the new nature within him, and calling it forth into exercise and action. By working such graces in him that he becomes "established" (2 Cor. 1:21). By keeping him conscious of his utter ruin and deep need of Christ. By bringing him to a concurrence with His gracious design, moving him to use appropriate means. But let us be more specific.

"Teach me, O LORD, the way of Thy statutes; and I shall keep it unto the end" (Ps. 119:33). We lost the way of true happiness when we fell in Adam, and ever since men have wandered up and down vainly seeking rest and satisfaction: "They are all gone out of the way" (Rom. 3:12). Nor can any man discover the way of holiness and happiness of himself: he must be taught it spiritually and supernaturally by God. Such teaching is earnestly desired by the regenerate, for they have been made painfully conscious of their perversity and insufficiency: "Surely I am more brutish than any man, and have not the understanding of a man" (Prov. 30:2) is their confession. It is by Divine and inward teaching that we are stirred into holy activity: "I will keep it"—that which is inwrought by the Spirit is outwrought by us. Thereby our final perseverance is accomplished: "I will keep it to the end"—because effectually taught of Jehovah.

"When wisdom entereth into thine heart, and knowledge is pleasant unto thy soul; discretion shall preserve thee, understanding shall keep thee" (Prov. 2:10, 11). For wisdom to enter into our hearts means that the things of God have such an influence upon us as to dominate our affections and move our wills. For knowledge to be pleasant to our souls signifies that we delight in the Law of God after the inward man (Rom. 7:22), that submission to God's will is not irksome but desirable. Now where such really be the case, the individual possesses a discernment which enables him to penetrate Satan's disguises and perceive the barb beneath the bait, and is endowed with a discretion which makes him prudent and cautious, so that he shuns those places where alluring temptations abound and avoids the company of evil men and women. Thereby is he delivered from danger and secured from making shipwreck of the faith: see also Proverbs 4:6; 6:22-24.

"I will make an Everlasting Covenant with them, that I will not turn away from them to do them good; but I will put My fear in their hearts, that they shall not depart from Me" (Jer. 32:40). This statement casts much light upon the means and method employed by God in the preserving of His people. The indwelling Spirit not only constrains the new nature by considerations drawn from the love of Christ (2 Cor. 5:14), but He also restrains the old nature by a sense of God's majesty. He often drops an awe on the believer's heart, which holds him back from running into that excess of riot which his lusts would carry him unto. The Spirit makes the soul to realize that God is not to be trifled with, and delivers from wickedly presuming upon His mercy. He stimulates a spirit of filial reverence in the saint, so that he shuns those things which would dishonor his Father. He causes us to heed such a word as, "Be not highminded, but fear: for if God spared not the natural branches, take heed lest He also spare not thee" (Rom. 11:20,21). By such means does God fulfill His promise "I will put My Spirit within you, and cause you to walk in My statutes" (Ezek. 36:27).

"For we through the Spirit wait for the hope of righteousness by faith" (Gal. 5:5). It is the stirrings of hope, however faint, which keeps the soul alive in seasons of disappointment and despondence. But for the renewings of the gracious Spirit, the believer would relinquish his hope and sink into abject despair. "Then the eyes of the blind shall be opened, and the ears of the deaf shall be unstopped. Then shall the lame man leap as a hart, and the tongue of the dumb sing: for in the wilderness shall waters break out, and streams in the desert" (Isa. 35:5, 6): it is by fresh supplies of the Spirit (Phil. 1:19) that there comes not only further light, but new strength and comfort. Amid the perturbations caused by indwelling sin and the anguish from our repeated defeats, it is one of the Spirit's greatest works to sustain the soul by the expectation of things to come.

"Who are kept by the power of God through faith" (1 Pet. 1:5). Here again we are shown how the preservation of the saint is effected: through the influences of an exercised faith—compare 1 John 5:4. Now faith implies not only the knowledge and belief of the Truth, but also those pious affections and dispositions and the performance of those spiritual duties which constitute practical holiness. Without faith no man can attain unto that holiness, and without the power of God none can exercise this faith. Faith is the channel through which the mighty works of God are wrought—as Hebrews 11 so clearly shows—not the least of which is the conducting of His people safely through the Enemy's land (1 John 5:19).

Perseverance in grace, or continuance in holiness, is not promoted by a blind confidence or carnal security, but by watchfulness, earnest effort and self-denial. So far from teaching that believers shall certainly reach Heaven whether or not they use the means of grace, Scripture affirms, "If ye live after the flesh ye shall die: but if ye through the Spirit do mortify the deeds of the body, ye shall live" (Rom. 8:13). God has not promised that, no matter how loosely a saint may live or what vile habits he may persist in, he shall not perish; but rather does He assure us that He will preserve from such looseness and wickedness as would expose him to His wrath. It is by working grace in our hearts, by calling into exercise the faculties of our souls, by exciting fear and hope, hatred and love, sorrow and joy, that the saint is preserved.

The Spirit Confirming

In view of the preceding chapter on the Spirit preserving, there is really no need for us to take up another aspect of the subject which so closely approximates thereto—yet a little reflection has persuaded us that it may be wise to do so. Some of our readers are fearful that the editor wavers on the blessed truth of the eternal security of the Christian. Some Arminians, because of our strong emphasis upon the absolute supremacy and sovereignty of God and the total impotency of fallen men unto holiness, have charged us with denying human responsibility, when the fact is that we go much farther than they do in the holding and proclaiming of man's accountability. On the other hand, some Calvinists, because we insist so emphatically and frequently on the imperative necessity of treading the Highway of Holiness in order to escape the everlasting burnings, have questioned our soundness on the final perseverance of the saints; when probably, as our writing on suicide shows, we believe this truth more fully than they do. Very few today hold the balance of the Truth.

The Holy Spirit as "Earnest"

That which we now desire to contemplate is the blessed Spirit viewed under the metaphor of an "earnest." This term is used of Him in the following passages: "Who hath also sealed us, and given the earnest of the Spirit in our hearts" (2 Cor. 1:22); "Now He that hath wrought us for the selfsame thing is God, who also hath given unto us the earnest of the Spirit" (2 Cor. 5:5); "After that ye believed, ye were sealed with that Holy Spirit of promise, which is the earnest of our inheritance until the redemption of the purchased possession, unto the praise of His glory" (Eph. 1:13, 14). The figure is taken from an ancient custom (which is by no means obsolete today) of the method used in the clinching of a commercial bargain or contract. The seller agrees to make delivery at some future date of what has been agreed upon, and as a guaranty of this the purchaser receives an "earnest," that is, a sample or token, an insignificant installment, of what has been contracted for.

An "earnest," then, supposes a contract wherein two parties are agreed, the one who is ultimately to come into possession of what has been agreed upon

The Holy Spirit

being given a token of the other's good faith that he will abide by the terms of the bargain. It is a part of the price given beforehand, to assure the one to whom the "earnest" is given that at the appointed season he shall receive the whole of that which is promised. Now the right which the believer has to eternal life and glory comes in a way of contract or covenant. On the one side, the believer agrees to the terms specified (the forsaking of sin and the serving of the Lord), and yields himself to God by repentance and faith. On the other side, God binds Himself to give the believer forgiveness of sins and an inheritance among them which are sanctified by faith. This is clearly enough stated in, "Incline your ear, and come unto Me: hear, and your soul shall live; and I will (then) make an Everlasting Covenant with you, even the sure mercies of David" (Isa. 55:3)—upon our hearty consent to the terms of the Gospel, God engages Himself to bestow upon us those inestimable blessings secured for His people by the spiritual or antitypical David.

An "earnest" intimates there is some delay before the thing bargained for is actually bestowed: in the case of goods, deliverance at once is not agreed upon, in the case of property possession is not immediately entered into. It is for this reason that the token of good faith or preliminary installment is given: because the promised deliverance is deferred, possession being delayed for a season, an "earnest" is bestowed as a pledge or confirmation of what is to follow. Now as soon as the believer really enters into covenant with God, he has a right to the everlasting inheritance, but his actual entrance into full blessedness is deferred. God does not remove us to Heaven the moment we believe, any more than He brought Israel into Canaan within a few days after delivering them from Egypt. Instead, we are left for a while in this world, and that for various reasons: one among them being that we may have opportunities for exercising faith and love; faith in "looking for that blessed hope and the glorious appearing of the great God and our Savior Jesus Christ" (Titus 2:13), hope in longing: "ourselves also, which have the firstfruits of the Spirit, even we ourselves groan within ourselves, waiting for the adoption" (Rom. 8:23).

An "earnest" is a part, though only a very small one, of the whole that has been agreed upon. If a contract was made for the delivery of a sum of money on a certain date, then a trifling installment thereof was given; if it were the transfer of a piece of land, then a square of turf was cut and handed to its future possessor, that being a symbolic guarantee to assure him during the interval of waiting. So too, those comforts which the Spirit communicates to believers are the same in kind as the joys of Heaven though they are vastly inferior in their degree. The saving gifts and graces of the Spirit are but a small beginning and part of that glory which shall yet be revealed in and to us. Grace is glory begun, and they differ from each other only as an infant does from a fully matured adult. Holiness or purity of heart is a pledge of that sinless estate and full conformity to Christ which is promised the Christian in the future. That present loosing of our bonds is but a sample of our perfect and final freedom.

An "earnest" is given for the security of the party who receives it, and not for the benefit of him that bestows it. He who gives the earnest is legally bound to complete his bargain, but the recipient has this guarantee in hand for the confirming and comforting of his mind while he is waiting—it being to him a tangible pledge and sample of what as yet is only promised. Here again we may see the aptness and accuracy of the figure, for the spiritual earnest which Christians receive is given solely for their benefit, for there is no danger whatever of backing out on God's part. "Wherein God, willing more abundantly to show unto the heirs of promise the immutability of His counsel, confirmed it by an oath: that by two immutable things, in which it was impossible for God to lie, we might have a strong consolation, who have fled for refuge to lay hold upon the hope set before us" (Heb. 6:17, 18)—and this because believers commonly are assailed by many doubts and fears.

More about "Earnest"

An "earnest" remains the irrevocable possession of its recipient until the bargain is consummated, and even then it is not taken from him. Therein an "earnest" differs from a "pledge," for when a pledged article is returned, the pledge is taken back again. So, too, the "earnest" which Christians receive is irrevocable and inalienable: "For the gifts and calling of God are without repentance" (Rom. 11:29). As the Lord Jesus declared, "I will pray the Father, and He shall give you another Comforter, that He may abide with you forever" (John 14:16). How blessedly and how positively this intimates the eternal security of God's elect! Jehovah has made with them "an Everlasting Covenant, ordered in all things and sure" (2 Sam. 23:5). Even now they have received "the firstfruits of the Spirit" (Rom. 8:23), and that is the Divine certification of the glorious harvest, the plentitude of God's favor yet to follow. Like Mary, the believer today, by yielding to the Lordship of Christ, has "chosen that good part, which shall not be taken away" (Luke 10:42).

"Now He which stablisheth us with you in Christ, and hath anointed us, is God; who hath also sealed us, and given the earnest of the Spirit in our hearts" (2 Cor. 1:21, 22). It is to be duly noted that both the sealing and the earnest are for our "stablishing." As one hymn-writer put it, "What more can He say than to you He hath said, to you who to Jesus for refuge hath fled?" And what more can He do, we may ask, than what He has done to assure His

The Holy Spirit

people of the glorious inheritance awaiting them? We have the Lord Jesus Christ in Heaven with our nature, to show that our nature shall yet come there: "Whither the Forerunner is for us entered, even Jesus" (Heb. 6:20). Nor is that all: we have the Holy Spirit sent down into our hearts as proof that we are not only children, but also the heirs of God: Romans 8:14-17.

"Now He that hath wrought us for the selfsame thing is God, who also hath given unto us the earnest of the Spirit" (2 Cor. 5:5). That "selfsame thing" is not to be restricted unto a resurrected body: it is the "far more exceeding and eternal weight of glory" of 2 Corinthians 4:17, the "things which are not seen" of 4:18. Having spoken of the everlasting bliss awaiting the saints on High, for which they now groan and earnestly long (5:4), the Apostle mentions two of the principal grounds on which such a hope rests. First, God has "wrought us for" the same, that is He has regenerated us, giving us a holy and heavenly nature which fully capacitates us to be with Himself. Second, He has given us "the earnest of the Spirit" as a guaranty of this glorious estate. Thus are we fitted for, and thus are we assured of the infinitely better life awaiting us.

"After that ye believed, ye were sealed with that Holy Spirit of promise, which is the earnest of our inheritance until the redemption of the purchased possession, unto the praise of His glory" (Eph. 1:13, 14). In this passage (1:3-14) the Apostle describes those wondrous and numerous blessings with which the saints are blest in Christ. Eternal election (v. 4), membership in God's family (v. 5), acceptance in the Beloved (v. 6), the forgiveness of sins (v. 7), and understanding of Divine mysteries (vv. 8, 9), predestined unto an inheritance (v. 11), sealed with the Holy Spirit (v. 13), and now the Spirit given to us as "the earnest of our inheritance"—a part-payment in promise and pledge of the whole. The dwelling of the Spirit in the believer's heart is the guaranty of his yet taking his place in that holy and joyous scene where all is according to the nature of God and where Christ is the grand Center.

According to the literal meaning of the figure, an "earnest" signifies the clinching of a bargain, that it is a sample of what has been agreed upon, that it confirms and ensures the consummation of the contract. And that is what the operations and presence of the Spirit in the believer connote. First, they supply proof that God has made a covenant with him "ordered in all things and sure." Second, the present work of the Spirit in him is a real foretaste and firstfruit of the coming harvest. Is there not something of the glorified eye in that faith which the Spirit has implanted? Do the pure in heart see God face to face in Heaven? Well, even now, faith enables us to endure "as seeing Him who is invisible" (Heb. 11:27). Is there not now something of that glorified joy wherein they in Heaven delight themselves in God: "In the multitude of my thoughts within me Thy comforts delight my soul" (Ps. 94:19). And is there not now a real though faint adumbration of that glorified transformation of soul into the image of Christ? Compare 2 Corinthians 3:18 with 1 John 3:2!

The "earnest" ensures the consummation of that contract. It is so here. The first operation of the Spirit in the elect is the guaranty of the successful completion of the same: "being confident of this very thing, that He which hath begun a good work in you will perform it until the day of Jesus Christ" (Phil. 1:6). Thus, God has given us something in hand that we may confidently anticipate the promised inheritance. And this, so that both our desire and our diligence may be stimulated. We are not asked to mortify sin, deny self, forsake the world, for nothing. If the "Earnest" be so blessed, what shall the Inheritance itself be! O what lively expectations of it should be cherished in our hearts! O what earnest efforts should be made in "reaching forth unto those things which are before" (Phil. 3:13)!

And what is the Inheritance of which the Spirit is the "Earnest" unto the believer? It is nothing less than God Himself! The blessed God, in the trinity of His Persons, is the everlasting portion of the saints. Is it not written, "If children, then heirs; heirs of God, and joint-heirs with Christ" (Rom. 8:17)? And what is Christ's "inheritance"? "The LORD is the portion of Mine inheritance" (Ps. 16:5), He declared. The future bliss of believers will consist in the fullness of the Spirit capacitating them to enjoy God to the full! And has not the believer already "tasted that the Lord is gracious" (1 Pet. 2:3)? Yes, by the Spirit. The Spirit is the utmost proof to us of God's love, the firstfruit of glory: "Because ye are sons, God hath sent forth the Spirit of his Son into your hearts" (Gal. 4:6).

God, then, grants His people a taste in this world of what He has prepared for them in the world to come. The gifts and graces of the Spirit in the elect affirm the certainty of the glory awaiting them: as surely as an "earnest" guarantees the whole sum, so do the "firstfruits of the Spirit" (Rom. 8:23) the coming harvest of bliss. The nature of the Christian's "earnest" intimates both the character and the greatness of what is in store for him: even now He bestows a measure of life, light, love, liberty—but what shall these be in their fullness! One ounce of real grace is esteemed by its possessor more highly than a ton of gold: what, then, will it be like to bathe in the ocean of God's favor? If now there are times when we experience that peace which "passeth all understanding" (Phil. 4:7) and are made to "rejoice with joy unspeakable and full of glory" (1 Pet. 1:8), how incapable we are of estimating the full value of our Inheritance, for an "earnest" is but a tiny installment of that which is promised. O that the realization of this, faint though it be, may move us to look and long for the heavenly glory with greater vehemence.

The Spirit Fructifying

In the Song of Solomon

Far more is said in Scripture upon this aspect of our many-sided subject than is generally supposed—different figures being used, especially in the Old Testament, to express the graces and virtues which the Spirit imparts to and develops in the elect. A considerable variety of emblems are employed to set them forth. They are frequently referred to as flowers and gardens of them, to beds of spices, and unto trees and orchards. For example, in Solomon's Song we hear Christ saying to His Spouse: "A garden enclosed is My sister, My Spouse; a spring shut up, a fountain sealed. Thy plants are an orchard of pomegranates, with pleasant fruits; camphor, with spikenard. Spikenard and saffron; calamus and cinnamon, with all trees of frankincense; myrrh and aloes, with all the chief spices: a fountain of gardens, a well of living waters, and streams from Lebanon" (Song. 4:12-15).

The figures used in the above passage are very beautiful and call for careful consideration. A "garden" is a piece of ground distinguished and separated from others, for the owner's use and delight; so the Church of Christ is distinguished and separated from all other people by electing, redeeming, and regenerating grace. In a garden is a great variety of plants, herbs, and flowers—so in the Church there are members differing much from each other, yet in all there is that which is delightful to their Lord. In a garden the plants and flowers do not grow up naturally of themselves, they do not spring forth spontaneously from its soil, but have to be set or sown, for nothing but weeds grow up of themselves; so in Christ's Church, those excellencies which are found in its members are not natural to them, but are the direct product of the Spirit's operations, for by nature nothing grows in their hearts but the weeds of sin and corruption.

The commentators are not agreed as to whether Christ is speaking to His Spouse in verse 15, or whether She is there heard replying to what He had said in verses 12-14. Personally, we strongly incline to the latter: that Christ having commended His Church as a fruitful garden, She now ascribes it all to Him: "A Fountain of gardens, a Well of living waters, and streams from

Lebanon." Yet, if we accept the former interpretation, it amounts to much the same thing, for He would there be explaining what it was that made His Garden so fertile. To be healthy and productive a garden must be well watered, otherwise its delicate plants will quickly wilt and wither; the same being true of trees and all vegetation: a plentiful supply of water is indispensable. Consequently, in keeping with the fact that believers are likened unto plants and trees, and their graces to flowers and fruits, the quickening, renewing, reviving, and fructifying operations of the Spirit are spoken of as "dew," as "showers," as "streams in the desert," etc.

Cultivating Christlikeness

The Holy Spirit not only imparts life and holiness, but He sustains the same in the soul; He not only communicates heavenly graces, but He cultivates and develops them. "That they might be called Trees of righteousness, the planting of the LORD, that He might be glorified ... For as the earth bringeth forth her bud, and as the garden causeth the things that are sown in it to spring forth; so the Lord GOD will cause righteousness and praise to spring forth before all the nations" (Isa. 61:3, 11). Yes, the same One who "planted" those "trees of righteousness" must also "cause them" to "spring forth" to grow and bear fruit. While the tendency of the new nature is ever Godwards, yet it has no power of its own, being entirely dependent upon its Creator and Giver. Hence, that fruit which is borne by the believer is expressly called "the fruit of the Spirit" so that the honor and glory may be ascribed alone unto Him. "From Me is thy fruit found" (Hosea 14:8).

"For I will pour water upon him that is thirsty, and floods upon the dry ground: I will pour My Spirit upon thy seed, and My blessing upon thine offspring: and they shall spring up as among the grass, as willows by the water courses" (Isa. 44:3, 4). Just as surely as a drought brings famine, so the absence of the Spirit's working leaves all in a state of spiritual death; but just as heavy rains renew a parched vegetation, so an outpouring of the Spirit brings new life. Then shall it indeed be said, "The wilderness and the solitary place shall be glad for them; and the desert shall rejoice, and blossom as the rose" (Isa. 35:1), which is expressly interpreted for us by the Spirit in, "For the LORD shall comfort Zion: He will comfort all her waste places; and He will make her wilderness like Eden, and her desert like the garden of the LORD; joy and gladness shall be found therein, thanksgiving, and the voice of melody" (Isa. 51:3). We have purposely added Scripture to Scripture because the spiritual meaning of these passages is commonly unperceived today, when carnal dispensationalists insist on the ignoring of all figures, and the interpreting of everything "literally."

The Holy Spirit

"My little children, of whom I travail in birth again until Christ be formed in you" (Gal. 4: 19)—that which the Apostle did ministerially, the Spirit does efficiently. This is how the Spirit makes the Christian fruitful, or rather, it is how He first fits him to be fruitful: by forming Christ in him! The metaphor is taken from the shaping of the child in its mother's womb, so that as its natural parents communicated the matter of its body, it is then framed and shaped into their likeness, limb for limb, answering to themselves. In like manner, the Spirit communicates to the heart an incorruptible "seed" (1 John 3:9) or spiritual nature, and then conforms the soul unto Christ's image: first to His graces, and then to His example: "That ye should show forth the praises of Him who hath called you" (1 Pet. 2:9)—which we could not do unless we had first received them. Ah, my reader, this is a solemn thing: we pass among men for genuine Christians, but the only coins which will pass the eye of God are those which bear stamped upon them the image of His Son.

In other words, then, the Spirit's fructifying of the believer is the conforming of him unto Christ, first in his heart, and then in his life. By nature we are totally unlike Christ, being born in the image of Adam and dominated by Satan; or, to revert to the figure in the opening paragraph, so far from resembling a beautiful and well-kept garden, we are like a barren desert, where nothing but useless shrubs and poisonous weeds are found. "I went by the field of the slothful, and by the vineyard of the man void of understanding; and, lo, it was all grown over with thorns, and nettles had covered the face thereof, and the stone wall thereof was broken down" (Prov. 24:30, 31). That is how we appeared unto the holy eye of God in our unregenerate state! It is only when a miracle of grace has been wrought in our hearts that Christ begins to be formed in us, and that we (in our measure) reproduce His graces; and this is due solely to the sovereign and effectual operations of the Holy Spirit.

Fruit of the Spirit (Graces of the Spirit)

"Even so every good tree bringeth forth good fruit; but a corrupt tree bringeth forth evil fruit. A good tree cannot bring forth evil fruit, neither can a corrupt tree bring forth good fruit ... Wherefore by their fruits ye shall know them" (Matthew 7:17, 18, 20). The fruit they bear is that which distinguishes the children of God from the children of the Devil. This "fruit" is the temper or disposition wrought in the elect by the Holy Spirit, which is manifested by them, severally, "according to the measure of the gift of Christ" (Eph. 4:7). The Spirit fructifies the regenerate by conforming them to the image of Christ: first to His graces, and then to His example. The lovely virtues found in them do not issue from the depraved nature of fallen man, but are supernaturally inwrought by God.

There are three leading passages in the New Testament on this subject. John 15 names the conditions of fruitfulness: union with Christ, purging by the Father, abiding in Christ, and Christ and His Word abiding in us. Galatians 5 furnishes a description of the fruit itself. 2 Peter 1:5-8 states the order of fruit or the process of its cultivation. "In the figure of the Vine, the Holy Spirit is not mentioned, but in comparing Himself to the Vine and His disciples to the Branches, the Tree corresponds to the Body, and the Life to His Spirit. The diffusion of life is the work of the Holy Spirit, and the fruit by which the Father is glorified is the fruit of the Spirit. Apart from Christ there is neither life nor fruit, but without the Spirit of Christ there can be neither union or abiding. Our Lord does not specify the fruit. What He emphasizes is the fact that it is fruit, and that it is fruit directly from Himself" (S. Chadwick).

"The fruit of the Spirit is love, joy, peace, longsuffering, gentleness, goodness, faith, meekness, temperance" (Gal. 5:22, 23). These are graces of the Spirit as distinguished from the gifts of the Spirit, enumerated in 1 Corinthians 12, and which will be considered in our next chapter. They are holy and heavenly dispositions with the conduct which results therefrom. The Apostle begins with the principal characteristics of the spiritual mind, and then passes on to its operation and manifestation in personal conduct, social virtues, and practical behavior. A threefold reason may be suggested why these spiritual graces are termed "fruit." First, because all grace is derived from the Spirit as fruit issues from the life of a plant. Second, to denote the pleasantness of grace, for what is more delightful than sweet and wholesome fruit? Third, to signify the advantage redounding to those who have the Spirit; as the owners are enriched by the fruit produced from their gardens and orchards, so believers are enriched by the fruits of holiness.

In the use of the singular number, "the fruit (rather than fruits) of the Spirit," emphasis is placed upon the unity of His operations: producing one harmonious whole—in contrast from the products of the flesh, which ever tend to discord and chaos. These virtues are not like so many separate flowers in a bouquet, as the variegated petals of one lovely flower exhibiting different shades and forms. A rainbow is one, yet in it all the primary colors are beautifully blended together. These graces which the Spirit imparts to a renewed soul are distinguishable, but they are inseparable. In some believers one grace predominates more than another—as meekness in Moses, patience in Job, love in John—yet all are present and to some extent active.

The Holy Spirit

Galatians 5:22, 23 enumerates nine of the graces communicated by the Spirit. Some have suggested that the last eight are but varied expressions of the first. That "Joy is love exulting, Peace is love in repose, Longsuffering is love on trial, Gentleness is love in society, Goodness is love in action, Faith is love in endurance, Meekness is love at school, and Temperance is love in discipline" (A. T. Pierson). But while love is, admittedly, the greatest of all the graces, yet 1 Corinthians 13:13 shows that it is but one of several. Personally, we prefer the older classification which divided the nine graces into three threes: the first three—love, joy, peace—being Godwards in their exercise; the second three—longsuffering, gentleness goodness—being exercised manwards; and the last three—fidelity, meekness, temperance—being exercised self-ward.

"Love": the Apostle begins with that which flows directly from God (Rom. 5:5), and without which there can be no fellowship with Him or pleasing of Him. "Joy" in God, in the knowledge of pardon, in communion with Christ, in the duties of piety, in the hope of Heaven. "Peace": of conscience, rest of heart, tranquillity of mind. "Longsuffering" when provoked and injured by others, exercising a magnanimous forbearance toward the faults and failing of our fellows. "Gentleness" rendered "kindness" in 2 Corinthians 6:6, a gracious benignity, the opposite of a harsh, crabbed, and brutal temper. "Goodness" or beneficence, seeking to help and benefit others, without expecting any return or reward. "Faith" or more accurately "faithfulness": being trustworthy, honest, keeping your promises. "Meekness" or yieldedness, the opposite of self-will and self-assertiveness. "Temperance" or self-control: being moderate in all things, ruling one's spirit, denying self

"In newspaper English, the passage would read something like this: The Fruit of the Spirit is an affectionate, lovable disposition, a radiant spirit and a cheerful temper, a tranquil mind and a quiet manner, a forbearing patience in provoking circumstances and with trying people, a sympathetic insight and tactful helpfulness, generous judgment and a big-souled charity, loyalty and reliableness under all circumstances, humility that forgets self in the joy of others, in all things self-mastered and self-controlled, which is the final mark of perfecting. This is the kind of character that is the Fruit of the Spirit. Everything is in the word Fruit. It is not by striving, but by abiding; not by worrying, but by trusting; not of works, but of faith" (S. Chadwick). And, as our passage goes on to say, "Against such there is no law" (Gal. 5:23): that which the Law enjoins the Spirit imparts, so that there is perfect harmony between the Law and the Gospel.

But here, too, there is to be a concurrence between the Christian and the Spirit; our responsibility is to cherish and cultivate our graces, and to resist and reject everything which opposes and hinders them. Fruit is neither our invention nor our product, nevertheless it requires our "diligence" as 2 Peter 1:5 plainly indicates. A neglected garden grows weeds in plenty, and then its flowers and fruits are quickly crowded out. The gardener has to be continually alert and active. Turn to and ponder Psalm 1 and see what has to be avoided, and what has to be done, if the believer is to "bring forth his fruit in his season." Re-read John 15 and note the conditions of fruitfulness, and then turn the same into earnest prayer. The Lord, in His grace, make both writer and reader successful horticulturists in the spiritual realm.

The Spirit Endowing

From the graces which the Spirit works in God's children, we turn now to consider the gifts which He bestows upon God's servants. This brings us to a comprehensive subject, and instead of devoting two brief papers thereto, a series of lengthy articles might well be written thereon. We can but here single out one or two aspects of it—those which we consider most need our attention today. Broadly speaking the fundamental principle underlying this branch of our theme may be expressed thus: when God calls any to the performance of special work in His service, He equips them by the gifts of His Spirit. For example we read, "The LORD hath called by name Bezaleel . . . and He hath filled him with the spirit of God, in wisdom, in understanding, and in knowledge, and in all manner of workmanship; and to devise curious works, to work in gold" etc. (Ex. 35:30-32).

Now just as men erred grievously concerning the being of God, grossly misrepresenting Him by images; and just as there have been the most horrible errors respecting the Person of the Mediator; so there has been fearful confusion upon the gifts of the Spirit, in fact it is at this point there pertains the most serious mistakes with regards to Him. Men have failed to distinguish between His extraordinary and His ordinary gifts, and have sought to generalize what was special and exceptional. Urging the rank and file of professing Christians to seek "power from on High," the "baptism of the Spirit," or His "filling for service," the wildest extravagances have been fostered and the door has been opened wide for Satan to enter and delude the souls and wreck the bodily health of thousands of people.

Gift of Prophecy

It was well said by John Owen nearly three centuries ago that, "The great deceit and abuse that hath been in all ages of the church under the pretense of the name and work of the Holy Spirit, make the thorough consideration of what we are taught concerning them exceedingly necessary." The most signal gift of the Spirit for the benefit of His people in Old Testament times was that of prophecy. The Prophets were men who spoke in the name and by the authority of God, giving forth a Divinely inspired message from Him. It is not surprising, then, that many pretended unto this gift who were never inspired by the Holy Spirit, but rather were filled by a lying spirit, Satan making use of them to accomplish his own designs: see 1 Kings 22:6, 7; Jeremiah 5:3 1, etc. Those facts are recorded for our warning!

This same gift of prophecy occupied a prominent place in the early days of the Christian dispensation, before the New Testament was written. The Gospel was at first declared from the immediate revelation of the Spirit, preached by His direct assistance, made effectual by His power, and accompanied in many instances by outward miraculous works, the whole of which is designated "the ministration of the Spirit" (2 Cor. 3:8). Those extraordinary manifestations of the Spirit were then so obvious and so acknowledged by all Christians that those who wished to impose and deceive found no more successful method than by claiming to be themselves immediately inspired by the Spirit. Consequently we find such warnings given by God as, "Despise not prophesyings. Prove all things; hold fast that which is good" (1 Thess. 5:20, 21); "But there were false prophets also among the people, even as there shall be false teachers among you" (2 Pet. 2:1); "Beloved, believe not every spirit, but try the spirits whether they are of God" (1 John 4:1).

Gift of Discernment

In order to preserve the church in truth and peace during those primitive times, and safeguard them from being imposed upon by the false prophets while there was a real communication of the extraordinary gifts of the Spirit (whereby the more occasion was afforded for charlatans to pretend unto the possession of them), God graciously endowed some of His people with the gift of "the discerning of spirits" (1 Cor. 12:10). The saints were thereby provided with some who were enabled in extraordinary manner to judge and determine those who claimed to be specially endowed by the Spirit—but when the extraordinary manifestations of the Spirit ceased, this particular gift was also withdrawn, so the Christians are now left with the Word alone by which to measure and try all who claim to be the mouthpiece of God.

Signs and Wonders

"How shall we escape, if we neglect so great salvation; which at the first began to be spoken by the Lord, and was confirmed unto us by them that heard Him; God also bearing them witness, both with signs and wonders, and with divers miracles, and gifts of the Holy Spirit" (Heb. 2:3, 4). This passage makes known to us God's design in the miraculous gifts of the Spirit at the beginning of this dispensation. They were for the purpose of confirming the preached Word—for none of the New Testament had then been written!

They were for the establishing of the Gospel; not to beget and strengthen faith, but to cause unbelievers to listen to the Truth—compare 1 Corinthians 14:22, 24, 25.

Nine Gifts

In 1 Corinthians 12:8-10 we are supplied with a list of those extraordinary gifts of the Spirit which then obtained—we use the word "extraordinary" in contrast from His ordinary gifts, or those which obtain in all ages and generations. "For to one is given by the Spirit the word of wisdom; to another the word of knowledge by the same Spirit; to another faith by the same Spirit; to another the gifts of healing by the same Spirit; to another the working of miracles; to another prophecy; to another discerning of spirits; to another divers kinds of tongues; to another the interpretation of tongues" (1 Cor. 12:8-10). It will be noted that just as "the fruit of the Spirit" is divided into nine graces (Gal. 5:22, 23), so "the ministration of the Spirit" is here described under nine distinct gifts. A very few words must now suffice upon them.

"The word of wisdom" (1 Cor. 12:8) was a special gift bestowed upon the Apostles (hence it heads this list of gifts) for the defense of the Gospel against powerful adversaries: see Luke 21:15! "The word of knowledge" was a special gift bestowed on all then called of God to preach the Gospel: it supernaturally qualified them to expound Divine mysteries without protracted study and lengthy experience: see Acts 4:13! "To another faith," a special gift which enabled its possessor to trust God in any emergency, and to boldly face a martyr's death: see Acts 6:5. The "gifts of healing" and "the working of miracles" are seen in their exercise by the Apostles in the Acts. "To another prophecy" or immediate inspiration and revelation from God. Upon "tongues" and their "interpretation" we shall have more to say later.

Non-continuance of Extraordinary Gifts

Now that all of these special impulses and extraordinary gifts of the Spirit were not intended to be perpetuated throughout this Christian dispensation, and that they have long since ceased, is clear from several conclusive considerations. Their non-continuance is hinted at in Mark 16:20 by the omission of Christ's, "and, lo, I am with you alway, even unto the end of the age" (Matthew 28:20). So, too, by the fact that God did not give faith to His servants to count upon the same throughout the centuries: it is unthinkable that the intrepid Reformers and the godly Puritans failed to appropriate God's promise if any had been given to that effect. "Love never fails. But whether there are prophecies, they will fail; whether there are tongues, they will cease; whether there is knowledge, it will vanish away" (1 Cor. 13:8).

The Apostle cannot there be contrasting Heaven with earth, for those on High possess more "knowledge" than we have; so the reference must be to the cessation of the miraculous gifts of 1 Corinthians 12. The qualifying language "which at the first began to be spoken by the Lord, and was confirmed to us . . . with signs and wonders" (Heb. 2:3, 4) points in the same direction, and clearly implies that those supernatural manifestations had even then ceased Finally, 2 Timothy 3:16, 17 proves conclusively that there is now no need for such gifts as prophecy and tongues: we are "thoroughly furnished" by the now complete Canon of Scripture.

Practice of Gifts in the Church Meeting

Our discussion upon the Person and work of the Holy Spirit would lack completeness if we ignored the fantastic and fanatical view which some have taken regarding 1 Corinthians 12 and 14 as the Divine pattern and ideal for "the open meeting" of the local church today. We refer to those who decry a "one-man ministry" and who encourage an "any-man minis-try" under the guise of allowing the Spirit full freedom to move and use any whom Christ has "gifted." It is insisted that here in 1 Corinthians 14 we behold different ones endowed with various gifts taking part in the same meeting, yet strange to say these very people readily acknowledge that the gift of tongues has ceased—but this very chapter prescribes how that gift was and was not to be used!

Now in the first place there is not a single statement in all the New Testament that the practice which obtained at Corinth prevailed generally in other churches of that day, still less that the assemblies of the saints in all generations were to be patterned after their order. Rather is there much to show that what obtained at Corinth was not the regular mode established by Christ and His Apostles. The fact is that not only were the conditions at Corinth merely transitory and exceptional, but they were fraught with much evil. In no other church of apostolic days was there such disorder and carnality. "Gifts" were valued there more highly than grace, knowledge than love, and the consequence was that the possessors of those miraculous gifts, by their pride and forwardness, neutralized whatever good those gifts accomplished. The reason for that is not far to seek: they had no governing head or heads and no Divinely authorized teacher or teachers. The absence of elders made them like an army without officers, or a school without masters. Where all were equal, none would submit; where all wanted to teach, none would learn.

So far from the Corinthian church supplying a pattern for all others to follow, it stands before us a most solemn warning and sample of what ensues when a company of Christians is left without a Divinely qualified leader. The most terrible laxity of discipline obtained: one member was living in adultery with his father's second wife (5:1), while others were getting drunk at the Lord's table (11:21). Those fearful sins (which would not be tolerated today in any Christian church worthy of the name) were winked at, because the assembly was split into parties through want of a controlling head (an under-shepherd of Christ), and because the sinning members belonged to the majority, the minority was powerless.

Besides the fearful laxity of discipline, the grossest irregularities prevailed at their public meetings for the worship of God. There was neither unity, order, edifying ministry, nor decorum. One had his "psalm," another his "doctrine," another his "tongue," another his "revelation," and yet another his "interpretation" (1 Cor. 14:26)—which is mentioned by the Apostle not by way of commendation, but as a rebuke for their disorder, as is quite evident from the final clause of that verse, as also from verse 40: carefully compare the opening words of verses 15 and 26! As another has said, "Here, then, all were charged, as it were, to the muzzle, and each wanting to have the first say, the longest say, and the loudest say. They did not wish to edify, but to show off."

Now it was in view of such a situation that the Apostle was moved of God to pen 1 Corinthians 14, in order to correct these abuses and to lay down rules for the regulation of those who possessed the extraordinary gifts of prophesying and speaking in tongues. But this very fact at once over-throws that theory which has been built on an erroneous conception of this chapter! Not only is there not a single statement elsewhere in the New Testament that the Holy Spirit is the President over assemblies, or that He is ever present in any other sense than that He dwells in individual believers, but 1 Corinthians 14 itself is very far from teaching that the Spirit presides over the local church, and requires those who have been "gifted" by Christ to wait on Him, and be governed entirely by His inward promptings. Surely it is perfectly obvious that inward promptings of the Spirit render quite needless such rules and regulations as are given here!

To affirm that "the spirits of the prophets are subject to the prophets" (v. 32), that is, their "gift" of prophecy is under the Prophet's own control, is a vastly different thing from saying that the prophets were to be subject to the Holy Spirit! No matter how strong was the impulse to speak, he could not rightly defy the command given, "Let the prophets speak two or three, and let the other judge" (v. 29) under the plea that the Spirit urged him to speak. So again, how easy it had been for the Apostle to affirm, "If the Spirit impel anyone to speak in a tongue, He will move some other brother to translate"; but so far from that, he commanded, "But if there be no interpreter, let him keep silence in the church" (v. 28), which utterly demolishes the idea that these Corinthians were being presided over by the Holy Spirit.

Nowhere in 1 Corinthians 14 is it stated that the Spirit conducted (or ought to conduct) their meetings, nor were the Corinthians rebuked for failing to look to Him for guidance. There is not a hint of their sinfulness in limiting His sovereign freedom among them! Instead, the Apostle says, "I would that ye all spake with tongues, but rather that ye prophesied" (v. 5), and, "I had rather speak five words with my understanding . . . than ten thousand words in an unknown tongue" (v. 19) which he most certainly had not said if his theme here was the Spirit's superintendence, for in that case the Apostle would have gladly and entirely subjected himself to His control. Throughout the entire chapter the Apostle presents action as coming from the side of the possessors of the gifts, and not from the side of the Spirit. It is not, "when ye come together the Spirit will move one to speak in a tongue, another to prophecy, etc." No, they are bidden to use good sense, to show their love to one another by subjection, and to beware of shocking visitors (vv. 20, 23). But enough.

As there were offices extraordinary (Apostle and Prophets) at the beginning of our dispensation, so there were gifts extraordinary; and as successors were not appointed for the former, so a continuance was never intended for the latter. The gifts were dependent upon the officers: see Acts 8:14-21; 10:44-46; 19:6; Romans 1:11; Galatians 3:5; 2 Timothy 1:6. We no longer have the Apostles with us, and therefore the supernatural gifts (the communication of which was an essential part of "the signs of an Apostle": 2 Cor. 12:12) are absent. None but a Prophet can "prophesy!" Let it be definitely noted that the "Prophet" and the "teacher" are quite distinct: 1 Corinthians 12:28, 29; Ephesians 2:20; 3:5—the one is no more, the latter still exists. A Prophet was inspired by God to give out an infallible communication of His mind: 2 Peter 1:21.

Surely it is a manifest absurdity, then, to take a chapter which was given for the express purpose of regulating the exercise of the extraordinary gifts of the Spirit, and apply it to a company today where none of those gifts exist! Furthermore, if 1 Corinthians 14 sets forth the Spirit's superintendence of the local assembly in worship, why is it that there is not a single mention of Him throughout the whole of its 40 verses? That is indeed a hard question to answer. Obviously, there has been read into it what is not there! But do we not still have the "word of wisdom" and "the word of knowledge"? Certainly not; they were among the spiritual gifts of 1 Corinthians 12:1, and that word "spiritual" is not used there in contrast from "carnal" (as is clear from 1 Cor. 3:1, for they were not spiritual in that sense), so that it must mean inspired, and "inspired" men ceased when the Canon of Scripture was closed!

It is true that the Spirit acts today, but it is in secret, and not in open manifestation as in the days of the Apostles; and by mixed agency. The Truth is taught, but not perfectly as the Apostles and their delegates preached it. The best sermon now preached or article written, is not a standard (as it would be if inspired by the Spirit), for it has blemishes in it; yet the Spirit is not responsible for them. What the Spirit does now is to bestow ordinary ministerial gifts, which the possessor must improve and develop by study and use. To "seek power from High" or a special "filling of the Spirit" is to run the serious risk of being controlled by evil spirits posing as angels of light.

Honoring The Spirit

It seems fitting that we should close this lengthy discussion upon the Person, office, and operations of the Holy Spirit by dwelling upon what is due Him from those in whom He has wrought so graciously, for it is very evident that some recognition and response must be made Him by us. There is, however, the more need for us to write something thereon, because there are quite a number who belong to a company which refrains from all direct worship of the Third Person in the Godhead, deeming it unscriptural and incongruous to do so. It seems strange that the very ones who claim to give the Spirit a freer and fuller place in their meetings than any branch of Christendom, should, at he same time, demur at prayer being immediately directed to Him. Yet it is so: some of them refuse to sing the Doxology because it ends with "Praise Father, Son, and Holy Ghost."

From time to time one and another of our readers have written, taking exception to occasional statements made by us, such as "what praise is due the Spirit for His grace and goodness unto us!" challenging us to point to any definite passage wherein we are bidden to worship or pray to the Spirit distinctively. First, let us point out that there are many things clearly implied in Scripture which are not formally and expressly stated, and to assert we must for that reason reject them is absurd—some have refused the canonicity of the book of Esther because the name of God is not found therein, yet His superintending Providence, His overruling power, His faithfulness and goodness, shine forth in each chapter! We build not our faith on any isolated texts, but on the Word of God as a whole, rightly and spiritually interpreted.

We have begun thus not because we are unable to find any definite statements in the Word which obviously warrant the position we have taken, but because we deemed it well to refute an erroneous principle. Even if there were no clear cases recorded of prayer and praise being offered immediately to the Holy Spirit, we should surely require some strong positive proof to show the Spirit is not to be supplicated. But where, we ask, is there anything in Holy Writ which informs us that one Person in the Godhead must be excluded from the praises that we make unto the Lord? Here we are meeting the objector on his own ground: if what we are about to advance fails to convince him, he must at least allow that he knows of no texts which refute or condemn us, no verse which warns us against rendering to the blessed Spirit that recognition and honor to which we consider He is fully entitled.

Worshipping the Spirit as a Member of the Trinity

"Thou shalt fear (worship—Matthew 4:10) the LORD thy God, and serve Him" (Deut. 6:13). Now the Lord our God is a Unity in Trinity, that is, He subsists in three Persons who are co-essential and co-glorious. Therefore the Holy Spirit, equally with the Father and the Son, is entitled to and must receive devout homage, for we are here commanded to render the same to Him. This is confirmed by the "holy, holy, holy," of Isaiah 6:3, where we find the seraphim owning separately and worshipping distinctively the Eternal Three. The words that follow in verse 8, "Who will go for Us?" make it quite clear that the threefold "holy" was ascribed to the Blessed Trinity. Still further confirmation is found in Acts 28:25, 26, where the Apostle prefaces his quotation of Isaiah 6:9 with "well spake the Holy Spirit by Isaiah the Prophet." If, then, the angels ascribe glory and render worship to the Holy Spirit, shall we, who have been regenerated by Him, do less!?

"O come, let us worship and bow down: let us kneel before the LORD our Maker" (Ps. 95:6). Who is our "Maker?" Perhaps you answer, Christ, the eternal Word, of whom it is said, "All things were made by Him; and without Him was not anything made that was made" (John 1:3 and cf. Col. 1:16). That is true, yet Christ is not our "Maker" (either naturally or spiritually) to the exclusion of the Holy Spirit. The Third Person of the Godhead, equally with the Father and the Son, is our "Maker." In proof of this assertion we quote, "The Spirit of God hath made me, and the Breath of the Almighty hath given me life" (Job 33:4). Let the reader carefully compare Job 26:13 with Psalm 33:6. Let it also be duly noted that this 95th Psalm (vv. 7-11) is quoted in Hebrews 3:7-11 and prefaced with, "Wherefore as the Holy Spirit saith." Thus not only may we worship the blessed Spirit, but here in Psalm 95:6 we are commanded to do so.

It does indeed seem strange that any professing Christian should raise any objection and question the propriety of worshipping the Spirit. Are we not to acknowledge our dependence upon and obligations unto the Holy Spirit? Surely! surely! He is as much the Object of faith as is the Father and the Son: He is so in His Being and perfections, His Deity and personality, His offices and operations. Moreover, there are particular acts of trust and confidence to be exercised on Him. As He is God, He is to be worshipped, and that cannot be done aright without faith. We are to trust Him for His help in prayer and the discharge of every duty! We are to exercise confidence that He will complete the good work which He has begun in us. Especially should ministers of the Word look to Him for His help in and blessing upon their labors.

"Then said He unto me, Prophesy unto the Wind (Breath), prophesy, son of man, and say to the wind, Thus saith the Lord GOD; Come from the four winds, O Breath, and breathe upon these slain, that they may live" (Ezek. 37:9). We sincerely trust that none of our readers will suppose that the Lord bade His servant to perform an idolatrous act by invoking the literal "wind." No, a comparison of verses 9 and 10 with verse 14 shows plainly that it was the Holy Spirit Himself who was referred to—see John 3:8. Nor does this passage stand alone. In Song of Solomon 4:16 we find the Spouse praying to the Spirit for renewal and revival: "Awake, O north Wind; and come, thou south; blow upon my garden, that the spices thereof may flow out." She expressed her desires metaphorically, but this is what she breathed after. It is the Spirit of life, then, we should always apply to for quickening, for the enlivening and exciting of His graces in us.

Worshipping the Spirit Directly

This subject is (alas) new to many. Not a few seem to have been misled through a wrong understanding of that word concerning the Spirit in John 16:13, as though, "He shall not speak of Himself," signified He shall never occupy the saints with His own Person and work, but always direct them to Christ. It is true that the Spirit is here to glorify Christ, yet that by no means exhausts His mission. His first work is to direct the attention of sinners to God as God, convicting them of rebellion against their Creator, Ruler, and Judge. Then, too, He occupies the saints with the Father: His love, grace, and providential care. But John 16:13 no more means that the Spirit does not magnify Himself than Christ's, "I have not spoken for Myself" (John 12:49) meant that He never occupied people with His own Person—His "come unto Me" (Matthew 11:28, John 7:37) proves otherwise.

Others create difficulty out of the fact that in the economy of redemption the Spirit now occupies the place of Servant of the Godhead, and as such it is incongruous to worship Him. Such a cavil hardly deserves reply. But lest some of our readers have been misled by this sophistry, let it be pointed out that during the days of His flesh, Christ occupied the place of "Servant," the One who came here not to be ministered unto, but to minister—nevertheless, even during that season of His humiliation we are told, "Behold there came a leper and worshipped Him" (Matthew 8:2). And have we not read that when the wise men from the east entered the house where He was, they "fell down and worshipped Him" (Matthew 2:11)? Thus, the fact that the Holy Spirit is the Executive of the Godhead by no means debars Him of His title to our love and homage. Some say that because the Spirit is in us, He is not a suitable Object of worship, as the Father and Son without us. But is the Spirit within the only relation He sustains to us? Is He not omnipresent, infinitely above us, and as such an appropriate Object of worship?

That the Holy Spirit is to be publicly owned and equally honored with the Father and the Son is very evident from the terms of the great commission, "Go ye therefore, and teach all nations, baptizing them in the name of the Father, and of the Son, and of the Holy Spirit" (Matthew 28:19). Now to be baptized in the name of the Holy Spirit is either a real act of worship, or otherwise it would be a mere formality—which of the two is not difficult to determine. In view of this verse, no one need have the slightest hesitation in rendering homage to the Spirit as he does to the Father and the Son. This is not a case of reasoning on our parts nor of drawing an inference, but is a part of Divinely-revealed Truth. If we praise and revere the Son for what He has done for us, shall not the Spirit be adored for what He has wrought in us!? The Spirit Himself loves us (Rom. 15:30), by whose authority, then, are we to stifle our love for Him!?

"The grace of the Lord Jesus Christ, and the love of God, and the communion of the Holy Spirit, be with you all. Amen" (2 Cor. 13:14). Here again the Holy Spirit is honored equally with the Father and the Son—the Apostles certainly did not slight Him as do some of our modems. Let it be duly weighed that "communion" is a mutual thing, a giving and receiving. In our communion with the Father we receive from Him, and then return to Him love and obedience. From the Son we receive life, and acknowledge it in our praises. From the Spirit we receive regeneration and sanctification, shall we render Him nothing in return? We understand this verse to signify, "O Lord Jesus Christ, let Thy grace be with us; O God the Father, let thy love be manifested unto us; O Holy Spirit, let Thy saints enjoy much of thy communion." This invocatory benediction revealed the longings of Paul's heart unto the Corinthian saints, and those longings prompted his petition on their behalf.

"And the Lord direct your hearts into the love of God, and into the patient waiting for Christ" (2 Thess. 3:5). What could be plainer? Here each of the three Divine Persons is distinguished, and the Apostle prays directly to the Lord the Spirit—obviously "the Lord" here cannot refer to the Son, for in such case it would signify "The Lord (Jesus) direct your hearts into the patient waiting for Christ." As it is the Spirit's office to "guide us into all truth" (John 16:13), to "lead us into the paths of righteousness" (Ps. 23:3), so to "direct" our hearts into the love of God and longings after Christ. He it is who communicates God's love to us (Rom. 5:50), and He it is who stirs us up to the performance of duty by inflaming our hearts with apprehensions of God's tenderness toward us—and for this we are to pray to Him! It is just as though the Apostle said, "O thou Lord the Spirit, warm our cold hearts with a renewed sense of God's tender regard for us, stabilize our fretful souls into a patient waiting for Christ."

"John to the seven churches which are in Asia: Grace be unto you, and peace, from Him which is, and which was, and which is to come; and from the seven Spirits which are before His throne; and from Jesus Christ, who is the faithful witness" (Rev. 1:4, 5). This is as much a prayer—an invocation of blessing—as that recorded in Numbers 6:24-26. The Apostle John desired and supplicated God the Father ("Him who is," etc.), God the Holy Spirit in the plenitude of His power ("the seven Spirits"), and God the Son, that the seven churches in Asia might enjoy Their grace and peace. When I say "The Lord bless you, dear brother," I should utter empty words unless I also pray the Lord to bless you. This "grace and peace be unto you," then, was far more that a pleasantry or courtesy: John was making known to the saints his deep longings for them, which found expression in ardent supplication for these very blessings to be conferred upon them. In conclusion let us say that every verse of the Bible which bids us "Praise the Lord" or "worship God" has reference to each of the Eternal Three.

"Pray ye therefore the Lord of the harvest, that He will send forth labourers into His harvest" (Matthew 9:38). Here is something very plain and expressive, the only point needing to be determined is, Who is "The Lord of the harvest"? During the days of His earthly ministry, Christ Himself sustained that office, as is clear from His calling and sending forth of the Twelve; but after His ascension, the Holy Spirit became such. As proof thereof, we refer to "The Holy Spirit said, Separate Me Barnabas and Saul for the work whereunto I have called them . . . so they, being sent forth by the Holy Spirit, departed" (Acts 13:2, 4)! So again we read, "Take heed therefore unto yourselves, and to all the flock, over the which the Holy Spirit hath made you overseers" (Acts 20:28). It is the Holy Spirit who now appoints the laborers, equips them, assigns their work, and blesses their efforts. In 1 Corinthians 12:5 and 2 Corinthians 3:17 the Holy Spirit expressly is designated "Lord."

The Holy Spirit

"Praise God from whom all blessings flow. Praise Him all you creatures here below. Praise Him above you heavenly hosts—praise Father, Son and Holy Ghost." Amen!

The Attributes of God

Table of Contents

Preface.	213
The Solitariness of God.	214
The Decrees of God.	218
The Knowledge of God.	223
The Foreknowledge of God.	228
The Supremacy of God.	234
The Sovereignty of God.	238
The Immutability of God.	243
The Holiness of God.	247
The Power of God.	252
The Faithfulness of God.	258
The Goodness of God.	264
The Patience of God.	268
The Grace of God.	273
The Mercy of God.	279
The Love of God.	284
The Wrath of God.	289
The Contemplation of God.	295

Preface

"Acquaint now thyself with Him, and be at peace: thereby good shall come unto thee" (Job 22:21). "Thus saith the Lord, Let not the wise man glory in his wisdom, neither let the mighty glory in his might, let not the rich glory in his riches: But let him that glorieth glory in this, that he understandeth, and knoweth Me, that I am the Lord" (Jer 9:23,24). A spiritual and saving knowledge of God is the greatest need of every human creature.

The foundation of all true knowledge of God must be a clear mental apprehension of His perfections as revealed in Holy Scripture. An unknown God can neither be trusted, served, nor worshipped. In this booklet an effort has been made to set forth some of the principal perfections of the Divine character. If the reader is to truly profit from his perusal of the pages that follow, he needs to definitely and earnestly beseech God to bless them to him, to apply His Truth to the conscience and heart, so that his life will be transformed thereby.

Something more than a theoretical knowledge of God is needed by us. God is only truly known in the soul as we yield ourselves to Him, submit to His authority, and regulate all the details of our lives by His holy precepts and commandments. "Then shall we know, if we follow on (in the path of obedience) to know the Lord" (Hosea 6:3). "If any man will do His will, he shall know" (John 7:17). "The people that do know their God shall be strong" (Dan. 11:32).

The Solitariness of God

The title of this article is perhaps not sufficiently explicit to indicate its theme. This is partly due to the fact that so few today are accustomed to meditate upon the personal perfections of God. Comparatively few of those who occasionally read the Bible are aware of the awe-inspiring and worship-provoking grandeur of the Divine character. That God is great in wisdom, wondrous in power, yet full of mercy, is assumed by many to be almost common knowledge; but, to entertain anything approaching an adequate conception of His being, His nature, His attributes, as these are revealed in Holy Scripture, is something which very, very few people in these degenerate times have attained unto. God is solitary in His excellency. "Who is like unto Thee, O Lord, among the gods? Who is like Thee, glorious in holiness, fearful in praises, doing wonders?" (Ex. 15:11).

"In the beginning, God" (Gen. 1:1). There was a time, if "time" is could be called, when God, in the unity of His nature (though subsisting equally in three Divine Persons), dwelt all alone. "In the beginning, God." There was no heaven, where His glory is now particularly manifested. There was no earth to engage His attention. There were no angels to hymn His praises; no universe to be upheld by the word of His power. There was nothing, no one, but God; and that, not for a day, a year, or an age, but "from everlasting." During a past eternity, God was alone: self-contained, self-sufficient, self-satisfied; in need of nothing. Had a universe, had angels, had human beings been necessary to Him in any way, they also had been called into existence from all eternity. The creating of them when He did, added nothing to God essentially. He changes not (Mal. 3:6), therefore His essential glory can be neither augmented nor diminished.

God was under no constraint, no obligation, no necessity to create. That He chose to do so was purely a sovereign act on His part, caused by nothing outside Himself, determined by nothing but His own mere good pleasure; for He "worketh all things after the counsel of His own will" (Eph. 1:11). That He did create was simply for His manifestative glory. Do some of our readers imagine that we have gone beyond what Scripture warrants? Then our appeal shall be to the Law and the Testimony: "Stand up and bless the Lord your God forever and ever: and blessed be Thy glorious name, which is exalted above all blessing and praise" (Neh. 9:5). God is no gainer even from our worship. He was in no need of that external glory of His grace which arises from His redeemed, for He is glorious enough in Himself without that. What was it moved Him to predestinate His elect to the praise of the glory of His grace? It was, as Ephesians 1:5 tells us, according to the good pleasure of His will.

We are well aware that the high ground we are here treading is new and strange to almost all of our readers; for that reason it is well to move slowly. Let our appeal again be to the Scriptures. At the end of Romans 11, where the apostle brings to a close his long argument on salvation by pure and sovereign grace, he asks, "For who hath known the mind of the Lord? Or who hath been His counsellor? Or who hath first given to Him, and it shall be recompensed to him again?" (vv. 34,35). The force of this is, it is impossible to bring the Almighty under obligations to the creature; God gains nothing from us. If thou be righteous, what givest thou Him? Or what receiveth He of thine hand? Thy wickedness may hurt a man as thou art; and thy righteousness may profit the son of man (Job 35:7,8), but it certainly cannot affect God, who is all-blessed in Himself. When ye shall have done all those things which are commanded you, say, We are unprofitable servants (Luke 17:10)—our obedience has profited God nothing.

Nay, we go further: our Lord Jesus Christ added nothing to God in His essential being and glory, either by what He did or suffered. True, blessedly and gloriously true, He manifested the glory of God to us, but He added nought to God. He Himself expressly declares so, and there is no appeal from His words: "My goodness extendeth not to Thee" (Ps. 16:2). The whole of that Psalm is a Psalm of Christ. Christ's goodness or righteousness reached unto His saints in the earth (Psa. 16:3), but God was high above and beyond it all, God only is the "Blessed One" (Mark 14:61, Gr.).

It is perfectly true that God is both honored and dishonored by men; not in His essential being, but in His official character. It is equally true that God has been "glorified" by creation, by providence, and by redemption. This we do not and dare not dispute for a moment. But all of this has to do with His manifestative glory and the recognition of it by us. Yet had God so pleased He might have continued alone for all eternity, without making known His glory unto creatures. Whether He should do so or not was determined solely by His own will. He was perfectly blessed in Himself before the first creature was called into being. And what are all the creatures of His hands unto Him even now? Let Scripture again make answer: "Behold, the nations are as a drop of a bucket, and are counted as the small dust of the balance: behold, He taketh up the isles as a very little thing. And Lebanon is not sufficient to burn, nor the beasts thereof sufficient for a burnt offering. All nations before Him are as nothing; and they are counted to Him less than nothing, and vanity. To whom then will ye liken God? or what likeness will ye compare unto Him?" (Isa. 40:15-18). That is the God of Scripture; alas, He is still "the unknown God" (Acts 17:23) to the heedless multitudes. "It is He that sitteth upon the circle of the earth, and the inhabitants thereof are as grasshoppers; that stretcheth out the heavens as a curtain, and spreadeth them out as a tent to dwell in: that bringeth the princes to nothing; He maketh the judges of the earth as vanity" (Isa. 40:22,23). How vastly different is the God of Scripture from the god of the average pulpit!

Nor is the testimony of the New Testament any different from that of the Old: how could it be, seeing that both have one and the same Author! There too we read, "Which in His times He shall show, who is the blessed and only Potentate, the King of kings, and Lord of lords: Who only hath immortality, dwelling in the light which no man can approach unto; whom no man hath seen, nor can see: to whom be honour and power everlasting, Amen" (1 Tim. 6:16). Such an One is to be revered, worshipped, adored. He is solitary in His majesty, unique

The Holy Spirit

in His excellency, peerless in His perfections. He sustains all, but is Himself independent of all. He gives to all, but is enriched by none.

Such a God cannot be found out by searching; He can be known, only as He is revealed to the heart by the Holy Spirit through the Word. It is true that creation demonstrates a Creator, and that, so plainly, men are "without excuse;" yet, we still have to say with Job, "Lo, these are parts of His ways: but how little a portion is heard of Him? but the thunder of His power who can understand?" (26:14). The so-called argument from design by well-meaning "Apologists" has, we believe, done much more harm than good, for it has attempted to bring down the great God to the level of finite comprehension, and thereby has lost sight of His solitary excellence.

Analogy has been drawn between a savage finding a watch upon the sands, and from a close examination of it he infers a watch-maker. So far so good. But attempt to go further: suppose that savage sits down on the sand and endeavors to form to himself a conception of this watch-maker, his personal affections and manners; his disposition, acquirements, and moral character—all that goes to make up a personality; could he ever think or reason out a real man—the man who made the watch, so that he could say, "I am acquainted with him?" It seems trifling to ask such questions, but is the eternal and infinite God so much more within the grasp of human reason? No, indeed! The God of Scripture can only be known by those to whom He makes Himself known.

Nor is God known by the intellect. "God is Spirit" (John 4:24), and therefore can only be known spiritually. But fallen man is not spiritual, he is carnal. He is dead to all that is spiritual. Unless he is born again supernaturally brought from death unto life, miraculously translated out of darkness into light, he cannot even see the things of God (John 3:3), still less apprehend them (1 Cor. 2:14). The Holy Spirit has to shine in our hearts (not intellects) in order to give us "the knowledge of the glory of God in the face of Jesus Christ" (2 Cor. 4:6). And even that spiritual knowledge is but fragmentary. The regenerated soul has to grow in grace and in the knowledge of the Lord Jesus (2 Pet. 3.18).

The principal prayer and aim of Christians should be that we "walk worthy of the Lord unto all pleasing, being fruitful in every good work and increasing in the knowledge of God" (Col. 1:10).

The Decrees of God

The decree of God is His purpose or determination with respect to future things. We have used the singular number as Scripture does (Rom 8:28, Eph 3:11), because there was only one act of His infinite mind about future things. But we speak as if there had been many, because our minds are only capable of thinking of successive revolutions, as thoughts and occasions arise, or in reference to the various objects of His decree, which being many seem to us to require a distinct purpose for each one. But an infinite understanding does not proceed by steps, from one stage to another: "Known unto God are all His works, from the beginning of the world" (Acts 15:18).

The Scriptures make mention of the decrees of God in many passages, and under a variety of terms. The word "decree" is found in Psalm 2:7, etc. In Ephesians 3:11 we read of His "eternal purpose." In Acts 2:23 of His "determinate counsel and foreknowledge." In Ephesians 1:9 of the mystery of His "will." In Romans 8:29 that He also did predestinate. In Ephesians 1:9 of His "good pleasure." God's decrees are called His "counsel" to signify they are consummately wise. They are called God's "will" to show He was under no control, but acted according to His own pleasure. When a man's will is the rule of his conduct, it is usually capricious and unreasonable; but wisdom is always associated with "will" in the Divine proceedings, and accordingly, God's decrees are said to be "the counsel of His own will" (Eph. 1:11).

The decrees of God relate to all future things without exception: whatever is done in time, was foreordained before time began. God's purpose was concerned with everything, whether great or small, whether good or evil, although with reference to the latter we must be careful to state that while God is the Orderer and Controller of sin, He is not the Author of it in the same way that He is the Author of good.

Sin could not proceed from a holy God by positive and direct creation, but only by decretive permission and negative action. God's decree is as comprehensive as His government, extending to all creatures and all events. It was concerned about our life and death; about our state in time, and our state in eternity. As God works all things after the counsel of His own will, we learn from His works what His counsel is (was), as we judge of an architect's plan by inspecting the building which was erected under his directions.

God did not merely decree to make man, place him upon the earth, and then leave him to his own uncontrolled guidance; instead, He fixed all the circumstances in the lot of individuals, and all the particulars which will comprise the history of the human race from its commencement to its close. He did not merely decree that general laws should be established for the government of the world, but He settled the application of those laws to all particular cases. Our days are numbered, and so are the hairs of our heads. We may learn what is the extent of the Divine decrees from the dispensations of providence, in which they are executed. The care of Providence reaches to the most insignificant creatures, and the most minute events—the death of a sparrow, and the fall of a hair.

Let us now consider some of the properties of the Divine decrees. First, they are eternal. To suppose any of them to be made in time, is to suppose that some new occasion has occurred, some unforeseen event or combination of circumstances has arisen, which has induced the Most High to form a new resolution. This would argue that the knowledge of the deity is limited, an that He is growing wiser in the progress of time—which would be horrible blasphemy. No man who believes that the Divine understanding is infinite, comprehending the past, the present, and the future, will ever assent to the erroneous doctrine of temporal decrees. God is not ignorant of future events which will be executed by human volitions; He has foretold them in innumerable instances, and prophecy is but the manifestation of His eternal prescience. Scripture affirms that believers were chosen in Christ before the world began (Eph. 1:4), yea, that grace was "given" to them then (2 Tim. 1:9).

Second, the decrees of God are wise. Wisdom is shown in the selection of the best possible ends and of the fittest means of accomplishing them. That this character belongs to the decrees of God is evident from what we know of them. They are disclosed to us by their execution, and every proof of wisdom in the works of God is a proof of the wisdom of the plan, in conformity to which they are performed. As the Psalmist declared, "O Lord, how manifold are Thy works! in wisdom hast Thou made them all" (Ps. 104:24). It is indeed but a very small part of them which falls under our observation, yet, we ought to proceed here as we do in other cases, and judge of the whole by the specimen, of what is unknown, by what is known. He who perceives the workings of admirable skill in the parts of a machine which he has an opportunity to examine, is naturally led to believe that the other parts are equally admirable. In like manner should we satisfy our minds as to God's works when doubts obtrude themselves upon us, and repel the objections which may be suggested by something which we cannot reconcile to our notions of what is good and wise. When we reach the bounds of the finite and gaze toward the mysterious realm of the infinite, let us exclaim. "O the depth of the riches! both of the wisdom and knowledge of God" (Rom. 11:33).

Third, they are free. "Who hath directed the Spirit of the Lord, or being His counselor hath taught Him? With whom took He counsel, and who instructed Him, and taught Him in the path of judgment, and taught Him knowledge, and showed to Him the way of understanding?" (Isa. 40:13,14). God was alone when He made His decrees, and His determinations were influenced by no external cause. He was free to decree or not to decree, and to decree one thing and not another. This liberty we must ascribe to Him who is supreme, independent, and sovereign in all His doings.

Fourth, they are absolute and unconditional. The execution of them is not suspended upon any condition which may, or may not be, performed. In every instance where God his decreed an end, He has also decreed every means to that end. The One who decreed the salvation of His elect also decreed to work faith in them (2 Thess. 2:13). "My counsel shall stand, and I will do all My pleasure" (Isa. 46:10): but that could not be, if His counsel depended upon a condition which might not be performed. But God "worketh all things after the counsel of His own will" (Eph. 1:11).

Side by side with the immutability and invincibility of God's decrees, Scripture plainly teaches that man is a responsible creature and answerable for his actions. And if our thoughts are formed from God's Word the maintenance of the one will not lead to the denial of the other. That there is a real difficulty in defining where the one ends and the other begins, is freely granted. This is ever the case where there is a conjunction of the Divine and the human. Real prayer is indited by the Spirit, yet it is also the cry of a human heart. The Scriptures are the inspired Word of God, yet were they written by men who were something more than machines in the hand of the Spirit. Christ is both God and man. He is Omniscient, yet "increased in wisdom" (Luke 2:52). He was Almighty, yet was "crucified through weakness" (2 Cor. 13:4). He was the Prince of life, yet He died. High mysteries are these, yet faith receives them unquestioningly.

It has often been pointed out in the past that every objection made against the eternal decrees of God applies with equal force against His eternal foreknowledge:

> Whether God has decreed all things that ever come to pass or not, all that own the being of a God, own that He knows all things beforehand. Now, it is self-evident that if He knows all things beforehand, He either doth approve of them or doth not approve of them; that is, He either is willing they should be, or He is not willing they should be. But to will that they should be is to decree them. (Jonathan Edwards).

Finally, attempt to assume and then contemplate the opposite. To deny the Divine decrees would be to predicate a world and all its concerns regulated by undesigned chance or blind fate. Then what peace, what assurance, what comfort would there be for our poor hearts and minds? What refuge would there be to fly to in the hour of need and trial? None at all. There would be nothing better than the black darkness and abject horror of atheism. O my reader, how thankful should we be that everything is determined by infinite wisdom and goodness! What praise and gratitude are due unto God for His Divine decrees. It is because of them that "we know that all things work together for good to them that love God, to them who are the called according to His purpose" (Rom. 8:28). Well may we exclaim, "For of Him, and through Him, and to Him, are all things: to whom he glory forever. Amen" (Rom 11:36).

The Knowledge of God

God is omniscient. He knows everything: everything possible, everything actual; all events, all creatures, God the past, the present and the future. He is perfectly acquainted with every detail in the life of every being in heaven, in earth and in hell. "He knoweth what is in the darkness" (Dan. 2:22). Nothing escapes Hs notice, nothing can be hidden from Him, nothing is forgotten by Him. Well may we say with the Psalmist, "Such knowledge is too wonderful for me; it is high, I cannot attain unto it" (Ps. 139:6). His knowledge is perfect. He never errs, never changes, never overlooks anything. "Neither is there any creature that is not manifest in His sight: but all things are naked and opened unto the eyes of Him with whom we have to do" (Heb. 4:13). Yes, such is the God with whom "we have to do!"

"Thou knowest my downsitting and mine uprising, Thou understandest my thoughts afar off. Thou compassest my path and my lying down, and art acquainted with all my ways. For there is not a word in my tongue but, lo, O Lord, Thou knowest it altogether" (Ps. 139:2-4). What a wondrous Being is the God of Scripture! Each of His glorious attributes should render Him honorable in our esteem. The apprehension of His omniscience ought to bow us in adoration before Him. Yet how little do we meditate upon this Divine perfection! Is it because the very thought of it fills us with uneasiness?

How solemn is this fact: nothing can be concealed from God! "For I know the things that come into your mind, every one of them" (Ezek. 11:5). Though He be invisible to us, we are not so to Him. Neither the darkness of night, the closest curtains, nor the deepest dungeon can hide any sinner from the eyes of Omniscience. The trees of the garden were not able to conceal our first parents. No human eye beheld Cain murder his brother, but his Maker witnessed his crime. Sarah might laugh derisively in the seclusion of her tent, yet was it heard by Jehovah. Achan stole a wedge of gold and carefully hid it in the earth, but God brought it to light. David was at much pains to cover up his wickedness, but ere long the all-seeing God sent one of His servants to say to him, "Thou art the man! And to writer and reader is also said, Be sure your sin will find you out" (Num. 32:23).

Men would strip Deity of His omniscience if they could—what a proof that "the carnal mind is enmity against God" (Rom. 8:7)! The wicked do as naturally hate this Divine perfection as much as they are naturally compelled to acknowledge it. They wish there might be no Witness of their sins, no Searcher of their hearts, no Judge of their deeds. They seek to banish such a God from their thoughts: "They consider not in their hearts that I remember all their wickedness" (Hosea 7:2). How solemn is Psalm 90:8! Good reason has every Christ-rejecter for trembling before it: Thou hast set our iniquities before Thee, our secret sins in the light of Thy countenance.

But to the believer, the fact of God's omniscience is a truth fraught with much comfort. In times of perplexity he says with Job, "But He knoweth the way that I take." (23:10). It may be profoundly mysterious to me, quite incomprehensible to my friends, but "He knoweth!" In times of weariness and weakness believers assure themselves "He knoweth our frame; He remembereth that we are dust" (Ps. 103:14). In times of doubt and suspicion they appeal to this very attribute saying, "Search me, O God, and know my heart: try me, and know my thoughts: and see if there be any wicked way in me, and lead me in the way everlasting" (Ps. 139:23,24). In time of sad failure, when our actions have belied our hearts, when our deeds have repudiated our devotion, and the searching question comes to us, "Lovest thou Me?;" we say, as Peter did, "Lord, Thou knowest all things; Thou knowest that I love Thee" (John 21:17).

Here is encouragement to prayer. There is no cause for fearing that the petitions of the righteous will not be heard, or that their sighs and tears shall escape the notice of God, since He knows the thoughts and intents of the heart. There is no danger of the individual saint being overlooked amidst the multitude of supplicants who daily and hourly present their various petitions, for an infinite Mind is as capable as paying the same attention to millions as if only one individual were seeking its attention. So too the lack of appropriate language, the inability to give expression to the deepest longing of the soul, will not jeopardize our prayers, for "It shall come to pass, that before they call, I will answer; and while they are yet speaking, I will hear" (Isa. 65:24).

"Great is our Lord, and of great power: His understanding is infinite" (Ps. 147:5). God not only knows whatsoever has happened in the past in every part of His vast domains, and He is not only thoroughly acquainted with everything that is now transpiring throughout the entire universe, but He is also perfectly cognizant with every event, from the least to the greatest, that ever will happen in the ages to come. God's knowledge of the future is as complete as is His knowledge of the past and the present, and that, because the future depends entirely upon Himself. Were it in anywise possible for something to occur apart from either the direct agency or permission of God, then that something would be independent of Him, and He would at once cease to be Supreme.

Now the Divine knowledge of the future is not a mere abstraction, but something which is inseparably connected with and accompanied by His purpose. God has Himself designed whatsoever shall yet be, and what He has designed must be effectuated. As His most sure Word affirms, "He doeth according to His will in the army of heaven, and the inhabitants of the earth: and none can stay His hand" (Dan. 4:35). And again, "There are many devices in a man's heart; nevertheless the counsel of the Lord, that shall stand" (Prov. 19:21). The wisdom and power of God being alike infinite, the accomplishment of whatever He hath purposed is absolutely guaranteed. It is no more possible for the Divine counsels to fail in their execution than it would be for the thrice holy God to lie.

Nothing relating to the future is in anywise uncertain so far as the actualization of God's counsels are concerned. None of His decrees are left contingent either on creatures or secondary causes. There is no future event which is only a mere possibility, that is, something which may or may not come to pass, "Known unto God are all His works from the beginning" (Acts 15:18). Whatever God has decreed is inexorably certain, for He is without variableness, or shadow, of turning. (James

1:17). Therefore we are told at the very beginning of that book which unveils to us so much of the future, of "Things which must shortly come to pass." (Rev. 1:1).

The perfect knowledge of God is exemplified and illustrated in every prophecy recorded in His Word. In the Old Testament are to be found scores of predictions concerning the history of Israel, which were fulfilled to their minutest detail, centuries after they were made. In them too are scores more foretelling the earthly career of Christ, and they too were accomplished literally and perfectly. Such prophecies could only have been given by One who knew the end from the beginning, and whose knowledge rested upon the unconditional certainty of the accomplishment of everything foretold. In like manner, both Old and New Testament contain many other announcements yet future, and they too "must be fulfilled" (Luke 24:44), must because foretold by Him who decreed them.

It should, however, be pointed out that neither God's knowledge nor His cognition of the future, considered simply in themselves, are causative. Nothing has ever come to pass, or ever will, merely because God knew it. The cause of all things is the will of God. The man who really believes the Scriptures knows beforehand that the seasons will continue to follow each other with unfailing regularity to the end of earth's history (Gen. 8:22), yet his knowledge is not the cause of their succession. So God's knowledge does not arise from things because they are or will be but because He has ordained them to be. God knew and foretold the crucifixion of His Son many hundreds of years before He became incarnate, and this, because in the Divine purpose, He was a Lamb slain from the foundation of the world: hence we read of His being "delivered by the determinate counsel and foreknowledge of God" (Acts 2:23).

A word or two by way of application. The infinite knowledge of God should fill us with amazement. How far exalted above the wisest man is the Lord! None of us knows what a day may bring forth, but all futurity is open to His omniscient gaze. The infinite knowledge of God ought to fill us with holy awe. Nothing we do, say, or even think, escapes the cognizance of Him with whom we have to do: "The eyes of the Lord are in every place, beholding the evil and the good" (Prov.

15:3). What a curb this would be unto us, did we but meditate upon it more frequently! Instead of acting recklessly, we should say with Hagar, "Thou God seest me" (Gen. 16:13). The apprehension of God's infinite knowledge should fill the Christian with adoration. The whole of my life stood open to His view from the beginning. He foresaw my every fall, my every sin, my every backsliding; yet, nevertheless, fixed His heart upon me. Oh, how the realization of this should bow me in wonder and worship before Him!

The Foreknowledge of God

What controversies have been engendered by this subject in the past! But what truth of Holy Scripture is there which has not been made the occasion of theological and ecclesiastical battles? The deity of Christ, His virgin birth, His atoning death, His second advent; the believer's justification, sanctification, security; the church, its organization, officers, discipline; baptism, the Lord's supper, and a score of other precious truths might be mentioned. Yet, the controversies which have been waged over them did not close the mouths of God's faithful servants; why, then, should we avoid the vexed question of God's Foreknowledge, because, forsooth, there are some who will charge us with fomenting strife? Let others contend if they will, our duty is to bear witness according to the light vouchsafed us.

There are two things concerning the Foreknowledge of God about which many are in ignorance: the meaning of the term, its Scriptural scope. Because this ignorance is so widespread, it is an easy matter for preachers and teachers to palm off perversions of this subject, even upon the people of God. There is only one safeguard against error, and that is to be established in the faith; and for that, there has to be prayerful and diligent study, and a receiving with meekness the engrafted Word of God. Only then are we fortified against the attacks of those who assail us. There are those today who are misusing this very truth in order to discredit and deny the absolute sovereignty of God in the salvation of sinners. Just as higher critics are repudiating the Divine inspiration of the Scriptures; evolutionists, the work of God in creation; so some pseudo Bible teachers are perverting His foreknowledge in order to set aside His unconditional election unto eternal life.

When the solemn and blessed subject of Divine foreordination is expounded, when God's eternal choice of certain ones to be conformed to the image of His Son is set forth, the Enemy sends along some man to argue that election is based upon the foreknowledge of God, and this "foreknowledge" is interpreted to mean that God foresaw certain ones would be more pliable than others, that they would respond more readily to the strivings of the Spirit, and that because God knew they would believe, He, accordingly, predestinated them unto salvation. But such a statement is radically wrong. It repudiates the truth of total depravity, for it argues that there is something good in some men. It takes away the independency of God, for it makes His decrees rest upon what He discovers in the creature. It completely turns things upside down, for in saying God foresaw certain sinners would believe in Christ, and that because of this, He predestinated them unto salvation, is the very reverse of the truth. Scripture affirms that God, in His high sovereignty, singled out certain ones to be recipients of His distinguishing favors (Acts 13:48), and therefore He determined to bestow upon them the gift of faith. False theology makes God's foreknowledge of our believing the cause of His election to salvation; whereas, God's election is the cause, and our believing in Christ is the effect.

Ere proceeding further with our discussion of this much misunderstood theme, let us pause and define our terms. What is meant by "foreknowledge?" "To know beforehand," is the ready reply of many. But we must not jump at conclusions, nor must we turn to Webster's dictionary as the final court of appeal, for it is not a matter of the etymology of the term employed. What is needed is to find out how the word is used in Scripture. The Holy Spirit's usage of an expression always defines its meaning and scope. It is failure to apply this simple, rule which is responsible for so much confusion and error. So many people assume they already know the signification of a certain word used in Scripture, and then they are too dilatory to test their assumptions by means of a concordance. Let us amplify this point.

Take the word "flesh." Its meaning appears to be so obvious that many would regard it as a waste of time to look up its various connections in Scripture. It is hastily assumed that the word is synonymous with the physical body, and so no inquiry is made. But, in fact, "flesh" in Scripture frequently includes far more than what is corporeal; all that is embraced by the term can only be ascertained by a diligent comparison of every occurrence of it and by a study of each separate context. Take the word "world." The average reader of the Bible imagines this word is the equivalent for the human race, and consequently, many passages where the term is found are wrongly interpreted. Take the word immortality. Surely it requires no study! Obviously it has reference to the indestructibility of the soul. Ah, my reader, it is foolish and wrong to assume anything where the Word of God is concerned. If the reader will take the trouble to carefully examine each passage where "mortal" and "immortal" are found, it will be seen these words are never applied to the soul, but always to the body.

Now what has just been said on "flesh," the "world," immortality, applies with equal force to the terms know and "foreknow." Instead of imagining that these words signify no more than a simple cognition, the different passages in which they occur require to be carefully weighed. The word "foreknowledge" is not found in the Old Testament. But know occurs there frequently. When that term is used in connection with God, it often signifies to regard with favour, denoting not mere cognition but an affection for the object in view. "I know thee by name" (Ex. 33:17). "Ye have been rebellious against the Lord from the day that I knew you" (Deut. 9:24). "Before I formed thee in the belly I knew thee" (Jer. 1:5). "They have made princes and I knew it not" (Hos. 8:4). "You only have I known of all the families of the earth" (Amos 3:2). In these passages knew signifies either loved or appointed.

In like manner, the word "know" is frequently used in the New Testament, in the same sense as in the Old Testament. "Then will I profess unto them, I never knew you" (Matt. 7:23). "I am the good shepherd and know My sheep and am known of Mine" (John 10:14). "If any man love God, the same is known of Him" (1 Cor. 8:3). "The Lord knoweth them that are His" (2 Tim. 2:19).

Now the word "foreknowledge" as it is used in the New Testament is less ambiguous than in its simple form "to know." If every passage in which it occurs is carefully studied, it will be discovered that it is a moot point whether it ever has reference to the mere perception of events which are yet to take place. The fact is that "foreknowledge" is never used in Scripture in connection with events or actions; instead, it always has reference to persons. It is persons God is said to "foreknow," not the actions of those persons. In proof of this we shall now quote each passage where this expression is found.

The first occurrence is in Acts 2:23. There we read, "Him being delivered by the determinate counsel and foreknowledge of God, ye have taken, and by wicked hands have crucified and slain." If careful attention is paid to the wording of this verse it will be seen that the apostle was not there speaking of God's foreknowledge of the act of the crucifixion, but of the Person crucified: "Him (Christ) being delivered by," etc.

The second occurrence is in Romans 8;29,30. "For whom He did foreknow, He also did predestinate to be conformed to the image, of His Son, that He might be the Firstborn among many brethren. Moreover whom He did predestinate, them He also called," etc. Weigh well the pronoun that is used here. It is not what He did foreknow, but whom He did. It is not the surrendering of their wills nor the believing of their hearts but the persons themselves, which is here in view.

"God hath not cast away His people which He foreknew" (Rom. 11:2). Once more the plain reference is to persons, and to persons only.

The last mention is in 1 Peter 1:2: "Elect according to the foreknowledge of God the Father." Who are elect according to the foreknowledge of God the Father? The previous verse tells us: the reference is to the "strangers scattered" i.e. the Diaspora, the Dispersion, the believing Jews. Thus, here too the reference is to persons, and not to their foreseen acts.

Now in view of these passages (and there are no more) what scriptural ground is there for anyone saying God "foreknew" the acts of certain ones, viz., their "repenting and believing," and that because of those acts He elected them unto salvation? The answer is, None whatever. Scripture never speaks of repentance and faith as being foreseen or foreknown by God. Truly, He did know from all eternity that certain ones would repent and believe, yet this is not what Scripture refers to as the object of God's "foreknowledge." The word uniformly refers to God's foreknowing persons; then let us "hold fast the form of sound words" (2 Tim. 1:13).

Another thing to which we desire to call particular attention is that the first two passages quoted above show plainly and teach implicitly that God's "foreknowledge" is not causative, that instead, something else lies behind, precedes it, and that something is His own sovereign decree. Christ was "delivered by the (1) determinate counsel and (2) foreknowledge of God." (Acts 2:23). His "counsel" or decree was the ground of His foreknowledge. So again in Romans 8:29. That verse opens with the word "for," which tells us to look back to what immediately precedes. What, then, does the previous verse say? This, "all things work together for good to them. . . .who are the called according to His purpose." Thus God's foreknowledge is based upon His purpose or decree (see Ps. 2:7).

God foreknows what will be because He has decreed what shall be. It is therefore a reversing of the order of Scripture, a putting of the cart before the horse, to affirm that God elects because He foreknows people. The truth is, He "foreknows" because He has elected. This removes the ground or cause of election from outside the creature, and places it in God's own sovereign will. God purposed in Himself to elect a certain people, not because of anything good in them or from them, either actual or foreseen, but solely out of His own mere pleasure. As to why He chose the ones He did, we do not know, and can only say, "Even so, Father, for so it seemed good in Thy sight." The plain truth of Romans 8:29 is that God, before the foundation of the world, singled out certain sinners and appointed them unto salvation (2 Thess. 2:13). This is clear from the concluding words of the verse: "Predestinated to be conformed to the image of His Son," etc. God did not predestinate those whom He foreknew were "conformed," but, on the contrary, those whom He "foreknew" (i.e., loved and elected) He predestinated to be conformed. Their conformity to Christ is not the cause, but the effect of God's foreknowledge and predestination.

God did not elect any sinner because He foresaw that he would believe, for the simple but sufficient reason that no sinner ever does believe until God gives him faith; just as no man sees until God gives him sight. Sight is God's gift, seeing is the consequence of my using His gift. So faith is God's gift (Eph. 1:8,9), believing is the consequence of my using His gift. If it were true that God had elected certain ones to be saved because in due time they would believe, then that would make believing a meritorious act, and in that event the saved sinner would have ground for "boasting," which Scripture emphatically denies: Ephesians 2:9.

Surely God's Word is plain enough in teaching that believing is not a meritorious act. It affirms that Christians are a people "who have believed through grace" (Acts 18:27). If then, they have believed "through grace," there is absolutely nothing meritorious about "believing," and if nothing meritorious, it could not be the ground or cause which moved God to choose them. No; God's choice proceeds not from anything in us, or anything from us, but solely from His own sovereign pleasure. Once more, in Romans 11:5, we read of "a remnant according to the election of grace." There it is, plain enough; election itself is of grace, and grace is unmerited favour something for which we had no claim upon God whatsoever.

It thus appears that it is highly important for us to have clear and scriptural views of the "foreknowledge" of God. Erroneous conceptions about it lead inevitably to thoughts most dishonoring to Him. The popular idea of Divine foreknowledge is altogether inadequate. God not only knew the end from the beginning, but He planned, fixed, predestinated everything from the beginning. And, as cause stands to effect, so God's purpose is the ground of His prescience. If then the reader be a real Christian, he is so because God chose him in Christ before the foundation of the world (Eph. 1:4), and chose not because He foresaw you would believe, but chose simply because it pleased Him to choose: chose you notwithstanding your natural unbelief. This being so, all the glory and praise belongs alone to Him. You have no ground for taking any credit to yourself. You have "believed through grace" (Acts 18:27), and that, because your very election was "of grace" (Rom. 11:5).

The Supremacy of God

In one of his letters to Erasmus, Luther said, "Your thoughts of God are too human." Probably that renowned scholar resented such a rebuke, the more so, since it proceeded from a miner's son; nevertheless, it was thoroughly deserved. We too, though having no standing among the religious leaders of this degenerate age, prefer the same charge against the majority of the preachers of our day, and against those who, instead of searching the Scriptures for themselves, lazily accept the teaching of others. The most dishonoring and degrading conceptions of the rule and reign of the Almighty are now held almost everywhere. To countless thousands, even among those professing to be Christians, the God of the Scriptures is quite unknown.

Of old, God complained to an apostate Israel, Thou thoughtest that I was altogether as thyself. (Ps. 50:21). Such must now be His indictment against an apostate Christendom. Men imagine that the Most High is moved by sentiment, rather than actuated by principle. They suppose that His omnipotency is such an idle fiction that Satan is thwarting His designs on every side. They think that if He has formed any plan or purpose at all, then it must be like theirs, constantly subject to change. They openly declare that whatever power He possesses must be restricted, lest He invade the citadel of man's "free will" and reduce him to a "machine." They lower the all efficacious Atonement, which has actually redeemed everyone for whom it was made, to a mere "remedy," which sin-sick souls may use if they feel disposed to; and they enervate the invincible work of the Holy Spirit to an "offer" of the Gospel which sinners may accept or reject as they please.

The "god" of this twentieth century no more resembles the Supreme Sovereign of Holy Writ than does the dim flickering of a candle the glory of the midday sun. The "god" who is now talked about in the average pulpit, spoken of in the ordinary Sunday School, mentioned in

The Holy Spirit 235

much of the religious literature of the day, and preached in most of the so-called Bible Conferences is the figment of human imagination, an invention of maudlin sentimentality. The heathen outside of the pale of Christendom form "gods" out of wood and stone, while the millions of heathen inside Christendom manufacture a "god" out of their own carnal mind. In reality, they are but atheists, for there is no other possible alternative between an absolutely supreme God, and no God at all. A "god" whose will is resisted, whose designs are frustrated, whose purpose is checkmated, possesses no title to Deity, and so far from being a fit object of worship, merits nought but contempt.

The supremacy of the true and living God might well be argued from the infinite distance which separates the mightiest creatures from the almighty Creator. He is the Potter, they are but the clay in His hands to be molded into vessels of honor, or to be dashed into pieces (Ps. 2-9) as He pleases. Were all the denizens of heaven and all the inhabitants of the earth to combine in revolt against Him, it would occasion Him no uneasiness, and would have less effect upon His eternal and unassailable Throne than has the spray of Mediterranean's waves upon the towering rocks of Gibraltar. So puerile and powerless is the creature to affect the Most High, Scripture itself tells us that when the Gentile heads unite with apostate Israel to defy Jehovah and His Christ, "He that sitteth in the heavens shall laugh" (Ps. 2:4).

The absolute and universal supremacy of God is plainly and positively affirmed in many scriptures. "Thine, O Lord, is the greatness, and the power, and the glory, and the victory and the majesty: for all in the heaven and all in the earth is Thine; Thine is the Kingdom, O Lord, and Thou art exalted as Head above all. . . .And Thou reignest over all" (1 Chron. 29:11, 12)—note reignest now, not "will do so in the Millennium." "O Lord God of our fathers, art not Thou, God in heaven? and rulest not Thou over all the kingdoms of the heathen? and in Thine hand is there not power and might, so that none (not even the Devil himself) is able to withstand Thee?" (2 Chron. 20:6). Before Him presidents and popes, kings and emperors, are less than grasshoppers.

"But He is in one mind, and who can turn Him? and what His soul desireth, even that He doeth" (Job 23:13). Ah, my reader, the God of

Scripture is no make-believe monarch, no mere imaginary sovereign, but King of kings, and Lord of lords. "I know that Thou canst do everything, and that no thought of Thine can be hindered" (Job 42:3, margin), or, as another translator, "no purpose of Thine can be frustrated." All that He has designed He does. All that He has decreed, He performs. "But our God is in the heavens: He hath done whatsoever He hath pleased" (Psa. 115.3); and why has He? Because "there is no wisdom, nor understanding, nor counsel against the Lord" (Prov 21:30).

God's supremacy over the works of His hands is vividly depicted in Scripture. Inanimate matter, irrational creatures, all perform their Maker's bidding. At His pleasure the Red Sea divided and its waters stood up as walls (Ex. 14); and the earth opened her mouth, and guilty rebels went down alive into the pit (Num. 14). When He so ordered, the sun stood still (Josh. 10); and on another occasion went backward ten degrees on the dial of Ahaz (Isa. 38:8). To exemplify His supremacy, He made ravens carry food to Elijah (1 Kings 17), iron to swim on top of the waters (2 Kings 6:5), lions to be tame when Daniel was cast into their den, fire to burn not when the three Hebrews were flung into its flames. Thus "Whatsoever the Lord pleased, that did He in heaven, and in earth, in the seas, and all deep places" (Psa. 135:6).

God's supremacy is also demonstrated in His perfect rule over the wills of men. Let the reader ponder carefully Ex. 34:24. Three times in the year all the males of Israel were required to leave their homes and go up to Jerusalem. They lived in the midst of hostile people, who hated them for having appropriated their lands. What, then, was to hinder the Canaanites from seizing their opportunity, and, during the absence of the men, slaying the women and children and taking possession of their farms? If the hand of the Almighty was not upon the wills even of wicked men, how could He make this promise beforehand, that none should so much as "desire" their lands? Ah, "The king's heart is in the hand of the Lord, as the rivers of water: He turneth it whithersoever He will" (Prov. 21:1).

But, it may be objected, do we not read again and again in Scripture how that men defied God, resisted His will, broke His commandments, disregarded His warnings, and turned a deaf ear to all His exhortations?

Certainly we do. And does this nullify all that we have said above? If it does, then the Bible plainly contradicts itself. But that cannot be. What the objector refers to is simply the wickedness of man against the external word of God, whereas what we have mentioned above is what God has purposed in Himself. The rule of conduct He has given us to walk by, is perfectly fulfilled by none of us; His own eternal "counsels" are accomplished to their minutest details.

The absolute and universal supremacy of God is affirmed with equal plainness and positiveness in the New Testament. There we are told that God "worketh all things after the counsel of His own will" (Eph. 1:11)—the Greek for "worketh" means to work effectually. For this reason we read, "For of Him, and through Him, and to Him are all things: to whom be glory forever. Amen" (Rom. 11:36). Men may boast that they are free agents, with a will of their own, and are at liberty to do as they please, but Scripture says to those who boast "we will go into such a city, and continue there a year, and buy and sell...Ye ought to say, If the Lord will" (Jas. 4:13,15)!

Here then is a sure resting-place for the heart. Our lives are neither the product of blind fate nor the result of capricious chance, but every detail of them was ordained from all eternity. and is now ordered by the living and reigning God. Not a hair of our heads can be touched without His permission. "A man's heart deviseth his way: but the Lord directeth his steps" (Prov. 16:9). What assurance, what strength, what comfort should this give the real Christian! "My times are in Thy hand" (Ps. 31:15). Then let me "Rest in the Lord, and wait patiently for Him" (Ps. 37:7).

The Sovereignty of God

The sovereignty of God may be defined as the exercise of His supremacy—(see Web Site on Supremacy). Being infinitely elevated above the highest creature, He is the Most High, Lord of heaven and earth. Subject to none, influenced by none, absolutely independent; God does as He pleases, only as He pleases always as He pleases. None can thwart Him, none can hinder Him. So His own Word expressly declares: "My counsel shall stand, and I will do all My pleasure" (Isa. 46:10); "He doeth according to His will in the army of heaven, and the inhabitants of the earth: and none can stay His hand" (Dan. 4:35). Divine sovereignty means that God is God in fact, as well as in name, that He is on the Throne of the universe, directing all things, working all things "after the counsel of His own will" (Eph. 1:11).

Rightly did the late Mr. Spurgeon say in his sermon on Matthew 20:15:

> There is no attribute more comforting to His children than that of God's Sovereignty. Under the most adverse circumstances, in the most severe trials, they believe that Sovereignty has ordained their afflictions, that Sovereignty overrules them, and that Sovereignty will sanctify them all. There is nothing for which the children ought more earnestly to contend than the doctrine of their Master over all creation—the Kingship of God over all the works of His own hands—the Throne of God and His right to sit upon that Throne. On the other hand, there is no doctrine more hated by worldings, no truth of which they have made such a football, as the great, stupendous, but yet most certain doctrine of the Sovereignty of the infinite Jehovah. Men will allow God to be everywhere except on His throne. They will allow Him to be in His workshop to fashion worlds and make stars. They will allow Him to be in His almonry to dispense His alms and

bestow His bounties. They will allow Him to sustain the earth and bear up the pillars thereof, or light the lamps of heaven, or rule the waves of the ever-moving ocean; but when God ascends His throne, His creatures then gnash their teeth, and we proclaim an enthroned God, and His right to do as He wills with His own, to dispose of His creatures as He thinks well, without consulting them in the matter; then it is that we are hissed and execrated, and then it is that men turn a deaf ear to us, for God on His throne is not the God they love. But it is God upon the throne that we love to preach. It is God upon His throne whom we trust.

"Whatsoever the Lord pleased, that did He in heaven, and in earth, in the seas, and all deep places" (Ps. 135:6). Yes, dear reader, such is the imperial Potentate revealed in Holy Writ. Unrivalled in majesty, unlimited in power, unaffected by anything outside Himself. But we are living in a day when even the most "orthodox" seem afraid to admit the proper Godhood of God. They say that to press excludes human responsibility; whereas human responsibility is based upon Divine sovereignty, and is the product of it.

"But our God is in the heavens: He hath done whatsoever He hath pleased" (Ps. 115:3). He sovereignly chose to place each of His creatures on that particular footing which seemed good in His sight. He created angels: some He placed on a conditional footing, others He gave an immutable standing before Him (1 Tim. 5:21), making Christ their head (Col. 2:10). Let it not be overlooked that the angels which sinned (2 Pet. 2:5),. were as much His creatures as the angels that sinned not. Yet God foresaw they would fall, nevertheless He placed them on a mutable creature, conditional footing, and suffered them to fall, though He was not the Author of their sin.

So too, God sovereignly placed Adam in the garden of Eden upon a conditional footing. Had He so pleased, He could have placed him upon an unconditional footing; He could have placed him on a footing as firm as that occupied by the unfallen angels, He could have placed him upon a footing as sure and as immutable as that which His saints have in Christ. But, instead, He chose to set him in Eden on the basis of creature responsibility, so that he stood or fell according as he measured or failed to measure up to his responsibility obedience to his

Maker. Adam stood accountable to God by the law which his Creator had given him. Here was responsibility, unimpaired responsibility, tested out under the most favorable conditions.

Now God did not place Adam upon a footing of conditional, creature responsibility, because it was right He should so place him. No, it was right because God did it. God did not even give creatures being because it was right for Him to do so, i. e., because He was under any obligations to create; but it was right because He did so. God is sovereign. His will is supreme. So far from God being under any law of "right," He is a law unto Himself, so that whatsoever He does is right. And woe be to the rebel that calls His sovereignty into question: "Woe unto him that striveth with his Maker. Let the potsherd strive with the potsherds of the earth. Shall the thing say to Him that fashioned it, What makest Thou?" (Isa. 45:9).

Again; the Lord God sovereignly placed Israel upon a conditional footing. The 19th, 20th and 24th chapters of Exodus afford a clear and full proof of this. They were placed under a covenant of works. God gave to them certain laws, and made national blessing for them depend upon their observance of His statutes. But Israel were stiffnecked and uncircumcised in heart. They rebelled against Jehovah, forsook His law, turned unto false gods, apostatized. In consequence, Divine judgment fell upon them, they were delivered into the hands of their enemies, dispersed abroad throughout the earth, and remain under the heavy frown of God's displeasure to this day.

It was God in the exercise of His high sovereignty that placed Satan and his angels, Adam, Israel, in their respective responsible positions. But so far from His sovereignty taking away responsibility from the creature, it was by the exercise thereof that He placed them on this conditional footing, under such responsibilities as He thought proper; by virtue of which sovereignty, He is seen to be God over all. Thus, there is perfect harmony between the sovereignty of God and the responsibility of the creature. Many have most foolishly said that it is quite impossible to show where Divine sovereignty ends and creature accountability begins. Here is where creature responsibility begins: in the sovereign ordination of the Creator. As to His sovereignty, there is not and never will be any "end" to it!

Let us give further proofs that the responsibility of the creature is based upon God's sovereignty. How many things are recorded in Scripture which were right because God commanded them, and which would not have been right had He not so commanded! What right had Adam to "eat" of the trees of the Garden? The permission of his Maker (Gen. 2:16), without such, he had been a thief! What right had Israel to "borrow" of the Egyptians' jewels and raiment (Ex. 12:35)? None, unless Jehovah had authorized it (Ex. 3:22). What right had Israel to slay so many lambs for sacrifice? None, except that God commanded it. What right had Israel to kill off all the Canaanites? None, save as Jehovah had bidden them. What right has the husband to require submission from his wife? None, unless God had appointed it. And so we might go on. Human responsibility is based upon Divine sovereignty.

One more example of the exercise of God's absolute sovereignty. God placed His elect upon a different footing from Adam or Israel. He placed them upon an unconditional footing. In the Everlasting Covenant Jesus Christ was appointed their Head, took their responsibilities upon Himself, and wrought out a righteousness for them which is perfect, indefeasible, eternal. Christ was placed upon a conditional footing, for He was "made under the law, to redeem them that were under the law," only with this infinite difference: the others failed, He did not and could not. And who placed Christ upon that conditional footing? The Triune God. It was sovereign will that appointed Him, sovereign love that sent Him, sovereign authority that assigned Him His work.

Certain conditions were set before the Mediator. He was to be made in the likeness of sin's flesh; He was to magnify the law and make it honorable; He was to bear all the sins of all God's people in His own body on the tree; He was to make full, atonement for them; He was to endure the outpoured wrath of God; He was to die and be buried. On the fulfillment of those conditions He was promised a reward: Isaiah 53:10-12. He was to be the Firstborn among many brethren; He was to have a people who should share His glory. Blessed be His name forever, He fulfilled those conditions, and because He did so, the Father stands pledged, on solemn oath, to preserve through time and bless throughout eternity every one of those for whom His incarnate Son mediated. Because He took their place, they now share His. His righteousness is theirs, His standing before God is theirs, His life is theirs. There is not a single condition for them to meet, not a single responsibility for them to discharge in order to attain their eternal bliss. "By one offering He hath perfected forever them that are set apart" (Heb. 10:14).

Here then is the sovereignty of God openly displayed before all, displayed in the different ways in which He has dealt with His creatures. Part of the angels, Adam, Israel, were placed upon a conditional footing, continuance in blessing being made dependent upon their obedience and fidelity to God. But in sharp contrast from them, the "little flock" (Luke 12:32), have been given an unconditional, an immutable standing in God's covenant, God's counsels, God's Son; their blessing being made dependent upon what Christ did for them. "The foundation of God standeth sure, having this seal: The Lord knoweth them that are His" (2 Tim. 1:19). The foundation on which God's elect stand is a perfect one: nothing can be added to it, nor anything taken from it (Eccl. 3:14). Here, then, is the highest and grandest display of the absolute sovereignty of God. Verily, He has "mercy on whom He will have mercy, and, whom He will He hardeneth" (Rom. 9:18).

The Immutability of God

This is one of the Divine perfections which is not sufficiently pondered. It is one of the excellencies of the Creator which distinguishes Him from all His creatures. God is perpetually the same: subject to no change in His being, attributes, or determinations. Therefore God is compared to a rock (Deut 32:4, etc.) which remains immovable, when the entire ocean surrounding it is continually in a fluctuating state; even so, though all creatures are subject to change, God is immutable. Because God has no beginning and no ending, He can know no change. He is everlastingly "the Father of lights, with whom is no variableness, neither shadow of turning" (Jas. 1:17).

First, God is immutable in His essence. His nature and being are infinite, and so, subject to no mutations. There never was a time when He was not; there never will come a time when He shall cease to be. God has neither evolved, grown, nor improved. All that He is today, He has ever been, and ever will be. "I am the Lord, I change not" (Mal. 3:6) is His own unqualified affirmation. He cannot change for the better, for He is already perfect; and being perfect, He cannot change for the worse. Altogether unaffected by anything outside Himself, improvement or deterioration is impossible. He is perpetually the same. He only can say, "I am that I am" (Ex. 3:14). He is altogether uninfluenced by the flight of time. There is no wrinkle upon the brow of eternity. Therefore His power can never diminish nor His glory ever fade.

Secondly, God is immutable in His attributes. Whatever the attributes of God were before the universe was called into existence, they are precisely the same now, and will remain so forever. Necessarily so; for they are the very perfections, the essential qualities of His being. Semper idem (always the same) is written across every one of them. His power is unabated, His wisdom undiminished, His holiness unsullied. The attributes of God can no more change than Deity can cease to be. His veracity is immutable, for His Word is "forever settled in heaven" (Ps. 119:89). His love is eternal: "I have loved thee with an everlasting love" (Jer. 31:3) and "Having loved His own which were in the world, He loved them unto the end" (John 13:1). His mercy ceases not, for it is "everlasting" (Ps. 100:5).

Thirdly, God is immutable in His counsel. His will never varies. Perhaps some are ready to object that we ought to read the following: "And it repented the Lord that He had made man" (Gen. 6:6). Our first reply is, Then do the Scriptures contradict themselves? No, that cannot be. Numbers 23:19 is plain enough: "God is not a man, that He should lie; neither the son of man, that He should repent." So also in 1 Samuel 15:19, "The strength of Israel will not lie nor repent: for He is not a man, that He should repent." The explanation is very simple. When speaking of Himself, God frequently accommodates His language to our limited capacities. He describes Himself as clothed with bodily members, as eyes, ears, hands, etc. He speaks of Himself as "waking" (Ps. 78:65), as "rising early" (Jer. 7:13); yet He neither slumbers nor sleeps. When He institutes a change in His dealings with men, He describes His course of conduct as "repenting."

Yes, God is immutable in His counsel. "The gifts and calling of God are without repentance" (Rom. 11:29). It must be so, for "He is in one mind, and who can turn Him? and what His soul desireth, even that He doeth" (Job 23:13). Change and decay in all around we see, may He who changeth not abide with thee. God's purpose never alters. One of two things causes a man to change his mind and reverse his plans: want of foresight to anticipate everything, or lack of power to execute them. But as God is both omniscient and omnipotent there is never any need for Him to revise His decrees. No. "The counsel of the Lord standeth forever, the thoughts of His heart to all generations" (Ps. 33:11). Therefore do we read of "the immutability of His counsel" (Heb. 6:17).

Herein we may perceive the infinite distance which separates the highest creature from the Creator. Creaturehood and mutability are correlative terms. If the creature was not mutable by nature, it would not be a creature; it would be God. By nature we tend to nothing, as we came from nothing. Nothing stays our annihilation but the will and sustaining power of God. None can sustain himself a single moment. We are entirely dependent on the Creator for every breath we draw. We gladly own with the Psalmist Thou "holdest our soul in life" (Ps. 66:9). The realization of this ought to make us lie down under a sense of our own nothingness in the presence of Him "in Whom we live and move, and have our being" (Acts 17:28).

As fallen creatures we are not only mutable, but everything in us is opposed to God. As such we are "wandering stars" (Jude 13), out of our proper orbit. The wicked are "like the troubled sea, when it cannot rest" (Isa. 57:20). Fallen man is inconstant. The words of Jacob concerning Reuben apply with full force to all of Adam's descendants: "unstable as water" (Gen. 49:4). Thus it is not only a mark of piety, but also the part of wisdom to heed that injunction, "cease ye from man" (Isa. 2:22). No human being is to be depended on. "Put not your trust in princes, in the son of man, in whom is no help" (Ps. 146:3). If I disobey God, then I deserve to be deceived and disappointed by my fellows. People who like you today, may hate you tomorrow. The multitude who cried "Hosanna to the Son of David," speedily changed to "Away with Him, Crucify Him."

Herein is solid comfort. Human nature cannot be relied upon; but God can! However unstable I may be, however fickle my friends may prove, God changes not. If He varied as we do, if He willed one thing today and another tomorrow, if He were controlled by caprice, who could confide in Him? But, all praise to His glorious name, He is ever the same. His purpose is fixed, His will stable, His word is sure. Here then is a rock on which we may fix our feet, while the mighty torrent is sweeping away everything around us. The permanence of God's character guarantees the fulfillment of His promises: "For the mountains shall depart, and the hills be removed; but my kindness shall not depart from thee, neither shall the covenant of My peace be removed, saith the Lord that hath mercy on thee" (Isa. 54:10).

Herein is encouragement to prayer: "What comfort would it be to pray to a god that, like the chameleon, changed color every moment? Who would put up a petition to an earthly prince that was so mutable as to grant a petition one day, and deny it another?" (S. Charnock,

1670). Should someone ask, But what is the use of praying to One whose will is already fixed? We answer, Because He so requires it. What blessings has God promised without our seeking them? "If we ask anything according to His will, He heareth us" (1 John 5:14), and He has willed everything that is for His child's good. To ask for anything contrary to His will is not prayer, but rank rebellion.

Herein is terror for the wicked. Those who defy Him, break His laws, have no concern for His glory, but live their lives as though He existed not, must not suppose that, when at the last they shall cry to Him for mercy, He will alter His will, revoke His word, and rescind His awful threatenings. No, He has declared, "Therefore will I also deal in fury: Mine eye shall not spare, neither will I have pity: and though they cry in Mine ears with a loud voice, yet will I not hear them" (Ezek. 8:18). God will not deny Himself to gratify their lusts. God is holy, unchangingly so. Therefore God hates sin, eternally hates it. Hence the eternality of the punishment of all who die in their sins.

The Divine immutability, like the cloud which interposed between the Israelites and the Egyptian army, has a dark as well as a light side. It insures the execution of His threatenings, as well as the performance of His promises; and destroys the hope which the guilty fondly cherish, that He will be all lenity to His frail and erring creatures, and that they will be much more lightly dealt with than the declarations of His own Word would lead us to expect. We oppose to these deceitful and presumptuous speculations the solemn truth, that God is unchanging in veracity and purpose, in faithfulness and justice. (J. Dick, 1850).

The Holiness of God

"Who shall not fear Thee, O Lord, and glorify Thy name? for Thou only art holy" (Rev. 15:4). He only is independently, infinitely, immutably holy. In Scripture He is frequently styled "The Holy One": He is so because the sum of all moral excellency is found in Him. He is absolute Purity, unsullied even by the shadow of sin. "God is light, and in Him is no darkness at all" (1 John 1:5). Holiness is the very excellency of the Divine nature: the great God is "glorious in holiness" (Ex. 15:11). Therefore do we read, "Thou art of purer eyes than to behold evil, and canst not look on iniquity" (Hab. 1:13). As God's power is the opposite of the native weakness of the creature, as His wisdom is in complete contrast from the least defect of understanding or folly, so His holiness is the very antithesis of all moral blemish or defilement. Of old God appointed singers in Israel "that they should praise for the beauty of holiness" (2 Chron. 20:21). "Power is God's hand or arm, omniscience His eye, mercy His bowels, eternity His duration, but holiness is His beauty" (S. Charnock). It is this, supremely, which renders Him lovely to those who are delivered from sin's dominion.

A chief emphasis is placed upon this perfection of God: God is oftener styled Holy than almighty, and set forth by this part of His dignity more than by any other. This is more fixed on as an epithet to His name than any other. You never find it expressed 'His mighty name' or 'His wise name,' but His great name, and most of all, His holy name. This is the greatest title of honour; in this latter doth the majesty and venerableness of His name appear (S. Charnock).

This perfection, as none other, is solemnly celebrated before the Throne of Heaven, the seraphim crying, "Holy, holy, holy, is the Lord of hosts" (Isa. 6:3). God Himself singles out this perfection, "Once have

I sworn by Thy holiness" (Ps. 89:35). God swears by His holiness because that is a fuller expression of Himself than anything else. Therefore are we exhorted, "Sing unto the Lord, O ye saints of His, and give thanks at the remembrance of His holiness" (Ps. 30:4). "This may be said to be a transcendental attribute, that, as it were, runs through the rest, and casts luster upon them. It is an attribute of attributes" (J. Howe, 1670). Thus we read of "the beauty of the Lord" (Ps. 27:4), which is none other than "the beauty of holiness" (Ps. 110:3).

As it seems to challenge an excellency above all His other perfections, so it is the glory of all the rest; as it is the glory of the Godhead, so it is the glory of every perfection in the Godhead; as His power is the strength of them, so His holiness is the beauty of them; as all would be weak without almightiness to back them, so all would be uncomely without holiness to adorn them. Should this be sullied, all the rest would lose their honour; as at the same instant the sun should lose its light, it would lose its heat, its strength, its generative and quickening virtue. As sincerity is the luster of every grace in a Christian, so is purity the splendor of every attribute in the Godhead. His justice is a holy justice, His wisdom a holy wisdom, His arm of power a "holy arm" (Ps. 98:1), His truth or promise a "holy promise" (Ps. 105:42). His name, which signifies all His attributes in conjunction, "is holy," Psalm 103:1 (S. Charnock).

God's holiness is manifested in His works. "The Lord is righteous in all His ways, and holy in all His works" (Ps. 145:17). Nothing but that which is excellent can proceed from Him. Holiness is the rule of all His actions. At the beginning He pronounced all that He made "very good" (Gen. 1:31), which He could not have done had there been anything imperfect or unholy in them. Man was made "upright" (Eccl. 7:29), in the image and likeness of his Creator. The angels that fell were created holy, for we are told that they "kept not their first habitation" (Jude 6). Of Satan it is written, "Thou wast perfect in thy ways from the day that thou wast created, till iniquity was found in thee" (Ezek. 28:15).

God's holiness is manifested in His law. That law forbids sin in all of its modifications: in its most refined as well as its grossest forms, the intent of the mind as well as the pollution of the body, the secret desire as well as the overt act. Therefore do we read, The law is holy, and "the commandment holy, and just, and good" (Rom. 7:12). Yes, "the commandment of the Lord is pure, enlightening the eyes. The fear of the Lord is clean, enduring forever: the judgments of the Lord are true and righteous altogether" (Ps. 19:8, 9).

God's holiness is manifested at the Cross. Wondrously and yet most solemnly does the Atonement display God's infinite holiness and abhorrence of sin. How hateful must sin be to God for Him to punish it to its utmost deserts when it was imputed to His Son!

Not all the vials of judgment that have or shall be poured out upon the wicked world, nor the flaming furnace of a sinner's conscience, nor the irreversible sentence pronounced against the rebellious demons, nor the groans of the damned creatures, give such a demonstration of God's hatred of sin, as the wrath of God let loose upon His Son. Never did Divine holiness appear more beautiful and lovely than at the time our Saviour's countenance was most marred in the midst of His dying groans. This Himself acknowledges in Psa. 22. When God had turned His smiling face from Him, and thrust His sharp knife into His heart, which forced that terrible cry from Him, "My God, My God, why hast Thou forsaken Me?" He adores this perfection—"Thou art holy," v. 3 (S. Charnock).

Because God is holy He hates all sin. He loves everything which is in conformity to His laws, and loathes everything which is contrary to it. His Word plainly declares, "The froward is an abomination to the Lord" (Prov. 3:32). And again, "The thoughts of the wicked are an abomination to the Lord" (Prov. 15:26). It follows, therefore, that He must necessarily punish sin. Sin can no more exist without demanding His punishment than without requiring His hatred of it. God has often forgiven sinners, but He never forgives sin; and the sinner is only forgiven on the ground of Another having borne his punishment; for "without shedding of blood is no remission" (Heb. 9:22). Therefore we are told, "The Lord will, take vengeance on His adversaries, and He reserveth Wrath for His enemies" (Nahum 1:2). For one sin God banished our first parents from Eden. For one sin all the posterity of Ham fell under a curse which remains over them to this day (Gen. 9:21). For one sin Moses was excluded from Canaan, Elisha's servant smitten with leprosy, Ananias and Sapphira cut off out of the land of the living.

Herein we find proof for the Divine inspiration of the Scriptures. The unregenerate do not really believe in the holiness of God. Their conception of His character is altogether one-sided. They fondly hope that His mercy will override everything else. "Thou thoughtest that I was altogether as thyself" (Ps. 50:21) is God's charge against them. They think only of a "god" patterned after their own evil hearts. Hence their continuance in a course of mad folly. Such is the holiness ascribed to the Divine nature and character in Scripture that it clearly demonstrates their superhuman origin. The character attributed to the "gods" of the ancients and of modern heathendom are the very reverse of that immaculate purity which pertains to the true God. An ineffably holy God, who has the utmost abhorrence of all sin, was never invented by any of Adam's fallen descendants! The fact is that nothing makes more manifest the terrible depravity of man's heart and his enmity against the living God than to have set before him One who is infinitely and immutably holy. His own idea of sin is practically limited to what the world calls "crime." Anything short of that, man palliates as "defects," "mistakes," "infirmities," etc. And even where sin is owned at all, excuses and extenuations are made for it.

The "god" which the vast majority of professing Christians "love," is looked upon very much like an indulgent old man, who himself has no relish for folly, but leniently winks at the "indiscretions" of youth. But the Word says, "Thou hatest all workers of iniquity "(Ps. 5:5). And again, "God is angry with the wicked every day" (Ps. 7:11). But men refuse to believe in this God, and gnash their teeth when His hatred of sin is faithfully pressed upon their attention. No, sinful man was no more likely to devise a holy God than to create the Lake of fire in which he will be tormented for ever and ever.

Because God is holy, acceptance with Him on the ground of creature doings is utterly impossible. A fallen creature could sooner create a world than produce that which would meet the approval of infinite Purity. Can darkness dwell with Light? Can the Immaculate One take pleasure in "filthy rags" (Isa. 64:6)? The best that sinful man brings forth is defiled. A corrupt tree cannot bear good fruit. God would deny

Himself, vilify His perfections, were He to account as righteous and holy that which is not so in itself; and nothing is so which has the least stain upon it contrary to the nature of God. But blessed be His name, that which His holiness demanded His grace has provided in Christ Jesus our Lord. Every poor sinner who has fled to Him for refuge stands "accepted in the Beloved" (Eph. 1:6). Hallelujah!

Because God is holy the utmost reverence becomes our approaches unto Him. "God is greatly to be feared in the assembly of the saints, and to be had in reverence of all about Him" (Ps. 89:7). Then "Exalt ye the Lord our God, and worship at His footstool; He is holy" (Ps. 99:5). Yes, "at His footstool," in the lowest posture of humility, prostrate before Him. When Moses would approach unto the burning bush, God said, "put off thy shoes from off thy feet" (Ex. 3:5). He is to be served "with fear" (Ps. 2:11). Of Israel His demand was, "I will be sanctified in them that come nigh Me, and before all the people I will be glorified" (Lev. 10:3). The more our hearts are awed by His ineffable holiness, the more acceptable will be our approaches unto Him.

Because God is holy we should desire to be conformed to Him. His command is, "Be ye holy, for I am holy" (1 Pet. 1:16). We are not bidden to be omnipotent or omniscient as God is, but we are to be holy, and that "in all manner of deportment" (1 Pet. 1:15).

This is the prime way of honoring God. We do not so glorify God by elevated admiration, or eloquent expressions, or pompous services of Him, as when we aspire to a conversing with Him with unstained spirits, end live to Him in living like Him (S. Charnock).

Then as God alone is the Source and Fount of holiness, let us earnestly seek holiness from Him; let our daily prayer be that He may "sanctify us wholly; and our whole spirit and soul and body be preserved blameless unto the coming of our Lord Jesus Christ" (1 Thess. 5:23).

The Power of God

We cannot have a right conception of God unless we think of Him as all-powerful, as well as all-wise. He who cannot do what he will and perform all his pleasure cannot be God. As God hath a will to resolve what He deems good, so has He power to execute His will.

The power of God is that ability and strength whereby He can bring to pass whatsoever He pleases, whatsoever His infinite wisdom may direct, and whatsoever the infinite purity of His will may resolve. . . . As holiness is the beauty of all God's attributes, so power is that which gives life and action to all the perfections of the Divine nature. How vain would be the eternal counsels, if power did not step in to execute them. Without power His mercy would be but feeble pity, His promises an empty sound, His threatenings a mere scarecrow. God's power is like Himself: infinite, eternal, incomprehensible; it can neither be checked, restrained, nor frustrated by the creature. (S. Charnock).

"God hath spoken once; twice have I heard this, that power belongeth unto God" (Ps. 62:11). "God hath spoken once": nothing more is necessary! Heaven and earth shall pass away, but His word abideth forever. God hath spoken once: how befitting His Divine majesty! We poor mortals may speak often and yet fail to be heard. He speaks but once and the thunder of His power is heard on a thousand hills. "The Lord also thundered in the heavens, and the Highest gave His voice; hailstones and coals of fire. Yea, He sent out His arrows, and scattered them; and He shot out lightnings, and discomfited them. Then the channels of waters were seen and the foundations of the world were discovered at Thy rebuke, O Lord, at the blast of the breath of Thy nostrils" (Ps. 18:13-15).

"God hath spoken once": behold His unchanging authority. "For who in the heaven can be compared unto the Lord? who among the sons of

The Holy Spirit 253

the mighty can be likened unto the Lord?" (Ps. 89:6). "And all the inhabitants of the earth are reputed as nothing: and He doeth according to His will in the army of heaven, and among the inhabitants of the earth: and none can stay His hand, or say unto Him, What dost Thou?" (Dan. 4:35). This was openly displayed when God became incarnate and tabernacled among men. To the leper He said, "I Will, be thou clean, and immediately his leprosy was cleansed" (Matt. 8:3). To one who had lain in the grave four days He cried, "Lazarus, come forth," and the dead came forth. The stormy wind and the angry wave were hushed at a single word from Him. A legion of demons could not resist His authoritative command.

"Power belongeth unto God," and to Him alone. Not a creature in the entire universe has an atom of power save what God delegates. But God's power is not acquired, nor does it depend upon any recognition by any other authority. It belongs to Him inherently.

God's power is like Himself, self-existent, self-sustained. The mightiest of men cannot add so much as a shadow of increased power to the Omnipotent One. He sits on no buttressed throne and leans on no assisting arm. His court is not maintained by His courtiers, nor does it borrow its splendor from His creatures. He is Himself the great central source and Originator of all power (C. H. Spurgeon).

Not only does all creation bear witness to the great power of God, but also to His entire independency of all created things. Listen to His own challenge: "Where wast thou when I laid the foundations of the earth? declare, if thou hast understanding. Who hath laid the measures thereof, if thou knowest? or who hath stretched the line upon it? Whereupon are the foundations thereof fastened or who laid the cornerstone thereof?" (Job 38:4-6). How completely is the pride of man laid in the dust!

Power is also used as a name of God, the Son of man sitting at the right hand of power (Mark 14:62), that is, at the right hand of God. God and power are so inseparable that they are reciprocated. As His essence is immense, not to be confined in place; as it is eternal, not to be measured in time; so it is almighty, not to be limited in regard of action (S. Charnock).

"Lo, these are parts of His ways:" but how little a portion is heard of Him? but the thunder of His power who can understand? (Job 26:14). Who is able to count all the monuments of His power? Even that which is displayed of His might in the visible creation is utterly beyond our powers of comprehension, still less are we able to conceive of omnipotence itself. There is infinitely more power lodged in the nature of God than is expressed in all His works.

"Parts of His ways" we behold in creation, providence, redemption, but only a "little part" of His might is seen in them. Remarkably is this brought out in Habakkuk 3:4: "and there was the hiding of His power." It is scarcely possible to imagine anything more grandiloquent than the imagery of this whole chapter, yet nothing in it surpasses the nobility of this statement. The prophet (in vision) beheld the mighty God scattering the hills and overturning the mountains, which one would think afforded an amazing demonstration of His power Nay, says our verse, that is rather the "hiding" than the displaying of His power. What is meant? This: so inconceivable, so immense, so uncontrollable is the power of Deity, that the fearful convulsions which He works in nature conceal more than they reveal of His infinite might!

It is very beautiful to link together the following passages: "He walketh upon the waves of the sea" (Job 9:8), which expresses God's uncontrollable power. "He walketh in the circuit of Heaven" (Job 22:14), which tells of the immensity of His presence. "He walketh upon the wings of the wind" (Ps. 104:3), which signifies the amazing swiftness of His operations. This last expression is very remarkable. It is not that "He flieth," or "runneth," but that He "walketh" and that, on the very "wings of the wind"—on the most impetuous of the elements, tossed into utmost rage, and sweeping along with almost inconceivable rapidity, yet they are under His feet, beneath His perfect control!

Let us now consider God's power in creation. "The heavens are Thine, the earth also is Thine, as for the world and the fulness thereof, Thou hast founded them. The north and the south Thou hast created them" (Ps. 89:11, 12). Before man can work be must have both tools and materials, but God began with nothing, and by His word alone out of nothing made all things. The intellect cannot grasp it. God "spake and it was done, He commanded and it stood fast" (Ps. 33:9). Primeval matter heard His voice. "God said, Let there be...and it was so" (Gen. 1). Well may we exclaim, "Thou hast a mighty arm: strong is Thy hand, high is Thy right hand" (Ps. 89:13).

Who, that looks upward to the midnight sky; and, with an eye of reason, beholds its rolling wonders; who can forbear inquiring, Of what were their mighty orbs formed? Amazing to relate, they were produced without materials. They sprung from emptiness itself. The stately fabric of universal nature emerged out of nothing. What instruments were used by the Supreme Architect to fashion the parts with such exquisite niceness, and give so beautiful a polish to the whole? How was it all connected into one finely-proportioned and nobly finished structure? A bare fiat accomplished all. Let them be, said God. He added no more; and at once the marvelous edifice arose, adorned with every beauty, displaying innumerable perfections, and declaring amidst enraptured seraphs its great Creator's praise. "By the word of the Lord were the heavens made, and all the host of them by the breath of His mouth," Psa. 150:1 (James Hervey, 1789).

Consider God's power in preservation. No creature has power to preserve itself. "Can the rush grow up without mire? can the flag grow up without water?" (Job 8:11). Both man and beast would perish if there were not herbs for food, and herbs would wither and die if the earth were not refreshed with fruitful showers. Therefore is God called the Preserver of "man and beast" (Ps. 36:6). "He upholdeth all things by the word of His power" (Heb 1:3). What a marvel of Divine power is the prenatal life of every human being! That an infant can live at all, and for so many months, in such cramped and filthy quarters, and that without breathing, is unaccountable without the power of God. Truly He "holdeth our soul in life" (Ps. 66:9).

The preservation of the earth from the violence of the sea is another plain instance of God's might. How is that raging element kept pent within those limits wherein He first lodged it, continuing its channel, without overflowing the earth and dashing in pieces the lower part of the creation? The natural situation of the water is to be above the earth, because it is lighter, and to be immediately under the air, because it is heavier. Who restrains the natural quality of it? certainly man does not, and cannot. It is the flat of its Creator which alone bridles it: And said, "Hitherto shalt thou come, but no further: and here shall thy proud waves be stayed" (Job 38:11). What a standing monument of the power of God is the preservation of the world!

Consider God's power in government. Take His restraining the malice of Satan. "The devil, as a roaring lion, walketh about, seeking whom he may devour" (1 Pet. 5:8). He is filled with hatred against God, and with fiendish enmity against men, particularly the saints. He that envied Adam in paradise, envies us the pleasure of enjoying any of God's blessings. Could he have his will, he would treat all the same way he treated Job: he would send fire from heaven on the fruits of the earth, destroying the cattle, cause a wind to overthrow our houses, and cover our bodies with boils. But, little as men may realize it, God bridles him to a large extent, prevents him from carrying out his evil designs, and confines him within His ordinations.

So too God restrains the natural corruption of men. He suffers sufficient outbreakings of sin to show what fearful havoc has been wrought by man's apostasy from his Maker, but who can conceive the frightful lengths to which men would go were God to remove His curbing hand? "Their mouth is full of cursing and bitterness their feet are swift to shed blood" (Rom. 3). This is the nature of every descendant of Adam. Then what unbridled licentiousness and headstrong folly would triumph in the world, if the power of God did not interpose to lock down the floodgates of it! See Psalm 93:3,4.

Consider God's power in judgment. When He smites, none can resist Him: see Ezekiel 22:14. How terribly this was exemplified at the Flood! God opened the windows of heaven and broke up the great fountains of the deep, and (excepting those in the ark) the entire human race, helpless before the storm of His wrath, was swept away. A shower of fire and brimstone from heaven, and the cities of the plain were exterminated. Pharaoh and all his hosts were impotent when God blew upon them at the Red Sea. What a terrific word is that in Romans 9:22: "What if God, willing to show wrath, and to make His power known, endured with much long-suffering the vessels of wrath fitted to destruction." God is going to display His mighty power upon the reprobate not merely by incarcerating them in Gehenna, but by supernaturally preserving their bodies as well as souls amid the eternal burnings of the Lake of Fire.

Well may all tremble before such a God! To treat with impunity One who can crush us more easily than we can a moth, is a suicidal policy. To openly defy Him who is clothed with omnipotence, who can rend us in pieces or cast into Hell any moment He pleases, is the very height of insanity. To put it on its lowest ground, it is but the part of wisdom to heed His command, "Kiss the Son. lest He be angry, and ye perish from the way, when His wrath is kindled but a little" (Ps. 2:12).

Well may the enlightened soul adore such a God! The wondrous and infinite perfections of such a Being call for fervent worship. If men of might and renown claim the admiration of the world, how much more should the power of the Almighty fill us with wonderment and homage. "Who is like unto Thee, O Lord, among the who is like Thee, glorious in holiness, fearful in praises, doing wonders?" (Ex. 15:11).

Well may the saint trust such a God! He is worthy of implicit confidence. Nothing is too hard for Him. If God were stinted in might and had a limit to His strength we might well despair. But seeing that He is clothed with omnipotence, no prayer is too hard for Him to answer, no need too great for Him to supply, no passion too strong for Him to subdue; no temptation too powerful for Him to deliver from, no misery too deep for Him to relieve. "The Lord is the strength of my life; of whom shall I be afraid?" (Ps. 27:1). "Now unto Him that is able to do exceeding abundantly above all that we ask or think, according to the power that worketh in us, unto Him be glory in the church by Christ Jesus throughout all ages, world without end. Amen" (Eph. 3:20,21).

The Faithfulness of God

Unfaithfulness is one of the most outstanding sins of these evil days. In the business world, a man's word is, with exceedingly rare exceptions, no longer his bond. In the social world, marital infidelity abounds on every hand, the sacred bonds of wedlock being broken with as little regard as the discarding of an old garment. In the ecclesiastical realm, thousands who have solemnly covenanted to preach the truth make no scruple to attack and deny it. Nor can reader or writer claim complete immunity from this fearful sin: in how many ways have we been unfaithful to Christ, and to the light and privileges which God has entrusted to us! How refreshing, then, how unspeakably blessed, to lift our eyes above this scene of ruin, and behold One who is faithful, faithful in all things, faithful at all times.

"Know therefore that the Lord thy God, He is God, the faithful God" (Deut. 7:9). This quality is essential to His being, without it He would not be God. For God to be unfaithful would be to act contrary to His nature, which were impossible: "If we believe not, yet He abideth faithful; He cannot deny Himself" (2 Tim. 2:13). Faithfulness is one of the glorious perfections of His being. He is as it were clothed with it: "O Lord God of hosts, who is a strong Lord like unto Thee? or to Thy faithfulness round about Thee?" (Ps. 89:8). So too when God became incarnate it was said, "Righteousness shall be the girdle of His loins, and faithfulness the girdle of His reins" (Isa. 11:5).

What a word is that in Psalm 36:5, Thy mercy, "O Lord, is in the heavens; and Thy faithfulness unto the clouds." Far above all finite comprehension is the unchanging faithfulness of God. Everything about God is great, vast, incomparable. He never forgets, never fails, never falters, never forfeits His word. To every declaration of promise or prophecy the Lord has exactly adhered, every engagement of covenant or threatening He will make good, for "God is not a man, that He should lie; neither the son of man, that He should repent: hath He said, and shall He not do it? or hath He spoken, and shall He not make it good?" (Num. 23:19). Therefore does the believer exclaim, "His compassions fail not, they are new every morning: great is Thy faithfulness" (Lam. 3:22, 23).

Scripture abounds in illustrations of God's faithfulness. More than four thousand years ago He said, "While the earth remaineth, seedtime and harvest, and cold and heat, and summer and winter, and day and night shall not cease" (Gen. 8:22). Every year that comes furnishes a fresh witness to God's fulfillment of this promise. In Genesis 15 we find that Jehovah declared unto Abraham, "Thy seed shall be a stranger in a land that is not theirs, and shall serve them. . . . But in the fourth generation they shall come hither again" (vv. 13-16). Centuries ran their weary course. Abraham's descendants groaned amid the brick-kilns of Egypt. Had God forgotten His promise? No, indeed. Read Exodus 12:41, "And it came to pass at the end of the four hundred and thirty years, even the selfsame day it came to pass, that all the hosts of the Lord went out from the land of Egypt." Through Isaiah the Lord declared, "Behold, a virgin shall conceive, and bear a son, and shall call His name Immanuel" (7:14). Again centuries passed, but "When the fulness of the time was come, God sent forth His Son, made of a woman" (Gal 4:4).

God is true. His Word of Promise is sure. In all His relations with His people God is faithful. He may be safely relied upon. No one ever yet really trusted Him in vain. We find this precious truth expressed almost everywhere in the Scriptures, for His people need to know that faithfulness is an essential part of the Divine character. This is the basis of our confidence in Him. But it is one thing to accept the faithfulness of God as a Divine truth, it is quite another to act upon it. God has given us many "exceeding great and precious promises," but are we really counting on His fulfillment of them? Are we actually expecting Him to do for us all that He has said? Are we resting with implicit assurance on these words, "He is faithful that promised" (Heb. 10:23)?

There are seasons in the lives of all when it is not easy, no not even for Christians, to believe that God is faithful. Our faith is sorely tried, our eyes bedimmed with tears, and we can no longer trace the outworkings of His love. Our ears are distracted with the noises of the world, harassed by the atheistic whisperings of Satan, and we can no longer hear the sweet accents of His still small voice. Cherished plans have been thwarted, friends on whom we relied have failed us, a profest brother or sister in Christ has betrayed us. We are staggered. We sought to be faithful to God, and now a dark cloud hides Him from us. We find it difficult, yea, impossible, for carnal reason to harmonize His frowning providence with His gracious promises. Ah, faltering soul, severely-tried fellow-pilgrim, seek grace to heed Isaiah 50:10, "Who is among you that feareth the Lord, that obeyeth the voice of His servant, that walketh in darkness and hath no light? let him trust in the name of the Lord, and stay upon his God."

When you are tempted to doubt the faithfulness of God, cry out, "Get thee hence, Satan." Though you cannot now harmonize God's mysterious dealings with the avowals of His love, wait on Him for more light. In His own good time He will make it plain to you. "What I do thou knowest not now, but thou shalt know hereafter" (John 13:7). The sequel will yet demonstrate that God has neither forsaken nor deceived His child. "And therefore will the Lord wait that He may be gracious unto you, and therefore will He be exalted, that He may have mercy upon you: for the Lord is a God of judgment: blessed are all they that wait for Him" (Isa. 30:18).

"Judge not the Lord by feeble sense,
But trust Him for His grace,
Behind a frowning providence
He hides a smiling face.
Ye fearful saints fresh courage take,
The clouds ye so much dread,
Are rich with mercy, and shall break
In blessing o'er your head."

"Thy testimonies which Thou hast commanded are righteous and very faithful" (Ps. 119:138). God has not only told us the best, but He has not withheld the worst. He has faithfully described the ruin which the Fall has effected. He has faithfully diagnosed the terrible state which sin has produced. He has faithfully made known his inveterate hatred of evil, and that He must punish the same. He has faithfully warned us that He is "a consuming fire" (Heb. 12:29). Not only does His Word abound in illustrations of His fidelity in fulfilling His promises, but it also records numerous examples of His faithfulness in making good His threatenings. Every stage of Israel's history exemplifies that solemn fact. So it was with individuals: Pharaoh, Korah, Achan and a host of others are so many proofs. And thus it will be with you, my reader: unless you have fled or do flee to Christ for refuge, the everlasting burning of the Lake of Fire will be your sure and certain portion. God is faithful.

God is faithful in preserving His people. "God is faithful, by whom ye are called unto the fellowship of His Son" (1 Cor. 1:9). In the previous verse promise was made that God would confirm unto the end His own people. The Apostle's confidence in the absolute security of believers was founded not on the strength of their resolutions or ability to persevere, but on the veracity of Him that cannot lie. Since God has promised to His Son a certain people for His inheritance, to deliver them from sin and condemnation, and to make them participants of eternal life in glory, it is certain that He will not allow any of them to perish.

God is faithful in disciplining His people. He is faithful in what He withholds, no less than in what He gives. He is faithful in sending sorrow as well as in giving joy. The faithfulness of god is a truth to be confessed by us not only when we are at ease, but also when we are smarting under the sharpest rebuke. Nor must this confession be merely of our mouths, but of our hearts, too. When God smites us with the rod of chastisement, it is faithfulness which wields it. To acknowledge this means that we humble ourselves before Him, own that we fully deserve His correction, and instead of murmuring, thank Him for it. God never afflicts without reason. "For this cause many are weak and sickly among you" (1 Cor. 11:30), says Paul, illustrating this principle. When His rod falls upon us let us say with Daniel, "O Lord, righteousness belongeth unto Thee, but unto us confusion of faces' (9:7)

"I know, O Lord, that Thy judgments are right, and that Thou in faithfulness hast afflicted me" (Ps. 119:15). Trouble and affliction are not only consistent with God's love pledged in the everlasting covenant, but they are parts of the administration of the same. God is not only faithful notwithstanding afflictions, but faithful in sending them. "The will I visit their transgression with the rod, and their iniquity with stripes: My lovingkindness will I not utterly take from him nor suffer My faithfulness to fail" (Ps. 89:32, 33). Chastening is not only reconcilable with God's lovingkindness, but it is the effect and expression of it. It would much quieten the minds of God's people if they would remember that His covenant love binds Him to lay on them seasonable correction. Afflictions are necessary for us: "In their affliction they will seek Me early" (Hos. 5:15)

God is faithful in glorifying His people. "Faithful is He which calleth you, who also will do" (1 Thess. 5:24). The immediate reference here is to the saints being preserved blameless unto the coming of our Lord Jesus Christ. God treats with us not on the ground of our merits (for we have none), but for His own great name's sake. God is constant to Himself and to His own purpose of grace whom He called. . .them He also glorified (Rom. 8:30). God gives a full demonstration of the constancy of His everlasting goodness toward His elect by effectually calling them out of darkness into His marvelous light, and this should fully assure them of the certain continuance of it. The foundation of God standeth sure (2 Tim. 2:19). Paul was resting on the faithfulness of God when he said, I know whom I have believed, and am persuaded that He is able to keep that which I have committed unto Him against that day (2 Tim 1:12).

The apprehension of this blessed truth will preserve us from worry. To be full of care, to view our situation with dark forebodings, to anticipate the morrow with sad anxiety, is to reflect upon the faithfulness of God. He who has cared for His child through all the years, will not forsake him in old age. He who has heard your prayers in the past, will not refuse to supply your need in the present emergency. Rest on Job 5:19, "He shall deliver thee in six troubles: yea, in seven there shall be no evil touch thee."

The apprehension of this blessed truth will check our murmurings. The Lord knows what is best for each of us, and one effect or resting on this truth will be the silencing of our petulant complainings. God is greatly honored when, under trial and chastening, we have good thoughts of Him, vindicate His wisdom and justice, and recognize His love in His very rebukes.

The apprehension of this blessed truth will beget increasing confidence in God. "Wherefore let them that suffer according to the will of God commit the keeping of their souls to Him in well to Him in well doing, as unto a faithful Creator" (1 Pet. 4:19). When we trustfully resign ourselves, and all our affairs into God's hands, fully persuaded of His love and faithfulness, the sooner shall we be satisfied with his providence and realize that "He doeth all things well."

The Goodness of God

"The goodness of God endureth continually" (Ps. 52:1) The "goodness" of God respects the perfection of His nature: "God is light, and in Him is no darkness at all" (1 John 1:5). There is such an absolute perfection in God's nature and being that nothing is wanting to it or defective in it, and nothing can be added to it to make it better.

He is originally good, good of Himself, which nothing else is; for all creatures are good only by participation and communication from God. He is essentially good; not only good, but goodness itself: the creature's good is a superadded quality, in God it is His essence. He is infinitely good; the creature's good is but a drop, but in God there is an infinite ocean or gathering together of good. He is eternally and immutably good, for He cannot be less good than He is; as there can be no addition made to Him, so no subtraction from Him. (Thos. Manton).

God is summum bonum, the chiefest good.

The original Saxon meaning of our English word "God" is "The Good." God is not only the Greatest of all beings, but the Best. All the goodness there is in any creature has been imparted from the Creator, but God's goodness is underived, for it is the essence of His eternal nature. As God is infinite in power from all eternity, before there was any display thereof, or any act of omnipotency put forth; so He was eternally good before there was any communication of His bounty, or any creature to whom it might be imparted or exercised. Thus, the first manifestation of this Divine perfection was in giving being to all things. "Thou art good, and doest good" (Ps. 119:68). God has in Himself an infinite and inexhaustible treasure of all blessedness enough to fill all things.

All that emanates from God—His decrees, His creation, His laws, His providences—cannot be otherwise than good: as it is written. "And

God saw everything that He had made, and, behold, it was very good" (Gen. 1:31). Thus, the "goodness" of God is seen, first, in Creation. The more closely the creature is studied, the more the beneficence of its Creator becomes apparent. Take the highest of God's earthly creatures, man. Abundant reason has he to say with the Psalmist, "I will praise Thee, for I am fearfully and wonderfully made: marvelous are Thy works, and that my soul knoweth right well" (139:14). Everything about the structure of our bodies attests the goodness of their Maker. How suited the bands to perform their allotted work! How good of the Lord to appoint sleep to refresh the wearied body! How benevolent His provision to give unto the eyes lids and brows for their protection! And so we might continue indefinitely.

Nor is the goodness of the Creator confined to man, it is exercised toward all His creatures. "The eyes of all wait upon Thee; and Thou givest them their meat in due season. Thou openest Thine hand, and satisfiest the desire of every living thing" (Ps. 145:15,16). Whole volumes might be written, yea have been, to amplify this fact. Whether it be the birds of the air, the beasts of the forest, or the fish in the sea, abundant provision has been made to supply their every need. God "giveth food to all flesh, for His mercy endureth forever" (Ps. 136:25). Truly, "The earth is full of the goodness of the Lord" (Ps. 33:5).

The goodness of God is seen in the variety of natural pleasures which He has provided for His creatures. God might have been pleased to satisfy our hunger without the food being pleasing to our palates—how His benevolence appears in the varied flavors which He has given to meats, vegetables, and fruits! God has not only given us senses, but also that which gratifies them; and this too reveals His goodness. The earth might have been as fertile as it is without its surface being so delightfully variegated. Our physical lives could have been sustained without beautiful flowers to regale our eyes, and exhale sweet perfumes. We might have walked the fields without our ears being saluted by the music of the birds. Whence, then, this loveliness, this charm, so freely diffused over the face of nature? Verily, "The tender mercies of the Lord are over all His works" (Ps. 145:9).

The goodness of God is seen in that when man transgressed the law of His Creator a dispensation of unmixed wrath did not at once commence. Well might God have deprived His fallen creatures of every blessing, every comfort, every pleasure. Instead, He ushered in a regime of a mixed nature, of mercy and judgment. This is very wonderful if it be duly considered, and the more thoroughly that regime be examined the more will it appear that "mercy rejoiceth against judgment" (Jas. 2:13). Notwithstanding all the evils which attend our fallen state, the balance of good greatly preponderates. With comparatively rare exceptions, men and women experience a far greater number of days of health, than they do of sickness and pain. There is much more creature—happiness than creature—misery in the world. Even our sorrows admit of considerable alleviation, and God has given to the human mind a pliability which adapts itself to circumstances and makes the most of them.

Nor can the benevolence of God be justly called into question because there is suffering and sorrow in the world. If man sins against the goodness of God, if he despises "the riches of His goodness and forbearance and longsuffering," and after the hardness and impenitency of his heart treasurest up unto himself wrath against the day of wrath (Rom 2:5,5), who is to blame but himself? Would God be "good" if He punished not those who ill-use His blessings, abuse His benevolence, and trample His mercies beneath their feet? It will be no reflection upon God's goodness, but rather the brightest exemplification of it, when He shall rid the earth of those who have broken His laws, defied His authority, mocked His messengers, scorned His Son, and persecuted those for whom He died.

The goodness of God appeared most illustriously when He sent forth His Son "made of a woman, made under the law, to redeem them that were under the law, that we might received the adoption of sons" (Gal. 4:4, 5) Then it was that a multitude of the heavenly host praised their Maker and said, "Glory to God in the highest and on earth peace, good-will toward men" (Luke 2:14). Yes, in the Gospel the "grace (Gk. benevolence or goodness) of God that bringeth salvation hath appeared to all men" (Titus 2:11). Nor can God's benignity be called into question because He has not made every sinful creature to be a subject of His redemptive grace. He did not the fallen angels. Had God left all to perish it had been no reflection on His goodness. To any who would challenge this statement we will remind him of our Lord's sovereign prerogative: "Is it not lawful for Me to do what I will with Mine own? Is thine eye evil, because I am good?" (Matt. 20:15).

"O that men would praise the Lord for His goodness, and for His wonderful works to the children of men" (Ps. 107:8). Gratitude is the return justly required from the objects of His beneficence; yet is it often withheld from our great Benefactor simply because His goodness is so constant and so abundant. It is lightly esteemed because it is exercised toward us in the common course of events. It is not felt because we daily experience it. "Despisest thou the riches of His goodness?" (Rom. 2:4). His goodness is "despised" when it is not improved as a means to lead men to repentance, but, on the contrary, serves to harden them from the supposition that God entirely overlooks their sin.

The goodness of God is the life of the believer's trust. It is this excellency in God which most appeals to our hearts. Because His goodness endureth forever, we ought never to be discouraged: "The Lord is good, a stronghold in the day of trouble, and He knoweth them that trust in Him" (Nahum 1:7).

When others behave badly to us, it should only stir us up the more heartily to give thanks unto the Lord, because He is good; and when we ourselves are conscious that we are far from being good, we should only the more reverently bless Him that He is good. We must never tolerate an instant's unbelief as to the goodness of the Lord; whatever else may be questioned, this is absolutely certain, that Jehovah is good; His dispensations may vary, but His nature is always the same. (C. H. Spurgeon).

The Patience of God

Far less has been written upon this than the other excellencies of the Divine character. Not a few of those who have expatiated at length upon the Divine attributes have passed over the patience of God without any comment. It is not easy to suggest a reason for this, for surely the longsuffering of God is as much one of the Divine perfections as His wisdom, power, or holiness, and as much to be admired and revered by us. True, the actual term will not be found in a concordance so frequently as the others, but the glory of this grace itself shines forth on almost every page of Scripture. Certain it is that we lose much if we do not frequently meditate upon the patience of God and earnestly pray that our hearts and ways may be more completely conformed thereto.

Most probably the principal reason why so many writers have failed to give us anything, separately, upon the patience of God was because of the difficulty of distinguishing this attribute from the Divine goodness and mercy, particularly the latter. God's longsuffering is mentioned in conjunction with His grace and mercy again and again, as may be seen by consulting Exodus 34:6, Numbers 14:18, Psalm 86:15, etc. That the patience of God is really a display of His mercy, in fact is one way in which it is frequently manifested, cannot be gainsaid; but that they are one and the same excellency, and are not to be separated, we cannot concede. It may not be easy to discriminate between them, nevertheless, Scripture fully warrants us, in predicating some things of the one which we cannot of the other.

Stephen Charnock, the Puritan, defines God's patience, in part, thus:

It is a part of the Divine goodness and mercy, yet differs from both. God being the greatest goodness, hath the greatest mildness; mildness is always the companion of true goodness, and the greater the goodness, the greater the mildness. Who so holy as Christ, and who so meek?

God's slowness to anger is a branch of His mercy: "the Lord is full of compassion, slow to anger" (Ps. 145:8). It differs from mercy in the formal consideration of the subject: mercy respects the creature as miserable, patience respects the creature as criminal; mercy pities him in his misery, patience bears with the sin which engendered the misery, and giving birth to more.

Personally we would define the Divine patience as that power of control which God exercises over Himself, causing Him to bear with the wicked and forebear so long in punishing them. In Nahum 1:3 we read, "The Lord is slow to anger and great in power," upon which Mr. Charnock said,

> Men that are great in the world are quick in passion, and are not so ready to forgive an injury, or bear with an offender, as one of a meaner rank. It is a want of power over that man's self that makes him do unbecoming things upon a provocation. A prince that can bridle his passions is a king over himself as well as over his subjects. God is slow to anger because great in power. He has no less power over Himself than over His creatures.

It is at the above point, we think, that God's patience is most clearly distinguished from His mercy. Though the creature is benefited thereby, the patience of God chiefly respects Himself, a restraint placed upon His acts by His will; whereas His mercy terminates wholly upon the creature. The patience of God is that excellency which causes Him to sustain great injuries without immediately avenging Himself. He has a power of patience as well as a power of justice. Thus the Hebrew word for the Divine longsuffering is rendered "slow to anger" in Nehemiah 9:17, Psalm 103:8, etc. Not that there are any passions in the Divine nature, but that God's wisdom and will is pleased to act with that stateliness and sobriety which becometh His exalted majesty.

In support of our definition above let us point out that it was to this excellency in the Divine character that Moses appealed, when Israel sinned so grievously at Kadesh-Barnea, and there provoked Jehovah so sorely. Unto His servant the Lord said, I will smite them with the pestilence and disinherit them. Then it was that the typical mediator pleaded, "I beseech Thee let the power of my Lord be great according as Thou hast spoken, saying, The Lord is longsuffering," etc. (Num. 14:17). Thus, His longsuffering is His "power" of self-restraint.

Again, in Romans 9:22 we read, "What if God, willing to show His wrath, and to make His power known, endured with much longsuffering the vessels of wrath fitted to destruction...?" Were God to immediately break these reprobate vessels into pieces, His power of self-control would not so eminently appear; by bearing with their wickedness and forebearing punishment so long, the power of His patience is gloriously demonstrated. True, the wicked interpret His longsuffering quite differently—"Because sentence against an evil work is not executed speedily, therefore the heart of the sons of men is fully set in them to do evil" (Eccl. 8:11)—but the anointed eye adores what they abuse.

"The God of patience" (Rom. 15:5) is one of the Divine titles. Deity is thus denominated, first, because God is both the Author and Object of the grace of patience in the saint. Secondly, because this is what He is in Himself: patience is one of His perfections. Thirdly, as a pattern for us: "Put on therefore, as the elect of God, holy and beloved, bowels of mercy, kindness, humbleness of mind, meekness, longsuffering" (Col. 3:12). And again, "Be ye therefore followers (emulators) of god, as dear children" (Eph. 5:2). When tempted to be disgusted at the dullness of another, or to be revenged on one who has wronged you, call to remembrance God's infinite patience and longsuffering with yourself.

The patience of God is manifested in His dealings with sinners. How strikingly was it displayed toward the antediluvians. When mankind was universally degenerate, and all flesh had corrupted his way, God did not destroy them till He had forewarned them. He "waited" (1 Pet. 3:20), probably no less than one hundred and twenty years (Gen. 6:3), during which time Noah was a "preacher of righteousness" (2 Pet. 2:5). So, later, when the Gentiles not only worshipped and served the creature more than the Creator, but also committed the vilest abominations contrary to even the dictates of nature (Rom. 1:19-26), and hereby filled up the measure of their iniquity; yet, instead of drawing His sword for the extermination of such rebels, God "suffered all nations to walk in their own ways," and gave them "rain from heaven and fruitful seasons"(Acts 14:16, 17).

Marvelously was God's patience exercised and manifested toward Israel. First, He "suffered their manners" for forty years in the wilderness (Acts 13:18). Later, when they had entered Canaan, but followed the evil customs of the nations around them, and turned to idolatry; though God chastened them sorely, He did not utterly destroy them, but in their distress, raised up deliverers for them. When their iniquity was raised to such a height that none but a God of infinite patience, could have borne them, He, notwithstanding, spared them many years before He allowed them to be carried down into Babylon. Finally, when their rebellion against Him reached its climax by crucifying His Son. He waited forty years ere He sent the Romans against them, and that only after they had judged themselves "unworthy of eternal life" (Acts 13:46).

How wondrous is God's patience with the world today. On every side people are sinning with a high hand. The Divine law is trampled under foot and God Himself openly despised. It is truly amazing that He does not instantly strike dead those who so brazenly defy Him. Why does He not suddenly cut off the haughty, infidel and blatant blasphemer, as He did Ananias and Sapphira? Why does He not cause the earth to open its mouth and devour the persecutors of his people, so that, like Dathan and Abiram, they shall go down alive into the Pit? And what of apostate Christendom, where every possible form of sin is now tolerated and practiced under cover of the holy name of Christ? Why does not the righteous wrath of Heaven make an end of such abominations? Only one answer is possible: because God bears with "much longsuffering the vessels of wrath fitted to destruction."

And what of the writer and the reader? Let us review our own lives. It is not long since we followed a multitude to do evil, had no concern for God's glory, and lived only to gratify self. How patiently He bore with our vile conduct! And now that grace has snatched us as brands from the burning, giving us a place in God's family, and begotten us unto an eternal inheritance in glory; how miserably we requite Him. How shallow our gratitude, how tardy our obedience, how frequent our backslidings! One reason why God suffers the flesh to remain in the believer is that He may exhibit His "longsuffering to usward" (2 Pet.

3:9). Since this Divine attribute is manifested only in this world, God takes advantage to display it toward His own.

May our meditation upon this Divine excellency soften our hearts, make our consciences tender, and may we learn in the school of holy experience the "patience of saints," namely, submission to the Divine will and continuance in well doing. Let us earnestly seek grace to emulate this Divine excellency. "Be ye therefore perfect, even as your Father which is in heaven is perfect" (Matt. 5:48): in the immediate context Christ exhorts us to love our enemies, bless them that curse us, do good to them that hate us. God bears long with the wicked notwithstanding the multitude of their sin, and shall we desire to be revenged because of a single injury?

The Grace of God

Grace is a perfection of the Divine character which is exercised only toward the elect. Neither in the Old Testament nor in the New is the grace of God ever mentioned in connection with mankind generally, still less with the lower orders of His creatures. In this it is distinguished from mercy, for the mercy of God is "over all His works" (Ps. 145-9). Grace is the alone source from which flows the goodwill, love, and salvation of God unto His chosen people. This attribute of the Divine character was defined by Abraham Booth in his helpful book, The Reign of Grace thus, "It is the eternal and absolute free favour of God, manifested in the vouchsafement of spiritual and eternal blessings to the guilty and the unworthy."

Divine grace is the sovereign and saving favour of God exercised in the bestowment of blessings upon those who have no merit in them and for which no compensation is demanded from them. Nay, more; it is the favour of God shown to those who not only have no positive deserts of their own, but who are thoroughly ill-deserving and hell-deserving. It is completely unmerited and unsought, and is altogether unattracted by anything in or from or by the objects upon which it is bestowed. Grace can neither be bought, earned, nor won by the creature. If it could be, it would cease to be grace. When a thing is said to be of grace we mean that the recipient has no claim upon it, that it was in nowise due him. It comes to him as pure charity, and, at first, unasked and undesired.

The fullest exposition of the amazing grace of God is to be found in the Epistles of the apostle Paul. In his writings "grace" stands in direct opposition to works and worthiness, all works and worthiness, of whatever kind or degree. This is abundantly clear from Romans 11:6, "And if by grace, then is it no more of works: otherwise grace is no more grace. If it be of works, then is it no more grace, otherwise work is no more work." Grace and works will no more unite than an acid and an alkali. "By grace are ye saved through faith; and that not of yourselves; it is the gift of God: not of works, lest any man should boast" (Eph. 2:8,9). The absolute favour of God can no more consist with human merit than oil and water will fuse into one: see also Romans 4:4,5.

There are three principal characteristics of Divine grace. First, it is eternal. Grace was planned before it was exercised, purposed before it was imparted: "Who hath saved us, and called us with a holy calling, not according to our works, but according to His own purpose and grace, which was given us in Christ Jesus before the world began" (2 Tim. 1:9). Second, it is free, for none did ever purchase it: "Being justified freely by His grace" (Rom. 3:24). Third, it is sovereign, because God exercises it toward and bestows it upon whom He pleases: "Even so might grace reign" (Rom. 5:21). If grace "reigns" then is it on the throne, and the occupant of the throne is sovereign. Hence "the throne of grace" (Heb. 4:16).

Just because grace is unmerited favour, it must be exercised in a sovereign manner. Therefore does the Lord declare, "I will be gracious to whom I will be gracious" (Ex 33:19). Were God to show grace to all of Adam's descendants, men would at once conclude that He was righteously compelled to take them to heaven as a meet compensation for allowing the human race to fall into sin. But the great God is under no obligation to any of His creatures, least of all to those who are rebels against Him.

Eternal life is a gift, therefore it can neither be earned by good works, nor claimed as a right. Seeing that salvation is a "gift," who has any right to tell God on whom He ought to bestow it? It is not that the Giver ever refuses this gift to any who seek it wholeheartedly, and according to the rules which He has prescribed. No! He refuses none who come to Him empty-handed and in the way of His appointing. But if out of a world of impenitent and unbelieving, God is determined to exercise His sovereign right by choosing a limited number to be saved, who is wronged? Is God obliged to force His gift on those who value it not? Is God compelled to save those who are determined to go their own way?

But nothing more riles the natural man and brings to the surface his innate and inveterate enmity against God than to press upon him the eternality, the freeness, and the absolute sovereignty of Divine grace. That God should have formed His purpose from everlasting without in anywise consulting the creature, is too abasing for the unbroken heart. That grace cannot be earned or won by any efforts of man is too self-emptying for self-righteousness. And that grace singles out whom it pleases to be its favored objects, arouses hot protests from haughty rebels. The clay rises up against the Potter and asks, "Why hast Thou made me thus?" A lawless insurrectionist dares to call into question the justice of Divine sovereignty.

The distinguishing grace of God is seen in saving that people whom He has sovereignly singled out to be His high favorites. By "distinguishing" we mean that grace discriminates, makes differences" chooses some and passes by others. It was distinguishing grace which selected Abraham from the midst of his idolatrous neighbors and made him "the friend of God." It was distinguishing grace which saved "publicans and sinners," but said of the religious Pharisees, "Let them alone" (Matt. 15:14). Nowhere does the glory of God's free and sovereign grace shine more conspicuously than in the unworthiness and unlikeness of its objects. Beautifully was this illustrated by James Hervey, (1751):

> Where sin has abounded, says the proclamation from the court of heaven, grace doth much more abound. Manasseh was a monster of barbarity, for he caused his own children to pass through the fire, and filled Jerusalem with innocent blood. Manasseh was an adept in iniquity, for he not only multiplied, and to an extravagant degree, his own sacrilegious impieties, but he poisoned the principles and perverted the manners of his subjects, making them do worse than the most detestable of the heathen idolators: see 2 Chronicles 33. Yet, through this superabundant grace he is humbled, he is reformed, and becomes a child of forgiving love, an heir of immortal glory.
>
> Behold that bitter and bloody persecutor, Saul; when, breathing out threatenings and bent upon slaughter, he worried the lambs and

put to death the disciples of Jesus. The havoc he had committed, the inoffensive families he had already ruined, were not sufficient to assuage his vengeful spirit. They were only a taste, which, instead of glutting the bloodhound, made him more closely pursue the track, and more eagerly pant for destruction. He still has a thirst for violence and murder. So eager and insatiable is his thirst, that be even breathes out threatening and slaughter (Acts 9:1). His words are spears and arrows, and his tongue a sharp sword. 'Tis as natural for him to menace the Christians as to breathe the air. Nay, they bled every hour in the purposes of his rancorous heart. It is only owing to want of power that every syllable he utters, every breath he draws, does not deal out deaths, and cause some of the innocent disciples to fall. Who, upon the principles of human judgment, would not nave pronounced him a vessel of wrath, destined to unavoidable damnation? Nay, would not have been ready to conclude that, if there were heavier chains and a deeper dungeon in the world of woe, they must surely be reserved for such an implacable enemy of true godliness? Yet, admire and adore the inexhaustible treasures of grace—this Saul is admitted into the goodly fellowship of the prophets, is numbered with the noble arm of martyrs and makes a distinguished figure among the glorious company of the apostles.

The Corinthians were flagitious even to a proverb. Some of them wallowing in such abominable vices, and habituated themselves to such outrageous acts of injustice, as were a reproach to human nature. Yet, even these sons of violence and slaves of sensuality were washed, sanctified, justified (1 Cor. 6:9-11). "Washed," in the precious blood of a dying Redeemer; "sanctified," by the powerful operations of the blessed Spirit; "justified," through the infinitely tender mercies of a gracious God. Those who were once the burden of the earth, are now the joy of heaven, the delight of angels.

Now the grace of God is manifested in and by and through the Lord Jesus Christ. "The law was given by Moses, grace and truth came by Jesus Christ" (John 1:17). This does not mean that God never exercised grace toward any before His Son became incarnate—Genesis 6:8, Exodus 33:19, etc., clearly show otherwise. But grace and truth were fully revealed and perfectly exemplified when the Redeemer came to this earth, and died for His people upon the cross. It is through Christ the Mediator alone that the grace of God flows to His elect. "Much more the grace of God, and the gift by grace, which is by one man, Jesus Christ...much more they which receive abundance of grace, and of the gift of righteousness, shall reign in life by one, Jesus Christ...so might grace reign, through righteousness, unto eternal life, by Jesus Christ our Lord" (Rom. 5:15, 17,21).

The grace of God is proclaimed in the Gospel (Acts 20:24), which is to the self-righteous Jew a "stumbling block," and to the conceited and philosophizing Greek "foolishness." And why so? Because there is nothing whatever in it that is adapted to gratify the pride of man. It announces that unless we are saved by grace, we cannot be saved at all. It declares that apart from Christ, the unspeakable Gift of God's grace, the state of every man is desperate, irremediable, hopeless. The Gospel addresses men as guilty, condemned, perishing criminals. It declares that the chastest moralist is in the same terrible plight as is the most voluptuous profligate; that the zealous professor, with all his religious performances, is no better off than the most profane infidel.

The Gospel contemplates every descendant of Adam as a fallen, polluted, hell-deserving and helpless sinner. The grace which the Gospel publishes is his only hope. All stand before God convicted as transgressors of His holy law, as guilty and condemned criminals; awaiting not sentence, but the execution of sentence already passed on them (John 3:18; Rom. 3:19). To complain against the partiality of grace is suicidal. If the sinner insists upon bare justice, then the Lake of Fire must be his eternal portion. His only hope lies in bowing to the sentence which Divine justice has passed upon him, owning the absolute righteousness of it, casting himself on the mercy of God, and stretching forth empty hands to avail himself of the grace of God now made known to him in the Gospel.

The third Person in the Godhead is the Communicator of grace, therefore is He denominated "the Spirit of grace" (Zech. 12:10). God the Father is the Fountain of all grace, for He purposed in Himself the everlasting covenant of redemption. God the Son is the only Channel of grace. The Gospel is the Publisher of grace. The Spirit is the Bestower. He is the One who applies the Gospel in saving power to the soul: quickening the elect while spiritually dead, conquering their rebellious wills, melting their hard hearts, opening their blind eyes, cleansing them from the leprosy of sin. Thus we may say with the late G. S. Bishop,

Grace is a provision for men who are so fallen that they cannot lift the axe of justice, so corrupt that they cannot change their own natures, so averse to God that they cannot turn to Him, so blind that they cannot see Him, so deaf that they cannot hear Him, and so dead that He Himself must open their graves and lift them into resurrection.

The Mercy of God

"O give thanks unto the Lord: for He is good, for His mercy endureth forever" (Ps. 136:1). For this perfection of the Divine character God is greatly to be praised. Three times over in as many verses does the Psalmist here call upon the saints to give thanks unto the Lord for this adorable attribute. And surely this is the least that can be asked for from those who have been such bounteous gainers by it. When we contemplate the characteristics of this Divine excellency, we cannot do otherwise than bless God for it. His mercy is "great" (1 Kings 3:6), "plenteous" (Ps. 86:5), "tender" (Luke 1:78), "abundant" (1 Pet. 1:3); it is "from everlasting to everlasting upon them that fear Him" (Ps. 103:17). Well may we say with the Psalmist, "I will sing aloud of Thy mercy" (59:16).

"I will make all My goodness pass before thee, and I will proclaim the name of the Lord before thee; and will be gracious to whom I will be gracious, and will show mercy on whom I will show mercy" (Ex. 33:19). Wherein differs the "mercy of God from His grace"? The mercy of God has its spring in the Divine goodness. The first issue of God's goodness is His benignity or bounty, by which He gives liberally to His creatures as creatures; thus has He given being and life to all things. The second issue of God's goodness is His mercy, which denotes the ready inclination of God to relieve the misery of fallen creatures. Thus, "mercy" presupposes sin.

Though it may not be easy at the first consideration to perceive a real difference between the grace and the mercy of God, it helps us thereto if we carefully ponder His dealings with the unfallen angels. He has never exercised mercy toward them, for they have never stood in any need thereof, not having sinned or come beneath the effects of the curse. Yet, they certainly are the objects of God's free and sovereign grace. First, because of His election of them from out of the whole angelic race (I Tim. 5:21). Second, and in consequence of their election, because of His preservation of them from apostasy, when Satan rebelled and dragged down with him one-third of the celestial hosts (Rev. 12:4). Third, in making Christ their Head (Col. 2:10; 1 Pet. 3:22), whereby they are eternally secured in the holy condition in which they were created. Fourth, because of the exalted position which has been assigned them: to live in God's immediate presence (Dan. 7:10), to serve Him constantly in His heavenly temple, to receive honorable commissions from Him (Heb. 1:14). This is abundant grace toward them but "mercy" it is not.

In endeavoring to study the mercy of God as it is set forth in Scripture, a threefold distinction needs to be made, if the Word of Truth is to be "rightly divided" thereon. First, there is a general mercy of God, which is extended not only to all men, believers and unbelievers alike, but also to the entire creation: "His tender mercies are over all His works" (Ps. 145:9): "He giveth to all life, and breath, and all things" (Acts 17:25). God has upon the brute creation in their needs, and supplies them with suitable provision. Second, there is a special mercy of God, which is exercised toward the children of men, helping and succouring them, notwithstanding their sins. To them also He communicates all the necessities of life: "for He maketh His sun to rise on the evil and on the good, and sendeth rain on the just and on the unjust" (Matt. 5:45). Third, there is a sovereign mercy which is reserved for the heirs of salvation, which is communicated to them in a covenant way, through the Mediator.

Following out a little further the difference between the second and third distinctions pointed out above, it is important to note that the mercies which God bestows on the wicked are solely of a temporal nature; that is to say, they are confined strictly to this present life. There will be no mercy extended to them beyond the grave: "It is a people of no understanding: therefore He that made them will not have mercy on them, and He that formed them will show them no favour" (Isa. 27:11). But at this point a difficulty may suggest itself to some of our readers, namely, Does not Scripture affirm that "His mercy endureth forever" (Ps. 136:1)? Two things need to be pointed out in

The Holy Spirit

that connection. God can never cease to be merciful, for this is a quality of the Divine essence (Ps. 116:5); but the exercise of His mercy is regulated by His sovereign will. This must be so, for there is nothing outside Himself which obliges Him to act; if there were, that "something" would be supreme, and God would cease to be God.

It is pure sovereign grace which alone determines the exercise of Divine mercy. God expressly affirms this fact in Romans 9:15, "For He saith to Moses, I will have mercy on whom I will have mercy." It is not the wretchedness of the creature which causes Him to show mercy, for God is not influenced by things outside of Himself as we are. If God were influenced by the abject misery of leprous sinners, He would cleanse and save all of them. But He does not. Why? Simply because it is not His pleasure and purpose so to do. Still less is it the merits of the creature which causes Him to bestow mercies upon them, for it is a contradiction in terms to speak of meriting "mercy." "Not by works of righteousness which we have done, but according to His mercy He saved us" (Titus 3:5)—the one standing in direct antithesis from the other. Nor is it the merits of Christ which moves God to bestow mercies on His elect: that would be putting the effect for the cause. It is "through" or because of the tender mercy of our God that Christ was sent here to His people (Luke 1:78). The merits of Christ make it possible for God to righteously bestow spiritual mercies on His elect, justice having been fully satisfied by the Surety! No, mercy arises solely from God's imperial pleasure.

Again; though it be true, blessedly and gloriously true, that God's mercy "endureth forever," yet we must observe carefully the objects to whom His "mercy" is shown. Even the casting of the reprobate into the Lake of Fire is an act of mercy. The punishment of the wicked is to be contemplated from a threefold viewpoint. From God's side, it is an act of justice, vindicating His honour. The mercy of God is never shown to the prejudice of His holiness and righteousness. From their side, it is an act of equity, when they are made to suffer the due reward of their iniquities. But from the standpoint of the redeemed, the punishment of the wicked is an act of unspeakable mercy. How dreadful would it be if the present order of things when the children of God are obliged to live in the midst of the children of the Devil, should continue forever!

Heaven would at once cease to be heaven if the ears of the saints still heard the blasphemous and filthy language of the reprobate. What a mercy that in the New Jerusalem "there shall in nowise enter into it any thing that defileth, neither worketh abomination" (Rev. 21:27)!

Lest the reader might think that in the last paragraph we have been drawing upon our imagination, let us appeal to Holy Scripture in support of what has been said. In Psalm 143:12 we find David praying, "And of Thy mercy cut off mine enemies, and destroy all them that afflict my soul: for I am Thy servant." Again; in Psalm 136:15 we read that God "overthrew Pharaoh and his hosts in the Red Sea: for His mercy endureth forever." It was an act of vengeance upon Pharaoh and his hosts, but it was an act of "mercy" unto the Israelites. Again, in Revelation 19:1-3 we read, "I heard a great voice of much people in heaven, saying, Alleluia; Salvation, and glory, and honour, and power, unto the Lord our God: for true and righteous are His judgments: for He hath judged the great whore, which did corrupt the earth with her fornication, and hath avenged the blood of His servants at her hand. And again they said, Alleluia. And her smoke rose up forever and ever."

From what has just been before us, let us note how vain is the presumptuous hope of the wicked, who, notwithstanding their continued defiance of God, nevertheless count upon His being merciful to them. How many there are who say, I do not believe that God will ever cast me into Hell; He is too merciful. Such a hope is a viper, which if cherished in their bosoms will sting them to death. God is a God of justice as well as mercy, and He has expressly declared that He will "by no means clear the guilty" (Ex. 34:7). Yea, He has said, "The wicked shall be turned into hell, all the nations that forget God" (Ps. 9:17). As well might men reason: I do not believe that if filth be allowed to accumulate and sewerage become stagnant and people deprive themselves of fresh air, that a merciful God will let them fall a prey to a deadly fever. The fact is that those who neglect the laws of health are carried away by disease, notwithstanding God's mercy. Equally true is it that those who neglect the laws of spiritual health shall forever suffer the Second Death.

The Holy Spirit

Unspeakably solemn is it to see so many abusing this Divine perfection. They continue to despise God's authority, trample upon His laws continue in sin, and yet presume upon His mercy. But God will not be unjust to Himself. God shows mercy to the truly penitent, but not to the impenitent (Luke 13:3). To continue in sin and yet reckon upon Divine mercy remitting punishment is diabolical. It is saying, "Let us do evil that good may come," and of all such it is written, whose "damnation is just" (Rom. 3:8). Presumption shall most certainly be disappointed; read carefully Deuteronomy 29:18-20. Christ is the spiritual Mercy-seat, and all who despise and reject His Lordship shall "perish from the way, when His wrath is kindled but a little" (Ps. 2:12).

But let our final thought be of God's spiritual mercies unto His own people. "Thy mercy is great unto the heavens" (Ps. 57:10). The riches thereof transcend our loftiest thought. "For as the heaven is high above the earth, so great is His mercy toward them that fear Him" (Ps. 103:11). None can measure it. The elect are designated "vessels of mercy" (Rom. 9:23). It is mercy that quickened them when they were dead in sins (Eph. 2:4,5). It is mercy that saves them (Titus 3:5). It is His abundant mercy which begat them unto an eternal inheritance (1 Peter 1:3). Time would fail us to tell of His preserving, sustaining, pardoning, supplying mercy. Unto His own, God is "the Father of mercies" (2 Cor. 1:3).

"When all Thy mercies, O my God,
My rising soul surveys,
Transported with the view I'm lost,
In wonder, love, and praise."

The Love of God

There are three things told us in Scripture concerning the nature of God. First, "God is spirit" (John 4:24). In the Greek there is no indefinite article, and to say "God is a spirit" is most objectionable, for it places Him in a class with others. God is "spirit" in the highest sense. Because He is "spirit" He is incorporeal, having no visible substance. Had God a tangible body, He would not be omnipresent, He would be limited to one place; because He is spirit He fills heaven and earth. Second, God is light (1 John 1:5), which is the opposite of "darkness." In Scripture "darkness" stands for sin, evil, death; and "light" for holiness, goodness, life. God is light, means that He is the sum of all excellency. Third, "God is love" (1 John 4:8). It is not simply that God "loves," but that He is Love itself. Love is not merely one of His attributes, but His very nature.

There are many today who talk about the love of God, who are total strangers to the God of love. The Divine love is commonly regarded as a species of amiable weakness, a sort of good-natured indulgence; it is reduced to a mere sickly sentiment, patterned after human emotion. Now the truth is that on this, as on everything else, our thoughts need to be formed and regulated by what is revealed thereon in Holy Scripture. That there is urgent need for this is apparent not only from the ignorance which so generally prevails, but also from the low state of spirituality which is now so sadly evident everywhere among professing Christians. How little real love there is for God. One chief reason for this is because our hearts are so little occupied with His wondrous love for His people. The better we are acquainted with His love—its character, fulness, blessedness—the more will our hearts be drawn out in love to Him.

The Holy Spirit

1. **The love of God is uninfluenced.** By this we mean, there was nothing whatever in the objects of His love to call it into exercise, nothing in the creature to attract or prompt it. The love which one creature has for another is because of something in them; but the love of God is free, spontaneous, uncaused. The only reason why God loves any is found in His own sovereign will: "The Lord did not set His love upon you, nor choose you because ye were more in number than any people; for ye were the fewest of all people: but because the Lord loved thee" (Deut. 7:7,8). God has loved His people from everlasting, and therefore nothing of the creature can be the cause of what is found in God from eternity. He loves from Himself: "according to His own purpose" (2 Tim. 1:9).

"We love Him, because He first loved us" (1 John 4:19). God did not love us because we loved Him, but He loved us before we had a particle of love for Him. Had God loved us in return for ours, then it would not be spontaneous on His part; but because He loved us when we were loveless, it is clear that His love was uninfluenced. It is highly important if God is to be honored and the heart of His child established, that we should be quite clear upon this precious truth. God's love for me, and for each of "His own," was entirely unmoved by anything in them. What was there in me to attract the heart of God? Absolutely nothing. But, to the contrary, everything to repel Him, everything calculated to make Him loathe me—sinful, depraved, a mass of corruption, with "no good thing" in me.

"What was there in me that could merit esteem,
Or give the Creator delight?
'Twas even so, Father, I ever must sing,
Because it seemed good, in Thy sight."

2. **It is eternal.** This of necessity. God Himself is eternal, and God is love; therefore, as God Himself had no beginning, His love had none. Granted that such a concept far transcends the grasp of our feeble minds, nevertheless, where we cannot comprehend, we can bow in adoring worship. How clear is the testimony of Jeremiah 31:3, "I have loved thee with an everlasting love, therefore with loving-kindness have I drawn thee." How blessed to know that the great and holy God loved His people before heaven and earth were called into existence,

that He had set His heart upon them from all eternity. Clear proof is this that His love is spontaneous, for He loved them endless ages before they had any being.

The same precious truth is set forth in Ephesians 1:4,5, "According as He hath chosen us in Him before the foundation of the world, that we should be holy and without blame before Him. In love having predestinated us." What praise should this evoke from each of His children! How tranquilizing for the heart: since God's love toward me had no beginning, it can have no ending! Since it be true that "from everlasting to everlasting" He is God, and since God is "love," then it is equally true that "from everlasting to everlasting" He loves His people.

3. It is sovereign. This also is self-evident. God Himself is sovereign, under obligations to none, a law unto Himself, acting always according to His own imperial pleasure. Since God be sovereign, and since He be love, it necessarily follows that His love is sovereign. Because God is God, He does as He pleases; because God is love, He loves whom He pleases. Such is His own express affirmation: "Jacob have I loved, but Esau have I hated" (Rom. 9:19). There was no more reason in Jacob why he should be the object of Divine love, than there was in Esau. They both had the same parents, and were born at the same time, being twins; yet God loved the one and hated the other! Why? Because it pleased Him to do so.

The sovereignty of God's love necessarily follows from the fact that it is uninfluenced by anything in the creature. Thus, to affirm that the cause of His love lies in God Himself, is only another way of saying, He loves whom He pleases. For a moment, assume the opposite. Suppose God's love were regulated by anything else than His will, in such a case He would love by rule, and loving by rule He would be under a law of love, and then so far from being free, God would Himself be ruled by law. "In love having predestinated us unto the adoption of children by Jesus Christ to Himself, according to"—what? Some excellency which He foresaw in them? No; what then? "According to the good pleasure of His will" (Eph. 1:4,5).

4. It is infinite. Everything about God is infinite. His essence fills heaven and earth. His wisdom is illimitable, for He knows everything

of the past, present and future. His power is unbounded, for there is nothing too hard for Him. So His love is without limit. There is a depth to it which none can fathom; there is a height to it which none can scale; there is a length and breadth to it which defies measurement, by any creature-standard. Beautifully is this intimated in Ephesians 2:4: But God, who is rich in mercy, for His great love wherewith He loved us: the word "great" there is parallel with the "God so loved" of John 3:16. It tells us that the love of God is so transcendent it cannot be estimated.

No tongue can fully express the infinitude of God's love, or any mind comprehend it: it "passeth knowledge" Eph. 3:19). The most extensive ideas that a finite mind can frame about Divine love, are infinitely below its true nature. The heaven is not so far above the earth as the goodness of God is beyond the most raised conceptions which we are able to form of it. It is an ocean which swells higher than all the mountains of opposition in such as are the objects of it. It is a fountain from which flows all necessary good to all those who are interested in it (John Brine, 1743).

5. It is immutable. As with God Himself there is "no variableness, neither shadow of turning" (James 1:17), so His love knows neither change or diminution. The worm Jacob supplies a forceful example of this: "Jacob have I loved," declared Jehovah, and despite all his unbelief and waywardness, He never ceased to love him. John 13:1 furnishes another beautiful illustration. That very night one of the apostles would say, "Show us the Father"; another would deny Him with cursings; all of them would be scandalized by and forsake Him. Nevertheless "having loved His own which were in the world, He love them unto the end." The Divine love is subject to no vicissitudes. Divine love is "strong as death ... many waters cannot quench it" (Song of Sol. 8:6,7). Nothing can separate from it: Romans 8:35-39.

"His love no end nor measure knows,
No change can turn its course,
Eternally the same it flows
From one eternal source."

6. It is holy. God's love is not regulated by caprice passion, or sentiment, but by principle. Just as His grace reigns not at the expense

of it, but "through righteousness" (Rom. 5:21), so His love never conflicts with His holiness. "God is light" (1 John 1:5) is mentioned before "God is love" (1 John 4:8). God's love is no mere amiable weakness, or effeminate softness. Scripture declares, "whom the Lord loveth He chasteneth, and scourgeth every son whom He receiveth" (Heb. 12:6). God will not wink at sin, even in His own people. His love is pure, unmixed with any maudlin sentimentality.

7. It is gracious. The love and favor of God are inseparable. This is clearly brought out in Romans 8:32-39. What that love is from which there can be no "separation," is easily perceived from the design and scope of the immediate context: it is that goodwill and grace of God which determined Him to give His Son for sinners. That love was the impulsive power of Christ's incarnation: "God so loved the world that He gave His only begotten Son" (John 3:16). Christ died not in order to make God love us, but because He did love His people, Calvary is the supreme demonstration of Divine love. Whenever you are tempted to doubt the love of God, Christian reader, go back to Calvary.

Here then is abundant cause for trust and patience under Divine affliction. Christ was beloved of the Father, yet He was not exempted from poverty, disgrace, and persecution. He hungered and thirsted. Thus, it was not incompatible with God's love for Christ when He permitted men to spit upon and smite Him. Then let no Christian call into question God's love when he is brought under painful afflictions and trials. God did not enrich Christ on earth with temporal prosperity, for "He had not where to lay His head." But He did give Him the Spirit "without measure" (John 3:34). Learn then that spiritual blessings are the principal gifts of Divine love. How blessed to know that when the world hates us ,God loves us!

The Wrath of God

It is sad to find so many professing Christians who appear to regard the wrath of God as something for which they need to make an apology, or at least they wish there were no such thing. While some would not go so far as to openly admit that they consider it a blemish on the Divine character, yet they are far from regarding it with delight, they like not to think about it, and they rarely hear it mentioned without a secret resentment rising up in their hearts against it. Even with those who are more sober in their judgment, not a few seem to imagine that there is a severity about the Divine wrath which is too terrifying to form a theme for profitable contemplation. Others harbor the delusion that God's wrath is not consistent with His goodness, and so seek to banish it from their thoughts.

Yes, many there are who turn away from a vision of God's wrath as though they were called to look upon some blotch in the Divine character, or some blot upon the Divine government. But what saith the Scriptures? As we turn to them we find that God has made no attempt to conceal the fact of His wrath. He is not ashamed to make it known that vengeance and fury belong unto Him. His own challenge is, "See now that I, even I, am He, and there is no god with Me: I kill, and I make alive; I wound, and I heal; neither is there any that can deliver out of My hand. For I lift up My hand to heaven, and say, I live forever, If I whet My glittering sword, and Mine hand take hold on judgment; I will render vengeance to Mine enemies, and will reward them that hate Me" (Deut. 32:39-41). A study of the concordance will show that there are more references in Scripture to the anger, fury, and wrath of God, than there are to His love and tenderness. Because God is holy, He hates all sin; And because He hates all sin, His anger burns against the sinner: Psalm 7:11.

Now the wrath of God is as much a Divine perfection as is His faithfulness, power, or mercy. It must be so, for there is no blemish whatever, not the slightest defect in the character of God; yet there would be if "wrath" were absent from Him! Indifference to sin is a moral blemish, and he who hates it not is a moral leper. How could He who is the Sum of all excellency look with equal satisfaction upon virtue and vice, wisdom and folly? How could He who is infinitely holy disregard sin and refuse to manifest His "severity" (Rom. 9:12) toward it? How could He who delights only in that which is pure and lovely, loathe and hate not that which is impure and vile? The very nature of God makes Hell as real a necessity, as imperatively and eternally requisite as Heaven is. Not only is there no imperfection in God, but there is no perfection in Him that is less perfect than another.

The wrath of God is His eternal detestation of all unrighteousness. It is the displeasure and indignation of Divine equity against evil. It is the holiness of God stirred into activity against sin. It is the moving cause of that just sentence which He passes upon evil-doers. God is angry against sin because it is a rebelling against His authority, a wrong done to His inviolable sovereignty. Insurrectionists against God's government shall be made to know that God is the Lord. They shall be made to feel how great that Majesty is which they despise, and how dreadful is that threatened wrath which they so little regarded. Not that God's anger is a malignant and malicious retaliation, inflicting injury for the sake of it, or in return for injury received. No; while God will vindicate His dominion as the Governor of the universe, He will not be vindictive.

That Divine wrath is one of the perfections of God is not only evident from the considerations presented above, but is also clearly established by the express declarations of His own Word. "For the wrath of God is revealed from heaven" (Rom. 1:18). Robert Haldane comments on this verse as follows:

> It was revealed when the sentence of death was first pronounced, the earth cursed, and man driven out of the earthly paradise; and afterwards by such examples of punishment as those of the Deluge and the destruction of the Cities of the Plain by fire from heaven; but especially by the reign of death throughout the world. It was proclaimed

in the curse of the law on every transgression, and was intimated in the institution of sacrifice. In the 8th of Romans, the apostle calls the attention of believers to the fact that the whole creation has become subject to vanity, and groaneth and travaileth together in pain. The same creation which declares that there is a God, and publishes His glory, also proclaims that He is the Enemy of sin and the Avenger of the crimes of men . . . But above all, the wrath of God was revealed from heaven when the Son of God came down to manifest the Divine character, and when that wrath was displayed in His sufferings and death, in a manner more awful than by all the tokens God had before given of His displeasure against sin. Besides this, the future and eternal punishment of the wicked is now declared in terms more solemn and explicit than formerly. Under the new dispensation there are two revelations given from heaven, one of wrath, the other of grace.

Again; that the wrath of God is a Divine perfection is plainly demonstrated by what we read of in Psalm 95:11, "Unto whom I sware in My wrath." There are two occasions of God "swearing": in making promises (Gen. 22:16), and in denouncing threatening (Deut. 1:34). In the former, He swares in mercy to His children; in the latter, He swares to terrify the wicked. An oath is for solemn confirmation: Hebrews 6:16. In Genesis 22:16 God said, "By Myself have I sworn." In Psalm 89:35 He declares, "Once have I sworn by My holiness." While in Psalm 95:11 He affirmed, "I swear in My wrath." Thus the great Jehovah Himself appeals to His "wrath" as a perfection equal to His "holiness": He swares by the one as much as by the other! Again; as in Christ "dwelleth all the fulness of the Godhead bodily" (Col. 2:9), and as all the Divine perfections are illustriously displayed by Him (John 1:18), therefore do we read of "the wrath of the Lamb" (Rev. 6:16).

The wrath of God is a perfection of the Divine character upon which we need to frequently meditate. First, that our hearts may be duly impressed by God's detestation of sin. We are ever prone to regard sin lightly, to gloss over its hideousness, to make excuses for it. But the more we study and ponder God's abhorrence of sin and His frightful vengeance upon it, the more likely are we to realize its heinousness. Second, to beget a true fear in our souls for God: "Let us have grace whereby we may serve God acceptably with reverence and godly fear:

for our God is a consuming fire" (Heb. 12:28,29). We cannot serve Him "acceptably" unless there is due "reverence" for His awful Majesty and "godly fear" of His righteous anger, and these are best promoted by frequently calling to mind that "our God is a consuming fire." Third, to draw out our souls in fervent praise for having delivered us from "the wrath to come" (1 Thess. 1:10).

Our readiness or our reluctancy to meditate upon the wrath of God becomes a sure test of how our hearts' really stand affected toward Him. If we do not truly rejoice in God, for what He is in Himself, and that because of all the perfections which are eternally resident in Him, then how dwelleth the love of God in us? Each of us needs to be most prayerfully on his guard against devising an image of God in our thoughts which is patterned after our own evil inclinations. Of old the Lord complained, "Thou thoughtest that I was altogether as thyself" (Ps. 50:21), If we rejoice not "at the remembrance of His holiness" (Ps. 97:12), if we rejoice not to know that in a soon coming Day God will make a most glorious display of His wrath, by taking vengeance on all who now oppose Him, it is proof positive that our hearts are not in subjection to Him, that we are yet in our sins, on the way to the everlasting burnings.

"Rejoice, O ye nations (Gentiles) His people, for He will avenge the blood of His servants, and will render vengeance to His adversaries" (Deut. 32:43). And again we read, "I heard a great voice of much people in heaven, saying Alleluia; Salvation, and glory, and honour, and power, unto the Lord our God; For true and righteous are His judgments: for He hath judged the great whore, which did corrupt the earth with her fornication, and hath avenged the blood of His servants at her hand. And again they said Alleluia." (Rev. 19:13). Great will be the rejoicing of the saints in that day when the Lord shall vindicate His majesty, exercise His awful dominion, magnify His justice, and overthrow the proud rebels who have dared to defy Him.

"If thou Lord, shouldest mark (impute) iniquities, O Lord, who shall stand?" (Ps. 130:3). Well may each of us ask this question, for it is written, "the ungodly shall not stand in the judgment" (Ps. 1:5). How sorely was Christ's soul exercised with thoughts of God's marking the iniquities of His people when they were upon Him! He was "amazed and very heavy" (Mark 14:33). His awful agony, His bloody sweat, His strong cries and supplications (Heb. 5:7), His reiterated prayers ("If it be possible, let this cup pass from Me"), His last dreadful cry, ("My God, My God, why hast Thou forsaken Me?") all manifest what fearful apprehensions He had of what it was for God to "mark iniquities." Well may poor sinners cry out, "Lord who shall stand" when the Son of God Himself so trembled beneath the weight of His wrath? If thou, my reader, hast not "fled for refuge" to Christ, the only Saviour, "how wilt thou do in the swelling of the Jordan?" (Jer. 12:5)?

When I consider how the goodness of God is abused by the greatest part of mankind, I cannot but be of his mind that said, The greatest miracle in the world is God's patience and bounty to an ungrateful world. If a prince hath an enemy got into one of his towns, he doth not send them in provision, but lays close siege to the place, and doth what he can to starve them. But the great God, that could wink all His enemies into destruction, bears with them, and is at daily cost to maintain them. Well may He command us to bless them that curse us, who Himself does good to the evil and unthankful. But think not, sinners, that you shall escape thus; God's mill goes slow, but grinds small; the more admirable His patience and bounty now is, the more dreadful and unsupportable will that fury be which ariseth out of His abused goodness. Nothing smoother than the sea, yet when stirred into a tempest, nothing rageth more. Nothing so sweet as the patience and goodness of God, and nothing so terrible as His wrath when it takes fire. (Wm Gurnall, 1660).

Then flee, my reader, flee to Christ; "flee from the wrath to come" (Matt. 3:7) ere it be too late. Do not, we earnestly beseech you, suppose that this message is intended for somebody else. It is to you! Do not be contented by thinking you have already fled to Christ. Make certain! Beg the Lord to search your heart and show you yourself.

A Word to Preachers. Brethren, do we in our oral ministry, preach on this solemn subject as much as we ought? The Old Testament prophets frequently told their hearers that their wicked lives provoked the Holy One of Israel, and that they were treasuring up to themselves wrath against the day of wrath. And conditions in the world are no better now than they were then! Nothing is so calculated to arouse the careless and cause carnal professors to search their hearts, as to enlarge upon the fact that "God is angry with the wicked every day" (Ps. 7:11). The forerunner of Christ warned his hearers to "flee from the wrath to come" (Matt. 3:7). The Saviour bade His auditors "Fear Him, which after He hath killed, hath power to cast into Hell; yea, I say unto you. Fear Him" (Luke 12:5). The apostle Paul said, "Knowing therefore the terror of the Lord, we persuade men" (2 Cor. 5:11). Faithfulness demands that we speak as plainly about Hell as about Heaven.

The Contemplation of God

In the previous chapters we have had in review some of the wondrous and lovely perfections of the Divine character. From this most feeble and faulty contemplation of His attributes, it should be evident to us all that God is, first, an incomprehensible Being, and, lost in wonder at His infinite greatness, we are constrained to adopt the words of Zophar, "Canst thou by searching find out God? canst thou find out the Almighty unto perfection? It is high as heaven; what canst thou do? deeper than hell; what canst thou know? The measure thereof is longer than the earth, and broader than the sea." (Job 11:7-9). When we turn our thoughts to God's eternity, His immateriality, His omnipresence, His almightiness, our minds are overwhelmed.

But the incomprehensibility of the Divine nature is not a reason why we should desist from reverent inquiry and prayerful strivings to apprehend what He has so graciously revealed of Himself in His Word. Because we are unable to acquire perfect knowledge, it would be folly to say we will therefore make no efforts to attain to any degree of it. It has been well said that, "Nothing will so enlarge the intellect, nothing so magnify the whole soul of man, as a devout, earnest, continued, investigation of the great subject of the Deity. The most excellent study for expanding the soul is the science of Christ and Him crucified and the knowledge of the Godhead in the glorious Trinity." (C. H. Spurgeon). Let us quote a little further from this prince of preachers.

The proper study of the Christian is the God-head. The highest science, the loftiest speculation, the mightiest philosophy, which can engage the attention of a child of God, is the name, the nature, the person, the doings, and the existence of the great God which he calls his Father. There is something exceedingly improving to the mind in a contemplation of the Divinity. It is a subject so vast, that all our thoughts are lost in its immensity; so deep, that our pride is drowned in its infinity. Other subjects we can comprehend and grapple with; in them we feel a kind of self-content, and go on our way with the thought, "Behold I am wise." But when we come to this master science, finding that our plumb-line cannot sound its depth, amid that our eagle eye cannot see its height, we turn away with the thought "I am but of yesterday and know nothing." (Sermon on Mal. 3:6).

Yes, the incomprehensibility of the Divine nature should teach us humility, caution and reverence. After all our searchings and meditations we have to say with Job, "Lo, these are parts of His ways: but how little a portion is heard of Him!" (26:14). When Moses besought Jehovah for a sight of His glory, He answered him "I will proclaim the name of the Lord before thee" (Ex. 33:19), and, as another has said, "the name is the collection of His attributes." Rightly did the Puritan John Howe declare:

> The notion therefore we can hence form of His glory, is only such as we may have of a large volume by a brief synopsis, or of a spacious country by a little landscape. He hath here given us a true report of Himself, but not a full; such as will secure our apprehensions—being guided thereby—from error, but not from ignorance. We can apply our minds to contemplate the several perfections whereby the blessed God discovers to us His being, and can in our thoughts attribute them all to Him, though we have still but low and defective conceptions of each one. Yet so far as our apprehensions can correspond to the discovery that He affords us of His several excellencies, we have a present view of His glory.

As the difference is indeed great between the knowledge of God which His saints have in this life and that which they shall have in Heaven, yet, as the former should not be undervalued because it is imperfect, so the latter is not to be magnified above its reality. True, the Scripture declares that we shall see "face to face" and "know" even as we are known (1 Cor. 13:12), but to infer from this that we shall then know God as fully as He knows us, is to be misled by the mere sound of words, and to disregard that restriction of the same which the subject necessarily requires. There is a vast difference between the saints being glorified and their being made Divine. In their glorified state, Christians will still be finite creatures, and therefore, never able to fully comprehend the infinite God.

The saints in heaven will see God with the eye of the mind, for He will be always invisible to the bodily eye; and will see Him more clearly than they could see Him by reason and faith, and more extensively than all His works and dispensations had hitherto revealed Him; but their minds will not be so enlarged as to be capable of contemplating at once, or in detail, the whole excellence of His nature. To comprehend infinite perfection, they must become infinite themselves. Even in Heaven, their knowledge will be partial, but at the same time their happiness will be complete, because their knowledge will be perfect in this sense, that it will be adequate to the capacity of the subject, although it will not exhaust the fulness of the object. We believe that it will be progressive, and that as their views expand, their blessedness will increase; but it will never reach a limit beyond which there is nothing to be discovered; and when ages after ages have passed away, He will still be the incomprehensible God. (John Dick, 1840).

Secondly, from a review of the perfections of God, it appears that He is an all-sufficient Being. He is all-sufficient in Himself and to Himself. As the First of beings, He could receive nothing from another, nor be limited by the power of another. Being infinite, He is possessed of all possible perfection. When the Triune God existed all alone, He was all to Himself. His understanding, His love, His energies, found an adequate object in Himself. Had He stood in need of anything external, He had not been independent, and therefore would not have been God. He created all things, and that "for Himself" (Col. 1:16), yet it was not in order to supply a lack, but that He might communicate life and happiness to angels and men, and admit them to the vision of His glory. True, He demands the allegiance and services of His intelligent creatures, yet He derives no benefit from their offices, all the advantage redounds to themselves: Job 22:2,3. He makes use of means and instruments to accomplish His ends, yet not from a deficiency of power, but often times to more strikingly display His power through the feebleness of the instruments.

The all-sufficiency of God makes Him to be the Supreme Object which is ever to be sought unto. True happiness consists only in the enjoyment of God. His favour is life, and His loving kindness is better than life. "The Lord is my portion, saith my soul; therefore will I hope in Him" (Lam. 3:24). His love, His grace, His glory, are the chief objects of the saints' desire and the springs of their highest satisfaction. "There be many that say, Who will show us any good? Lord, lift Thou up the light of Thy countenance upon us. Thou hast put gladness in my heart, more than in the time that their corn and their wine increased" (Ps. 4:6,7). Yea, the Christian, when in his right mind, is able to say, "Although the fig tree shall not blossom, neither shall fruit be in the vines; the labour of the olive shall fail, and the fields shall yield no meat; the flock shall be cutoff from the fold, and there shall be no herd in the stalls: yet I will rejoice in the Lord, I will joy in the God of my salvation" (Hab. 3:17,18).

Thirdly, from a review of the perfections of God, it appears that He is the Supreme Sovereign of the universe. It has been rightly said:

No dominion is so absolute as that which is founded on creation. He who might not have made any thing, had a right to make all things according to His own pleasure. In the exercise of His uncontrolled power, He has made some parts of the creation mere inanimate matter, of grosser or more refined texture, and distinguished by different qualities, but all inert and unconscious. He has given organization to other parts, and made them susceptible of growth and expansion, but still without life in the proper sense of the term. To others He has given not only organization, but conscious existence, organs of sense and self-motive power. To these He has added in man the gift of reason, and an immortal spirit, by which he is allied to a higher order of beings who are placed in the superior regions. Over the world which He has created, He sways the scepter of omnipotence. "I praised and honored Him that liveth forever, whose dominion is an everlasting dominion, and His kingdom is from generation to generation: and all the inhabitants of the earth are reputed as nothing: and He doeth according to His will in the army of heaven, and among the inhabitants of the earth: and none can stay His hand, or say unto Him, What doeth Thou?"—Daniel 4:34, 35. (John Dick).

A creature, considered as such, has no rights. He can demand nothing from his Maker; and in whatever manner he may be treated, has no title to complain. Yet, when thinking of the absolute dominion of God over all, we ought never to lose sight of His moral perfections. God is just and good, and ever does that which is right. Nevertheless, He exercises His sovereignty according to His own imperial and righteous pleasure. He assigns each creature his place as seemeth good in His own sight. He orders the varied circumstances of each according to His own counsels. He moulds each vessel according to His own uninfluenced determination. He has mercy on whom He will, and whom He will He hardens. Wherever we are, His eye is upon us. Whoever we are, our life and everything is held at His disposal. To the Christian, He is a tender Father; to the rebellious sinner He will yet be a consuming fire. "Now unto the King eternal, immortal, invisible, the only wise God, be honour and glory for ever and ever. Amen" (1 Tim. 1:17).

The Sovereignty of God

Table of Contents

Foreword..301
Introduction..303
God's Sovereignty Defined.................................310
The Sovereignty of God in Creation........................317
The Sovereignty of God in Administration..................321
The Sovereignty of God in Salvation.......................333
The Sovereignty of God in Reprobation.....................359
The Sovereignty of God in Operation.......................382
God's Sovereignty and the Human Will......................396
God's Sovereignty and Human Responsibility................410
God's Sovereignty and Prayer..............................427
Our Attitude Towards God's Sovereignty....................438
Difficulties and Objections...............................449
The Value of this Doctrine................................465
Conclusion..478
Appendix 1. The Will of God...............................490
Appendix 2. The Case of Adam..............................494
Appendix 3. The Meaning of "Kosmos" in John 3:16..........499
Appendix 4. 1 John 2:2....................................502

Foreword to the First Edition

In the following pages an attempt has been made to examine anew in the light of God's Word some of the profoundest questions which can engage the human mind. Others have grappled with these mighty problems in days gone by and from their labors we are the gainers. While making no claim for originality the writer, nevertheless, has endeavored to examine and deal with his subject from an entirely independent viewpoint. We have studied diligently the writings of such men as Augustine and Acquinas, Calvin and Melancthon, Jonathan Edwards and Ralph Erskine, Andrew Fuller and Robert Haldane. And sad it is to think that these eminent and honored names are almost entirely unknown to the present generation. Though, of course, we do not endorse all their conclusions, yet we gladly acknowledge our deep indebtedness to their works. We have purposely refrained from quoting freely from these deeply taught theologians, because we desired that the faith of our readers should stand not in the wisdom of men but in the power of God. For this reason we have quoted freely from the Scriptures and have sought to furnish proof-texts for every statement we have advanced.

It would be foolish for us to expect that this work will meet with general approval. The trend of modern theology—if theology it can be called—is ever toward the deification of the creature rather than the glorification of the Creator, and the leaven of present-day Rationalism is rapidly permeating the whole of Christendom. The malevolent effects of Darwinianism are more far reaching than most are aware. Many of those among our religious leaders who are still regarded as orthodox would, we fear, be found to be very heterodox if they were weighed in the balances of the Sanctuary. Even those who are clear, intellectually, upon other truth, are rarely sound in doctrine. Few, very few, today, really believe in the complete ruin and total depravity of man. Those who speak of man's "free will," and insist upon his inherent power to either accept or reject the Saviour, do but voice their ignorance of the real condition of Adam's fallen children. And if there are few who believe that, so far as he is concerned, the condition of the sinner is entirely hopeless, there are fewer still who really believe in the absolute Sovereignty of God.

In addition to the widespread effects of unscriptural teaching, we also have to reckon with the deplorable superficiality of the present generation. To announce that a certain book is a treatise on doctrine is quite sufficient to prejudice against it the great bulk of church-members and most of our preachers as well. The craving today is for something light and spicy, and few have patience, still less desire, to examine carefully that which would make a demand both upon their hearts and their mental powers. We remember, also, 'how that it is becoming increasingly difficult in these strenuous days for those who are desirous of studying the deeper things of God to find the time which such study requires. Yet, it is still true that "Where there's a will, there's a way," and in spite of the discouraging features referred to, we believe there is even now a godly remnant who will take pleasure in giving this little work a careful consideration, and such will, we trust, find in it "Meat in due season."

We do not forget the words of one long since passed away, namely, that "Denunciation is the last resort of a defeated opponent." To dismiss this book with the contemptuous epithet—"Hyper-Calvinism"! will not be worthy of notice. For controversy we have no taste, and we shall not accept any challenge to enter the lists against those who might desire to debate the truths discussed in these pages. So far as our personal reputation is concerned, that we leave our Lord to take care of, and unto Him we would now commit this volume and whatever fruit it may bear, praying Him to use it for the enlightening of His own dear people (insofar as it is in accord with His Holy Word) and to pardon the writer for and preserve the reader from the injurious effects of any false teaching that may have crept into it. If the joy and comfort which have come to the author while penning these pages are shared by those who may scan them, then we shall be devoutly thankful to the One whose grace alone enables us to discern spiritual things.

June 1918.
Arthur W. Pink.

Introduction

Who is regulating affairs on this earth today—God, or the Devil? That God reigns supreme in Heaven, is generally conceded; that He does so over this world, is almost universally denied—if not directly, then indirectly. More and more are men in their philosophizing and theorizing, relegating God to the background. Take the material realm. Not only is it denied that God created everything, by personal and direct action, but few believe that He has any immediate concern in regulating the works of His own hands. Everything is supposed to be ordered according to the (impersonal and abstract) "laws of Nature". Thus is the Creator banished from His own creation. Therefore we need not be surprised that men, in their degrading conceptions, exclude Him from the realm of human affairs. Throughout Christendom, with an almost negligible exception, the theory is held that man is "a free agent", and therefore, lord of his fortunes and the determiner of his destiny. That Satan is to be blamed for much of the evil which is in the world, is freely affirmed by those who, though having so much to say about "the responsibility of man", often deny their own responsibility, by attributing to the Devil what, in fact, proceeds from their own evil hearts (Mark 7:21-23).

But who is regulating affairs on this earth today—God, or the Devil? Attempt to take a serious and comprehensive view of the world. What a scene of confusion and chaos confronts us on every side! Sin is rampant; lawlessness abounds; evil men and seducers are waxing "worse and worse" (2 Tim. 3:13). Today, everything appears to be out of joint. Thrones are creaking and tottering, ancient dynasties are being overturned, democracies are revolting, civilization is a demonstrated failure; half of Christendom was but recently locked-together in a death grapple; and now that the titanic conflict is over, instead of the world having been made "safe for democracy", we have discovered that democracy is very unsafe for the world. Unrest, discontent, and lawlessness are rife every where, and none can say how soon another great war will be set in motion. Statesmen are perplexed and staggered. Men's hearts are "failing them for fear, and for looking after those things which are coming on the earth" (Luke 21:26). Do these things look as though God had full control?

But let us confine our attention to the religious realm. After nineteen centuries of Gospel preaching, Christ is still "despised and rejected of men". Worse still, He (the Christ of Scripture) is proclaimed and magnified by very few. In the majority of modern pulpits He is dishonored and disowned. Despite frantic efforts to attract the crowds, the majority of the churches are being emptied rather than filled. And what of the great masses of non-church goers? In the light of Scripture we are compelled to believe that the "many" are on the Broad Road that leadeth to destruction, and that only "few" are on the Narrow Way that leadeth unto life. Many are declaring that Christianity is a failure, and despair is settling on many faces. Not a few of the Lord's own people are bewildered, and their faith is being severely tried. And what of God? Does He see and hear? Is He impotent or indifferent? A number of those who are regarded as leaders of Christian-thought told us that, God could not help the coming of the late awful War, and that He was unable to bring about its termination. It was said, and said openly, that conditions were beyond God's control. Do these things look as though God were ruling the world?

Who is regulating affairs on this earth today—God, or the Devil? What impression is made upon the minds of those men of the world who, occasionally, attend a Gospel service? What are the conceptions formed by those who hear even those preachers who are counted as "orthodox"? Is it not that a disappointed God is the One whom Christians believe in? From what is heard from the average evangelist today, is not any serious hearer obliged to conclude that he professes to represent a God who is filled with benevolent intentions, yet unable to carry them out; that He is earnestly desirous of blessing men, but that they will not let Him? Then, must not the average hearer draw the inference that the Devil has gained the upper hand, and that God is to be pitied rather than blamed?

But does not everything seem to show that the Devil has far more to do with the affairs of earth than God has? Ah, it all depends upon whether we are walking by faith, or walking by sight. Are your thoughts, my reader, concerning this world and God's relation to it, based upon what you see? Face this question seriously and honestly. And if you are a Christian, you will, most probably, have cause to bow your head with shame and sorrow, and to acknowledge that it is so. Alas, in reality, we walk very little "by faith". But what does "walking by faith" signify? It means that our thoughts are formed, our actions regulated, our lives molded by the Holy Scriptures, for, "faith cometh by hearing, and hearing by the Word of God" (Rom. 10:17). It is from the Word of Truth, and that alone, that we can learn what is God's relation to this world.

Who is regulating affairs on this earth today—God or the Devil? What saith the Scriptures? Ere we consider the direct reply to this query, let it be said that, the Scriptures predicted just what we now see and hear. The prophecy of Jude is in course of fulfillment. It would lead us too far astray from our present inquiry to fully amplify this assertion, but what we have particularly in mind is a sentence in verse 8—"Likewise also these dreamers defile the flesh, despise dominion and speak evil of dignities." Yes, they "speak evil" of the Supreme Dignity, the "Only Potentate, the King of kings, and Lord of lords." Ours is peculiarly an age of irreverence, and as the consequence, the spirit of lawlessness, which brooks no restraint and which is desirous of casting off everything which interferes with the free course of self-will, is rapidly engulfing the earth like some giant tidal wave. The members of the rising generation are the most flagrant offenders, and in the decay and disappearing of parental authority we have the certain precursor of the abolition of civic authority. Therefore, in view of the growing disrespect for human law and the refusal to "render honor to whom honor is due," we need not be surprised that the recognition of the majesty, the authority, the sovereignty of the Almighty Law-giver should recede more and more into the background, and that the masses have less and less patience with those who insist upon them. And conditions will not improve; instead, the more sure Word of Prophecy makes known to us that they will grow worse and worse. Nor do we expect to be able to stem the tide—it has already risen much too high for that. All we can now hope to do is warn our fellow-saints against the spirit of the age, and thus seek to counteract its baneful influence upon them.

Who is regulating affairs on this earth today—God, or the Devil? What saith the Scriptures? If we believe their plain and positive declarations, no room is left for uncertainty. They affirm, again and again, that God is on the throne of the universe; that the sceptre is in His hands; that He is directing all things "after the counsel of His own will". They affirm, not only that God created all things, but also that God is ruling and reigning over all the works of His hands. They affirm that God is the "Almighty", that His will is irreversible, that He is absolute sovereign in every realm of all His vast dominions. And surely it must be so. Only two alternatives are possible: God must either rule, or be ruled; sway, or be swayed; accomplish His own will, or be thwarted by His creatures. Accepting the fact that He is the "Most High", the only Potentate and King of kings, vested with perfect wisdom and illimitable power, and the conclusion is irresistible that He must be God in fact, as well as in name.

It is in view of what we have briefly referred to above. that we say, Present-day conditions call loudly for a new examination and new presentation of God's omnipotency, God's sufficiency, God's sovereignty. From every pulpit in the land it needs to be thundered forth that God still lives, that God still observes, that God still reigns. Faith is now in the crucible, it is being tested by fire, and there is no fixed and sufficient resting-place for the heart and mind but in the Throne of God. What is needed now, as never before, is a full, positive, constructive setting forth of the Godhood of God. Drastic diseases call for drastic remedies. People are weary of platitudes and mere generalizations—the call is for something definite and specific. Soothing-syrup may serve for peevish children, but an iron tonic is better suited for adults, and we know of nothing which is more calculated to infuse spiritual vigor into our frames than a scriptural apprehension of the full character of God. It is written, "The people that do know their God shall be strong and do exploits" (Dan. 11:32).

Without a doubt a world-crisis is at hand, and everywhere men are alarmed. But God is not! He is never taken by surprise. It is no unexpected emergency which now confronts Him, for He is the One who "worketh all things after the counsel of His own will" (Eph. 1:11). Hence, though the world is panic-stricken, the word to the believer is, "Fear not"! "All things" are subject to His immediate control: "all things" are moving in accord with His eternal purpose, and therefore, "all things" are "working together for good to them that love God, to them who are the called according to His purpose." It must be so, for "of Him, and through Him, and to Him are all things" (Rom. 11:36). Yet how little is this realized today even by the people of God! Many suppose that He is little more than a far-distant Spectator, taking no immediate hand in the affairs of earth. It is true that man has a will, but so also has God. It is true that man is endowed with power, but God is all-powerful. It is true that, speaking generally, the material world is regulated by law, but behind that law is the law-Giver and law-Administrator. Man is but the creature. God is the Creator, and endless ages before man first saw the light "the mighty God" (Isa. 9:6) existed, and ere the world was founded, made His plans; and being infinite in power and man only finite, His purpose and plan cannot be withstood or thwarted by the creatures of His own hands.

We readily acknowledge that life is a profound problem, and that we are surrounded by mystery on every side; but we are not like the beasts of the field—ignorant of their origin, and unconscious of what is before them. No: "We have also a more sure Word of Prophecy", of which it is said ye do well that ye "take heed, as unto a light that shineth in a dark place, until the day dawn, and the day star arise in your hearts" (2 Pet. 1:19). And it is to this Word of Prophecy we indeed do well to "take heed," to that Word which had not its origin in the mind of man but in the Mind of God, for, "the prophecy came not at any time by the will of man: but holy men of God spake moved by the Holy Spirit." We say again, it is to this "Word" we do well to take heed. As we turn to this Word and are instructed there, we discover a fundamental principle which must be applied to every problem: Instead of beginning with man and his world and working back to God, we must begin with God and work down to man—"In the beginning God"! Apply this principle to the present situation. Begin with the world as it is today and try and work back to God, and everything will seem to show that God has no connection with the world at all. But begin with God and work down to the world and light, much light, is cast on the problem. Because God is holy His anger burns against sin; because God is righteous His judgments fall upon those who rebel against Him; because God is faithful the solemn threatenings of His Word are fulfilled; because God is omnipotent none can successfully resist Him, still less overthrow His counsel; and because God is omniscient no problem can master Him and no difficulty baffle His wisdom. It is just because God is who He is and what He is that we are now beholding on earth what we do—the beginning of His out-poured judgments: in view of His inflexible justice and immaculate holiness we could not expect anything other than what is now spread before our eyes.

But let it be said very emphatically that the heart can only rest upon and enjoy the blessed truth of the absolute sovereignty of God as faith is in exercise. Faith is ever occupied with God. That is the character of it: that is what differentiates it from intellectual theology. Faith endures "as seeing Him who is invisible" (Heb. 11:27) : endures the disappointments, the hardships, and the heart-aches of life, by recognizing that all comes from the hand of Him who is too wise to err and too loving to be unkind. But so long as we are occupied with any other object than God Himself, there will be neither rest for the heart nor peace for the mind. But when we receive all that enters our lives as from His hand, then, no matter what may be our circumstances or surroundings—whether in a hovel, a prison-dungeon, or a martyr's stake—we shall be enabled to say, "The lines are fallen unto me in pleasant places" (Ps. 16:6). But that is the language of faith, not of sight or of sense.

But if instead of bowing to the testimony of Holy Writ, if instead of walking by faith, we follow the evidence of our eyes, and reason therefrom, we shall fall into a quagmire of virtual atheism. Or, if we are regulated by the opinions and views of others, peace will be at an end. Granted that there is much in this world of sin and, suffering which appalls and saddens us; granted that there is much in the providential dealings of God which startle and stagger us; that is no reason why we should unite with the unbelieving worldling who says, "If I were God, I would not allow this or tolerate that" etc. Better far, in the presence of bewildering mystery, to say with one of old, "I was dumb, I opened not my mouth; because Thou didst it" (Ps. 39:9). Scripture tells us that God's judgments are "unsearchable", and His ways "past finding out" (Rom. 11:33). It must be so if faith is to be tested, confidence in His wisdom and righteousness strengthened, and submission to His holy will fostered.

Here is the fundamental difference between the man of faith and the man of unbelief. The unbeliever is "of the world," judges everything by worldly standards, views life from the standpoint of time and sense, and weighs everything in the balances of his own carnal making. But the man of faith brings in God, looks at everything from His standpoint, estimates values by spiritual standards, and views life in the light of eternity. Doing this, he receives whatever comes as from the hand of God. Doing this, his heart is calm in the midst of the storm. Doing this, he rejoices in hope of the glory of God.

In these opening paragraphs we have indicated the lines of thought followed out in this book. Our first postulate is that because God is God, He does as He pleases, only as He pleases, always as He pleases; that His great concern is the accomplishment of His own pleasure and the promotion of His own glory; that He is the Supreme Being, and therefore Sovereign of the universe. Starting with this postulate we have contemplated the exercise of God's Sovereignty, first in Creation, second in Governmental Administration over the works of His hands, third in the Salvation of His own elect, fourth in the Reprobation of the wicked, and fifth in Operation upon and within men. Next we have viewed the Sovereignty of God as it relates to the human will in particular and human Responsibility in general, and have sought to show what is the only becoming attitude for the creature to take in view of the majesty of the Creator. A separate chapter has been set apart for a consideration of some of the difficulties which are involved, and to answering the questions which are likely to be raised in the minds of our readers; while one chapter has been devoted to a more careful yet brief examination of God's Sovereignty in relation to prayer. Finally, we have sought to show that the Sovereignty of God is a truth revealed to us in Scripture for the comfort of our hearts, the strengthening of our souls, and the blessing of our lives. A due apprehension of God's Sovereignty promotes the spirit of worship, provides an incentive to practical godliness, and inspires zeal in service. It is deeply humbling to the human heart, but in proportion to the degree that it brings man into the dust before his Maker, to that extent is God glorified.

We are well aware that what we have written is in open opposition to much of the teaching that is current both in religious literature and in the representative pulpits of the land. We freely grant that the postulate of God's Sovereignty with all its corollaries is at direct variance with the opinions and thoughts of the natural man, but the truth is, we are quite unable to think upon these matters: we are incompetent for forming a proper estimate of God's character and ways, and it is because of this that God has given us a revelation of His mind, and in that revelation He plainly declares, "My thoughts are not your thoughts, neither are your ways My ways, saith the Lord. For as the heavens are higher than the earth, so are My ways higher than your ways, and My thoughts than your thoughts" (Is. 55:8,9). In view of this scripture, it is only to be expected that much of the contents of the Bible conflicts with the sentiments of the carnal mind, which is enmity against God. Our appeal then is not to the popular beliefs of the day, nor to the creeds of the churches, but to the Law and Testimony of Jehovah. All that we ask for is an impartial and attentive examination of what we have written, and that, made prayerfully in the light of the Lamp of Truth. May the reader heed the Divine admonition to "prove all things; hold fast that which is good" (1 Thess. 5:21).

God's Sovereignty Defined

"Thine, O Lord, is the greatness, and the power, and the glory, and the victory, and the majesty: for all that is in the heaven and in the earth is Thine; Thine is the kingdom, O Lord, and Thou art exalted as Head above all"

1 Chronicles 29:11

The Sovereignty of God is an expression that once was generally understood. It was a phrase commonly used in religious literature. It was a theme frequently expounded in the pulpit. It was a truth which brought comfort to many hearts, and gave virility and stability to Christian character. But, today, to make mention of God's sovereignty is, in many quarters, to speak in an unknown tongue. Were we to announce from the average pulpit that the subject of our discourse would be the sovereignty of God, it would sound very much as though we had borrowed a phrase from one of the dead languages. Alas! that it should be so. Alas! that the doctrine which is the key to history, the interpreter of Providence, the warp and woof of Scripture, and the foundation of Christian theology, should be so sadly neglected and so little understood.

The sovereignty of God. What do we mean by this expression? We mean the supremacy of God, the kingship of God, the godhood of God. To say that God is sovereign is to declare that God is God. To say that God is sovereign is to declare that He is the Most High, doing according to His will in the army of heaven, and among the inhabitants of the earth, so that none can stay His hand or say unto Him what doest Thou? (Dan. 4:35). To say that God is sovereign is to declare that He is the Almighty, the Possessor of all power in heaven and earth, so that none can defeat His counsels, thwart His purpose, or resist His will (Ps. 115:3). To say that God is sovereign is to declare that He is "The Governor among the nations" (Ps. 22:28), setting up kingdoms, overthrowing empires, and determining the course of dynasties as pleaseth Him best. To say that God is sovereign is to declare that He is the "Only Potentate, the King of kings, and Lord of lords" (1 Tim. 6:15). Such is the God of the Bible.

The Holy Spirit

How different is the God of the Bible from the God of modern Christendom! The conception of Deity which prevails most widely today, even among those who profess to give heed to the Scriptures, is a miserable caricature, a blasphemous travesty of the Truth. The God of the twentieth century is a helpless, effeminate being who commands the respect of no really thoughtful man. The God of the popular mind is the creation of a maudlin sentimentality. The God of many a present-day pulpit is an object of pity rather than of awe-inspiring reverence.' To say that God the Father has purposed the salvation of all mankind, that God the Son died with the express intention of saving the whole human race, and that God the Holy Spirit is now seeking to win the world to Christ; when, as a matter of common observation, it is apparent that the great majority of our fellow-men are dying in sin, and passing into a hopeless eternity: is to say that God the Father is disappointed, that God the Son is dissatisfied, and that God the Holy Spirit is defeated. We have stated the issue baldly, but there is no escaping the conclusion. To argue that God is "trying His best" to save all mankind, but that the majority of men will not let Him save them, is to insist that the will of the Creator is impotent, and that the will of the creature is omnipotent. To throw the blame, as many do, upon the Devil, does not remove the difficulty, for if Satan is defeating the purpose of God, then, Satan is Almighty and God is no longer the Supreme Being.

To declare that the Creator's original plan has been frustrated by sin, is to dethrone God. To suggest that God was taken by surprise in Eden and that He is now attempting to remedy an unforeseen calamity, is to degrade the Most High to the level of a finite, erring mortal. To argue that man is a free moral agent and the determiner of his own destiny, and that therefore he has the power to checkmate his Maker, is to strip God of the attribute of Omnipotence. To say that the creature has burst the hounds assigned by his Creator, and that God is now practically a helpless Spectator before the sin and suffering entailed by Adam's fall, is to repudiate the express declaration of Holy Writ, namely, "Surely the wrath of man shall praise Thee: the remainder of wrath shalt Thou restrain" (Ps. 76:10). In a word, to deny the sovereignty of God is to enter upon a path which, if followed to its logical terminus, is to arrive at blank atheism.

The sovereignty of the God of Scripture is absolute, irresistible, infinite. When we say that God is sovereign we affirm His right to govern the universe, which He has made for His own glory, just as He pleases. We affirm that His right is the right of the Potter over the clay, i.e., that He may mould that clay into whatsoever form He chooses, fashioning out of the same lump one vessel unto honor and another unto dishonor. We affirm that He is under no rule or law outside of His own will and nature, that God is a law unto Himself, and that He is under no obligation to give an account of His matters to any.

Sovereignty characterizes the whole Being of God. He is sovereign in all His attributes. He is sovereign in the exercise of His power. His power is exercised as He wills, when He wills, where He wills. This fact is evidenced on every page of Scripture. For a long season that power appears to be dormant, and then it is put forth in irresistible might. Pharaoh dared to hinder Israel from going forth to worship Jehovah in the wilderness—what happened? God exercised His power, His people were delivered and their cruel task-masters slain. But a little later, the Amalekites dared to attack these same Israelites in the wilderness, and what happened? Did God put forth His power on this occasion and display His hand as He did at the Red Sea? Were these enemies of His people promptly overthrown and destroyed? No, on the contrary, the Lord swore that He would "have war with Amalek from generation to generation" (Ex. 17:16). Again, when Israel entered the land of Canaan, God's power was signally displayed. The city of Jericho barred their progress—what happened? Israel did not draw a bow nor strike a blow: the Lord stretched forth His hand and the walls fell down flat. But the miracle was never repeated! No other city fell after this manner. Every other city had to be captured by the sword!

Many other instances might be adduced illustrating the sovereign exercise of God's power. Take one other example. God put forth His power and David was delivered from Goliath, the giant; the mouths of the lions were closed and Daniel escaped unhurt; the three Hebrew children were cast into the burning fiery furnace and came forth unharmed and unscorched. But God's power did not always interpose for the deliverance of His people, for we read: "And others had trial of cruel mockings and scourgings, yea, moreover of bonds and imprisonment: they were stoned, they were sawn asunder, were tempted, were slain with the sword; they wandered about in sheepskins and goatskins; being destitute, afflicted, tormented" (Heb. 11:36, 37). But why? Why were not these men of faith delivered like the others? Or, why were not the others suffered to be killed like these? Why should God's power interpose and rescue some and not the others? Why allow Stephen to be stoned to death, and then deliver Peter from prison?

God is sovereign in the delegation of His power to others. Why did God endow Methuselah with a vitality which enabled him to outlive all his contemporaries? Why did God impart to Samson a physical strength which

The Holy Spirit

no other human has ever possessed? Again; it is written, "But thou shalt remember the Lord thy God: for it is He that giveth thee power to get wealth" (Deut. 8:18), but God does not bestow this power on all alike. Why not? Why has He given such power to men like Morgan, Carnegie, Rockefeller? The answer to all of these questions, is, Because God is Sovereign, and being Sovereign He does as He pleases.

God is sovereign in the exercise of His mercy. Necessarily so, for mercy is directed by the will of Him that showeth mercy. Mercy is not a right to which man is entitled. Mercy is that adorable attribute of God by which He pities and relieves the wretched. But under the righteous government of God no one is wretched who does not deserve to be so. The objects of mercy, then, are those who are miserable, and all misery is the result of sin, hence the miserable are deserving of punishment not mercy. To speak of deserving mercy is a contradiction of terms.

God bestows His mercies on whom He pleases and withholds them as seemeth good unto Himself. A remarkable illustration of this fact is seen in the manner that God responded to the prayers of two men offered under very similar circumstances. Sentence of death was passed upon Moses for one act of disobedience, and he besought the Lord for a reprieve. But was his desire gratified? No; he told Israel, "The Lord is wroth with me for your sakes, and would not hear me: and the Lord said unto me, Let it suffice thee" (Deut. 3:26). Now mark the second case

those days was Hezekiah sick unto death. And the prophet Isaiah the son of Amoz came to him, and said unto him, Thus saith the Lord, Set thine house in order; for thou shalt die, and not live. Then he turned his face to the wall, and prayed unto the Lord, saying, I beseech Thee, O Lord, remember now how I have walked before Thee in truth and with a perfect heart, and have done that which is good in Thy sight. And Hezekiah wept sore. And it came to pass, afore Isaiah was gone out into the middle court, that the word of the Lord came to him, saying, Turn again, and tell Hezekiah the captain of my people, Thus saith the Lord, the God of David thy father, I have heard thy prayer, I have seen thy tears: behold, I will heal thee: on the third day thou shalt go up unto the house of the Lord. And I will add unto thy days fifteen years" (2 Kings 20:1-6). Both of these men had the sentence of death in themselves, and both prayed earnestly unto the Lord for a reprieve: the one wrote: "The Lord would not hear me," and died; but to the other it was said, "I have heard thy prayer", and his life was spared. What an illustration and exemplification of the truth expressed in Romans 9:15!—"For

He saith to Moses, I will have mercy on whom I will have mercy, and I will have compassion on whom I will have compassion."

The sovereign exercise of God's mercy—pity shown to the wretched—was displayed when Jehovah became flesh and tabernacled among men. Take one illustration. During one of the Feasts of the Jews, the Lord Jesus went up to Jerusalem. He came to the Pool of Bethesda, where lay "a great multitude of impotent folk, of blind, halt, withered, waiting for the moving of the water." Among this "great multitude" there was "a certain man which had an infirmity thirty and eight years." What happened? "When Jesus saw hint lie, and knew that he had been now a long time in that case, he saith unto him, Wilt thou be made whole? The impotent man answered Him, Sir, I have no man, when the water is troubled, to put me into the pool: but while I am coming, another steppeth down before me. Jesus saith unto him, Rise, take up thy bed, and walk. And immediately the man was made whole, and took up his bed, and walked" (John 5:3-9). Why was this one man singled out from all the others? We are not told that he cried "Lord, have mercy on me." There is not a word in the narrative which intimates that this man possessed any qualifications which entitled him to receive special favor. Here then was a case of the sovereign exercise of Divine mercy, for it was just as easy for Christ to heal the whole of that "great multitude" as this one "certain man." But lie did not. He put forth His power and relieved the wretchedness of this one particular sufferer, and for some reason known only to Himself, He declined to do the same for the others. Again, we say, what an illustration and exemplification of Romans 9:15!—"I will have mercy on whom I will have mercy, and I will have compassion on whom I will have compassion."

God is sovereign in the exercise of His love. Ah! that is a hard saying, who then can receive it? It is written, "A man can receive nothing, except it be given him from heaven" (John 3:27). When we say that God is sovereign in the exercise of His love, we mean that He loves whom He chooses. God does not love everybody;' if He did, He would love the Devil. Why does not God love the Devil? Because there is nothing in him to love; because there is nothing in him to attract the heart of God. Nor is there anything to attract God's love in any of the fallen sons of Adam, for all of them are, by nature, "children of wrath" (Eph. 2:3). If then there is nothing in any member of the human race to attract God's love, and if, notwithstanding, He does love some, then it necessarily follows that the cause of His love must be found in Himself, which is only another way of saying that the exercise of God's love towards the fallen sons of men is according to His own good pleasure.'

In the final analysis, the exercise of God's love must be traced back to His sovereignty, or, otherwise, He would love by rule; and if He loved by rule, then is He under a law of love, and if He is under a law of love then is He not supreme, but is Himself ruled by law. "But," it may be asked, "Surely you do not deny that God loves the entire human family?" We reply, it is written, "Jacob have I loved, but Esau have I hated" (Rom. 9:13). If then God loved Jacob and hated Esau, and that before they were born or had done either good or evil, then the reason for His love was not in them, but in Himself.

That the exercise of God's love is according to His own sovereign pleasure is also clear from the language of Ephesians 1:3-5, where we read, "Blessed be the God and Father of our Lord Jesus Christ, who hath blessed us with all spiritual blessings in heavenly places in Christ: According as He hath chosen us in Him before the foundation of the world, that we should be holy and without blame before Him. In love having predestinated us unto the adoption of children by Jesus Christ to Himself according to the good pleasure of His will." It was "in love" that God the Father predestined His chosen ones unto the adoption of children by Jesus Christ to Himself, "according"—according to what? According to some excellency He discovered in them? No. What then? According to what He foresaw they would become? No; mark carefully the inspired answer—"According to the good pleasure of His will."

God is sovereign in the exercise of His grace. This of necessity, for grace is favor shown to the undeserving, yea, to the Hell-deserving. Grace is the antithesis of justice. Justice demands the impartial enforcement of law. Justice requires that each shall receive his legitimate due, neither more nor less. Justice bestows no favors and is no respecter of persons. Justice, as such, shows no pity and knows no mercy. But after justice has been fully satisfied, grace flows forth. Divine grace is not exercised at the expense of justice, but "grace reigns through righteousness" (Rom. 5:21), and if grace "reigns", then is grace sovereign.

Grace has been defined as the unmerited favor of God;' and if unmerited, then none can claim it as their inalienable right. If grace is unearned and undeserved, then none are entitled to it. If grace is a gift, then none can demand it. Therefore, as salvation is by grace, the free gift of God, then He bestows it on whom He pleases. Because salvation is by grace, the very chief of sinners is not beyond the reach of Divine mercy. Because salvation is by grace, boasting is excluded and God gets all the glory.

The sovereign exercise of grace is illustrated on nearly every page of Scripture. The Gentiles are left to walk in their own ways, while Israel becomes the covenant people of Jehovah. Ishmael the firstborn is cast out comparatively unblessed, while Isaac the son of his parents' old age is made the child of promise. Esau the generous-hearted and forgiving-spirited is denied the blessing, though he sought it carefully with tears, while the worm Jacob receives the inheritance and is fashioned into a vessel of honor. So in the New Testament. Divine truth is hidden from the wise and prudent, but is revealed to babes. The Pharisees and Sadducees are left to go their own way, while publicans and harlots are drawn by the cords of love.

In a remarkable manner Divine grace was exercised at the time of the Saviour's birth. The incarnation of God's Son was one of the greatest events in the history of the universe, and yet its actual occurrence was not made known to all mankind; instead, it was specially revealed to the Bethlehem shepherds and wise men of the East. And this was prophetic and indicative of the entire course of this dispensation, for even today Christ is not made known to all. It would have been an easy matter f or God to have sent a company of angels to every nation and announced the birth of His Son. But He did not. God could have readily attracted the attention of all mankind to the "star;" but He did not. Why? Because God is sovereign and dispenses His favors as He pleases. Note particularly the two classes to whom the birth of the Saviour was made known, namely, the most unlikely classes—illiterate shepherds and heathen from a far country. No angel stood before the Sanhedrin and announced the advent of Israel's Messiah! No "star" appeared unto the scribes and lawyers as they, in their pride and self-righteousness, searched the Scriptures! They searched diligently to find out where He should be born, and yet it was not made known to them when He was actually come. What a display of Divine sovereignty—the illiterate shepherds singled out for peculiar honor, and the learned and eminent passed by! And why was the birth of the Saviour revealed to these foreigners, and not to those in whose midst He was born? See in this a wonderful foreshadowing of God's dealings with our race throughout the entire Christian dispensation—sovereign in the exercise of His grace, bestowing His favors on whom He pleases, often on the most unlikely and unworthy.'

The Sovereignty of God in Creation

"Thou art worthy, O Lord, to receive glory, and honor, and power: for Thou hast created all things, and

for Thy pleasure they are and were created"
Revelation 4:11

Having shown that sovereignty characterizes the whole Being of God, let us now observe how it marks all His ways and dealings.

In the great expanse of eternity, which stretches behind Genesis 1:1, the universe was unborn and creation existed only in the mind of the great Creator. In His sovereign majesty God dwelt all alone. We refer to that far distant period before the heavens and the earth were created. There were then no angels to hymn God's praises, no creatures to occupy His notice, no rebels to be brought into subjection. The great God was all alone amid the awful silence of His own vast universe. But even at that time, if time it could be called, God was sovereign. He might create or not create according to His own good pleasure. He might create this way or that way; He might create one world or one million worlds, and who was there to resist His will? He might call into existence a million different creatures and place them on absolute equality, endowing them with the same faculties and placing them in the same environment; or, He might create a million creatures each differing from the others, and possessing nothing in common save their creaturehood, and who was there to challenge His right? If He so pleased, He might call into existence a world so immense that its dimensions were utterly beyond finite computation; and were He so disposed, He might create an organism so small that nothing but the most powerful microscope could reveal its existence to human eyes. It was His sovereign right to create, on the one hand, the exalted seraphim to burn around His throne, and on the other hand, the tiny insect which dies the same hour that it is born. If the mighty God chose to have one vast gradation in His universe, from loftiest seraph to creeping reptile, from revolving worlds to floating atoms, from macrocosm to microcosm, instead of making everything uniform, who was there to question His sovereign pleasure?

Behold then the exercise of Divine sovereignty long before man ever saw the light. With whom took God counsel in the creation and disposition of His creatures. See the birds as they fly through the air, the beasts as they roam the earth, the fishes as they swim in the sea, and then ask, Who was it that made them to differ? Was it not their Creator who sovereignly assigned their various locations and adaptations to them!

Turn your eye to the heavens and observe the mysteries of Divine sovereignty which there confront the thoughtful beholder: "There is one glory of the sun, and another glory of the moon, and another glory of the stars: for one star differeth from another star in glory" (1 Cor. 15:41). But why should they? Why should the sun be more glorious than all the other planets? Why should there be stars of the first magnitude and others of the tenth? Why such amazing inequalities? Why should some of the heavenly bodies be more favorably placed than others in their relation to the sun? And why should there be "shooting stars," "falling stars," "wandering stars" (Jude 13), in a word, ruined stars? And the only possible answer is, "For Thy pleasure they are and were created" (Rev. 4:11).

Come now to our own planet. Why should two thirds of its surface be covered with water, and why should so much of its remaining third be unfit for human cultivation or habitation? Why should there be vast stretches of marshes, deserts and ice-fields? Why should one country be so inferior, topographically, from another? Why should one be fertile, and another almost barren? Why should one be rich in minerals and another own none? Why should the climate of one be congenial and healthy, and another uncongenial and unhealthy? Why should one abound in rivers and lakes, and another be almost devoid of them? Why should one be constantly troubled with earthquakes, and another be almost entirely free from them? Why? Because thus it pleased the Creator and Upholder of all things.

Look at the animal kingdom and note the wondrous variety. What comparison is possible between the lion and the lamb, the bear and the kid, the elephant and the mouse? Some, like the horse and the dog, are gifted with great intelligence; while others, like sheep and swine, are almost devoid of it. Why? Some are designed to be beasts of burden, while others enjoy a life of freedom. But why should the mule and the donkey be shackled to a life of drudgery, while the lion and tiger are allowed to roam the jungle at their pleasure? Some are fit for food, others unfit; some are beautiful, others ugly; some are endowed with great strength, others are quite helpless; some are fleet of foot, others can scarcely crawl—contrast the hare and the tortoise; some are of use to man, others appear to be quite valueless; some live for centuries, others a few months at most; some are tame, others fierce. But why all these variations and differences?

What is true of the animals is equally true of the birds and fishes. But consider now the vegetable kingdom. Why should roses have thorns, and lilies grow without them? Why should one flower emit a fragrant aroma and another have none? Why should one tree bear fruit which is wholesome and another that which is poisonous? Why should one vegetable be capable of enduring frost and another wither under it? Why should one apple tree be loaded with fruit, and another tree of the same age and in the same orchard be almost barren? Why should one plant flower a dozen times in a year and another bear blossoms but once a century? Truly, "whatsoever the Lord pleased, that did He in heaven, and in the earth, in the seas, and all deep places" (Ps. 135:6).

Consider the angelic hosts. Surely we shall find uniformity here. But no; there, as elsewhere, the same sovereign pleasure of the Creator is displayed. Some are higher in rank than others; some are more powerful than others; some are nearer to God than others. Scripture reveals a definite and well-defined gradation in the angelic orders. From arch-angel, past seraphim and cherubim, we come to "principalities and powers" (Eph. 3:10), and from principalities and powers to "rulers" (Eph. 6:12), and then to the angels themselves, and even among them we read of "the elect angels" (1 Tim. 5:21). Again we ask, Why this inequality, this difference in rank and order? And all we can say is "Our God is in the heavens, He hath done whatsoever He hath pleased" (Ps. 115:3).

If then we see the sovereignty of God displayed throughout all creation why should it be thought a strange thing if we behold it operating in the midst of the human family? Why should it be thought strange if to one God is pleased to give five talents and to another only one? Why should it be thought strange if one is born with a robust constitution and another of the same parents is frail and sickly? Why should it be thought strange if Abel is cut off in his prime, while Cain is suffered to live on for many years? Why should it be thought strange that some should be born black and others white; some be born idiots and others with high intellectual endowments; some be born constitutionally lethargic and others full of energy; some be born with a temperament that is selfish, fiery, egotistical, others who are naturally self-sacrificing, submissive and meek? Why should it be thought strange if some are qualified by nature to lead and rule, while others are only fitted to follow and serve? Heredity and environment cannot account for all these variations and inequalities. No; it is God who maketh one to differ from another. Why should He? "Even so, Father, for so it seemed good in Thy sight" must be our reply.

Learn then this basic truth, that the Creator is absolute Sovereign, executing His own will, performing His own pleasure, and considering nought but His own glory. "The Lord hath made all things for Himself" (Prov. 16:4). And had He not a perfect right to? Since God is God, who dare challenge His prerogative? To murmur against Him is rank rebellion. To question His ways is to impugn His wisdom. To criticize Him is sin of the deepest dye. Have we forgotten who He is? Behold, "All nations before Him are as nothing; and they are counted to Him less than nothing, and vanity. To whom then will ye liken God ?" (Isa. 40:17, 18).

The Sovereignty of God in Administration

"The Lord hath prepared His Throne in the heavens; and His Kingdom ruleth over all"
Psalm 103:19

First, a word concerning the need for God to govern the material world. Suppose the opposite for a moment. For the sake of argument, let us say that God created the world, designed and fixed certain laws (which men term "the laws of Nature"), and that He then withdrew, leaving the world to its fortune and the out-working of these laws. In such a case, we should have a world over which there was no intelligent, presiding Governor, a world controlled by nothing more than impersonal laws—a concept worthy of gross Materialism and blank Atheism. But, I say, suppose it for a moment; and in the light of such a supposition, weigh well the following question:—What guaranty have we that some day ere long the world will not be destroyed? A very superficial observation of "the laws of Nature" reveals the fact that they are not uniform in their working. The proof of this is seen in the fact that no two seasons are alike. If then Nature's laws are irregular in their operations, what guaranty have we against some dreadful catastrophe striking our earth? "The wind bloweth where it listeth" (pleaseth), which means that man can neither harness nor hinder it. Sometimes the wind blows with great fury, and it might be that it should suddenly gather in volume and velocity, until it became a hurricane earth-wide in its range. If there is nothing more than the laws of Nature regulating the wind, then, perhaps tomorrow, there may come a terrific tornado and sweep everything from the surface of the earth! What assurance have we against such a calamity? Again; of late years we have heard and read much about clouds bursting and flooding whole districts, working fearful havoc in the destruction of both property and life. Man is helpless before them, for science can devise no means to prevent clouds bursting. Then how do we know that these bursting-clouds will not be multiplied indefinitely and the whole earth be deluged by their downpour?

This would be nothing new: why should not the Flood of Noah's day be repeated? And what of earthquakes? Every few years, some island or some great city is swept out of existence by one of them—and what can man do? Where is the guaranty that ere long a mammoth earthquake will not destroy the whole world? Science tells us of great subterranean fires burning beneath the comparatively thin crust of our earth, how do we know but what these fires will not suddenly burst forth and consume our entire globe? Surely every reader now sees the point we are seeking to make: Deny that God is governing matter, deny that He is "upholding all things by the word of His power" (Heb. 1:3), and all sense of security is gone!

Let us pursue a similar course of reasoning in connection with the human race. Is God governing this world of ours? Is He shaping the destinies of nations, controlling the course of empires, determining the limits of dynasties? Has He described the limits of evil-doers, saying, Thus far shalt thou go and no further? Let us suppose the opposite for a moment. Let us assume that God has delivered over the helm into the hand of His creatures, and see where such a supposition leads us. For the sake of argument we will say that every man enters this world endowed with a will that is absolutely free, and that it is impossible to compel or even coerce him without destroying his freedom. Let us say that every man possesses a knowledge of right and wrong, that he has the power to choose between them, and that he is left entirely free to make his own choice and go his own way. Then what? Then it follows that man is sovereign, for he does as he pleases and is the architect of his own fortune. But in such a case we can have no assurance that ere long every man will reject the good and choose the evil. In such a case we have no guaranty against the entire human race committing moral suicide. Let all Divine restraints be removed and man be left absolutely free, and all ethical distinctions would immediately disappear, the spirit of barbarism would prevail universally, and pandemonium would reign supreme. Why not? If one nation deposes its rulers and repudiates its constitution, what is there to prevent all nations from doing the same? If little more than a century ago the streets of Paris ran with the blood of rioters, what assurance have we that before the present century closes every city throughout the world will not witness a similar sight? What is there to hinder worldwide lawlessness and universal anarchy? Thus we have sought to show the need, the imperative need, for God to occupy the Throne, take the government upon His shoulder, and control the activities and destinies of His creatures.

But has the man of faith any difficulty in perceiving the government of God over this world? Does not the anointed eye discern, even amid much seeming confusion and chaos, the hand of the Most High controlling and shaping the affairs of men, even in the common concerns of every day life? Take for example farmers and their crops. Suppose God left them to themselves: what would then prevent them, one and all, from grassing their arable lands and devoting themselves exclusively to the rearing of cattle and dairying? In such a case there would be a world-famine of wheat and corn! Take the work of the post-office. Suppose that everybody decided to write letters on Mondays only, could the authorities cope with the mail on Tuesdays? and how would they occupy their time the balance of the week? So again with storekeepers. What would happen if every housewife did her shopping on Wednesday, and stayed at home the rest of the week? But instead of such things happening, farmers in different countries both raise sufficient cattle and grow enough grain of various kinds to supply the almost incalculable needs of the human race; the mails are almost evenly distributed over the six days of the week; and some women shop on Monday, some on Tuesday, and so on. Do not these things clearly evidence the overruling and controlling hand of God!

Having shown, in brief, the imperative need for God to reign over our world, let us now observe still further the fact that God does rule, actually rule, and that His government extends to and is exercised over all things and all creatures. And,

1. God Governs Inanimate Matter.

That God governs inanimate matter, that inanimate matter performs His bidding and fulfils His decrees, is clearly shown on the very frontispiece of Divine revelation. God said, Let there be light, and we read, "There was light." God said, "Let the waters under the heaven be gathered together unto one place, and let the dry land appear," and "it was so." And again, "God said, Let the earth bring forth grass, the herb yielding seed, and the fruit tree yielding fruit after his kind, whose seed is in itself, upon the earth: and it was so." As the Psalmist declares, "He spake, and it was done; He commanded, and it stood fast."

What is stated in Genesis one is afterwards illustrated all through the Bible. After the creation of Adam, sixteen centuries went by before ever a shower of rain fell upon the earth, for before Noah "there went up a mist from the earth, and watered the whole face of the ground" (Gen. 2:6). But, when the iniquities of the antediluvians had come to the full, then God said, "And, behold, I, even. I, do bring a flood of waters upon the earth, to destroy all flesh, wherein is the breath of life, from under heaven; and everything that is in the earth shall die;" and in fulfillment of this we read, "In the six hundredth year of Noah's life, in the second month, the seventeenth day of the month, the same day were all the fountains of the great deep broken up, and the windows of heaven were opened. And the rain was upon the earth forty days and forty nights" (Gen. 6:17 and 7:11, 12).

Witness God's absolute (and sovereign) control of inanimate matter in connection with the plagues upon Egypt. At His bidding the light was turned into darkness and rivers into blood; hail fell, and death came down upon the godless land of the Nile, until even its haughty monarch was compelled to cry out for deliverance. Note particularly how the inspired record here emphasizes God's absolute control over the elements—"And Moses stretched forth his rod toward heaven: and the Lord sent thunder and hail, and the fire ran along upon the ground; and the Lord rained hail upon the land of Egypt." So there was hail, and fire mingled with the hail, very grievous, such as there was none like it in all the land of Egypt since it became a nation. And the hail smote throughout all the land of Egypt all that was in the field, both man and beast; and the hail smote every herb of the field, and brake every tree of the field. Only in the land of Goshen, where the children of Israel were, was there no hail" (Ex. 9:23-26). The same distinction was observed in connection with the ninth plague: "And the Lord said unto Moses, Stretch out thine hand toward heaven, that there may be darkness over the land of Egypt, even darkness which may be felt. And Moses stretched forth his hand toward heaven; and there was a thick darkness in all the land of Egypt three days: They saw not one another, neither rose any from his place for three days: but all the children of Israel had light in their dwellings" (Ex. 10:21-23).

The above examples are by no means isolated cases. At God's decree fire and brimstone descended from heaven and the cities of the Plain were destroyed, and a fertile valley was converted into a loathsome sea of death. At His bidding the waters of the Red Sea parted asunder so that the Israelites passed over dry shod, and at His word they rolled back again and destroyed the Egyptians who were pursuing them. A word from Him, and the earth opened her mouth and Korah and his rebellious company were swallowed up. The furnace of Nebuchadnezzar was heated seven times beyond its normal temperature, and into it three of God's children were cast, but the fire did not so much as scorch their clothes, though it slew the men who cast them into it.

What a demonstration of the Creator's governmental control over the elements was furnished when He became flesh and tabernacled among men! Behold Him asleep in the boat. A storm arises. The winds roar and the waves are lashed into fury. The disciples who are with Him, fearful lest their little craft should founder, awake their Master, saying, "Carest Thou not that we perish?" And then we read, "And He arose, and rebuked the wind, and said unto the sea, Peace, be still. And the wind ceased, and there was a great calm" (Mark 4:39). Mark again, the sea, at the will of its Creator, bore Him up upon its waves. At a word from Him the fig-tree withered; at His touch disease fled instantly.

The heavenly bodies are also ruled by their Maker and perform His sovereign pleasure. Take two illustrations. At God's bidding the sun went back ten degrees on the dial of Ahaz to help the weak faith of Hezekiah. In New Testament times, God caused a star to herald the incarnation of His Son—the star which appeared unto the wise men of the East. This star, we are told, "went before them till it came and stood over where the young Child was" (Matt. 2:9).

What a declaration is this—"He sendeth forth His commandment upon earth: His word runneth very swiftly. He giveth snow like wool: He scattereth the hoar frost like ashes. He casteth forth His ice like morsels: who can stand before His cold? He sendeth out His word, and melteth them: He causeth His wind to blow, and the waters flow" (Ps. 147:15-18). The mutations of the elements are beneath God's sovereign control. It is God who withholds the rain, and it is God who gives the rain when He wills, where He wills, as He wills, and on whom He wills. Weather Bureaus may attempt to give forecasts of the weather, but how frequently God mocks their calculations! Sun 'spots,' the varying activities of the planets, the appearing and disappearing of comets (to which abnormal weather is sometimes attributed), atmospheric disturbances, are merely secondary causes, for behind them all is God Himself. Let His Word speak once more: "And also I have withholden the rain from you, when there were yet three months to the harvest: and I caused it to rain upon one city, and caused it not to rain upon another city: one piece was rained upon, and the piece whereon it rained not withered. So two or three cities wandered unto one city, to drink water; but they were not satisfied: yet have ye not returned unto Me, saith the Lord. I have smitten you with blasting and mildew: when your gardens and your vineyards and your fig trees and your olive trees increased, the palmerworm devoured them: yet have ye not returned unto Me, saith the Lord. I have sent among you the pestilence after the manner of Egypt: your young men have I slain with the sword, and have taken away your horses; and I have made the stink of your camps to come up into your nostrils: yet have ye not returned unto Me, saith the Lord" (Amos 4:7-10).

Truly, then, God governs inanimate matter. Earth and air, fire and water, hail and snow, stormy winds and angry seas, all perform the word of His power and fulfil His sovereign pleasure. Therefore, when we complain about the weather, we are, in reality, murmuring against God.

2. God Governs Irrational Creatures.

What a striking illustration of God's government over the animal kingdom is found in Genesis 2:19! "And out of the ground the Lord God formed every beast of the field, and every fowl of the air; and brought them unto Adam to see what he would call them: and whatsoever Adam called every living creature, that was the name thereof." Should it be said that this occurred in Eden, and took place before the fall of Adam and the consequent curse which was inflicted on every creature, then our next reference fully meets the objection: God's control of the beasts was again openly displayed at the Flood. Mark how God caused to "come unto" Noah every specie of living creature "of every living thing of all flesh, two of every sort shalt thou bring into the ark, to keep them alive with thee; they shall be male and female. Of fowls after their kind, of every creeping thing after his kind: two of every sort shall come unto thee" (Gen. 6:19, 20)—all were beneath God's sovereign control. The lion of the jungle, the elephant of the forest, the bear of the polar regions; the ferocious panther, the untameable wolf, the fierce tiger; the high-soaring eagle and the creeping crocodile—see them all in their native fierceness, and yet, quietly submitting to the will of their Creator, and coming two by two into the ark!

We referred to the plagues sent upon Egypt as illustrating God's control of inanimate matter, let us now turn to them again to see how they demonstrate His perfect ruler-ship over irrational creatures. At His word the river brought forth frogs abundantly, and these frogs entered the palace of Pharaoh and the houses of his servants and, contrary to their natural instincts, they entered the beds, the ovens and the kneadingtroughs (Ex. 8:13). Swarms of flies invaded the land of Egypt, but there were no flies in the land of Goshen! (Ex. 8:22). Next, the cattle were stricken. and we read, "Behold, the hand of the Lord is upon thy cattle which is in the field, upon the horses, upon the asses, upon the camels, upon the oxen, and upon the sheep: there shall be a very grievous murrain. And the Lord shall sever between the cattle of Israel and the cattle of Egypt: and there shall nothing die of all that is the children's of Israel. And the Lord appointed a set time, saying, Tomorrow the Lord shall do this thing in the land. And the Lord did that thing on the morrow, and all the cattle of Egypt died: but of the cattle of the children of Israel died not one" (Ex. 9:3-6). In like manner God sent clouds of locusts to plague Pharaoh and his land, appointing the time of their visitation, determining the course and assigning the limits of their depredations.

Angels are not the only ones who do God's bidding. The brute beasts equally perform His pleasure. The sacred ark, the ark of the covenant, is in the country of the Philistines. How is it to be brought back to its home land? Mark the servants of God's choice, and how completely they were beneath His control: "And the Philistines called for the priests and the diviners saying, What shall we do to the ark of the Lord? tell us wherewith we shall send it to his place. And they said. . . . Now therefore make a new cart, and take two milch kine, on which there hath come no yoke, and tie the kine to the cart, and bring their calves home from them: And take the ark of the Lord, and lay it upon the cart; and put the jewels of gold, which ye return Him for a trespass offering, in a coffer by the side thereof, and send it away that it may go. And see, if it goeth up by the way of his own coast to Bethshemesh, then He hath done us this great evil: but if not, then we shall know that it is not His hand that smote us; it was a chance that happened to us." And what happened? How striking the sequel! "And the kine took the straight way to the way of Bethshemesh, and went along the highway, lowing as they went, and turned not aside to the right hand or to the left" (1 Sam. 6:12). Equally striking is the case of Elijah: "And the word of the Lord came unto him, saying, Get thee hence, and hide thyself by the brook Cherith, that is before Jordan. And it shall be, that thou shalt drink of the brook; and I have commanded the ravens to feed thee there." (1 Kings 17:2-4). The natural instinct of these birds of prey was held in subjection, and instead of consuming the food themselves, they carried it to Jehovah's servant in his solitary retreat.

Is further proof required? then it is ready to hand. God makes a dumb ass to rebuke the prophet's madness. He sends forth two she-bears from the woods to devour forty and two of Elijah's tormentors. In fulfillment of His word, He causes the dogs to lick up the blood of the wicked Jezebel. He seals the mouths of Babylon's lions when Daniel is cast into the den, though, later, He causes them to devour the prophet's accusers. He prepares a great fish to swallow the disobedient Jonah and then, when His ordained hour struck, compelled it to vomit him forth on dry land. At His bidding a fish carries a coin to Peter for tribute money, and in order to fulfil His word He makes the cock to crow twice after Peter's denial. Thus we see that God reigns over irrational creatures: beasts of the field, birds of the air, fishes of the sea, all perform His sovereign bidding.

3. God Governs the Children of Men.

We fully appreciate the fact that this is the most difficult part of our subject, and, accordingly, it will be dealt with at greater length in the pages that follow; but at present we consider the fact of God's government over men in general, before we attempt to deal with the problem in detail.

Two alternatives confront us, and between them we obliged to choose: either God governs, or He is governed: either God rules, or He is ruled; either God has His way, or men have theirs. And is our choice between these alternatives hard to make? Shall we say that in man we behold a creature so unruly that he is beyond God's control? Shall we say that sin has alienated the sinner so far from the thrice Holy One that he is outside the pale of His jurisdiction? Or, shall we say that man has been endowed with moral responsibility, and therefore God must leave him entirely free, at least during the period of his probation? Does it necessarily follow because the natural man is an outlaw against heaven, a rebel against the Divine government, that God is unable to fulfil His purpose through him? We mean, not merely that He may overrule the effects of the actions of evil-doers, nor that He will yet bring the wicked to stand before His judgment-bar so that sentence of punishment may be passed upon them—multitudes of non-Christians believe these things—but, we mean, that every action of the most lawless of His subjects is entirely beneath His control, yea that the actor is, though unknown to himself, carrying out the secret decrees of the Most High. Was it not thus with Judas? and is it possible to select a more extreme case? If then the arch-rebel was performing the counsel of God is it any greater tax upon our faith to believe the same of all rebels?

Our present object is not philosophic inquiry nor metaphysical causistry, but to ascertain the teaching of Scripture upon this profound theme. To the Law and the Testimony, for there only can we learn of the Divine government—its character, its design, its modus operandi, its scope. What then has it pleased God to reveal to us in His blessed Word concerning His rule over the works of His hands, and particularly, over the one who originally was made in His own image and likeness?

"In Him we live, and move, and have our being" (Acts 17:28). What a sweeping assertion is this! These words, be it noted, were addressed, not to one of the churches of God, not to a company of saints who had reached an exalted plane of spirituality, but to a heathen audience, to those who worshipped "the unknown God" and who "mocked" when they heard of the resurrection of the dead. And yet, to the Athenian philosophers, to the Epicureans and Stoics, the apostle Paul did not hesitate to affirm that they lived and moved and had their being in God, which signified not only that they owed their existence and preservation to the One who made the world and all things therein, but also that their very actions were encompassed and therefore controlled by the Lord of heaven and earth. Compare Dan. 5:23, last clause!

"The disposings (margin) of the heart, and the answer of the tongue is from the Lord" (Prov. 16:1). Mark that the above declaration is of general application—it is of "man," not simply of believers, that this is predicated. "A man's heart deviseth his way: but the Lord directeth his steps" (Prov. 16:9). If the Lord directs the steps of a man, is it not proof that he is being controlled or governed by God? Again; "There are many devices in a man's heart; nevertheless the counsel of the Lord, that shall stand" (Prov. 19:21). Can this mean anything less than, that no matter what man may desire and plan, it is the will of his Maker which is executed? As an illustration take the "Rich Fool" The "devices" of his heart are made known to us—"And he thought within himself, saying, What shall I do, because I have no room where to bestow my fruits? And he said, This will I do: I will pull down my barns, and build greater; and there I will bestow all my fruits and my goods. And I will say to my soul, Soul, thou hast much goods laid up for many years; take thine ease, eat, drink, and be merry." Such were the "devices" of his heart, nevertheless it was "the counsel of the Lord" that stood. The "I will's" of the rich man came to nought, for "God said unto him, Thou fool, this night shall thy soul be required of thee" (Luke 12:17-20).

"The king's heart is in the hand of the Lord, as the rivers of water: He turneth it whithersoever He will" (Prov. 21:1). What could be more explicit? Out of the heart are "the issues of life" (Prov. 4:23), for as a man "thinketh in his heart, so is he" (Prov. 23:7). If then the heart is in the hand of the Lord, and if "He turneth it whithersoever He will," then is it not clear that men, yea, governors and rulers, and so all men, are completely beneath the governmental control of the Almighty!

No limitations must be placed upon the above declarations. To insist that some men, at least, do thwart God's will and overturn His counsels, is to repudiate other scriptures equally explicit. Weigh well the following: "But He is in one mind, and who can turn Him? and what His soul desireth, even that He doeth" (Job 23:13). "The counsel of the Lord standeth for ever, the thoughts of His heart to all generations" (Ps. 33:11). "There is no wisdom nor understanding nor counsel against the Lord" (Prov. 21:30). "For the Lord of hosts hath purposed, and who shall disannul it? And His hand is stretched out, and who shall turn it back?" (Isa. 14:27). "Remember the former things of old: for I am God, and there is none else! I am God, and there is none like Me, declaring the end from the beginning, and from ancient times the things that are not yet done, saying, My counsel shall stand, and I will do all My pleasure" (Isa. 46:9, 10). There is no ambiguity in these passages. They affirm in the most unequivocal and unqualified terms that it is impossible to bring to naught the purpose of Jehovah.

We read the Scriptures in vain if we fail to discover that the actions of men, evil men as well as good, are governed by the Lord God. Nimrod and his fellows determined to erect the tower of Babel, but ere their task was accomplished God frustrated their plans. God called Abraham "alone" (Isa. 51:2), but his kinsfolk accompanied him as he left Ur of the Chaldees. Was then the will of the Lord defeated? Nay, verily. Mark the sequel. Terah died before Canaan was reached (Gen. 11:31), and though Lot accompanied his uncle into the land of promise, he soon separated from him and settled down in Sodom. Jacob was the child to whom the inheritance was promised, and though Isaac sought to reverse Jehovah's decree and bestow the blessing upon Esau, his efforts came to naught. Esau again swore vengeance upon Jacob, but when next they met they wept for joy instead of fighting in hate. The brethren of Joseph determined his destruction, but their evil counsels were overthrown. Pharaoh refused to let Israel carry out the instructions of Jehovah and perished in the Red Sea for his pains. Balak hired Balaam to curse the Israelites, but God compelled him to bless them. Haman erected a gallows for Mordecai but was hanged upon it himself. Jonah resisted the revealed will of God, but what became of his efforts?

Ah, the heathen may "rage" and the people imagine a "vain thing"; the kings of the earth may "set themselves", and the rulers take counsel together against the Lord and against His Christ, saying, "Let us break Their bands asunder, and cast away Their cords from us" (Ps. 2:1-3). But is the great God perturbed or disturbed by the rebellion of His puny creatures? No, indeed: "He that sitteth in the heavens shall laugh: the Lord shall have them in derision" (v. 4). He is infinitely exalted above all, and the greatest confederacies of earth's pawns, and their most extensive and vigorous preparations to defeat His purpose are, in His sight, altogether purile. He looks upon their puny efforts, not only without any alarm, but He "laughs" at their folly; He treats their impotency with "derision." He knows that He can crush them like moths when He pleases, or consume them in a moment with the breath of His mouth. Ah, it is but "a vain thing" for the potsherds of the earth to strive with the glorious Majesty of Heaven. Such is our God; worship ye Him.

Mark, too, the sovereignty which God displayed in His dealings with men! Moses who was slow of speech, and not Aaron his elder brother who was not slow of speech, was the one chosen to be His ambassador in demanding from

The Holy Spirit

Egypt's monarch the release of His oppressed people. Moses again, though greatly beloved utters one hasty word and was excluded from Canaan; whereas Elijah, passionately murmurs and suffers but a mild rebuke, and was afterwards taken to heaven without seeing death! Uzzah merely touched the ark and was instantly slain, whereas the Philistines carried it off in insulting triumph and suffered no immediate harm. Displays of grace which would have brought a doomed Sodom to repentance, failed to move an highly privileged Capernaum. Mighty works which would have subdued Tyre and Sidon, left the upbraided cities of Galilee under the curse of a rejected Gospel. If they would have prevailed over the former, why were they not wrought there? If they proved ineffectual to deliver the latter then why perform them? What exhibitions are these of the sovereign will of the Most High!

4. God Governs Angels: Both Good and Evil Angels.

The angels are God's servants, His messengers, His chariots. They ever hearken to the word of His mouth and do His commands. "And God sent an angel unto Jerusalem to destroy it: and as he was destroying, the Lord beheld, and He repented Him of the evil, and said to the angel that destroyed, It is enough, Stay now thine hand. . . . And the Lord commanded the angel; and he put his sword again into the sheath thereof" (1 Chron. 21:15, 27). Many other scriptures might be cited to show that the angels are in subjection to the will of their Creator and perform His bidding—"And when Peter was come to himself, he said, Now I know of a surety, that the Lord hath sent His angel, and hath delivered me out of the hand of Herod" (Acts 12:11). "And the Lord God of the holy prophets sent His angel to shew unto His servants the things which must shortly be done" (Rev. 22:6). So it will be when our Lord returns: "The Son of Man shall send forth His angels and they shall gather out of His kingdom all things that offend, and them which do iniquity" (Matt. 13:41). Again, we read, "He shall send His angels with a great sound of a trumpet, and they shall gather together His elect from the four winds, from one end of heaven to the other" (Matt. 24:31).

The same is true of evil spirits: they, too, fulfil God's sovereign decrees. An evil spirit is sent by God to stir up rebellion in the camp of Abimelech: "Then God sent an evil spirit between Abimelech and the men of Shechem,. . . which aided him in the killing of his brethren" (Judges 9:23). Another evil spirit He sent to be a lying spirit in the mouth of Ahab's prophets—"Now therefore, behold, the Lord hath put a lying spirit in the mouth of all these thy prophets, and the Lord hath spoken evil concerning thee" (1 Kings 22:23). And yet another was sent by the Lord to trouble Saul—"But the Spirit of the Lord departed from Saul, and an evil spirit from the Lord troubled him"

(1 Sam. 16:14). So, too, in the New Testament: a whole legion of the demons go not out of their victim until the Lord gave them permission to enter the herd of swine.

It is clear from Scripture, then, that the angels, good and evil, are under God's control, and willingly or unwillingly carry out God's purpose. Yea, Satan himself is absolutely subject to God's control. When arraigned in Eden, he listened to the awful sentence, but answered not a word. He was unable to touch Job until God granted him leave. So, too, he had to gain our Lord's consent before he could "sift" Peter. When Christ commanded him to depart— "Get thee hence, Satan"—we read, "Then the Devil leaveth Him" (Matt. 4:11). And, in the end, he will be cast into the Lake of Fire, which has been prepared for him and his angels.

The Lord God omnipotent reigneth. His government is exercised over inanimate matter, over the brute beasts, over the children of men, over angels good and evil, and over Satan himself. No revolving world, no shining of star, no storm, no creature moves, no actions of men, no errands of angels, no deeds of Devil—nothing in all the vast universe can come to pass otherwise than God has eternally purposed. Here is a foundation for faith. Here is a resting place for the intellect. Here is an anchor for the soul, both sure and steadfast. It is not blind fate, unbridled evil, man or Devil, but the Lord Almighty who is ruling the world, ruling it according to His own good pleasure and for His own eternal glory.

"Ten thousand ages ere the skies
Were into motion brought;
All the long years and worlds to come,
Stood present to His thought:
There's not a sparrow nor a worm,
But's found in His decrees,
He raises monarchs to their thrones
And sinks as He may please."

The Sovereignty of God in Salvation

"O the depths of the riches both of the wisdom and knowledge of God! how unsearchable are His judgments, and His ways past finding out"
Romans 11:33

"Salvation is of the Lord" (Jonah 2:9); but the Lord does not save all. Why not? He does save some; then if He saves some, why not others? Is it because they are too sinful and depraved? No; for the apostle wrote, "This is a faithful saying, and worthy of all acceptation, that Christ Jesus came into the world to save sinners; of whom 1 am chief" (1 Tim. 1:15). Therefore, if God saved the "chief" of sinners, none are excluded because of their depravity. Why then does not God save all? Is it because some are too stony-hearted to be won? No; because of the most stony-hearted people of all it is written, that God will yet "take the stony heart out of their flesh, and will give them a heart of flesh" (Ezek. 11:19). Then is it because some are so stubborn, so intractable, so defiant that God is unable to woo them to Himself? Before we answer this question let us ask another; let us appeal to the experience of the Christian reader.

Friend; was there not a time when you walked in the counsel of the ungodly, stood in the way of sinners, sat in the seat of the scorners, and with them said, "We will not have this Man to reign over us" (Luke 19:14)? Was there not a time when you "would not come to Christ that you might have life" (John 5:40)? Yea, was there not a time when you mingled your voice with those who said unto God, "Depart from us; for we desire not the knowledge of Thy ways. What is the Almighty, that we should serve Him? and what profit should we have, if we pray unto Him?" (Job 21:14, 15)? With shamed face you have to acknowledge there was. But how is it that all is now changed? What was it that brought you from haughty self-sufficiency to a humble suppliant, from one that was at enmity with God to one that is at peace with Him, from lawlessness to subjection, from hate to love? And, as one 'born of the Spirit,' you will readily reply, "By the grace of God I am what I am" (1 Cor. 15:10). Then do you not see that it is due to no lack of power in God, nor to His refusal to coerce man, that other rebels are not saved too?

If God was able to subdue your will and win your heart, and that without interfering with your moral responsibility, then is He not able to do the same for others? Assuredly He is. Then how inconsistent, how illogical, how foolish of you, in seeking to account for the present course of the wicked and their ultimate fate, to argue that God is unable to save them, that they will not let Him. Do you say, "But the time came when I was willing, willing to receive Christ as my Saviour"? True, but it was the Lord who made you willing (Ps. 110:3; Phil. 2:13) why then does He not make all sinners willing? Why, but for the fact that He is sovereign and does as He pleases! But to return to our opening inquiry.

Why is it that all are not saved, particularly all who hear the Gospel? Do you still answer, Because the majority refuse to believe? Well, that is true, but it is only a part of the truth. It is the truth from the human side. But there is a Divine side too, and this side of the truth needs to be stressed or God will be robbed of His glory. The unsaved are lost because they refuse to believe; the others are saved because they believe. But why do these others believe? What is it that causes them to put their trust in Christ? Is it because they are more intelligent than their fellows, and quicker to discern their need of salvation? Perish the thought—"Who maketh thee to differ from another? And what hast thou that thou didst not receive? Now if thou didst receive it, why dost thou glory, as if thou hadst not received it?" (1 Cor. 4:7). It is God Himself who maketh the difference between the elect and the non-elect, for of His own it is written, "And we know that the Son of God is come, and hath given us an understanding, that we may know Him that is true" (1 John 5:20).

Faith is God's gift, and "all men have not faith" (2 Thess. 3:2); therefore, we see that God does not bestow this gift upon all. Upon whom then does He bestow this saving favor? And we answer, upon His own elect—"As many as were ordained to eternal life believed" (Acts 13:48). Hence it is that we read of "the faith of God's elect" (Titus 1:1). But is God partial in the distribution of His favors? Has He not the right to be? Are there still some who 'murmur against the Good-Man of the house'? Then His own words are sufficient reply—"Is it not lawful for Me to do what I will with Mine own?" (Matt. 20:15). God is sovereign in the bestowment of His gifts, both in the natural and in the spiritual realms. So much then for a general statement, and now to particularize.

1. The Sovereignty of God the Father in Salvation.

Perhaps the one Scripture which most emphatically of all asserts the absolute sovereignty of God in connection with His determining the destiny

The Holy Spirit

of His creatures, is the ninth of Romans. We shall not attempt to review here the entire chapter, but will confine ourselves to verses 21-23—"Hath not the potter power over the clay of the same lump, to make one vessel unto honor, and another unto dishonor? What if God, willing to show His wrath, and to make His power known, endured with much long-suffering the vessels of wrath fitted to destruction: And that He might make known the riches of His glory on the vessels of mercy, which He had afore prepared unto glory?" These verses represent fallen mankind as inert and as impotent as a lump of lifeless clay. This Scripture evidences that there is "no difference," in themselves, between the elect and the non-elect: they are clay of "the same lump," which agrees with Ephesians 2:3, where we are told, that all are by nature "children of wrath." It teaches us that the ultimate destiny of every individual is decided by the will of God, and blessed it is that such be the case; if it were left to our wills, the ultimate destination of us all would be the Lake of Fire. It declares that God Himself does make a difference in the respective destinations to which He assigns His creatures, for one vessel is made "unto honor and another unto dishonor;" some are "vessels of wrath fitted to destruction," others are "vessels of mercy, which He had afore prepared unto glory."

We readily acknowledge that it is very humbling to the proud heart of the creature to behold all mankind in the hand of God as the clay is in the potter's hand, yet this is precisely how the Scriptures of Truth represent the case. In this day of human boasting, intellectual pride, and deification of man, it needs to be insisted upon that the potter forms his vessels for himself. Let man strive with his Maker as he will, the fact remains that he is nothing more than clay in the Heavenly Potter's hands, and while we know that God will deal justly with His creatures, that the Judge of all the earth will do right, nevertheless, He shapes His vessels for His own purpose and according to His own pleasure. God claims the indisputable right to do as He wills with His own.

Not only has God the right to do as He wills with the creatures of His own hands, but He exercises this right, and nowhere is that seen more plainly than in His predestinating grace. Before the foundation of the world God made a choice, a selection, an election. Before His omniscient eye stood the whole of Adam's race, and from it He singled out a people and predestinated them "unto the adoption of children," predestinated them "to be conformed to the image of His Son," "ordained" them unto eternal life. Many are the Scriptures which set forth this blessed truth, seven of which will now engage our attention.

"As many as were ordained to eternal life, believed" (Acts 13:48). Every artifice of human ingenuity has been employed to blunt the sharp edge of this Scripture and to explain away the obvious meaning of these words, but it has been employed in vain, though nothing will ever be able to reconcile this and similar passages to the mind of the natural man. "As many as were ordained to eternal life, believed." Here we learn four things: First, that believing is the consequence and not the cause of God's decree. Second, that a limited number only are "ordained to eternal life," for if all men without exception were thus ordained by God, then the words "as many as are a meaningless qualification. Third, that this "ordination" of God is not to mere external privileges but to "eternal life," not to service but to salvation itself. Fourth, that all—"as many as," not one less—who are thus ordained by God to eternal life will most certainly believe.

The comments of the beloved Spurgeon on the above passage are well worthy of our notice. Said he, "Attempts have been made to prove that these words do not teach predestination, but these attempts so clearly do violence to language that I shall not waste time in answering them. I read: 'As many as were ordained to eternal life believed', and I shall not twist the text but shall glorify the grace of God by ascribing to that grace the faith of every man. Is it not God who gives the disposition to believe? If men are disposed to have eternal life, does not He—in every case—dispose them? Is it wrong for God to give grace? If it be right for Him to give it, is it wrong for Him to purpose to give it? Would you have Him give it by accident? If it is right for Him to purpose to give grace today, it was right for Him to purpose it before today—and, since He changes not—from eternity."

"Even so then at this present time also there is a remnant according to the election of grace. And if by grace, then it is no more of works: otherwise grace is no more grace. But if it be of works, then is it no more grace: otherwise work is no more work" (Rom. 11:5, 6). The words "Even so" at the beginning of this quotation refer us to the previous verse where we are told, "I have reserved to Myself seven thousand men who have not bowed the knee to Baal." Note particularly the word "reserved." In the days of Elijah there were seven thousand—a small minority—who were Divinely preserved from idolatry and brought to the knowledge of the true God. This preservation and illumination was not from anything in themselves, but solely by God's special influence and agency. How highly favored such individuals were to be thus "reserved" by God! Now says the apostle, Just as there was a "remnant" in Elijah's days "reserved by God", even so there is in this present dispensation.

"A remnant according to the election of grace." Here the cause of election is traced back to its source. The basis upon which God elected this "remnant" was not faith foreseen in them, because a choice founded upon the foresight of good works is just as truly made on the ground of works as any choice can be, and in such a case, it would not be "of grace;" for, says the apostle, "if by grace, then it is no more of works: otherwise grace is no more grace;" which means that grace and works are opposites, they have nothing in common, and will no more mingle than will oil and water. Thus the idea of inherent good foreseen in those chosen, or of anything meritorious performed by them, is rigidly excluded. "A remnant according to the election of grace," signifies an unconditional choice resulting from the sovereign favor of God; in a word, it is absolutely a gratuitous election.

"For ye see your calling, brethren, how that not many wise men after the flesh, not many mighty, not many noble, are called: But God hath chosen the foolish things of the world to confound the wise; and God hath chosen the weak things of the world to confound the things which are mighty: and base things of the world, and things which are despised, hath God chosen, yea, and things which are not, to bring to nought things that are: That no flesh should glory in His presence" (1 Cor. 1:26-29). Three times over in this passage reference is made to God's choice, and choice necessarily supposes a selection, the taking of some and the leaving of others. The Chooser here is God Himself, as said the Lord Jesus to the apostles, "Ye have not chosen Me, but I have chosen you" (John 15:16). The number chosen is strictly defined—"not many wise men after the flesh, not many noble," etc., which agrees with Matthew 20:16, "So the last shall be first, and the first last; for many be called, but few chosen." So much then for the fact of God's choice; now mark the objects of His choice.

The ones spoken of above as chosen of God are "the weak things of the world, base things of the world, and things which are despised." But why? To demonstrate and magnify His grace. God's ways as well as His thoughts are utterly at variance with man's. The carnal mind would have supposed that a selection had been made from the ranks of the opulent and influential, the amiable and cultured, so that Christianity might have won the approval and applause of the world by its pageantry and fleshly glory. Ah! but "that which is highly esteemed among men is abomination in the sight of God" (Luke 16:15). God chooses the "base things." He did so in Old Testament times. The nation which He singled out to be the depository of His holy oracles and the channel through which the promised Seed should come, was not the ancient Egyptians, the imposing Babylonians, nor the highly civilized and cultured Greeks. No; that people upon whom Jehovah set His love and regarded as 'the apple of His eye', were the despised, nomadic Hebrews. So it was when our Lord tabernacled among men. The ones whom He took into favored intimacy with Himself and commissioned to go forth as His ambassadors, were, for the most part, unlettered fishermen. And so it has been ever since. So it is today: at the present rates of increase, it will not be long before it is manifested that the Lord has more in despised China who are really His, than He has in the highly favored U. S. A.; more among the uncivilized blacks of Africa, than He has in cultured (?) Germany! And the purpose of God's choice, the raison d'etre of the selection He has made is, "that no flesh should glory in His presence"—there being nothing whatever in the objects of His choice which should entitle them to His special favors, then, all the praise will be freely ascribed to the exceeding riches of His manifold grace.

"Blessed be the God and Father of our Lord Jesus Christ, who hath blessed us with all spiritual blessings in the heavenlies in Christ: According as He hath chosen us in Him before the foundation of the world, that we should be holy and without blame before Him; In love having predestinated us unto the adoption of children by Jesus Christ to Himself, according to the good pleasure of His will. . . .In whom also we have obtained an inheritance, being predestinated according to the purpose of Him who worketh all things after the counsel of His own will" (Eph. 1:3-5, 11). Here again we are told at what point in time—if time it could be called—when God made choice of those who were to be His children by Jesus Christ. It was not after Adam had fallen and plunged his race into sin and wretchedness, but long ere Adam saw the light, even before the world itself was founded, that God chose us in Christ. Here also we learn the purpose which God had before Him in connection with His own elect: it was that they "should be holy and without blame before Him;" it was "unto the adoption of children;" it was that they should "obtain an inheritance." Here also we discover the motive which prompted Him. It was "in love that He predestinated us unto the adoption of children by Jesus Christ to Himself"—a statement which refutes the oft made and wicked charge that, for God to decide the eternal destiny of His creatures before they are born, is tyrannical and unjust. Finally, we are informed here, that in this matter He took counsel with none, but that we are "predestinated according to the good pleasure of His will."

"But we are bound to give thanks always to God for you, brethren beloved of the Lord, because God hath from the beginning chosen you to salvation through sanctification of the Spirit and belief of the truth" (2 Thess. 2:13).

The Holy Spirit

There are three things here which deserve special attention. First, the fact that we are expressly told that God's elect are "chosen to salvation." Language could not be more explicit. How summarily do these words dispose of the sophistries and equivocations of all who would make election refer to nothing but external privileges or rank in service! It is to "salvation" itself that God hath chosen us. Second, we are warned here that election unto salvation does not disregard the use of appropriate means: salvation is reached through "sanctification of the Spirit and belief of the truth." It is not true that because God has chosen a certain one to salvation that he will be saved willy-nilly, whether he believes or not: nowhere do the Scriptures so represent it. The same God who predestined the end, also appointed the means; the same God who "chose unto salvation", decreed that His purpose should be realized through the work of the Spirit and belief of the truth. Third, that God has chosen us unto salvation is a profound cause for fervent praise. Note how strongly the apostle expresses this—"we are bound to give thanks always to God for you, brethren beloved of the Lord, because God hath from the beginning chosen you to salvation," etc. Instead of shrinking back in horror from the doctrine of predestination, the believer, when he sees this blessed truth as it is unfolded in the Word, discovers a ground for gratitude and thanksgiving such as nothing else affords, save the unspeakable gift of the Redeemer Himself.

"Who hath saved us, and called us with an holy calling, not according to our works, but according to His own purpose and grace, which was given us in Christ Jesus before the world began" (2 Tim. 1:9). How plain and pointed is the language of Holy Writ! It is man who, by his words, darkeneth counsel. It is impossible to state the case more clearly, or strongly, than it is stated here. Our salvation is not "according to our works;" that is to say, it is not due to anything in us, nor the rewarding of anything from us; instead, it is the result of God's own "purpose and grace;" and this grace was given us in Christ Jesus before the world began. It is by grace we are saved, and in the purpose of God this grace was bestowed upon us not only before we saw the light, not only before Adam's fall, but even before that far distant "beginning" of Genesis 1:1. And herein lies the unassailable comfort of God's people. If His choice has been from eternity it will last to eternity! "Nothing can survive to eternity but what came from eternity, and what has so come, will" (G. S. Bishop).

"Elect according to the foreknowledge of God the Father, through sanctification of the Spirit, unto obedience and sprinkling of the blood of Jesus Christ" (1 Pet. 1:2). Here again election by the Father precedes the work of the Holy Spirit in, and the obedience of faith by, those who are saved; thus taking it entirely off creature ground, and resting it in the sovereign pleasure of the Almighty. The "foreknowledge of God the Father" does not here refer to His prescience of all things, but signifies that the saints were all eternally present in Christ before the mind of God. God did not "foreknow" that certain ones who heard the Gospel would believe it apart from the fact that He had "ordained" these certain ones to eternal life. What God's prescience saw in all men was, love of sin and hatred of Himself. The "foreknowledge" of God is based upon His own decrees as is clear from Acts 2:23—"Him, being delivered by the determinate counsel and foreknowledge of God, ye have taken, and by wicked hands have crucified and slain"—note the order here: first God's "determinate counsel" (His decree), and second His "foreknowledge." So it is again in Romans 8:28, 29, "For whom He did foreknow, He also did predestinate to be conformed to the image of His Son," but the first word here, "for," looks back to the preceding verse and the last clause of it reads, "to them who are the called according to His purpose"—these are the ones whom He did "foreknow and predestinate." Finally, it needs to be pointed out that when we read in Scripture of God "knowing" certain people, the word is used in the sense of knowing with approbation and love: "But if any man love God, the same is known of Him" (1 Cor. 8:3). To the hypocrites Christ will yet say "I never knew you"—He never loved them. "Elect according to the foreknowledge of God the Father" signifies, then, chosen by Him as the special objects of His approbation and love.

Summarizing the teaching of these seven passages we learn that, God has "ordained to eternal life" certain ones, and that in consequence of His ordination they, in due time, "believe;" that God's ordination to salvation of His own elect, is not due to any good thing in them nor to anything meritorious from them, but solely of His "grace;" that God has designedly selected the most unlikely objects to be the recipients of His special favors, in order that "no flesh should glory in His presence;" that God chose His people in Christ before the foundation of the world, not because they were so, but in order that they "should be, holy and without blame before him"; that having selected certain ones to salvation, He also decreed the means by which His eternal counsel should be made good; that the very "grace" by which we are saved was, in God's purpose, "given us in Christ Jesus before the world began;" that long before they were actually created, God's elect stood present before His mind, were "foreknown" by Him, i.e., were the definite objects of His eternal love.

Before turning to the next division of this chapter, a further word concerning the subjects of God's predestinating grace. We go over this ground again because it is at this point that the doctrine of God's sovereignty in predestining certain ones to salvation is most frequently assaulted. Perverters of this truth invariably seek to find some cause outside God's own will, which moves Him to bestow salvation on sinners; something or other is attributed to the creature which entitles him to receive mercy at the hands of the Creator. We return then to the question, Why did God choose the ones He did?

What was there in the elect themselves which attracted God's heart to them? Was it because of certain virtues they possessed? because they were generous-hearted, sweet tempered, truth-speaking? in a word, because they were "good," that God chose them? No; for our Lord said, "There is none good but one, that is God" (Matt. 19:17). Was it because of any good works they had performed? No; for it is written, "There is none that doeth good, no, not one" (Rom. 3:12). Was it because they evidenced an earnestness and zeal in inquiring after God? No; for it is written again, "There is none that seeketh after God" (Rom. 3:11). Was it because God foresaw they would believe? No; for how can those who are "dead in trespasses and sins" believe in Christ? How could God foreknow some men as believers when belief was impossible to them? Scripture declares that we "believe through grace" (Acts 18:27). Faith is God's gift, and apart from this gift none would believe. The cause of His choice then lies within Himself and not in the objects of His choice. He chose the ones He did simply because He chose to choose them.

"Sons we are by God's election
Who on Jesus Christ believe,
By eternal destination,
Sovereign grace we now receive,
Lord Thy mercy,
Doth both grace and glory give!"

2. The Sovereignty of God the Son in Salvation.

For whom did Christ die? It surely does not need arguing that the Father had an express purpose in giving Him to die, or that God the Son had a definite design before Him in laying down His life—"Known unto God are all His works from the beginning of the world" (Acts 15:18). What then was the purpose of the Father and the design of the Son? We answer, Christ died for "God's elect."

We are not unmindful of the fact that the limited design in the death of Christ has been the subject of much controversy—what great truth revealed in Scripture has not? Nor do we forget that anything which has to do with the person and work of our blessed Lord requires to be handled with the utmost reverence, and that a "Thus saith the Lord" must be given in support of every assertion we make. Our appeal shall be to the Law and to the Testimony.

For whom did Christ die? Who were the ones He intended to redeem by His blood-shedding? Surely the Lord Jesus had some absolute determination before Him when He went to the Cross. If He had, then it necessarily follows that the extent of that purpose was limited, because an absolute determination or purpose must be effected. If the absolute determination of Christ included all mankind, then all mankind would most certainly be saved. To escape this inevitable conclusion many have affirmed that there was no such absolute determination before Christ, that in His death a merely conditional provision of salvation has been made for all mankind. The refutation of this assertion is found in the promises made by the Father to His Son before He went to the Cross, yea, before He became incarnate. The Old Testament Scriptures represent the Father as promising the Son a certain reward for His sufferings on behalf of sinners. At this stage we shall confine ourselves to one or two statements recorded in the well known fifty-third of Isaiah. There we find God saying, "When Thou shalt make His soul an offering for sin, He shall see His seed," that "He shall see of the travail of His soul, and shall be satisfied," and that God's righteous Servant "should justify many" (vv. 10 and 11). But here we would pause and ask, How could it be certain that Christ should "see His seed," and "see of the travail of His soul and be satisfied," unless the salvation of certain members of the human race had been Divinely decreed, and therefore was sure? How could it be certain that Christ should "justify many," if no effectual provision was made that any should receive Him as their Saviour? On the other hand, to insist that the Lord Jesus did expressly purpose the salvation of all mankind, is to charge Him with that which no intelligent being should be guilty of, namely, to design that which by virtue of His omniscience He knew would never come to pass. Hence, the only alternative left us is that, so far as the pre-determined purpose of His death is concerned, Christ died for the elect only. Summing up in a sentence, which we trust will be intelligible to every reader, we would say, Christ died not merely to make possible the salvation of all mankind, but to make certain the salvation of all that the Father had given to Him. Christ died not simply to render sins pardonable, but "to put away sin by the sacrifice of Himself" (Heb. 9:26). As to who's "sin" (i.e., guilt, as in 1 John 1:7, etc.) has been "put away," Scripture leaves us in no doubt—it was that of the elect, the "world" (John 1:29) of God's people!

(1.) The limited design in the Atonement follows, necessarily, from the eternal choice of the Father of certain ones unto salvation. The Scriptures inform us that, before the Lord became incarnate He said, "Lo, I come, to do Thy will O God" (Heb. 10:7), and after He had become incarnate He declared, "For I came down from heaven, not to do Mine own will, but the will of Him that sent Me" (John 6:38). If then God had from the beginning chosen certain ones to salvation, then, because the will of Christ was in perfect accord with the will of the Father, He would not seek to enlarge upon His election. What we have just said is not merely a plausible deduction of our own, but is in strict harmony with the express teaching of the Word. Again and again our Lord referred to those whom the Father had "given" Him, and concerning whom He was particularly exercised. Said He, "All that the Father giveth Me shall come to Me; and him that cometh to Me I will in no wise cast out. . . . And this is the Father's will which hath sent Me, that of all which He hath given Me I should lose nothing, but should raise it up again at the last day" (John 6:37, 39). And again, "These words spake Jesus, and lifted up His eyes to heaven, and said, Father, the hour is come; glorify Thy Son, that Thy Son also may glorify Thee; As Thou hast given Him power over all flesh, that He should give eternal life to as many as Thou hast given Him. . . .I have manifested Thy name unto the men which Thou gavest Me out of the world: Thine they were, and Thou gavest them Me; and they have kept Thy Word. . . . I pray for them: I pray not for the world, but for them which Thou hast given Me; for they are Thine. . . . Father, I will that they also, whom Thou hast given Me, be with Me where I am; that they may behold My glory, which Thou hast given Me: for Thou lovest Me before the foundation of the world" (John 17:1, 2, 6, 9, 24). Before the foundation of the world the Father predestinated a people to be conformed to the image of His Son, and the death and resurrection of the Lord Jesus was in order to the carrying out of the Divine purpose.

(2.) The very nature of the Atonement evidences that, in its application to sinners, it was limited in the purpose of God. The Atonement of Christ may be considered from two chief viewpoints—Godward and manward. Godwards, the Cross-work of Christ was a propitiation, an appeasing of Divine wrath, a satisfaction rendered to Divine justice and holiness; manwards, it was a substitution, the Innocent taking the place of the guilty, the Just dying for the unjust. But a strict substitution of a Person for persons, and the infliction upon Him of voluntary sufferings, involve the definite recognition on the part of the Substitute and of the One He is to propitiate of the persons for whom He acts, whose sins He bears, whose legal obligations He discharges. Furthermore, if the Law-giver accepts the satisfaction which is made by the Substitute then those for whom the Substitute acts, whose place He takes, must necessarily be acquitted. If I am in debt and unable to discharge it and another comes forward and pays my creditor in full and receives a receipt in acknowledgment, then, in the sight of the law, my creditor no longer has any claim upon me. On the Cross the Lord Jesus gave Himself a ransom, and that it was accepted by God was attested by the open grave three days later; the question we would here raise is, For whom was this ransom offered? If it was offered for all mankind then the debt incurred by every man has been cancelled. If Christ bore in His own body on the tree the sins of all men without exception, then none will perish. If Christ was "made a curse" for all of Adam's race then none are now "under condemnation." "Payment God cannot twice demand, first at my bleeding Surety's hand and then again at mine." But Christ did not discharge the debt of all men without exception, for some there are who will be "cast into prison" (cf. 1 Pet. 3:19 where the same Greek word for "prison" occurs), and they shall "by no means come out thence, till they have paid the uttermost farthing" (Matt. 5:26), which, of course, will never be. Christ did not bear the sins of all mankind, for some there are who "die in their sins" (John 8:21), and whose "sin remaineth" (John 9:41). Christ was not "made a curse" for all of Adam's race, for some there are to whom He will yet say, "Depart from Me ye cursed" (Matt. 25:41). To say that Christ died for all alike, to say that He became the Substitute and Surety of the whole human race, to say that He suffered on behalf of and in the stead of all mankind, is to say that He "bore the curse for many who are now bearing the curse for themselves; that He suffered punishment for many who are now lifting up their own eyes in Hell, being in torments; that He paid the redemption price for many who shall yet pay in their own eternal anguish 'the wages of sin, which is death'" (G. S. Bishop). But, on the other hand, to say as Scripture says, that Christ was stricken for the transgressions of God's people, to say that He gave His life for the sheep, to say that He gave His life a ransom for many, is to say that He made an atonement which fully atones; it is to say He paid a price which actually ransoms; it is to say He was set forth a propitiation which really propitiates; it is to say He is a Saviour who truly saves.

(3.) Closely connected with, and confirmatory of what we have said above, is the teaching of Scripture concerning our Lord's priesthood. It is as the great High Priest that Christ now makes intercession. But for whom does He intercede? for the whole human race, or only for His own people? The answer furnished by the New Testament to this question is clear as a sunbeam. Our Saviour has entered into heaven itself "now to appear in the presence of God for us" (Heb. 9:24), that is, for those who are "partakers of the heavenly calling" (Heb. 3:1). And again it is written, "Wherefore He is able also to save them to the uttermost that come unto God by Him, seeing He ever liveth to make intercession for them" (Heb. 7:25). This is in strict accord with the Old Testament type. After slaying the sacrificial animal, Aaron went into the holy of holies as the representative and on behalf of the people of God: it was the names of Israel's tribes which were engraven on his breastplate, and it was in their interests he appeared before God. Agreeable to this are our Lord's words in John 17:9—"I pray for them: I pray not for the world, but for them which Thou hast given Me; for they are Thine." Another Scripture which deserves careful attention in this connection is found in Romans 8. In verse 33 the question is asked, "Who shall lay anything to the charge of God's elect?" and then follows the inspired answer— "It is God that justifieth. Who is he that condemneth? It is Christ that died, yea, rather that is risen again, who is even at the right hand of God, who also maketh intercession for us." Note particularly that the death and intercession of Christ have one and the same objects! As it was in the type so it is with the antitype—expiation and supplication are co-extensive. If then Christ intercedes for the elect only, and "not for the world," then He died for them only. And observe further, that the death, resurrection, exaltation and intercession of the Lord Jesus, are here assigned as the reason why none can lay any "charge" against God's elect. Let those who would still take issue with what we are advancing weigh carefully the following question—If the death of Christ extends equally to all, how does it become security against a "charge," seeing that all who believe not are "under condemnation"? (John 3:18).

(4.) The number of those who share the benefits of Christ's death is determined not only by the nature of the Atonement and the priesthood of Christ but also by His power. Grant that the One who died upon the cross was God manifest in the flesh, and it follows inevitably that what Christ has purposed that will He perform; that what He has purchased that will He possess; that what He has set His heart upon that will He secure. If the Lord Jesus possesses all power in heaven and earth, then none can successfully resist His will. But it may be said, This is true in the abstract, nevertheless, Christ refuses to exercise this power, inasmuch as He will never force anyone to receive Him as their Saviour. In one sense that is true, but in another sense it is positively untrue. The salvation of any sinner is a matter of Divine power. By nature the sinner is at enmity with God, and naught but Divine power operating within him, can overcome this enmity; hence it is written, "No man can come unto Me, except the Father which hath sent Me draw him" (John 6:44). It is the Divine power overcoming the sinner's innate enmity which makes him willing to come to Christ that he might have life. But this "enmity" is not overcome in all—why? Is it because the enmity is too strong to be overcome? Are there some hearts so steeled against Him that Christ is unable to gain entrance? To answer in the affirmative is to deny His omnipotence. In the final analysis it is not a question of the sinner's willingness or unwillingness, for by nature all are unwilling. Willingness to come to Christ is the finished product of Divine power operating in the human heart and will in overcoming man's inherent and chronic "enmity," as it is written, "Thy people shall be willing in the day of Thy power" (Ps. 110:3). To say that Christ is unable to win to Himself those who are unwilling is to deny that all power in heaven and earth is His. To say that Christ cannot put forth His power without destroying man's responsibility is a begging of the question here raised, for He has put forth His power and made willing those who have come to Him, and if He did this without destroying their responsibility, why "cannot" He do so with others? If He is able to win the heart of one sinner to Himself, why not that of another? To say, as is usually said, the others will not let Him is to impeach His sufficiency. It is a question of His will. If the Lord Jesus has decreed, desired, purposed the salvation of all mankind, then the entire human race will be saved, or, otherwise, He lacks the power to make good His intentions; and in such a case it could never be said, "He shall see of the travail of His soul and be satisfied." The issue raised involves the deity of the Saviour, for a defeated Saviour cannot be God.

Having reviewed some of the general principles which require us to believe that the death of Christ was limited in its design, we turn now to consider some of the explicit statements of Scripture which expressly affirm it. In that wondrous and matchless fifty-third of Isaiah God tells us concerning His Son, "He was taken from prison and from judgment: and who shall declare His generation? for He was cut off out of the land of the living: for the transgression of My people was He stricken" (v. 8). In perfect harmony with this was the word of the angel to Joseph, "Thou shalt call His name Jesus, for He shall save His people from their sins" (Matt. 1:21) i.e. not merely Israel, but all whom the Father had "given" Him. Our Lord Himself declared, "The Son of Man came not to be ministered unto, but to minister, and to give His life a ransom for many" (Matt. 20:28), but why have said "for many" if all without exception were included? It was "His people" whom He "redeemed" (Luke 1:68). It was for "the sheep," and not the "goats", that the Good Shepherd gave His life (John 10:11). It was the "Church of God" which He purchased with His own blood (Acts 20:28).

If there is one Scripture more than any other upon which we should be willing to rest our case it is John 11:49-52. Here we are told, "And one of them, named Caiaphas, being the high priest that same year, said unto them, Ye know nothing at all, nor consider that it is expedient for us, that one man should die for the people, and that the whole nation perish not. And this spake he not of himself: but being high priest that year, he prophesied that Jesus should die for that nation; And not for that nation only, but that also He should gather together in one the children of God that were scattered abroad." Here we are told that Caiaphas "prophesied not of himself," that is, like those employed by God in Old Testament times (see 2 Pet. 1:21), his prophecy originated not with himself, but he spake as he was moved by the Holy Spirit; thus is the value of his utterance carefully guarded, and the Divine source of this revelation expressly vouched for. Here, too, we are definitely informed that Christ died for "that nation," i.e., Israel, and also for the One Body, His Church, for it is into the Church that the children of God—"scattered" among the nations—are now being "gathered together in one." And is it not remarkable that the members of the Church are here called "children of God" even before Christ died, and therefore before He commenced to build His Church! The vast majority of them had not then been born, yet were they regarded as "children of God;" children of God because they had been chosen in Christ before the foundation of the world, and therefore "predestinated unto the adoption of children by Jesus Christ to Himself" (Eph. 1:4, 5). In like manner, Christ said, "Other sheep I have (not "shall have") which are not of this fold" (John 10:16).

If ever the real design of the Cross was uppermost in the heart and speech of our blessed Saviour it was during the last week of His earthly ministry. What then do the Scriptures which treat of this portion of His ministry record in connection with our present inquiry? They say, "When Jesus knew that His hour was come that He should depart out of this world unto the Father, having loved His own which were in the world, He loved them unto the end" (John 13:1). They tell us how He said, "Greater love hath no man than this, that a man lay down His life for His friends" (John 15:13). They record His word, "For their sakes I sanctify Myself, that they also might be sanctified through the truth" (John 17:19); which means, that for the sake of His own, those "given" to Him by the Father, He separated Himself unto the death of the Cross. One may well ask, Why such discrimination of terms if Christ died for all men indiscriminately?

Ere closing this section of the chapter we shall consider briefly a few of those passages which seem to teach most strongly an unlimited design in the death of Christ. In 2 Corinthians 5:14 we read, "One died for all." But that is not all this Scripture affirms. If the entire verse and passage from which these words are quoted be carefully examined, it will be found that instead of teaching an unlimited atonement, it emphatically argues a limited design in the death of Christ. The whole verse reads, "For the love of Christ constraineth us; because we thus judge, that if One died for all, then were all dead." It should be pointed out that in the Greek there is the definite article before the last "all," and that the verb here is in the aorist tense, and therefore should read, "We thus judge: that if One died for all, then they all died." The apostle is here drawing a conclusion as is clear from the words "we thus judge, that if . . . then were." His meaning is, that those for whom the One died are regarded, judicially, as having died too. The next verse goes on to say, "And He died for all, that they which live should not henceforth live unto themselves, but unto Him which died for them, and rose again." The One not only died but "rose again," and so, too, did the "all" for whom He died, for it is here said they "live." Those for whom a substitute acts are legally regarded as having acted themselves. In the sight of the law the substitute and those whom he represents are one. So it is in the sight of God. Christ was identified with His people and His people were identified with Him, hence when He died they died (judicially) and when He rose they rose also. But further we are told in this passage (v. 17), that if any man be in Christ he is a new creation; he has received a new life in fact as well as in the sight of the law, hence the "all" for whom Christ died are here bidden to live henceforth no more unto themselves, "but unto Him which died for them, and rose again." In other words, those who belonged to this "all" for whom Christ died, are here exhorted to manifest practically in their daily lives what is true of them judicially: they are to "live unto Christ who died for them." Thus the "One died for all" is defined for us. The "all" for which Christ died are the they which "live," and which are here bidden to live "unto Him." This passage then teaches three important truths, and the better to show its scope we mention them in their inverse order: certain ones are here bidden to live no more unto themselves but unto Christ; the ones thus admonished are "they which live," that is live spiritually, hence, the children of God, for they alone of mankind possess spiritual life, all others being dead in trespasses and sins; those who do thus live are the ones, the "all," the "them," for whom Christ died and rose again. This passage therefore teaches that Christ died for all His people, the elect, those given to Him by the Father; that as the result of His death (and rising again "for them") they "live"—and the elect are the only ones who do thus "live;" and this life which is theirs through Christ must be lived "unto Him," Christ's love must now "constrain" them.

"For there is one God, and one Mediator, between God and men (not "man", for this would have been a generic term and signified mankind. O the accuracy of Holy Writ!), the Man Christ Jesus; who gave Himself a ransom for all, to be testified in due time" (1 Tim. 2:5, 6). It is upon the words "who gave Himself a ransom for all" we would now comment. In Scripture the word "all" (as applied to humankind) is used in two senses—absolutely and relatively. In some passages it means all without exception; in others it signifies all without distinction. As to which of these meanings it bears in any particular passage, must be determined by the context and decided by a comparison of parallel Scriptures. That the word "all" is used in a relative and restricted sense, and in such case means all without distinction and not all without exception, is clear from a number of Scriptures, from which we select two or three as samples. "And there went out unto him all the land of Judea, and they of Jerusalem, and were all baptized of him in the river Jordan, confessing their sins" (Mark 1:5). Does this mean that every man, woman and child from "all the land of Judea and they of Jerusalem" were baptized of John in Jordan? Surely not. Luke 7:30 distinctly says, "But the Pharisees and lawyers rejected the counsel of God against themselves, being not baptized of him." Then what does "all baptized of him" mean? We answer it does not mean all without exception, but all without distinction, that is, all classes and conditions of men. The same explanation applies to Luke 3:21. Again we read, "And early in the morning He came again into the Temple, and all the people came unto Him; and He sat down, and taught them" (John 8:2); are we to understand this expression absolutely or relatively? Does "all the people" mean all without exception or all without distinction, that is, all classes and conditions of people? Manifestly the latter; for the Temple was not able to accommodate everybody that was in Jerusalem at this time, namely, the Feast of Tabernacles. Again, we read in Acts 22:15, "For thou (Paul) shalt be His witness unto all men of what thou hast seen and heard." Surely "all men" here does not mean every member of the human race. Now we submit that the words "who gave Himself a ransom for all" in 1 Timothy 2:6 mean all without distinction, and not all without exception. He gave Himself a ransom for men of all nationalities, of all generations, of all classes;

in a word, for all the elect, as we read in Revelation 5:9, "For Thou wast slain, and hast redeemed us to God by Thy blood out of every kindred, and tongue, and people, and nation." That this is not an arbitrary definition of the "all" in our passage is clear from Matthew 20:28 where we read, "The Son of Man came not to be ministered unto, but to minister, and to give His life a ransom for many", which limitation would be quite meaningless if He gave Himself a ransom for all without exception. Furthermore, the qualifying words here, "to be testified in due time", must be taken into consideration. If Christ gave Himself a ransom for the whole human race, in what sense will this be "testified in due time"? seeing that multitudes of men will certainly be eternally lost. But if our text means that Christ gave Himself a ransom for God's elect, for all without distinction, without distinction of nationality, social prestige, moral character, age or sex, then the meaning of these qualifying words is quite intelligible, for in "due time" this will be "testified" in the actual and accomplished salvation of every one of them.

"But we see Jesus, who was made a little lower than the angels for the suffering of death, crowned with glory and honor; that He by the grace of God should taste death for every man" (Heb. 2:9). This passage need not detain us long. A false doctrine has been erected here on a false translation. There is no word whatever in the Greek corresponding to "man" in our English version. In the Greek it is left in the abstract—"He tasted death for every." The Revised Version has correctly omitted "man" from the text, but has wrongly inserted it in italics. Others suppose the word "thing" should be supplied—"He tasted death for every thing" —but this, too, we deem a mistake. It seems to us that the words which immediately follow explain our text: "For it became Him, for whom are all things, and by whom are all things, in bringing many sons unto glory, to make the captain of their salvation perfect through sufferings." It is of "sons" the apostle is here writing, and we suggest an ellipsis of "son"—thus: "He tasted death for every"—and supply son in italics. Thus instead of teaching the unlimited design of Christ's death, Hebrews 2:9, 10 is in perfect accord with the other Scriptures we have quoted which set forth the restricted purpose in the Atonement: it was for the "sons" and not the human race our Lord "tasted death" (1 John 2:2 will be examined in detail in Appendix 4).

In closing this section of the chapter let us say that the only limitation in the Atonement we have contended for arises from pure sovereignty; it is a limitation not of value and virtue, but of design and application. We turn now to consider—

3. The Sovereignty of God the Holy Spirit in Salvation.

Since the Holy Spirit is one of the three Persons in the blessed Trinity, it necessarily follows that He is in full sympathy with the will and design of the other Persons of the Godhead. The eternal purpose of the Father in election, the limited design in the death of the Son, and the restricted scope of the Holy Spirit's operations are in perfect accord. If the Father chose certain ones before the foundation of the world and gave them to His Son, and if it was for them that Christ gave Himself a ransom, then the Holy Spirit is not now working to "bring the world to Christ." The mission of the Holy Spirit in the world today is to apply the benefits of Christ's redemptive sacrifice. The question which is now to engage us is not the extent of the Holy Spirit's power—on that point there can be no doubt, it is infinite—but what we shall seek to show is that, His power and operations are directed by Divine wisdom and sovereignty.

We have just said that the power and operations of the Holy Spirit are directed by Divine wisdom and indisputable sovereignty. In proof of this assertion we appeal first to our Lord's words to Nicodemus in John 3:8—"The wind bloweth where it listeth, and thou hearest the sound thereof, but canst not tell whence it cometh, and whither it goeth; so is every one that is born of the Spirit." A comparison is here drawn between the wind and the Spirit. The comparison is a double one: first, both are sovereign in their actions, and second, both are mysterious in their operations. The comparison is pointed out in the word "so." The first point of analogy is seen in the words "where it listeth" or "pleaseth"; the second is found in the words "canst not tell." With the second point of analogy we are not now concerned, but upon the first we would comment further.

"The wind bloweth where it pleaseth . . . so is every one that is born of the Spirit." The wind is an element which man can neither harness nor hinder. The wind neither consults man's pleasure nor can it be regulated by his devices. So it is with the Spirit. The wind blows when it pleases, where it pleases, as it pleases. So it is with the Spirit. The wind is regulated by Divine wisdom, yet, so far as man is concerned, it is absolutely sovereign in its operations. So it is with the Spirit. Sometimes the wind blows so softly it scarcely rustles a leaf; at other times it blows so loudly that its roar can be heard for miles. So it is in the matter of the new birth; with some the Holy Spirit deals so gently, that His work is imperceptible to human onlookers; with others His action is so powerful, radical, revolutionary, that His operations are patent to many. Sometimes the wind is purely local in its reach, at other times wide-spread in its scope. So it is with the Spirit: today He acts on one or two souls, tomorrow He may, as at Pentecost, "prick in the heart" a whole multitude. But whether He works on few or many, He consults not man. He acts as He pleases. The new birth is due to the sovereign will of the Spirit.

Each of the three Persons in the blessed Trinity is concerned with our salvation: with the Father it is predestination; with the Son propitiation; with the Spirit regeneration. The Father chose us; the Son died for us; the Spirit quickens us. The Father was concerned about us; the Son shed His blood for us, the Spirit performs His work within us. What the One did was eternal, what the Other did was external, what the Spirit does is internal. It is with the work of the Spirit we are now concerned, with His work in the new birth, and particularly His sovereign operations in the new birth. The Father purposed our new birth; the Son has made possible (by His "travail") the new birth; but it is the Spirit who effects the new birth—"Born of the Spirit" (John 3:6).

The new birth is solely the work of God the Spirit and man has no part or lot in it. This from the very nature of the case. Birth altogether excludes the idea of any effort or work on the part of the one who is born. Personally we have no more to do with our spiritual birth than we had with our natural birth. The new birth is a spiritual resurrection, a "passing from death unto life" (John 5:24) and, clearly, resurrection is altogether outside of man's province. No corpse can reanimate itself. Hence it is written, "It is the Spirit that quickeneth; the flesh profiteth nothing" (John 6:63). But the Spirit does not "quicken" everybody—why? The usual answer returned to this question is, Because everybody does not trust in Christ. It is supposed that the Holy Spirit quickens only those who believe. But this is to put the cart before the horse. Faith is not the cause of the new birth, but the consequence of it. This ought not to need arguing. Faith (in God) is an exotic, something that is not native to the human heart. If faith were a natural product of the human heart, the exercise of a principle common to human nature, it would never have been written, "All men have not faith" (2 Thess. 3:2). Faith is a spiritual grace, the fruit of the spiritual nature, and because the unregenerate are spiritually dead—"dead in trespasses and sins"—then it follows that faith from them is impossible, for a dead man cannot believe anything. "So then they that are in the flesh cannot please God" (Rom. 8:8)—but they could if it were possible for the flesh to believe. Compare with this last-quoted Scripture Hebrews 11:6—"But without faith it is impossible to please Him." Can God be "pleased" or satisfied with any thing which does not have its origin in Himself?

The Holy Spirit

That the work of the Holy Spirit precedes our believing is unequivocally established by 2 Thessalonians 2:13—"God hath from the beginning chosen you to salvation through sanctification of the Spirit and belief of the truth." Note that "sanctification of the Spirit" comes before and makes possible "belief of the truth." What then is the "sanctification of the Spirit"? We answer, the new birth. In Scripture "sanctification" always means "separation," separation from something and unto something or someone. Let us now amplify our assertion that the "sanctification of the Spirit" corresponds to the new birth and points to the positional effect of it.

Here is a servant of God who preaches the Gospel to a congregation in which are an hundred unsaved people. He brings before them the teaching of Scripture concerning their ruined and lost condition; he speaks of God, His character and righteous demands; he tells of Christ meeting God's demands, and dying the Just for the unjust, and declares that through "this Man" is now preached the forgiveness of sins; he closes by urging the lost to believe what God has said in His Word and receive His Son as their own personal Saviour. The meeting is over; the congregation disperses; ninety-nine of the unsaved have refused to come to Christ that they might have life, and go out into the night having no hope, and without God in the world. But the hundredth heard the Word of life; the Seed sown fell into ground which had been prepared by God; he believed the Good News, and goes home rejoicing that his name is written in heaven. He has been "born again," and just as a newly-born babe in the natural world begins life by clinging instinctively, in its helplessness, to its mother, so this newborn soul has clung to Christ. Just as we read, "The Lord opened" the heart of Lydia "that she attended unto the things which were spoken of Paul" (Acts 16:14), so in the case supposed above, the Holy Spirit quickened that one before he believed the Gospel message. Here then is the "sanctification of the Spirit:" this one soul who has been born again has, by virtue of his new birth, been separated from the other ninety-nine. Those born again are, by the Spirit, set apart from those who are dead in trespasses and sins.

A beautiful type of the operations of the Holy Spirit antecedent to the sinner's "belief of the truth", is found in the first chapter of Genesis. We read in verse 2, "And the earth was without form, and void; and darkness was upon the face of the deep." The original Hebrew here might be literally rendered thus: "And the earth had become a desolate ruin, and darkness was upon the face of the deep." In "the beginning" the earth was not created in the condition described in verse 2. Between the first two verses of Genesis 1 some awful catastrophe had occurred [the Gap Theory-ed.]—possibly the fall of Satan—and, as the consequence, the earth had been blasted and blighted, and had become a "desolate ruin", lying beneath a pall of "darkness." Such also is the history of man. Today, man is not in the condition in which he left the hands of his Creator: an awful catastrophe has happened, and now man is a "desolate ruin" and in total "darkness" concerning spiritual things. Next we read in Genesis 1 how God refashioned the ruined earth and created new beings to inhabit it. First we read, "And the Spirit of God moved upon the face of the waters." Next we are told, "And God said, Let there be light; and there was light." The order is the same in the new creation: there is first the action of the Spirit, and then the Word of God giving light. Before the Word found entrance into the scene of desolation and darkness, bringing with it the light, the Spirit of God "moved." So it is in the new creation. "The entrance of Thy words giveth light" (Ps. 119:130), but before it can enter the darkened human heart the Spirit of God must operate upon it. '

To return to 2 Thessalonians 2:13: "But we are bound to give thanks always to God for you, brethren beloved of the Lord, because God hath from the beginning chosen you to salvation through sanctification of the Spirit and belief of the truth." The order of thought here is most important and instructive. First, God's eternal choice; second, the sanctification of the Spirit; third, belief of the truth. Precisely the same order is found in 1 Peter 1:2—"Elect according to the foreknowledge of God the Father, through sanctification of the Spirit, unto obedience and sprinkling of the blood of Jesus Christ." We take it that the "obedience" here is the "obedience of faith" (Rom. 1:5), which appropriates the virtues of the sprinkled blood of the Lord Jesus. So then before the "obedience" (of faith, cf. Heb. 5:9), there is the work of the Spirit setting us apart, and behind that is the election of God the Father. The ones "sanctified of the Spirit" then, are they whom "God hath from the beginning chosen to salvation" (2 Thess. 2:13), those who are "elect according to the foreknowledge of God the Father" (1 Pet. 1:2).

But, it may be said, is not the present mission of the Holy Spirit to "convict the world of sin"? And we answer, It is not. The mission of the Spirit is threefold; to glorify Christ, to vivify the elect, to edify the saints. John 16:8-11 does not describe the "mission" of the Spirit, but sets forth the significance of His presence here in the world. It treats not of His subjective work in sinners, showing them their need of Christ, by searching their consciences and striking terror to their hearts; what we have there is entirely objective. To illustrate. Suppose I saw a man hanging on the gallows, of what would that "convince" me? Why, that he was a murderer. How would I thus be convinced? By reading the record of his trial? by hearing a confession from his own lips? No; but by the fact that he was hanging there. So the fact that the Holy Spirit is here furnishes proof of the world's guilt, of God's righteousness, and of the Devil's judgment.

The Holy Spirit ought not to be here at all. That is a startling statement, but we make it deliberately. Christ is the One who ought to be here. He was sent here by the Father, but the world did not want Him, would not have Him, hated Him, and cast Him out. And the presence of the Spirit here instead evidences its guilt. The coming of the Spirit was a proof to demonstration of the resurrection, ascension, and glory of the Lord Jesus. His presence on earth reverses the world's verdict, showing that God has set aside the blasphemous judgment in the palace of Israel's high priest and in the hall of the Roman governor. The "reproof" of the Spirit abides, and abides altogether irrespective of the world's reception or rejection of His testimony.

Had our Lord been referring here to the gracious work which the Spirit would perform in those who should be brought to feel their need of Him, He had said that the Spirit would convict men of their unrighteousness, their lack of righteousness. But this is not the thought here at all. The descent of the Spirit from heaven establishes God's righteousness, Christ's righteousness. The proof of that is, Christ has gone to the Father. Had Christ been an Imposter, as the religious world insisted when they cast Him out, the Father had not received Him. The fact that the Father did exalt Him to His own right hand, demonstrates that He was innocent of the charges laid against Him; and the proof that the Father has received Him, is the presence now of the Holy Spirit on earth, for Christ has sent Him from the Father (John 16:7)! The world was unrighteous in casting Him out, the Father righteous in glorifying Him; and this is what the Spirit's presence here establishes.

"Of judgment, because the Prince of this world is judged" (v. 11). This is the logical and inevitable climax. The world is brought in guilty for their rejection of, for their refusal to receive, Christ. Its condemnation is exhibited by the Father's exaltation of the spurned One. Therefore nothing awaits the world, and its Prince, but judgment. The "judgment" of Satan is already established by The Spirit's presence here, for Christ, through death, set at nought him who had the power of death, that is, the Devil (Heb. 2:14). When God's time comes for the Spirit to depart from the earth, then His sentence will be executed, both on the world and its Prince. In the light of this unspeakably solemn passage, we need not be surprised to find Christ saying, "The Spirit of truth, whom the world cannot receive, because it seeth Him not, neither knoweth Him". No, the world wants Him not; He condemns the world.

"And when He is come, He will reprove (or, better, "convict"—bring in guilty) the world of sin, and of righteousness, and of judgment: Of sin, because they believe not on Me; Of righteousness, because I go to My Father, and ye see Me no more; Of judgment, because the prince of this world is judged" (John 16:8-11). Three things, then, the presence of the Holy Spirit on earth demonstrates to the world: first, its sin, because the world refused to believe on Christ; second, God's righteousness in exalting to His own right hand the One cast out, and now no more seen by the world; third, judgment, because Satan the world's prince is already judged, though execution of his judgment is yet future. Thus the Holy Spirit's presence here displays things as they really are.

The Holy Spirit is sovereign in His operations and His mission is confined to God's elect: they are the ones He "comforts," "seals," guides into all truth, shews things to come, etc. The work of the Spirit is necessary in order to the complete accomplishment of the Father's eternal purpose. Speaking hypothetically, but reverently, be it said, that if God had done nothing more than given Christ to die for sinners, not a single sinner would ever have been saved. In order for any sinner to see his need of a Saviour and be willing to receive the Saviour he needs, the work of the Holy Spirit upon and within him were imperatively required. Had God done nothing more than given Christ to die for sinners and then sent forth His servants to proclaim salvation through Christ, leaving sinners entirely to themselves to accept or reject as they pleased, then every sinner would have rejected, because at heart every man hates God and is at enmity with Him. Therefore the work of the Holy Spirit was needed to bring the sinner to Christ, to overcome his innate opposition, and compel him to accept the provision God has made. We say "compel" the sinner, for this is precisely what the Holy Spirit does, has to do, and this leads us to consider at some length, though as briefly as possible, the parable of the "Marriage Supper."

In Luke 14:16 we read, "A certain man made a great supper, and bade many." By comparing carefully what follows here with Matthew 22:2-10 several important distinctions will be observed. We take it that these passages are two independent accounts of the same parable, differing in detail according to the distinctive purpose and design of the Holy Spirit in each Gospel. Matthew's account—in harmony with the Spirit's presentation there of Christ as the Son of David, the King of the Jews—says, "A certain king made a marriage for his son." Luke's account—where the Spirit presents Christ as the Son of Man—says, "A certain man made a great supper and bade many." Matthew 22:3 says, "And sent forth His servants;" Luke 14:17

The Holy Spirit

says, "And sent His servant." Now what we wish particularly to call attention to is, that all through Matthew's account it is "servants," whereas in Luke it is always "servant." The class of readers for whom we are writing are those that believe, unreservedly, in the verbal inspiration of the Scriptures, and such will readily acknowledge there must be some reason for this change from the plural number in Matthew to the singular number in Luke. We believe the reason is a weighty one and that attention to this variation reveals an important truth. We believe that the "servants" in Matthew, speaking generally, are all who go forth preaching the Gospel, but that the "Servant" in Luke 14 is the Holy Spirit Himself. This is not incongruous, or derogatory to the Holy Spirit, for God the Son, in the days of His earthly ministry, was the Servant of Jehovah (Isa. 42:1). It will be observed that in Matthew 22 the "servants" are sent forth to do three things: first, to "call" to the wedding (v. 3); second, to "tell those which are bidden . . . all things are ready: come unto the marriage" (v. 4); third, to "bid to the marriage" (v. 9); and these three are the things which those who minister the Gospel today are now doing. In Luke 14 the Servant is also sent forth to do three things: first, He is "to say to them that were bidden, Come: for all things are now ready" (v. 17) ; second, He is to "bring in the poor, and the maimed, and the halt, and the blind" (v. 21); third, He is to "compel them to come in" (v. 23), and the last two of these the Holy Spirit alone can do!

In the above Scripture we see that "the Servant," the Holy Spirit, compels certain ones to come in to the "supper" and herein is seen His sovereignty, His omnipotency, His Divine sufficiency. The clear implication from this word "compel" is, that those whom the Holy Spirit does "bring in" are not willing of themselves to come. This is exactly what we have sought to show in previous paragraphs. By nature, God's elect are children of wrath even as others (Eph. 2:3), and as such their hearts are at enmity with God. But this "enmity" of theirs is overcome by the Spirit and He "compels" them to come in. Is it not clear then that the reason why others are left outside, is not only because they are unwilling to go in, but also because the Holy Spirit does not "compel" them to come in? Is it not manifest that the Holy Spirit is sovereign in the exercise of His power, that as the wind "bloweth where it pleaseth", so the Holy Spirit operates where He pleases?

And now to sum up. We have sought to show the perfect consistency of God's ways: that each Person in the Godhead acts in sympathy and harmony with the Others. God the Father elected certain ones to salvation, God the Son died for the elect, and God the Spirit quickens the elect. Well may we sing,

Praise God from whom all blessings flow,
Praise Him all creatures here below,
Praise Him above ye heavenly host,
Praise Father, Son, and Holy Ghost.

The Sovereignty of God in Reprobation

"Behold therefore the goodness and the severity of God"
Romans. 11:22

In the last chapter when treating of the Sovereignty of God the Father in Salvation, we examined seven passages which represent Him as making a choice from among the children of men, and predestinating certain ones to be conformed to the image of His Son. The thoughtful reader will naturally ask, And what of those who were not "ordained to eternal life?" The answer which is usually returned to this question, even by those who profess to believe what the Scriptures teach concerning God's sovereignty, is, that God passes by the non-elect, leaves them alone to go their own way, and in the end casts them into the Lake of Fire because they refused His way, and rejected the Saviour of His providing. But this is only a part of the truth; the other part—that which is most offensive to the carnal mind—is either ignored or denied.

In view of the awful solemnity of the subject here before us, in view of the fact that today almost all—even those who profess to be Calvinists—reject and repudiate this doctrine, and in view of the fact that this is one of the points in our book which is calculated to raise the most controversy, we feel that an extended enquiry into this aspect of God's Truth is demanded. That this branch of the subject of God's sovereignty is profoundly mysterious we freely allow, yet, that is no reason why we should reject it. The trouble is that, nowadays, there are so many who receive the testimony of God only so far as they can satisfactorily account for all the reasons and grounds of His conduct, which means they will accept nothing but that which can be measured in the petty scales of their own limited capacities.

Stating it in its baldest form the point now to be considered is, Has God fore-ordained certain ones to damnation? That many will be eternally damned is clear from Scripture, that each one will be judged according to his works and reap as he has sown, and that in consequence his "damnation is just" (Rom. 3:8), is equally sure, and that God decreed that the non-elect should choose the course they follow we now undertake to prove.

From what has been before us in the previous chapter concerning the election of some to salvation, it would unavoidably follow, even if Scripture had been silent upon it, that there must be a rejection of others. Every choice, evidently and necessarily implies a refusal, for where there is no leaving out there can be no choice. If there be some whom God has elected unto salvation (2 Thess. 2:13), there must be others who are not elected unto salvation. If there are some that the Father gave to Christ (John 6:37), there must be others whom He did not give unto Christ. If there are some whose names are written in the Lamb's book of Life (Rev. 21:27), there must be others whose names are not written there. That this is the case we shall fully prove below.

Now all will acknowledge that from the foundation of the world God certainly fore-knew and fore-saw who would and who would not receive Christ as their Saviour, therefore in giving being and birth to those He knew would reject Christ, He necessarily created them unto damnation. All that can be said in reply to this is, No, while God did foreknow these ones would reject Christ, yet He did not decree that they should. But this is a begging of the real question at issue. God had a definite reason why He created men, a specific purpose why He created this and that individual, and in view of the eternal destination of His creatures, He purposed either that this one should spend eternity in Heaven or that this one should spend eternity in the Lake of Fire. If then He foresaw that in creating a certain person that that person would despise and reject the Saviour, yet knowing this beforehand He, nevertheless, brought that person into existence, then it is clear He designed and ordained that that person should be eternally lost. Again; faith is God's gift, and the purpose to give it only to some, involves the purpose not to give it to others. Without faith there is no salvation—"He that believeth not shall be damned"— hence if there were some of Adam's descendants to whom He purposed not to give faith, it must be because He ordained that they should be damned.

Not only is there no escape from these conclusions, but history confirms them. Before the Divine Incarnation, for almost two thousand years, the vast majority of mankind were left destitute of even the external means of grace, being favored with no preaching of God's Word and with no written revelation of His will. For many long centuries Israel was the only nation to whom the Deity vouchsafed any special discovery of Himself—"Who in times past suffered all nations to walk in their own ways" (Acts 14:16)—"You only (Israel) have I known of all the families of the earth" (Amos 3:2). Consequently, as all other nations were deprived of the preaching of God's

Word, they were strangers to the faith that cometh thereby (Rom. 10:17). These nations were not only ignorant of God Himself, but of the way to please Him, of the true manner of acceptance with Him, and the means of arriving at the everlasting enjoyment of Himself.

Now if God had willed their salvation, would He not have vouchsafed them the means of salvation? Would He not have given them all things necessary to that end? But it is an undeniable matter of fact that He did not. If, then, Deity can, consistently, with His justice, mercy, and benevolence, deny to some the means of grace, and shut them up in gross darkness and unbelief (because of the sins of their forefathers, generations before), why should it be deemed incompatible with His perfections to exclude some persons, many, from grace itself, and from that eternal life which is connected with it? seeing that He is Lord and sovereign Disposer both of the end to which the means lead, and the means which lead to that end?

Coming down to our own day, and to those in our own country—leaving out the almost innumerable crowds of unevangelized heathen—is it not evident that there are many living in lands where the Gospel is preached, lands which are full of churches, who die strangers to God and His holiness? True, the means of grace were close to their hand, but many of them knew it not. Thousands are born into homes where they are taught from infancy to regard all Christians as hypocrites and preachers as arch-humbugs. Others, are instructed from the cradle in Roman Catholicism, and are trained to regard Evangelical Christianity as deadly heresy, and the Bible as a book highly dangerous for them to read. Others, reared in "Christian Science" families, know no more of the true Gospel of Christ than do the unevangelized heathen. The great majority of these die in utter ignorance of the Way of Peace. Now are we not obliged to conclude that it was not God's will to communicate grace to them? Had His will been otherwise, would He not have actually communicated His grace to them? If, then, it was the will of God, in time, to refuse to them His grace, it must have been His will from all eternity, since His will is, as Himself, the same yesterday, and today and forever. Let it not be forgotten that God's providences are but the manifestations of His decrees: what God does in time is only what He purposed in eternity—His own will being the alone cause of all His acts and works. Therefore from His actually leaving some men in final impenitency and unbelief we assuredly gather it was His everlasting determination so to do; and consequently that He reprobated some from before the foundation of the world.

In the Westminster Confession it is said, "God from all eternity did by the most wise and holy counsel of His own will, freely and unchangeably foreordain whatsoever comes to pass". The late Mr. F. W. Grant—a most careful and cautious student and writer—commenting on these words said: "It is perfectly, divinely true, that God hath ordained for His own glory whatsoever comes to pass." Now if these statements are true, is not the doctrine of Reprobation established by them? What, in human history, is the one thing which does come to pass every day? What, but that men and women die, pass out of this world into a hopeless eternity, an eternity of suffering and woe. If then God has foreordained whatsoever comes to pass then He must have decreed that vast numbers of human beings should pass out of this world unsaved to suffer eternally in the Lake of Fire. Admitting the general premise, is not the specific conclusion inevitable?

In reply to the preceding paragraphs the reader may say, All this is simply reasoning, logical no doubt, but yet mere inferences. Very well, we will now point out that in addition to the above conclusions there are many passages in Holy Writ, which are most clear and definite in their teaching on this solemn subject; passages which are too plain to be misunderstood and too strong to be evaded. The marvel is that so many good men have denied their undeniable affirmations.

"Joshua made war a long time with all those kings. There was not a city that made peace with the children of Israel, save the Hivites the inhabitants of Gibeon: all other they took in battle. For it was of the Lord to harden their hearts, that they should come against Israel in battle, that He might destroy them utterly, and that they might have no favour, but that He might destroy them, as the Lord commanded Moses" (Josh. 11:18-20). What could be plainer than this? Here was a large number of Canaanites whose hearts the Lord hardened, whom He had purposed to utterly destroy, to whom He showed "no favour". Granted that they were wicked, immoral, idolatrous; were they any worse than the immoral, idolatrous cannibals of the South Sea Islands (and many other places), to whom God gave the Gospel through John G. Paton! Assuredly not. Then why did not Jehovah command Israel to teach the Canaanites His laws and instruct them concerning sacrifices to the true God? Plainly, because He had marked them out for destruction, and if so, that from all eternity.

"The Lord hath made all things for Himself: yea, even the wicked for the day of evil." (Prov. 16:4). That the Lord made all, perhaps every reader of this book will allow: that He made all for Himself is not so widely believed. That God made us, not for our own sakes, but for Himself; not for our own happiness, but for His glory; is, nevertheless, repeatedly affirmed in Scripture—Revelation 4:11. But Proverbs 16:4 goes even farther: it expressly declares that the Lord made the wicked for the Day of Evil: that was His design in giving them being. But why? Does not Romans 9:17 tell us, "For the Scripture saith unto Pharaoh, Even for this purpose have I raised thee up, that I might shew My power in thee, and that My name might be declared throughout all the earth"! God has made the wicked that, at the end, He may demonstrate "His power"—demonstrate it by showing what an easy matter it is for Him to subdue the stoutest rebel and to overthrow His mightiest enemy.

"And then will I profess unto them, I never knew you: Depart from Me, ye that work iniquity" (Matt. 7:23). In the previous chapter it has been shown that, the words "know" and "foreknowledge" when applied to God in the Scriptures, have reference not simply to His prescience (i.e. His bare knowledge beforehand), but to His knowledge of approbation. When God said to Israel, "You only have I known of all the families of the earth" (Amos 3:2), it is evident that He meant, "You only had I any favorable regard to." When we read in Romans 11:2 "God hath not cast away His people (Israel) whom He foreknew," it is obvious that what was signified is, "God has not finally rejected that people whom He has chosen as the objects of His love—cf. Deuternomy 7:7, 8. In the same way (and it is the only possible way) are we to understand Matthew 7:23. In the Day of Judgment the Lord will say unto many, "I never knew you". Note, it is more than simply "I know you not". His solemn declaration will be, "I never knew you"—you were never the objects of My approbation. Contrast this with "I know (love) My sheep, and am known (loved) of Mine" (John 10:14). The "sheep", His elect, the "few", He does "know"; but the reprobate, the non-elect, the "many" He knows not—no, not even before the foundation of the world did He know them—He "NEVER" knew them!

In Romans 9 the doctrine of God's sovereignty in its application to both the elect and the reprobate is treated of at length. A detailed exposition of this important chapter would be beyond our present scope; all that we can essay is to dwell upon the part of it which most clearly bears upon the aspect of the subject which we are now considering.

Verse 17: "For the Scripture saith unto Pharaoh, Even for this same purpose have I raised thee up, that I might show My power in thee, and that My name might be declared throughout all the earth." These words refer us back to verses 13 and 14. In verse 13 God's love to Jacob and His hatred to Esau are declared. In verse 14 it is asked "Is there unrighteousness with

God?" and here in verse 17 the apostle continues his reply to the objection. We cannot do better now than quote from Calvin's comments upon this verse. "There are here two things to be considered,—the predestination of Pharaoh to ruin, which is to be referred to the past and yet the hidden counsel of God,—and then, the design of this, which was to make known the name of God. As many interpreters, striving to modify this passage, pervert it, we must first observe, that for the word 'I have raised thee up', or stirred up, in the Hebrew is, 'I have appointed', by which it appears, that God, designing to show that the contumacy of Pharaoh would not prevent Him to deliver His people, not only affirms that his fury had been foreseen by Him, and that He had prepared means for restraining it, but that He had also thus designedly ordained it and indeed for this end,—that he might exhibit a more illustrious evidence of His own power." It will be observed that Calvin gives as the force of the Hebrew word which Paul renders "For this purpose have I raised thee up,"—"I have appointed". As this is the word on which the doctrine and argument of the verse turns we would further point out that in making this quotation from Exodus 9:16 the apostle significantly departs from the Septuagint—the version then in common use, and from which he most frequently quotes—and substitutes a clause for the first that is given by the Septuagint: instead of "On this account thou hast been preserved", he gives "For this very end have I raised thee up"!

But we must now consider in more detail the case of Pharaoh which sums up in concrete example the great controversy between man and his Maker. "For now I will stretch out My hand, that I may smite thee and thy people with pestilence; and thou shalt be cut off from the earth. And in very deed for this cause have I raised thee up, for to show in thee My power; and that My name may be declared throughout all the earth" (Ex. 9:15, 16). Upon these words we offer the following comments:

First, we know from Exodus 14 and 15 that Pharaoh was "cut off", that he was cut off by God, that he was cut off in the very midst of his wickedness, that he was cut off not by sickness nor by the infirmities which are incident to old age, nor by what men term an accident, but cut off by the immediate hand of God in judgment.

Second, it is clear that God raised up Pharaoh for this very end—to "cut him off," which in the language of the New Testament means "destroyed." God never does anything without a previous design. In giving him being, in preserving him through infancy and childhood, in raising him to the throne of Egypt, God had one end in view. That such was God's purpose is clear from His words to Moses before he went down to Egypt, to demand of Pharaoh that Jehovah's people should be allowed to go a three days' journey into the wilderness to worship Him—"And the Lord said unto Moses, When thou goest to return into Egypt, see that thou do all these wonders before Pharaoh, which I have put in thine hand: but I will harden his heart, that he shall not let the people go" (Ex. 4:21). But not only so, God's design and purpose was declared long before this. Four hundred years previously God had said to Abraham, "Know of a surety that thy seed shall be a stranger in a land that is not theirs, and shall serve them; and they shall afflict them four hundred years; and also that nation, whom they shall serve, will I judge" (Gen. 15:13, 14). From these words it is evident (a nation and its king being looked at as one in the O. T.) that God's purpose was formed long before He gave Pharaoh being.

Third, an examination of God's dealings with Pharaoh makes it clear that Egypt's king was indeed a "vessel of wrath fitted to destruction." Placed on Egypt's throne, with the reins of government in his hands, he sat as head of the nation which occupied the first rank among the peoples of the world. There was no other monarch on earth able to control or dictate to Pharaoh. To such a dizzy height did God raise this reprobate, and such a course was a natural and necessary step to prepare him for his final fate, for it is a Divine axiom that "pride goeth before destruction and a haughty spirit before a fall." Further,—and this is deeply important to note and highly significant—God removed from Pharaoh the one outward restraint which was calculated to act as a check upon him. The bestowing upon Pharaoh of the unlimited powers of a king was setting him above all legal influence and control. But besides this, God removed Moses from his presence and kingdom. Had Moses, who not only was skilled in all the wisdom of the Egyptians but also had been reared in Pharaoh's household, been suffered to remain in close proximity to the throne, there can be no doubt but that his example and influence had been a powerful check upon the king's wickedness and tyranny. This, though not the only cause, was plainly one reason why God sent Moses into Midian, for it was during his absence that Egypt's inhuman king framed his most cruel edicts. God designed, by removing this restraint, to give Pharaoh full opportunity to fill up the full measure of his sins, and ripen himself for his fully-deserved but predestined ruin.

Fourth, God "hardened" his heart as He declared He would (Ex. 4:21). This is in full accord with the declarations of Holy Scripture—"The preparations of the heart in man, and the answer of the tongue, is from the Lord" (Prov. 16:1); "The king's heart is in the hand of the Lord, as the rivers of water, He turneth it whithersoever He will" (Prov. 21:1). Like all other kings, Pharaoh's heart was in the hand of the Lord; and God had both the right and the power to turn it whithersoever He pleased. And it pleased Him to turn it against all good. God determined to hinder Pharaoh from granting his request through Moses to let Israel go, until He had fully prepared him for his final overthrow, and because nothing short of this would fully fit him, God hardened his heart.

Finally, it is worthy of careful consideration to note how the vindication of God in His dealings with Pharaoh has been fully attested. Most remarkable it is to discover that we have Pharaoh's own testimony in favor of God and against himself! In Exodus 9:15 and 16 we learn how God had told Pharaoh for what purpose He had raised him up, and in verse 27 of the same chapter we are told that Pharaoh said, "I have sinned this time: the Lord is righteous, and I and my people are wicked." Mark that this was said by Pharaoh after he knew that God had raised him up in order to "cut him off", after his severe judgments had been sent upon him, after he had hardened his own heart. By this time Pharaoh was fairly ripened for judgment, and fully prepared to decide whether God had injured him, or whether he had sought to injure God; and he fully acknowledges that he had "sinned" and that God was "righteous". Again; we have the witness of Moses who was fully acquainted with God's conduct toward Pharaoh. He had heard at the beginning what was God's design in connection with Pharaoh; he had witnessed God's dealings with him; he had observed his "long-sufferance" toward this vessel of wrath fitted to destruction; and at last he had beheld him cut off in Divine judgment at the Red Sea. How then was Moses impressed?

Does he raise the cry of injustice? Does he dare to charge God with unrighteousness? Far from it. Instead, he says, "Who is like unto Thee, O Lord, among the gods? "Who is like Thee, glorious in holiness, fearful in praises, doing wonders!" (Ex. 15:11).

Was Moses moved by a vindictive spirit as he saw Israel's arch-enemy "cut off" by the waters of the Red Sea? Surely not. But to remove forever all doubt upon this score, it remains to be pointed out how that saints in heaven, after they have witnessed the sore judgments of God, join in singing "the song of Moses the servant of God, and the song of the Lamb saying, Great and marvelous are Thy works, Lord God Almighty; just and true are Thy ways, Thou King of Nations" (Rev. 15:3). Here then is the climax, and the full and final vindication of God's dealings with Pharaoh. Saints in heaven join in singing the Song of Moses, in which that servant of God celebrated Jehovah's praise in overthrowing Pharaoh and his hosts, declaring that in so acting God was not unrighteous but just and true. We must believe, therefore, that the

Judge of all the earth did right in creating and destroying this vessel of wrath, Pharaoh.

The case of Pharaoh establishes the principle and illustrates the doctrine of Reprobation. If God actually reprobated Pharaoh, we may justly conclude that He reprobates all others whom He did not predestinate to be conformed to the image of His Son. This inference the apostle Paul manifestly draws from the fate of Pharaoh, for in Romans 9, after referring to God's purpose in raising up Pharaoh, he continues, "therefore". The case of Pharaoh is introduced to prove the doctrine of Reprobation as the counterpart of the doctrine of Election.

In conclusion, we would say that in forming Pharaoh God displayed neither justice nor injustice, but only His bare sovereignty. As the potter is sovereign in forming vessels, so God is sovereign in forming moral agents.

Verse 18: "Therefore hath He mercy on whom He will have mercy, and whom He will He hardeneth". The "therefore" announces the general conclusion which the apostle draws from all he had said in the three preceding verses in denying that God was unrighteous in loving Jacob and hating Esau, and specifically it applies the principle exemplified in God's dealings with Pharaoh. It traces everything back to the sovereign will of the Creator. He loves one and hates another, He exercises mercy toward some and hardens others, without reference to anything save His own sovereign will.

That which is most repellant to the carnal mind in the above verse is the reference to hardening—"Whom He will He hardeneth"—and it is just here that so many commentators and expositors have adulterated the truth. The most common view is that the apostle is speaking of nothing more than judicial hardening, i.e., a forsaking by God because these subjects of His displeasure had first rejected His truth and forsaken Him. Those who contend for this interpretation appeal to such scriptures as Romans 1:19-26—"God gave them up", that is (see context) those who "knew God" yet glorified Him not as God (v. 21). Appeal is also made to 2 Thessalonians 2:10-12. But it is to be noted that the word "harden" does not occur in either of these passages. But further. We submit that Romans 9:18 has no reference whatever to judicial "hardening". The apostle is not there speaking of those who had already turned their backs on God's truth, but instead, he is dealing with God's sovereignty, God's sovereignty as seen not only in showing mercy to whom He wills, but also in hardening whom He pleases. The exact words are "Whom He will"—not "all who have rejected His truth"—"He hardeneth", and this, coming immediately after the mention of Pharaoh, clearly fixes their meaning. The case of Pharaoh is plain enough, though man by his glosses has done his best to hide the truth.

Verse 18: "Therefore hath He mercy on whom He will have mercy, and whom He will He hardeneth". This affirmation of God's sovereign "hardening" of sinners' hearts—in contradistinction from judicial hardening—is not alone. Mark the language of John 12:37-40, "But though He had done so many miracles before them, yet they believed not on Him: that the saying of Isaiah the prophet might be fulfilled, which he spake, Lord, who hath believed our report? and to whom hath the arm of the Lord been revealed? Therefore they could not believe (why?), because that Isaiah said again, He hath blinded their eyes, and hardened their hearts (why? Because they had refused to believe on Christ? This is the popular belief, but mark the answer of Scripture) that they should not see with their eyes, nor understand with their heart, and be converted, and I should heal them." Now, reader, it is just a question as to whether or not you will believe what God has revealed in His Word. It is not a matter of prolonged searching or profound study, but a childlike spirit which is needed, in order to understand this doctrine.

Verse 19: "Thou wilt say then unto me, Why doth He yet find fault? For who hath resisted His will?" Is not this the very objection which is urged today? The force of the apostle's questions here seems to be this: Since everything is dependent on God's will, which is irreversible, and since this will of God, according to which He can do everything as sovereign—since He can have mercy on whom He wills to have mercy, and can refuse mercy and inflict punishment on whom He chooses to do so—why does He not will to have mercy on all, so as to make them obedient, and thus put finding of fault out of court? Now it should be particularly noted that the apostle does not repudiate the ground on which the objection rests. He does not say God does not find fault. Nor does he say, Men may resist His will. Furthermore; he does not explain away the objection by saying: You have altogether misapprehended my meaning when I said 'Whom He wills He treats kindly, and whom He wills He treats severely'. But he says, "first, this is an objection you have no right to make; and then, This is an objection you have no reason to make" (vide Dr. Brown). The objection was utterly inadmissible, for it was a replying against God. It was to complain about, argue against, what God had done!

Verse 19: "Thou wilt say then unto me, Why doth He yet find fault? For who hath resisted His will?" The language which the apostle here puts into the mouth of the objector is so plain and pointed, that misunderstanding ought to be impossible. Why doth He yet find fault? Now, reader, what can

The Holy Spirit

these words mean? Formulate your own reply before considering ours. Can the force of the apostle's question be any other than this: If it is true that God has "mercy" on whom He wills, and also "hardens" whom He wills, then what becomes of human responsibility? In such a case men are nothing better than puppets, and if this be true then it would be unjust for God to "find fault" with His helpless creatures. Mark the word "then"—Thou wilt say then unto me—he states the (false) inference or conclusion which the objector draws from what the apostle had been saying. And mark, my reader, the apostle readily saw the doctrine he had formulated would raise this very objection, and unless what we have written throughout this book provokes, in some at least, (all whose carnal minds are not subdued by divine grace) the same objection, then it must be either because we have not presented the doctrine which is set forth in Romans 9, or else because human nature has changed since the apostle's day. Consider now the remainder of the verse (19). The apostle repeats the same objection in a slightly different form—repeats it so that his meaning may not be misunderstood—namely, "For who hath resisted His will?" It is clear then that the subject under immediate discussion relates to God's "will", i.e., His sovereign ways, which confirms what we have said above upon verses 17 and 18, where we contended that it is not judicial hardening which is in view (that is, hardening because of previous rejection of the truth), but sovereign "hardening", that is, the "hardening" of a fallen and sinful creature for no other reason than that which inheres in the sovereign will of God. And hence the question, "Who hath resisted His will?" What then does the apostle say in reply to these objections?

Verse 20: "Nay but, O man, who art thou that repliest against God? Shall the thing formed say to him that formed it, Why hast thou made me thus?" The apostle, then, did not say the objection was pointless and groundless, instead, he rebukes the objector for his impiety. He reminds him that he is merely a "man", a creature, and that as such it is most unseemly and impertinent for him to "reply (argue, or reason) against God". Furthermore, he reminds him that he is nothing more than a "thing formed", and therefore, it is madness and blasphemy to rise up against the Former Himself. Ere leaving this verse it should be pointed out that its closing words, "Why hast thou made me thus" help us to determine, unmistakably, the precise subject under discussion. In the light of the immediate context what can be the force of the "thus"? What, but as in the case of Esau, why hast thou made me an object of "hatred"? What, but as in the case of Pharaoh, Why hast thou made me simply to "harden" me? What other meaning can, fairly, be assigned to it?

It is highly important to keep clearly before us that the apostle's object throughout this passage is to treat of God's sovereignty in dealing with, on the one hand, those whom He loves—vessels unto honor and vessels of mercy, and also, on the other hand, with those whom He "hates" and "hardens"—vessels unto dishonor and vessels of wrath.

Verses 21-23: "Hath not the potter power over the clay, of the same lump, to make one vessel unto honour, and another unto dishonour? What if God, willing to shew His wrath, and to make His power known, endured with much longsuffering the vessels of wrath fitted to destruction: And that He might make known the riches of His glory on the vessels of mercy, which He had afore prepared unto glory." In these verses the apostle furnishes a full and final reply to the objections raised in verse 19. First, he asks, "Hath not the potter power over the clay?" etc. It is to be noted the word here translated "power" is a different one in the Greek from the one rendered "power" in verse 22 where it can only signify His might; but here in verse 21, the "power" spoken of must refer to the Creator's rights or sovereign prerogatives; that this is so, appears from the fact that the same Greek word is employed in John 1:12—"As many as received Him, to them gave He power to become the sons of God"—which, as is well known, means the right or privilege to become the sons of God. The R. V. employs "right" both in John 1:12 and Romans 9:21.

Verse 21: "Hath not the potter power over the clay of the same lump, to make one vessel unto honour, and another unto dishonour?" That the "potter" here is God Himself is certain from the previous verse, where the apostle asks "Who art thou that repliest against God?" and then, speaking in the terms of the figure he was about to use, continues, "Shall the thing formed say to Him that formed it" etc. Some there are who would rob these words of their force by arguing that while the human potter makes certain vessels to be used for less honorable purposes than others, nevertheless, they are designed to fill some useful place. But the apostle does not here say, Hath not the potter power over the clay of the same lump, to make one vessel unto an honorable use and another to a less honorable use, but he speaks of some "vessels" being made "unto dishonour". It is true, of course, that God's wisdom will yet be fully vindicated, inasmuch as the destruction of the reprobate will promote His glory—in what way the next verse tells us.

Ere passing to the next verse let us summarize the teaching of this and the two previous ones. In verse 19 two questions are asked, "Thou wilt say then unto me, Why doth He yet find fault? For who hath resisted His will?" To those questions a threefold answer is returned. First, in verse 20 the apostle denies the creature the right to sit in judgment upon the ways of the

Creator—"Nay but, O man who art thou that repliest against God? Shall the thing formed say to Him that formed it, Why hast Thou made me thus?" The apostle insists that the rectitude of God's will must not be questioned. Whatever He does must be right. Second, in verse 21 the apostle declares that the Creator has the right to dispose of His creatures as He sees fit—"Hath not the Potter power over the clay, of the same lump, to make one vessel unto honor, and another unto dishonor?" It should be carefully noted that the word for "power" here is exousia—an entirely different word from the one translated "power" in the following verse ("to make known His power"), where it is dunaton. In the words "Hath not the Potter power over the clay?" it must be God's power justly exercised, which is in view—the exercise of God's rights consistently with His justice,—because the mere assertion of His omnipotency would be no such answer as God would return to the questions asked in verse 19. Third, in verses 22, 23, the apostle gives the reasons why God proceeds differently with one of His creatures from another: on the one hand, it is to "shew His wrath" and to "make His power known"; on the other hand, it is to "make known the riches of His glory."

"Hath not the potter power over the clay of the same lump, to make one vessel unto honour, and another unto dishonour?" Certainly God has the right to do this because He is the Creator. Does He exercise this right? Yes, as verses 13 and 17 clearly show us—"For this same purpose have I raised thee (Pharaoh) up".

Verse 22: "What if God, willing to shew His wrath, and to make His power known, endured with much longsuffering the vessels of wrath fitted to destruction". Here the apostle tells us in the second place, why God acts thus, i.e., differently with different ones—having mercy on some and hardening others, making one vessel "unto honour" and another "unto dishonour". Observe, that here in verse 22 the apostle first mentions "vessels of wrath", before he refers in verse 23 to the "vessels of mercy". Why is this? The answer to this question is of first importance: we reply, Because it is the "vessels of wrath" who are the subjects in view before the objector in verse 19. Two reasons are given why God makes some "vessels unto dishonour": first, to "shew His wrath", and secondly "to make His power known"—both of which were exemplified in the case of Pharaoh.

One point in the above verse requires separate consideration—"Vessels of wrath fitted to destruction". The usual explanation which is given of these words is that the vessels of wrath fit themselves to destruction, that is, fit themselves by virtue of their wickedness; and it is argued that there is no need for God to "fit them to destruction", because they are already fitted by their own depravity, and that this must be the real meaning of this expression. Now if by "destruction" we understand punishment, it is perfectly true that the non-elect do "fit themselves", for every one will be judged "according to his works"; and further, we freely grant that subjectively the non-elect do fit themselves for destruction. But the point to be decided is, Is this what the apostle is here referring to? And, without hesitation, we reply it is not. Go back to verses 11-13: did Esau fit himself to be an object of God's hatred, or was he not such before he was born? Again; did Pharaoh fit himself for destruction, or did not God harden his heart before the plagues were sent upon Egypt?—see Exodus 4:21!

Romans 9:22 is clearly a continuation in thought of verse 21, and verse 21 is part of the apostle's reply to the questions raised in verse 20: therefore, to fairly follow out the figure, it must be God Himself who "fits" unto destruction the vessels of wrath. Should it be asked how God does this, the answer, necessarily, is, objectively,—He fits the non-elect unto destruction by His fore-ordinating decrees. Should it be asked why God does this, the answer must be, To promote His own glory, i.e., the glory of His justice, power and wrath. "The sum of the apostle's answer here is, that the grand object of God, both in the election and the reprobation of men, is that which is paramount to all things else in the creation of men, namely, His own glory" (Robert Haldane).

Verse 23: "And that He might make known the riches of His glory on the vessels of mercy, which He had afore prepared unto glory." The only point in this verse which demands attention is the fact that the "vessels of mercy" are here said to be "afore prepared unto glory". Many have pointed out that the previous verse does not say the vessels of wrath were afore prepared unto destruction, and from this omission they have concluded that we must understand the reference there to the non-elect fitting themselves in time, rather than God ordaining them for destruction from all eternity. But this conclusion by no means follows. We need to look back to verse 21 and note the figure which is there employed. "Clay" is inanimate matter, corrupt, decomposed, and therefore a fit substance to represent fallen humanity. As then the apostle is contemplating God's sovereign dealings with humanity in view of the Fall, He does not say the vessels of wrath were "afore" prepared unto destruction, for the obvious and sufficient reason that, it was not until after the Fall that they became (in themselves) what is here symbolized by the "clay". All that is necessary to refute the erroneous conclusion referred to above, is to point out that what is said of the vessels of wrath is not that they are fit for destruction (which is the word that would have been used if the reference had been to them fitting themselves by their own wickedness), but fitted to destruction; which, in the light of the whole context, must mean a sovereign ordination to destruction by the Creator. We quote here the pointed words of Calvin on this passage—"There are vessels prepared for destruction, that is, given up and appointed to destruction; they are also vessels of wrath, that is, made and formed for this end, that they may 'be examples of God's vengeance and displeasure.' Though in the second clause the apostle asserts more expressly, that it is God who prepared the elect for glory, as he had simply said before that the reprobate are vessels prepared for destruction, there is yet no doubt but that the preparation of both is connected with the secret counsel of God. Paul might have otherwise said, that the reprobate gave up or cast themselves into destruction, but he intimates here, that before they are born they are destined to their lot". With this we are in hearty accord. Romans 9:22 does not say the vessels of wrath fitted themselves, nor does it say they are fit for destruction, instead, it declares they are "fitted to destruction", and the context shows plainly it is God who thus "fits" them—objectively by His eternal decrees.

Though Romans 9 contains the fullest setting forth of the doctrine of Reprobation, there are still other passages which refer to it, one or two more of which we will now briefly notice: —

"What then? That which Israel seeketh for, that he obtained not, but the election obtained it, and the rest were hardened" (Rom. 11:7 R. V.). Here we have two distinct and clearly defined classes which are set in sharp antithesis: the "election" and "the rest"; the one "obtained", the other is "hardened". On this verse we quote from the comments of John Bunyan of immortal memory:—"These are solemn words: they sever between men and men—the election and the rest, the chosen and the left, the embraced and the refused. By 'rest' here must needs be understood those not elect, because set the one in opposition to the other, and if not elect, whom then but reprobate?"

Writing to the saints at Thessalonica the apostle declared "For God hath not appointed us to wrath, but to obtain salvation by our Lord Jesus Christ" (1 Thess. 5:9). Now surely it is patent to any impartial mind that this statement is quite pointless if God has not "appointed" any to wrath. To say that God "hath not appointed us to wrath", clearly implies that there are some whom He has "appointed to wrath", and were it not that the minds of so many professing Christians are so blinded by prejudice, they could not fail to clearly see this.

"A Stone of stumbling, and a Rock or offence, even to them who stumble at the Word, being disobedient, whereunto also they were appointed" (1 Pet.

2:8). The "whereunto" manifestly points back to the stumbling at the Word, and their disobedience. Here, then, God expressly affirms that there are some who have been "appointed" (it is the same Greek word as in 1 Thess. 5:9) unto disobedience. Our business is not to reason about it, but to bow to Holy Scripture. Our first duty is not to understand, but to believe what God has said.

"But these, as natural brute beasts, made to be taken and destroyed, speak evil of the things that they understand not; and shall utterly perish in their own corruption" (2 Pet. 2:12). Here, again, every effort is made to escape the plain teaching of this solemn passage. We are told that it is the "brute beasts" who are "made to be taken and destroyed", and not the persons here likened to them. All that is needed to refute such sophistry is to inquire wherein lies the point of analogy between the "these" (men) and the "brute beasts"? What is the force of the "as"—but "these as brute beasts"? Clearly, it is that "these" men as brute beasts, are the ones who, like animals, are "made to be taken and destroyed": the closing words confirming this by reiterating the same sentiment—"and shall utterly perish in their own corruption."

"For there are certain men crept in unawares, who were before of old ordained to this condemnation; ungodly men, turning the grace of our God into lasciviousness, and denying the only Lord God, and our Lord Jesus Christ" (Jude 4). Attempts have been made to escape the obvious force of this verse by substituting a different translation. The R.V. gives: "But there are certain men crept in privily, even they who were of old written of beforehand unto this condemnation." But this altered rendering by no means gets rid of that which is so distasteful to our sensibilities. The question arises, Where were these "of old written of beforehand"? Certainly not in the Old Testament, for nowhere is there any reference there to wicked men creeping into Christian assemblies. If "written of" be the best translation of "prographo", the reference can only be to the book of the Divine decrees. So whichever alternative be selected there can be no evading the fact that certain men are "before of old" marked out by God "unto condemnation."

"And all that dwell on the earth shall worship him (viz. the Antichrist), every one whose name hath not been written from the foundation of the world in the Book of Life of the Lamb that hath been slain" (Rev. 13:8, R. V. compare Rev. 17:8). Here, then, is a positive statement affirming that there are those whose names were not written in the Book of Life. Because of this they shall render allegiance to and bow down before the Antichrist.

Here, then, are no less than ten passages which most plainly imply or expressly teach the fact of reprobation. They affirm that the wicked are made for the Day of Evil; that God fashions some vessels unto dishonor; and by His eternal decree (objectively) fits them unto destruction; that they are like brute beasts, made to be taken and destroyed, being of old ordained unto this condemnation. Therefore in the face of these scriptures we unhesitatingly affirm (after nearly twenty years careful and prayerful study of the subject) that the Word of God unquestionably teaches both Predestination and Reprobation, or to use the words of Calvin, "Eternal Election is God's predestination of some to salvation, and others to destruction".

Having thus stated the doctrine of Reprobation, as it is presented in Holy Writ, let us now mention one or two important considerations to guard it against abuse and prevent the reader from making any unwarranted deductions:—

First, the doctrine of Reprobation does not mean that God purposed to take innocent creatures, make them wicked, and then damn them. Scripture says, "God hath made man upright, but they have sought out many inventions" (Eccl. 7:29). God has not created sinful creatures in order to destroy them, for God is not to be charged with the sin of His creatures. The responsibility and criminality is man's.

God's decree of Reprobation contemplated Adam's race as fallen, sinful, corrupt, guilty. From it God purposed to save a few as the monuments of His sovereign grace; the others He determined to destroy as the exemplification of His justice and severity. In determining to destroy these others, God did them no wrong. They had already fallen in Adam, their legal representative; they are therefore born with a sinful nature, and in their sins He leaves them. Nor can they complain. This is as they wish; they have no desire for holiness; they love darkness rather than light. Where, then, is there any injustice if God "gives them up to their own hearts' lusts" (Ps. 81:12)!

Second, the doctrine of Reprobation does not mean that God refuses to save those who earnestly seek salvation. The fact is that the reprobate have no longing for the Saviour: they see in Him no beauty that they should desire Him. They will not come to Christ—why then should God force them to? He turns away none who do come—where then is the injustice of God fore-determining their just doom? None will be punished but for their iniquities; where then, is the supposed tyrannical cruelty of the Divine procedure? Remember that God is the Creator of the wicked, not of their wickedness; He is the Author of their being, but not the Infuser of their sin.

God does not (as we have been slanderously reported to affirm) compel the wicked to sin, as the rider spurs on an unwilling horse. God only says in effect that awful word, "Let them alone" (Matt. 15:14). He needs only to slacken the reins of providential restraint, and withhold the influence of saving grace, and apostate man will only too soon and too surely, of his own accord, fall by his iniquities. Thus the decree of reprobation neither interferes with the bent of man s own fallen nature, nor serves to render him the less inexcusable.

Third, the decree of Reprobation in nowise conflicts with God's goodness. Though the non-elect are not the objects of His goodness in the same way or to the same extent as the elect are, yet are they not wholly excluded from a participation of it. They enjoy the good things of Providence (temporal blessings) in common with God's own children, and very often to a higher degree. But how do they improve them? Does the (temporal) goodness of God lead them to repent? Nay, verily, they do but "despise His goodness, and forbearance, and longsuffering, and after their hardness and impenitency of heart treasure up unto themselves wrath against the day of wrath" (Rom. 2:4, 5). On what righteous ground, then, can they murmur against not being the objects of His benevolence in the endless ages yet to come? Moreover, if it did not clash with God's mercy and kindness to leave the entire body of the fallen angels (2 Pet. 2:4) under the guilt of their apostasy; still less can it clash with the Divine perfections to leave some of fallen mankind in their sins and punish them for them.

Finally, let us interpose this necessary caution: It is utterly impossible for any of us, during the present life, to ascertain who are among the reprobate. We must not now so judge any man, no matter how wicked he may be. The vilest sinner, may, for all we know, be included in the election of grace and be one day quickened by the Spirit of grace. Our marching orders are plain, and woe be unto us if we disregard them—"Preach the Gospel to every creature". When we have done so our skirts are clear. If men refuse to heed, their blood is on their own heads; nevertheless "we are unto God a sweet savour of Christ, in them that are saved, and in them that perish. To the one we are a savor of death unto death; and to the other we are a savour of life unto life" (2 Cor. 2:15, 16).

We must now consider a number of passages which are often quoted with the purpose of showing that God has not fitted certain vessels to destruction or ordained certain ones to condemnation. First, we cite Ezekiel 18:31—"Why will ye die, O house of Israel?" On this passage we cannot do better than quote from the comments of Augustas Toplady:—"This is a passage very frequently, but very idly, insisted upon by Arminians, as if it were a hammer which would at one stroke crush the whole fabric to powder. But it so happens that the "death" here alluded to is neither spiritual nor eternal death: as is abundantly evident from the whole tenor of the chapter. The death intended by the prophet is a political death; a death of national prosperity, tranquillity, and security. The sense of the question is precisely this: What is it that makes you in love with captivity, banishment, and civil ruin? Abstinence from the worship of images might, as a people, exempt you from these calamities, and once more render you a respectable nation. Are the miseries of public devastation so alluring as to attract your determined pursuit? Why will ye die? die as the house of Israel, and considered as a political body? Thus did the prophet argue the case, at the same time adding—"For I have no pleasure in the death of him that dieth saith the Lord God, wherefore, turn yourselves, and live ye." This imports: First, the national captivity of the Jews added nothing to the happiness of God. Second, if the Jews turned from idolatry, and flung away their images, they should not die in a foreign, hostile country, but live peaceably in their own land and enjoy their liberties as an independent people." To the above we may add: political death must be what is in view in Ezekiel 18:31, 32 for the simple but sufficient reason that they were already spiritually dead!

Matthew 25:41 is often quoted to show that God has not fitted certain vessels to destruction—"Depart from Me, ye cursed, into everlasting fire, prepared for the Devil and his angels." This is, in fact, one of the principal verses relied upon to disprove the doctrine of Reprobation. But we submit that the emphatic word here is not "for" but "Devil." This verse (see context) sets forth the severity of the judgment which awaits the lost. In other words, the above Scripture expresses the awfulness of the everlasting fire rather than the subjects of it—if the fire be "prepared for the Devil and his angels" then how intolerable it will be! If the place of eternal torment into which the damned shall be cast is the same as that in which God's arch-enemy will suffer, how dreadful must that place be!

Again: if God has chosen only certain ones to salvation, why are we told that God "now commandeth all men everywhere to repent" (Acts 17:30)? That God commandeth "all men" to repent is but the enforcing of His righteous claims as the moral Governor of the world. How could He do less, seeing that all men everywhere have sinned against Him? Furthermore; that God commandeth all men everywhere to repent argues the universality of creature responsibility. But this Scripture does not declare that it is God's pleasure to "give repentance" (Acts 5:31) to all men everywhere. That the apostle Paul did not believe God gave repentance to every soul is clear from his words in 2 Timothy 2:25—"In meekness instructing those that oppose themselves; if God peradventure will give them repentance to the acknowledging of the truth."

Again, we are asked, if God has "ordained" only certain ones unto eternal life, then why do we read that He "will have all men to be saved, and come to the knowledge of the truth" (1 Tim. 2:4)? The reply is, that the words "all" and "all men", like the term "world," are often used in a general and relative sense. Let the reader carefully examine the following passages: Mark 1:5; John 6:45; 8:2; Acts 21:28; 22:15; 2 Corinthians 3:2 etc., and he will find full proof of our assertion. 1 Timothy 2:4 cannot teach that God wills the salvation of all mankind, or otherwise all mankind would be saved—"What His soul desireth even that He doeth" (Job 23:13)!

Again; we are asked, Does not Scripture declare, again and again, that God is no "respecter of persons"? We answer, it certainly does, and God's electing grace proves it. The seven sons of Jesse, though older and physically superior to David, are passed by, while the young shepherd-boy is exalted to Israel's throne. The scribes and lawyers pass unnoticed, and ignorant fishermen are chosen to be the apostles of the Lamb. Divine truth is hidden from the wise and prudent and is revealed to babes instead. The great majority of the wise and noble are ignored, while the weak, the base, the despised, are called and saved. Harlots and publicans are sweetly compelled to come in to the gospel feast, while self-righteous Pharisees are suffered to perish in their immaculate morality. Truly, God is "no respecter" of persons or He would not have saved me.

That the Doctrine of Reprobation is a "hard saying" to the carnal mind is readily acknowledged—yet, is it any "harder" than that of eternal punishment? That it is clearly taught in Scripture we have sought to demonstrate, and it is not for us to pick and choose from the truths revealed in God's Word. Let those who are inclined to receive those doctrines which commend themselves to their judgment, and who reject those which they cannot fully understand, remember those scathing words of our Lord's, "O fools, and slow of heart to believe all that the prophets have spoken" (Luke 24:25): fools because slow of heart; slow of heart, not dull of head!

Once more we would avail ourselves of the language of Calvin: "But, as I have hitherto only recited such things as are delivered without any obscurity or ambiguity in the Scriptures, let persons who hesitate not to brand with ignominy those Oracles of heaven, beware what kind of opposition they make. For, if they pretend ignorance, with a desire to be commended for their modesty, what greater instance of pride can be conceived, than to oppose one little word to the authority of God! as, 'It appears otherwise to me,' or 'I would rather not meddle with this subject.' But if they openly censure, what will they gain by their puny attempts against heaven? Their petulance, indeed, is no novelty; for in all ages there have been impious and profane men, who have virulently opposed this doctrine. But they shall feel the truth of what the Spirit long ago declared by the mouth of David, that God 'is clear when He judgeth' (Ps. 51 :4). David obliquely hints at the madness of men who display such excessive presumption amidst their insignificance, as not only to dispute against God, but to arrogate to themselves the power of condemning Him. In the meantime, he briefly suggests, that God is unaffected by all the blasphemies which they discharge against heaven, but that He dissipates the mists of calumny, and illustriously displays His righteousness; our faith, also, being founded on the Divine Word, and therefore, superior to all the world, from its exaltation looks down with contempt upon those mists" (John Calvin).

In closing this chapter we propose to quote from the writings of some of the standard theologians since the days of the Reformation, not that we would buttress our own statements by an appeal to human authority, however venerable or ancient, but in order to show that what we have advanced in these pages is no novelty of the twentieth century, no heresy of the 'latter days' but, instead, a doctrine which has been definitely formulated and commonly taught by many of the most pious and scholarly students of Holy Writ.

"Predestination we call the decree of God, by which He has determined in Himself, what He would have to become of every individual of mankind. For they are not all created with a similar destiny: but eternal life is foreordained for some, and eternal damnation for others. Every man, therefore, being created for one or the other of these ends, we say, he is predestinated either to life or to death"—from John Calvin's "Institutes" (1536 A. D.) Book III, Chapter XXI entitled "Eternal Election, or God's Predestination of Some to Salvation and of Others to Destruction."

We ask our readers to mark well the above language. A perusal of it should show that what the present writer has advanced in this chapter is not "Hyper-Calvinism" but real Calvinism, pure and simple. Our purpose in making this remark is to show that those who, not acquainted with Calvin's writings, in their ignorance condemn as ultra-Calvinism that which is simply a reiteration of what Calvin himself taught—a reiteration because that prince of theologians as well as his humble debtor have both found this doctrine in the Word of God itself.

Martin Luther is his most excellent work "De Servo Arbitrio" (Free will a Slave), wrote: "All things whatsoever arise from, and depend upon, the Divine appointments, whereby it was preordained who should receive the

Word of Life, and who should disbelieve it, who should be delivered from their sins, and who should be hardened in them, who should be justified and who should be condemned. This is the very truth which razes the doctrine of freewill from its foundations, to wit, that God's eternal love of some men and hatred of others is immutable and cannot be reversed."

John Fox, whose Book of Martyrs was once the best known work in the English language (alas that it is not so today, when Roman Catholicism is sweeping upon us like a great destructive tidal wave!), wrote:—"Predestination is the eternal decreement of God, purposed before in Himself, what should befall all men, either to salvation, or damnation".

The "Larger Westminster Catechism" (1688)—adopted by the General Assembly of the Presbyterian Church—declares, "God, by an eternal and immutable decree, out of His mere love, for the praise of His glorious grace, to be manifested in due time, hath elected some angels to glory, and in Christ hath chosen some men to eternal life, and the means thereof; and also, according to His sovereign power, and the unsearchable counsel of His own will (whereby He extendeth or withholdeth favor as He pleases), hath passed by, and fore-ordained the rest to dishonour and wrath, to be for their sin inflicted, to the praise of the glory of His justice".

John Bunyan, author of "The Pilgrim's Progress," wrote a whole volume on "Reprobation". From it we make one brief extract:—"Reprobation is before the person cometh into the world, or hath done good or evil. This is evidenced by Romans 9:11. Here you find twain in their mother's womb, and both receiving their destiny, not only before they had done good or evil, but before they were in a capacity to do it, they being yet unborn—their destiny, I say, the one unto, the other not unto the blessing of eternal life; the one elect, the other reprobate; the one chosen, the other refused". In his "Sighs from Hell", John Bunyan also wrote: "They that do continue to reject and slight the Word of God are such, for the most part, as are ordained to be damned".

Commenting upon Romans 9:22, "What if God willing to shew His wrath, and to make His power known, endured with much longsuffering the vessels of wrath fitted to destruction" Jonathan Edwards (Vol. 4, p. 306—1743 A.D.) says, "How awful doth the majesty of God appear in the dreadfulness of His anger! This we may learn to be one end of the damnation of the wicked."

Augustus Toplady, author of "Rock of Ages" and other sublime hymns, wrote: "God, from all eternity decreed to leave some of Adam's fallen posterity in their sins, and to exclude them from the participation of Christ and His benefits". And again; "We, with the Scriptures, assert: That there is a predestination of some particular persons to life, for the praise of the glory of Divine grace; and also a predestination of other particular persons to death for the glory of Divine justice—which death of punishment they shall inevitably undergo, and that justly, on account of their sins

George Whitefield, that stalwart of the eighteenth century, used by God in blessing to so many, wrote: "Without doubt, the doctrine of election and reprobation must stand or fall together. . . . I frankly acknowledge I believe the doctrine of Reprobation, that God intends to give saving grace, through Jesus Christ, only to a certain number; and that the rest of mankind, after the fall of Adam, being justly left of God to continue in sin, will at last suffer that eternal death which is its proper wages

"Fitted to destruction" (Rom. 9:22). After declaring this phrase admits of two interpretations, Dr. Hodge—perhaps the best known and most widely read commentator on Romans—says, "The other interpretation assumes that the reference is to God and that the Greek word for 'fitted' has its full participle force; prepared (by God) for destruction." This, says Dr. Hodge, "Is adopted not only by the majority of Augustinians, but also by many Lutherans".

Were it necessary we are prepared to give quotations from the writings of Wycliffe, Huss, Ridley, Hooper, Cranmer, Ussher, John Trapp, Thomas Goodwin, Thomas Manton (Chaplain to Cromwell), John Owen, Witsius, John Gill (predecessor of Spurgeon), and a host of others. We mention this simply to show that many of the most eminent saints in bye-gone days, the men most widely used of God, held and taught this doctrine which is so bitterly hated in these last days, when men will no longer "endure sound doctrine"; hated by men of lofty pretensions, but who, notwithstanding their boasted orthodoxy and much advertised piety, are not worthy to unfasten the shoes of the faithful and fearless servants of God of other days.

"O the depth of the riches both of the wisdom and knowledge of God! How unsearchable are His judgments and His ways past finding out! For who hath known the mind of the Lord? or who hath been His counsellor? or who hath first given to Him, and it shall be recompensed unto him again? For of Him, and through Him, and to Him, are all things: to whom be glory forever, Amen" (Rom. 11:33-36).'

The Sovereignty of God in Operation

"For of Him, and thro' Him, and to Him, are all things: to whom be glory for ever. Amen" (Romans 11:36).

Has God foreordained everything that comes to pass? Has He decreed that what is, was to have been? In the final analysis this is only another way of asking, Is God now governing the world and everyone and everything in it? If God is governing the world, then is He governing it according to a definite purpose, or aimlessly and at random? If He is governing it according to some purpose, then when was that purpose made? Is God continually changing His purpose and making a new one every day, or was His purpose formed from the beginning? Are God's actions, like ours, regulated by the change of circumstances, or are they the outcome of His eternal purpose? If God formed a purpose before man was created, then is that purpose going to be executed according to His original designs and is He now working toward that end? What saith the Scriptures? They declare God is One "who worketh all things after the counsel of His own will" (Eph. 1:11).

Few who read this book are likely to call into question the statement that God knows and foreknows all things, but perhaps many would hesitate to go further than this. Yet is it not self-evident that if God foreknows all things, He has also fore-ordained all things? Is it not clear that God foreknows what will be because He has decreed what shall be? God's foreknowledge is not the cause of events, rather are events the effects of His eternal purpose. When God has decreed a thing shall be, He knows it will be. In the nature of things there cannot be anything known as what shall be, unless it is certain to be, and there is nothing certain to be unless God has ordained it shall be. Take the Crucifixion as an illustration. On this point the teaching of Scripture is as clear as a sunbeam. Christ as the Lamb whose blood was to be shed, was "foreordained before the foundation of the world" (1 Pet. 1:20). Having then "ordained" the slaying of the Lamb, God knew He would be "led to the slaughter", and therefore made it known accordingly through Isaiah the prophet. The Lord Jesus was not "delivered" up by God fore-knowing it before it took place, but by His fixed counsel and fore-ordination (Acts 2:23).

Fore-knowledge of future events then is founded upon God's decrees, hence if God foreknows everything that is to be, it is because He has determined in Himself from all eternity everything which will be—"Known unto God are all His works from the beginning of the world" (Acts 15:18), which shows that God has a plan, that God did not begin His work at random or without a knowledge of how His plan would succeed.

God created all things. This truth no one, who bows to the testimony of Holy Writ, will question; nor would any such be prepared to argue that the work of creation was an accidental work. God first formed the purpose to create, and then put forth the creative act in fulfillment of that purpose. All real Christians will readily adopt the words of the Psalmist and say, "O Lord, how manifold are Thy works! in wisdom hast Thou made them all." Will any who endorse what we have just said, deny that God purposed to govern the world which He created? Surely the creation of the world was not the end of God's purpose concerning it. Surely He did not determine simply to create the world and place man in it. and then leave both to their fortunes. It must be apparent that God has some great end or ends in view, worthy of His infinite perfections, and that He is now governing the world so as to accomplish these ends—"The counsel of the Lord standeth for ever, the thoughts of His heart to all generations" (Ps. 33:11).

"Remember the former things of old: for I am God, and there is none else; I am God, and there is none like Me, declaring the end from the beginning, and from ancient times the things that are not yet done, saying, My counsel shall stand, and I will do all My pleasure" (Isa. 46:9, 10). Many other passages might be adduced to show that God has many counsels concerning this world and concerning man, and that all these counsels will most surely be realized. It is only when they are thus regarded that we can intelligently appreciate the prophecies of Scripture. In prophecy the mighty God has condescended to take us into the secret chamber of His eternal counsels, and make known to us what He has purposed to do in the future. The hundreds of prophecies which are found in the Old and New Testaments are not so much predictions of what will come to pass, as they are revelations to us of what God has purposed shall come to pass. Do we know from prophecy that this present age, like all preceding ones, is to end with a full demonstration of man's failure; do we know that there is to be a universal turning away from the truth, a general apostasy; do we know that the Antichrist is to be manifested, and that he will succeed in deceiving the whole world; do we know that Antichrist's career will be cut short, and an end made of man's miserable attempts to govern himself, by the return of God's Son; then it is all because these and a hundred other things are included among God's eternal decrees, now made known to us in the sure Word of Prophecy, and because it is infallibly certain that all God has purposed "must shortly come to pass" (Rev. 1:1).

What then was the great purpose for which this world and the human race were created? The answer of Scripture is, "The Lord hath made all things for Himself" (Prov. 16:4). And again, "Thou hast created all things, and for Thy pleasure they are and were created" (Rev. 4:11). The great end of creation was the manifestation of God's glory. The heavens declare the glory of God and the firmament sheweth His handiwork; but it was by man, originally made in His own image and likeness, that God designed chiefly to manifest His glory. But how was the great Creator to be glorified by man? Before his creation, God foresaw the fall of Adam and the consequent ruin of his race, therefore He could not have designed that man should glorify Him by continuing in a state of innocency. Accordingly, we are taught that Christ was "fore-ordained before the foundation of the world" to be the Saviour of fallen men. The redemption of sinners by Christ was no mere after-thought of God: it was no expediency to meet an unlooked-for calamity. No; it was a Divine provision, and therefore when man fell, he found mercy walking hand in hand with justice.

From all eternity God designed that our world should be the stage on which He would display His manifold grace and wisdom in the redemption of lost sinners: "To the intent that now unto the principalities and powers in heavenly places might be known by the Church the manifold wisdom of God, according to the eternal purpose which He purposed in Christ Jesus our Lord" (Eph. 3:11). For the accomplishment of this glorious design God has governed the world from the beginning, and will continue it to the end. It has been well said, "We can never understand the providence of God over our world, unless we regard it as a complicated machine having ten thousand parts, directed in all its operations to one glorious end—the display of the manifold wisdom of God in the salvation of the Church," i.e., the "called out" ones. Everything else down here is subordinated to this central purpose. It was the apprehension of this basic truth that the apostle, moved by the Holy Spirit, was led to write, "Wherefore I endure all things for the elect's sake, that they may also obtain the salvation which is in Christ Jesus with eternal glory" (2 Tim. 2:10). What we would now contemplate is the operation of God's sovereignty in the government of this world.

In regard to the operation of God's government over the material world little needs now be said. In previous chapters we have shown that inanimate matter and all irrational creatures are absolutely subject to their Creator's pleasure. While we freely admit that the material world appears to be governed by laws that are stable and more or less uniform in their operations, yet Scripture, history, and observation, compel us to recognize the fact that God suspends these laws and acts apart from them whenever it pleaseth Him to do so. In sending His blessings or judgments upon His creatures He may cause the sun itself to stand still, and the stars in their courses to fight for His people (Judges 5:20) He may send or withhold "the early and the latter rains" according to the dictates of His own infinite wisdom; He may smite with plague or bless with health; in short, being God, being absolute Sovereign, He is bound and tied by no laws of Nature, but governs the material world as seemeth Him best.

But what of God's government of the human family? What does Scripture reveal in regard to the modus operandi of the operations of His governmental administration over mankind? To what extent and by what influences does God control the sons of men? We shall divide our answer to this question into two parts and consider first God's method of dealing with the righteous, His elect; and then His method of dealing with the wicked.

God's Method of Dealing with the Righteous:

1. God exerts upon His own elect a quickening influence or power.

By nature they are spiritually dead, dead in trespasses and sins, and their first need is spiritual life, for "Except a man be born again, he cannot see the kingdom of God" (John 3:3). In the new birth God brings us from death unto life (John 5:24). He imparts to us His own nature (2 Pet. 1:4). He delivers us from the power of darkness and translates us into the kingdom of His dear Son (Col. 1:13). Now, manifestly, we could not do this ourselves, for we were "without strength" (Rom. 5:6), hence it is written, "we are His workmanship created in Christ Jesus" (Eph. 2:10).

In the new birth we are made partakers of the Divine nature: a principle, a "seed," a life, is communicated to us which is "born of the Spirit," and therefore "is spirit;" is born of the Holy Spirit, and therefore is holy. Apart from this Divine and holy nature which is imparted to us at the new birth, it is utterly impossible for any man to generate a spiritual impulse, form a spiritual concept, think a spiritual thought, understand spiritual things, still less engage in spiritual works. "Without holiness no man shall see the Lord," but the natural man has no desire for holiness, and the provision that God has made he does not want. Will then a man pray for, seek for, strive after, that which he dislikes? Surely not. If then a man does "follow after" that which by nature he cordially dislikes, if he does now love the One he once hated, it is because a miraculous change has taken place within him; a power outside of himself has operated upon him, a nature entirely different from his old one has been imparted to him, and hence it is written, "Therefore if any man be in Christ, he is a new creation: old things are passed away, behold all things are become new" (2 Cor. 5:17). Such an one as we have just described has passed from death unto life, has been turned from darkness to light, and from the power of Satan unto God (Acts 26:18). In no other way can the great change be accounted for.

The new birth is very, very much more than simply shedding a few tears due to a temporary remorse over sin. It is far more than changing our course of life, the leaving off of bad habits and the substituting of good ones. It is something different from the mere cherishing and practicing of noble ideals. It goes infinitely deeper than coming forward to take some popular evangelist by the hand, signing a pledge-card, or "joining the church." The new birth is no mere turning over a new leaf, but is the inception and reception of a new life. It is no mere reformation but a Complete transformation. In short, the new birth is a miracle, the result of the supernatural operation of God. It is radical, revolutionary, lasting.

Here then is the first thing, in time, which God does in His own elect. He lays hold of those who are spiritually dead and quickens them into newness of life. He takes up one who was shapen in iniquity and conceived in sin, and conforms him to the image of His Son. He seizes a captive of the Devil and makes him a member of the household of faith. He picks up a beggar and makes him joint-heir with Christ. He comes to one who is full of enmity against Him, and gives him a new heart that is full of love for Him. He stoops to one who by nature is a rebel, and works in him both to will and to do of His good pleasure. By His irresistible power He transforms a sinner into a saint, an enemy into a friend, a slave of the Devil into a child of God. Surely then we are moved to say,

"When all Thy mercies O my God
My wondering soul surveys,
Transported with the view I'm lost
In wonder, love and praise."

2. God exerts upon His own elect an energizing influence or power.

The apostle prayed to God for the Ephesian saints that the eyes of their understanding might be enlightened in order that, among other things, they might know "what is the exceeding greatness of His power to usward who believe" (Eph. 1:18), and that they might be "strengthened with might "by His Spirit in the inner man" (3:16). It is thus that the children of God are enabled to fight the good fight of faith, and battle with the adverse forces which constantly war against them. In themselves they have no strength: they are but "sheep," and sheep are one of the most defenceless animals there is; but the promise is sure—"He giveth power to the faint, and to them that have no might He increaseth strength" (Isa. 40:29).

It is this energizing power that God exerts upon and within the righteous which enables them to serve Him acceptably. Said the prophet of old, "But truly I am full of power by the Spirit of the Lord" (Micah 3:8). And said our Lord to His apostles, "Ye shall receive power after that the Holy Spirit is come upon you" (Acts 1:8), and thus it proved, for of these same men we read subsequently, "And with great power gave the apostles witness of the resurrection of the Lord Jesus: and great grace was upon them all" (Acts 4:33). So it was, too, with the apostle Paul, "And my speech and my preaching was not with enticing words of man's wisdom, but in demonstration of the Spirit and of power" (1 Cor. 2:4). But the scope of this power is not confined to service, for we read in 2 Peter 1:3, "According as His Divine power bath given unto us all things that pertain unto life and godliness, through the knowledge of Him that hath called us to glory and virtue." Hence it is that the various graces of the Christian character, "love, joy, peace, long-suffering, gentleness, goodness, faith, meekness, temperance," are ascribed directly to God Himself, being denominated "the fruit of the Spirit" (Gal. 5:22). Compare Ephesians 5:9.

3. God exerts upon His own elect a directing influence or power.

Of old He led His people across the wilderness, and directing their steps by a pillar of cloud by day and a pillar of fire by night; and today He still directs His saints, though now from within rather than from without. "For this God is our God for ever and ever: He will be our Guide even unto death" (Ps. 48:14), but He "guides" us by working in us both to will and to do of His good pleasure. That He does so guide us is clear from the words of the apostle in Ephesians 2:10—"For we are His workmanship, created in Christ Jesus unto good works, which God hath before ordained that we should walk in them." Thus all ground for boasting is removed, and God gets all the glory, for with the prophet we have to say, "Lord, Thou wilt ordain peace for us: for Thou also hast wrought all our works in us" (Isa. 26:12). How true then that "A man's heart deviseth his way: hut the Lord directeth his steps" (Prov. 16:9)! Compare Psalm 65:4, Ezekiel 36:27.

4. God exerts upon His own elect a preserving influence or power.

Many are the scriptures which set forth this blessed truth. "He preserveth the souls of His saints; He delivereth them out of the hand of the wicked" (Ps. 97:10). "For the Lord loveth judgment, and forsaketh not His saints; they are preserved for ever: but the seed of the wicked shall be cut off" (Ps. 37:28). "The Lord preserveth all them that love Him: but all the wicked will He destroy" (Ps. 145:20). It is needless to multiply texts or to raise an argument at this point respecting the believer's responsibility and faithfulness—we can no more "persevere" without God preserving us, than we can breathe when God ceases to give us breath; we are "kept by the power of God through faith unto salvation ready to be revealed in the last time" (1 Pet. 1:5). Compare 1 Chronicles 18:6. It remains for us now to consider,

God's Method of Dealing with the Wicked:

In contemplating God's governmental dealings with the non-elect we find that He exerts upon them a fourfold influence or power. We adopt the clear-cut divisions suggested by Dr. Rice:

1. God exerts upon the wicked a restraining influence by which they are prevented from doing what they are naturally inclined to do.

A striking example of this is seen in Abimelech king of Gerar. Abraham came down to Gerar and fearful lest he might be slain on account of his wife he instructed her to pose as his sister. Regarding her as an unmarried woman, Abimelech sent and took Sarah unto himself; and then we learn how God put forth His power to protect her honor—"And God said unto him in a dream, Yea, I know that thou didst this in the integrity of thy heart; for I also withheld thee from sinning against Me: therefore suffered I thee not to touch her" (Gen. 20:6). Had not God interposed, Abimelech would have grievously wronged Sarah, but the Lord restrained him and allowed him not to carry out the intentions of his heart.

A similar instance is found in connection with Joseph and his brethren's treatment of Him. Owing to Jacob's partiality for Joseph, his brethren "hated him," and when they thought they had him in their power, "they conspired against him to slay him" (Gen. 37:18). But God did not allow them to carry out their evil designs. First He moved Reuben to deliver him out of their hands, and next he caused Judah to suggest that Joseph should be sold to the passing Ishmaelites, who carried him down into Egypt. That it was God who thus restrained them is clear from the words of Joseph himself, when some years later he made known himself to his brethren: said he, "So now it was not you that sent me hither, but God" (Gen. 45:8)!

The restraining influence which God exerts upon the wicked was strikingly exemplified in the person of Balaam, the prophet hired by Balak to curse the

Israelites. One cannot read the inspired narrative without discovering that, left to himself, Balaam had readily and certainly accepted the offer of Balak. How evidently God restrained the impulses of his heart is seen from his own acknowledgment—"How shall I curse, whom God hath not cursed? or how shall I defy, whom the Lord hath not defied? Behold I have received commandment to bless: and He bath blessed; and I cannot reverse it" (Num. 23:8, 20).

Not only does God exert a restraining influence upon wicked individuals, but He does so upon whole peoples as well. A remarkable illustration of this is found in Ex. 34:24—"For I will cast out the nations before thee, and enlarge thy borders: neither shall any man desire thy land, when thou shalt go up to appear before the Lord thy God thrice in the year." Three times every male Israelite, at the command of God, left his home and inheritance and journeyed to Jerusalem to keep the Feasts of the Lord; and in the above scripture we learn He promised them that, while they were at Jerusalem, He would guard their unprotected homes by restraining the covetous designs and desires of their heathen neighbors.

2. God exerts upon the wicked a softening influence disposing them contrary to their natural inclinations to do that which will promote His cause.

Above, we referred to Joseph's history as an illustration of God exerting a restraining influence upon the wicked, let us note now his experiences in Egypt as exemplifying our assertion that God also exerts a softening influence upon the unrighteous. We are told that while he was in the house of Potiphar, "The Lord was with Joseph, and his master saw the Lord was with him," and in consequence, "Joseph found favor in his sight and he made him overseer over his house" (Gen. 39:3, 4). Later, when Joseph was unjustly cast into prison, we are told, "But the Lord was with Joseph, and shewed him mercy, and gave him favor in the sight of the keeper of the prison" (Gen. 39:21), and in consequence the prison-keeper shewed him much kindness and honor. Finally, after his release from prison, we learn from Acts 7:10 that the Lord "gave him favor and wisdom in the sight of Pharaoh king of Egypt; and he made him governor over Egypt and all his house."

An equally striking evidence of God's power to melt the hearts of his enemies, was seen in Pharaoh's daughter's treatment of the infant Moses. The incident is well known. Pharaoh had issued an edict commanding the destruction of every male child of the Israelites. A certain Levite had a son born to him who for three months was kept hidden by his mother. No longer able to conceal the infant Moses, she placed him in an ark of bulrushes, and laid him by the river's brink. The ark was discovered by none less than the king's daughter who had come down to the river to bathe, but instead of heeding her father's wicked decree and casting the child into the river, we are told that "she hod compassion on him" (Ex. 2:6)! Accordingly, the young life was spared and later Moses became the adopted son of this princess!

God has access to the hearts of all men and He softens or hardens them according to His sovereign purpose. The profane Esau swore vengeance upon his brother for the deception which he had practiced upon his father, yet when next he met Jacob, instead of slaying him we are told that Esau "fell on his neck and kissed him" (Gen. 32:4)! Ahab, the weak and wicked consort of Jezebel, was highly enraged against Elijah the prophet, at whose word the heavens had been shut up for three years and a half: so angry was he against the one whom he regarded as his enemy that, we are told he searched for him in every nation and kingdom, and when he could not be found "he took an oath" (1 Kings 18:10). Yet, when they met, instead of killing the prophet, Ahab meekly obeyed Elijah's behest and "sent unto all the children of Israel and gathered the prophets together unto Mount Carmel" (v. 20). Again; Esther the poor Jewess is about to enter the presence-chamber of the august Medo-Persian monarch which, said she, "is not according to the law" (Est. 4:16). She went in expecting to "perish," but we are told "She obtained favor in his sight, and the king held out to Esther the golden scepter" (5:2). Yet again; the boy Daniel is a captive in a foreign court. The king "appointed" a daily provision of meat and drink for Daniel and his fellows. But Daniel purposed in his heart that he would not defile himself with the allotted portion, and accordingly made known his purpose to his master, the prince of the eunuchs. What happened? His master was a heathen, and "feared" the king. Did he turn then upon Daniel and angrily demand that his orders be promptly carried out? No; for we read, "Now God had brought Daniel into favor and tender love with the prince of the eunuchs" (Dan. 1:9)!

"The king's heart is in the hand of the Lord, as the rivers of water: He turneth it whithersoever He will" (Prov. 21:1). A remarkable illustration of this is seen in Cyrus, the heathen king of Persia. God's people were in captivity, but the predicted end of their captivity was almost reached. Meanwhile the Temple at Jerusalem lay in ruins, and, as we have said, the Jews were in bondage in a distant land. What hope was there then that the Lord's house would be re-built? Mark now what God did, "Now in the first year of Cyrus king of Persia, that the word of the Lord by the mouth of Jeremiah might be fulfilled, the Lord stirred up the spirit of Cyrus king of Persia, that he made a proclamation throughout all his kingdom, and put it in writing, saying, Thus saith Cyrus king of Persia, The Lord God of heaven hath given me all the kingdoms of the earth; and He hath charged me to build Him a house at Jerusalem, which is in Judah" (Ezra 1:1, 2). Cyrus, be it remembered, was a pagan, and as secular history bears witness, a very wicked man, yet the Lord moved him to issue this edict, that His Word through Jeremiah seventy years before might be fulfilled. A similar and further illustration is found in Ezra 7:27, where we find Ezra returning thanks for what God had caused king Artaxerxes to do in completing and beautifying the house which Cyrus had commanded to be erected—"Blessed be the Lord God of our fathers which hath put such a thing as this in the king's heart, to beautify the house of the Lord which is in Jerusalem" (Ezra 7:27).

3. God exerts upon the wicked a directing influence so that good is made to result from their intended evil.

Once more we revert to the history of Joseph as a case in point. In selling Joseph to the Ishmaelites, his brethren were actuated by cruel and heartless motives. Their object was to make away with him, and the passing of these travelling traders furnished an easy way out for them. To them the act was nothing more than the enslaving of a noble youth for the sake of gain. But now observe how God was secretly working and over-ruling their wicked actions. Providence so ordered it that these Ishmaelites passed by just in time to prevent Joseph being murdered, for his brethren had already taken counsel together to put him to death. Further; these Ishmaelites were journeying to Egypt, which was the very country to which God had purposed to send Joseph, and He ordained they should purchase Joseph just when they did. That the hand of God was in this incident, that it was something more than a fortunate co-incidence, is clear from the words of Joseph to his brethren at a later date, "God sent me before you to preserve you a posterity in the earth, and to save your lives by a great deliverance" (Gen. 45:7).

Another equally striking illustration of God directing the wicked is found in Isaiah 10:5-7—"O Assyrian, the rod of Mine anger, and the staff in their hand is Mine indignation. I will send him against a hypocritical nation, and against the people of My wrath will I give him a charge, to take the spoil, and to take the prey, and to tread them down like the mire of the streets. Howbeit he meaneth not so, neither doth his heart think so; but it is in his heart to destroy and cut off nations not a few." Assyria's king had determined to be a world-conqueror, to "cut off nations not a few." But God directed and controlled his military lust and ambition, and caused him to confine his attention to the conquering of the insignificant nation of Israel. Such a task was not in the proud king's heart—"he meant it not so"—but God gave him this charge and he could do nothing but fulfill it. Compare also Judges 7:22.

The supreme example of the controlling, directing influence, which God exerts upon the wicked, is the Cross of Christ with all its attending circumstances. If ever the superintending providence of God was witnessed, it was there. From all eternity God had predestined every detail of that event of all events. Nothing was left to chance or the caprice of man. God had decreed when and where and how His blessed Son was to die. Much of what He had purposed concerning the Crucifixion had been made known through the Old Testament prophets, and in the accurate and literal fulfillment of these prophecies we have clear proof, full demonstration, of the controlling and directing influence which God exerts upon the wicked. Not a thing occurred except as God had ordained, and all that He had ordained took place exactly as He purposed. Had it been decreed (and made known in Scripture) that the Saviour should be betrayed by one of His own disciples—by His "familiar friend"—see Psalm 41:9 and compare Matthew 26:50—then the apostle Judas is the one who sold Him. Had it been decreed that the betrayer should receive for his awful perfidy thirty pieces of silver, then are the chief priests moved to offer him this very sum. Had it been decreed that this betrayal sum should be put to a particular use, namely, purchase the potter's field, then the hand of God directs Judas to return the money to the chief priests and so guided their "counsel" (Matt. 27:7) that they did this very thing. Had it been decreed that there should be those who bore "false witness" against our Lord (Ps. 35:11), then accordingly such were raised up. Had it been decreed that the Lord of glory should be "spat upon and scourged" (Is. 50:6), then there were not found wanting those who were vile enough to do so. Had it been decreed that the Saviour should be "numbered with the transgressors," then unknown to himself, Pilate, directed by God, gave orders for His crucifixion along with two thieves. Had it been decreed that vinegar and gall should be given Him to drink while He hung upon the Cross, then this decree of God was executed to the very letter. Had it been decreed that the heartless soldiers should gamble for His garments, then sure enough they did this very thing. Had it been decreed that not a bone of Him should be broken (Ps. 34:20), then the controlling hand of God which suffered the Roman soldier to break the legs of the thieves, prevented him from doing the same with our Lord. Ah! there were not enough soldiers in all the Roman legions, there were not sufficient demons in all the hierarchies of Satan, to break one bone in the body of Christ. And why? Because the Almighty Sovereign had decreed that not a bone should be broken. Do we need to extend this paragraph any farther? Does not the accurate and literal fulfillment of all that Scripture had predicted in connection with the Crucifixion, demonstrate beyond all controversy that an Almighty power was directing and superintending everything that was done on that Day of days?

4. God also hardens the hearts of wicked men and blinds their minds.

"God hardens men's hearts! God blinds men's minds!" Yes, so Scripture represents Him. In developing this theme of the sovereignty of God in Operation we recognize that we have now reached its most solemn aspect of all, and that here especially, we need to keep very close indeed to the words of Holy Writ. God forbid that we should go one fraction further than His Word goes; but may He give us grace to go as far as His Word goes. It is true that secret things belong unto the Lord, but it is also true that those things which are revealed in Scripture belong unto us and to our children.

"He turned their heart to hate His people, to deal subtly with His servants" (Ps. 105:25). The reference here is to the sojourn of the descendants of Jacob in the land of Egypt when, after the death of the Pharaoh who had welcomed the old patriarch and his family, there "arose up a new king who knew not Joseph;" and in his days the children of Israel had "increased greatly" so that they outnumbered the Egyptians; then it was that God "turned their heart to hate His people."

The consequence of the Egyptians' "hatred" is well known: they brought them into cruel bondage and placed them under merciless taskmasters, until their lot became unendurable. Helpless and wretched the Israelites cried unto Jehovah, and in response, He appointed Moses to be their deliverer. God revealed Himself unto His chosen servant, gave him a number of miraculous signs which he was to exhibit at the Egyptian court, and then bade him go to Pharaoh, and demand that the Israelites should be allowed to go a three days journey into the wilderness, that they might worship the Lord. But before Moses started out on his journey God warned him concerning Pharaoh, "I will harden his heart that he shall not let the people go" (Ex. 4:21). If it be asked, Why did God harden Pharaoh's heart? the answer furnished by Scripture itself is, In order that God might show forth His power in him (Rom. 9:17); in other words, it was so that the Lord might demonstrate that it was just as easy for Him to overthrow this haughty and powerful monarch as it was for Him to crush a worm. If it should be pressed further, Why did God select such a method of displaying His power? then the answer must be, that being sovereign God reserves to Himself the right to act as He pleases.

Not only are we told that God hardened the heart of Pharaoh so that he would not let the Israelites go, but after God had plagued his land so severely that he reluctantly gave a qualified permission, and after that the first-born of all the Egyptians had been slain, and Israel had actually left the land of bondage, God told Moses, "And I, behold, I will harden the hearts of the Egyptians, and they shall follow them: and I will get Me honor upon Pharaoh, upon his chariots, and upon his horsemen. And the Egyptians shall know that I am the Lord, when I have gotten Me honor upon Pharaoh, upon his chariots, and upon his horsemen" (Ex. 14:17, 18).

The same thing happened subsequently in connection with Sihon king of Heshbon, through whose territory Israel had to pass on their way to the promised Land. When reviewing their history, Moses told the people, "But Sihon king of Heshbon would not let us pass by him: for the Lord thy God hardened his spirit, and made his heart obstinate, that He might deliver him into thy hand" (Deut. 2:30)!

So it was also after that Israel had entered Canaan. We read, "There was not a city that made peace with the children of Israel, save the Hivites the inhabitants of Gibeon: all other they took in battle. For it was of the Lord to harden their hearts, that they should come against Israel in battle, that He might destroy them utterly, and that they might have no favor, but that He might destroy them, as the Lord commanded Moses" (Josh. 11:19,20). From other scriptures we learn why God purposed to "destroy utterly" the Canaanites—it was because of their awful wickedness and corruption.

Nor is the revelation of this solemn truth confined to the Old Testament. In John 12:37-40 we read, "But though He had done so many miracles before them, yet they believed not on Him: that (in order that) the saying of Isaiah the prophet might be fulfilled, which he spake, Lord, who hath believed our report? and to whom hath the arm of the Lord been revealed? Therefore they could not believe, because that Isaiah said again, HE hath blinded their eyes, and hardened their heart; that they should not see with their eyes, nor understand with their heart, and be converted, and I should heal them." It needs to be carefully noted here that these whose eyes God "blinded" and whose heart He "hardened," were men who had deliberately scorned the Light and rejected the testimony of God's own Son.

Similarly we read in 2 Thessalonians 2:11, 12, "And for this cause God shall send them strong delusion, that they should believe a lie: that they all might be damned who believed not the truth, but had pleasure in unrighteousness". The fulfillment of this scripture is yet future. What God did unto the Jews of old He is yet going to do unto Christendom. Just as the Jews of Christ's day despised His testimony, and in consequence, were "blinded," so a guilty Christendom which has rejected the Truth shall yet have sent them from God a "strong delusion" that they may believe a lie.

Is God really governing the world? Is He exercising rule over the human family? What is the modus operandi of His governmental administration over mankind? To what extent and by what means does He control the sons of men? How does God exercise an influence upon the wicked, seeing their hearts are at enmity against Him? These are some of the questions we have sought to answer from Scripture in the previous sections of this chapter. Upon His own elect God exerts a quickening, an energizing, a directing, and a preserving power. Upon the wicked God exerts a restraining, softening, directing, and hardening and blinding power, according to the dictates of His own infinite wisdom and unto the outworking of His own eternal purpose. God's decrees are being executed. What He has ordained is being accomplished. Man's wickedness is bounded. The limits of evil-doing and of evil-doers has been Divinely defined and cannot be exceeded. Though many are in ignorance of it, all men, good and bad, are under the jurisdiction of and are absolutely subject to the administration of the Supreme Sovereign.—"Alleluia: for the Lord God omnipotent reigneth" (Rev. 19:6)—reigneth over all.

The Sovereignty of God and the Human Will

"It is God which worketh in you both to will and to do of His good pleasure"
Philippians 2:13

Concerning the nature and the power of fallen man s will, the greatest confusion prevails today, and the most erroneous views are held, even by many of God's children. The popular idea now prevailing, and which is taught from the great majority of pulpits, is that man has a "free will", and that salvation comes to the sinner through his will co-operating with the Holy Spirit. To deny the "free will" of man, i.e. his power to choose that which is good, his native ability to accept Christ, is to bring one into disfavor at once, even before most of those who profess to be orthodox. And yet Scripture emphatically says, "It is not of him that willeth, nor of him that runneth, but of God that showeth mercy" (Rom. 9:16). Which shall we believe: God, or the preachers?

But some one may reply, Did not Joshua say to Israel, "Choose you this day whom ye will serve"? Yes, he did; but why not complete his sentence?—"whether the gods that your fathers served which were on the other side of the flood, or the gods of the Amorites, in whose land ye dwell" (Josh. 24:15)! But why attempt to pit scripture against scripture? The Word of God never contradicts itself, and the Word expressly declares, "There is none that seeketh after God" (Rom. 3:11). Did not Christ say to the men of His day, "Ye will not come to Me, that ye might have life" (John 5:40)? Yes, but some did "come" to Him, some did receive Him. True and who were they? John 1:12, 13 tells us; "But as many as received Him, to them gave He power to become the sons of God, to them that believe on His name: which were born, not of blood, nor of the will of the flesh, nor of the will of man, but of God"!

But does not Scripture say, "Whosoever will may come"? It does, but does this signify that everybody has the will to come? What of those who won't come? "Whosoever will may come" no more implies that fallen man has the power (in himself) to come, than "Stretch forth thine hand" implied that the man with the withered arm had ability (in himself) to comply. In and of himself the natural man has power to reject Christ; but in and of himself he has not the power to receive Christ. And why? Because he has a mind that is "enmity against" Him (Rom. 8:7); because he has a heart that hates Him (John 15:18). Man chooses that which is according to his nature, and therefore before he will ever choose or prefer that which is divine and spiritual, a new nature must be imparted to him; in other words, he must be born again.

Should it be asked, But does not the Holy Spirit overcome a man's enmity and hatred when He convicts the sinner of his sins and his need of Christ; and does not the Spirit of God produce such conviction in many that perish? Such language betrays confusion of thought: were such a man's enmity really "overcome", then he would readily turn to Christ; that he does not come to the Saviour, demonstrates that his enmity is not overcome. But that many are, through the preaching of the Word, convicted by the Holy Spirit, who nevertheless die in unbelief, is solemnly true. Yet, it is a fact which must not be lost sight of that, the Holy Spirit does something more in each of God's elect than He does in the non-elect: He works in them "both to will and to do of God's good pleasure" (Phil. 2:13).

In reply to what we have said above, Arminians would answer, No; the Spirit's work of conviction is the same both in the converted and in the unconverted, that which distinguishes the one class from the other is that the former yielded to His strivings, whereas the latter resist them. But if this were the case, then the Christian would make himself to "differ", whereas the Scripture attributes the "differing" to God's discriminating grace (1 Cor. 4:7). Again; if such were the case, then the Christian would have ground for boasting and self-glorying over his cooperation with the Spirit; but this would flatly contradict Ephesians 2:8, "For by grace are ye saved through faith; and that not of yourselves: it is the gift of God".

Let us appeal to the actual experience of the Christian reader. Was there not a time (may the remembrance of it bow each of us into the dust) when you were unwilling to come to Christ? There was. Since then you have come to Him. Are you now prepared to give Him all the glory for that (Ps. 115:1)? Do you not acknowledge you came to Christ because the Holy Spirit brought you from unwillingness to willingness? You do. Then is it not also a patent fact that the Holy Spirit has not done in many others what He has in you! Granting that many others have heard the Gospel, been shown their need of

Christ, yet, they are still unwilling to come to Him. Thus He has wrought more in you, than in them. Do you answer, Yet I remember well the time when the Great Issue was presented to me, and my consciousness testifies that my will acted and that I yielded to the claims of Christ upon me. Quite true. But before you "yielded", the Holy Spirit overcame the native enmity of your mind against God, and this "enmity" He does not overcome in all. Should it be said, That is because they are unwilling for their enmity to be overcome. Ah, none are thus "willing" till He has put forth His all-mighty power and wrought a miracle of grace in the heart.

But let us now inquire, What is the human Will? Is it a self-determining agent, or is it, in turn, determined by something else? Is it sovereign or servant? Is the will superior to every other faculty of our being so that it governs them, or is it moved by their impulses and subject to their pleasure? Does the will rule the mind, or does the mind control the will? Is the will free to do as it pleases, or is it under the necessity of rendering obedience to something outside of itself? "Does the will stand apart from the other great faculties or powers of the soul, a man within a man, who can reverse the man and fly against the man and split him into segments, as a glass snake breaks in pieces? Or, is the will connected with the other faculties, as the tail of the serpent is with his body, and that again with his head, so that where the head goes, the whole creature goes, and, as a man thinketh in his heart, so is he? First thought, then heart (desire or aversion), and then act. Is it this way, the dog wags the tail? Or, is it the will, the tail, wags the dog? Is the will the first and chief thing in the man, or is it the last thing—to be kept subordinate, and in its place beneath the other faculties? and, is the true philosophy of moral action and its process that of Gen. 3:6: 'And when the woman saw that the tree was good for food' (sense-perception, intelligence), 'and a tree to be desired' (affections), 'she took and ate thereof' (the will)." (G. S. Bishop). These are questions of more than academical interest. They are of practical importance. We believe that we do not go too far when we affirm that the answer returned to these questions is a fundamental test of doctrinal soundness.'

1. The Nature of the Human Will.

What is the Will? We answer, the will is the faculty of choice, the immediate cause of all action. Choice necessarily implies the refusal of one thing and the acceptance of another. The positive and the negative must both be present to the mind before there can be any choice. In every act of the will there is a preference—the desiring of one thing rather than another. Where there is no preference, but complete indifference, there is no volition.

To will is to choose, and to choose is to decide between two or more alternatives. But there is something which influences the choice; something which determines the decision. Hence the will cannot be sovereign because it is the servant of that something. The will cannot be both sovereign and servant. It cannot be both cause and effect. The will is not causative, because, as we have said, something causes it to choose, therefore that something must be the causative agent. Choice itself is affected by certain considerations, is determined by various influences brought to bear upon the individual himself, hence, volition is the effect of these considerations and influences, and if the effect, it must be their servant; and if the will is their servant then it is not sovereign, and if the will is not sovereign, we certainly cannot predicate absolute "freedom" of it. Acts of the will cannot come to pass of themselves—to say they can, is to postulate an uncaused effect. Ex nihilo nihil fit—nothing cannot produce something.

In all ages, however, there have been those who contended for the absolute freedom or sovereignty of the human will. Men will argue that the will possesses a self-determining power. They say, for example, I can turn my eyes up or down, the mind is quite indifferent which I do, the will must decide. But this is a contradiction in terms. This case supposes that I choose one thing in preference to another, while I am in a state of complete indifference. Manifestly, both cannot be true. But it may be replied, the mind was quite indifferent until it came to have a preference. Exactly; and at that time the will was quiescent, too! But the moment indifference vanished, choice was made, and the fact that indifference gave place to preference, overthrows the argument that the will is capable of choosing between two equal things. As we have said, choice implies the acceptance of one alternative and the rejection of the other or others.

That which determines the will is that which causes it to choose. If the will is determined, then there must be a determiner. What is it that determines the will? We reply, The strongest motive power which is brought to bear upon it. What this motive power is, varies in different cases. With one it may be the logic of reason, with another the voice of conscience, with another the impulse of the emotions, with another the whisper of the Tempter, with another the power of the Holy Spirit; whichever of these presents the strongest motive power and exerts the greatest influence upon the individual himself, is that which impels the will to act. In other words, the action of the will is determined by that condition of mind (which in turn is influenced by the world, the flesh, and the Devil, as well as by God), which has the greatest degree of tendency to excite volition. To illustrate what we have just said let us analyze a simple example—On a certain Lord's day afternoon a friend of ours was suffering from a severe headache. He was anxious to visit the sick, but feared that if he did so his own condition would grow worse, and as the consequence, be unable to attend the preaching of the Gospel that evening. Two alternatives confronted him: to visit the sick that afternoon and risk being sick himself, or, to take a rest that afternoon (and visit the sick the next day), and probably arise refreshed and fit for the evening service. Now what was it that decided our friend in choosing between these two alternatives? The will? Not at all. True, that in the end, the will made a choice, but the will itself was moved to make the choice. In the above case certain considerations presented strong motives for selecting either alternative; these motives were balanced the one against the other by the individual himself, i.e., his heart and mind, and the one alternative being supported by stronger motives than the other, decision was formed accordingly, and then the will acted. On the one side, our friend felt impelled by a sense of duty to visit the sick; he was moved with compassion to do so, and thus a strong motive was presented to his mind. On the other hand, his judgment reminded him that he was feeling far from well himself, that he badly needed a rest, that if he visited the sick his own condition would probably be made worse, and in such case he would be prevented from attending the preaching of the Gospel that night; furthermore, he knew that on the morrow, the Lord willing, he could visit the sick, and this being so, he concluded he ought to rest that afternoon. Here then were two sets of alternatives presented to our Christian brother: on the one side was a sense of duty plus his own sympathy, on the other side was a sense of his own need plus a real concern for God's glory, for he felt that he ought to attend the preaching of the Gospel that night. The latter prevailed. Spiritual considerations outweighed his sense of duty. Having formed his decision the will acted accordingly, and he retired to rest. An analysis of the above case shows that the mind or reasoning faculty was directed by spiritual considerations, and the mind regulated and controlled the will. Hence we say that, if the will is controlled, it is neither sovereign nor free, but is the servant of the mind.

It is only as we see the real nature of freedom and mark that the will is subject to the motives brought to bear upon it, that we are able to discern there is no conflict between two statements of Holy Writ which concern our blessed Lord. In Matthew 4:1 we read, "Then was Jesus led up of the Spirit into the wilderness to be tempted of the Devil;" but in Mark 1:12, 13 we are told, "And immediately the Spirit driveth Him into the wilderness. And He was there in the wilderness forty days, tempted of Satan". It is utterly impossible to harmonize these two statements by the Arminian conception of the will. But really there is no difficulty. That Christ was "driven", implies it was by a forcible motive or powerful impulse, such as was not to be resisted or refused; that He was "led" denotes His freedom in going. Putting the two together we learn, that He was driven, with a voluntary condescension thereto. So, there is the liberty of man's will and the victorious efficacy of God's grace united together: a sinner may be "drawn" and yet "come" to Christ—the "drawing" presenting to him the irresistible motive, the "coming" signifying the response of his will—as Christ was "driven" and "led" by the Spirit into the wilderness.

Human philosophy insists that it is the will which governs the man, but the Word of God teaches that it is the heart which is the dominating center of our being. Many scriptures might be quoted in substantiation of this. "Keep thy heart with all diligence; for out of it are the issues of life" (Prov. 4:23). "For from within, out of the heart of men, proceed evil thoughts, adulteries, fornications, murders," etc. (Mark 7:21). Here our Lord traces these sinful acts back to their source, and declares that their fountain is the "heart," and not the will! Again; "This people draweth nigh unto Me with their lips, but their heart is far from Me" (Matt. 15:8). If further proof were required we might call attention to the fact that the word "heart" is found in the Bible more than three times oftener than is the word "will," even though nearly half of the references to the latter refer to God's will!

When we affirm that it is the heart and not the will which governs the man, we are not merely striving about words, but insisting on a distinction that is of vital importance. Here is an individual before whom two alternatives are placed; which will he choose? We answer, the one which is most agreeable to himself, i.e., his "heart"—the innermost core of his being. Before the sinner is set a life of virtue and piety, and a life of sinful indulgence; which will he follow? The latter. Why? Because this is his choice. But does that prove the will is sovereign? Not at all. Go back from effect to cause. Why does the sinner choose a life of sinful indulgence? Because he prefers it—and he does prefer it, all arguments to the contrary notwithstanding, though of course he does not enjoy the effects of such a course. And why does he prefer it? Because his heart is sinful. The same alternatives, in like manner, confront the Christian, and he chooses and strives after a life of piety and virtue. Why? Because God has given him a new heart or nature. Hence we say it is not the will which makes the sinner impervious to all appeals to "forsake his way," but his corrupt and evil heart.

He will not come to Christ, because be does not want to, and he does not want to because his heart hates Him and loves sin: see Jeremiah 17:9!

In defining the will we have said above, that "the will is the faculty of choice, the immediate cause of all action." We say the immediate cause, for the will is not the primary cause of any action, any more than the hand is. Just as the hand is controlled by the muscles and nerves of the arm, and the arm by the brain; so the will is the servant of the mind, and the mind, in turn, is affected by various influences and motives which are brought to bear upon it. But, it may be asked, Does not Scripture make its appeal to man's will? Is it not written, "And whosoever will, let him take the water of life freely" (Rev. 22:17)? And did not our Lord say, "ye will not come to Me that ye might have life" (John 5:40)? We answer; the appeal of Scripture is not always made to man's "will"; other of his faculties are also addressed. For example: "He that hath ears to hear, let him hear." "Hear and your soul shall live." "Look unto Me and be ye saved." "Believe on the Lord Jesus Christ and thou shalt be saved." "Come now and let us reason together," "with the heart man believeth unto righteousness," etc., etc.

2. The Bondage of the Human Will.

In any treatise that proposes to deal with the human will, its nature and functions, respect should be had to the will in three different men, namely, unfallen Adam, the sinner, and the Lord Jesus Christ. In unfallen Adam the will was free, free in both directions, free toward good and free toward evil. Adam was created in a state of Innocency, but not in a state of holiness, as is so often assumed and asserted. Adam's will was therefore in a condition of moral equipoise: that is to say, in Adam there was no constraining bias in him toward either good or evil, and as such, Adam differed radically from all his descendants, as well as from "the Man Christ Jesus." But with the sinner it is far otherwise. The sinner is born with a will that is not in a condition of moral equipoise, because in him there is a heart that is "deceitful above all things and desperately wicked," and this gives him a bias toward evil. So, too, with the Lord Jesus it was far otherwise: He also differed radically from unfallen Adam. The Lord Jesus Christ could not sin because He was "the Holy One of God." Before He was born into this world it was said to Mary, "The Holy Spirit shall come upon thee, and the power of the Highest shall overshadow thee: therefore also that Holy Thing which shall be born of thee shall be called the Son of God" (Luke 1:35). Speaking reverently then, we say, that the will of the Son of Man was not in a condition of moral equipoise, that is, capable of turning toward either good or evil. The will of the Lord Jesus was biased toward that which is good because, side by side with His sinless, holy, perfect humanity, was His eternal Deity. Now in contradistinction from the will of the Lord Jesus which was biased toward good, and Adam's will which, before his fall, was in a condition of moral equipoise—capable of turning toward either good or evil—the sinner's will is biased toward evil, and therefore is free in one direction only, namely, in the direction of evil. The sinner's will is enslaved because it is in bondage to and is the servant of a depraved heart.

In what does the sinner's freedom consist? This question is naturally suggested by what we have just said above. The sinner is 'free' in the sense of being unforced from without. God never forces the sinner to sin. But the sinner is not free to do either good or evil, because an evil heart within is ever inclining him toward sin. Let us illustrate what we have in mind. I hold in my hand a book. I release it; what happens? It falls. In which direction? Downwards; always downwards. Why? Because, answering the law of gravity, its own weight sinks it. Suppose I desire that book to occupy a position three feet higher; then what? I must lift it; a power outside of that book must raise it. Such is the relationship which fallen man sustains toward God. Whilst Divine power upholds him, he is preserved from plunging still deeper into sin; let that power be withdrawn, and he falls—his own weight (of sin) drags him down. God does not push him down, anymore than I did that book. Let all Divine restraint be removed, and every man is capable of becoming, would become, a Cain, a Pharaoh, a Judas. How then is the sinner to move heavenwards? By an act of his own will? Not so. A power outside of himself must grasp hold of him and lift him every inch of the way. The sinner is free, but free in one direction only—free to fall, free to sin. As the Word expresses it: "For when ye were the servants of sin, ye were free from righteousness" (Rom. 6:20). The sinner is free to do as he pleases, always as he pleases (except as he is restrained by God), but his pleasure is to sin.

In the opening paragraph of this chapter we insisted that a proper conception of the nature and function of the will is of practical importance, nay, that it constitutes a fundamental test of theological orthodoxy or doctrinal soundness. We wish to amplify this statement and attempt to demonstrate its accuracy. The freedom or bondage of the will was the dividing line between Augustinianism and Pelagianism, and in more recent times between Calvinism and Arminianism. Reduced to simple terms, this means, that the difference involved was the affirmation or denial of the total depravity of man. In taking the affirmative we shall now consider,

3. The Impotency of the Human Will.

Does it lie within the province of man's will to accept or reject the Lord Jesus Christ as Saviour? Granted that the Gospel is preached to the sinner, that the Holy Spirit convicts him of his lost condition, does it, in the final analysis, lie within the power of his own will to resist or to yield himself up to God? The answer to this question defines our conception of human depravity. That man is a fallen creature all professing Christians will allow, but what many of them mean by "fallen" is often difficult to determine. The general impression seems to be that man is now mortal, that he is no longer in the condition in which he left the hands of his Creator, that he is liable to disease, that he inherits evil tendencies; but, that if he employs his powers to the best of his ability, somehow he will be happy at last. O, how far short of the sad truth! Infirmities, sickness, even corporeal death, are but trifles in comparison with the moral and spiritual effects of the Fall! It is only by consulting the Holy Scriptures that we are able to obtain some conception of the extent of that terrible calamity.

When we say that man is totally depraved, we mean that the entrance of sin into the human constitution has affected every part and faculty of man's being. Total depravity means that man is, in spirit and soul and body, the slave of sin and the captive of the Devil—walking "according to the prince of the power of the air, the spirit that now worketh in the children of disobedience" (Eph. 2:2). This statement ought not to need arguing: it is a common fact of human experience. Man is unable to realize his own aspirations and materialize his own ideals. He cannot do the things that he would. There is a moral inability which paralyzes him. This is proof positive that he is no free man, but instead, the slave of sin and Satan. "Ye are of your father the Devil, and the lusts (desires) of your father ye will do" (John 8:44). Sin is more than an act or a series of acts; it is a state or condition: it is that which lies behind and produces the acts. Sin has penetrated and permeated the whole of man's make-up. It has blinded the understanding, corrupted the heart, and alienated the mind from God. And the will has not escaped. The will is under the dominion of sin and Satan. Therefore, the will is not free. In short, the affections love as they do and the will chooses as it does because of the state of the heart, and because the heart is deceitful above all things and desperately wicked "There is none that seeketh after God" (Rom. 3:11).

We repeat our question; Does it lie within the power of the sinner's will to yield himself up to God? Let us attempt an answer by asking several others: Can water (of itself) rise above its own level? Can a clean thing come out of an unclean? Can the will reverse the whole tendency and strain of human nature? Can that which is under the dominion of sin originate that which is pure and holy? Manifestly not. If ever the will of a fallen and depraved creature is to move Godwards, a Divine power must be brought to bear upon it which will overcome the influences of sin that pull in a counter direction. This is only another way of saying, "No man can come to Me, except the Father which hath sent Me, draw him" (John 6:44). In other words, God's people must be made willing in the day of His power (Ps. 110:3). As said Mr. Darby, "If Christ came to save that which is lost, free will has no place. Not that God prevents men from receiving Christ—far from it. But even when God uses all possible inducements, all that is capable of exerting influence in the heart of man, it only serves to show that man will have none of it, that so corrupt is his heart, and so decided his will not to submit to God (however much it may be the devil who encourages him to sin) that nothing can induce him to receive the Lord, and to give up sin. If by the words, 'freedom of man,' they mean that no one forces him to reject the Lord, this liberty fully exists. But if it is said that, on account of the dominion of sin, of which he is the slave, and that voluntarily, he cannot escape from his condition, and make choice of the good—even while acknowledging it to be good, and approving of it—then he has no liberty whatever (italics ours). He is not subject to the law, neither indeed can be; hence, they that are in the flesh cannot please God." The will is not sovereign; it is a servant, because influenced and controlled by the other faculties of man's being. The sinner is not a free agent because he is a slave of sin—this was clearly implied in our Lord's words, "If the Son shall therefore make you free, ye shall be free indeed" (John 8:36). Man is a rational being and as such responsible and accountable to God, but to affirm that he is a free moral agent is to deny that he is totally depraved—i.e., depraved in will as in everything else. Because man's will is governed by his mind and heart, and because these have been vitiated and corrupted by sin, then it follows that if ever man is to turn or move in a Godward direction, God Himself must work in him "both to will and to do of His good pleasure" (Phil. 2:13). Man's boasted freedom is in truth "the bondage of corruption"; he "serves divers lusts and pleasures." Said a deeply taught servant of God, "Man is impotent as to his will. He has no will favorable to God. I believe in free will; but then it is a will only free to act according to nature (italics ours). A dove has no will to eat carrion; a raven no will to eat the clean food of the dove. Put the nature of the dove into the raven and it will eat the food of the dove. Satan could have no will for holiness. We speak it with reverence, God could have no will for evil. The sinner in his sinful nature could never have a will according to God. For this he must be born again" (J. Denham Smith). This is just what we have contended for throughout this chapter—the will is regulated by the nature.

Among the "decrees" of the Council of Trent (1563), which is the avowed standard of Popery, we find the following:—

"If any one shall affirm, that man's free-will, moved and excited by God, does not, by consenting, co-operate with God, the mover and exciter, so as to prepare and dispose itself for the attainment of justification; if moreover, anyone shall say, that the human will cannot refuse complying, if it pleases, but that it is inactive, and merely passive; let such an one be accursed"!

"If anyone shall affirm, that since the fall of Adam, man's free-will is lost and extinguished; or, that it is a thing titular, yea a name, without a thing, and a fiction introduced by Satan into the Church; let such an one be accursed"!

Thus, those who today insist on the free-will of the natural man believe precisely what Rome teaches on the subject! That Roman Catholics and Arminians walk hand in hand may be seen from others of the decrees issued by the Council of Trent:—"If any one shall affirm that a regenerate and justified man is bound to believe that he is certainly in the number of the elect (which, 1 Thess. 1:4, 5 plainly teaches. A.W.P.) let such an one be accursed"! "If any one shall affirm with positive and absolute certainty, that he shall surely have the gift of perseverance to the end (which John 10:28-30 assuredly guarantees, A.W.P.); let him be accursed"!

In order for any sinner to be saved three things were indispensable: God the Father had to purpose his salvation, God the Son had to purchase it, God the Spirit has to apply it. God does more than "propose" to us: were He only to "invite", every last one of us would be lost. This is strikingly illustrated in the Old Testament. In Ezra 1:1-3 we read, "Now in the first year of Cyrus king of Persia, that the word of the Lord by the mouth of Jeremiah might be fulfilled, the Lord stirred up the spirit of Cyrus king of Persia, that he made a proclamation throughout all his kingdom, and put it also in writing saying, Thus saith Cyrus king of Persia, the Lord God of heaven hath given me all the kingdoms of the earth, and He hath charged me to build Him an house at Jerusalem, which is in Judah. Who is there among you of all His people? his God be with him, and let him go up to Jerusalem which is in Judah, and build the house of the Lord God of Israel." Here was an "offer" made, made to a people in captivity, affording them opportunity to leave and return to Jerusalem—God's dwelling-place. Did all Israel eagerly respond to this offer? No indeed. The vast majority were content to remain in the enemy's land. Only an insignificant "remnant" availed themselves of this overture of mercy!

And why did they? Hear the answer of Scripture: "Then rose up the chief of the fathers of Judah and Benjamin, and the priests, and the Levites, with all whose spirit God had stirred up, to go up to build the house of the Lord which is in Jerusalem" (Ezra I :5) ! In like manner, God "stirs up" the spirits of His elect when the effectual call comes to them, and not till then do they have any willingness to respond to the Divine proclamation.

The superficial work of many of the professional evangelists of the last fifty years is largely responsible for the erroneous views now current upon the bondage of the natural man, encouraged by the laziness of those in the pew in their failure to "prove all things" (1 Thess. 5:21). The average evangelical pulpit conveys the impression that it lies wholly in the power of the sinner whether or not he shall be saved. It is said that "God has done His part, now man must do his." Alas, what can a lifeless man do, and man by nature is "dead in trespasses and sins" (Eph. 2:1)! If this were really believed, there would be more dependence upon the Holy Spirit to come in with His miracle-working power, and less confidence in our attempts to "win men for Christ."

When addressing the unsaved, preachers often draw an analogy between God's sending of the Gospel to the sinner, and a sick man in bed, with some healing medicine on a table by his side: all he needs to do is reach forth his hand and take it. But in order for this illustration to be in any wise true to the picture which Scripture gives us of the fallen and depraved sinner, the sick man in bed must be described as one who is blind (Eph. 4:18) so that he cannot see the medicine, his hand paralyzed (Rom. 5:6) so that he is unable to reach forth for it, and his heart not only devoid of all confidence in the medicine but filled with hatred against the physician himself (John 15:18). O what superficial views of man's desperate plight are now entertained! Christ came here not to help those who were willing to help themselves, but to do for His people what they were incapable of doing for themselves: "To open the blind eyes, to bring out the prisoners from the prison, and them that sit in darkness out of the prison house" (Isa. 42:7).

Now in conclusion let us anticipate and dispose of the usual and inevitable objection—Why preach the Gospel if man is powerless to respond? Why bid the sinner come to Christ if sin has so enslaved him that he has no power in himself to come? Reply:—We do not preach the Gospel because we believe that men are free moral agents, and therefore capable of receiving Christ, but we preach it because we are commanded to do so (Mark 16:15); and though to them that perish it is foolishness, yet, "unto us which are saved it is the power of God" (1 Cor. 1:18). "The foolishness of God is wiser than men; and the weakness of God is stronger than men" (1 Cor. 1:25). The sinner is dead in trespasses and sins (Eph. 2:1), and a dead man is utterly incapable of willing anything, hence it is that "they that are in the flesh (the unregenerate) cannot please God" (Rom. 8:8).

To fleshly wisdom it appears the height of folly to preach the Gospel to those that are dead, and therefore beyond the reach of doing anything themselves. Yes, but God's ways are different from ours. It pleases God "by the foolishness of preaching to save them that believe" (1 Cor. 1:21). Man may deem it folly to prophesy to "dead bones" and to say unto them, "O, ye dry bones, hear the Word of the Lord" (Ezek. 37:4). Ah! but then it is the Word of the Lord, and the words He speaks "they are spirit, and they are life" (John 6:63). Wise men standing by the grave of Lazarus might pronounce it an evidence of insanity when the Lord addressed a dead man with the words, "Lazarus, Come forth." Ah! but He who thus spake was and is Himself the Resurrection and the Life, and at His word even the dead live! We go forth to preach the Gospel, then, not because we believe that sinners have within themselves the power to receive the Saviour it proclaims, but because the Gospel itself is the power of God unto salvation to everyone that believeth, and because we know that "as many as were ordained to eternal life" (Acts 13:48), shall believe (John 6:37; 10:16—note the "shall's"!) in God's appointed time, for it is written, "Thy people shall be willing in the day of Thy power" (Ps. 110:3)!

What we have set forth in this chapter is not a product of "modern thought"; no indeed, it is at direct variance with it. It is those of the past few generations who have departed so far from the teachings of their scripturally-instructed fathers. In the thirty-nine Articles of the Church of England we read, "The condition of man after the fall of Adam is such, that he cannot turn and prepare himself by his own natural strength and good works to faith, and calling upon God: Wherefore we have no power to do good works, pleasant and acceptable to God, without the grace of God by Christ preventing us (being before-hand with us), that we may have a good will, and working with us, when we have that good will" (Article 10). In the Westminster Catechism of Faith (adopted by the Presbyterians) we read, "The sinfulness of that state whereinto man fell, consisteth in the guilt of Adam's first sin, the wont of that righteousness wherein he was created, and the corruption of his nature, whereby he is utterly indisposed, disabled, and made opposite unto all that is spiritually good, and wholly inclined to all evil, and that continually" (Answer to question 25). So in the Baptists' Philadelphian Confession of Faith, 1742, we read, "Man, by his fall into a state of sin, hath wholly lost all ability of will to any spiritual good accompanying salvation; so as a natural man, being altogether averse from good, and dead in sin, is not able by his own strength to convert himself, or to prepare himself thereunto" (Chapter 9).

' Since writing the above we have read an article by the late J. N. Darby entitled, "Man's so-called freewill," that opens with these words: "This re-appearance of the doctrine of freewill serves to support that of the pretension of the natural man to be not irremediably fallen, for this is what such doctrine tends to. All who have never been deeply convicted of sin, all persons in whom this conviction is based on gross external sins, believe more or less in freewill."

God's Sovereignty and Human Responsibility

"So then every one of us shall give account of himself to God"
Romans 14:12

In our last chapter we considered at some length the much debated and difficult question of the human will. We have shown that the will of the natural man is neither sovereign nor free but, instead, a servant and slave. We have argued that a right conception of the sinner's will— its servitude— is essential to a just estimate of his depravity and ruin. The utter corruption and degradation of human nature is something which man hates to acknowledge, and which he will hotly and insistently deny, until he is "taught of God." Much, very much, of the unsound doctrine which we now hear on every hand is the direct and logical outcome of man's repudiation of God's expressed estimate of human depravity. Men are claiming that they are "increased with goods, and have need of nothing," and know not that they are "wretched and miserable, and poor, and blind, and naked" (Rev. 3:17). They prate about the 'Ascent of Man,' and deny his Fall. They put darkness for light and light for darkness. They boast of the 'free moral agency' of man when, in fact, he is in bondage to sin and enslaved by Satan—"taken captive by him at his will" (2 Tim. 2:26). But if the natural man is not a 'free moral agent,' does it also follow that he is not accountable?

'Free moral agency' is an expression of human invention and, as we have said before, to talk of the freedom of the natural man is to flatly repudiate his spiritual ruin. Nowhere does Scripture speak of the freedom or moral ability of the sinner, on the contrary, it insists on his moral and spiritual inability.

This is, admittedly, the most difficult branch of our subject. Those who have ever devoted much study to this theme have uniformly recognized that the harmonizing of God's Sovereignty with Man's Responsibility is the gordian knot' of theology.

The main difficulty encountered is to define the relationship between God's sovereignty and man's responsibility. Many have summarily disposed of the difficulty by denying its existence. A certain class of theologians, in their anxiety to maintain man's responsibility, have magnified it beyond all due proportions, until God's sovereignty has been lost sight of, and in not a few instances flatly denied. Others have acknowledged that the Scriptures present both the sovereignty of God and the responsibility of man, but affirm that in our present finite condition and with our limited knowledge it is impossible to reconcile the two truths, though it is the bounden duty of the believer to receive both. The present writer believes that it has been too readily assumed that the Scriptures themselves do not reveal the several points which show the conciliation of God's sovereignty and man's responsibility. While perhaps the Word of God does not clear up all the mystery (and this is said with reserve), it does throw much light upon the problem, and it seems to us more honoring to God and His Word to prayerfully search the Scriptures for the complete solution of the difficulty, and even though others have thus far searched in vain, that ought only to drive us more and more to our knees. God has been pleased to reveal many things out of His Word during the last century which were hidden from earlier students. Who then dare affirm that there is not much to be learned yet respecting our present inquiry!

As we have said above, our chief difficulty is to determine the meeting-point of God's sovereignty and man's responsibility. To many it has seemed that for God to assert His sovereignty, for Him to put forth His power and exert a direct influence upon man, for Him to do anything more than warn or invite, would be to interfere with man's freedom, destroy his responsibility, and reduce him to a machine. It is sad indeed to find one like the late Dr. Pierson—whose writings are generally so scriptural and helpful—saying, "It is a tremendous thought that even God Himself cannot control my moral frame, or constrain my moral choice. He cannot prevent me defying and denying Him, and would not exercise His power in such directions if He could, and could not if He would" (A Spiritual Clinique). It is sadder still to discover that many other respected and loved brethren are giving expression to the same sentiments. Sad, because directly at variance with the Holy Scriptures.

It is our desire to face honestly the difficulties involved, and to examine them carefully in what light God has been pleased to grant us. The chief difficulties might be expressed thus: first, How is it possible for God to so bring His power to bear upon men that they are prevented from doing what they desire to do, and impelled to do other things they do not desire to do, and yet to preserve their responsibility? Second, How can the sinner be held responsible for the doing of what he is unable to do? And how can he be justly condemned for not doing what he could not do? Third, How is it possible for God to decree that men shall commit certain sins, hold them responsible in the committal of them, and adjudge them guilty because they committed them? Fourth, How can the sinner be held responsible to receive Christ, and be damned for rejecting Him, when God had foreordained him to condemnation? We shall now deal with these several problems in the above order. May the Holy Spirit Himself be our Teacher, so that in His light we may see light.

I. How is it possible for God to so bring His power to bear upon men that they are PREVENTED from doing what they desire to do, and IMPELL to do other things they do not desire to do, and yet to preserve their responsibility?

It would seem that if God put forth His power and exerted a direct influence upon men their freedom would be interfered with. It would appear that if God did anything wore than warn and invite men their responsibility would be infringed upon. We are told that God must not coerce man, still less compel him, or otherwise he would be reduced to a machine. This sounds very plausible; it appears to be good philosophy, and based upon sound reasoning; it has been almost universally accepted as an axiom in ethics; nevertheless, it is refuted by Scripture!

Let us turn first to Genesis 20:6—"And God said unto him in a dream, Yea, I know that thou didst this in the integrity of thy heart; for I also withheld thee from sinning against Me: therefore suffered I thee not to touch her." It is argued, almost universally, that God must not interfere with man's liberty, that he must not coerce or compel him, lest he be reduced to a machine. But the above scripture proves, unmistakably proves, that it is not impossible for God to exert His power upon man without destroying his responsibility. Here is a case where God did exert His power, restrict man's freedom, and prevent him from doing that which he otherwise would have done.

Ere turning from this scripture, let us note how it throws light upon the case of the first man. Would-be philosophers, who sought to be wise above that which was written, have argued that God could not have prevented Adam's fall without reducing him to a mere automaton. They tell us, constantly, that God must not coerce or compel His creatures, otherwise He would destroy their accountability. But the answer to all such philosophizing is, that Scripture records a number of instances where we are expressly told God did prevent certain of His creatures from sinning both against Himself and against His people, in view of which all men's reasonings are utterly worthless. If God could "withhold" Abimelech from sinning against Him, then why was He unable to do the same with Adam? Should someone ask, Then why did not God do so? we might return the question by asking, Why did not God "withhold" Satan from falling? or, Why did not God "withhold" the Kaiser from starting the recent War? The usual reply is, as we have said, God could not without interfering with man's "freedom" and reducing him to a machine. But the case of Abimelech proves conclusively that such a reply is untenable and erroneous—we might add wicked and blasphemous, for who are we to limit the Most High! How dare any finite creature take it upon him to say what the Almighty can and cannot do? Should we be pressed further as to why God refused to exercise His power and prevent Adam's fall, we should say, Because Adam's fall better served His own wise and blessed purpose—among other things, it provided an opportunity to demonstrate that where sin had abounded grace could much more abound. But we might ask further; Why did God place in the garden the tree of the knowledge of good and evil, when He foresaw that man would disobey His prohibition and eat of it; for mark, it was God and not Satan who made that tree. Should someone respond, Then is God the Author of Sin? We would have to ask, in turn, What is meant by "Author"? Plainly it was God's will that sin should enter this world, otherwise it would not have entered, for nothing happens save as God has eternally decreed. Moreover, there was more than a bare permission, for God only permits that which He has purposed. But we leave now the origin of sin, insisting once more, however, that God could have "withheld" Adam from sinning without destroying his responsibility.

The case of Abimelech does not stand alone. Another illustration of the same principle is seen in the history of Balaam, already noticed in the last chapter, but concerning which a further word is in place. Balak the Moabite sent for this heathen prophet to "curse" Israel. A handsome reward was offered for his services, and a careful reading of Numbers 22-24 will show that Balaam was willing, yea, anxious, to accept Balak's offer and thus sin against God and His people. But Divine power "withheld" him. Mark his own admission, "And Balaam said unto Balak, Lo, I am come unto thee: have I now any power at all to say anything? the word that God putteth in my mouth, that shall I speak" (Num. 22:38). Again, after Balak had remonstrated with Balaam, we read, "He answered and said, Must I not take heed to speak that which the Lord hath put in my mouth? . . . Behold, I have received commandment to bless: and He hath blessed; and I cannot reverse it" (23:12, 20). Surely these verses show us God's power, and Balaam's powerlessness: man's will frustrated, and God's will performed. But was

Balaam's "freedom" or responsibility destroyed? Certainly not, as we shall yet seek to show.

One more illustration: "And the fear of the Lord fell upon all the kingdoms of the lands that were round about Judah, so that they made no war against Jehoshaphat" (2 Chron. 17:10). The implication here is clear. Had not the "fear of the Lord" fallen upon these kingdoms, they would have made war upon Judah. God's restraining power alone prevented them. Had their own will been allowed to act, "war" would have been the consequence. Thus we see that Scripture teaches that God "withholds" nations as well as individuals, and that when it pleaseth Him to do so He interposes and prevents war. Compare further Genesis 35:5.

The question which now demands our consideration is, How is it possible for God to "withhold" men from sinning and yet not to interfere with their liberty and responsibility—a question which so many say is incapable of solution in our present finite condition. This question causes us to ask, In what does moral "freedom," real moral freedom, consist? We answer, it is the being delivered from the bondage of sin. The more any soul is emancipated from the thralldom of sin, the more does he enter into a state of freedom—"If the Son therefore shall make you free, ye shall be free indeed" (John 8:36). In the above instances God "withheld" Abimelech, Balaam, and the heathen kingdoms from sinning, and therefore we affirm that He did not in anywise interfere with their real freedom. The nearer a soul approximates to sinlessness, the nearer does he approach to God's holiness. Scripture tells us that God "cannot lie," and that He "cannot be tempted," but is He any the less free because He cannot do that which is evil? Surely not. Then is it not evident that the more man is raised up to God, and the more he be "withheld" from sinning, the greater is his real freedom!

A pertinent example setting forth the meeting-place of God's sovereignty and man's responsibility, as it relates to the question of moral freedom, is found in connection with the giving to us of the Holy Scriptures. In the communication of His Word God was pleased to employ human instruments, and in the using of them He did not reduce them to mere mechanical amanuenses: "Knowing this first, that no prophecy of the Scripture is of any private interpretation (Greek: of its own origination). For the prophecy came not at any time by the will of man: but holy men of God spake moved by the Holy Spirit" (2 Pet. 1:20, 21). Here we have man's responsibility and God's sovereignty placed in juxtaposition. These holy men were moved" (Greek: "borne along") by the Holy Spirit, yet was not their moral responsibility disturbed nor their "freedom" impaired. God enlightened their minds, enkindled their hearts, revealed to them His truth, and so controlled them that error on their part was, by Him, made impossible, as they communicated His mind and will to men. But what was it that might have, would have, caused error, had not God controlled as He did the instruments which He employed? The answer is sin, the sin which was in them. But as we have seen, the holding in check of sin, the preventing of the exercise of the carnal mind in these "holy men," was not a destroying of their "freedom," rather was it the inducting of them into real freedom.

A final word should be added here concerning the nature of true liberty. There are three chief things concerning which men in general greatly err: misery and happiness, folly and wisdom, bondage and liberty. The world counts none miserable but the afflicted, and none happy but the prosperous, because they judge by the present ease of the flesh. Again; the world is pleased with a false show of wisdom (which is "foolishness" with God), neglecting that which makes wise unto salvation. As to liberty, men would be at their own disposal, and live as they please. They suppose the only true liberty is to be at the command and under the control of none above themselves, and live according to their heart's desire. But this is a thralldom and bondage of the worst kind. True liberty is not the power to live as we please, but to live as we ought! Hence, the only One Who has ever trod this earth since Adam's fall that has enjoyed perfect freedom was the Man Christ Jesus, the Holy Servant of God, Whose meat it ever was to do the will of the Father.

We now turn to consider the question.

II. How can the sinner be held responsible FOR the doing of what he is UNABLE to do? And how can he be justly condemned for NOT DOING what he COULD NOT do?

As a creature the natural man is responsible to love, obey, and serve God; as a sinner he is responsible to repent and believe the Gospel. But at the outset we are confronted with the fact that the natural man is unable to love and serve God, and that the sinner, of himself, cannot repent and believe. First, let us prove what we have just said. We begin by quoting and considering John 6:44 "No man can come to Me, except the Father which bath sent Me draw him". The heart of the natural man (every man) is so "desperately wicked" that if he is left to himself he will never 'come to Christ.' This statement would not be questioned if the full force of the words "Coming to Christ" were properly apprehended. We shall therefore digress a little at this point to define and consider what is implied and involved in the words "No man can come to Me"—cf. John 5:40, "Ye will not come to Me that ye might have life."

For the sinner to come to Christ that he might have life, is for him to realize the awful danger of his situation; is for him to see that the sword of Divine justice is suspended over his head; is to awaken to the fact that there is but a step betwixt him and death, and that after death is the "judgment;" and in consequence of this discovery, is for him to be in real earnest to escape, and in such earnestness that he shall flee from the wrath to come, cry unto God for mercy, and agonize to enter in at the "strait gate."

To come to Christ for life, is for the sinner to feel and acknowledge that he is utterly destitute of any claim upon God's favor; is to see himself as "without strength," lost and undone; is to admit that he is deserving of nothing but eternal death, thus taking side with God against himself; it is for him to cast himself into the dust before God, and humbly sue for Divine mercy.

To come to Christ for life, is for the sinner to abandon his own righteousness and be ready to be made the righteousness of God in Christ; it is to disown his own wisdom and be guided by His; it is to repudiate his own will and be ruled by His; it is to unreservedly receive the Lord Jesus as his Saviour and Lord, as his All in all.

Such, in part and in brief, is what is implied and involved in "Coming to Christ." But is the sinner willing to take such an attitude before God? No; for in the first place, he does not realize the danger of his situation, and in consequence is not in real earnest after his escape; instead, men are for the most part at ease, and apart from the operations of the Holy Spirit whenever they are disturbed by the alarms of conscience or the dispensations of providence, they flee to any other refuge but Christ. In the second place, they will not acknowledge that all their righteousnesses are as filthy rags but, like the Pharisee, will thank God they are not as the Publican. And in the third place, they are not ready to receive Christ as their Saviour and Lord, for they are unwilling to part with their idols: they had rather hazard their soul's eternal welfare than give them up. Hence we say that, left to himself, the natural man is so depraved at heart that he cannot come to Christ.

The words of our Lord quoted above by no means stand alone. Quite a number of Scriptures set forth the moral and spiritual inability of the natural man. In Joshua 24:19 we read, "And Joshua said unto the people, Ye cannot serve the Lord: for He is a holy God." To the Pharisees Christ said, "Why do ye not understand My speech? Even because ye cannot hear My word" (John 8:43). And again: "The carnal mind is enmity against God: for it is not

The Holy Spirit

subject to the law of God, neither indeed can be. So then they that are in the flesh cannot please God" (Rom. 8:7, 8).

But now the question returns, How can God hold the sinner responsible for failing to do what he is unable to do? This necessitates a careful definition of terms. Just what is meant by "unable" and "cannot"?

Now let it be clearly understood that, when we speak of the sinner's inability, we do not mean that if men desired to come to Christ they lack the necessary power to carry out their desire. No; the fact is that the sinner's inability or absence of power is itself due to lack of willingness to come to Christ, and this lack of willingness is the fruit of a depraved heart. It is of first importance that we distinguish between natural inability and moral and spiritual inability. For example, we read, "But Abijah could not see; for his eyes were set by reason of his age" (1 Kings 14:4); and again, "The men rowed hard to bring it to the land; but they could not: for the sea wrought, and was tempestuous against them" (Jonah 1:13). In both of these passages the words "could not" refer to natural inability. But when we read, "And when his brethren saw that their father loved him (Joseph) more than all his brethren, they hated him, and could not speak peaceably unto him" (Gen. 37:4), it is clearly moral inability that is in view. They did not lack the natural ability to "speak peaceably unto him", for they were not dumb. Why then was it that they "could not speak peaceably unto him"? The answer is given in the same verse: it was because "they hated him." Again; in 2 Peter 2:14 we read of a certain class of wicked men "having eyes full of adultery, and that cannot cease from sin." Here again it is moral inability that is in view. Why is it that these men "cannot cease from sin"? The answer is, Because their eyes were full of adultery. So of Romans 8:8.—"They that are in the flesh cannot please God": here it is spiritual inability. Why is it that the natural man "cannot please God"? Because he is "alienated from the life of God" (Eph. 4:18). No man can choose that from which his heart is averse—"O generation of vipers how can ye, being evil, speak good things?" (Matt. 12:34). "No man can come to Me, except the Father which hath sent Me draw him" (John 6:44). Here again it is moral and spiritual inability which is before us. Why is it the sinner cannot come to Christ unless he is "drawn"? The answer is, Because his wicked heart loves sign and hates Christ.

We trust we have made it clear that the Scriptures distinguish sharply between natural inability and moral and spiritual inability. Surely all can see the difference between the blindness of Bartimeus, who was ardently desirous of receiving his sight, and the Pharisees, whose eyes were closed, "lest at any time they should see with their eyes, and hear with their ears, and should understand with their heart, and should be converted" (Matt. 13:15). But should it be said, The natural man could come to Christ if he wished to do so, we answer, Ah! but in that IF lies the hinge of the whole matter. The inability of the sinner consists of the want of moral power to wish and will so as to actually perform.

What we have contended for above is of first importance. Upon the distinction between the sinner's natural Ability, and his moral and spiritual Inability, rests his Responsibility. The depravity of the human heart does not destroy man's accountability to God; so far from this being the case the very moral inability of the sinner only serves to increase his guilt. This is easily proven by a reference to the scriptures cited above. We read that Joseph's brethren "could not speak peaceably unto him," and why? It was because they "hated" Him. But was this moral inability of theirs any excuse? Surely not: in this very moral inability consisted the greatness of their sin. So of those concerning whom it is said, "They cannot cease from sin" (2 Pet. 2:14), and why? Because "their eyes were full of adultery," but that only made their case worse. It was a real fact that they could not cease from sin, yet this did not excuse them—it only made their sin the greater.

Should some sinner here object, I cannot help being born into this world with a depraved heart, and therefore I am not responsible for my moral and spiritual inability which accrue from it, the reply would be, Responsibility and Culpability lie in the indulgence of the depraved propensities, the free indulgence, for God does not force any to sin. Men might pity me, but they certainly would not excuse me if I gave vent to a fiery temper, and then sought to extenuate myself on the ground of having inherited that temper from my parents. Their own common sense is sufficient to guide their judgment in such a case as this. They would argue I was responsible to restrain my temper. Why then cavil against this same principle in the case supposed above? "Out of thine own mouth will I judge thee thou wicked servant" surely applies here! What would the reader say to a man who had robbed him, and who later argued in defence, "I cannot help being a thief, that is my nature"? Surely the reply would be, Then the penitentiary is the proper place for that man. What then shall be said to the one who argues that he cannot help following the bent of his sinful heart? Surely, that the Lake of Fire is where such an one must go. Did ever murderer plead that he hated his victim so much that he could not go near him without slaying him. Would not that only magnify the enormity of his crime! Then what of the one who loves sin so much that he is "at enmity against God"!

The fact of man's responsibility is almost universally acknowledged. It is inherent in man's moral nature. It is not only taught in Scripture but witnessed to by the natural conscience. The basis or ground of human responsibility is human ability. What is implied by this general term "ability" must now be defined. Perhaps a concrete example will be more easily grasped by the average reader than an abstract argument.

Suppose a man owed me $100 and could find plenty of money for his own pleasures but none for me, yet pleaded that he was unable to pay me. What would I say? I would say that the only ability that was lacking was an honest heart. But would it not be an unfair construction of my words if a friend of my dishonest debtor should say I had stated that an honest heart was that which constituted the ability to pay the debt? No; I would reply: the ability of my debtor lies in the power of his hand to write me a check, and this he has, but what is lacking is an honest principle. It is his power to write me a check which makes him responsible to do so, and the fact that he lacks an honest heart does not destroy his accountability.'

Now, in like manner, the sinner while altogether lacking in moral and spiritual ability does, nevertheless, possess natural ability, and this it is which renders him accountable unto God. Men have the same natural faculties to love God with as they have to hate Him with, the same hearts to believe with which they disbelieve, and it is their failure to love and believe which constitutes their guilt. An idiot or an infant is not personally responsible to God, because lacking in natural ability. But the normal man who is endowed with rationality, who is gifted with a conscience that is capable of distinguishing between right and wrong, who is able to weigh eternal issues is a responsible being, and it is because he does possess these very faculties that he will yet have to "give account of himself to God" (Rom. 14:12).

We say again that the above distinction between the natural ability and the moral and spiritual inability of the sinner is of prime importance. By nature he possesses natural ability but lacks moral and spiritual ability. The fact that he does not possess the latter, does not destroy his responsibility, because his responsibility rests upon the fact that he does possess the former. Let me illustrate again. Here are two men guilty of theft: the first is an idiot, the second perfectly sane but the offspring of criminal parents. No just judge would sentence the former; but every right-minded judge would the latter. Even though the second of these thieves possessed a vitiated moral nature inherited from criminal parents, that would not excuse him, providing he was a normal rational being. Here then is the ground of human accountability—the possession of rationality plus the gift of conscience. It is because the sinner is endowed with these natural faculties that he is a responsible creature; because he does not use his natural powers for God's glory, constitutes his guilt.

How can it remain consistent with His mercy that God should require the debt of obedience from him that is not able to pay? In addition to what has been said above, it should be pointed out that God has not lost His right, even though man has lost his power. The creature's impotence does not cancel his obligation. A drunken servant is a servant still, and it is contrary to all sound reasoning to argue that his master loses his rights through his servant's default. Moreover, it is of first importance that we should ever bear in mind that God contracted with us in Adam, who was our federal head and representative, and in him, God gave us a power which we lost through our first parent's fall; but though our power be gone, nevertheless, God may justly demand His due of obedience and of service.

We turn now to ponder,

III. How is it possible for God to DECREE that men SHOULD commit certain sins, hold them RESPONSIBLE in the committal of them, and adjudge them GUILTY because they committed them?

Let us now consider the extreme case of Judas. We hold that it is clear from Scripture that God decreed from all eternity that Judas should betray the Lord Jesus. If anyone should challenge this statement we refer him to the prophecy of Zechariah, through whom God declared that His Son should be sold for "Thirty pieces of silver" (Zech. 11:12). As we have said in earlier pages, in prophecy God makes known what will be, and in making known what will be, He is but revealing to us what He has ordained shall be. That Judas was the one through whom the prophecy of Zechariah was fulfilled needs not to be argued. But now the question we have to face is, Was Judas a responsible agent in fulfilling this decree of God? We reply that he was. Responsibility attaches mainly to the motive and intention of the one committing the act. This is recognized on every hand. Human law distinguishes between a blow inflicted by accident (without evil design), and a blow delivered with 'malice aforethought.' Apply then this same principle to the case of Judas. What was the design of his heart when he bargained with the priests? Manifestly he had no conscious desire to fulfil any decree of God, though unknown to himself he was actually doing so. On the contrary, his intention was evil only, and therefore, though God had decreed and directed his act, nevertheless, his own evil intention rendered him justly guilty as he afterwards acknowledged himself—"I have betrayed innocent blood." It was the same with the Crucifixion of Christ. Scripture plainly declares that He was "delivered up by the determinate counsel and foreknowledge of God" (Acts 2:23), and that though "the kings of the earth stood up, and the rulers were gathered together against the Lord, and against His Christ" yet, notwithstanding, it was but "for to do whatsoever Thy hand and Thy counsel determined before to be done" (Acts 4:26, 28); which verses teach very much more than a bare permission by God, declaring, as they do, that the Crucifixion and all its details had been decreed by God. Yet, nevertheless, it was by "wicked hands," not merely "human hands", that our Lord was "crucified and slain" (Acts 2:23). "Wicked" because the intention, of His crucifiers was only evil.

But it might be objected that, if God had decreed that Judas should betray Christ, and that the Jews and Gentiles should crucify Him, they could not do otherwise, and therefore, they were not responsible for their intentions. The answer is, God had decreed that they should perform the acts they did, but in the actual perpetration of these deeds they were justly guilty, because their own purposes in the doing of them was evil only. Let it be emphatically said that God does not produce the sinful dispositions of any of His creatures, though He does restrain and direct them to the accomplishing of His own purposes. Hence He is neither the Author nor the Approver of sin. This distinction was expressed thus by Augustine: "That men sin proceeds from themselves; that in sinning they perform this or that action, is from the power of God who divideth the darkness according to His pleasure." Thus it is written, "A man's heart deviseth his way: but the Lord directeth his steps" (Prov. 16:9). What we would here insist upon is, that God's decrees are not the necessitating cause of the sins of men, but the fore-determined and prescribed boundings and directings of men's sinful acts. In connection with the betrayal of Christ, God did not decree that He should be sold by one of His creatures and then take up a good man, instill an evil desire into his heart and thus force him to perform the terrible deed in order to execute His decree. No; not so do the Scriptures represent it. Instead, God decreed the act and selected the one who was to perform the act, but He did not make him evil in order that he should perform the deed; on the contrary, the betrayer was a "devil" at the time the Lord Jesus chose him as one of the twelve (John 6:70), and in the exercise and manifestation of his own devilry God simply directed his actions, actions which were perfectly agreeable to his own vile heart, and performed with the most wicked intentions. Thus it was with the Crucifixion.

IV. How can the sinner be held responsible to receive Christ, and be damned for rejecting Him, when God FOREORDAINED him TO condemnation?

Really, this question has been covered in what has been said under the other queries, but for the benefit of those who are exercised upon this point we give it a separate, though brief, examination. In considering the above difficulty the following points should be carefully weighed:

In the first place, no sinner, while he is in this world, knows for certain, nor can he know, that he is a "vessel of wrath fitted to destruction". This belongs to the hidden counsels of God, to which he has not access. God's secret will is no business of his; God's revealed will (in the Word) is the standard of human responsibility. And God's revealed will is plain. Each sinner is among those whom God now "commandeth to repent" (Acts 17:30). Each sinner who hears the Gospel is "commanded" to believe (1 John 3:23). And all who do truly repent and believe are saved. Therefore, is every sinner responsible to repent and believe.

In the second place, it is the duty of every sinner to search the Scriptures which "are able to make wise unto salvation" (2 Tim. 3:15). It is the sinner's "duty" because the Son of God has commanded him to search the Scriptures (John 5:39). If he searches them with a heart that is seeking after God, then does he put himself in the way where God is accustomed to meet with sinners. Upon this point the Puritan Manton has written very helpfully.

"I cannot say to every one that ploweth, infallibly, that he shall have a good crop; but this I can say to him, It is God's use to bless the diligent and provident. I cannot say to every one that desireth posterity, Marry, and you shall have children; I cannot say infallibly to him that goeth forth to battle for his country's good that he shall have victory and success; but I can say, as Joab, (1 Chron. 19:13) 'Be of good courage, and let us behave ourselves valiantly for our people and the cities of our God, and let the Lord do what is good in His sight'. I cannot say infallibly you shall have grace; but I can say to every one, Let him use the means, and leave the success of his labor and his own salvation to the will and good pleasure of God. I cannot say this infallibly, for there is no obligation upon God. And still this work is made the fruit of God's will and mere arbitrary dispensation—'Of His own will begat He us by the Word of Truth' (James 1:18). Let us do what God hath commanded, and let God do what He will. And I need not say so; for the whole world in all their actings are and should be guided by this principle. Let us do our duty, and refer the success to God, Whose ordinary practice it is to meet with the creature that seeketh after Him; yea, He is with us already; this earnest importunity in the use of means proceeding from the earnest impression of His grace. And therefore, since He is beforehand with us, and bath not showed any backwardness to our good, we have no reason to despair of His goodness and mercy, but rather to hope for the best" (Vol. XXI, page 312).

God has been pleased to give to men the Holy Scriptures which "testify" of the Saviour, and make known the way of salvation. Every sinner has the same natural faculties for the reading of the Bible as he has for the reading of the newspaper; and if he is illiterate or blind so that he is unable to read, he has the same mouth with which to ask a friend to read the Bible to him, as he has to inquire concerning other matters. If, then, God has given to men His Word, and in that Word has made known the way of salvation, and if men are commanded to search those Scriptures which are able to make them wise unto salvation, and they refuse to do so, then is it plain that they are justly censurable, that their blood lies on their own heads, and that God can righteously cast them into the Lake of Fire.

In the third place, should it be objected, Admitting all you have said above, Is it not still a fact that each of the non-elect is unable to repent and believe? The reply is, Yes. Of every sinner it is a fact that, of himself, he cannot come to Christ. And from God's side the "cannot" is absolute. But we are now dealing with the responsibility of the sinner (the sinner foreordained to condemnation, though he knows it not), and from the human side the inability of the sinner is a moral one, as previously pointed out. Moreover, it needs to be borne in mind that in addition to the moral inability of the sinner there is a voluntary inability, too. The sinner must be regarded not only as impotent to do good, but as delighting in evil. From the human side, then, the "cannot" is a will not; it is a voluntary impotence. Man's impotence lies in his obstinacy. Hence, is everyone left "without excuse", And hence, is God "clear" when He judgeth (Ps. 51:4), and righteous in damning all who "love darkness rather than light".

That God does require what is beyond our own power to render is clear from many scriptures. God gave the Law to Israel at Sinai and demanded a full compliance with it, and solemnly pointed out what would be the consequences of their disobedience (see Deut. 28). But will any readers be so foolish as to affirm that Israel were capable of fully obeying the Law! If they do, we would refer them to Romans 8:3 where we are expressly told, "For what the law could not do, in that it was weak through the flesh, God sending His own Son in the likeness of sinful flesh, and for sin, condemned sin in the flesh".

Come now to the New Testament. Take such passages as Matthew 5:48, "Be ye therefore perfect, even as your Father which is in heaven is perfect". 1 Corinthians 15:34, "Awake to righteousness and sin not". 1 John 2:1, "My little children, these things I write unto you, that ye sin not". Will any reader say he is capable in himself of complying with these demands of God? If so, it is useless for us to argue with him.

But now the question arises, Why has God demanded of man that which he is incapable of performing? The first answer is, Because God refuses to lower His standard to the level of our sinful infirmities. Being perfect, God must set a perfect standard before us. Still we must ask, if man is incapable of measuring up to God's standard, wherein lies his responsibility? Difficult as seems the problem it is nevertheless capable of a simple and satisfactory solution.

Man is responsible to (1st) acknowledge before God his inability, and (2nd) to cry unto Him for enabling grace. Surely this will be admitted by every Christian reader. It is my bounden duty to own before God my ignorance, my weakness, my sinfulness, my impotence to comply with His holy and just requirements. It is also my bounden duty, as well as blessed privilege, to earnestly beseech God to give me the wisdom, strength, grace, which will enable me to do that which is pleasing in His sight; to ask Him to work in me "both to will and to do of His good pleasure" (Phil. 2:13).

In like manner, the sinner, every sinner, is responsible to call upon the Lord. Of himself he can neither repent nor believe. He can neither come to Christ, nor turn from his sins. God tells him so; and his first duty is to "set to his seal that God is true". His second duty is to cry unto God for His enabling power—to ask God in mercy to overcome his enmity, and "draw" him to Christ; to bestow upon him the gifts of repentance and faith. If he will do so, sincerely from the heart, then most surely God will respond to his appeal, for it is written—"For whosoever shall call upon the name of the Lord shall be saved" (Rom. 10:13).

Suppose, I had slipped on the icy pavement, late at night, and had broken my hip. I am unable to arise; if I remain on the ground, I must freeze to death. What, then, ought I to do? If I am determined to perish, I shall lie there silent—but I shall be to blame for such a course. If I am anxious to be rescued, I shall lift up my voice and cry for help. So the sinner, though unable of himself to rise and take the first step toward Christ, is responsible to cry to God, and if he does (from the heart), there is a Deliverer to hand. God is "not far from every one of us" (Acts 17:27); yea, "He is a very present help in trouble" (Ps. 46:1). But if the sinner refuses to cry unto the

The Holy Spirit 425

Lord, if he is determined to perish, then his blood is on his own head, and his "damnation is just" (Rom. 3:8).

A brief word now concerning the extent of human responsibility.

It is obvious that the measure of human responsibility varies in different cases, and is greater or less with particular individuals. The standard of measurement was given in the Saviour's words, "For unto whomsoever much is given, of him shall much be required" (Luke 12:48). Surely God did not require as much from those living in Old Testament times as He does from those who have been born during the Christian dispensation. Surely God will not require as much from those who lived during the 'dark ages,' when the Scriptures were accessible to but a few, as He will from those of this generation, when practically every family in the land own a copy of His Word for themselves. In the same way, God will not demand from the heathen what He will from those in Christendom. The heathen will not perish because they have not believed in Christ, but because they failed to live up to the light which they did have—the testimony of God in nature and conscience.

To sum up. The fact of man's responsibility rests upon his natural ability, is witnessed to by conscience, and is insisted on throughout the Scriptures. The ground of man's responsibility is that he is a rational creature capable of weighing eternal issues, and that he possesses a written Revelation from God, in which his relationship with and duty toward his Creator is plainly defined. The measure of responsibility varies in different individuals, being determined by the degree of light each has enjoyed from God. The problem of human responsibility receives at least a partial solution in the Holy Scriptures, and it is our solemn obligation as well as privilege to search them prayerfully and carefully for further light, looking to the Holy Spirit to guide us "into all truth." It is written, "The meek will He guide in judgment: and the meek will He teach His way" (Ps. 25:9).

In conclusion it remains to point out that it is the responsibility of every man to use the means which God has placed to his hand. An attitude of fatalistic inertia, because I know that God has irrevocably decreed whatsoever comes to pass, is to make a sinful and hurtful use of what God has revealed for the comfort of my heart. The same God who has decreed that a certain end shall be accomplished, has also decreed that that end shall be attained through and as the result of His own appointed means. God does not disdain the use of means, nor must I. For example: God has decreed that "while the earth remaineth, seed-time and harvest... shall not cease" (Gen. 8:22); but that does not mean man's ploughing of the ground and sowing of the seed are needless. No; God moves men to do those very things, blesses their labours, and so fulfills His own ordination. In like manner, God has, from the beginning, chosen a people unto salvation; but that does not mean there is no need for evangelists to preach the Gospel, or for sinners to believe it; it is by such means that His eternal counsels are effectuated.

To argue that, because God has irrevocably determined the eternal destiny of every man, relieves us of all responsibility for any concern about our souls, or any diligent use of the means to salvation, would be on a par with refusing to perform my temporal duties because God has fixed my earthly lot. And that He has is clear from Acts 17:26, Job 7:1; 14:5, etc. If then the foreordination of God may consist with the respective activities of man in present concerns, why not in the future? What God has joined together we must not cut asunder. Whether we can or cannot see the link which unites the one to the other, our duty is plain: "The secret things belong unto the Lord our God: but those things which are revealed belong unto us and to our children forever, that we may do all the words of this law" (Deut. 29:29).

In Acts 27:22 God made known that He had ordained the temporal preservation of all who accompanied Paul in the ship; yet the apostle did not hesitate to say, "Except these abide in the ship, ye cannot be saved" (v. 31); God appointed that means for the execution of what He had decreed. From 2 Kings 20 we learn that God was absolutely resolved to add fifteen years to Hezekiah's life, yet he must take a lump of figs and lay it on his boil! Paul knew that he was eternally secure in the hand of Christ (John 10:28), yet he "kept under his body" (1 Cor. 9:26). The apostle John assured those to whom he wrote, "Ye shall abide in Him", yet in the very next verse he exhorted them, "And now, little children, abide in Him" (1 John 2:27, 28). It is only by taking heed to this vital principle, that we are responsible to use the means of God's appointing, that we shall be enabled to preserve the balance of Truth, and be saved from a paralyzing fatalism.

God's Sovereignty and Prayer

"If we ask anything according to His will, He heareth us"
1 John 5:14

Throughout this book it has been our chief aim to exalt the Creator and abase the creature. The well-nigh universal tendency, now, is to magnify man and dishonor and degrade God. On every hand it will be found that, when spiritual things are under discussion, the human side and element is pressed and stressed, and the Divine side, if not altogether ignored, is relegated to the background. This holds true of very much of the modern teaching about prayer. In the great majority of the books written and in the sermons preached upon prayer, the human element fills the scene almost entirely: it is the conditions which we must meet, the promises we must "claim", the things we must do, in order to get our requests granted; and God's claims, God's rights, God's glory are disregarded.

As a fair sample of what is being given out today we subjoin a brief editorial which appeared recently in one of the leading religious weeklies entitled "Prayer, or Fate?"

"God in His sovereignty has ordained that human destinies may be changed and moulded by the will of man. This is at the heart of the truth that prayer changes things, meaning that God changes things when men pray. Some one has strikingly expressed it this way: 'There are certain things that will happen in a man's life whether he prays or not. There are other things that will happen if he prays, and will not happen if he does not pray'. A Christian worker was impressed by these sentences as he entered a business office, and he prayed that the Lord would open the way to speak to some one about Christ, reflecting that things would be changed because he prayed. Then his mind turned to other things and the prayer was forgotten. The opportunity came to speak to the business man on whom he was calling, but he did not grasp it, and was on his way out when he remembered his prayer of a half hour before, and God's answer. He promptly returned and had a talk with the business man, who, though a church-member, had never in his life been asked whether he was saved. Let us give ourselves to prayer, and open the way for God to change things. Let us beware lest we become virtual fatalists by failing to exercise our God-given wills in praying".

The above illustrates what is now being taught on the subject of prayer, and the deplorable thing is that scarcely a voice is lifted in protest. To say that "human destinies may be changed and moulded by the will of man" is rank infidelity—that is the only proper term for it. Should any one challenge this classification, we would ask them whether they can find an infidel anywhere who would dissent from such a statement, and we are confident that such an one could not be found. To say that "God has ordained that human destinies may be changed and moulded by the will of man", is absolutely untrue. "Human destiny" is settled not by "the will of man," but by the will of God. That which determines human destiny is whether or not a man has been born again, for it is written, "Except a man be born again he cannot see the kingdom of God". And as to whose will, whether God's or man's, is responsible for the new birth is settled, unequivocally, by John 1:13—"Which were born, not of blood, nor of the will of the flesh, nor of the will of man, but OF GOD". To say that "human destiny" may be changed by the will of man, is to make the creature's will supreme, and that is, virtually, to dethrone God. But what saith the Scriptures? Let the Book answer: "The Lord killeth, and maketh alive: He bringeth down to the grave, and bringeth up. The Lord maketh poor, and maketh rich: He bringeth low, and lifteth up. He raiseth up the poor out of the dust, and lifteth up the beggar from the dunghill, to set them among princes, and to make them inherit the throne of glory" (1 Sam. 2:6-8).

Turning back to the Editorial here under review, we are next told, "This is at the heart of the truth that prayer changes things, meaning that God changes things when men pray." Almost everywhere we go today one comes across a motto-card bearing the inscription "Prayer Changes Things". As to what these words are designed to signify is evident from the current literature on prayer—we are to persuade God to change His purpose. Concerning this we shall have more to say below.

Again, the Editor tells us, "Some one has strikingly expressed it this way: 'There are certain things that will happen in a man's life whether he prays or not. There are other things that will happen if he prays, and will not happen if he does not pray.'" That things happen whether a man prays or not is exemplified daily in the lives of the unregenerate, most of whom never pray at all. That 'other things will happen if he prays' is in need of qualification. If a believer prays in faith and asks for those things which are according to God's will, he will most certainly obtain that for which he has asked. Again, that other things will happen if he prays, is also true in respect to the subjective benefits derived from prayer: God will become more real to him and His promises more precious. That other things 'will not happen if he does not pray' is true so far as his own life is concerned—a prayerless life means a life lived out of communion with God and all that is involved by this. But to affirm that God will not and cannot bring to pass His eternal purpose unless we pray, is utterly erroneous, for the same God who has decreed the end has also decreed that His end shall be reached through His appointed means, and one of these is prayer. The God who has determined to grant a blessing, also gives a spirit of supplication which first seeks the blessing.

The example cited in the above Editorial of the Christian Worker and the business man is a very unhappy one to say the least, for according to the terms of the illustration the Christian Worker's prayer was not answered by God at all, inasmuch as, apparently, the way was not opened to speak to the business man about his soul. But on leaving the office and recalling his prayer the Christian Worker (perhaps in the energy of the flesh) determined to answer the prayer for himself, and instead of leaving the Lord to "open the way" for him, took matters into his own hand.

We quote next from one of the latest books issued on Prayer. In it the author says, "The possibilities and necessity of prayer, its power and results, are manifested in arresting and changing the purposes of God and in relieving the stroke of His power". Such an assertion as this is a horrible reflection upon the character of the Most High God, who "doeth according to His will in the army of heaven, and among the inhabitants of the earth: and none can stay His hand, or say unto Him, What doest Thou?"(Dan. 4:35). There is no need whatever for God to change His designs or alter His purpose, for the all-sufficient reason that these were framed under the influence of perfect goodness and unerring wisdom. Men may have occasion to alter their purposes, for in their short-sightedness they are frequently unable to anticipate what may arise after their plans are formed. But not so with God, for He knows the end from the beginning. To affirm that God changes His purpose is either to impugn His goodness or to deny His eternal wisdom.

In the same book we are told, "The prayers of God's saints are the capital stock in heaven by which Christ carries on His great work upon earth. The great throes and mighty convulsions on earth are the results of these prayers. Earth is changed, revolutionized, angels move on more powerful, more rapid wing, and God's policy is shaped as the prayers are more numerous, more efficient". If possible, this is even worse, and we have no hesitation in denominating it as blasphemy. In the first place, it flatly denies Ephesians

3:11, which speaks of God's having an "eternal purpose". If God's purpose is an eternal one, then His "policy" is not being "shaped" today. In the second place, it contradicts Ephesians 1:11 which expressly declares that God "worketh all things after the counsel of His own will," therefore it follows that, "God's policy" is not being "shaped" by man's prayers. In the third place, such a statement as the above makes the will of the creature supreme, for if our prayers shape God's policy, then is the Most High subordinate to worms of the earth. Well might the Holy Spirit ask through the apostle, "For who hath known the mind of the Lord? or who hath been His counsellor?" (Rom. 11:34).

Such thoughts on prayer as we have been citing are due to low and inadequate conceptions of God Himself. It ought to be apparent that there could be little or no comfort in praying to a God that was like the chameleon, which changes its color every day. What encouragement is there to lift up our hearts to One who is in one mind yesterday and another today? What would be the use of petitioning an earthly monarch, if we knew he was so mutable as to grant a petition one day and deny it another? Is it not the very unchangeableness of God which is our greatest encouragement to pray? It is because He is "without variableness or shadow of turning" we are assured that if we ask anything according to His will we are most certain of being heard. Well did Luther remark, "Prayer is not overcoming God's reluctance, but laying hold of His willingness."

And this leads us to offer a few remarks concerning the design of prayer. Why has God appointed that we should pray? The vast majority of people would reply, In order that we may obtain from God the things which we need. While this is one of the purposes of prayer, it is by no means the chief one. Moreover, it considers prayer only from the human side, and prayer sadly needs to be viewed from the Divine side. Let us look, then, at some of the reasons why God has bidden us to pray.

First and foremost, prayer has been appointed that the Lord God Himself should be honored. God requires we should recognize that He is, indeed, "the high and lofty One that inhabiteth eternity" (Isa. 57:17). God requires that we shall own His universal dominion: in petitioning God for rain, Elijah did but confess His control over the elements; in praying to God to deliver a poor sinner from the wrath to come, we acknowledge that "salvation is of the Lord" (Jonah 2:9) ; in supplicating His blessing on the Gospel unto the uttermost parts of the earth, we declare His rulership over the whole world.

Again; God requires that we shall worship Him, and prayer, real prayer, is an act of worship. Prayer is an act of worship inasmuch as it is the prostrating of the soul before Him; inasmuch as it is a calling upon His great and holy name; inasmuch as it is the owning of His goodness, His power, His immutability, His grace, and inasmuch as it is the recognition of His sovereignty, owned by a submission to His will. It is highly significant to notice in this connection that the Temple was not termed by Christ the House of Sacrifice, but instead, the House of Prayer.

Again; prayer redounds to God's glory, for in prayer we do but acknowledge our dependency upon Him. When we humbly supplicate the Divine Being we cast ourselves upon His power and mercy. In seeking blessings from God we own that He is the Author and Fountain of every good and perfect gift. That prayer brings glory to God is further seen from the fact that prayer calls faith into exercise, and nothing from us is so honoring and pleasing to Him as the confidence of our hearts.

In the second place, prayer is appointed by God for our spiritual blessing, as a means for our growth in grace. When seeking to learn the design of prayer, this should ever occupy us before we regard prayer as a means for obtaining the supply of our need. Prayer is designed by God for our humbling. Prayer, real prayer, is a coming into the Presence of God, and a sense of His awful majesty produces a realization of our nothingness and unworthiness. Again; prayer is designed by God for the exercise of our faith. Faith is begotten in the Word (Rom. 10:17), but it is exercised in prayer; hence, we read of "the prayer of faith". Again; prayer calls love into action. Concerning the hypocrite the question is asked, "Will he delight himself in the Almighty? Will he always call upon God?" (Job 27:10). But they that love the Lord cannot be long away from Him, for they delight in unburdening themselves to Him. Not only does prayer call love into action, but through the direct answers vouchsafed to our prayers, our love to God is increased—"I love the Lord, because He hath heard my voice and my supplications" (Ps. 116:1). Again; prayer is designed by God to teach us the value of the blessings we have sought from Him, and it causes us to rejoice the more when He has bestowed upon us that for which we supplicate Him.

Third, prayer is appointed by God for our seeking from Him the things which we are in need of. But here a difficulty may present itself to those who have read carefully the previous chapters of this book. If God has foreordained, before the foundation of the world, everything which happens in time, what is the use of prayer? If it is true that "of Him and through Him and to Him are all things" (Rom. 11:36), then why pray? Ere replying directly to these queries it should be pointed out how that there is just as much reason to ask, What is the use of me coming to God and telling Him what He already knows? wherein is the use of me spreading before Him my need, seeing He is already acquainted with it? as there is to object, What is the use of praying for anything when everything has been ordained beforehand by God? Prayer is not for the purpose of informing God, as if He were ignorant, (the Saviour expressly declared "for your Father knoweth what things ye have need of, before ye ask Him"—Matt. 6:8), but it is to acknowledge He does know what we are in need of. Prayer is not appointed for the furnishing of God with the knowledge of what we need, but it is designed as a confession to Him of our sense of the need. In this, as in everything, God's thoughts are not as ours. God requires that His gifts should be sought for. He designs to be honored by our asking, just as He is to be thanked by us after He has bestowed His blessing.

However, the question still returns on us, If God be the Predestinator of everything that comes to pass, and the Regulator of all events, then is not prayer a profitless exercise? A sufficient answer to these questions is, that God bids us to pray—"Pray without ceasing" (1 Thess. 5:17). And again, "men ought always to pray" (Luke 18:1). And further: Scripture declares that, "the prayer of faith shall save the sick", and, "the effectual fervent prayer of a righteous man availeth much" (James 5:15, 16); while the Lord Jesus Christ—our perfect Example in all things—was pre-eminently a Man of Prayer. Thus, it is evident, that prayer is neither meaningless nor valueless. But still this does not remove the difficulty nor answer the question with which we started out. What then is the relationship between God's sovereignty and Christian prayer?

First of all, we would say with emphasis, that prayer is not intended to change God's purpose, nor is it to move Him to form fresh purposes. God has decreed that certain events shall come to pass, but He has also decreed that these events shall come to pass through the means He has appointed for their accomplishment. God has elected certain ones to be saved, but He has also decreed that these ones shall be saved through the preaching of the Gospel. The Gospel, then, is one of the appointed means for the working out of the eternal counsel of the Lord; and prayer is another. God has decreed the means as well as the end, and among the means is prayer. Even the prayers of His people are included in His eternal decrees. Therefore, instead of prayers being in vain, they are among the means through which God exercises His decrees. "If indeed all things happen by a blind chance, or a fatal necessity, prayers in that case could be of no moral efficacy, and of no use; but since they are regulated by the direction of Divine wisdom, prayers have a place in the order of events" (Haldane).

That prayers for the execution of the very things decreed by God are not meaningless, is clearly taught in the Scriptures. Elijah knew that God was about to give rain, but that did not prevent him from at once betaking himself to prayer, (James 5:17, 18). Daniel "understood" by the writings of the prophets that the captivity was to last but seventy years, yet when these seventy years were almost ended, we are told that he "set his face unto the Lord God, to seek by prayer and supplications, with fasting and sackcloth and ashes" (Dan. 9:2, 3). God told the prophet Jeremiah "For I know the thoughts that I think toward you, saith the Lord, thoughts of peace, and not of evil, to give you an expected end"; but instead of adding, there is, therefore, no need for you to supplicate Me for these things, He said, "Then shall ye call upon Me, and ye shall go and pray unto Me, and I will hearken unto you" (Jer. 29:12).

Once more; in Ezekiel 36 we read of the explicit, positive, and unconditional promises which God has made concerning the future restoration of Israel, yet in verse 37 of this same chapter we are told, "Thus saith the Lord God; I will yet for this be enquired of by the house of Israel, to do it for then;"! Here then is the design of prayer: not that God's will may be altered, but that it may be accomplished in His own good time and way. It is because God has promised certain things, that we can ask for them with the full assurance of faith. It is God's purpose that His will shall be brought about by His own appointed means, and that He may do His people good upon His own terms, and that is, by the 'means' and 'terms' of entreaty and supplication. Did not the Son of God know for certain that after His death and resurrection He would be exalted by the Father? Assuredly He did. Yet we find Him asking for this very thing: "O Father, glorify Thou Me with Thine Own Self with the glory which I had with Thee before the world was" (John 17:5)! Did not He know that none of His people could perish? yet He besought the Father to "keep" them (John 17:11)!

Finally; it should be said that God's will is immutable, and cannot be altered by our crying. When the mind of God is not toward a people to do them good, it cannot be turned to them by the most fervent and importunate prayers of those who have the greatest interest in Him—"Then said the Lord unto me, Though Moses and Samuel stood before Me, yet My mind could not be toward this people: cast them out of My sight, and let them go forth" (Jer. 15:1). The prayers of Moses to enter the promised land is a parallel case.

Our views respecting prayer need to be revised and brought into harmony with the teaching of Scripture on the subject. The prevailing idea seems to be, that I come to God and ask Him for something that I want, and that I expect Him to give me that which I have asked. But this is a most dishonoring and degrading conception. The popular belief reduces God to a servant, our servant: doing our bidding, performing our pleasure, granting our desires. No; prayer is a coming to God, telling Him my need, committing my way unto the Lord, and leaving Him to deal with it as seemeth Him best. This makes my will subject to His, instead of, as in the former case, seeking to bring His will into subjection to mine. No prayer is pleasing to God unless the spirit actuating it is, "not my will, but thine be done". "When God bestows blessings on a praying people, it is not for the sake of their prayers, as if He was inclined and turned by them; but it is for His own sake, and of His own sovereign will and pleasure. Should it be said, to what purpose then is prayer? it is answered, This is the way and means God has appointed, for the communication of the blessing of His goodness to His people. For though He has purposed, provided, and promised them, yet He will be sought unto, to give them, and it is a duty and privilege to ask. When they are blessed with a spirit of prayer, it forebodes well, and looks as if God intended to bestow the good things asked, which should be asked always with submission to the will of God, saying, Not my will but Thine be done" (John Gill).

The distinction just noted above is of great practical importance for our peace of heart. Perhaps the one thing that exercises Christians as much as anything else is that of unanswered prayers. They have asked God for something: so far as they are able to judge, they have asked in faith believing they would receive that for which they had supplicated the Lord: and they have asked earnestly and repeatedly, but the answer has not come. The result is that, in many cases, faith in the efficacy of prayer becomes weakened, until hope gives way to despair and the closet is altogether neglected. Is it not so?

Now will it surprise our readers when we say that every real prayer of faith that has ever been offered to God has been answered? Yet we unhesitatingly affirm it. But in saying this we must refer back to our definition of prayer. Let us repeat it. Prayer is a coming to God, telling Him my need (or the need of others), committing my way unto the Lord, and then leaving Him to deal with the case as seemeth Him best. This leaves God to answer the prayer in whatever way He sees fit, and often, His answer may be the very opposite of what would be most acceptable to the flesh; yet, if we have really LEFT our need in His hands, it will be His answer, nevertheless. Let us look at two examples.

In John 11 we read of the sickness of Lazarus. The Lord "loved" him, but He was absent from Bethany. The sisters sent a messenger unto the Lord acquainting Him of their brother's condition. And note particularly how their appeal was worded—"Lord, behold, he whom Thou lovest is sick." That was all. They did not ask Him to heal Lazarus. They did not request Him to hasten at once to Bethany. They simply spread their need before Him, committed the case into His hands, and left Him to act as He deemed best! And what was our Lord's reply? Did He respond to their appeal and answer their mute request? Certainly He did, though not, perhaps, in the way they had hoped. He answered by abiding "two days still in the same place where He was" (John 11:6), and allowing Lazarus to die! But in this instance, that was not all. Later, He journeyed to Bethany and raised Lazarus from the dead. Our purpose in referring here to this case, is to illustrate the proper attitude for the believer to take before God in the hour of need. The next example will emphasize, rather, God's method of responding to His needy child.

Turn to 2 Corinthians 12. The apostle Paul had been accorded an unheard-of privilege. He had been transported into Paradise. His ears have listened to and his eyes have gazed upon that which no other mortal had heard or seen this side of death. The wondrous revelation was more than the apostle could endure. He was in danger of becoming "puffed up" by his extraordinary experience. Therefore, a thorn in the flesh, the messenger of Satan, was sent to buffet him lest he be exalted above measure. And the apostle spreads his need before the Lord; he thrice beseeches Him that this thorn in the flesh should be removed. Was his prayer answered? Assuredly, though not in the manner he had desired. The "thorn" was not removed, but grace was given to bear it. The burden was not lifted, but strength was vouchsafed to carry it.

Does someone object that it is our privilege to do more than spread our need before God? Are we reminded that God has, as it were, given us a blank check and invited us to fill it in? Is it said that the promises of God are all-inclusive, and that we may ask God for what we will? If so, we must call attention to the fact that it is necessary to compare scripture with scripture if we are to learn the full mind of God on any subject, and that as this is done we discover God has qualified the promises given to praying souls by saying, "If we ask anything according to His will He heareth us" (1 John 5:14). Real prayer is communion with God, so that there will be common thoughts between His mind and ours. What is needed is for Him to fill our hearts with His thoughts, and then His desires will become our desires flowing back to Him. Here then is the meeting-place between God's sovereignty and Christian prayer: If we ask anything according to His will He heareth us, and if we do not so ask, He does not hear us; as saith the apostle James, "Ye ask, and receive not, because ye ask amiss, that ye might consume it upon your lusts" or desires (4:3)

But did not the Lord Jesus tell His disciples, "Verily, verily, I say unto you, Whatsoever ye shall ask the Father in My name, He will give it you" (John 16:23)? He did; but this promise does not give praying souls carte blanche. These words of our Lord are in perfect accord with those of the apostle John—"If we ask anything according to His will He heareth us." What is it to ask "in the name of Christ"? Surely it is very much more than a prayer formula, the mere concluding of our supplications with the words "in the name of Christ." To apply to God for anything in the name of Christ, it must needs be in keeping with what Christ is! To ask God in the name of Christ is as though Christ Himself were the suppliant. We can only ask God for what Christ would ask. To ask in the name of Christ, is therefore, to set aside our own wills, accepting God's!

Let us now amplify our definition of prayer. What is prayer? Prayer is not so much an act as it is an attitude— an attitude of dependency, dependency upon God. Prayer is a confession of creature weakness, yea, of helplessness. Prayer is the acknowledgment of our need and the spreading of it before God. We do not say that this is all there is in prayer, it is not: but it is the essential, the primary element in prayer. We freely admit that we are quite unable to give a complete definition of prayer within the compass of a brief sentence, or in any number of words. Prayer is both an attitude and an act, a human act, and yet there is the Divine element in it too, and it is this which makes an exhaustive analysis impossible as well as impious to attempt. But admitting this, we do insist again, that prayer is fundamentally an attitude of dependency upon God. Therefore, prayer is the very opposite of dictating to God. Because prayer is an attitude of dependency, the one who really prays is submissive, submissive to the Divine will; and submission to the Divine will means, that we are content for the Lord to supply our need according to the dictates of His own sovereign pleasure. And hence it is that we say, every prayer that is offered to God in this spirit is sure of meeting with an answer or response from Him.

Here then is the reply to our opening question, and the scriptural solution to the seeming difficulty. Prayer is not the requesting of God to alter His purpose or for Him to form a new one. Prayer is the taking of an attitude of dependency upon. God, the spreading of our need before Him, the asking for those things which are in accordance with His will, and therefore there is nothing whatever inconsistent between Divine sovereignty and Christian prayer.

In closing this chapter we would utter a word of caution to safeguard the reader against drawing a false conclusion from what has been said. We have not here sought to epitomize the whole teaching of Scripture on the subject of prayer, nor have we even attempted to discuss in general the problem of prayer; instead, we have confined ourselves, more or less, to a consideration of the relationship between God's Sovereignty and Christian Prayer. What we have written is intended chiefly as a protest against much of the modern teaching, which so stresses the human element in prayer, that the Divine side is almost entirely lost sight of.

In Jeremiah 10:23 we are told "It is not in man that walketh to direct his steps" (cf. Prov. 16:9); and yet in many of his prayers, man impiously presumes to direct the Lord as to His way, and as to what He ought to do: even implying that if only he had the direction of the affairs of the world and of the Church, he would soon have things very different from what they are. This cannot be denied: for anyone with any spiritual discernment at all could not fail to detect this spirit in many of our modern prayer-meetings where the flesh holds sway. How slow we all are to learn the lesson that the haughty creature needs to be brought down to his knees and humbled into the dust. And this is where the very act of prayer is intended to put us. But man (in his usual perversity) turns the footstool into a throne, from whence he would fain direct the Almighty as to what He ought to do! giving the onlooker the impression that if God had half the compassion that those who pray (?) have, all would quickly be put right! Such is the arrogance of the old nature even in a child of God.

Our main purpose in this chapter has been to emphasize the need for submitting, in prayer, our wills to God's. But it must also be added, that prayer is much more than a pious exercise, and far otherwise than a mechanical performance. Prayer is, indeed, a Divinely appointed means whereby we may obtain from God the things we ask, providing we ask for those things which are in accord with His will. These pages will have been penned in vain unless they lead both writer and reader to cry with a deeper earnestness than heretofore, "Lord, teach us to pray" (Luke 11:1).

Our Attitude Toward God's Sovereignty

"Even so, Father: for so it seemed good in Thy sight"
(Matthew 11:26

In the present chapter we shall consider, somewhat briefly, the practical application to ourselves of the great truth which we have pondered in its various ramifications in earlier pages. In chapter twelve we shall deal more in detail with the value of this doctrine, but here we would confine ourselves to a definition of what ought to be our attitude toward the sovereignty of God.

Every truth that is revealed to us in God's Word is there not only for our information but also for our inspiration. The Bible has been given to us not to gratify an idle curiosity but to edify the souls of its readers. The sovereignty of God is something more than an abstract principle which explains the rationale of the Divine government: it is designed as a motive for godly fear, it is made known to us for the promotion of righteous living, it is revealed in order to bring into subjection our rebellious hearts. A true recognition of God's sovereignty humbles as nothing else does or can humble, and brings the heart into lowly submission before God, causing us to relinquish our own self-will and making us delight in the perception and performance of the Divine will.

When we speak of the sovereignty of God we mean very much more than the exercise of God's governmental power, though, of course, that is included in the expression. As we have remarked in an earlier chapter, the sovereignty of God means the Godhood of God. In its fullest and deepest meaning the title of this book signifies the Character and Being of the One whose pleasure is performed and whose will is executed. To truly recognize the sovereignty of God is, therefore, to gaze upon the Sovereign Himself. It is to come into the presence of the august "Majesty on High." it is to have a sight of the thrice holy God in His excellent glory. The effects of such a sight may be learned from those scriptures which describe the experience of different ones who obtained a view of the Lord God.

The Holy Spirit

Mark the experience of Job—the one of whom the Lord Himself said, "There is none like him in the earth, a perfect and an upright man, one that feareth God, and escheweth evil" (Job 1:8). At the close of the book which bears his name we are shown Job in the Divine presence, and how does he carry himself when brought face to face with Jehovah? Hear what he says: "I have heard of Thee by the hearing of the ear; but now mine eye seeth Thee: Wherefore I abhor myself, and repent in dust and ashes" (Job 42:5, 6). Thus, a sight of God, God revealed in awesome majesty, caused Job to abhor himself, and not only so, but to abase himself before the Almighty.

Take note of Isaiah. In the sixth chapter of his prophecy a scene is brought before us which has few equals even in Scripture. The prophet beholds the Lord upon the Throne, a Throne, "high and lifted up." Above this Throne stood the seraphim with veiled faces, crying, "Holy, holy, holy, is the Lord of hosts." What is the effect of this sight upon the prophet? We read, "Then said I, Woe is me! for I am undone; because I am a man of unclean lips, and I dwell in the midst of a people of unclean lips: for mine eyes have seen the King, the Lord of hosts" (Isa. 6:5). A sight of the Divine King humbled Isaiah into the dust, bringing him, as it did, to a realization of his own nothingness.

Once more. Look at the prophet Daniel. Toward the close of his life this man of God beheld the Lord in theophanic manifestation. He appeared to His servant in human form "clothed in linen" and with loins "girded with fine gold"—symbolic of holiness and Divine glory. We read that, "His body also was like the beryl, and His face as the appearance of lightning, and His eyes as lamps of fire, and His arms and His feet like in color to polished brass, and the voice of His words like the voice of a multitude." Daniel then tells the effect this vision had upon him and those who were with him—"And I Daniel alone saw the vision: for the men that were with me saw not the vision; but a great quaking fell upon them, so that they fled to hide themselves. Therefore I was left alone, and saw this great vision, and there remained no strength in me: for my comeliness was turned in me into corruption, and I retained no strength. Yet heard I the voice of His words: and when I heard the voice of His words, then was I in a deep sleep on my face, and my face toward the ground" (Dan. 10:6-9). Once more, then, we are shown that to obtain a sight of the Sovereign God is for creature strength to wither up, and results in man being humbled into the dust before his Maker. What then ought to be our attitude toward the Supreme Sovereign? We reply,

1. One of Godly fear.

Why is it that, today, the masses are so utterly unconcerned about spiritual and eternal things, and that they are lovers of pleasure more than lovers of

God? Why is it that even on the battlefields multitudes were so indifferent to their soul's welfare? Why is it that defiance of heaven is becoming more open, more blatant, more daring? The answer is, Because "There is no fear of God before their eyes" (Rom. 3:18). Again; why is it that the authority of the Scriptures has been lowered so sadly of late? Why is it that even among those who profess to be the Lord's people there is so little real subjection to His Word, and that its precepts are so lightly esteemed and so readily set aside? Ah! what needs to be stressed to-day is that God is a God to be feared.

"The fear of the Lord is the beginning of wisdom" (Pro. 1:7). Happy the soul that has been awed by a view of God's majesty, that has had a vision of God's awful greatness, His ineffable holiness, His perfect righteousness, His irresistible power, His sovereign grace. Does someone say, "But it is only the unsaved, those outside of Christ, who need to fear God"? Then the sufficient answer is that the saved, those who are in Christ, are admonished to work out their own salvation with "fear and trembling." Time was, when it was the general custom to speak of a believer as a "God-fearing man"—that such an appellation has become nearly extinct only serves to show whither we have drifted. Nevertheless, it still stands written, "Like as a father pitieth his children, so the Lord pitieth them that fear Him" (Ps. 103:13)!

When we speak of godly fear, of course, we do not mean a servile fear, such as prevails among the heathen in connection with their gods. No; we mean that spirit which Jehovah is pledged to bless, that spirit to which the prophet referred when he said, "To this man will I (the Lord) look, even to him that is poor and of a contrite spirit, and trembleth at My Word" (Isa. 66:2). It was this the apostle had in view when he wrote, "Honor all men. Love the brotherhood. Fear God. Honor the king" (1 Pet. 2:17). And nothing will foster this godly fear like a recognition of the sovereign Majesty of God.

What ought to be our attitude toward the Sovereignty of God? We answer again,

2. One of Implicit Obedience.

A sight of God leads to a realization of our littleness and nothingness, and issues in a sense of dependency and of casting ourselves upon God. Or, again; a view of the Divine Majesty promotes the spirit of godly fear and this, in turn, begets an obedient walk. Here then is the Divine antidote for the native evil of our hearts. Naturally, man is filled with a sense of his own importance, with his greatness and self-sufficiency; in a word, with pride and rebellion. But, as we remarked, the great corrective is to behold the Mighty God, for this alone will really humble him. Man will glory either in himself or in God.

Man will live either to serve and please himself, or he will seek to serve and please the Lord. None can serve two masters.

Irreverence begets disobedience. Said the haughty monarch of Egypt, "Who is the Lord that I should obey His voice to let Israel go? I know not the Lord; neither will I let Israel go" (Ex. 5:2). To Pharaoh, the God of the Hebrews was merely a god, one among many, a powerless entity who needed not to be feared or served. How sadly mistaken he was, and how bitterly he had to pay for his mistake, he soon discovered; but what we are here seeking to emphasize is that, Pharaoh's defiant spirit was the fruit of irreverence, and this irreverence was the consequence of his ignorance of the majesty and authority of the Divine Being.

Now if irreverence begets disobedience, true reverence will produce and promote obedience. To realize that the Holy Scriptures are a revelation from the Most High, communicating to us His mind and defining for us His will, is the first step toward practical godliness. To recognize that the Bible is God's Word, and that its precepts are the precepts of the Almighty, will lead us to see what an awful thing it is to despise and ignore them. To receive the Bible as addressed to our own souls, given to us by the Creator Himself, will cause us to cry with the Psalmist, "Incline my heart unto Thy testimonies....Order my steps in Thy Word" (Ps. 119:36, 133). Once the sovereignty of the Author of the Word is apprehended, it will no longer be a matter of picking and choosing from the precepts and statutes of that Word, selecting those which meet with our approval; but it will be seen that nothing less than an unqualified and whole-hearted submission becomes the creature.

What ought to be our attitude toward the Sovereignty of God? We answer, once more,

3. One of entire resignation.

A true recognition of God's Sovereignty will exclude all murmuring. This is self-evident, yet the thought deserves to be dwelt upon. It is natural to murmur against afflictions and losses. It is natural to complain when we are deprived of those things upon which we had set our hearts. We are apt to regard our possessions as ours unconditionally. We feel that when we have prosecuted our plans with prudence and diligence that we are entitled to success; that when by dint of hard work we have accumulated a 'competence,' we deserve to keep and enjoy it; that when we are surrounded by a happy family, no power may lawfully enter the charmed circle and strike down a loved one; and if in any of these cases disappointment, bankruptcy, death, actually comes, the perverted instinct of the human heart is to cry out against God. But in the one who, by grace, has recognized God's sovereignty, such murmuring is silenced, and instead, there is a bowing to the Divine will, and an acknowledgment that He has not afflicted us as sorely as we deserve.

A true recognition of God's sovereignty will avow God's perfect right to do with us as He wills. The one who bows to the pleasure of the Almighty will acknowledge His absolute right to do with us as seemeth Him good. If He chooses to send poverty, sickness, domestic bereavements, even while the heart is bleeding at every pore, it will say, Shall not the Judge of all the earth do right! Often there will be a struggle, for the carnal mind remains in the believer to the end of his earthly pilgrimage. But though there may be a conflict within his breast, nevertheless, to the one who has really yielded himself to this blessed truth, there will presently be heard that Voice saying, as of old it said to the turbulent Gennesareth, "Peace be still"; and the tempestuous flood within will be quieted and the subdued soul will lift a tearful but confident eye to heaven and say, "Thy will be done."

A striking illustration of a soul bowing to the sovereign will of God is furnished by the history of Eli the high priest of Israel. In 1 Samuel 3 we learn how God revealed to the young child Samuel that He was about to slay Eli's two sons for their wickedness, and on the morrow Samuel communicates this message to the aged priest. It is difficult to conceive of more appalling intelligence for the heart of a pious parent. The announcement that his child is going to be stricken down by sudden death is, under any circumstances, a great trial to any father, but to learn that his two sons—in the prime of their manhood, and utterly unprepared to die—were to be cut off by a Divine judgment, must have been overwhelming. Yet, what was the effect upon Eli when he learned from Samuel the tragic tidings? What reply did he make when he heard the awful news? "And he said, It is the Lord: let Him do what seemeth Him good" (1 Sam. 3:18). And not another word escaped him. Wonderful submission! Sublime resignation! Lovely exemplification of the power of Divine grace to control the strongest affections of the human heart and subdue the rebellious will, bringing it into unrepining acquiescence to the sovereign pleasure of Jehovah.

Another example, equally striking, is seen in the life of Job. As is well known, Job was one that feared God and eschewed evil. If ever there was one who might reasonably expect Divine providence to smile upon him—we speak as a man—it was Job. Yet, how fared it with him? For a time, the lines fell unto him in pleasant places. The Lord filled his quiver by giving him seven sons and three daughters. He prospered him in his temporal affairs until he owned great possessions. But of a sudden, the sun of life was hidden behind dark clouds. In a single day Job lost not only his flocks and herds, but his sons and daughters as well. News arrived that his cattle had been carried off by robbers, and his children slain by a cyclone. And how did he receive this intelligence? Hearken to his sublime words: "The Lord gave, and the Lord hath taken away." He bowed to the sovereign will of Jehovah. He traced his afflictions back to their First Cause. He looked behind the Sabeans who had stolen his cattle, and beyond the winds that had destroyed his children, and saw the hand of God. But not only did Job recognize God's sovereignty, he rejoiced in it, too. To the words, "The Lord gave, and the Lord bath taken away," he added, "Blessed be the name of the Lord" (Job 1:21). Again we say, Sweet submission! Sublime resignation!

A true recognition of God's sovereignty causes us to hold our every plan in abeyance to God's will. The writer well recalls an incident which occurred in England over twenty years ago. Queen Victoria was dead, and the date for the coronation of her eldest son, Edward, had been set for April 1902. In all the announcements which were sent out, two little letters were omitted—D. V.—Deo Volente: God willing. Plans were made and all arrangements completed for the most imposing celebrations that England had ever witnessed. Kings and emperors from all parts of the earth had received invitations to attend the royal ceremony. The Prince's proclamations were printed and displayed, but, so far as the writer is aware, the letters D. V. were not found on a single one of them. A most imposing program had been arranged, and the late Queen's eldest son was to be crowned Edward the Seventh at Westminster Abbey at a certain hour on a fixed day. And then God intervened, and all man's plans were frustrated. A still small voice was heard to say, "You have reckoned without Me," and Prince Edward was stricken down with appendicitis, and his coronation postponed for months!

As remarked, a true recognition of God's sovereignty causes us to hold our plans in abeyance to God's will. It makes us recognize that the Divine Potter has absolute power over the clay and moulds it according to his own imperial pleasure. It causes us to heed that admonition—now, alas! so generally disregarded—"Go to now, ye that say, Today or tomorrow we will go into such a city, and continue there a year, and buy and sell, and get gain: Whereas ye know not what shall be on the morrow. For what is your life? It is even a vapor, that appeareth for a little time, and then vanisheth away. For that ye ought to say, If the Lord will, we shall live, and do this, or that" (James 4:13-15). Yes, it is to the Lord's will we must bow. It is for Him to say where I shall live—whether in America or Africa. It is for Him to determine under what circumstances I shall live—whether amid wealth or poverty, whether in health or sickness. It is for Him to say how long I shall live—whether I shall be cut down in youth like the flower of the field, or whether I shall continue for three score and ten years. To really learn this lesson is, by grace, to attain unto a high form in the school of God, and even when we think we have learnt it, we discover, again and again, that we have to relearn it.

4. One if deep thankfulness and joy.

The heart's apprehension of this most blessed truth of the sovereignty of God, produces something far different than a sullen bowing to the inevitable. The philosophy of this perishing world knows nothing better than to "make the best of a bad job". But with the Christian it should be far other wise. Not only should the recognition of God's supremacy beget within us godly fear, implicit obedience, and entire resignation, but it should cause us to say with the Psalmist, "Bless the Lord, O my soul: and all that is within me, bless His holy name". Does not the apostle say, "Giving thanks always for all things unto God and the Father in the name of our Lord Jesus Christ" (Eph. 5:20)? Ah, it is at this point the state of our souls is so often put to the test. Alas, there is so much self-will in each of us. When things go as we wish them, we appear to be very grateful to God; but what of those occasions when things go contrary to our plans and desires?

We take it for granted when the real Christian takes a train-journey that, upon reaching his destination, he devoutly returns thanks unto God—which, of course, argues that He controls everything; otherwise, we ought to thank the engine-driver, the stoker, the signalmen etc. Or, if in business, at the close of a good week, gratitude is expressed unto the Giver of every good (temporal) and of every perfect (spiritual) gift—which again, argues that He directs all customers to your shop. So far, so good. Such examples occasion no difficulty. But imagine the opposites. Suppose my train was delayed for hours, did I fret and fume; suppose another train ran into it, and I am injured! Or, suppose I have had a poor week in business, or that lightning struck my shop and set it on fire, or that burglars broke in and rifled it—then what: do I see the hand of God in these things?

Take the case of Job once more. When loss after loss came his way, what did he do? Bemoan his "bad luck"? Curse the robbers? Murmur against God? No; he bowed before Him in worship. Ah, dear reader, there is no real rest for your poor heart until you learn to see the hand of God in everything. But for that, faith must be in constant exercise. And what is faith? A blind credulity? A fatalistic acquiescence? No, far from it. Faith is a resting on the sure Word of the living God, and therefore says, "We know that all things work together for good to them that love God, to them who are the called according to His

The Holy Spirit 445

purpose" (Rom. 8:28); and therefore faith will give thanks "always for all things". Operative faith will "Rejoice in the Lord alway" (Phil. 4:4).

We turn now to mark how this recognition of God's sovereignty which is expressed in godly fear, implicit obedience, entire resignation, and deep thankfulness and joy was supremely and perfectly exemplified by the Lord Jesus Christ.

In all things the Lord Jesus has left us an example that we should follow His steps. But is this true in connection with the first point made above? Are the words "godly fear" ever linked with His peerless name? Remembering that 'godly fear' signifies not a servile terror, but rather a filial subjection and reverence, and remembering too that "the fear of the Lord is the beginning of wisdom," would it not rather be strange if no mention at all were made of godly fear in connection with the One who was wisdom incarnate! What a wonderful and precious word is that of Hebrews 5:7—"Who in the days of His flesh, having offered up prayers and supplications with strong crying and tears unto Him that was able to save Him from death, and having been heard for His godly fear" (R. V.). What was it but 'godly fear' which caused the Lord Jesus to be "subject" unto Mary and Joseph in the days of His childhood? Was it not 'godly fear'—a filial subjection to and reverence for God—that we see displayed, when we read, "And He came to Nazareth where He had been brought up: and, as His custom was, He went into the synagogue on the Sabbath day" (Luke 4:16)? Was it not 'godly fear' which caused the incarnate Son to say, when tempted by Satan to fall down and worship him, "It is written, thou shalt worship the Lord thy God and Him only shalt thou serve"? Was it not 'godly fear' which moved Him to say to the cleansed leper, "Go thy way, shew thyself to the priest, and offer the gift that Moses commanded" (Matt. 8:4)? But why multiply illustrations? ' How perfect was the obedience that the Lord Jesus offered to God the Father! And in reflecting upon this let us not lose sight of that wondrous grace which caused Him, who was in the very form of God, to stoop so low as to take upon Him the form of a Servant, and thus be brought into the place where obedience was becoming. As the perfect Servant He yielded complete obedience to His Father. How absolute and entire that obedience was we may learn from the words, He "became obedient unto death, even the death of the Cross" (Phil. 2:8). That this was a conscious and intelligent obedience is clear from His own language—"Therefore doth My Father love Me, because I lay down My life, that I might take it again. No man taketh it from Me, but I lay it down of Myself. I have power to lay it down, and I have power to take it again. This commandment have I received from My Father" (John 10:17, 18).

And what shall we say of the absolute resignation of the Son to the Father's will—what, but, between Them there was entire oneness of accord. Said He, "For I came down from heaven, not to do Mine own will, but the will of Him that sent Me" (John 6:38), and how fully He substantiated that claim all know who have attentively followed His path as marked out in the Scriptures. Behold Him in Gethsemane! The bitter 'cup,' held in the Father's hand, is presented to His view. Mark well His attitude. Learn of Him who was meek and lowly in heart. Remember that there in the Garden we see the Word become flesh—a perfect Man. His body is quivering at every nerve, in contemplation of the physical sufferings which await Him; His holy and sensitive nature is shrinking from the horrible indignities which shall be heaped upon Him; His heart is breaking at the awful "reproach" which is before Him; His spirit is greatly troubled as He foresees the terrible conflict with the Power of Darkness; and above all, and supremely, His soul is filled with horror at the thought of being separated from God Himself—thus and there He pours out His soul to the Father, and with strong crying and tears He sheds, as it were, great drops of blood. And now observe and listen. Still the beating of thy heart, and hearken to the words which fall from His blessed lips—"Father, if Thou be willing, remove this cup from Me: nevertheless, not My will, but Thine be done" (Luke 22:42). Here is submission personified. Here is resignation to the pleasure of a sovereign God superlatively exemplified. And He has left us an example that we should follow His steps. He who was God became man, and was tempted in all points like as we are—sin apart—to show us how to wear our creature nature!

Above we asked, What shall we say of Christ's absolute resignation to the Father's will? We answer further, This,—that here, as everywhere, He was unique, peerless. In all things He has the pre-eminence. In the Lord Jesus there was no rebellious will to be broken. In His heart there was nothing to be subdued. Was not this one reason why, in the language of prophecy, He said, "I am a worm, and no man" (Ps. 22:6)—a worm has no power of resistance! It was because in Him there was no resistance that He could say, "My meat is to do the will of Him that sent Me" (John 4:34). Yea, it was because He was in perfect accord with the Father in all things that He said, "I delight to do Thy will, O God; yea, Thy law is within My heart" (Ps. 40:8). Note the last clause here and behold His matchless excellency. God has to put His laws into our minds, and write them in our hearts (see Heb. 8:10), but His law was already in Christ's heart!

What a beautiful and striking illustration of Christ's thankfulness and joy is found in Matthew 11. There we behold, first, the failure in the faith of His forerunner (vv. 22, 23). Next, we learn of the discontent of the people: satisfied neither with Christ's joyous message, nor with John's solemn one (vv. 16-20). Third, we have the non-repentance of those favored cities in which our Lord's mightiest works were done (vv. 21-24). And then we read, "At that time Jesus answered and said, I thank Thee, O Father, Lord of heaven and earth, because Thou hast hid these things from the wise and prudent, and hast revealed them unto babes" (v. 25)! Note the parallel passage in Luke 10:21 opens by saying, "In that hour Jesus rejoiced in spirit, and said, I thank Thee" etc. Ah, here was submission in its purest form. Here was One by which the worlds were made, yet, in the days of His humiliation, and in the face of His rejection, thankfully and joyously bowing to the will of the "Lord of heaven and earth".

What ought to be our attitude towards God's sovereignty? Finally,

5. One of adoring worship.

It has been well said that "true worship is based upon recognized GREATNESS, and greatness is superlatively seen in Sovereignty, and at no other footstool will men really worship" (J. B. Moody). In the presence of the Divine King upon His throne even the seraphim 'veil their faces.'

Divine sovereignty is not the sovereignty of a tyrannical Despot, but the exercised pleasure of One who is infinitely wise and good! Because God is infinitely wise He cannot err, and because He is infinitely righteous He will not do wrong. Here then is the preciousness of this truth. The mere fact itself that God's will is irresistible and irreversible fills me with fear, but once I realize that God wills only that which is good, my heart is made to rejoice.

Here then is the final answer to the question of this chapter—What ought to be our attitude toward the sovereignty of God? The becoming attitude for us to take is that of godly fear, implicit obedience, and unreserved resignation and submission. But not only so: the recognition of the sovereignty of God, and the realization that the Sovereign Himself is my Father, ought to overwhelm the heart and cause me to bow before Him in adoring worship. At all times I must say, "Even so, Father, for so it seemeth good in Thy sight." We conclude with an example which well illustrates our meaning.

Some two hundred years ago the saintly Madam Guyon, after ten years spent in a dungeon lying far below the surface of the ground, lit only by a candle at meal-times, wrote these words,

"A little bird I am,
Shut from the fields of air;
Yet in my cage I sit and sing

To Him who placed me there;
Well pleased a prisoner to he,
Because, my God, it pleases Thee.

Nought have I else to do
I sing the whole day long;
And He whom most I love to please,
Doth listen to my song;
He caught and bound my wandering wing
But still He bends to hear me sing.

My cage confines me round;
Abroad I cannot fly;
But though my wing is closely bound,
My heart's at liberty.
My prison walls cannot control
The flight, the freedom of the soul.

Ah! it is good to soar
These bolts and bars above,
To Him whose purpose I adore,
Whose Providence I love;
And in Thy mighty will to find
The joy, the freedom of the mind."

Difficulties and Objections

"Yet ye say, The way of the Lord is not equal. Hear now, O house of Israel; Is not My way equal? are not your ways unequal?"
Ezekiel 18:25

A convenient point has been reached when we may now examine, more definitely, some of the difficulties encountered and the objections which might be advanced against what we have written in previous pages. The author deemed it better to reserve these for a separate consideration, rather than deal with them as he went along, requiring as that would have done the breaking of the course of thought and destroying the strict unity of each chapter, or else cumbering our pages with numerous and lengthy footnotes.

That there are difficulties involved in an attempt to set forth the truth of God's sovereignty is readily acknowledged. The hardest thing of all, perhaps, is to maintain the balance of truth. It is largely a matter of perspective. That God is sovereign is explicitly declared in Scripture: that man is a responsible creature is also expressly affirmed in Holy Writ. To define the relationship of these two truths, to fix the dividing line betwixt them, to show exactly where they meet, to exhibit the perfect consistency of the one with the other, is the weightiest task of all. Many have openly declared that it is impossible for the finite mind to harmonize them. Others tell us it is not necessary or even wise to attempt it. But, as we have remarked in an earlier chapter, it seems to us more honoring to God to seek in His Word the solution to every problem. What is impossible to man is possible with God, and while we grant that the finite mind is limited in its reach, yet, we remember that the Scriptures are given to us that the man of God may be "thoroughly furnished," and if we approach their study in the spirit of humility and of expectancy, then, according unto our faith will it be unto us.

As remarked above, the hardest task in this connection is to preserve the balance of truth while insisting on both the sovereignty of God and the responsibility of the creature. To some of our readers it may appear that in pressing the sovereignty of God to the lengths we have, man is reduced to a mere puppet. Hence, to guard against this, they would modify their definitions and statements relating to God's sovereignty, and thus seek to blunt the keen edge of what is so offensive to the carnal mind. Others, while refusing to weigh the evidence that we have adduced in support of our assertions, may raise objections which to their minds are sufficient to dispose of the whole subject. We would not waste time in the effort to refute objections made in a carping and contentious spirit, but we are desirous of meeting fairly the difficulties experienced by those who are anxious to obtain a fuller knowledge of the truth. Not that we deem ourselves able to give a satisfactory and final answer to every question that might be asked. Like the reader, the writer knows but "in part" and sees through a glass "darkly." All that we can do is to examine these difficulties in the light we now have, in dependence upon the Spirit of God that we may follow on to know the Lord better.

We propose now to retrace our steps and pursue the same order of thought as that followed up to this point. As a part of our "definition" of God's sovereignty we affirmed: "To say that God is sovereign is to declare that He is the Almighty, the Possessor of all power in heaven and earth, so that none can defeat His counsels, thwart His purpose, or resist His will. . . The sovereignty of the God of Scripture is absolute, irresistible, infinite." To put it now in its strongest form, we insist that God does as He pleases, only as He pleases, always as He pleases: that whatever takes place in time is but the outworking of that which He decreed in eternity. In proof of this assertion we appeal to the following scriptures—"But our God is in the heavens:

He hath done whatsoever He hath pleased" (Ps. 115:3). "For the Lord of hosts hath purposed, and who shall disannul it? and His hand is stretched out, and who shall turn it back?" (Isa. 14:27). "And all the inhabitants of the earth are reputed as nothing: and He doeth according to His will in the army of heaven, and among the inhabitants of the earth: and none can stay His hand or say unto Him, What doest thou?" (Dan. 4:35). "For of Him, and through Him, and to Him, are all things: to whom be glory for ever. Amen" (Rom. 11:36).

The above declarations are so plain and positive that any comments of ours upon them would simply be darkening counsel by words without knowledge. Such express statements as those just quoted, are so sweeping and so dogmatic that all controversy concerning the subject of which they treat ought for ever to be at an end. Yet, rather than receive them at their face value, every device of carnal ingenuity is resorted to so as to neutralize their force. For example, it has been asked, If what we see in the world today is but the outworking of God's eternal purpose, if God's counsel is NOW being accomplished, then why did our Lord teach His disciples to pray, "Thy will be done on earth as it is in heaven"? Is it not a clear implication from these words that God's will is not now being done on earth? The answer is very simple. The emphatic word in the above clause is "as." God's will is being done on earth today, if it is not, then our earth is not subject to God's rule, and if it is not subject to His rule then He is not, as Scripture proclaims Him to be, "The Lord of all the earth" (Josh. 3:13). But God's will is not being done on earth as it is in heaven. How is God's will "done in heaven"?—consciously and joyfully. How is it "done on earth"?—for the most part, unconsciously and sullenly. In heaven the angels perform the bidding of their Creator intelligently and gladly, but on earth the unsaved among men accomplish His will blindly and in ignorance. As we have said in earlier pages, when Judas betrayed the Lord Jesus and when Pilate sentenced Him to be crucified, they had no conscious intention of fulfilling God's decrees yet, nevertheless, unknown to themselves they did do so!

But again. It has been objected: If everything that happens on earth is the fulfilling of the Almighty's pleasure, if God has fore-ordained—before the foundation of the world—everything which comes to pass in human history, then why do we read in Genesis 6:6, "It repented the Lord that He had made man on the earth, and it grieved Him at His heart"? Does not this language intimate that the antediluvians had followed a course which their Maker had not marked out for them, and that in view of the fact they had "corrupted" their way upon the earth, the Lord regretted that He had ever brought such a creature into existence? Ere drawing such a conclusion let us note what is involved in such an inference. If the words "It repented the Lord that He had made man" are regarded in an absolute sense, then God's omniscience would be denied, for in such a case the course followed by man must have been unforeseen by God in the day that He created him. Therefore it must be evident to every reverent soul that this language bears some other meaning. We submit that the words, "It repented the Lord" is an accommodation to our finite intelligence, and in saying this we are not seeking to escape a difficulty or cut a knot, but are advancing an interpretation which we shall seek to show is in perfect accord with the general trend of Scripture.

The Word of God is addressed to men, and therefore it speaks the language of men. Because we cannot rise to God's level He, in grace, comes down to ours and converses with us in our own speech. The apostle Paul tells us of how he was "caught up into Paradise and heard unspeakable words which it is not possible (margin) to utter" (2 Cor. 12:4) Those on earth could not understand the vernacular of heaven. The finite cannot comprehend the

Infinite, hence the Almighty deigns to couch His revelation in terms we may understand. It is for this reason the Bible contains many anthropomorphisms—i.e., representations of God in the form of man. God is Spirit, yet the Scriptures speak of Him as having eyes, ears, nostrils, breath, hands etc., which is surely an accommodation of terms brought down to the level of human comprehension.

Again; we read in Genesis 18:20, 21, "And the Lord said, Because the cry of Sodom and Gomorrah is great, and because their sin is very grievous, I will go down now, and see whether they have done altogether according to the cry of it, which is come up unto Me; and if not, I will know." Now, manifestly, this is an anthropologism—God, speaking in human language. God knew the conditions which prevailed in Sodom, and His eyes had witnessed its fearful sins, yet He is pleased to use terms here that are taken from our own vocabulary.

Again; in Genesis 22:12 we read, "And He (God) said, Lay not thine hand upon the lad, neither do thou anything unto him: for now I know that thou fearest God, seeing thou hast not withheld thy son, thine only son, from Me." Here again, God is speaking in the language of men, for He "knew" before He tested Abram exactly how the patriarch would act. So too the expression used of God so often in Jeremiah (7:13 etc.), of Him "rising up early", is manifestly an accommodation of terms.

Once more: in the parable of the vineyard Christ Himself represents its Owner as saying, "Then said the Lord of the vineyard, What shall I do? I will send My beloved Son: it may be they will reverence Him when they see Him" (Luke 20:13), and yet, it is certain that God knew perfectly well that the "husbandmen" of the vineyard—the Jews—would not "reverence His Son" but, instead, would "despise and reject" Him, as His own Word had declared!

In the same way we understand the words in Genesis 6:6— "It repented the Lord that He had made man on the earth"—as an accommodation of terms to human comprehension. This verse does not teach that God was confronted with an unforeseen contingency, and therefore regretted that He had made man, but it expresses the abhorrence of a holy God at the awful wickedness and corruption into which man had fallen. Should there be any doubt remaining in the minds of our readers as to the legitimacy and soundness of our interpretation, a direct appeal to Scripture should instantly and entirely remove it—"The Strength of Israel (a Divine title) will not lie nor repent: for He is not a man, that He should repent" (1 Sam. 15:29)! "Every good and perfect gift is from above, and cometh down from the Father

The Holy Spirit

of lights, with Whom is no variableness, neither shadow of turning" (James 1:17)!

Careful attention to what we have said above will throw light on numerous other passages which, if we ignore their figurative character and fail to note that God applies to Himself human modes of expression, will be obscure and perplexing. Having commented at such length upon Genesis 6:6 there will be no need to give such a detailed exposition of other passages which belong to the same class, yet, for the benefit of those of our readers who may be anxious for us to examine several other scriptures, we turn to one or two more.

One scripture which we often find cited in order to overthrow the teaching advanced in this book is our Lord's lament over Jerusalem: "O Jerusalem, Jerusalem, thou that killest the prophets, and stonest them that are sent unto thee, how often would I have gathered thy children together, even as a hen gathereth her chickens under her wings, and ye would not!" (Matt. 23:37). The question is asked, Do not these words show that the Saviour acknowledged the defeat of His mission, that as a people the Jews resisted all His gracious overtures toward them? In replying to this question, it should first be pointed out that our Lord is here referring not so much to His own mission, as He is upbraiding the Jews for having in all ages rejected His grace—this is clear from His reference to the "prophets." The Old Testament bears full witness of how graciously and patiently Jehovah dealt with His people, and with what extreme obstinacy, from first to last, they refused to be "gathered" unto Him, and how in the end He (temporarily) abandoned them to follow their own devices, yet, as the same Scriptures declare, the counsel of God was not frustrated by their wickedness, for it had been foretold (and therefore, decreed) by Him—see, for example, 1 Kings 8:33.

Matthew 23:37 may well be compared with Isaiah 65:2 where the Lord says, "I have spread out My hands all the day unto a rebellious people, which walketh in a way that was not good, after their own thoughts." But, it may be asked, Did God seek to do that which was in opposition to His own eternal purpose? In words borrowed from Calvin we reply, "Though to our apprehension the will of God is manifold and various, yet He does not in Himself will things at variance with each other, but astonishes our faculties with His various and 'manifold' wisdom, according to the expression of Paul, till we shall be enabled to understand that He mysteriously wills what now seems contrary to His will." As a further illustration of the same principle we would refer the reader to Isaiah 5:1-4: "Now will I sing to my well Beloved a song of my Beloved touching His vineyard. My well Beloved hath a vineyard in a very fruitful hill: And He fenced it, and gethered out the stones thereof, and planted it with the choicest vine and built a tower in the midst of it, and also made a winepress therein: and He looked that it should bring forth grapes, and it brought forth wild grapes. And now,) inhabitants of Jerusalem, and men of Judah, judge, I pray you, betwixt Me and My vineyard. What could have been done more to My vineyard, that I have not done in it? wherefore, when I looked that it should bring forth grapes, brought it forth wild grapes?" Is it not plain from this language that God reckoned Himself to have done enough for Israel to warrant an expectation—speaking after the manner of men—of better returns? Yet, is it not equally evident when Jehovah says here "He looked that it should bring forth grapes" that He is accommodating Himself to a form of finite expression? And, so also when He says "What could have been done more to My vineyard, that I have not done in it ?" we need to take note that in the previous enumeration of what He had done—the "fencing" etc.—He refers only to external privileges, means, and opportunities, which had been bestowed upon Israel, for, of course, He could even then have taken away from them their stony heart and given them a new heart, even a heart of flesh, as He will yet do, had He so pleased.

Perhaps we should link up with Christ's lament over Jerusalem in Matthew 23:37, His tears over the City, recorded in Luke 19:41: "He beheld the city, and wept over it." In the verses which immediately follow, we learn what it was that occasioned His tears: "Saying, If thou hadst known, even thou, at least in this thy day, the things which belong unto thy peace! but now they are hid from thine eyes. For the days shall come upon thee, that thine enemies shall cast a trench about thee, and compass thee round, and keep thee in on every side." It was the prospect of the fearful judgment which Christ knew was impending. But did those tears make manifest a disappointed God? Nay, verily. Instead, they displayed a perfect Man. The Man Christ Jesus was no emotionless stoic, but One "filled with compassion." Those tears expressed the sinless sympathies of His real and pure humanity. Had He not "wept", He had been less than human. Those "tears" were one of many proofs that "in all things it behooved Him to be made like unto His brethren" (Heb. 2:17).

In chapter one we have affirmed that God is sovereign in the exercise of His love, and in saying this we are fully aware that many will strongly resent the statement and that, furthermore, what we have now to say will probably meet with more criticism than anything else advanced in this book. Nevertheless, we must be true to our convictions of what we believe to be the teaching of Holy Scripture, and we can only ask our readers to examine diligently in the light of God's Word what we here submit to their attention.

One of the most popular beliefs of the day is that God loves everybody, and the very fact that it is so popular with all classes ought to be enough to arouse the suspicions of those who are subject to the Word of Truth. God's Love toward all His creatures is the fundamental and favorite tenet of Universalists, Unitarians, Theosophists, Christian Scientists, Spiritualists, Russellites, etc. No matter how a man may live—in open defiance of Heaven, with no concern whatever for his soul's eternal interests, still less for God's glory, dying, perhaps with an oath on his lips,—notwithstanding, God loves him, we are told. So widely has this dogma been proclaimed, and so comforting is it to the heart which is at enmity with God, we have little hope of convincing many of their error. That God loves everybody, is, we may say, quite a modern belief. The writings of the church-fathers, the Reformers or the Puritans will (we believe) be searched in vain for any such concept. Perhaps the late D. L. Moody—captivated by Drummond's "The Greatest Thing in the World"—did more than anyone else last century to popularize this concept.

It has been customary to say God loves the sinner, though He hates his sin. ' But that is a meaningless distinction. What is there in a sinner but sin? Is it not true that his "whole head is sick", and his "whole heart faint", and that "from the sole of the foot even unto the head there is no soundness" in him? (Isa. 1:5,6). Is it true that God loves the one who is despising and rejecting His blessed Son? God is Light as well as Love, and therefore His love must be a holy love. To tell the Christ-rejector that God loves him is to cauterize his conscience, as well as to afford him a sense of security in his sins. The fact is, that the love of God, is a truth for the saints only, and to present it to the enemies of God is to take the children's bread and cast it to the dogs. With the exception of John 3:16, not once in the four Gospels do we read of the Lord Jesus—the perfect Teacher— telling sinners that God loved them! In the book of Acts, which records the evangelistic labors and messages of the apostles, God's love is never referred to at all! But, when we come to the Epistles, which are addressed to the saints, we have a full presentation of this precious truth—God's love for His own. Let us seek to rightly divide the Word of God and then we shall not be found taking truths which are addressed to believers and misapplying them to unbelievers. That which sinners need to have brought before them is, the ineffable holiness, the exacting righteousness, the inflexible justice and the terrible wrath of God. Risking the danger of being mis-understood, let us say—and we wish we could say it to every evangelist and preacher in the country—there is far too much presenting of Christ to sinners today (by those sound in the faith), and far too little showing sinners their need of Christ, i.e., their absolutely ruined and lost condition, their imminent and awful danger of suffering the wrath to come, the fearful guilt resting upon them in the sight of God—to present Christ to those who have never been shown their need of Him, seems to us to be guilty of casting pearls before swine. '

If it be true that God loves every member of the human family then why did our Lord tell His disciples, "He that hath My commandments, and keepeth them, he it is that loveth Me: and he that loveth Me shall be loved of My Father..... If a man love Me, he will keep My words: and My Father will love him" (John 14:21,23)? Why say "he that loveth Me shall be loved of My Father" if the Father loves everybody? The same limitation is found in Proverbs 8:17: "I love them that love Me." Again; we read, "Thou hatest all workers of iniquity"—not merely the works of iniquity. Here, then, is a flat repudiation of present teaching that, God hates sin but loves the sinner; Scripture says, "Thou hatest all workers of iniquity" (Ps. 5:5)! "God is angry with the wicked every day." "He that believeth not the Son shall not see life, but the wrath of God"—not "shall abide," but even now—"abideth on him" (Ps. 5:5; 7:11 John 3:36). Can God "love" the one on whom His "wrath" abides? Again; is it not evident that the words "The love of God which is in Christ Jesus" (Rom. 8:39) mark a limitation, both in the sphere and objects of His love? Again; is it not plain from the words "Jacob have I loved, but Esau have I hated" (Rom. 9:13) that God does not love everybody? Again; it is written, "For whom the Lord loveth He chasteneth, and scourgeth every son whom He receiveth" (Heb. 12:6). Does not this verse teach that God's love is restricted to the members of His own family? If He loves all men without exception, then the distinction and limitation here mentioned is quite meaningless. Finally, we would ask, Is it conceivable that God will love the damned in the Lake of Fire? Yet, if He loves them now He will do so then, seeing that His love knows no change—He is "without variableness or shadow of turning"!

Turning now to John 3:16, it should be evident from the passages just quoted, that this verse will not bear the construction usually put upon it. "God so loved the world". Many suppose that this means, The entire human race. But "the entire human race," includes all mankind from Adam till the close of the earth's history: it reaches backward as well as forward! Consider, then, the history of mankind before Christ was born. Unnumbered millions lived and died before the Saviour came to the earth, lived here "having no hope and without God in the world", and therefore passed out into an eternity of woe. If God "loved" them, where is the slightest proof thereof?

The Holy Spirit

Scripture declares, "Who (God) in times past (from the tower of Babel till after Pentecost) suffered all nations to walk in their own ways" (Acts 14:16). Scripture declares that, "And even as they did not like to retain God in their knowledge, God gave them over to a reprobate mind, to do those things which are not convenient" (Rom. 1:28). To Israel God said, "You only have I known of all the families of the earth" (Amos 3:2). In view of these plain passages, who will be so foolish as to insist that God in the past loved all mankind! The same applies with equal force to the future. Read through the book of Revelation, noting especially chapters 8 to 19, where we have described the judgments which will yet be poured out from heaven on this earth. Read of the fearful woes, the frightful plagues, the vials of God's wrath, which shall be emptied on the wicked. Finally, read the 20th chapter of the Revelation, the great white throne judgment, and see if you can discover there the slightest trace of love.

But the objector comes back to John 3:16 and says, "World means world". True, but we have shown that "the world" does not mean the whole human family. The fact is that "the world" is used in a general way. When the brethren of Christ said, "Shew Thyself to the world" (John 7:4), did they mean "shew Thyself to all mankind"? When the Pharisees said, "Behold, the world is gone after Him" (John 12:19), did they mean that "all the human family" were flocking after Him? When the apostle wrote, "Your faith is spoken of throughout the whole world" (Rom. 1:8), did he mean that the faith of the saints at Rome was the subject of conversation by every man, woman, and child on the earth? When Revelation 13:3 informs us that "all the world wondered after the beast", are we to understand that there will be no exceptions? What of the godly Jewish Remnant, who will be slain (Rev. 20:4) rather than submit? These, and other passages which might be quoted, show that the term "the world" often has a relative rather than an absolute force.

Now the first thing to note in connection with John 3:16 is that our Lord was there speaking to Nicodemus—a man who believed that God's mercies were confined to his own nation. Christ there announced that God's love in giving His Son had a larger object in view, that it flowed beyond the boundary of Palestine, reaching out to "regions beyond". In other words, this was Christ's announcement that God had a purpose of grace toward Gentiles as well as Jews. "God so loved the world", then, signifies, God's love is international in its scope. But does this mean that God loves every individual among the Gentiles? Not necessarily, for as we have seen, the term "world" is general rather than specific, relative rather than absolute. The term "world" in itself is not conclusive. To ascertain who are the objects of God's love other passages where His love is mentioned must be consulted.

In 2 Peter 2:5 we read of "the world of the ungodly". If then, there is a world of the ungodly there must also be a world of the godly. It is the latter who are in view in the passages we shall now briefly consider. "For the bread of God is He which cometh down from heaven, and giveth life unto the world" (John 6:33). Now mark it well, Christ did not say, "offereth life unto the world", but "giveth". What is the difference between the two terms? This: a thing which is "offered" may be refused, but a thing "given", necessarily implies its acceptance. If it is not accepted, it is not "given", it is simply proffered. Here, then, is a scripture that positively states Christ giveth life (spiritual, eternal life) "unto the world." Now He does not give eternal life to the "world of the ungodly" for they will not have it, they do not want it. Hence, we are obliged to understand the reference in John 6:33 as being to "the world of the godly", i.e., God's own people.

One more: in 2 Corinthians 5:19 we read, "To wit that God was in Christ, reconciling the world unto Himself". What is meant by this is clearly defined in the words immediately following, "not imputing their trespasses unto them". Here again, "the world" cannot mean "the world of the ungodly", for their "trespasses" are "imputed" to them, as the judgment of the Great White Throne will yet show. But 2 Corinthians 5:19 plainly teaches there is a "world" which are "reconciled", reconciled unto God, because their trespasses are not reckoned to their account, having been borne by their Substitute. Who then are they? Only one answer is fairly possible—the world of God's people!

In like manner, the "world" in John 3:16 must, in the final analysis, refer to the world of God's people. Must we say, for there is no other alternative solution. It cannot mean the whole human race, for one half of the race was already in hell when Christ came to earth. It is unfair to insist that it means every human being now living, for every other passage in the New Testament where God's love is mentioned limits it to His own people—search and see! The objects of God's love in John 3:16 are precisely the same as the objects of Christ's love in John 13:1: "Now before the Feast of the Passover, when Jesus knew that His time was come, that He should depart out of this world unto the Father, having loved His own which were in the world, He loved them unto the end". We may admit that our interpretation of John 3:16 is no novel one invented by us, but one almost uniformly given by the Reformers and Puritans, and many others since them. '

The Holy Spirit

Coming now to chapter three—The Sovereignty of God in Salvation—innumerable are the questions which might be raised here. It is strange, yet it is true, that many who acknowledge the sovereign rule of God over material things, will cavil and quibble when we insist that God is also sovereign in the spiritual realm. But their quarrel is with God and not with us. We have given scripture in support of everything advanced in these pages, and if that will not satisfy our readers it is idle for us to seek to convince them. What we write now is designed for those who do bow to the authority of Holy Writ, and for their benefit we propose to examine several other scriptures which have purposely been held over for this chapter.

Perhaps the one passage which has presented the greatest difficulty to those who have seen that passage after passage in Holy Writ plainly teaches the election of a limited number unto salvation is 2 Peter 3:9: "not willing that any should perish, but that all should come to repentance".

The first thing to be said upon the above passage is that, like all other scripture, it must be understood and interpreted in the light of its context. What we have quoted in the preceding paragraph is only part of the verse, and the last part of it at that! Surely it must be allowed by all that the first half of the verse needs to be taken into consideration. In order to establish what these words are supposed by many to mean, viz., that the words "any" and "all" are to be received without any qualification, it must be shown that the context is referring to the whole human race! If this cannot be shown, if there is no premise to justify this, then the conclusion also must be unwarranted. Let us then ponder the first part of the verse.

"The Lord is not slack concerning His promise". Note "promise" in the singular number, not "promises." What promise is in view? The promise of salvation? Where, in all Scripture, has God ever promised to save the whole human race!! Where indeed? No, the "promise" here referred to is not about salvation. What then is it? The context tells us.

"Knowing this, first, that there shall come in the last days scoffers, walking after their own lusts, and saying, Where is the promise of His coming?" (vv. 3,4). The context then refers to God's promise to send back His beloved Son. But many long centuries have passed, and this promise has not yet been fulfilled. True, but long as the delay may seem to us, the interval is short in the reckoning of God. As the proof of this we are reminded, "But, beloved, be not ignorant of this one thing, that one day is with the Lord as a thousand years, and a thousand years as one day" (v. 8). In God's reckoning of time, less than two days have yet passed since He promised to send back Christ.

But more, the delay in the Father sending back His beloved Son is not only due to no "slackness" on His part, but it is also occasioned by His "longsuffering". His long-suffering to whom? The verse we are now considering tells us: "but is longsuffering to usward". And whom are the "usward"?—the human race, or God's own people? In the light of the context this is not an open question upon which each of us is free to form an opinion. The Holy Spirit has defined it. The opening verse of the chapter says, "This second Epistle, beloved, I now write unto you". And, again, the verse immediately preceding declares, "But, beloved, be not ignorant of this one thing etc.," (v. 8). The "usward" then are the "beloved" of God. They to whom this Epistle is addressed are "them that have obtained (not "exercised", but "obtained" as God's sovereign gift) like precious faith with us through the righteousness of God and our Saviour Jesus Christ" (2 Pet. 1:11). Therefore we say there is no room for a doubt, a quibble or an argument—the "usward" are the elect of God.

Let us now quote the verse as a whole: "The Lord is not slack concerning His promise, as some men count slackness; but is longsuffering to usward, not willing that any should perish, but that all should come to repentance." Could anything be clearer? The "any" that God is not willing should perish, are the "usward" to whom God is "longsuffering", the "beloved" of the previous verses. 2 Peter 3:9 means, then, that God will not send back His Son until "the fulness of the Gentiles be come in" (Rom. 11:25). God will not send back Christ till that "people" whom He is now "taking out of the Gentiles" (Acts 15:14) are gathered in. God will not send back His Son till the Body of Christ is complete, and that will not be till the ones whom He has elected to be saved in this dispensation shall have been brought to Him. Thank God for His "longsuffering to us-ward". Had Christ come back twenty years ago the writer had been left behind to perish in His sins. But that could not be, so God graciously delayed the Second Coming. For the same reason He is still delaying His Advent. His decreed purpose is that all His elect will come to repentance, and repent they shall. The present interval of grace will not end until the last of the "other sheep" of John 10:16 are safely folded,—then will Christ return,

In expounding the sovereignty of God the Spirit in Salvation we have shown that His power is irresistible, that, by His gracious operations upon and within them, He "compels" God's elect to come to Christ. The sovereignty of the Holy Spirit is set forth not only in John 3:8 where we are told "The wind bloweth where it pleaseth. . . . . .so is every one that is born of the Spirit," but is affirmed in other passages as well. In 1 Corinthians 12:11 we read, "But all these worketh that one and the self same Spirit, dividing to every man severally as He will." And again; we read in Acts 16:6, 7— "Now when they had gone throughout Phrygia and the region of Galatia, and were forbidden of the Holy Spirit to preach the Word in Asia. After they were come to Mysia, they assayed to go in to Bithynia: but the Spirit suffered them not." Thus we see how the Holy Spirit interposed His imperial will in opposition to the determination of the apostles.

But, it is objected against the assertion that the will and power of the Holy Spirit are irresistible that there are two passages, one in the Old Testament and the other in the New, which appear to militate against such a conclusion. God said of old, "My Spirit shall not always strive with man" (Gen. 6:3), and to the Jews Stephen declared, "Ye stiffnecked and uncircumcised in heart and ears, ye do always resist the Holy Spirit: as your fathers did, so do ye. Which of the prophets have not your fathers persecuted?" (Acts 7:51, 52). If then the Jews "resisted" the Holy Spirit, how can we say His power is irresistible? The answer is found in Nehemiah 9:30—"Many years didst Thou forbear them, and testifiedst against them by Thy Spirit in Thy Prophets: yet would they not give ear." It was the external operations of the Spirit which Israel "resisted." It was the Spirit speaking by and through the prophets to which they "would not give ear." It was not anything which the Holy Spirit wrought in them that they "resisted," but the motives presented to them by the inspired messages of the prophets. Perhaps it will help the reader to catch our thought better if we compare Matthew 11:20-24—"Then began He to upbraid the cities wherein most of His mighty works were done, because they repented not. Woe unto thee Chorazin!" etc. Our Lord here pronounces woe upon these cities for their failure to repent because of the "mighty works" (miracles) which He had done in their sight, and not because of any internal operations of His grace! The same is true of Genesis 6:3. By comparing 1 Peter 3:18-20 it will be seen that it was by and through Noah that God's Spirit "strove" with the antediluvians. The distinction noted above was ably summarized by Andrew Fuller (another writer long deceased from whom our moderns might learn much) thus: "There are two kinds of influences by which God works on the minds of men. First, That which is common, and which is effected by the ordinary use of motives presented to the mind for consideration; Secondly, That which is special and supernatural. The one contains nothing mysterious, anymore than the influence of our words and actions on each other; the other is such a mystery that we know nothing of it but by its effects—The former ought to be effectual; the latter is so." The work of the Holy Spirit upon or towards men is always "resisted," by them;

His work within is always successful. What saith the scriptures? This: "He which hath begun a good work IN you, will finish it" (Phil. 1:6)

The next question to be considered is: Why preach the Gospel to every creature? If God the Father has predestined only a limited number to be saved, if God the Son died to effect the salvation of only those given to Him by the Father, and if God the Spirit is seeking to quicken none save God's elect, then what is the use of giving the Gospel to the world at large, and where is the propriety of telling sinners that "Whosoever believeth in Christ shall not perish but have everlasting life"?

First; it is of great importance that we should be clear upon the nature of the Gospel itself. The Gospel is God's good news concerning Christ and not concerning sinners,— "Paul a servant of Jesus Christ, called to be an apostle, separated unto the Gospel of God . . . . concerning His Son, Jesus Christ our Lord" (Rom. 1:1-3). God would have proclaimed far and wide the amazing fact that His own blessed Son "became obedient unto death, even the death of the cross." A universal testimony must be borne to the matchless worth of the person and work of Christ. Note the word "witness" in Matthew 22:14. The Gospel is God's "witness" unto the perfections of His Son. Mark the words of the apostle: "For we are unto God a sweet savor of Christ, in them that are saved, and in them that perish" (2 Cor. 2:15)!

Concerning the character and contents of the Gospel the utmost confusion prevails today. The Gospel is not an "offer" to be bandied around by evangelistic peddlers. The Gospel is no mere invitation, but a proclamation, a proclamation concerning Christ; true, whether men believe it or no. No man is asked to believe that Christ died for him in particular. The Gospel, in brief, is this: Christ died for sinners, you are a sinner, believe in Christ, and you shall be saved. In the Gospel, God simply announces the terms upon which men may be saved (namely, repentance and faith) and, indiscriminately, all are commanded to fulfill them.

Second; repentance and remission of sins are to be preached in the name of the Lord Jesus "unto all the nations" (Luke 24:47), because God's elect are "scattered abroad" (John 11:52) among all nations, and it is by the preaching and hearing of the Gospel that they are called out of the world. The Gospel is the means which God uses in the saving of His own chosen ones. By nature God's elect are children of wrath "even as others"; they are lost sinners needing a Saviour, and apart from Christ there is no salvation for them. Hence, the Gospel must be believed by them before they can rejoice in the knowledge of sins forgiven. The Gospel is God's winnowing fan: it separates the chaff from the wheat, and gathers the latter into His garner.

Third; it is to be noted that God has other purposes in the preaching of the Gospel than the salvation of His own elect. The world exists for the elect's sake, yet others have the benefit of it. So the Word is preached for the elect's sake, yet others have the benefit of an external call. The sun shines, though blind men see it not. The rain falls upon rocky mountains and waste deserts, as well as on the fruitful valleys; so also, God suffers the Gospel to fall on the ears of the non-elect. The power of the Gospel is one of God's agencies for holding in check the wickedness of the world. Many who are never saved by it are reformed, their lusts are bridled, and they are restrained from becoming worse. Moreover, the preaching of the Gospel to the non-elect is made an admirable test of their characters. It exhibits the inveteracy of their sin: it demonstrates that their hearts are at enmity against God: it justifies the declaration of Christ that "men loved darkness rather than light, because their deeds were evil" (John 3:19).

Finally; it is sufficient for us to know that we are bidden to preach the Gospel to every creature. It is not for us to reason about the consistency between this and the fact that "few are chosen." It is for us to obey. It is a simple matter to ask questions relating to the ways of God which no finite mind can fully fathom. We, too, might turn and remind the objector that our Lord declared, "Verily I say unto you, All sins shall be forgiven unto the sons of men, and blasphemies wherewith soever they shall blaspheme. But he that shall blaspheme against the Holy Spirit hath never forgiveness" (Mark 3:28, 29), and there can be no doubt whatever but that certain of the Jews were guilty of this very sin (see Matt. 12:24 etc.), and hence their destruction was inevitable. Yet, notwithstanding, scarcely two months later, He commanded His disciples to preach the Gospel to every creature. When the objector can show us the consistency of these two things—the fact that certain of the Jews had committed the sin for which there is never forgiveness, and the fact that to them the Gospel was to be preached—we will undertake to furnish a more satisfactory solution than the one given above to the harmony between a universal proclamation of the Gospel and a limitation of its saving power to those only that God has predestined to be conformed to the image of His Son.

Once more, we say, it is not for us to reason about the Gospel; it is our business to preach it. When God ordered Abraham to offer up his son as a burnt-offering, he might have objected that this command was inconsistent with His promise "In Isaac shall thy seed be called." But instead of arguing he obeyed, and left God to harmonize His promise and His precept. Jeremiah might have argued that God had bade him do that which was altogether unreasonable when He said, "Therefore thou shalt speak all these words unto them; but they will not hearken to thee; thou shalt also call unto them; but they will not answer thee" (Jer. 7:27), but instead, the prophet obeyed. Ezekiel, too, might have complained that the Lord was asking of him a hard thing when He said, "Son of man, go, get thee unto the House of Israel, and speak with My words unto them. For thou art not sent to a people of a strange speech and of an hard language, but to the House of Israel; Not to many people of a strange speech and of a hard language, whose words thou cans't not understand. Surely, had I sent thee to them, they would have hearkened unto thee. But the House of Israel will not hearken unto thee; for they will not hearken unto Me; for all the House of Israel are impudent and hard hearted" (Ezek. 3:4-7).

"But, O my soul, if truth so bright
Should dazzle and confound thy sight,
Yet still His written Word obey,
And wait the great decisive day."—Watts.

It has been well said, "The Gospel has lost none of its ancient power. It is, as much today as when it was first preached, 'the power of God unto salvation'. It needs no pity, no help, and no handmaid. It can overcome all obstacles, and break down all barriers. No human device need be tried to prepare the sinner to receive it, for if God has sent it no power can hinder it; and if He has not sent it, no power can make it effectual." (Dr. Bullinger).

This chapter might be extended indefinitely, but it is already too long, so a word or two more must suffice. A number of other questions will be dealt with in the pages yet to follow, and those that we fail to touch upon the reader must take to the Lord Himself who has said, "If any of you lack wisdom, let him ask of God, that giveth to all liberally, and upbraideth not" (James 1:5).

The Value of this Doctrine

"All Scripture is given by inspiration of God, And is profitable for doctrine, For reproof, for correction, for instruction in righteousness: That the man of God may be perfect, Throughly furnished unto all good works"
2 Timothy 3:16, 17

"All Scripture is given by inspiration of God, and is profitable for doctrine, for reproof, for correction, for instruction in righteousness: that the man of God may be perfect, throughly furnished unto all good works" (2 Tim. 3:16, 17). "Doctrine" means "teaching," and it is by doctrine or teaching that the great realities of God and of our relation to Him—of Christ, the Spirit, salvation, grace, glory, are made known to us. It is by doctrine (through the power of the Spirit) that believers are nourished and edified, and where doctrine is neglected, growth in grace and effective witnessing for Christ necessarily cease. How sad then that doctrine is now decried as "unpractical" when, in fact, doctrine is the very base of the practical life. There is an inseparable connection between belief and practice—"As he thinketh in his heart, so is he" (Pro. 23:7). The relation between Divine truth and Christian character is that of cause to effect—"And ye shall know the truth, and the truth shall make you free" (John 8:32)—free from ignorance, free from prejudice, free from error, free from the wiles of Satan, free from the power of evil; and if the truth is not "known" then such freedom will not be enjoyed. Observe the order of mention in the passage with which we have opened. All Scripture is profitable first for "doctrine"! The same order is observed throughout the Epistles, particularly in the great doctrinal treatises of the apostle Paul. Read the Epistle of "Romans" and it will be found that there is not a single admonition in the first five chapters. In the Epistle of "Ephesians" there are no exhortations till the fourth chapter is reached. The order is first doctrinal exposition and then admonition or exhortation for the regulation of the daily walk.

The substitution of so-called "practical" preaching for the doctrinal exposition which it has supplanted is the root cause of many of the evil maladies which now afflict the church of God. The reason why there is so little depth, so little intelligence, so little grasp of the fundamental verities of Christianity, is because so few believers have been established in the faith, through hearing expounded and through their own personal study of the doctrines of grace. While the soul is unestablished in the doctrine of the Divine Inspiration of the Scriptures—their full and verbal inspiration—there can be no firm foundation for faith to rest upon. While the soul is ignorant of the doctrine of Justification there can be no real and intelligent assurance of its acceptance in the Beloved. While the soul is unacquainted with the teaching of the Word upon Sanctification it is open to receive all the crudities and errors of the Perfectionists or "Holiness" people. While the soul knows not what Scripture has to say upon the doctrine of the New Birth there can be no proper grasp of the two natures in the believer, and ignorance here inevitably results in loss of peace and joy. And so we might go on right through the list of Christian doctrine. It is ignorance of doctrine that has rendered the professing church helpless to cope with the rising tide of infidelity. It is ignorance of doctrine which is mainly responsible for thousands of professing Christians being captivated by the numerous fallacies of the day. It is because the time has now arrived when the bulk of our churches "will not endure sound doctrine" (2 Tim. 4:3) that they so readily receive false doctrines. Of course it is true that doctrine, like anything else in Scripture, may be studied from a merely cold intellectual viewpoint, and thus approached, doctrinal teaching and doctrinal study will leave the heart untouched, and will naturally be "dry" and profitless. But, doctrine properly received, doctrine studied with an exercised heart, will ever lead into a deeper knowledge of God and of the unsearchable riches of Christ.

The doctrine of God's sovereignty then is no mere metaphysical dogma which is devoid of practical value, but is one that is calculated to produce a powerful effect upon Christian character and the daily walk. The doctrine of God's sovereignty lies at the foundation of Christian theology, and in importance is perhaps second only to the Divine Inspiration of the Scriptures. It is the center of gravity in the system of Christian truth—the sun around which all the lesser orbs are grouped. It is the golden milestone to which every highway of knowledge leads and from which they all radiate. It is the cord upon which all other doctrines are strung like so many pearls, holding them in place and giving them unity. It is the plumb-line by which every creed needs to be measured, the balance in which every human dogma must be weighed. It is designed as the sheet-anchor for our souls amid the storms of life. The doctrine of God's sovereignty is a Divine cordial to refresh our spirits. It is designed and adapted to mould the affections of the heart and to give a right direction to conduct. It produces gratitude in prosperity and patience in adversity. It affords comfort for the present and a sense of security respecting the unknown future. It is, and it does all, and much more than we have just said, because it ascribes to God—Father, Son, and Holy Spirit—the glory which is His due, and places the creature in his proper place before Him—in the dust.

We shall now consider the Value of the doctrine in detail.

1. It deepens our veneration of the Divine Character.

The doctrine of God's sovereignty as it is unfolded in the Scriptures affords an exalted view of the Divine perfections. It maintains His creatorial rights. It insists that "to us there is but one God, the Father, of whom are all things, and we in Him; and one Lord Jesus Christ, by whom are all things, and we by Him" (1 Cor. 8:6). It declares that His rights are those of the "potter" who forms and fashions the clay into vessels of whatever type and for whatever use He may please. Its testimony is, "Thou hast created all things, and for Thy pleasure they are and were created" (Rev. 4:11). It argues that none has any right to "reply" against God, and that the only becoming attitude for the creature to take is one of reverent submission before Him. Thus the apprehension of the absolute supremacy of God is of great practical importance, for unless we have a proper regard to His high sovereignty He will never be honored in our thoughts of Him, nor will He have His proper place in our hearts and lives.

It exhibits the inscrutableness of His wisdom. It shows that while God is immaculate in His holiness, He has permitted evil to enter His fair creation; that while He is the Possessor of all power, He has allowed the Devil to wage war against Him for six thousand years at least; that while He is the perfect embodiment of love, He spared not His own Son; that while He is the God of all grace, multitudes will be tormented for ever and ever in the Lake of Fire. High mysteries are these. Scripture does not deny them, but acknowledge their existence—"O the depth of the riches both of the wisdom and knowledge of God! how unsearchable are His judgments, and His ways past finding out!" (Rom. 11:33).

It makes known the irreversibleness of His will. "Known unto God are all His works from the beginning of the world" (Acts 15:18). From the beginning God purposed to glorify Himself "in the Church by Christ Jesus, throughout all ages, world without end" (Eph. 3:21). To this end, He created the world, and formed man. His all-wise plan was not defeated when man fell, for in the Lamb "slain from the foundation of the world" (Rev. 13:8) we behold the Fall anticipated. Nor will God's purpose be thwarted by the wickedness of men since the Fall, as is clear from the words of the Psalmist, "Surely the wrath of man shall praise Thee: the remainder of wrath shalt Thou restrain" (Ps. 76:10). Because God is the Almighty His will cannot be withstood. "His purposes originated in eternity, and are carried forward without change to eternity. They extend to all His works, and control all events. He 'worketh all things after the counsel of His own will.'" (Dr. Rice). Neither man nor devil can successfully resist Him, therefore is it written, "The Lord reigneth; let the people tremble." (Ps. 99:1).

It magnifies His grace. Grace is unmerited favor, and because grace is shown to the undeserving and Hell-deserving, to those who have no claim upon God, therefore is grace free and can be manifested toward the chief of sinners. But because grace is exercised toward those who are destitute of worthiness or merit, grace is sovereign; that is to say, God bestows grace upon whom He pleases. Divine sovereignty has ordained that some shall be cast into the Lake of Fire to show that all deserved such a doom. But grace comes in like a drag-net and draws out from a lost humanity a people for God's name, to be throughout all eternity the monuments of His inscrutable favor. Sovereign grace reveals God breaking down the opposition of the human heart, subduing the enmity of the carnal mind, and bringing us to love Him because He first loved us.

2. It is the solid foundation of all true religion.

This naturally follows from what we have said above under the first head. If the doctrine of Divine sovereignty alone gives God His rightful place, then it is also true that it alone can supply a firm base for practical religion to build upon. There can be no progress in Divine things until there is the personal recognition that God is Supreme, that He is to be feared and revered, that He is to be owned and served as Lord. We read the Scriptures in vain unless we come to them earnestly desiring a better knowledge of God's will for us—any other motive is selfish and utterly inadequate and unworthy. Every prayer we send up to God is but carnal presumption unless it be offered "according to His will"— anything short of this is to ask 'amiss,' that we might consume upon our own lusts the thing requested. Every service we engage in is but a "dead work" unless it be done for the glory of God. Experimental religion consists mainly in the perception and performance of the Divine will—performance both active and passive. We are predestinated to be "conformed to the image of God's Son", whose meat it ever was to do the will of the One that sent Him, and the measure in which each saint is becoming "conformed" practically, in his daily life, is largely determined by his response to our Lord's word—"Take My yoke upon you, and learn of Me; for I am meek and lowly in heart."

3. It repudiates the heresy of salvation by works.

"There is a way which seemeth right unto a man; but the end thereof are the ways of death" (Prov. 14:12). The way which "seemeth right" and which ends in "death," death eternal, is salvation by human effort and merit. The belief in salvation by works is one that is common to human nature. It may not always assume the grosser form of Popish penances, or even of Protestant "repentance"—i.e., sorrowing for sin, which is never the meaning of repentance in Scripture—anything which gives man a place at all is but a variety of the same evil genus. To say, as alas! many preachers are saying, God is willing to do His part if you will do yours, is a wretched and excuseless denial of the Gospel of His grace. To declare that God helps those who help themselves, is to repudiate one of the most precious truths taught in the Bible, and in the Bible alone; namely, that God helps those who are unable to help themselves, who have tried again and again only to fail. To say that the sinner's salvation turns upon the action of his own. will, is another form of the God-dishonoring dogma of salvation by human efforts. In the final analysis, any movement of the will is a work: it is something from me, something which I do. But the doctrine of God's sovereignty lays the axe at the root of this evil tree by declaring, "it is not of him that willeth, nor of him that runneth, but of God that sheweth mercy" (Rom. 9:16). Does some one say, Such a doctrine will drive sinners to despair. The reply is, Be it so; it is just such despair the writer longs to see prevail. It is not until the sinner despairs of any help from himself, that he will ever fall into the arms of sovereign mercy; but if once the Holy Spirit convicts him that there is no help in himself, then he will recognize that he is lost, and will cry, "God be merciful to me a sinner," and such a cry will be heard. If the author may be allowed to bear personal witness, he has found during the course of his ministry that, the sermons he has preached on human depravity, the sinner's helplessness to do anything himself, and the salvation of the soul turning upon the sovereign mercy of God, have been those most owned and blessed in the salvation of the lost. We repeat, then, a sense of utter helplessness is the first prerequisite to any sound conversion. There is no salvation for any soul until it looks away from itself, looks to something, yea, to Someone, outside of itself.

4. It is deeply humbling to the creature.

This doctrine of the absolute sovereignty of God is a great battering-ram against human pride, and in this it is in sharp contrast from "the doctrines of men." The spirit of our age is essentially that of boasting and glorying in the flesh. The achievements of man, his development and progress, his greatness and self-sufficiency, are the shrine at which the world worships today. But the truth of God's sovereignty, with all its corollaries, removes every ground for human boasting and instills the spirit of humility in its stead. It declares that salvation is of the Lord—of the Lord in its origination, in its operation, and in its consummation. It insists that the Lord has to apply as well as supply, that He has to complete as well as begin His saving work in our souls, that He has not only to reclaim but to maintain and sustain us to the end. It teaches that salvation is by grace through faith, and that all our works (before conversion), good as well as evil, count for nothing toward salvation. It tells us we are "born, not of the will of the flesh, nor of the will of man, but of God" (John 1:13). And all this is most humbling to the heart of man, who wants to contribute something to the price of his redemption and do that which will afford ground for boasting and self-satisfaction.

But if this doctrine humbles us, it results in praise to God. If, in the light of God's sovereignty, we have seen our own worthlessness and helplessness, we shall indeed cry with the Psalmist, "All my springs are in Thee" (Ps. 87:7). If by nature we were "children of wrath," and by practice rebels against the Divine government and justly exposed to the "curse" of the Law, and if God was under no obligation to rescue us from the fiery indignation and yet, notwithstanding, He delivered up His well-beloved Son for us all; then how such grace and love will melt our hearts, how the apprehension of it will cause us to say in adoring gratitude, "Not unto us, O Lord, not unto us, but unto Thy name give glory, for Thy mercy, and for Thy truth's sake" (Ps. 115:1)! How readily shall each of us acknowledge, "By the grace of God I am what I am"! With what wondering praise shall we exclaim—

"Why was I made to hear His voice,
And enter while there's room,
When thousands make a wretched choice,
And rather starve than come?
'Twas the same love that spread the feast,
That sweetly forced us in;
Else we had still refused to taste
And perished in our sin."

5. It affords a sense of absolute security.

God is infinite in power, and therefore it is impossible to withstand His will or resist the outworking of His decrees. Such a statement as that is well calculated to fill the sinner with alarm, but from the saint it evokes naught but praise. Let us add a word and see what a difference it makes:—My God is infinite in power! then "I will not fear what man can do unto me." My God is infinite in power, then "what time I am afraid I will trust in Him." My God is infinite in power, then "I will both lay me down in peace, and sleep: for Thou, Lord, only makest me dwell in safety" (Ps. 4:8). Right down the ages this has been the source of the saints' confidence. Was not this the assurance of Moses when, in his parting words to Israel, he said—"There is none like unto the God of Jeshurun (Israel), who rideth upon the heaven in Thy help, and in His excellency on the sky. The eternal God is thy refuge, and underneath are the everlasting arms" (Deut. 33:26, 27)? Was it not this sense of security that caused the Psalmist, moved by the Holy Spirit, to write—"He that dwelleth in the secret place of the Most High shall abide under the shadow of the Almighty. I will say of the Lord, He is my refuge and my fortress: my God: in Him will I trust. Surely He shall deliver thee from the snare of the fowler, and from the noisome pestilence. He shall cover thee with His feathers, and under His wings shalt thou trust: His truth shall be thy shield and buckler: Thou shalt not be afraid for the terror by night; nor for the arrow that flieth by day; Nor for the pestilence that walketh in darkness; nor for the destruction that wasteth at noonday. A thousand shall fall at thy side, and ten thousand at thy right hand, but it shall not come nigh thee. Because thou hast made the Lord, which is my refuge, even the Most High thy Habitation; There shall no evil befall thee (instead, all things will work together for good), neither shall any plague come nigh thy dwelling" (Ps. 91)?

"Death and plagues around me fly,
Till He bid, I cannot die;
Not a single shaft can hit,
Till the God of love sees fit."

O the preciousness of this truth! Here am I, a poor, helpless, senseless "sheep," yet am I secure in the hand of Christ. And why am I secure there? None can pluck me thence because the hand that holds me is that of the Son of God, and all power in heaven and earth is His! Again; I have no strength of my own: the world, the flesh, and the Devil, are arrayed against me, so I commit myself into the care and keeping of the Lord and say with the apostle, "I know Whom I have believed, and am persuaded that He is able to keep that which I have committed unto Him against that day" (2 Tim. 1:12). And what is the ground of my confidence? How do I know that He is able to keep that which I have committed unto Him? I know it because God is almighty, the King of kings and Lord of lords.

6. It supplies comfort in sorrow.

The doctrine of God's sovereignty is one that is full of consolation and imparts great peace to the Christian. The sovereignty of God is a foundation that nothing can shake and is more firm than the heavens and earth. How blessed to know there is no corner of the universe that is out of His reach! as said the Psalmist, "Whither shall I go from Thy Spirit? or whither shall I flee from Thy presence? If I ascend up into heaven, Thou art there: if I make my bed in hell, behold, Thou art there. If I take the wings of the morning, and dwell in the uttermost parts of the sea; even there shall Thy hand lead me, and Thy right hand shall hold me. If I say surely the darkness shall cover me; even the night shall be light about me. Yea, the darkness hideth not from Thee: but the night shineth as the day: the darkness and the light are both alike to Thee" (Ps. 139:7-12). How blessed it is to know that God's strong hand is upon every one and every thing! How blessed to know that not a sparrow falleth to the ground without His notice! How blessed to know that our very afflictions come not by chance, nor from the Devil, but are ordained and ordered by God:— "That no man should be moved by these afflictions: for yourselves know that we are appointed thereunto" (1 Thess. 3:3)!

But our God is not only infinite in power, He is infinite in wisdom and goodness too. And herein is the preciousness of this truth. God wills only that which is good and His will is irreversible and irresistible! God is too wise to err and too loving to cause His child a needless tear. Therefore if God be perfect wisdom and perfect goodness how blessed is the assurance that everything is in His hand, and moulded by His will according to His eternal purpose! "Behold, He taketh away, who can hinder Him? who will say unto Him what doest Thou?" (Job 9:12). Yet, how comforting to learn that it is "He", and not the Devil, who "taketh away" our loved ones! Ah! what peace for our poor frail hearts to be told that the number of our days is with Him (Job 7:1; 14:5); that disease and death are His messengers, and always march under His orders; that it is the Lord who gives and the Lord who takes away!

7. It begets a spirit of sweet resignation.

To bow before the sovereign will of God is one of the great secrets of peace and happiness. There can be no real submission with contentment until we are broken in spirit, that is, until we are willing and glad for the Lord to have His way with us. Not that we are insisting upon a spirit of fatalistic acquiescence; far from it. The saints are exhorted to "prove what is that good, and acceptable, and perfect will of God" (Rom. 12:2).

We touched upon this subject of resignation to God's will in the chapter upon our Attitude towards God's Sovereignty, and there, in addition to the supreme Pattern, we cited the examples of Eli and Job: we would now supplement their cases with further examples. What a word is that in Leviticus 10:3—"And Aaron held his peace." Look at the circumstances: "And Nadab and Abihu, the sons of Aaron, took either of them his censer, and put fire therein, and put incense thereon, and offered strange fire before the Lord, which He commanded them not. And there went out fire from the Lord, and devoured them, and they died before the Lord. . . . . And Aaron held his peace." Two of the high priests' sons were slain, slain by a visitation of Divine judgment, and they were probably intoxicated at the time; moreover, this trial came upon Aaron suddenly, without anything to prepare him for it; yet, he "held his peace." Precious exemplification of the power of God's all-sufficient grace!

Consider now an utterance which fell from the lips of David: "And the king said unto Zadok, Carry back the ark of God into the city: if I shall find favor in the eyes of the Lord, He will bring me again, and shew me both it, and His habitation. But if He thus say, I have no delight in thee; behold, here am I, let Him do to me as seemeth good unto Him" (2 Sam. 15:25, 26). Here, too, the circumstances which confronted the speaker were exceedingly trying to the human heart. David was sore pressed with sorrow. His own son was driving him from the throne, and seeking his very life. Whether he would ever see Jerusalem and the Tabernacle again he knew not. But he was so yielded up to God, he was so fully assured that His will was best, that even though it meant the loss of the throne and the loss of his life he was content for Him to have His way—"let Him do to me as seemeth Him good."

There is no need to multiply examples, but a reflection upon the last case will be in place. If amid the shadows of the Old Testament dispensation, David was content for the Lord to have His way, now that the heart of God has been fully revealed at the Cross, how much more ought we to delight in the execution of His will! Surely we shall have no hesitation in saying—

"Ill that He blesses is our good,
And unblest good is ill,
And all is right that seems most wrong,
If it he His sweet will."

8. It evokes a song of praise.

It could not be otherwise. Why should I, who am by nature no different from the careless and godless throngs all around, have been chosen in Christ before the foundation of the world and now blest with all spiritual blessings in the heavenlies in Him! Why was I, that once was an alien and a rebel, singled out for such wondrous favors! Ah, that is something I cannot fathom. Such grace, such love, "passeth knowledge." But if my mind is unable to discern a reason, my heart can express its gratitude in praise and adoration. But not only should I be grateful to God for His grace toward me in the past, His present dealings will fill me with thanksgivings. What is the force of that word "Rejoice in the Lord alway" (Phil. 4:4)? Mark it is not "Rejoice in the Saviour," but we are to "Rejoice in the Lord," as "Lord," as the Master of every circumstance. Need we remind the reader that when the apostle penned these words he was himself a prisoner in the hands of the Roman government. A long course of affliction and suffering lay behind him. Perils on land and perils on sea, hunger and thirst, scourging and stoning, had all been experienced. He had been persecuted by those within the church as well as by those without: the very ones who ought to have stood by him had forsaken him. And still he writes, "Rejoice in the Lord alway"! What was the secret of his peace and happiness? Ah! had not this same apostle written, "And we know that all things work together for good to them that love God, to them who are the called according to His purpose" (Rom. 8:28). But how did he, and how do we, "know," that all things work together for good? The answer is, Because all things are under the control of and are being regulated by the Supreme Sovereign, and because He has naught but thoughts of love toward His own, then "all things" are so ordered by Him that they are made to minister to our ultimate good. It is for this cause we are to give "thanks always for all things unto God and the Father in the name of our Lord Jesus Christ" (Eph. 5:20). Yes, give thanks for "all things" for, as it has been well said "Our disappointments are but His appointments." To the one who delights in the sovereignty of God the clouds not only have a 'silver lining' but they are silvern all through, the darkness only serving to offset the light—

"Ye fearful saints fresh courage take
The clouds ye so much dread,
Are big with mercy and shall break
In blessings o'er your head."

9. It guarantees the final triumph of good over evil.

Ever since the day that Cain slew Abel, the conflict on earth between good and evil, has been a sore problem to the saints. In every age the righteous have been hated and persecuted, whilst the unrighteous have appeared to defy God with impugnity. The Lord's people, for the most part, have been poor in this world's goods, whereas the wicked in their temporal prosperity have flourished like the green bay tree. As one looks around and beholds the oppression of believers and the earthly success of unbelievers, and notes how few are the former and how numerous the latter; as he sees the apparent defeat of the right, and the triumphing of might and the wrong; as he hears the roar of battle, the cries of the wounded, and the lamentations of the bereaved; as he discovers that almost everything down here is in confusion, chaos, and ruins, it seems as though Satan were getting the better of the conflict. But as one looks above, instead of around, there is plainly visible to the eye of faith a Throne, a Throne unaffected by the storms of earth, a Throne that is "set," stable and secure; and upon it is seated One whose name is the Almighty, and who "worketh all things after the counsel of His own will" (Eph. 1:11). This then is our confidence—God is on the Throne. The helm is in His hand, and being Almighty His purpose cannot fail, for "He is in one mind, and who can turn Him? and what His soul desireth, even that He doeth" (Job 23:13). Though God's governing hand is invisible to the eye of sense, it is real to faith, that faith which rests with sure confidence upon His Word, and therefore is assured He cannot fail. What follows below is from the pen of our brother Mr. Gaebelein.

"There can be no failure with God. 'God is not a man, that He should lie, neither the Son of man, that He should repent; bath He said and shall He not do it? or bath He spoken, and shall He not make it good?' (Num. 23:19). All will be accomplished. The promise made to His own beloved people to come for them and take them from hence to glory will not fail. He will surely come and gather them in His own presence. The solemn words spoken to the nations of the earth by the different prophets will also not fail. 'Come near, ye nations, to hear; and hearken ye people; let the earth hear, and all that is therein; the world, and all things that come forth of it. For the indignation of the Lord is upon all nations, and His fury upon all armies; He bath utterly destroyed them, He hath delivered them to the slaughter' (Isa. 34:1, 2). Nor will that day fail in which 'the lofty looks of man shall be humbled and the haughtiness of men shall be bowed down and the Lord alone shall be exalted' (Isa. 2:11). The day in which He is manifested, when His glory shall cover the heavens and His feet will stand again upon this earth, will surely come. His kingdom will not fail, nor all the promised events connected with the end of the age and the consummation.

"In these dark and trying times bow well it is to remember that He is on the throne, the throne which cannot be shaken, and that He will not fail in doing all He has spoken and promised. 'Seek ye out of the book of the Lord and read: Not one of these shall fail' (Isa. 34:16). In believing, blessed anticipation, we can look on to the glory-time when His Word and His Will is accomplished, when through the coming of the Prince of Peace, righteousness and peace comes at last. And while we wait for the supreme and blessed moment when His promise to us is accomplished, we trust Him, walking in His fellowship and daily find afresh, that He does not fail to sustain and keep us in all our ways.

10. It provides a resting place for the heart.

Much that might have been said here has already been anticipated under previous heads. The One seated upon the Throne of Heaven, the One who is Governor over the nations and who has ordained and now regulates all events, is infinite not only in power but in wisdom and goodness as well. He who is Lord over all creation is the One that was "manifest in the flesh" (1 Tim. 3:16). Ah! here is a theme no human pen can do justice to. The glory of God consists not merely in that He is Highest, but in that being high He stooped in lowly love to bear the burden of His own sinful creatures, for it is written "God was in Christ, reconciling the world unto Himself" (2 Cor. 5:19). The Church of God was purchased "with His own Blood" (Acts 20:28). It is upon the gracious self-humiliation of the King Himself that His kingdom is established. O wondrous Cross! By it He who suffered upon it has become not the Lord of our destinies (He was that before), but the Lord of our hearts. Therefore, it is not in abject terror that we bow before the Supreme Sovereign, but in adoring worship we cry, "Worthy is the Lamb that was slain to receive power, and riches, and wisdom, and strength, and honor, and glory, and blessing" (Rev. 5:12).

Here then is the refutation of the wicked charge that this doctrine is a horrible calumny upon God and dangerous to expound to His people. Can a doctrine be "horrible" and "dangerous" that gives God His true place, that maintains His rights, that magnifies His grace, that ascribes all glory to Him and removes every ground of boasting from the creature? Can a doctrine be "horrible" and "dangerous" which affords the saints a sense of security in danger, that supplies them comfort in sorrow, that begets patience within them in adversity, that evokes from them praise at all times? Can a doctrine be "horrible" and "dangerous" which assures us of the certain triumph of good over evil, and which provides a sure resting-place for our hearts, and that place, the perfections of the Sovereign Himself? No; a thousand times, no. Instead of being "horrible and dangerous" this doctrine of the Sovereignty of God is glorious and edifying, and a due apprehension of it will but serve to make us exclaim with Moses, "Who is like unto thee, O Lord, among the gods? who is like Thee, glorious in holiness, fearful in praises, doing wonders?" (Ex. 15:11).

Conclusion

"Halleluia: for the Lord God omnipotent reigneth" - Revelation 19:6

In our Foreword to the second edition we acknowledge the need for preserving the balance of Truth. Two things are beyond dispute: God is sovereign, man is responsible. In this book we have sought to expound the former; in our other works we have frequently pressed the latter. That there is real danger of over-emphasizing the one and ignoring the other, we readily admit; yea, history furnishes numerous examples of cases of each. To emphasize the sovereignty of God, without also maintaining the accountability of the creature tends to fatalism; to be so concerned in maintaining the responsibility of man, as to lose tight of the sovereignty of God, is to exalt the creature and dishonor the Creator.

Almost all doctrinal error, is, really, Truth perverted, Truth wrongly divided, Truth disproportionately held and taught. The fairest face on earth, with the most comely features, would soon become ugly and unsightly, if one member continued growing while the others remained undeveloped. Beauty is, primarily, a matter of proportion. Thus it is with the Word of God: its beauty and blessedness are best perceived when its manifold wisdom is exhibited in its true proportions. Here is where so many have failed in the past. A single phase of God's Truth has so impressed this man or that, that he has concentrated his attention upon it, almost to the exclusion of everything else. Some portion of God's Word has been made a "pet doctrine", and often this has become the distinctive badge of some party. But it is the duty of each servant of God to "declare all the counsel of God" (Acts 20:27).

It is true that the degenerate days in which our lot is cast, when on every side man is exalted, and "superman" has become a common expression, there is real need for a special emphasis upon the glorious fact of God's supremacy. The more so where this is expressly denied. Yet even here much wisdom is required, lest our zeal should not be according to knowledge." The words "meat in due season" should ever be before the servant of God. What is needed, primarily, by one congregation, may not be specifically needed by another. If called to labor where Arminian preachers have preceded, then the neglected truth of God's sovereignty should be expounded—though with caution and care, lest too much "strong meat" be given to "babes". The example of Christ in John 16:12, "I have yet many things to say unto you, but ye cannot hear them now", must be borne in mind. On the other hand, if I am called to take charge of a distinctly Calvinistic pulpit, then the truth of human responsibility (in its many aspects) may be profitably set forth. What the preacher needs to give-out is not what his people most like to hear, but what they most need, i.e. those aspects of truth they are least familiar with, or least exhibiting in their walk.

To carry into actual practice what we have inculcated above will, most probably, lay the preacher open to the charge of being a Turncoat. But what matters that if he has his Master's approval? He is not called upon to be "consistent" with himself, nor with any rules drawn up by man; his business is to be consistent with Holy Writ. And in Scripture each part or aspect of truth is balanced by another aspect of truth. There are two sides to everything, even to the character of God, for He is "light" (1 John 1:5) as well as "love" (1 John 4:8), and therefore are we called upon to "Behold, therefore the goodness and severity of God" (Rom. 11:22). To be all the time preaching on the one to the exclusion of the other, caricatures the Divine character.

When the Son of God became incarnate He came here in "the form of a servant" (Phil. 2:6); nevertheless, in the manger He was "Christ the Lord" (Luke 2:11)! All things are possible with God (Matt. 19:26), yet God "cannot lie" (Titus 1:2). Scripture says, "Bear ye one another's burdens (Gal. 6:2), yet the same chapter insists "every man shall bear his own burden" (Gal. 6:5). We are enjoined to take "no thought for the morrow" (Matt. 6:34), yet "if any provide not for his own, and specially for those of his own house, he hath denied the faith, and is worse than an infidel" (1 Tim. 5:8). No sheep of Christ's can perish (John 10:28, 29), yet the Christian is bidden to make his "calling and election sure" (2 Pet. 1:10). And so we might go on multiplying illustrations. These things are not contradictions, but complementaries: the one "balances the other". Thus, the Scriptures set forth both the sovereignty of God and the responsibility of man. So too should every servant of God, and that, in their proper proportions.

But we return now to a few closing reflections upon our present theme. "And Jehoshaphat stood in the congregation of Judah and Jerusalem, in the house of the Lord, before the new court, And said, O Lord God of our fathers, art not Thou God in heaven? and rulest not Thou over all the kingdoms of the heathen? and in Thine hand is there not power and might, so that none is able to withstand Thee?" (2 Chron. 20:5, 6). Yes, the Lord is

God, ruling over all the kingdoms of men, ruling in supreme majesty and might. Yet in our day, a day of boasted enlightenment and progress, this is denied on every hand. A materialistic science and an atheistic philosophy have bowed God out of His own world, and everything is regulated, forsooth, by (impersonal) laws of nature. So in human affairs: at best God is a far-distant spectator, and a helpless one at that. God could not help the launching of the dreadful war, and though He longed to put a stop to it He was unable to do so—and this in the face of 1 Chronicles 5:22; 2 Chronicles 24:24! Having endowed man with "free agency God is obliged to let man make his own choice and go his own way, and He cannot interfere with him, or otherwise his moral responsibility would be destroyed. Such are the popular beliefs of the day. One is not surprised to find these sentiments emanating from German neologians (coiners of new words), but how sad that they should be taught in many of our Seminaries, echoed from many of our pulpits, and accepted by many of the rank and file of professing Christians.

One of the most flagrant sins of our age is that of irreverence—the failure to ascribe the glory which is due the august majesty of God. Men limit the power and activities of the Lord in their degrading concepts of His being and character. Originally, man was made in the image and likeness of God, but today we are asked to believe in a god made in the image and likeness of man. The Creator is reduced to the level of the creature: His omniscience is called into question, His omnipotency is no longer believed in, and His absolute sovereignty is flatly denied. Men claim to be the architects of their own fortunes and the determiners of their own destiny. They know not that their lives are at the disposal of the Divine Despot. They know not they have no more power to thwart Hs secret decrees than a worm has to resist the tread of an elephant. They know not that "The Lord hath prepared His throne in the heavens; and His kingdom ruleth over all" (Ps. 103:19).

In the foregoing pages we have sought to repudiate such paganistic views as the above-mentioned, and have endeavored to show from Scripture that God is God, on the Throne, and that so far from the recent war being an evidence that the helm had slipped out of His hand, it was a sure proof that He still lives and reigns, and is now bringing to pass that which He had fore-determined and fore-announced (Matt. 24:6-8 etc.). That the carnal mind is enmity against God, that the unregenerate man is a rebel against the Divine government, that the sinner has no concern for the glory of his Maker, and little or no respect for His revealed will, is freely granted. But, nevertheless, behind the scenes, God is ruling and over-ruling, fulfilling His eternal purpose, not only in spite of but, also by means of, those who are His enemies.

How earnestly are the claims of man contended for against the claims of God! Has not man power and knowledge, but what of it? Has God no will, or power, or knowledge? Suppose man's will conflicts with God's—then what? Turn to the Scripture of Truth for answer. Men had a will on the plains of Shinar and determined to build a tower whose top should reach unto heaven, but what came of their purpose? Pharaoh had a will when he hardened his heart and refused to allow Jehovah's people to go and worship Him in the wilderness, but what came of his rebellion? Balak had a will when he hired Balaam to come and curse the Hebrews, but of what avail was it? The Canaanites had a will when they determined to prevent Israel occupying the land of Canaan, but how far did they succeed? Saul had a will when he hurled his javelin at David, but it entered the wall instead! Jonah had a will when he refused to go and preach to the Ninevites, but what came of it? Nebuchadnezzar had a will when he thought to destroy the three Hebrew children, but God had a will too, and the fire did not harm them. Herod had a will when he sought to slay the Child Jesus, and had there been no living, reigning God, his evil desire would have been effected; but in daring to pit his puny will against the irresistible will of the Almighty, his efforts came to nought. Yes, my reader, and you, too, had a will when you formed your plans without first seeking counsel of the Lord, therefore did He overturn them! "There are many devices in a man s heart: nevertheless the counsel of the Lord, that shall stand" (Prov. 19:21).

What a demonstration of the irresistible sovereignty of God is furnished by that wonderful statement found in Revelation 17:17—"For God hath put in their hearts to fulfill His will, and to agree, and give their kingdom unto the Beast, until the words of God shall be fulfilled." The fulfillment of any single prophecy is but the sovereignty of God in operation. It is the demonstration that what He has decreed He is able also to perform. It is proof that none can withstand the execution of His counsel or prevent the accomplishment of His pleasure. It is the evidence that God inclines men to fulfill that which He has ordained and perform that which He has fore-determined. If God were not absolute Sovereign, then Divine prophecy would be valueless, for in such case no guarantee would be left that what He had predicted would surely come to pass.

"For God hath put in their hearts to fulfill His will and, to agree, and give their kingdom unto the Beast, until the words of God shall he fulfilled" (Rev. 17:17). Even in that terrible time, when Satan has been cast down to the earth itself (Rev. 12:9), when the Antichrist is reigning in full power (Rev. 13), when the basest passions of men are let loose (Rev. 6:4), even then God is supreme above all, working "through all" (Eph. 4:6), controlling men's hearts and directing their counsels to the fulfilling of His own purpose. We cannot do better than quote here the excellent comments of our esteemed friend Mr. Walter Scott upon this verse—"God works unseen, but not the less truly, in all the political changes of the day. The astute statesman. the clever diplomatist, is simply an agent in the Lord's hands. He knows it not. Self-will and motives of policy may influence to action, but God is steadily working toward an end— to exhibit the heavenly and earthly glories of His Son. Thus, instead of kings and statesmen thwarting God's purpose, they unconsciously forward it. God is not indifferent, but is behind the scenes of human action. The doings of the future ten kings in relation to Babylon and the Beast— the ecclesiastical and secular powers—are not only under the direct control of God, but all is done in fulfillment of His words."

Closely connected with Revelation 17:17 is that which is brought before us in Micah 4:11, 12—"Now also many nations are gathered against thee, that say, Let her be defiled, and let our eye look upon Zion. But they know not the thoughts of the Lord, neither understand they His counsel: for He shall gather them as the sheaves into the floor." Here is another instance which demonstrates God's absolute control of the nations, of His power to fulfill His secret counsel or decrees through and by them, and of His inclining men to perform His pleasure though it be performed blindly and unwittingly by them.

Once more. What a word was that of the Lord Jesus as He stood before Pilate! Who can depict the scene! There was the Roman official, and there also was the Servant of Jehovah standing before him. Said Pilate, "Whence art Thou?" And we read, "Jesus gave him no answer. Then said Pilate unto Him, "Speakest Thou not unto me? Knowest Thou not that I have power to crucify Thee, and have power to release Thee?" (John 19:10). Ah! that is what Pilate thought. That is what many another has thought. He was merely voicing the common conviction of the human heart—the heart which leaves God out of its reckoning. But hear the Lord Jesus as He corrects Pilate, and at the same time repudiates the proud boasting of men in general—"thou couldest have no power against Me, except it were given thee from above" (John 19:11). How sweeping is this assertion! Man—even though he be a prominent official in the most influential empire of his day—has no power except that which is given him from above, no power, even, to do that which is evil, i.e., carry out his own evil designs, unless God empowers him so that

His purpose may be forwarded. It was God who gave Pilate the power to sentence to death His well-beloved Son! And how this rebukes the sophistries and reasonings of men, who argue that God does nothing more than permit evil! Why, go right back to the very first words spoken by the Lord God to man after the Fall, and hear Him saying, "I will put ENMITY between thee and the woman, and between thy seed and her seed" (Gen. 3:15)! Bare permission of sin does not cover all the facts which are revealed in Scripture touching this mystery. As Calvin succinctly remarked, "But what reason shall we assign for His permitting it but because it is His will?"

At the close of chapter eleven we promised to give attention to one or two other Difficulties which were not examined at that time. To them we now turn. If God has not only pre-determined the salvation of His own, but has also fore-ordained the good works which they are to walk 'in (Eph. 2:10), then what incentive remains for us to strive after practical godliness? If God has fixed the number of those who are to be saved, and the others are vessels of wrath fitted to destruction, then what encouragement have we to preach the Gospel to the lost? Let us take up these questions in the order of mention.

1. God's Sovereignty and the believer's growth in grace.

If God has fore-ordained everything that comes to pass, of what avail is it for us to "exercise" ourselves "unto godliness" (1 Tim. 4:7)? If God has before ordained the good works in which we are to walk (Eph. 2:10), then why should we be "careful to maintain good works" (Titus 3:8)? This only raises once more the problem of human responsibility. Really, it should be enough for us to reply, God has bidden us do so. Nowhere does Scripture inculcate or encourage a spirit of fatalistic indifference. Contentment with our present attainments is expressly disallowed. The word to every believer is, "Press toward the mark for the prize of the high calling of God in Christ Jesus" (Phil. 3:14). This was the apostle's aim, and it should be ours. Instead of hindering the development of Christian character, a proper apprehension and appreciation of God's sovereignty will forward it. Just as the sinner's despair of any help from himself is the first prerequisite of a sound conversion, so the loss of all confidence in himself is the first essential in the believer's growth in grace; and just as the sinner despairing of help from himself will cast him into the arms of sovereign mercy, so the Christian, conscious of his own frailty, will turn unto the Lord for power. It is when we are weak, we are strong (2 Cor. 12:10): that is to say, there must be consciousness of our weakness before we shall turn to the Lord for help. While the Christian allows the thought that he is sufficient in himself, while he imagines that by mere force of will he shall resist temptation, while he has any confidence in the flesh then, like Peter who boasted that though all forsook the Lord yet should not he, so we shall certainly fail and fall. Apart from Christ we can do nothing (John 15:5). The promise of God is, "He giveth power to the faint; and to them that have no might (of their own) He increaseth strength" (Isa. 40:29).

The question now before us is of great practical importance, and we are deeply anxious to express ourselves clearly and simply. The secret of development of Christian character is the realization of our own powerlessness, acknowledged powerlessness, and the consequent turning unto the Lord for help. The plain fact is that of ourselves we are utterly unable to practice a single precept or obey a single command that is set before us in the Scriptures. For example: "Love your enemies"—but of ourselves we cannot do this, or make ourselves do it. "In nothing be anxious"—but who can avoid and prevent anxiety when things go wrong? "Awake to righteousness and sin not"—but who can help sinning? These are merely examples selected at random from scores of others. Does then God mock us by bidding us do what He knows we are unable to do? The answer of Augustine to this question is the best we have met with—"God gives commands we cannot perform, that we may know what we ought to request from Him." A consciousness of our powerlessness should cast us upon Him who has all power. Here then is where a vision and view of God's sovereignty helps, for it reveals His sufficiency and shows us our insufficiency.

2. God's Sovereignty and Christian service.

If God has determined before the foundation of the world the precise number of those who shall be saved, then why should we concern ourselves about the eternal destiny of those with whom we come into contact? What place is left for zeal in Christian service? Will not the doctrine of God's sovereignty, and its corollary of predestination, discourage the Lord's servants from faithfulness in evangelism? No; instead of discouraging His servants, a recognition of God's sovereignty is most encouraging to them. Here is one, for example, who is called upon to do the work of an evangelist, and he goes forth believing in the freedom of the will and in the sinner's own ability to come to Christ. He preaches the Gospel as faithfully and zealously as he knows how; but, he finds the vast majority of his hearers are utterly indifferent and have no heart at all for Christ. He discovers that men are, for the most part, thoroughly wrapt up in the things of the world, and that few have any concern about the world to come. He beseeches men to be reconciled to God, and pleads with them over their soul's salvation. But it is of no avail. He becomes thoroughly disheartened, and asks himself, What is

The Holy Spirit

the use of it all? Shall he quit, or had he better change his mission and message? If men will not respond to the Gospel, had he not better engage in that which is more popular and acceptable to the world? Why not occupy himself with humanitarian efforts, with social uplift work, with the purity campaign? Alas! that so many men who once preached the Gospel are now engaged in these activities instead.

What then is God's corrective for His discouraged servant? First, he needs to learn from Scripture that God is not now seeking to convert the world, but that in this Age He is "taking out of the Gentiles" a people for His name (Acts 15:14). What then is God's corrective for His discouraged servant? This—a proper apprehension of God's plan for this Dispensation. Again: what is God's remedy for dejection at apparent failure in our labors? This—the assurance that God's purpose cannot fail, that God's plans cannot miscarry, that God's will must be done. Our labors are not intended to bring about that which God has not decreed. Once more: what is God's word of cheer for the one who is thoroughly disheartened at the lack of response to his appeals and the absence of fruit for his labors? This— that we are not responsible for results: that is God's side, and God's business. Paul may "plant," and Apollos may "water," but it is God who "gave the increase" (1 Cor. 3:6). Our business is to obey Christ and preach the Gospel to every creature, to emphasize the "Whosoever believeth", and then to leave the sovereign operations of the Holy Spirit to apply the Word in quickening power to whom He wills, resting on the sure promise of Jehovah—"For as the rain cometh down, and the snow from heaven, and returneth not thither, but watereth the earth, and maketh it bring forth and bud, that it may give seed to the sower, and bread to the eater: So shall My Word be that goeth forth out of My mouth: it shall not return unto Me void, but it shall accomplish that which I please (it may not that which we please), and it shall prosper in the thing whereto I sent it" (Isa. 55:10, 11). Was it not this assurance that sustained the beloved apostle when he declared "Therefore (see context) I endure all things for the elect's sake" (2 Tim.2:10)! Yea, is not this same lesson to be learned from the blessed example of the Lord Jesus! When we read that He said to the people, "Ye also have seen Me, and believe not", He fell back upon the sovereign pleasure of the One who sent Him, saying, "All that the Father giveth Me shall come to Me, and him that cometh to Me I will in no wise cast out" (John 6:36, 37). He knew that His labor would not be in vain. He knew God's Word would not return unto Him "void." He knew that "God's elect" would come to Him and believe on Him. And this same assurance fills the soul of every servant who intelligently rests upon the blessed truth of God's sovereignty.

Ah fellow-Christian-worker, God has not sent us forth to "draw a bow at a venture". The success of the ministry which He has committed into our hands is not left contingent on the fickleness of the wills in those to whom we preach. How gloriously encouraging, how soul-sustaining the assurance are those words of our Lord's, if we rest on them in simple faith: "And other sheep I have ("have" mark you, not "will have"; "have," because given to Him by the Father before the foundation of the world), which are not of this fold (i.e. the Jewish fold then existing) : them also I must bring, and they shall hear My voice" (John 10:16). Not simply, "they ought to hear My voice," not simply "they may hear My voice", not "they will do so if they are willing." There is no "if", no "perhaps", no uncertainty about it. "They shall hear My voice" is His own positive, unqualified, absolute promise. Here then, is where faith is to rest! Continue your quest, dear friend, after the "other sheep" of Christ's. Be not discouraged because the "goats" heed not His voice as you preach the Gospel. Be faithful, be scriptural, be persevering, and Christ may use even you to be His mouthpiece in calling some of His lost sheep unto Himself. "Therefore, my beloved brethren, be ye stedfast, unmoveable, always abounding in the work of the Lord, forasmuch as ye know that your labor is not in vain in the Lord" (1 Cor. 15:58).

It now remains for us to offer a few closing reflections and our happy task is finished.

God's sovereign election of certain ones to salvation is a MERCIFUL provision. The sufficient answer to all the wicked accusations that the doctrine of Predestination is cruel, horrible, and unjust, is that, unless God had chosen certain ones to salvation, none would have been saved, for "there is none that seeketh after God" (Rom. 3:11). This is no mere inference of ours but the definite teaching of Holy Scripture. Attend closely to the words of the apostle in Romans 9, where this theme is fully discussed—"Though the number of the children of Israel be as the sand of the sea, a remnant shall be saved. . . . And as Isaiah said before, Except the Lord of hosts had left us a seed, we had been as Sodom, and been made like unto Gomorrah" (Rom. 9:27, 29). The teaching of this passage is unmistakable: but for Divine interference, Israel would have become as Sodom and Gomorrah. Had God left Israel alone, human depravity would have run its course to its own tragic end. But God left Israel a "remnant" or "seed." Of old the cities of the plain had been obliterated for their sin, and none was left to survive them; and so it would have been in Israel's case had not God "left" or spared a remnant.

Thus it is with the human race: but for God's sovereign grace in sparing a remnant, all of Adam's descendants had perished in their sins. Therefore, we say that God's sovereign election of certain ones to salvation is a merciful provision. And, be it noted, in choosing the ones He did, God did no injustice to the others who were passed by, for none had any right to salvation. Salvation is by grace, and the exercise of grace is a matter of pure sovereignty—God might save all or none, many or few, one or ten thousand, just as He saw best. Should it be replied, But surely it were "best" to save all. The answer would be: We are not capable of judging. We might have thought it "best" never to have created Satan, never to have allowed sin to enter the world, or having entered, to have brought the conflict between good and evil to an end long before now. Ah! God's ways are not ours, and His ways are "past finding out."

God fore-ordains everything which comes to pass. His sovereign rule extends throughout the entire Universe and is over every creature. "For of Him, and through Him, and to Him, are all things" (Rom. 11:36). God initiates all things, regulates all things, and all things are working unto His eternal glory. "There is but one God, the Father, of whom are all things, and we in Him; and one Lord Jesus Christ, by whom are all things, and we by Him" (1 Cor. 8:6). And again, "According to the purpose of Him who worketh all things after the counsel of His own will" (Eph. 1:11). Surely if anything could be ascribed to chance it is the drawing of lots, and yet the Word of God expressly declares, "The lot is cast into the lap; but the whole disposing thereof is of the Lord" (Prov. 16:33)!!

God's wisdom in the government of our world shall yet be completely vindicated before all created intelligences. God is no idle Spectator, looking on from a distant world at the happenings on our earth, but is Himself shaping everything to the ultimate promotion of His own glory. Even now He is working out His eternal purpose, not only in spite of human and Satanic opposition, but by means of them. How wicked and futile have been all efforts to resist His will shall one day be as fully evident as when of old He overthrew the rebellious Pharaoh and his hosts at the Red Sea.

It has been well said, "The end and object of all is the glory of God. It is perfectly, divinely true, that 'God hath ordained for His own glory whatsoever comes to pass.' In order to guard this from all possibility of mistake, we have only to remember who is this God, and what the glory that He seeks. It is He who is the God and Father of our Lord Jesus Christ,—of Him in whom divine love came seeking not her own, among us as 'One that serveth.' It is He who, sufficient in Himself, can receive no real accession of glory from His creatures, but from whom—'Love', as He is 'Light,'—cometh down every good and every perfect gift, in whom is no variableness nor shadow of turning. Of His own alone can His creatures give to Him."

"The glory of such an one is found in the display of His own goodness, righteousness, holiness, truth; in manifesting Himself as in Christ He has manifested Himself and will forever. The glory of this God is what of necessity all things must serve—adversaries and evil as well as all else. He has ordained it; His power will insure it; and when all apparent clouds and obstructions are removed, then shall He rest—'rest in His love' forever, although eternity only will suffice for the apprehension of the revelation. 'God shall be all in all' (italics ours throughout this paragraph) gives in six words the ineffable result" (F. W. Grant on "Atonement").

That what we have written gives but an incomplete and imperfect presentation of this most important subject we must sorrowfully confess. Nevertheless, if it results in a clearer apprehension of the majesty of God and His sovereign mercy we shall be amply repaid for our labors. If the reader has received blessing from the perusal of these pages, let him not fail to return thanks to the Giver of every good and every perfect gift, ascribing all praise to His inimitable and sovereign grace.

"The Lord, our God, is clothed with might,
The winds and waves obey His will;
He speaks, and in the shining height
The sun and rolling worlds stand still.
Rebel ye waves, and o'er the land
With threatening aspect foam and roar,
The Lord hath spoken His command
That breaks your rage upon the shore.
Ye winds of night, your force combine—
Without His holy high behest
You shall not in a mountain pine
Disturb the little swallow's nest.
His voice sublime is heard afar;
In distant peals it fades and dies;
He binds the cyclone to His car
And sweeps the howling murky skies.
Great God! how infinite art Thou,
What weak and worthless worms are we,
Let all the race of creatures bow

And seek salvation now from Thee.
Eternity, with all its years
Stands ever-present to Thy view,
To Thee there's nothing old appears
Great God! There can be nothing new.
Our lives through varied scenes are drawn,
And vexed with mean and trifling cares;
While Thine eternal thought moves on
Thy fixed and undisturbed affairs."

"Halleluia: for the Lord God omnipotent reigneth" (Rev. 19:6).

The Will of God

In treating of the Will of God some theologians have differentiated between His decretive will and His permissive will, insisting that there are certain things which God has positively fore-ordained, but other things which He merely suffers to exist or happen. But such a distinction is really no distinction at all, inasmuch as God only permits that which is according to His will. No such distinction would have been invented had these theologians discerned that God could have decreed the existence and activities of sin without Himself being the Author of sin. Personally, we much prefer to adopt the distinction made by the older Calvinists between God's secret and revealed will, or, to state it in another way, His disposing and His preceptive will.

God's revealed will is made known in His Word, but His secret will is His own hidden counsels. God's revealed will is the definer of our duty and the standard of our responsibility. The primary and basic reason why I should follow a certain course or do a certain thing is because it is God's will that I should, His will being clearly defined for me in His Word. That I should not follow a certain course, that I must refrain from doing certain things, is because they are contrary to God's revealed will. But suppose I disobey God's Word, then do I not cross His will? And if so, how can it still be true that God's will is always done and His counsel accomplished at all times? Such questions should make evident the necessity for the distinction here advocated. God's revealed will is frequently crost, but His secret will is never thwarted. That it is legitimate for us to make such a distinction concerning God's will is clear from Scripture. Take these two passages: "For this is the will of God, even your sanctification" (1 Thess. 4:3); "For who hath resisted His will?" (Rom. 9:19). Would any thoughtful reader declare that God's "will" has precisely the same meaning in both of these passages? We surely hope not. The first passage refers to God's revealed will, the latter to His secret will. The first passage concerns our duty, the latter declares that God's secret purpose is immutable and must come to pass notwithstanding the creature's insubordination. God's revealed will is never done perfectly or fully by any of us, but His secret will never fails of accomplishment even in the minutest particular. His secret will mainly concerns future events; His revealed will, our present duty: the one has to do with His irresistible purpose, the other with His manifested pleasure: the one is wrought upon us and accomplished through us, the other is to be done by us.

The secret will of God is His eternal, unchanging purpose concerning all things which He bath made, to be brought about by certain means to their appointed ends: of this God expressly declares "My counsel shall stand, and I will do all My pleasure" (Isa. 46:10). This is the absolute, efficacious will of God, always effected, always fulfilled. The revealed will of God contains not His purpose and decree but our duty,—not what He will do according to His eternal counsel, but what we should do if we would please Him, and this is expressed in the precepts and promises of His Word. Whatever God has determined within Himself, whether to do Himself, or to do by others, or to suffer to be done, whilst it is in His own breast, and is not made known by any event in providence, or by precept, or by prophecy, is His secret will. Such are the deep things of God, the thoughts of His heart, the counsels of His mind, which are impenetrable to all creatures. But when these are made known they become His revealed will: such is almost the whole of the book of Revelation, wherein God has made known to us "things which must shortly come to pass (Rev. 1:1—"must" because He has eternally purposed that they should).

It has been objected by Arminian theologians that the division of God's will into secret and revealed is untenable, because it makes God to have two different wills, the one opposed to the other. But this is a mistake, due to their failure to see that the secret and revealed will of God respect entirely different objects. If God should require and forbid the same thing, or if He should decree the same thing should and should not exist, then would His secret and revealed will be contradictory and purposeless. If those who object to the secret and revealed will of God being inconsistent would only make the same distinction in this case that they do in many other cases, the seeming inconsistency would at once disappear. How often do men draw a sharp distinction between what is desirable in its own nature. and what is not desirable all things considered. For example, the fond parent does not desire simply considered to punish his offending child, but, all things considered, he knows it is his bounden duty, and so corrects his child. And though he tells his child he does not desire to punish him, but that he is satisfied it is for the best all things considered to do so, then an intelligent child would see no inconsistency in what his father says and does. Just so the All-wise Creator may consistently decree to bring to pass things which He hates, forbids and condemns. God chooses that some things shall exist which He thoroughly hates (in their intrinsic nature), and He also chooses that some things shall not yet exist which He perfectly loves (in their intrinsic nature). For example: He commanded that Pharaoh should let His people go, because that was right in the nature of things, yet, He had secretly declared that Pharaoh should not let His people go, not because it was right in Pharaoh to refuse, but because it was best all things considered that he should not let them go—i.e. best because it subserved God's larger purpose.

Again; God commands us to be perfectly holy in this life (Matt. 5:48), because this is right in the nature of things, but He has decreed that no man shall be perfectly holy in this life, because this is best all things considered that none shall be perfectly holy (experimentally) before they leave this world. Holiness is one thing, the taking place of holiness is another; so, sin is one thing, the taking place of sin is another. When God requires holiness His preceptive or revealed will respects the nature or moral excellence of holiness; but when He decrees that holiness shall not take place (fully and perfectly) His secret or decretive will respects only the event of it not taking place. So, again, when He forbids sin, His preceptive or revealed will respects only the nature or moral evil of sin; but when He decrees that sin shall take place, His secret will respects only its actual occurrence to serve His good purpose. Thus the secret and revealed will of God respect entirely different objects.

God's will of decree is not His will in the same sense as His will of command is. Therefore, there is no difficulty in supposing that one may be contrary to the other. His will, in both senses, is His inclination. Everything that concerns His revealed will is perfectly agreeable to His nature, as when He commands love, obedience, and service from His creatures. But that which concerns His secret will has in view His ultimate end, that to which all things are now working. Thus, He decreed the entrance of sin into His universe, though His own holy nature hates all sin with infinite abhorrence, yet, because it is one of the means by which His appointed end is to be reached He suffered it to enter. God's revealed will is the measure of our responsibility and the determiner of our duty. With God's secret will we have nothing to do: that is His concern. But, God knowing that we should fail to perfectly do His revealed will ordered His eternal counsels accordingly, and these eternal counsels, which make up His secret will, though unknown to us are, though unconsciously, fulfilled in and through us.

Whether the reader is prepared to accept the above distinction in the will of God or not he must acknowledge that the commands of Scripture declare

God's revealed will, and he must also allow that sometimes God wills not to hinder a breach of those commands, because He does not as a fact so hinder it. God wills to permit sin as is evident, for He does permit it. Surely none will say that God Himself does what He does not will to do.

Finally, let it be said again that, my responsibility with regard to the will of God is measured by what He has made known in His Word. There I learn that it is my duty to use the means of His providing, and to humbly pray that He may be pleased to bless them to me. To refuse so to do on the ground that I am ignorant of what may or may not be His secret counsels concerning me, is not only absurd, but the height of presumption. We repeat: the secret will of God is none of our business; it is His revealed will which measures our accountability. That there is no conflict whatever between the secret and the revealed will of God is made clear from the fact that, the former is accomplished by my use of the means laid down in the latter.

The Case of Adam

In our chapter on God's Sovereignty and Human Responsibility we dealt only with the responsibility of man considered as a fallen creature, and at the close of the discussion it was pointed out how that the measure and extent of our responsibility varies in different individuals, according to the advantages they have received and the privileges they have enjoyed, which is a truth clearly established by the declaration of the Saviour recorded in Luke 12:47, 48, "And that servant, which knew his lord's will, and prepared not himself, neither did according to his will, shall be beaten with many stripes. But he that knew not, and did not commit things worthy of stripes, shall be beaten with few stripes. For unto whomsoever much is given, of him shall be much required: and to whom men have committed much, of him they will ask the more".

Now, strictly speaking, there are only two men who have ever walked this earth which were endowed with full and unimpaired responsibility, and they were the first and last Adam's. The responsibility of each of the rational descendants of Adam, while real, and sufficient to establish them accountable to their Creator is, nevertheless, limited in degree, limited because impaired through the effects of the Fall.

Not only is the responsibility of each descendant of Adam sufficient to constitute him, personally an accountable creature (that is, as one so constituted that he ought to do right and ought not to do wrong), but originally every one of us was also endowed, judicially, with full and unimpaired responsibility, not in ourselves, but, in Adam. It should ever be borne in mind that not only was Adam the father of the human race seminally, but he was also the head of the race legally. When Adam was placed in Eden he stood there as our representative, so that what he did is reckoned to the account of each for whom he acted.

It is beside our present purpose to enter here into a lengthy discussion of the Federal Headship of Adam (Though there is deep and widespread need for this, and we hope ere long to write upon this subject in another book.), suffice it now to refer the reader to Romans 5:12-19 where this truth is dealt with by the Holy Spirit. In the heart of this most important passage we are told that Adam was "the figure of Him that was to come" (v. 14), that is, of Christ. In what sense, then, was Adam "the figure" of Christ? The answer must be, In that he was a Federal Head; in that he acted on the behalf of a race of men; in that he was one who has legally, as well as vitally, affected all connected with him. It is for this reason that the Lord Jesus is in 1 Corinthians 15:45 denominated "the last Adam", that is, the Head of the new creation, as the first Adam was the Head of the old creation.

In Adam, then, each of us stood. As the representative of the human race the first man acted. As then Adam was created with full and unimpaired responsibility, unimpaired because there was no evil nature within him; and as we were all "in Adam", it necessarily follows that all of us, originally, were also endowed with full and unimpaired responsibility. Therefore, in Eden, it was not merely the responsibility of Adam as a single person that was tested, but it was Human Responsibility, the Responsibility of the Race, as a whole and in part, which was on trial.

Webster defines responsibility first, as "liable to account"; second, as "able to discharge an obligation". Perhaps the meaning and scope of the term responsibility might be expressed and summed up in the one word oughtness. Godwards, responsibility respects that which is due the Creator from the creature, and which the creature is under moral obligations to render.

In the light of the above definition it is at once apparent that responsibility is something that must be placed on trial. And as a fact, this is, as we learn from the Inspired Record, exactly what transpired in Eden. Adam was placed on probation. His obligations to God were put to the test. His loyalty to the Creator was tried out. The test consisted of obedience to his Maker's command. Of a certain tree he was forbidden to eat.

But right here a very formidable difficulty confronts us. From God's standpoint the result of Adam's probation was not left in uncertainty. Before He formed him out of the dust of the ground and breathed into his nostrils the breath of life, God knew exactly how the appointed test would terminate. With this statement every Christian reader must be in accord, for, to deny God's foreknowledge is to deny His omniscience, and this is to repudiate one of the fundamental attributes of Deity. But we must go further: not only had God a perfect foreknowledge of the outcome of Adam's trial, not only did His omniscient eye see Adam eating of the forbidden fruit, but He decreed beforehand that he should do so. This is evident not only from the general fact that nothing happens save that which the Creator and Governor of the universe has eternally purposed, but also from the express declaration of

Scripture that Christ as a Lamb "verily was foreordained before the foundation of the world" (1 Pet. 1:20). If, then, God had foreordained before the foundation of the world that Christ should, in due time, be offered as a Sacrifice for sin, then it is unmistakably evident that God had also foreordained sin should enter the world, and if so, that Adam should transgress and fall. In full harmony with this, God Himself placed in Eden the tree of the knowledge of good and evil, and also allowed the Serpent to enter and deceive Eve.

Here then is the difficulty: If God has eternally decreed that Adam should eat of the tree, how could he be held responsible not to eat of it? Formidable as the problem appears, nevertheless, it is capable of a solution, a solution, moreover, which can be grasped even by the finite mind. The solution is to be found in the distinction between God's secret will and His revealed will. As stated in Appendix I, human responsibility is measured by our knowledge of God's revealed will; what God has told us, not what He has not told us, is the definer of our duty. So it was with Adam.

That God had decreed sin should enter this world through the disobedience of our first parents was a secret hid in His own breast. Of this Adam knew nothing, and that made all the difference so far as his responsibility was concerned. Adam was quite unacquainted with the Creator's hidden counsels. What concerned him was God's revealed will. And that was plain! God had forbidden him to eat of the tree, and that was enough. But God went further: He even warned Adam of the dire consequences which would follow should he disobey—death would be the penalty. Transgression, then, on the part of Adam was entirely excuseless. Created with no evil nature in him, with a will in perfect equipoise, placed in the fairest environment, given dominion over all the lower creation, allowed full liberty with only a single restriction upon him, plainly warned of what would follow an act of insubordination to God, there was every possible inducement for Adam to preserve his innocence; and, should he fail and fall, then by every principle of righteousness his blood must lie upon his own head, and his guilt be imputed to all in whose behalf he acted.

Had God disclosed to Adam His purpose that sin would enter this world, and that He had decreed Adam should eat of the forbidden fruit, it is obvious that Adam could not have been held responsible for the eating of it. But in that God withheld the knowledge of His counsels from Adam, his accountability was not interfered with.

Again; had God created Adam with a bias toward evil, then human responsibility had been impaired and man's probation merely one in name.

But inasmuch as Adam was included among that which God, at the end of the sixth day, pronounced "Very good", and, inasmuch as man was made "upright" (Eccl. 7:29), then every mouth must be "stopped" and "the whole world" must acknowledge itself "guilty before God" (Rom. 3:19).

Once more, it needs to be carefully borne in mind that God did not decree that Adam should sin and then inject into Adam an inclination to evil, in order that His decree might be carried out. No; "God cannot be tempted, neither tempteth He any man" (James 1:13). Instead, when the Serpent came to tempt Eve, God caused her to remember His command forbidding to eat of the tree of the knowledge of good and evil and of the penalty attached to disobedience! Thus, though God had decreed the Fall, in no sense was He the Author of Adam's sin, and at no point was Adam's responsibility impaired. Thus may we admire and adore the "manifold wisdom of God", in devising a way whereby His eternal decree should be accomplished, and yet the responsibility of His creatures be preserved intact.

Perhaps a further word should be added concerning the decretive will of God, particularly in its relation to evil. First of all we take the high ground that, whatever things God does or permits, are right, just, and good, simply because God does or permits them. When Luther gave answer to the question, "Whence it was that Adam was permitted to fall, and corrupt his whole posterity; when God could have prevented him from falling, etc", he said, "God is a Being whose will acknowledges no cause: neither is it for us to prescribe rules to His sovereign pleasure, or call Him to account for what He does. He has neither superior nor equal; and His will is the rule of all things. He did not thus will such and such things because they were right, and He was bound to will them; but they are therefore equitable and right because He wills them. The will of man, indeed, may be influenced and moved; but God's will never can. To assert the contrary is to undeify Him" (De Servo, Arb. c/ 153).

To affirm that God decreed the entrance of sin into His universe, and that He foreordained all its fruits and activities, is to say that which, at first may shock the reader; but reflection should show that it is far more shocking to insist that sin has invaded His dominions against His will, and that its exercise is outside His jurisdiction: for in such a case where would be His omnipotency? No; to recognize that God has foreordained all the activities of evil, is to see that He is the Governor of sin: His will determines its exercise, His power regulates its bounds (Ps. 76:10). He is neither the Inspirer nor the Infuser of sin in any of His creatures, but He is its Master, by which we mean God's management of the wicked is so entire that, they can do nothing save that which His hand and counsel, from everlasting, determined should be done.

Though nothing contrary to holiness and righteousness can ever emanate from God, yet He has, for His own wise ends, ordained His creatures to fall into sin. Had sin never been permitted, how could the justice of God have been displayed in punishing it? How could the wisdom of God have been manifested in so wondrously over-ruling it? How could the grace of God have been exhibited in pardoning it? How could the power of God have been exercised in subduing it? A very solemn and striking proof of Christ's acknowledgment of God's decretal of sin is seen in His treatment of Judas. The Saviour knew full well that Judas would betray Him, yet we never read that He expostulated with him! Instead, He said to him, "That thou doest, do quickly" (John 13 :27)! Yet, mark this was said after he had received the sop and Satan had taken possession of his heart. Judas was already prepared for and determined on his traitorous work, therefore did Christ permissively (bowing to His Father's ordination) bid him go forth to his awful work.

Thus, though God is not the Author of sin, and though sin is contrary to His holy nature, yet the existence and operations of it are not contrary to His will, but subservient to it. God never tempts man to sin, but He has, by His eternal counsels (which He is now executing), determined its course. Moreover, as we have shown in chapter 8, though God has decreed man's sins, yet is man responsible not to commit them, and blamable because he does. Strikingly were these two sides of this awful subject brought together by Christ in that statement of His: "Woe unto the world because of offences! for it must needs be that offences come (because God has foreordained them); but woe to that man by whom the offence cometh" (Matt. 18:7). So, too, though all which took place at Calvary was by the "determinate counsel and foreknowledge of God" (Acts 2:23), nevertheless, "wicked hands" crucified the Lord of glory, and, in consequence, His blood has righteously rested upon them and on their children. High mysteries are these, yet it is both our happy privilege and bounden duty to humbly receive whatsoever God has been pleased to reveal concerning them in His Word of Truth.

The Meaning of "Kosmos" in John 3:16

It may appear to some of our readers that the exposition we have given of John 3:16 in the chapter on "Difficulties and Objections" is a forced and unnatural one, inasmuch as our definition of the term "world" seems to be out of harmony with the meaning and scope of this word in other passages, where, to supply the world of believers (God's elect) as a definition of "world" would make no sense. Many have said to us, "Surely, 'world' means world, that is, you, me, and everybody." In reply we would say: We know from experience how difficult it is to set aside the "traditions of men" and come to a passage which we have heard explained in a certain way scores of times, and study it carefully for ourselves without bias Nevertheless, this is essential if we would learn the mind of God.

Many people suppose they already know the simple meaning of John 3:16, and therefore they conclude that no diligent study is required of them to discover the precise teaching of this verse. Needless to say, such an attitude shuts out any further light which they otherwise might obtain on the passage. Yet, if anyone will take a Concordance and read carefully the various passages in which the term "world" (as a translation of "kosmos") occurs, he will quickly perceive that to ascertain the precise meaning of, the word "world" in any given passage is not nearly so easy as is popularly supposed. The word "kosmos," and its English equivalent "world," is not used with a uniform significance in the New Testament. Very far from it. It is used in quite a number of different ways. Below we will refer to a few passages where this term occurs, suggesting a tentative definition in each case:

"Kosmos" is used of the Universe as a whole: Acts 17:24 - "God that made the world and all things therein seeing that He is Lord of heaven and earth."

"Kosmos" is used of the earth: John 13:1; Ephesians 1:4, etc., etc.- "When Jesus knew that his hour was come that He should depart out of this world unto the Father, having loved His own which were in the world He loved them unto the end." "Depart out of this world" signifies, leave this earth. "According as He hath chosen us in Him before the foundation of the world." This expression signifies, before the earth was founded—compare Job 38:4 etc.

"Kosmos" is used of the world-system: John 12:31 etc. "Now is the judgment of this world: now shall the Prince of this world be cast out"—compare Matthew 4:8 and 1 John 5:19, R. V.

"Kosmos" is used of the whole human race: Romans 3:19, etc.—"Now we know that what things soever the law saith, it saith to them who are under the law: that every mouth may be stopped, and all the world may become guilty before God."

"Kosmos" is used of humanity minus believers: John 15:18; Romans 3:6 "If the world hate you, ye know that it hated Me before it hated you." Believers do not "hate" Christ, so that "the world" here must signify the world of unbelievers in contrast from believers who love Christ. "God forbid: for then how shall God judge the world." Here is another passage where "the world" cannot mean "you, me, and everybody," for believers will not be "judged" by God, see John 5:24. So that here, too, it must be the world of unbelievers which is in view.

"Kosmos" is used of Gentiles in contrast from Jews: Romans 11:12 etc. "Now if the fall of them (Israel) be the riches of the world, and the diminishing of them (Israel) the riches of the Gentiles; how much more their (Israel's) fulness." Note how the first clause in italics is defined by the latter clause placed in italics. Here, again, "the world" cannot signify all humanity for it excludes Israel!

"Kosmos" is used of believers only: John 1:29; 3:16, 17; 6:33; 12:47; 1 Corinthians 4:9; 2 Corinthians 5:19. We leave our readers to turn to these passages, asking them to note, carefully, exactly what is said and predicated of "the world" in each place.

Thus it will be seen that "kosmos" has at least seven clearly defined different meanings in the New Testament. It may be asked, Has then God used a word thus to confuse and confound those who read the Scriptures? We answer, No! nor has He written His Word for lazy people who are too dilatory, or too busy with the things of this world, or, like Martha, so much occupied with "serving," they have no time and no heart to "search" and "study" Holy Writ! Should it be asked further, But how is a searcher of the Scriptures to know which of the above meanings the term "world" has in any given passage? The answer is: This may be ascertained by a careful study of the context, by diligently noting what is predicated of "the world" in each passage, and by prayer fully consulting other parallel passages to the one being studied. The principal subject of John 3:16 is Christ as the Gift of God. The first clause tells us what moved God to "give" His only begotten Son, and that was His great "love;" the second clause informs us for whom God "gave" His Son, and that is for, "whosoever (or, better, 'every one') believeth;" while the last clause makes known why God "gave" His Son (His purpose), and that is, that everyone that believeth "should not perish but have everlasting life." That "the world" in John 3:16 refers to the world of believers (God's elect), in contradistinction from "the world of the ungodly" (2 Pet. 2:5), is established, unequivocally established, by a comparison of the other passages which speak of God's "love." "God commendeth His love toward US"—the saints, Romans 5:8. "Whom the Lord loveth He chasteneth"—every son, Hebrews 12:6. "We love Him, because He first loved US"—believers, 1 John 4:19. The wicked God "pities" (see Matt. 18:33). Unto the unthankful and evil God is "kind" (see Luke 6:35). The vessels of wrath He endures "with much long-suffering" (see Rom. 9:22). But "His own" God "loves"!!

1 John 2:2

There is one passage more than any other which is appealed to by those who believe in universal redemption, and which at first sight appears to teach that Christ died for the whole human race. We have therefore decided to give it a detailed examination and exposition.

"And He is the propitiation for our sins: and not for ours only, but also for the sins of the whole world" (1 John 2:2). This is the passage which, apparently, most favors the Arminian view of the Atonement, yet if it be considered attentively it will be seen that it does so only in appearance, and not in reality. Below we offer a number of conclusive proofs to show that this verse does not teach that Christ has propitiated God on behalf of all the sins of all men.

In the first place, the fact that this verse opens with "and" necessarily links it with what has gone before. We, therefore, give a literal word for word translation of 1 John 2:1 from Bagster's Interlinear: "Little children my, these things I write to you, that ye may not sin; and if any one should sin, a Paraclete we have with the Father, Jesus Christ (the) righteous". It will thus be seen that the apostle John is here writing to and about the saints of God. His immediate purpose was two-fold: first, to communicate a message that would keep God's children from sinning; second, to supply comfort and assurance to those who might sin, and, in consequence, be cast down and fearful that the issue would prove fatal. He, therefore, makes known to them the provision which God has made for just such an emergency. This we find at the end of verse 1 and throughout verse 2. The ground of comfort is twofold: let the downcast and repentant believer (1 John 1:9) be assured that, first, he has an "Advocate with the Father"; second, that this Advocate is "the propitiation for our sins". Now believers only may take comfort from this, for they alone have an "Advocate", for them alone is Christ the propitiation, as is proven by linking the Propitiation ("and") with "the Advocate"!

In the second place, if other passages in the New Testament which speak of "propitiation," be compared with 1 John 2:2, it will be found that it is strictly limited in its scope. For example, in Romans 3:25 we read that God

The Holy Spirit

set forth Christ "a propitiation through faith in His blood". If Christ is a propitiation "through faith", then He is not a "propitiation" to those who have no faith! Again, in Hebrews 2:17 we read, "To make propitiation for the sins of the people" (Heb. 2:17, R. V.).

In the third place, who are meant when John says, "He is the propitiation for our sins"? We answer, Jewish believers. And a part of the proof on which we base this assertion we now submit to the careful attention of the reader.

In Galatians 2:9 we are told that John, together with James and Cephas, were apostles "unto the circumcision" (i.e. Israel). In keeping with this, the Epistle of James is addressed to "the twelve tribes, which are scattered abroad" (1:1). So, the first Epistle of Peter is addressed to "the elect who are sojourners of the Dispersion" (1 Pet.1:1, R. V.). And John also is writing to saved Israelites, but for saved Jews and saved Gentiles.

Some of the evidences that John is writing to saved Jews are as follows.

(a) In the opening verse he says of Christ, "Which we have seen with our eyes .... and our hands have handled". How impossible it would have been for the Apostle Paul to have commenced any of his epistles to Gentile saints with such language!

(b) "Brethren, I write no new commandment unto you, but an old commandment which ye had from the beginning" (1 John 2:7). The "beginning" here referred to is the beginning of the public manifestation of Christ—in proof compare 1:1; 2:13, etc. Now these believers the apostle tells us, had the "old commandment" from the beginning. This was true of Jewish believers, but it was not true of Gentile believers.

(c) "I write unto you, fathers, because ye have known Him from the beginning" (2:13). Here, again, it is evident that it is Jewish believers that are in view.

(d) "Little children, it is the last time: and as ye have heard that Antichrist shall come, even now are there many antichrists; whereby we know that it is the last time. They went out from us, but they were not of us" (2:18, 19).

These brethren to whom John wrote had "heard" from Christ Himself that Antichrist should come (see Matt. 24). The "many antichrists" whom John declares "went out from us" were all Jews, for during the first century none but a Jew posed as the Messiah. Therefore, when John says "He is the propitiation for our sins" he can only mean for the sins of Jewish believers. '

In the fourth place, when John added, "And not for ours only, but also for the whole world", he signified that Christ was the propitiation for the sins of Gentile believers too, for, as previously shown, "the world" is a term contrasted from Israel. This interpretation is unequivocally established by a careful comparison of 1 John 2:2 with John 11:51,52, which is a strictly parallel passage: "And this spake he not of himself: but being high priest that year, he prophesied that Jesus should die for that nation; And not for that nation only, but that also He should gather together in one the children of God that were scattered abroad". Here Caiaphas, under inspiration, made known for whom Jesus should "die". Notice now the correspondency of his prophecy with this declaration of John's:

1 John 2:2

John 11:51, 52
"He is the propitiation for our (believing Israelites) sins".

"He prophesied that Jesus should die for that) nation".
"And not for ours only".

"And not for that nation only".
"But also for the whole world"— That is, Gentile believers scattered throughout the) earth.

"He should gather together in one the children of God that were scattered abroad".

In the fifth place, the above interpretation is confirmed by the fact that no other is consistent or intelligible. If the "whole world" signifies the whole human race, then the first clause and the "also" in the second clause are absolutely meaningless. If Christ is the propitiation for everybody, it would be idle tautology to say, first, "He is the propitiation for our sins and also for everybody". There could be no "also" if He is the propitiation for the entire human family. Had the apostle meant to affirm that Christ is a universal propitiation he had omitted the first clause of verse 2, and simply said, "He is the propitiation for the sins of the whole world." Confirmatory of "not for ours (Jewish believers) only, but also for the whole world"—Gentile believers, too; compare John 10:16; 17:20.

In the sixth place, our definition of "the whole world" is in perfect accord with other passages in the New Testament. For example: "Whereof ye heard before in the word of the truth of the Gospel; which is come unto you, as it is in all the world" (Col. 1:5, 6). Does "all the world" here mean, absolutely and unqualifiedly, all mankind? Had all the human family heard the Gospel?

No; the apostle's obvious meaning is that, the Gospel, instead of being confined to the land of Judea, had gone abroad, without restraint, into Gentile lands. So in Romans 1:8: "First, I thank my God through Jesus Christ for you all, that your faith is spoken of throughout the whole world". The apostle is here referring to the faith of these Roman saints being spoken of in a way of commendation. But certainly all mankind did not so speak of their faith! It was the whole world of believers that he was referring to! In Revelation 12:9 we read of Satan "which deceiveth the whole world". But again this expression cannot be understood as a universal one, for Matthew 24:24 tells us that Satan does not and cannot "deceive" God's elect. Here it is "the whole world" of unbelievers.

In the seventh place, to insist that "the whole world" in 1 John 2:2 signifies the entire human race is to undermine the very foundations of our faith. If Christ is the propitiation for those that are lost equally as much as for those that are saved, then what assurance have we that believers too may not be lost? If Christ is the propitiation for those now in hell, what guarantee have I that I may not end in hell? The blood-shedding of the incarnate Son of God is the only thing which can keep any one out of hell, and if many for whom that precious blood made propitiation are now in the awful place of the damned, then may not that blood prove inefficacious for me! Away with such a God-dishonoring thought.

However men may quibble and wrest the Scriptures, one thing is certain: The Atonement is no failure. God will not allow that precious and costly sacrifice to fail in accomplishing, completely, that which it was designed to effect. Not a drop of that holy blood was shed in vain. In the last great Day there shall stand forth no disappointed and defeated Saviour, but One who "shall see of the travail of His soul and be satisfied" (Isa. 53:11). These are not our words, but the infallible assertion of Him who declares, "My counsel shall stand, and I will do all My pleasure" (Isa. 64:10). Upon this impregnable rock we take our stand. Let others rest on the sands of human speculation and twentieth-century theorizing if they wish. That is their business. But to God they will yet have to render an account. For our part we had rather be railed at as a narrow-minded, out-of-date, hyper-Calvinist, than be found repudiating God's truth by reducing the Divinely-efficacious atonement to a mere fiction.

www.ingramcontent.com/pod-product-compliance
Lightning Source LLC
Chambersburg PA
CBHW020344170426
43200CB00005B/47